THE 1-MINUTE
BIBLE
GUIDE

THE 1-MINUTE
BIBLE
GUIDE

More Than 1,250
Quick, Easy-to-Read Entries on
People, Places, Events, and More

BARBOUR
PUBLISHING

ISBN 978-1-63609-018-4

Published by Barbour Publishing, Inc., 1810 Barbour Drive, Uhrichsville, Ohio 44683, www.barbourbooks.com

Our mission is to inspire the world with the life-changing message of the Bible.

 Member of the
Evangelical Christian
Publishers Association

Printed in the United States of America.

CONTENTS ────────────────

WANT A BETTER GRASP OF SCRIPTURE? ——

The 1-Minute Bible Guide offers just that.

This easy-to-read guide covers more than 1,250 of the most important elements of God's Word, within seven overall categories:

- Names of God
- People
- Places
- Events
- Ideas
- Questions
- Figures of Speech

Each entry includes

- a representative verse
- a concise description you can read and digest in 60 seconds or less
- and, as a bonus, additional references if you want to dig deeper.

You'll learn why each person, place, thing, or idea plays an important role in the larger story of the Bible—the ultimate story of God's love for humanity.

THE 1-MINUTE
BIBLE
GUIDE

180 Key Names of God

An alphabetical listing of the 180 most important
names and titles of God the Father,
Jesus Christ, and the Holy Spirit.

Written by George W. Knight
Edited by Paul Kent

ABBA, FATHER

And he said, Abba, Father. MARK 14:36

This is the name with which Jesus the Son addressed God the Father in His agonizing prayer in the garden of Gethsemane. *Abba* is an Aramaic word of affection for "Father," similar in meaning to "Papa" in the English language.

The Jewish people generally avoided such affectionate terms for God. They thought of Him as an exalted and larger-than-life being who demanded respect. He was to be spoken of in hushed reverence rather than addressed as if He were a member of the family.

But it was appropriate for Jesus to address the Father as *Abba*. As God's Son, He knew the Father more intimately than anyone has ever known Him. Jesus Himself declared, "As the Father knoweth me, even so know I the Father" (John 10:15).

Through His death on the cross, Jesus made it possible for us to know God as a loving, forgiving Father. The apostle Paul declared, "And because ye are sons, God hath sent forth the spirit of his Son into your hearts, crying, Abba, Father" (Galatians 4:6).

Learn More: Matthew 6:9 / Mark 9:7 / Luke 10:21 / John 3:35; 10:37–38

ADVOCATE

We have an advocate with the Father. 1 JOHN 2:1

This is the only place in the Bible where Jesus is called by this name. It expresses the idea that He stands before God on our behalf. He serves as our "defense attorney" to represent us before the Father in heaven when Satan, the accuser, charges us with sin. Jesus' argument on our behalf is solid because it is based on His own atoning work—His death on the cross for our sins.

Any attorney will tell you that his client must be totally honest about the charges that have brought him into court. Unless the advocate knows everything about the circumstances of the case, he cannot represent his client adequately before the judge and jury.

In the same way, if we expect Jesus to serve as our Advocate before God, we as believers must be honest with Him when sin creeps into our lives. Full disclosure, also known as confession, is essential. As the apostle John wrote, "If we confess our sins, he is faithful and just to forgive us our sins, and to cleanse us from all unrighteousness" (1 John 1:9).

Learn More: Romans 10:9 / 1 John 4:15

ALIVE FOR EVERMORE

I am alive for evermore, Amen. REVELATION 1:18

These words are among the first that Jesus spoke when He revealed Himself to the apostle John on the isle of Patmos. This revelation occurred about fifty or sixty years after Jesus' death and resurrection. He assured John that He was not only alive but "alive for evermore."

During His brief ministry of about three years, Jesus predicted His death and resurrection on more than one occasion (Matthew 16:21–28; Mark 10:32–34; Luke 9:43–45). But even His disciples had a hard time believing this would happen.

Even after Jesus appeared to them in His resurrection body, they had doubts. To prove that they were not seeing a ghost or a vision, Jesus encouraged the disciples to touch His hands and feet, showing that He had flesh and bones. He even ate a piece of fish and a honeycomb as they looked on, confirming that He had a physical body just like theirs (Luke 24:37–43).

Since Jesus experienced a physical resurrection and is alive for evermore, we as believers have His assurance that death is not the end of life but a glorious new beginning.

Learn More: Acts 1:3 / 1 Thessalonians 4:17

ALL, AND IN ALL

Christ is all, and in all. COLOSSIANS 3:11

Jesus was born into a divided world. Jews looked down on Gentiles. Greeks considered themselves superior in education and culture to the Jews. But the apostle Paul declared in this famous passage that the coming of Jesus changed all that. He is the "All in All"—the great unifier—who brings all people together at the foot of the cross.

To those who know Jesus, worldly distinctions and social status are no longer important. The only thing that really matters is Christ. He is the sum and substance of life—the absolute and the center of our existence. Because He gave His all to purchase our salvation, our purpose in life is to bring honor and glory to Him. As Jesus expressed it in His Sermon on the Mount, "Let your light so shine before men, that they may see your good works, and glorify your Father which is in heaven" (Matthew 5:16).

Learn More: Matthew 28:19–20 / Acts 10:34–35 / Romans 3:29 / Ephesians 4:4–6

ALMIGHTY GOD

I am the Almighty God. GENESIS 17:1

God had already promised Abram (later renamed Abraham) that He would make his descendants a great nation and give them a land of their own (Genesis 12:1–3; 13:15–17). But Abraham had no son through whom this promise could be fulfilled. The Lord, by identifying Himself as "the Almighty God" in this verse, declared to Abraham that He had the power to make this happen.

The Hebrew words behind this divine compound name also express the idea of plenty. Some interpreters suggest that they may be rendered as "the All-Sufficient One" or "the All-Bountiful One." God not only has the power to bless His people, but He *will* do so abundantly. The apostle Paul put it like this: God is "able to do exceedingly abundantly above all that we ask or think" (Ephesians 3:20).

Learn More: Psalm 45:3 / Isaiah 1:24; 49:26 / Jeremiah 32:18 / 2 Corinthians 6:18 / Revelation 15:3; 19:6

ALPHA AND OMEGA

I am Alpha and Omega. REVELATION 22:13

This is one of four places in the book of Revelation where Jesus is called by this name (see also 1:8, 11; 21:6). In all four places, Jesus uses this name of Himself.

The alpha and the omega were the first and last letters of the Greek alphabet—the language in which most of the New Testament was originally written. Thus this name is a poetic way of declaring that Jesus is the beginning and the end of all things. We might put it this way in modern terms: "Jesus is the A and Z of life and everything in between."

No letter stands before the alpha, and no letter follows the omega. This shows that Jesus defines truth and reality. All other gods that people worship are counterfeit deities. He encompasses all things and rejects all limitations.

Jesus also declared that He is the "first and the last" (Revelation 1:17)—a name that means basically the same thing as Alpha and Omega. As the first, He was present with God the Father before the creation (John 1:2). In the last days, He will bring the world to its appointed end (Revelation 22:10–12). See also *Beginning of the Creation of God*.

Learn More: Revelation 2:8

AMEN

These things saith the Amen. REVELATION 3:14

This verse was spoken by Jesus as He prepared to deliver a special message to the church at Laodicea. By designating Himself as "the Amen," He claimed to be speaking a truthful, authoritative word for this church.

The word *amen* has a rich biblical history. In the Old Testament, it was used to confirm an oath or consent to an agreement. For example, Nehemiah called on the people of his time not to cheat and defraud one another. The people responded with "amen" to pledge their agreement with his proposal (Nehemiah 5:13).

Jesus often used the word *verily* (or *amen*) in His teachings to show that He was about to speak God's words of truth (Matthew 16:28). In modern translations, this Greek word is rendered as "Truly I tell you" (NIV) or "I assure you" (HCSB). The early church used *amen* to declare "let it be so" or "let it be true" at the close of prayers (2 Thessalonians 3:18), just as we do today.

Because Jesus is the great Amen, we can trust His words and His leadership. He is the sum and substance of truth (John 14:6). He will never say or do anything that will cause us to stumble or go astray. He has promised that if we follow Him, we will know the truth, and this truth will make us free (John 8:32).

Learn More: 1 Kings 1:36 / Jeremiah 28:6 / Romans 16:20

ANCIENT OF DAYS

The Ancient of days did sit. DANIEL 7:9

This name of God is used only by the prophet Daniel (see also 7:13, 22). He had a vision of four world empires that rose to great power and prominence, only to eventually fall and crumble into insignificance.

In contrast to the short life of these world powers was One who had always existed and always would. Daniel's use of the imagery of old age to describe God suggests His eternality. Unlike humans and worldly affairs, God is not limited by time. Everything around us changes, but He remains the same. The only real security we have in this world is to place our trust in the Ancient of Days.

"King of old," a title used by the psalmist (Psalm 74:12), expresses basically the same idea about God.

Learn More: Genesis 21:33 / Deuteronomy 33:27 / Psalm 90:2 / Isaiah 40:28 / Habakkuk 1:12

ANOINTED

. . .against the Lord, and against his anointed. . . PSALM 2:2–3

Psalm 2 is a "messianic psalm," one that predicts the coming of the Messiah. Rebellion against the Lord by the nations of the world is futile, the psalmist declared, because God has appointed Christ, "his anointed," as the King of the earth.

This name of Jesus reflects the anointing custom of the Old Testament. Priests and kings were anointed by having oil poured on their heads. This ritual showed that a person had been especially chosen or set apart to perform the responsibilities of his office.

As God's anointed, Jesus Christ was set apart for His role as the divine mediator and redeemer. Through Him we find forgiveness for our sins and the abundant life that God intends for His people.

Jesus in turn has anointed us as believers for the task of declaring His message of hope in a desperate world. The apostle Paul put it like this: "We are therefore Christ's ambassadors, as though God were making his appeal through us. We implore you in Christ's behalf: Be reconciled to God" (2 Corinthians 5:20 NIV).

Learn More: Leviticus 8:10–12 / 1 Samuel 16:13 / Luke 4:18

Consider the Apostle and High Priest of our profession. HEBREWS 3:1

Jesus selected twelve apostles (Mark 3:14; 6:30) to learn from Him and to carry on His work after He was gone. But here Jesus Himself is called "the Apostle." This is the only place in the Bible where this name of Jesus occurs.

The basic meaning of the word *apostle* is a person sent on a special mission with delegated authority and power. Jesus sent out the Twelve to teach and heal, and He gave them the ability to succeed in this mission (Mark 6:7–13). They continued this teaching and healing ministry even after Jesus' resurrection and ascension to the Father (Acts 2:38–43).

But Jesus was the ultimate Apostle. Under the authority of His Father, He came into the world on a mission of love and grace. He did not falter in His task. From the cross He declared triumphantly, "It is finished" (John 19:30). His provision for our salvation was complete, but the Good News about His death and resurrection—the gospel—rolls on across the ages.

Learn More: Matthew 10:2 / Acts 4:33 / Ephesians 2:20

AUTHOR AND FINISHER OF OUR FAITH

Looking unto Jesus the author and finisher of our faith. HEBREWS 12:2

Jesus is called "author" in this verse from Hebrews, as well as in Hebrews 5:9: "And being made perfect, he became the author of eternal salvation unto all them that obey him." In one modern translation, He is also called "the author of [our] salvation" (Hebrews 2:10 NASB).

An author is someone who creates. Jesus is the author of our faith or salvation in that He has provided us with the only flawless example of what the life of faith is like. The New Revised Standard Version expresses this idea by calling Him the "pioneer" of our faith. He blazed the trail for all others who seek to follow His example.

But Jesus not only *started* the journey—He brought it to *completion* as the "finisher" ("perfecter," NRSV) of faith. He did not stop until He guaranteed our final redemption, making it possible for us to enjoy eternal life with Him in heaven.

Learn More: John 19:30 / Hebrews 10:12

BEGINNING OF THE CREATION OF GOD

. . .the beginning of the creation of God. REVELATION 3:14

The affirmation of this verse is that Jesus has always been. Before He was born into the world in human form, He existed with God the Father. The Nicene Creed, a famous statement of faith formulated by the church in AD 325, put it like this: "I believe in one Lord, Jesus Christ. . .born of the Father before all ages." Thus He is called the "beginning of the creation of God."

Not only has Jesus existed eternally; the Bible affirms that He participated with God in the creation. On the sixth day of creation the Lord declared, "Let us make man in *our* image, after *our* likeness" (Genesis 1:26, emphasis added). The plural *our* probably refers to God in His trinitarian existence: God the Father, God the Son, and God the Holy Spirit.

This creative force in the universe has promised that believers will live with Him in eternity. The apostle Paul declared, "we have a building of God, an house not made with hands, eternal in the heavens" (2 Corinthians 5:1).

Learn More: Genesis 1:1 / John 1:1–3 / Colossians 1:16–17 / Ephesians 3:9

BELOVED SON

This is my beloved Son, in whom I am well pleased. Matthew 3:17

In graphic terms, these verses describe what happened when Jesus was baptized by John the Baptist at the beginning of His public ministry. The heavens opened, the Holy Spirit settled on Jesus, and God identified Him clearly as His "beloved Son" who brought Him joy. God was pleased with Jesus because He had waited patiently on the Father's timing. Now Jesus was ready to begin the work for which He had been sent into the world.

God the Father repeated these words near the end of Jesus' public ministry following His transfiguration (Matthew 17:1–5). His words on this occasion showed He was pleased with what His beloved Son had done. Only Jesus' death and resurrection to follow could top the divine work He had already accomplished.

Because Jesus was God's beloved Son, we as believers in Jesus are also known as the Father's beloved (Romans 1:7). We hold a special place in His heart because we have been cleansed by Jesus' blood and are committed to the work of His everlasting kingdom.

Learn More: Matthew 3:17 / Luke 9:35 / 2 Peter 1:17

BREAD

My Father giveth you the true bread from heaven. John 6:32

John 6 might be called the "bread chapter" of the New Testament. In this long narrative, Jesus uses four different names for Himself involving the imagery of bread: "bread from heaven" (verse 32), "bread of God" (verse 33), "bread of life" (verse 35), and "living bread" (verse 51).

Bread made from wheat or barley was the staple food of Jesus' day, so the common people could identify with these names. Bread was also closely identified with some of the major events from Israel's history. When the Israelites left Egypt in the Exodus, they baked their bread without leaven because they didn't have time to wait for the bread to rise (Exodus 12:30–34). The Lord also kept His people alive in the wilderness after the Exodus by providing manna, a bread substitute, for them to eat (Numbers 11:6–9).

Just as God provided food in the wilderness, He also provides spiritual sustenance for His people. As the living bread and the bread of life, Jesus provides eternal life for those who claim Him as their Lord and Savior.

Learn More: Matthew 26:26 / Luke 22:19 / 1 Corinthians 10:17

BREATH OF THE ALMIGHTY

The breath of the Almighty hath given me life. Job 33:4

This name of the Holy Spirit comes from the long speech that the young man Elihu addressed to Job. He spoke after Job's three friends—Eliphaz, Bildad, and Zophar (Job 2:11)—had ended their speeches.

Elihu stated that he owed his life to the breath of God. This is a reference to God's creation of the first man in the garden of Eden. The Lord "breathed into his nostrils the breath of life; and man became a living soul" (Genesis 2:7). It was God's own breath that brought Adam to life. Even today, our ability to inhale life-giving oxygen into our lungs is evidence of God's care of the physical world through the agency of His Spirit.

The Holy Spirit, or the "breath of the Almighty," also energizes believers in a spiritual sense. Just before His ascension to the Father, Jesus empowered His followers to carry on His work by breathing on them and charging them to receive the Holy Spirit (John 20:22). This is the same life-giving Spirit that enables believers in our time to witness to others about God's transforming power.

Learn More: Job 4:9 / Psalm 33:6 / Isaiah 42:5 / Daniel 5:23 / Acts 17:25

BRIDEGROOM

...when the bridegroom shall be taken from them. MATTHEW 9:15

Jesus responded with these words when the followers of John the Baptist asked why He and His disciples did not participate in the ritual of fasting. His answer picked up imagery from a Jewish wedding, with Jesus referring to Himself as the bridegroom and His disciples as the wedding guests.

It would not be appropriate, Jesus said, for His disciples to fast or mourn while He as the bridegroom was physically present with them. They should save their fasting for the time after His death and resurrection, when Jesus would be taken up to heaven by God the Father.

Perhaps Jesus was looking ahead to the birth of the church, which is spoken of symbolically as His bride (Revelation 21:9). The apostle Paul pointed out that just as "the husband is head of the wife," so "Christ is the head of the church" (Ephesians 5:23). Jesus loved the church so much that He laid down His life for it (Ephesians 5:25). Every single member of His kingdom has experienced this sacrificial love.

Learn More: Luke 5:34–35 / Revelation 21:2

BRIGHT AND MORNING STAR

...the bright and morning star. REVELATION 22:16

This is one of the last names of Jesus mentioned in scripture, since it appears in the final chapter of the last book of the Bible. How appropriate that He should call Himself the "bright and morning star," a name associated with a heavenly body and its light.

The people of ancient times did not know as much about stars and planets as we know today. To them the last star to disappear in the eastern sky as the sun began to rise was known as the "morning star." Astronomers of modern times have identified this "star" as the planet Venus, earth's closest neighbor. Because of its closeness, Venus is the third brightest object in the sky, outshone only by the sun and the moon.

When the light from all the other stars disappeared in the early morning, this star twinkled on, signaling the beginning of a new day. The birth of Jesus also marked the beginning of a new day, a truth that should bring joy to our hearts. What better way to greet the dawning of each new day than to breathe a prayer of thanks to God for sending His bright and morning star into the world?

Learn More: Numbers 24:17 / Matthew 2:2 / 2 Peter 1:19 / Revelation 2:27–28

CAPTAIN OF SALVATION

...to make the captain of their salvation perfect through sufferings. HEBREWS 2:10

This is the only place in the Bible where Jesus is called by this name. The Greek word behind *captain* in this verse is rendered as "author" in Hebrews 12:2. Other meanings of this word are "prince" and "leader."

This verse from Hebrews goes on to say that Jesus was made "perfect through sufferings." A genuine leader does not ask his followers to do something that he is not willing to do himself. He sets the example for those he leads. This is what Jesus did when He died on the cross for us. We as believers will never suffer more by following Him than He did to make it possible for us to be cleansed of our sins.

A leader also guides, encourages, inspires, and motivates the people in his charge. We can rest assured that we are in good hands when we follow our captain of salvation.

Learn More: Psalm 48:14 / Isaiah 63:5 / John 16:13 / Hebrews 1:14

CHIEF CORNERSTONE

Jesus Christ himself being the chief corner stone. EPHESIANS 2:20

With these words the apostle Paul assured believers in the church at Ephesus that they were recipients of God's grace. Their faith in Christ had brought them into God's kingdom, because He was the "chief corner stone" on which this kingdom was built.

This image is rooted in a famous messianic passage that was written several centuries before Jesus was born. In Psalm 118:22, the psalmist declared, "The stone which the builders rejected is become the head stone of the corner."

Jesus identified with this passage during the final days of His ministry. He knew that He would be rejected as the Messiah by His own people. So he told the disciples that His offer of salvation would pass to the non-Jewish (Gentile) nations that would accept Him as Lord and Savior (Matthew 21:42–43).

In the stone buildings of Bible times, a cornerstone was used to hold two opposing rows of stones together at the point where they came together in a corner. Jesus as the chief cornerstone is the force on which our faith is based. Though He may be rejected by the non-believing world, He is our hope in this life and the life to come.

Learn More: Isaiah 28:16 / Mark 12:10 / Acts 4:11 / 1 Peter 2:7

CHOSEN OF GOD

Christ, the chosen of God. LUKE 23:35

Religious leaders and other people around the cross called Jesus by this name as He was dying. The irony is that their ridicule was a perfect description of Him and the divine mission from His Father that brought Jesus into the world.

For generations the Jewish people had looked for a messiah who would deliver God's people. Jesus was that chosen one, but He was not the type of champion they expected. He came not as a military conqueror but as a spiritual savior who died to rescue people from their sin. His work as the "chosen of God" continues to this day as He calls people to follow Him (Matthew 16:24).

Jesus was the chosen of God in a special sense. But He followed in the tradition of many people in the Bible who were said to be chosen of God. These included the descendants of Jacob, also called the Israelites (1 Chronicles 16:13), King Solomon (1 Chronicles 29:1), Moses (Psalm 106:23), Zerubbabel (Haggai 2:23), the apostle Paul (Acts 9:15), and all believers (Ephesians 1:4).

Learn More: Psalm 33:12 / Isaiah 42:1 / Matthew 12:18 / 1 Peter 2:4, 9

CHRIST

Thou art the Christ, the Son of the living God. MATTHEW 16:16

This verse is part of the account of Peter's confession of Jesus as the Messiah (or "anointed one") in the Gospel of Matthew (16:13–20). Peter declared that Jesus was the anointed one, a special agent who had been sent into the world by God Himself. He was the Son of God, the Messiah, the great deliverer for whom the Jewish people had been looking for many years.

Jesus commended Peter for recognizing Him as God's anointed. But He went on to caution the disciples not to tell anyone "that he was Jesus the Christ" (Matthew 16:20). He probably gave this command because the Jewish people expected their messiah to be a military and political champion. Jesus could not live up to these expectations because He was a spiritual messiah. He had been sent to teach about the kingdom of God, to heal the sick, and to deliver the people from their sin. He would eventually reveal Himself as the Messiah (Luke 22:70–71), but only after He had completed the spiritual mission on which He had been sent.

Because Jesus was the anointed one of God, we as His followers are also commissioned to continue His work in the world (2 Corinthians 1:21–22).

Learn More: Luke 9:20 / Romans 3:24 / 1 Corinthians 1:2

CHRIST CRUCIFIED

But we preach Christ crucified. 1 CORINTHIANS 1:23

This is the only place in the Bible where this name of Jesus appears. The word *Christ* means "the anointed one" or "the messiah," so the literal meaning of the name is "the messiah crucified."

In Jewish tradition, the coming messiah was to be a powerful leader who would defeat all their enemies and rule over a restored Israel. That this messiah would die on a Roman cross like a common criminal was something they found totally unacceptable—a "stumblingblock" that prevented them from accepting Jesus as the Messiah.

A crucified Savior who died in our place to set us free from bondage to sin is still a foreign concept to many people. Like the rich young ruler of Jesus' day, they want to know "what good thing" (Matthew 19:16) they must do to obtain eternal life. But there is nothing we can do that will buy God's favor. We must accept by faith the provision that God has already made for our salvation through the death of His Son.

The apostle Paul put it like this: "For by grace are ye saved through faith; and that not of yourselves: it is the gift of God: not of works, lest any man should boast" (Ephesians 2:8–9).

Learn More: Matthew 27:35 / Acts 2:36 / Galatians 2:20

COMFORTER

I will pray the Father, and he shall give you another Comforter. JOHN 14:16

Jesus spoke these words after He had told the disciples that His death was drawing near. He would no longer be with them in a physical sense, but He was not leaving them alone: He would send a "Comforter," the Holy Spirit, to fill the void caused by His return to the Father in heaven after His resurrection.

Jesus referred to the Holy Spirit as "another" Comforter. The Greek word He used means "another of the same kind." Jesus Himself was the chief Comforter of His disciples, and He was sending another like Himself to serve as His stand-in. So close and personal would be the presence of the Holy Spirit that it would seem as if Jesus had never left.

The Greek word behind Comforter is *parakletos,* meaning "one called alongside." This is the same word translated as "Advocate," another name of Jesus (1 John 2:1).

When Jesus promised that the Comforter will come "alongside" us, He meant that the Holy Spirit will help us in our times of need. His presence will sustain us through the tough times of life.

Learn More: Isaiah 40:1 / John 14:26; 15:26; 16:7 / Acts 9:31

CONSOLATION OF ISRAEL

. . .waiting for the consolation of Israel. LUKE 2:25

A few days after Jesus was born, Joseph and Mary took Him to the temple in Jerusalem to be dedicated to the Lord. A man named Simeon was moved by the Holy Spirit to come to the temple at the same time. He immediately recognized the infant Jesus as the "consolation of Israel."

The word *consolation* means "comfort" or "relief." In the Old Testament, God had promised that He would send His Messiah to His people. Simeon was convinced that he would not die before he had seen this come to pass. God apparently showed Simeon by divine revelation that the baby Jesus was the fulfilment of this promise.

This good news had a dark side, though. Simeon went on to tell Mary and Joseph that many people would accept their Son as the Messiah but many would not. He also revealed to Mary that "a sword shall pierce through thy own soul also" (Luke 2:35)—a hint of Jesus' future crucifixion.

Jesus' birth was good news for those who accepted His messiahship and bad news for those who refused to believe in Him. The task of Christians is to help others find the consolation that Jesus can bring into their lives.

Learn More: Job 15:11 / Romans 15:5 / 2 Thessalonians 2:16 / Hebrews 6:18

CONSUMING FIRE

Our God is a consuming fire. HEBREWS 12:29

God is often associated with fire in the Bible. Sometimes fire symbolizes His guidance and protection. For example, He spoke to Moses from a burning bush (Exodus 3:2). He guided the Israelites through the wilderness at night by a pillar of fire (Exodus 13:21).

But this verse from the book of Hebrews shows that fire is also a symbol of God's wrath. To those who are disrespectful or disobedient, He is a searing flame of judgment. For example, when the Israelites complained against Moses in the wilderness, God sent His fire of judgment upon the troublemakers (Numbers 11:1–3). Years earlier, He also rained fire and brimstone from heaven against the evil people of the cities of Sodom and Gomorrah (Genesis 19:24)

All people must decide for themselves whether the Lord will be a guiding light or a consuming fire in their lives. See also *Wall of Fire*.

Learn More: Numbers 26:10 / Deuteronomy 5:24–25 / 1 Kings 18:38 / Psalm 21:9

COUNSELLOR

His name shall be called Wonderful, Counsellor. ISAIAH 9:6

This verse is probably the most familiar messianic prophecy in the book of Isaiah. It is especially quoted at Christmastime when believers gather to celebrate the birth of Jesus.

The word *counsel* refers to guidance, advice, or instruction. The Bible is filled with models of good and bad counsel and counselors who fall into both of these categories.

For example, on the good side, Daniel provided wise counsel to an aide to King Nebuchadnezzar of Babylon, after the king had issued an order to have all his wise men put to death (Daniel 2:10–16). But on the foolish side, King Rehoboam of Judah rejected the wise counsel of the older leaders of the nation and listened to the foolish counsel of his young associates (1 Kings 12:6–8). This led to the rebellion of the northern tribes and the division of the united kingdom of Solomon into two separate nations (1 Kings 12:16–19).

We can depend on Jesus, our wise Counsellor, to always provide us with good instruction. He guides us with grace and righteousness. He will never give us bad advice that would cause us to go astray.

Learn More: Psalm 73:24 / Proverbs 19:21 / Isaiah 11:2

CREATOR

The everlasting God, the Lord, the Creator of the ends of the earth. ISAIAH 40:28

The prophet Isaiah was amazed that the people of Judah were rejecting the one true God and worshiping false gods instead. The Creator God had brought the universe into being by the power of His word (Hebrews 11:3). These pagan idols were weak and puny by comparison.

From the first chapter of the Bible we learn several important truths about God's creation of the world and its inhabitants. (1) He created the world from nothing; He is the ultimate cause of all that exists. (2) The creation was accomplished in orderly fashion, in six successive days. This means that God has placed order and design into the universe. (3) Man is the crown of God's creation. (4) The Lord has given us the responsibility to take care of His world.

As Isaiah reminded the people of his nation, the one-and-only Creator God is solely worthy of our loyalty and worship. See also *Maker*.

Learn More: Ecclesiastes 12:1 / Romans 1:22–25 / 1 Peter 4:19

DAYSMAN

Neither is there any daysman betwixt us. Job 9:33

This verse is part of Job's complaint that God was punishing him without cause. Job was convinced that he had done nothing to deserve his suffering. To make matters worse, God was all-powerful and Job was simply a weak human being. Job had no right to question God, so he longed for a daysman—a referee, mediator, or impartial judge—who could speak to God on his behalf.

Job's desire for someone to represent him before God the Father was eventually fulfilled with the coming of Jesus Christ into the world. As the God-man, He is fully human and fully divine. He communicates directly with the Father, because He is God's Son. But He identifies with us humans in our frailties because He came to earth in human form.

It's difficult for us to comprehend how Jesus could be both human and divine at the same time. But our lack of understanding doesn't make the fact untrue. The apostle Paul attempted to explain it like this: Although Jesus was equal with God and had the nature of God, He emptied Himself of these divine attributes to become a man who was "obedient unto death, even the death of the cross" (Philippians 2:8).

Learn More: Job 8:3 / Psalm 72:2; 89:14 / Isaiah 9:7; 33:22

DAYSPRING FROM ON HIGH

The dayspring from on high hath visited us. Luke 1:78

This verse is part of a passage in the Gospel of Luke known as the "Benedictus" (Luke 1:68–79)—a prayer uttered by Zacharias, after the birth of his son, John the Baptist. An angel had revealed to Zacharias before John's birth that the boy would become the forerunner of the Messiah. Zacharias praised God for sending the Messiah, Jesus, whom he called the "dayspring from on high."

The English term *dayspring* comes from a Greek word that means "a rising up." It is generally used to describe the rising of the sun in the morning and the appearance of stars in the night sky. Thus Zacharias thought of Jesus the Messiah as a bright light that God was preparing to send into a dark world.

The words *on high* reveal the origin of this dayspring. Jesus did not come into the world on His own as a solitary agent. He was on a mission of redemption from God the Father.

The prophet Malachi used a similar name for Jesus in his prophecy about the coming Messiah. He called Him the "Sun of righteousness" who would "arise with healing in his wings" (Malachi 4:2).

Learn More: Job 38:12 / Psalm 84:11

DELIVERER

There shall come out of Sion the Deliverer. Romans 11:26

In this verse the apostle Paul referred to a portion of Psalm 14:7. This is a messianic psalm attributed to David, who declared that the salvation of God's people would come from Zion, or Jerusalem.

This is an unusual reference to the Messiah, because Jesus was born in Bethlehem, not Jerusalem. But Jesus was crucified and resurrected in Jerusalem. This is also the place where the church was born on the day of Pentecost (Acts 2:1–41) following Jesus' ascension. These facts are probably what Paul had in mind when he declared that Jesus as our Deliverer came out of Jerusalem.

God is also referred to in the Old Testament as our Deliverer. This was one of King David's favorite words for God, perhaps because God had delivered him from danger many times throughout his life (1 Samuel 18:10–11; 19:11–12).

As Deliverer, the great work that Jesus performs is rescue from sin. He sets us free from our sin that separates us from God (Isaiah 59:2). He delivers us from the power of Satan, who temps us constantly to fall back into sin (Ephesians 6:11–13). And He will deliver His followers from a world filled with sin when He returns to claim us as His own.

Learn More: 2 Samuel 22:2 / Psalm 18:2; 31:2; 40:17

DESIRE OF ALL NATIONS

The desire of all nations shall come. HAGGAI 2:7

The prophet Haggai spoke these words to the Jewish exiles who had returned to Jerusalem after their period of captivity in Babylonia and Persia. He challenged them to get busy with the task of rebuilding the Jewish temple that had been destroyed several decades before by the invading Babylonian army. The temple is apparently the "house" referred to in this verse.

But Haggai's words looked beyond his time to the distant future when Israel's Messiah would become the "desire of all nations." At Jesus' return in glory in the end time, all nations will pay Him homage and recognize His universal rule throughout the earth. One modern translation renders this name as the "wealth of all nations" (NIV).

Jesus is not only the desire of believers, He is the hope of the entire world. As the apostle Paul declared, "At the name of Jesus every knee should bow. . .every tongue confess that Jesus Christ is Lord, to the glory of God the Father" (Philippians 2:10–11 NIV).

Learn More: Psalm 22:27; 72:17 / Isaiah 11:10 / Matthew 28:19 / Galatians 3:8 / Revelation 7:9

DOOR

I am the door. JOHN 10:9

This is one of several "I Am" statements of Jesus in the Gospel of John. A door is an opening or entryway into a building or a shelter. By affirming that He was the door, Jesus made it clear that He was the only way to salvation and eternal life.

In His sermon on the mount, Jesus also addressed this topic by talking about two gates (Matthew 7:13–14). The broad gate, representing the way of the world, was so wide that people could drift through it without any conscious thought about what they were doing. But the narrow gate, representing Jesus and His teachings, required commitment and sacrifice from those who wanted to enter this way and follow Him.

Maybe you have heard people say, "It doesn't matter what you believe as long as you're sincere," or "All religions are basically the same; they just take us to heaven by different paths." Don't believe it. Jesus declared, "I am the way, the truth, and the life: no man cometh unto the Father but by me" (John 14:6).

Learn More: John 10:7–8 / Acts 4:12

DWELLING PLACE

Lord, thou hast been our dwelling place in all generations. PSALM 90:1

This psalm may be the oldest in the entire book of Psalms, since it is attributed to Moses (see psalm title). He led the Israelites during their years of wandering in the wilderness. This was before they settled in Canaan, so they lived in tents and moved from place to place.

It's interesting that Moses would call God the people's "dwelling place" at a time when they did not have permanent homes. In spite of their primitive living arrangements, they still thought of God as their ultimate dwelling place. His presence followed them wherever they moved, and His faithfulness continued from one generation to the next.

When the psalmist considered the Lord's promise to protect His people, he declared, "There shall no evil befall thee, neither shall any plague come nigh thy dwelling" (Psalm 91:10). God is still a dwelling place for His people. Whether we live in an apartment, a mobile home, a condominium, a gated community, or a mansion, we find in Him all the joys and comforts of home.

Learn More: Psalm 4:8; 23:6; 91:1 / 2 Corinthians 5:1 / Revelation 21:3

END OF THE LAW

For Christ is the end of the law for righteousness. ROMANS 10:4

This is the only place in the Bible where Jesus is referred to by this name. The New International Version clarifies the meaning of this verse by stating that He is the "culmination of the law so that there may be righteousness for everyone who believes." This name of Jesus has a double meaning.

First, Jesus is the end of the law because He did everything required by the Old Testament law to become a righteous person. He lived a sinless life and obeyed all of God's commandments, although He was tempted to do wrong, like any person in a human body (Hebrews 4:15).

Second, Jesus is the end of the law because He brought an end to law-keeping as the way for people to find justification in God's sight. Belief in Jesus as Lord and Savior is the only way to deal with sin and eliminate the separation that exists between God and man.

Some things outlive their usefulness and ought to be brought to an end or transformed into something better. We should be grateful that Jesus—as the end of the law—offers all believers a glorious new beginning.

Learn More: Jeremiah 31:31–33 / Romans 6:14 / Galatians 2:16 / Hebrews 7:19

ETERNAL LIFE

This is the true God, and eternal life. 1 JOHN 5:20

In several places in the New Testament, Jesus is described as the provider of eternal life. For example:

- "The gift of God is eternal life through Jesus Christ our Lord" (Romans 6:23).
- "This is the promise that he hath promised us, even eternal life" (1 John 2:25).
- "Looking for the mercy of our Lord Jesus Christ unto eternal life" (Jude 21).

But this verse from 1 John is the only place in the Bible where Jesus Himself is given the name *eternal life*. The apostle John was probably thinking about the resurrection of Jesus, His ascension to the Father, and His declaration, "I am alive for evermore" (Revelation 1:18).

Jesus tasted death like all mortal human beings. But He was gloriously raised and restored to His place of honor with God the Father in heaven. As the perfect model of eternal life, He promises that all who place their trust in Him will live in eternal fellowship with Him.

Learn More: John 3:16; 17:3 / 1 Corinthians 15:22 / 1 John 2:25

ETERNAL SPIRIT

. . .who through the eternal Spirit offered himself without spot to God. HEBREWS 9:14

The Holy Spirit empowered Jesus throughout His public ministry. Jesus was led by the Spirit into the region of Galilee, where He began to teach and heal (Luke 4:14). Jesus cast demons out of people "by the spirit of God" (Matthew 12:28). And this verse from the book of Hebrews shows that the Holy Spirit—described here as "the eternal spirit"—gave Jesus the strength to offer His life as a sacrifice for sin.

This is the only place in the Bible where the phrase "eternal spirit" appears. It clearly identifies the Holy Spirit as a divine being. Only the three persons of the Trinity—Father, Son, and Holy Spirit—are eternal. Everything else is created matter.

The eternality of the Holy Spirit is evident in the very first book of the Bible. As God began to mold and shape the universe, "the spirit of God moved upon the face of the waters" (Genesis 1:2). Thus, the Spirit existed with God before time began and participated with Him in the creation of the world.

Learn More: Job 33:4 / Psalm 33:6; 104:30 / John 14:26 / Acts 2:1–3

EVERLASTING FATHER

...the everlasting Father. ISAIAH 9:6

We are accustomed to making a distinction between God and Jesus by referring to God as the Father and to Jesus as the Son. But in this famous passage, the prophet Isaiah seems to blur these neat lines by referring to *Jesus* as "The everlasting Father."

This name of Jesus shows the dilemma we face in trying to explain the Trinity, or God's existence in three different modes or essences—Father, Son, and Holy Spirit.

Some people explain the Trinity by using the analogy of water. We know that water is one substance, but it can exist in three different forms—liquid, ice, and vapor. In the same way, so this analogy goes, God exists in the three different modes known as the Trinity—one substance in three different forms.

Rather than resorting to analogies like this, we are better off if we admit that there is no rational way to explain the Trinity. Faith takes over where reasoning ends. Jesus was separate from God but one with Him at the same time because He Himself declared: "I and my Father are one" (John 10:30).

Learn More: Genesis 21:33 / Isaiah 40:28 / Romans 16:26

EVERLASTING GOD

...the Lord, the everlasting God. GENESIS 21:33

Abraham had moved from place to place for several years in the land of Canaan, the territory that God had promised to his descendants (Genesis 12:1–5). Finally, the patriarch decided to make a site known as Beersheba the center of the territory where he would graze his flocks and herds. Here Abraham dug a well and planted a grove of trees to mark the site as his permanent dwelling place.

At Beersheba it was appropriate that Abraham should call on the name of "the everlasting God," the One without beginning and end who would never cease to be. He would guide Abraham into the future and fulfill His promise that Abraham's offspring would eventually populate this entire region.

God kept His promise, but it took a while. More than five centuries would pass after Abraham's time before the Israelites conquered the land and made it their own.

We should remember that the everlasting God never gets in a hurry; He is not limited by time as we humans are.

Learn More: Psalm 90:1–2 / Isaiah 40:28 / Romans 16:26

EXPRESS IMAGE OF GOD

...being the brightness of his glory, and the express image of his person. HEBREWS 1:3

This name occurs at the beginning of the book of Hebrews, where the writer declared that Jesus is the climax of God's revelation of Himself. In the past He had communicated to His people through the prophets, but now He has "spoken unto us by his Son" (Hebrews 1:2).

The Greek word behind "express image" refers to engravings in wood, impressions in clay, or stamped images on coins. The word picture implies that Jesus was an exact duplicate of His Father in His attitudes, character, and actions. Physical features are not included in this resemblance, because God is a spiritual being (John 4:24).

This name tells us that Christ perfectly represents God His Father. If we want to know what God is like, we should examine the life and ministry of His Son.

Have you ever heard someone say, "That boy is just like his father"? Sometimes, because of a youngster's bad behavior, this pronouncement can cause embarrassment for a father. But God was always pleased with the actions of His Son (Luke 3:22).

Learn More: 2 Corinthians 4:4 / Colossians 1:15

FAITHFUL AND TRUE

. . .called Faithful and True. Revelation 19:11

In this verse near the end of the book of Revelation, the heavens were opened and the apostle John saw Jesus. The white horse on which He was seated symbolized His triumph over all His enemies. As the "Faithful and True," Jesus was coming to earth in judgment against unrighteousness and injustice.

This verse contains images that are similar to the portrayal of God as the divine judge in the Old Testament. The psalmist looked forward to the time when God would judge the earth with righteousness and its people with His truth (Psalm 96:13). Since God is the standard of truth, He has the right to set the standards by which the world will be judged.

God has delegated to His Son the authority to judge the world. Jesus is faithful to God's promise of judgment, and He is the true One who will judge by God's standard of ultimate truth.

In an unjust and unrighteous world, we have to admit that truth does not always win out. But the final work of judgment belongs to Him who is called Faithful and True.

Learn More: 1 Corinthians 1:9 / 2 Thessalonians 3:3 / 1 John 1:9 / Revelation 3:14

FATHER OF GLORY

. . .the Father of glory. Ephesians 1:17

This is the only place in the Bible where God is called "the Father of glory." The apostle Paul used this name while assuring the believers at Ephesus that he was praying to the Father on their behalf.

The word *glory* appears many times throughout the Bible, usually in reference to God's splendor, moral beauty, and perfection. At times His glory was revealed visibly—for example, shortly after the construction of the tabernacle and temple (Exodus 40:34; 1 Kings 8:11). Jesus' glory or splendor was revealed in a special way at His transfiguration before His disciples Peter, James, and John (Matthew 17:2).

The prophet Isaiah declared of the Lord, "The whole earth is full of his glory" (Isaiah 6:3). To put it another way, the beauty and majesty of the physical world gives evidence of God's presence in His creation.

Just as God is the Father of glory, believers should bring glory to Him by becoming living examples of His goodness in the world

Learn More: Isaiah 28:5 / Matthew 16:27 / Acts 7:2 / Romans 6:4

FATHER OF LIGHTS

. . .the Father of lights, with whom is no variableness. James 1:17

With this name of God, James probably had in mind the creation account in the book of Genesis. On the fourth day of creation God created the sun, moon, and stars and "set them in the firmament of the heaven to give light upon the earth" (Genesis 1:17).

The pagan people of many ancient cultures thought of the heavenly bodies as gods. But James declared that they were created things, brought into being by the one true God of the universe. Only the "Father of lights" is worthy of worship.

This God who created the light-giving bodies of the heavens is also dependable and trustworthy. As the New International Version translates it, He "does not change like shifting shadows." God's presence is an unwavering light that guides His people through this life and beyond.

Those who follow the Lord should carry His light as a witness to others. The apostle Peter declared "Ye are a chosen generation. . .that ye should shew forth the praises of him who hath called you out of darkness into his marvellous light" (1 Peter 2:9).

Learn More: Genesis 1:3 / Isaiah 2:5 / John 8:12 / 2 Corinthians 4:6

FATHER OF MERCIES

...the Father of mercies, and the God of all comfort. 2 CORINTHIANS 1:3

This is another of the apostle Paul's names for God that appears in only one verse in the Bible. In this case, he used "Father of mercies" in his prayer for the believers in the church he founded at Corinth.

The dictionary defines *mercy* as "compassionate treatment of those in distress." Because of the original disobedience of Adam and Eve in the garden of Eden, humankind is caught in a web of sin. But we can be grateful that God refuses to abandon us in this perilous situation.

If the Lord gave us what we deserved, we would be destitute and lost. But His love and patience won't let us go. God the Father sent His Son, Jesus, into the world to deliver us from our sin. This is the supreme example of His mercy and love.

Because God is the originator—or Father—of mercies, He expects His people to show this attribute of His character to others. Jesus declared, "Be ye therefore merciful, as your Father also is merciful" (Luke 6:36).

Learn More: Deuteronomy 4:31 / Psalm 86:15; 136:2 / Micah 6:8 / 1 Peter 1:3

FATHER OF OUR LORD JESUS CHRIST

We give thanks to God and the Father of our Lord Jesus Christ. COLOSSIANS 1:3

This name of God used by the apostle Paul draws attention to the miraculous birth of Jesus the Son. He did not have a human father but was miraculously conceived in the womb of Mary by God the Father, acting through the Holy Spirit (Luke 1:34–35).

Jesus was sent by God to fulfill the Father's work of redemption in the world. When He was only twelve years old, Jesus stated that this was His divine mission (Luke 2:48–49). His declaration from the cross, "It is finished" (John 19:30), shows that He accomplished the purpose for which He was sent—our salvation.

This verse is one of several in the New Testament in which these three names of Jesus—*Lord, Jesus,* and *Christ*—appear in succession. This happens especially in the book of Acts and the writings of the apostle Paul. He urged the Christians at Rome to "glorify God, even the Father of our Lord Jesus Christ" with "one mind and one mouth" (Romans 15:6).

Learn More: Acts 16:31; 20:21; 28:31 / Romans 1:7 / 1 Corinthians 1:3 / Galatians 6:14

FATHER OF SPIRITS

...be in subjection unto the Father of spirits. HEBREWS 12:9

This is one of those places in the Bible where the addition of one word makes all the difference in its meaning. Rather than "Father of spirits," the New Living Translation renders this name of God as "Father of *our* spirits" (emphasis added). This rendering makes it clear that the writer of Hebrews was contrasting physical fathers ("fathers of our flesh") with God as our Father in a spiritual sense.

Earthly fathers discipline their children, teaching them right from wrong and respect for others. God our spiritual Father teaches us to obey Him as the ultimate authority, to follow His commands, and to present our lives as living sacrifices for His honor and glory. The next verse in the New International Version says our fathers "disciplined us for a little while as they thought best; but God disciplines us for our good, in order that we may share in his holiness" (Hebrews 12:10).

Most fathers admit they are far from perfect, but the heavenly Father is an always-right, never-failing guide and provider. "In all thy ways acknowledge him," the writer of Proverbs declared, "and he shall direct thy paths" (Proverbs 3:6).

Learn More: Matthew 5:45; 6:8 / Luke 11:2 / John 6:32 / Romans 8:15

FIRSTBEGOTTEN

When he bringeth in the firstbegotten into the world... Hebrews 1:6

The word *he* in this verse refers to God the Father, and *firstbegotten* refers to His Son, Jesus Christ. But because Jesus has existed from eternity with the Father, how could He be the firstborn or "firstbegotten into the world"?

The term refers to Jesus' incarnation, or His appearance in human flesh. True, He has existed with the Father from the beginning. But there was a specific point in time when He was conceived by the Holy Spirit in Mary's womb and then born nine months later like any human infant (Luke 1:35; 2:7). This is one sense in which the title "firstbegotten" is applied to Jesus.

The word also refers to rank or order. To say that Jesus is God's firstbegotten is to declare that He ranks above all other beings except the Father Himself. This verse from Hebrews makes the point that Jesus is higher than all of God's angels, because they are told to bow down and worship Him.

As God's firstbegotten (or firstborn), Jesus is worthy of our honor and praise. The apostle Peter declared that all believers should glorify Jesus Christ, "to whom be praise and dominion for ever and ever" (1 Peter 4:11).

Learn More: Psalm 89:27 / Romans 8:29 / Colossians 1:15

FIRSTBORN FROM THE DEAD

...the firstborn from the dead. Colossians 1:18

The apostle Paul applied this name to Jesus in his description of Jesus as head of the church. "Firstborn from the dead" expresses basically the same meaning as the name "first begotten of the dead" (Revelation 1:5).

This name refers to Jesus' resurrection. But in what sense was He the "firstborn from the dead"? Jesus was not the first person in the Bible to be brought back to life following physical death. The prophet Elisha raised a boy back to life (2 Kings 4:18–37). Jesus Himself raised three people from the dead: the daughter of Jairus (Matthew 9:18–26), the son of a widow in the village of Nain (Luke 7:11–15), and His friend Lazarus (John 11:41–44).

But all these resurrections were temporary stays of death. These people eventually died again. Jesus rose from the grave, never to die again. He was the first person to overcome death and to appear in a glorified body (Luke 24:36–39). Jesus has the authority and power to provide bodily resurrection and eternal life for all who commit their lives to Him (1 Corinthians 15:12–26).

Learn More: Romans 8:29 / Colossians 1:15

FIRSTFRUITS

...the firstfruits of them that slept. 1 Corinthians 15:20

This name of Jesus occurs in the apostle Paul's famous passage about the resurrection of Jesus and His promise of a similar resurrection for all believers (1 Corinthians 15:12–57). Paul based his argument for Jesus' resurrection on the fact that He had been seen by many other believers during the days after He rose from the dead (1 Corinthians 15:3–7). He was the "firstfruits" of the resurrection, the model that had blazed the trail for others.

The Jewish people thought of the firstfruits (the first of their crops to be gathered) as God's harvest. These were presented as offerings to God on the day of the firstfruits, a part of the celebration of the festival known as Pentecost (2 Chronicles 31:5).

To Paul, Jesus through His resurrection was the firstfruits of a spiritual harvest known as eternal life. Believers were the rest of the harvest that would be gathered in at the appointed time. Just as Jesus had been raised from the dead to reign with His Father in glory, so their bodies would be "raised incorruptible" (1 Corinthians 15:52) at His second coming, and they would live with Him forever in heaven.

Learn More: Leviticus 23:10 / Proverbs 3:9 / 1 Corinthians 15:23 / Revelation 14:4

FORERUNNER

. . .the forerunner is for us entered, even Jesus. HEBREWS 6:20

A forerunner is an advance agent, the lead person on a team. He goes ahead on a scouting mission to spot possible dangers and prepare the way for others who will follow. Good examples of forerunners in the Bible are the twelve spies sent by Moses to investigate the land of Canaan (Numbers 13:1–3) and the forerunner of Jesus, John the Baptist (Mark 1:1–8).

But the ultimate forerunner, according to the author of Hebrews, was Jesus Christ Himself. He came to prepare the way so we could become citizens of God's kingdom. Following His death and resurrection, He returned to His Father in heaven (Acts 1:9). Here He has prepared a place for us. We as believers have His word that we will live there with Him forever. "If I go and prepare a place for you," He promised, "I will come again, and receive you unto myself, that where I am, there ye may be also" (John 14:3).

Learn More: Genesis 45:5–7 / Luke 1:76

FORTRESS

O Lord, my strength and my fortress. JEREMIAH 16:19

A fortress was any heavily fortified place that provided protection from enemy attacks. In Bible times, a defensive wall around a city, with reinforced towers and gates, was considered the ultimate fortress.

In this verse Jeremiah portrayed the Lord as his fortress. The prophet's unpopular message that Judah would fall to its enemies subjected him to ridicule, imprisonment, and charges of treason. At the beginning of Jeremiah's ministry, God promised that He would make him "a defenced city, and an iron pillar, and brasen walls against the whole land" (Jeremiah 1:18). The Lord had made good on His promise.

A phrase in the Bible that means basically the same thing as fortress is "strong hold." The prophet Nahum declared: "The LORD is good, a strong hold in the day of trouble; and he knoweth them that trust in him" (Nahum 1:7).

Like these two prophets, all of us need a fortress or stronghold at times. This advice from Peter can help us persevere when troubles seem to fall like the spring rain: "Cast all your anxiety on him because he cares for you" (1 Peter 5:7 NIV). See also *Strong Tower*.

Learn More: 2 Samuel 22:2 / Psalm 91:2 / Jeremiah 16:19

FOUNDATION

Other foundation can no man lay than that is laid, which is Jesus Christ. 1 CORINTHIANS 3:11

In his first letter to the believers at Corinth, the apostle Paul dealt with divisions in the church (1 Corinthians 1:10–15). The people were following four different authority figures—Paul, Apollos, Cephas, and Christ. Paul made it clear in this verse (3:11) that the one foundation on which they should be basing their faith was Jesus Christ.

Jesus Himself addressed this issue during His earthly ministry. In the parable of the two foundations, He described men who built houses on different sites (Matthew 7:24–27). The house built on sand collapsed in a storm. But the second house stood firm in violent weather because "it was founded upon a rock" (verse 25).

The message of this parable is that almost any foundation will do when the weather is good. But only a faith based on the solid foundation known as Jesus Christ can withstand the gales and floods of life.

Several centuries before Jesus was born, the prophet Isaiah looked ahead to the coming of the Messiah and referred to Him as the "sure foundation" (Isaiah 28:16).

Learn More: Job 4:19 / Psalm 16:8 / Ephesians 2:20

FOUNTAIN OF LIVING WATERS

They have forsaken me the fountain of living waters. JEREMIAH 2:13

This name of God appears in Jeremiah's prophecy in connection with the Lord's condemnation of the people of Judah for their idolatry. God found it hard to believe that they had rejected the waters of a flowing spring—or worship of the one true God. Instead they chose to drink stagnant water from a broken cistern—that is, to worship the pagan gods of surrounding nations that were untrustworthy and powerless.

This situation is not unique to Jeremiah's time. When we allow anything besides the Lord to take first place in our lives, it's like drinking contaminated water from a muddy pond. God wants only the best for us. He gives water in abundance from "the fountain of the water of life" to all who will come and drink (Revelation 21:6).

Jesus also used the imagery of refreshing water in His conversation with the woman at the well. He was the "living water" that could satisfy her spiritual thirst and bring meaning and purpose to her life (John 4:10).

Learn More: Psalm 36:9 / Jeremiah 17:13 / John 7:37–39 / Revelation 7:17

FREE SPIRIT

Uphold me with thy free spirit. PSALM 51:12

David's plea for forgiveness in Psalm 51 is one of the most eloquent prayers in the Bible. He had plotted the murder of Uriah, the husband of Bathsheba, to cover up his sin of adultery that had resulted in her pregnancy (2 Samuel 11:1–17). David's sin had separated him from God. He prayed for the restoration of this relationship ("a right spirit," Psalm 51:10) through a movement of the Holy Spirit, which he described as God's "free spirit."

The Holy Spirit is free in the sense that He is not bound by our expectations. God is sovereign; He does not have to wait for our permission before He acts in His world. Sometimes His actions take us by surprise.

For example, it took a while for the early church to realize that the gospel was meant for all people, not just the Jews. The apostle Peter's famous vision, on the roof of Simon the tanner's house, convinced him that he "should not call any man common or unclean" (Acts 10:28). This insight came to Peter from the Holy Spirit, who brought many Gentiles to saving faith in Jesus Christ.

Learn More: John 16:13 / Acts 2:1–12

FRIEND OF PUBLICANS AND SINNERS

. . .a friend of publicans and sinners. MATTHEW 11:19

The Pharisees criticized Jesus for associating with people whom they considered unworthy of God's love. But Jesus took their complaint as a compliment. He had been sent into the world to become the Savior of people like these.

In addition to befriending all sinners, Jesus was also a special friend to His disciples—the twelve ordinary men He trained to carry on the work after His earthly ministry came to an end. In Jesus' long farewell address in the Gospel of John, He told them, "Henceforth I call you not servants. . .but I have called you friends; for all things that I have heard of my Father I have made known unto you" (John 15:15).

Among the people whom we consider friends, one stands out above all others—our Lord Jesus Christ. He is the Friend who made the ultimate sacrifice on our behalf. "Greater love hath no man than this," He declared, "that a man lay down his life for his friends" (John 15:13).

Learn More: Mark 2:17 / Luke 5:30; 7:34; 15:1 / Romans 5:8 / 1 Timothy 1:15

FULLERS' SOAP

He is like a refiner's fire, and like fullers' soap. MALACHI 3:2

This verse refers to the coming Messiah. The Jewish people expected Him to be a conquering hero. But the prophet Malachi declared that He would come in judgment against the sinful nation of Israel.

A fuller made his living by washing and dyeing clothes or the cloth used to make items to wear. Soap as we know it did not exist in Bible times, so the fuller used a strong alkaline substance to get the material clean. This cleaning agent was made from a plant that was reduced to ashes to form potash or lye. The imagery of a fuller is applied to Jesus' dazzling clothes at His transfiguration. They were whiter than any "fuller on earth [could] white them" (Mark 9:3).

The prophet Jeremiah pointed out that physical soap was useless against the sins of the wayward people of Judah. "For though thou wash thee with nitre, and take thee much soap," he declared, "yet thine iniquity is marked before me, saith the Lord GOD" (Jeremiah 2:22).

The name "fullers' soap" emphasizes the judgment side of Jesus' ministry. He will return to earth in judgment against those who refuse to accept Him as Lord and Savior (2 Corinthians 5:10).

Learn More: Psalm 51:2, 7 / Isaiah 1:16; 7:3 / Mark 1:41

GIFT OF GOD

If thou knewest the gift of God. . . JOHN 4:10

Jesus spoke these words to the Samaritan woman at the well (John 4:5–26). He made it clear that He was the "gift of God" who had been sent into the world by the Father as His agent of salvation.

A gift is something a person gives to others without expecting anything in return. In spiritual terms, the element of grace should be added to this definition: God through His Son gave us a gift that we could never earn and certainly did not deserve.

Most of us have received gifts that we couldn't use or that had to be returned because they were the wrong size or color. But this is never so with God's gift of His Son. It was selected with great care, it was given in love, and we needed this gift more than anything in the world.

This familiar verse from the Gospel of John says it all: "For God so loved the world, that he gave his only begotten Son, that whosoever believeth in him should not perish, but have everlasting life" (John 3:16).

Learn More: Matthew 7:11 / Romans 6:23 / 2 Corinthians 9:15 / Ephesians 2:8

GLORY OF ISRAEL

. . .the glory of thy people Israel. LUKE 2:32

These verses are part of the prayer of Simeon when he recognized the infant Jesus as Messiah in the temple. Simeon realized that Jesus would grow up to become not only a light to the Gentiles but the glory of Israel as well.

As God's chosen people, the nation of Israel was commissioned to lead other nations to come to know Him as the one true God. Jesus was born into the world as a Jew and a native of Israel. In this sense, He was the glory of Israel, showing that God had not given up on His promise to bless the entire world through Abraham and his descendants (Genesis 12:1–3).

The tragedy is that Jesus was not accepted by many of His own people. They expected a Messiah who would restore Israel to its golden days as a political power. But God's purpose was not thwarted by their rejection. The glory of one nation, Israel, went on to become a light to the Gentiles, as Simeon predicted. At His return he will become the glorified One among all the peoples of the world (Philippians 2:11).

Learn More: Psalm 29:3 / Acts 7:2 / Colossians 1:27

And Thomas answered and said unto him, My Lord and my God. John 20:28

This verse from the Gospel of John describe an appearance of Jesus to His disciples after the resurrection. Jesus had revealed Himself to them once before, at a time when Thomas was not present. Thomas had declared that he would not believe Jesus was alive unless he could see Him with his own eyes.

When Thomas finally saw the Lord, he not only believed the resurrection—he acknowledged Jesus as God in the flesh. This is one of the clearest statements in all the New Testament of the divinity of Jesus and His oneness with God the Father.

Thomas, like all the other disciples, had lived and worked with Jesus for about three years. They had seen His miracles and heard His teachings. They had observed firsthand that Jesus had the power and authority to forgive sin. But they were slow to understand that Jesus was actually God come to earth in human form.

As the God-man, Jesus is both the all-powerful deity for whom nothing is impossible and the man of sorrows who can sympathize with us in our human weakness. He is the all-sufficient Savior.

Learn More: Matthew 9:2 / John 1:1; 10:30; 14:9 / 1 Timothy 3:16

GOD OF ABRAHAM, ISAAC, AND JACOB ──────────────────

. . .the God of Abraham, the God of Isaac, and the God of Jacob. Exodus 3:15

God used this name for Himself when He called Moses to lead the Israelites out of slavery in Egypt. The Lord assured Moses that He had promised the land of Canaan to Abraham and his descendants many years before. God had not changed; He was the same God who would finally lead the Israelites to take the land and make it their own.

This promise had been renewed with Abraham's son Isaac, and then renewed again with Isaac's son Jacob. In Moses' time this promise had been all but forgotten. The Israelites had been in Egypt for more than four hundred years, suffering as slaves for part of that time (Exodus 12:40).

The message of this divine name is that God keeps His promises. Their fulfillment may take a while, but He will make good on what He is determined to do for His people.

Learn More: Exodus 3:6 / Matthew 22:32 / Acts 3:13

GOD OF ALL COMFORT ──────────────────────────────

. . .the God of all comfort. 2 Corinthians 1:3

The context of this verse makes it clear that the apostle Paul—when he spoke of the Lord as the "God of all comfort"—was thinking of the sufferings that believers endure We as Christians are often ridiculed by the world for our beliefs and the stands we take. But our persecution should not lead us to despair. God's comforting presence enables us to remain joyful and optimistic in spite of our pain (James 1:2).

Jesus described the Holy Spirit as a Comforter who would strengthen the disciples after He was no longer with them in the flesh (John 14:16–26). "And I will pray the Father, and he shall give you another Comforter," Jesus promised, "that he may abide with you for ever" (John 14:16).

Because we know and feel God's presence, we are expected to serve as agents of God's comfort in the lives of others. The apostle Paul declared that we should "comfort them which are in any trouble, by the comfort wherewith we ourselves are comforted of God" (2 Corinthians 1:4).

Learn More: Psalm 23:4; 119:76 / Isaiah 12:1; 49:13; 61:2 / Zechariah 1:17

GOD OF GODS

Your God is a God of gods, and a Lord of kings. Daniel 2:47

King Nebuchadnezzar of Babylon had a disturbing dream about a huge statue. None of his pagan wizards could interpret the dream. But the prophet Daniel told the king what the dream meant after declaring that it would be revealed to him by the one true God.

This pagan king was so impressed by this interpretation of his dream that he declared Daniel's God to be the "God of gods"—or the God above all the other deities in the kingdom of Babylon. This was a shocking admission, since the Babylonians had a god for every need and purpose—war, fertility, science, literature, and so on. This type of worship—known as polytheism, or belief in many deities—was typical of all the pagan nations during Bible times.

As Christians, we know that the one true God is capable of mighty acts. But like King Nebuchadnezzar, sometimes even we are overwhelmed with His awesome deeds.

Two other divine names that express the superiority of the Lord to all false gods are "King of kings" and "Lord of lords" (Revelation 17:14).

Learn More: Joshua 22:22 / Psalm 136:2 / Daniel 11:36

GOD OF HEAVEN

. . and prayed before the God of heaven. Nehemiah 1:4

This verse describes Nehemiah's reaction when he heard disturbing news about the Jewish exiles who had gone back to their homeland. The Persian king had allowed them to return to rebuild the city of Jerusalem. But the work was at a standstill, and the Jews were being persecuted by their enemies.

Nehemiah's name for God in this verse appears multiple times in his book (Nehemiah 1:5; 2:4, 20) as well as the book of Ezra (Ezra 5:12; 6:9–10; 7:21, 23). These two books describe the bleak conditions of God's people after the exile. They had lived for several decades as captives of the pagan nations of Babylon and Persia. They had to start life all over again when they were finally allowed to return to their homeland.

Perhaps the Israelites had a hard time seeing God at work among them during these turbulent times. But Ezra and Nehemiah assured them that God was still in His heaven and had not forsaken His people. We as believers have this same assurance.

Learn More: Genesis 24:3 / 2 Chronicles 36:23 / Psalm 136:26 / Jonah 1:9

GOD OF MY SALVATION

I will joy in the God of my salvation. Habakkuk 3:18

This passage from the little-known prophet Habakkuk is one of the most beautiful in the Bible. It is filled with agricultural imagery from the prophet's time, including crop failures and the loss of livestock. But Habakkuk's faith allowed him to see beyond the troubles of the moment to the deeper reality that the God of his salvation was in charge. He would not let the prophet down.

Rephrased in modern terms, Habakkuk's sentiments might read something like this: "Although the grocery money is gone, energy prices are going through the ceiling, our mortgage payment just jumped by four hundred dollars a month, and I don't know where the next meal is coming from, I will rejoice in the Lord and continue to trust in the God of my salvation."

Learn More: Exodus 15:2 / Job 13:16 / Micah 7:7

GOD OF PEACE

The God of peace, that brought again from the dead our Lord Jesus... Hebrews 13:20

The author of the epistle to the Hebrews brought his book to a close with a request for the blessings of "the God of peace" to rest upon His people. This is one of the most beautiful benedictions in the Bible.

Some people think of peace as the absence of conflict. But peace, according to the New Testament, is the inner tranquility of those who have placed their trust in Jesus Christ and have been reconciled to God because their sins have been forgiven.

The Lord is the God of peace because He sent His own Son to allow us to experience this sense of well-being. This is how the apostle Paul expressed it: "Therefore being justified by faith, we have peace with God through our Lord Jesus Christ" (Romans 5:1).

Learn More: Romans 15:33; 16:20 / Philippians 4:9

GOD OF THE WHOLE EARTH

The God of the whole earth shall he be called. Isaiah 54:5

This name of God from the prophet Isaiah emphasizes the Lord's unlimited jurisdiction. There is no place on earth where His authority is limited. This idea is the opposite of the view of most pagan nations of Bible times, which believed their gods were local or regional in scope. These deities existed to serve certain people's needs and protect them from their enemies, so their authority as gods did not extend beyond national borders.

This is why the Syrian military commander Naaman, after he was healed by the prophet Elisha in Israelite territory, wanted to carry dirt from Israel back to his own country (2 Kings 5:17). Naaman thought this miracle-working God was a regional deity whose power he could transfer to his own people.

The Lord's presence doesn't have to be carried back and forth from one country to another. He already exists in every place, as the supreme God over all the world. The psalmist declared, "The earth is the Lord's, and the fulness thereof; the world, and they that dwell therein" (Psalm 24:1).

Learn More: Genesis 14:19; 18:25 / Joshua 3:13 / Psalm 47:2 / Micah 4:3

GOD WHO SEES

Thou God seest me. Genesis 16:13

Sarah's servant, Hagar, called God by this name when the angel of the Lord appeared to her in the wilderness. After conceiving a child by Abraham, Hagar had been driven away by Sarah, Abraham's wife. The Lord assured Hagar that He was aware of her plight, and He would bless her and others through the life of her unborn child.

After Hagar gave birth, she named the boy Ishmael, meaning "God hears." Her experience shows that the Lord is not a distant and detached God who refuses to get involved in our lives. He sees our needs, hears our prayers, and comes to our aid in times of trouble.

The Bible speaks often of the Lord as the all-seeing One who knows what is going on in His world and who keeps watch over His people. The psalmist declared, "The eyes of the Lord are upon the righteous, and his ears are open unto their cry" (Psalm 34:15).

Learn More: 2 Chronicles 16:9 / Proverbs 15:3 / Jeremiah 7:11 / Amos 9:8 / 1 Peter 3:12

GOOD MASTER

Good Master, what shall I do that I may inherit eternal life? Mark 10:17

This account of Jesus' encounter with a man seeking eternal life appears in the three Synoptic Gospels: Matthew tells us he was young (Matthew 19:22); Mark reveals that he was rich (Mark 10:22); Luke adds that he was a ruler (Luke 18:18). Thus, he is known as the "rich young ruler."

This young man called Jesus "Good Master" and bowed before Him. He respected Jesus and recognized Him as a teacher of authority. But Jesus corrected him for calling Him "good." "There is none good but one," He replied, "that is, God" (Mark 10:18).

Why did Jesus resist this name? Perhaps He saw "good" as meaningless flattery. Or this may have been His way of testing the young man's commitment to God the Father, who held the keys to eternal life—the very thing he was seeking. The rich young ruler wanted to know what he could *do* to have eternal life. Jesus made it clear that this is a gift that God bestows on those who follow His commands.

This young man was more committed to his riches than he was to following the Lord. Tragically, this kept him from finding what he was searching for.

Learn More: Matthew 8:19 / Mark 9:5 / Luke 8:24

GOOD SHEPHERD

I am the good shepherd. John 10:11

This verse is part of a long monologue of Jesus in which He compares His followers to sheep and identifies Himself as the Shepherd who leads His flock (John 10:1–16).

In the Old Testament, God is also known by the name "shepherd" (Psalm 23:1). Sheep were helpless animals that had no natural defenses against predators such as wolves and lions. Unless they were watched constantly, sheep would wander away from the flock and find themselves in danger. They had to be led from one area to another to find new sources of food and water. Sheep needed a vigilant leader—a shepherd—to provide all these resources.

But Jesus is more than just another shepherd. He is the "*good* shepherd." He deliberately set Himself apart from the religious leaders of Israel—the scribes and Pharisees—who were leading people astray. They were like "hirelings" (John 10:12), hired hands who were paid to do a job but had no personal interest in the sheep they were leading. Jesus loved His sheep—that includes you and me—and He eventually gave His life for our salvation.

Learn More: John 10:7 / Hebrews 13:20 / 1 Peter 2:25; 5:4

GOOD SPIRIT

Thou gavest also thy good spirit to instruct them. Nehemiah 9:20

This verse describes the provision of God for the Israelites in the wilderness after their release from slavery in Egypt. These words were spoken in Nehemiah's time by Levites who led the people to renew the covenant with God the Father. They described the Holy Spirit as God's "good spirit."

Because the very essence of God is goodness, He showered His people with goodness during the perilous years of wandering in the wilderness. He led them by His presence in a cloud and fire, encouraged them with His promise of a land of their own, and gave them instructions for life in the laws He delivered to Moses. Through His "good spirit," God provided many good things for His people.

The Lord is still the God of goodness who provides abundantly for believers through His Spirit. He expects us to exemplify this spirit of goodness to others. The apostle Paul told the believers at Rome that he was "persuaded of you, my brethren, that ye also are full of goodness, filled with all knowledge, able also to admonish one another" (Romans 15:14).

Learn More: John 16:13 / Romans 8:11 / Galatians 5:22

GOVERNOR

Out of thee shall come a Governor, that shall rule my people Israel. MATTHEW 2:6

The world into which Jesus was born knew all about governors, or rulers. These officials were agents set over the provinces—territories similar to states—into which the Roman government had divided its empire. A provincial governor was responsible for collecting taxes for the Roman treasury, keeping the peace, and administering the rule of Rome. Three Roman governors are mentioned in the New Testament: Cyrenius (Luke 2:2), Pontius Pilate (Matthew 27:2), and Felix (Acts 23:24).

But Jesus is a Governor of a different type. He was sent as a spiritual ruler to guide and direct His people in the ways of the Lord. He rules by love and not by force. As believers, our lives should reflect more of His rule every day as we grow in our commitment to Him and His teachings.

Governors of states and nations come and go, but Jesus' rule over His followers is eternal. As the prophet Isaiah declared, "Of the increase of his government and peace there shall be no end" (Isaiah 9:7).

Learn More: Isaiah 40:10; 55:4 / Micah 5:2

GREAT HIGH PRIEST

We have a great high priest, that is passed into the heavens. HEBREWS 4:14

Priests of the Bible offered various types of sacrifices on behalf of the people to atone for their sins. This name of Jesus from the book of Hebrews reflects this priestly imagery of the Jewish religious system.

At the top of the priestly hierarchy stood the high priest. His job was to see that all the functions of the priesthood were carried out appropriately (2 Chronicles 19:11). Below him were other priests who performed sacrificial rituals at the altar. On the lower end of the priesthood were the Levites, who performed menial jobs as assistants to the priests.

The writer of Hebrews adds another level to this priestly hierarchy by referring to Jesus as the "great high priest." He stands above even the high priest of Israel because He laid down His own life as the perfect sacrifice for sin.

In modern terms, a priest is a religious leader who intercedes between God and man on behalf of sinful people. As believers, we need no human intermediary to represent us before God. We can come directly into His presence through "one mediator between God and men, the man Christ Jesus" (1 Timothy 2:5). See also *High Priest after the Order of Melchisedec.*

Learn More: Hebrews 2:17; 3:1; 6:20; 7:17

GREAT PROPHET

A great prophet is risen up among us. LUKE 7:16

This verse describes the reaction of the people of Nain when Jesus raised the son of a widow from the dead. Perhaps they were comparing Jesus to Elijah, the famous prophet of Old Testament times, who also brought back from the dead the son of a poor widow (1 Kings 17:17–24).

The classic definition of a prophet in the Jewish tradition is that he should declare God's message to the people and he should foretell the future. Jesus fit this definition perfectly. He was the ultimate Prophet in a long line of prophets whom God had sent to His people, the Israelites, across many centuries.

A true prophet must be committed to declaring God's truth, no matter how his message is received. He accepts the fact that he will never be the most popular person in town. It was no different with Jesus. Some of the saddest words He ever uttered were spoken after He was rejected by the people of His own hometown: "A prophet is not without honour, save in his own country, and in his own house" (Matthew 13:57).

Learn More: Matthew 21:11 / Luke 24:19 / John 6:14

GUIDE UNTO DEATH

He will be our guide even unto death. PSALM 48:14

The unknown author of this psalm made the same declaration that King David did when he wrote the Twenty-third Psalm. God will abide with us and continue to lead us, even through the experience of death itself. As David expressed it, "Yea, though I walk through the valley of the shadow of death, I will fear no evil: for thou art with me" (Psalm 23:4).

A guide is a person who can lead us safely on a trip or an adventure because he knows the best path to follow. He can help us avoid any obstacles on the way to our destination. With the Lord as our guide, we don't have to fear death. He will take us to dwell in glory with Him when our days on earth come to an end.

The prophet Jeremiah spoke of God as "the guide of my youth" (Jeremiah 3:4). It is comforting to know that whether our life is just beginning or coming to an end, we can trust God as our never-failing guide.

Learn More: Job 30:23 / Psalm 119:105 / Romans 8:38–39 / 1 Corinthians 15:55 / Revelation 21:4

HEAD OF ALL PRINCIPALITY AND POWER

. . .complete in him, which is the head of all principality and power. COLOSSIANS 2:10

In this verse the apostle Paul dealt with a false teaching in the church at Colossae. Some members of this congregation were claiming that Jesus was a member of an order of angels, thus a created being like all other things made by God. Paul declared that Jesus was actually the "head of all principality and power," or a non-created being who was above all heavenly beings, with the exception of God Himself. And even in His relationship to God, Jesus reflected "all the fulness of the Godhead."

Just as Jesus is supreme in the heavens, He also exercises dominion over all the earth. As the apostle Paul expressed it, "For by him were all things created, that are in heaven, and that are in earth, visible and invisible, whether they be thrones, or dominions, or principalities, or powers: all things were created by him, and for him" (Colossians 1:16). This truth should drive us to our knees in worship and praise.

Learn More: Ephesians 1:21–22 / Revelation 17:14

HEAD OF THE CHURCH

Christ is the head of the church. EPHESIANS 5:23

The word *disciple* means "learner"—and that's exactly what Jesus' disciples were. They learned from Jesus—who He was, about the mission on which He had been sent, and of God's love for all people. Jesus trained these ordinary men to carry on His work through the church He brought into being.

On one occasion Jesus told Peter, "Upon this rock I will build my church" (Matthew 16:18). Peter had just declared his belief that Jesus was the long-awaited Messiah and "the Son of the living God" (Matthew 16:16). Jesus was saying that His church would be built on confessions of faith just like the one Peter had made. The church would consist of people who accepted Jesus as Savior and Lord and committed themselves to His work of redemption in the world.

Jesus is the "head of the church," and we as believers make up the body. A body without a head is useless, but a body joined to a head becomes a living, breathing, working organism. The church is still the key element in Jesus' strategy to bring the world into God's kingdom.

Learn More: Ephesians 1:22; 5:24 / Colossians 1:18

HEAD OF THE CORNER

The stone which the builders rejected, the same is become the head of the corner. MATTHEW 21:42

Jesus directed these words to the religious leaders who were questioning His authority. He quoted Psalm 118:22–23, an Old Testament passage that they probably knew well. His point was that He, as the Messiah, was destined to be rejected by them.

But Jesus, the rejected stone, would become the centerpiece of a new building that would include all people who accepted Him as Savior and Lord. This building would be the church, a fresh, new organism that would be born out of the ashes of the old religious order based on the Jewish law.

The apostle Peter also referenced this same verse from the Psalms (1 Peter 2:7). Peter went on to say that Jesus, the rejected stone, was also "a stone of stumbling, and a rock of offence" (1 Peter 2:8) to those people who thought the Messiah would be a political and military leader. It was unthinkable to them that He would come as a spiritual deliverer who would suffer and die on the cross.

Learn More: Isaiah 28:16 / Mark 12:10 / Luke 20:17 / Acts 4:11 / Ephesians 2:19–20

HEIR OF ALL THINGS

. . .his Son, whom he hath appointed heir of all things. HEBREWS 1:2

The dictionary defines an heir as "one who receives some endowment or quality from a parent or predecessor." Many heirs receive only a portion of the property or cash that their parents have accumulated during a lifetime. But the writer of Hebrews declared that Jesus was the "heir of all things," and these were granted to Him by none other than God the Father.

The heirship of Jesus is both material and spiritual. He participated with God in the creation of the world (John 1:3), so God has granted Jesus dominion over the universe. In the spiritual sense, He sets the terms by which all people will be judged for their sins. Then He Himself became the means by which people could be made righteous in God's sight. This was accomplished through His death on the cross.

The great thing about Jesus' spiritual heirship is that He shares His inheritance with us. As the apostle Paul expressed it, we are "joint-heirs with Christ" (Romans 8:17) because He lives eternally with the Father and He has made it possible for us to enjoy eternal life with Him.

Learn More: Galatians 3:29; 4:7 / Titus 3:7 / James 2:5

HIDING PLACE

Thou art my hiding place. PSALM 32:7

This name of God appears in a psalm attributed to David, king of Israel. During his early years, he had to flee for his life because the jealous King Saul was trying to kill him. Once David hid in a cave, and he later wrote about this experience in one of his psalms (1 Samuel 22:1; Psalm 142 title).

The problem with a physical hiding place is that it can't last forever. David eventually had to come out of his cave for food and water. But he found the Lord to be his ultimate "hiding place." He kept David safe until Saul was killed in a battle with the Philistines and David became the unchallenged king of the nation of Israel.

There's no safer place for any of us to be than under the protective hand of a loving, benevolent God. As the psalmist expressed it, "I will both lay me down in peace, and sleep: for thou, LORD, only makest me dwell in safety" (Psalm 4:8).

Learn More: Psalm 17:8; 27:5; 143:9 / Proverbs 29:25

HIGH PRIEST AFTER THE ORDER OF MELCHISEDEC

...an high priest after the order of Melchisedec. HEBREWS 5:10

This name refers to one of the most mysterious personalities of the Bible. Melchisedec was the king of Salem—an ancient name for Jerusalem—and a priest of the Most High God. He appeared to Abraham after the patriarch had defeated several kings who had carried his nephew Lot away as a captive.

When Abraham returned from battle with the spoils of war, Melchisedec blessed him and provided food for him and his hungry men. In return, Abraham presented Melchisedec with a tithe—one-tenth of the booty they had taken (Genesis 14:12–20).

The author of Hebrews called Jesus a "high priest after the Order of Melchisedec" because Melchisedec did not become a priest by virtue of his birth. He was not a descendant of Aaron, the first high priest of Israel through whose family line all succeeding priests of Israel emerged.

Just like Melchisedec, Jesus did not inherit His priestly responsibilities. He was appointed to this role by God the Father. His priesthood has no beginning or end, so it is superior to the inherited priesthood and the sacrificial system of the Old Testament (Hebrews 7:23–24). See also *Great High Priest*.

Learn More: Hebrews 2:17; 3:1; 6:20; 7:17

HOLY ONE

I am the Lord, your Holy One. ISAIAH 43:15

This divine name is one of the few in the Bible that is applied to all three persons of the Trinity—Father (Isaiah 43:15), Son (Acts 3:14), and Holy Spirit (1 John 2:20). Holiness xpresses the idea of separation. The Lord exists on a different level than all earthly things—He is perfect in His moral excellence, unlike sinful people.

The apostle Peter called Jesus "the Holy One" to contrast the righteousness of Jesus with the unrighteousness of Barabbas, a criminal whom the crowd released instead of Jesus on the day of His crucifixion (Acts 13:4). Jesus is also the Holy One because He resisted sin through His close relationship with God the Father.

The apostle John declared that one role of the Holy Spirit as the Holy One was to keep believers from erroneous thinking about the nature of Jesus. Some false teachers in John's time were claiming that Jesus was the divine Son of God but denying that He had come to earth in human form. The Holy Spirit filled believers with the truth about Jesus (1 John 2:20).

We as believers will never achieve complete holiness in this life. We will always struggle with temptation and our sinful nature. But we ought to be growing more and more like Jesus in this dimension of the Christian life.

Learn More: Isaiah 12:6; 29:23; 60:9

HOLY SPIRIT OF GOD

Grieve not the holy Spirit of God. EPHESIANS 4:30

These words from the apostle Paul to the believers at Ephesus emphasize several important truths about the Holy Spirit.

The Holy Spirit can be grieved or pained by the sinful actions of believers. This shows that the Holy Spirit is not a vague force but a person. Only a person can experience emotions like grief and sorrow; thus, the Spirit is not an "it" but a "He." He is as much a person as God the Father and Jesus the Son.

This verse also emphasizes the "sealing" work of the Holy Spirit. A seal symbolizes ownership and security. The seal of the Holy Spirit marks believers as God's property until the day of our final redemption in the end time (Romans 8:23).

If some actions by believers grieve the Holy Spirit, it follows that certain acts and attitudes bring Him joy and pleasure. These include the fruits of the Spirit in the apostle Paul's famous list in Galatians 5:22–23.

Learn More: Psalm 51:11 / Luke 11:13 / John 14:26 / 1 Thessalonians 4:8

HOPE OF GLORY

Christ in you, the hope of glory. COLOSSIANS 1:27

The apostle Paul is known as the "apostle to the Gentiles," but he could also be called the "apostle of hope." His writings abound with the theme of the hope that believers have in the promises of Jesus Christ.

In this verse from his letter to the Colossian believers, Paul called Jesus the "hope of glory." If we know Christ as our Savior and Lord, we are assured that we will live with Him in His full glory when we reach our heavenly home.

The writer of Hebrews described our hope in Jesus as an "anchor of the soul" (Hebrews 6:19). He is the great stabilizing force that helps us live victoriously in spite of the difficulties and problems of life.

To hope in something is to look forward to its fulfillment with confident expectation. Notice that Paul said in this verse that "Christ in you" is our hope of glory. With Jesus as a constant presence in our lives, we are as certain of heaven as if we were already there.

Learn More: Romans 15:13 / Colossians 1:23 / Titus 3:7

HORN OF MY SALVATION

. . .the horn of my salvation. PSALM 18:2

David wrote this psalm to express his praise to God for saving him from "all his enemies, and from the hand of Saul" (Psalm 18 title). In Bible times the horn of an animal was a symbol of strength. To lift one's horn in arrogance like an ox was to show pride and power (Psalm 75:4–5). Thus, God had been a "horn of salvation" on David's behalf by delivering him from those who were trying to kill him.

This imagery from the Old Testament was picked up in the New Testament and applied to Jesus in a spiritual sense. Zacharias, the father of John the Baptist, declared that God through His Son had "raised up an horn of salvation for us in the house of his servant David" (Luke 1:69).

This verse is part of the song of praise known as the "Benedictus" that Zacharias sang at the birth of his son John, the forerunner of Jesus (Luke 1:67–79). Zacharias stated that Jesus was the king of salvation from the kingly line of David. The horn imagery as applied to Jesus declared that He would be a powerful Savior.

Learn More: Exodus 15:2 / 2 Samuel 22:3 / Job 13:16 / Micah 7:7

HUSBAND

I was an husband unto them, saith the Lord. JEREMIAH 31:31–32

This name of God appears in the prophet Jeremiah's description of the new covenant that God will make with His people. The Lord had led the Israelites out of Egypt and through the wilderness like a loving husband takes care of his wife. But He would provide even more abundantly for His people by sending the Messiah, who would save them from their sins.

The imagery of God as a husband appears in only one other place in the Bible. The prophet Isaiah told the people of Israel: "Thy Maker is thine husband; the LORD of hosts is his name" (Isaiah 54:5).

The role of a husband involves more than providing for the physical needs of his family. He should also be an encourager, a listener, an emotional support, and a protector for his wife and children. God as a loving husband provides all of these things in abundance for His people.

Learn More: 2 Corinthians 11:2 / Revelation 21:2

I AM

Before Abraham was, I am. John 8:58

This name that Jesus called Himself is the equivalent of the name with which God identified Himself to Moses at the burning bush. Just like the great "I Am" of the Old Testament, Jesus was claiming to be eternal, timeless, and unchanging. He had always been and He would always be. In other words, He was of the same divine essence as God the Father.

This claim of divinity was blasphemy to the Jewish religious leaders, so they picked up stones to execute Him—the penalty for such a crime spelled out in the Old Testament law (Leviticus 24:16). But Jesus' escape proved the claim He was making. He easily avoided their death threat as He slipped miraculously "through the midst of them." Only when the time was right in accordance with God's plan would He allow Himself to be captured and crucified.

Other "I Am" statements of Jesus appear throughout John's Gospel (see Learn More passages below).

Learn More: John 6:35; 8:12; 10:7, 11, 36; 11:25; 14:6; 15:1

I AM THAT I AM

And God said unto Moses, I Am That I Am. Exodus 3:14

When God appeared in the burning bush, Moses wanted to know who was sending him back to Egypt to lead the Israelites out of slavery. Moses may have been puzzled by the Lord's reply that "I Am That I Am" was behind this plan.

This name for God is a form of the verb "to be" in the Hebrew language. It expresses God's self-existence and the unchangeable nature of His character. He transcends the past, the present, and the future. We might express the meaning of this name like this: He has always been in the past, He is in the present, and He will always be in the future.

This is the only place in the Bible where this name appears. But Jehovah or Yahweh, generally rendered as "Lord," is a closely related name that also comes from the Hebrew form of "to be." This name appears hundreds of times throughout the Old Testament. In most translations of the Bible, it appears with a large capital "L" and smaller capital letters like this: Lord.

Learn More: Deuteronomy 33:27 / Psalm 90:2 / 1 Timothy 1:17

IMMANUEL / EMMANUEL

. . .and shall call his name Immanuel. Isaiah 7:14

This prophecy from Isaiah was fulfilled with the birth of Jesus (Matthew 1:22–23). The name, meaning "God with us," was given to Jesus even before He was born by an angel who appeared to Joseph. He needed divine assurance that Mary's pregnancy was an act of the Holy Spirit and that he should proceed to take her as his wife.

The promise of God's presence among His people goes back to Old Testament times. For example, He assured Moses of His presence (Exodus 3:12) when giving him the task to free the Israelites from their slavery in Egypt. King David declared that God's presence would follow him wherever he went (Psalm 139:9–10).

These promises reach their peak in God's Son, Jesus Christ. He came to earth in the form of the God-man to show that God is for us in our weak, sinful, and helpless condition. As man, He understands our temptations and shortcomings. As God, He can meet all these needs through His love and grace.

Just as Matthew's Gospel begins with the affirmation that God is with us, so it ends with Jesus' promise of His abiding presence: "Lo, I am with you always, even unto the end of the world" (Matthew 28:20).

Learn More: Exodus 33:14 / Psalm 139:7 / John 14:18 / Romans 8:35 / Hebrews 13:5

JEHOVAH

By my name Jehovah was I not known to them. Exodus 6:3

With these words the Lord reassured Moses that He would stand with him and give him the strength and power to lead the Israelites out of Egyptian slavery. He had already given Moses this promise at the burning bush (Exodus 3:2, 12). But Moses needed encouragement after Pharaoh rejected his first request to release the Israelites.

God declared to Moses that He was prepared to perform miracles for His people, things they had never seen before. As Jehovah, He was the infinite and self-existent God who caused everything to happen and to whom all things must eventually be traced. He would not fail in His determination to bring freedom to His people.

In his messages to the wayward people of Judah, the prophet Isaiah declared, "Trust ye in the LORD for ever: for in the LORD JEHOVAH is everlasting strength (Isaiah 26:4).

Learn More: Psalm 83:18 / Isaiah 12:2

JEHOVAH-JIREH

Abraham called the name of that place Jehovahjireh. Genesis 22:14

Abraham called God by this name and assigned it to the site where he was told to sacrifice his son, Isaac, as a burnt offering to the Lord. This was God's way of testing Abraham's faith and obedience.

When Abraham raised a knife to take Isaac's life, God stopped him. Then Abraham noticed a ram that had been trapped in a nearby thicket. He offered this ram as a sacrifice instead of Isaac. It was clear to him that God had provided a sacrificial animal for this purpose—thus the name *Jehovahjireh*, or "The Lord Will Provide" as rendered by modern translations.

God still delights in providing for His people. Jesus assured us of this in His sermon on the mount. "Behold the fowls of the air," He declared, "for they sow not, neither do they reap, nor gather into barns; yet your heavenly Father feedeth them. Are ye not much better than they" (Matthew 6:26).

Learn More: Psalm 37:4 / Matthew 6:8 / Philippians 4:19

JEHOVAH-NISSI

Moses built an altar, and called the name of it Jehovahnissi. Exodus 17:15

Moses gave this name to an altar that he built in the wilderness near Rephidim. The altar memorialized an Israelite victory over the Amalekites because of God's miraculous intervention on their behalf. Most modern translations render these two Hebrew words as "The LORD Is My Banner."

In Bible times, armies fought under a banner or battle flag that identified their tribe or nation. "Jehovah-nissi" was Moses' way of saying that the Israelites in the wilderness did not need such a flag. The Lord was the banner under which they fought, and He had given the victory.

When the Israelites entered the land of Canaan, the Lord gave them many victories, beginning with the capture of Jericho. They conquered this fortified city without firing a single arrow because the Lord caused the defensive walls to collapse (Joshua 6:20).

In a messianic passage in his book, the prophet Isaiah looked forward to the coming of the Messiah, whom he described as an "ensign," or battle flag (Isaiah 11:10).

Learn More: Psalm 20:5 / Song of Solomon 2:4 / Isaiah 5:26

JEHOVAH-SHALOM

Gideon built an altar there unto the Lord, and called it Jehovahshalom. JUDGES 6:24

Gideon was given the task of delivering God's people from Midianite raiders who were destroying their crops and stealing their livestock. The Lord assured Gideon of His presence and guidance by burning up a sacrificial offering that Gideon placed on an altar.

This display frightened Gideon. But God showed that His intentions were peaceful and that Gideon had nothing to fear. With this assurance, Gideon gave God a special name, *ehovahshalom*—translated as "The Lord Is Peace" by modern translations—and also applied this name to the altar he had built.

"Peace to you and your house" was a common greeting of Bible times, just as we greet people today with "Good morning" or "How are you?" With this divine name, Gideon expressed his confidence that God intended to bless him and to strengthen him for the task to which he had been called.

God extends this same promise to His people today. The psalmist declared, "The LORD will give strength unto his people; the LORD will bless his people with peace" (Psalm 29:11).

Learn More: Isaiah 9:6 / Romans 15:33 / Hebrews 13:20

JESUS

His name was called Jesus. LUKE 2:21

Jewish custom dictated that a male child be circumcised and named on the eighth day after he was born. Mary and Joseph followed this custom with Jesus. They had been told by an angel even before the birth that His name would be Jesus. They followed the angel's instruction by giving Him this name.

The name *Jesus* is the equivalent of the Old Testament name rendered variously as Jehoshua (Numbers 13:16), Jeshua (Ezra 2:2), and Joshua (Exodus 17:9). It means "Jehovah (or Yahweh) Is Salvation." Thus Jesus' personal name indicated from the very beginning that He was to be God's agent of salvation in a dark and sinful world.

When the Lord was born, *Jesus* was actually a common name among the Jewish people, similar to "John" or "Robert" in our society. But His life and ministry have made the name a synonym for self-giving love. In the words of the apostle Paul, it is the "name which is above every name" (Philippians 2:9).

Learn More: Matthew 1:21, 25 / Luke 1:31

JUDGE OF ALL THE EARTH

Shall not the Judge of all the earth do right? GENESIS 18:25

Abraham called the Lord by this name when they discussed God's decision to destroy the city of Sodom. The residents of this city, along with Gomorrah, had grown so wicked that God was determined to wipe them from the face of the earth. Abraham believed that God was just in all His actions. Surely "the Judge of all the earth" would not destroy the righteous people of Sodom along with the wicked.

God did follow through on His plan to destroy the city. But He sent an angel to warn the only righteous people in Sodom—Lot and his family—to flee before the judgment fell (Genesis 19:1, 15–17). This proved that the Lord is fair and equitable in His dispensing of justice in this world. The psalmist declared, "Justice and judgment are the habitation of thy throne: mercy and truth shall go before thy face" (Psalm 89:14).

Learn More: 1 Chronicles 16:33 / Psalm 94:2 / Hebrews 12:23

JUDGE OF QUICK AND DEAD

. . .ordained of God to be the Judge of quick and dead. ACTS 10:42

This name of Jesus appears in a sermon that the apostle Peter preached to the Roman centurion Cornelius (Acts 10:25–43). Peter declared that Jesus had been appointed by God the Father as the supreme Judge of all things—the living ("quick") and the dead.

God's activity as Judge is one of the key themes of the Old Testament. But after God sent Jesus into the world, He established a new way of rendering judgment. Jesus is now the agent through whom divine judgment is handed down (John 5:22).

As the divine Judge, Jesus is the great dividing line in history. At the "great white throne" judgment in the end times, those who have refused to accept Him as Savior and Lord will be consigned to eternal separation from God (Revelation 20:11–15). Believers will escape this judgment because they have accepted the sacrifice that Jesus has made on their behalf.

Christians will be subjected to an evaluation known as the "judgment seat of Christ." The service they have rendered for Jesus Christ will be judged and rewarded accordingly. This principle of accountability should motivate us to loyal service in His name.

Learn More: Romans 4:17; 6:11; 8:11 / 2 Timothy 4:8

JUST MAN

Have thou nothing to do with that just man. MATTHEW 27:19

Pontius Pilate, the Roman governor who condemned Jesus to death, received this message from his wife while Jesus was on trial. It had been revealed to her in a dream that Jesus was innocent of the charges against Him, so she tried to get Pilate to release Him.

Pilate also knew that Jesus was not guilty, but he caved in to political pressure from the Jewish religious leaders and pronounced the death penalty against Him. The governor washed his own hands before the crowd and declared, "I am innocent of the blood of this just person" (Matthew 27:24).

The word *just* as applied to Jesus by Pilate and his wife means "innocent." Jesus, the sinless and righteous One, was not guilty of any crime or wrongdoing. This makes His death on our behalf all the more meaningful. He willingly laid down His life on the cross as the sacrifice for our sin.

Learn More: Luke 23:47 / Acts 3:14; 7:52; 22:14

KEEPER

The Lord is thy keeper. PSALM 121:5

This is the only place in the Bible where God is referred to as our "keeper." This name refers to His protection, provision, and watchfulness. The New International Version renders the meaning of the name as "the LORD watches over you."

No matter where we are or what we are doing, God has His watchful eye on us. This can be either comforting or disturbing. As the writer of Proverbs said, "The eyes of the LORD are in every place, beholding the evil and the good" (Proverbs 15:3).

Just as God promises to keep us in His care, so we as believers are instructed to stay close to Him and keep His commandments. Psalm 119, the longest chapter in the Bible, pays tribute to God's written Word. It is filled with vows from the psalmist to stay true to God's commands in the Bible. "Give me understanding, and I shall keep thy law," he declared. "Yea, I shall observe it with my whole heart" (Psalm 119:34).

Learn More: Psalm 17:8; 25:20; 34:15; 91:11

KING ETERNAL, IMMORTAL, INVISIBLE

...the King eternal, immortal, invisible, the only wise God. 1 TIMOTHY 1:17

This benediction from the apostle Paul, in his first letter to Timothy, the only place in the Bible where God is called by this name. The adjectives "eternal, immortal, invisible" express three of God's characteristics, or attributes.

God is eternal because He has always existed—and He always will. Unlike man, who is mortal, God is not subject to sickness and death. And He is invisible because He is a spiritual being who exists everywhere at the same time (John 4:24).

The prophet Jeremiah also referred to God as the "everlasting king" (Jeremiah 10:10). Both he and Paul were familiar with earthly kings who ruled for a few years, then were succeeded by other members of the royal family. Even the long reign of fifty-five years achieved by King Manasseh of Judah (2 Kings 21:1) is like the blink of an eye when compared to God's eternal kingship over the nations of the world.

Learn More: Deuteronomy 33:27 / John 4:23 / Romans 1:20 / 2 Corinthians 4:18 / 1 Timothy 6:16 / Colossians 1:15 / Hebrews 11:27

KING OF GLORY

The King of glory shall come in. PSALM 24:7

Psalm 24 is the only place in the Bible where God is called the "King of glory," and the name appears five times in its ten verses. The title of the psalm ascribes it to David.

The exuberant joy of Psalm 24 leads some interpreters to speculate that it may have been sung when the ark of the covenant was moved to the city of Jerusalem in David's time. On this occasion David danced in celebration as trumpets sounded and the people shouted with joy (2 Samuel 6:14–16).

Two choirs, singing responsively, may have accompanied the ark. One choir sang, "Who is this King of glory?" And the other choir responded by identifying Him as Yahweh, the strong and mighty God of the Israelites.

As the King of glory, God is worthy of our praise. The psalmist declared, "Not unto us, O LORD, not unto us, but unto thy name give glory" (Psalm 115:1).

Learn More: Psalm 29:3 / Daniel 2:37 / 1 Corinthians 2:8

KING OF KINGS

King of Kings and Lord of Lords. REVELATION 19:16

Chapter 19 of the book of Revelation describes the return of Christ to earth in the end time. According to this verse, He will wear a banner emblazoned with the phrase "King of Kings." This name, emphasizing His supreme rule over all the earth, will be prominently displayed for everyone to see.

In Old Testament times, the title "king of kings" was assigned to a ruler with an empire that covered a wide territory. Often a king of an empire would allow the rulers of conquered nations to keep their royal titles for political and economic reasons. But it was clear that he as "king of kings" was the undisputed ruler of his vast domain. Thus, the Persian ruler Artaxerxes referred to himself as "king of kings" in a letter that he sent to Jerusalem with Ezra the priest (Ezra 7:12).

When Jesus returns in glory, He will be the sole ruler of the universe. Meanwhile, He rules over His kingdom known as the church. If we belong to Him, we are subjects of His kingdom. He is the King of kings over our lives.

Learn More: Psalm 89:27; 102:15 / Zechariah 14:9 / Revelation 17:14

KING OF THE JEWS

Art thou the King of the Jews? MATTHEW 27:11

This question of Pontius Pilate, the Roman governor who condemned Jesus to death, appears in all four Gospels (see also Mark 15:12; Luke 23:3; John 18:33). The Gospel writers considered this name important because it was the basis of the charge that led to Jesus' execution.

The Jewish religious leaders who turned Jesus over to Pilate were enraged by what they considered blasphemy, His claim to be the Son of God (Matthew 26:63–66). But they knew the Romans would never condemn Jesus to death on the basis of their religious laws alone (John 18:29–32). So they claimed that Jesus was guilty of sedition against the Roman government by claiming to be a king (Luke 23:2). The implication of this charge was that Jesus was plotting to overthrow Roman rule.

Jesus refused to answer Pilate's question because He knew the time for His sacrificial death had arrived. He would allow events to run their course without protest because it was His destiny to die on the cross. Jesus would sacrifice Himself willingly to provide salvation for the entire world.

Learn More: Matthew 2:2 / John 1:49; 12:13

LAMB OF GOD

Behold the Lamb of God. JOHN 1:29

Of all the names John the Baptist could have used for Jesus, he chose to identify Him as the "Lamb of God." Lambs were choice young sheep used as sacrificial animals in Jewish worship rituals (Leviticus 14:11–13). Thus, here at the very beginning of Jesus' ministry, John realized the sacrificial role Jesus was destined to fill.

The use of lambs as sacrifices began with the deliverance of the Israelites from slavery in Egypt. The Lord commanded the people to smear the blood of lambs on the doorposts of their houses. This indicated that they would be passed over when God struck the land with the death of the firstborn (Exodus 12:21–23).

On the night before His crucifixion, Jesus picked up on the sacrificial lamb imagery. He gathered His disciples for a meal that was part of the observance of the Jewish festival of Passover. As Jesus passed the cup among the disciples, He told them, "This is my blood of the new testament, which is shed for many for the remission of sins" (Matthew 26:28).

Learn More: Ephesians 2:13 / Hebrews 9:12 / 1 Peter 1:18–19 / 1 John 1:7

LAST ADAM

The last Adam was made a quickening spirit. 1 CORINTHIANS 15:45

The apostle Paul in this verse drew a contrast between Jesus as the "last Adam" and the Adam of the book of Genesis who was the first man created. This contrast appears at several points throughout the fifteenth chapter of 1 Corinthians.

After God placed the man in the garden of Eden, He told Adam that he could eat the fruit from every tree in the garden except one—"the tree of the knowledge of good and evil" (Genesis 2:17). But Adam disobeyed God and ate the forbidden fruit anyway (Genesis 3:6). This act of rebellion placed Adam and all his descendants—everyone born since Adam's time—under the curse of sin and death.

But there was good news for those who were tainted by Adam's sin. God sent another Adam—the last Adam, Jesus Christ—to undo what the first Adam had caused. The apostle Paul expressed it like this: "As in Adam all die, even so in Christ shall all be made alive" (1 Corinthians 15:22). The first Adam's legacy of death has been canceled by the last Adam's perfect obedience to God the Father, and His sacrificial death on our behalf.

Learn More: Genesis 2:19 / Job 31:33 / Romans 5:14

LAWGIVER

The Lord is our lawgiver. ISAIAH 33:22

This name of the Lord reflects His delivery of the Ten Commandments to Moses on Mount Sinai (Exodus 20:1–17). There was no doubt about the divine origin of these laws, because they were "written with the finger of God" (Exodus 31:18).

These commandments were a moral code to guide the behavior of God's people, the Israelites, whom He had delivered from slavery in Egypt. The Lord is sovereign over His creation, and He is the source of truth, righteousness, and holiness. He alone has the authority to make the laws and set the standards by which His people should live.

Many people have a strictly negative view of God's laws. They think of them only in binding and restrictive terms. But these laws are actually given for our benefit: following God's directives and commands is the key to joy and contentment in life. The psalmist focused on this positive side of God's laws when he declared, "Thou art good, and doest good; teach me thy statutes" (Psalm 119:68).

Learn More: Nehemiah 9:13 / Psalm 105:45 / Daniel 9:10 / Hebrews 8:10 / James 4:12

LIFE

. . .Christ, who is our life. COLOSSIANS 3:4

We are accustomed to thinking of Jesus in terms of the eternal life that He promises to believers. But in this verse from the apostle Paul's letter to the Colossian believers, he describes Jesus as the "life" of believers in the here-and-now. In the previous verse, Paul declared that the Colossians had been trapped hopelessly in their sin before Christ gave them a glorious new life as His followers.

The message of this divine name is that we don't have to wait until we die to enjoy life with Jesus. He is our life today—in this present world. The apostle John stated it like this: "The Word gave life to everything that was created, and his life brought light to everyone" (John 1:4 NLT).

With Jesus as our life, we can live each day with joy in spite of the problems and frustrations that come our way. He is the very essence of the truly good life, and He promises the same to those who follow Him. Jesus himself declared, "I am come that they might have life, and that they might have it more abundantly" (John 10:10).

Learn More: John 1:4; 20:31 / Acts 3:14–15 / 1 John 1:1

LIGHT OF ISRAEL

And the light of Israel shall be for a fire. ISAIAH 10:17

This name of God was used by the prophet Isaiah in connection with his prophecy about the nation of Assyria. The Assyrians overran the nation of Israel (the northern Jewish kingdom) about 722 BC. Isaiah predicted that Assyria would eventually be punished by the Lord for their mistreatment of His people. God—the "light of Israel"—would become a blazing fire that would consume this pagan nation. This prophecy was fulfilled about a century after Isaiah's time when Assyria fell to the Babylonians.

These images of light and fire show two different sides of God's nature. It is always better to experience the light of His love than the fire of His wrath.

This imagery of the light of Israel was also applied by Simeon to the infant Jesus at His dedication in the temple. Simeon described Jesus as "a light to lighten the Gentiles, and the glory of thy people Israel" (Luke 2:32).

Learn More: Exodus 13:21 / 2 Kings 8:19 / 2 Chronicles 21:7 / Psalm 27:1 / Isaiah 60:19 / John 8:12

LIGHT OF THE WORLD

I am the light of the world. JOHN 8:12

The Jewish religious leaders to whom Jesus addressed this comment were filled with pride. They thought of God's favor on the Jewish people as something they deserved because of their moral superiority. But they forgot that God had blessed them because He wanted them to serve as His witnesses to the rest of the world.

Jesus was sent by God the Father as a Savior for all people. This is one reason He was rejected by the religious elite of His time. How could God the Father possibly love the pagan peoples of the world as much as He loved the Jewish leadership? They wanted to put limits on God's love and concern.

This problem is still with us today. Some people want to make Jesus into the light of the middle class, or the light of Western society, or the light of the beautiful. But He refuses to be bound by such restrictions. He is also the light of the poor, the light of the Third World, and the light of the homely. No matter what your earthly circumstances, He is *your* light.

Learn More: Genesis 1:3 / Isaiah 42:6 / John 1:6–7; 9:5

LION OF THE TRIBE OF JUDAH

Behold, the Lion of the tribe of Judah. REVELATION 5:5

This verse declares that only Jesus, as "the Lion of the tribe of Judah," is worthy to open the scroll that contains God's end-time judgment against the world. This name of Jesus probably reflects a prophecy of Jacob in the book of Genesis: he declared that his son Judah was destined to become the greatest among all his twelve sons, whose descendants would become the Israelites, God's chosen people. Jacob described Judah symbolically as a lion, a fearless ruler, who would lead God's people (Genesis 49:8–12).

This prophecy was fulfilled dramatically throughout the Bible. The tribe of Judah took the lead on the Israelites' trek through the wilderness after they left Egypt (Numbers 10:14). Moses' census of the people in the wilderness revealed that the tribe of Judah was the largest of the twelve (Numbers 26:22).

Most significantly of all, Jesus the Messiah sprang from the line of Judah. The genealogy of Jesus in the Gospel of Matthew traces His lineage back to Judah (Matthew 1:2–3; *Judas*: KJV). Thus Jesus is the Lion of the tribe of Judah who rules among His people as supreme Savior and Lord.

Learn More: Numbers 1:26–27 / Psalm 78:67–72

LIVING GOD

O Daniel, servant of the living God. . . DANIEL 6:20

King Darius of Persia was one of several people who used this name for the Lord. It was spoken when Darius went to the lion's den to see if Daniel had survived the night among the ferocious animals. Even a pagan king recognized that it would take the "living God" to deliver Daniel from this holding pen that had been turned into an execution chamber.

God is referred to as the *living* God several times throughout the Bible (Joshua 3:10; 1 Samuel 17:26; Jeremiah 10:10; Hebrews 10:31). This title contrasts the one true God—the One who actually exists—with pagan idols that are lifeless counterfeits. The prophet Isaiah claimed that the pagan deities of the ancient world were not gods at all but "the work of men's hands, wood and stone" that could be easily destroyed (Isaiah 37:19).

Unlike pagan deities, the living God is capable of acting on behalf of His people. Just as He saved Daniel from the lions, He hears our prayers and stands beside us in our time of need.

Learn More: Deuteronomy 5:26 / Psalm 42:2 / Daniel 6:26 / Romans 9:26

LIVING STONE

To whom coming, as unto a living stone. . . 1 PETER 2:4

In this verse the apostle Peter compared Jesus to a stone used in the construction of a building. The imagery of a stone is applied to Jesus in other New Testament passages. But Peter referred to Jesus here as a "living stone," emphasizing His resurrection from the dead and His close relationship with believers as the living Christ.

Peter went on in the next verse to describe believers as "lively stones" (1 Peter 2:5). Just as Jesus is the living and breathing Head of the church, so believers make up the body of the church. Thus the church is a living organism devoted to the service of Jesus and His kingdom.

Peter summarized the mission of the church by stating that believers are "a chosen generation, a royal priesthood, an holy nation, a peculiar people; that ye should show forth the praises of him who hath called you out of darkness into his marvellous light" (1 Peter 2:9).

We who belong to Jesus have the spirit of the "living stone" in our lives. We bring honor to Him when we serve as "lively stones" in the world.

Learn More: Psalm 118:22 / Matthew 21:42 / Ephesians 2:19–20 / 1 Peter 2:7

LORD

. . .always abounding in the work of the Lord. 1 CORINTHIANS 15:58

Sometimes the name *Lord* was used of Jesus as a term of respect. For example, a man once told Him, "Lord, I will follow thee whithersoever thou goest" (Luke 9:57). This man respected Jesus, but he did not reply when Jesus told him about the sacrifice He required of His followers (Luke 9:58).

Even Jesus' disciples sometimes called Him "Lord" in this polite, respectful sense. For example, Jesus once told a parable about the need for people to watch expectantly for His return. Peter asked Him, "Lord, speakest thou this parable unto us, or even to all?" (Luke 12:41).

As Jesus' earthly ministry unfolded, the polite title *Lord* that people used of Him was transformed into a declaration of faith in Him as the divine son of God. This is the sense in which the apostle Paul called Jesus "Lord" in the verse above.

After His resurrection and ascension, Jesus became the Lord of history, the Lord of the church, and the Lord of individual believers. When we declare that "Jesus is Lord," we submit to His leadership and crown Him as the supreme ruler over our lives.

Learn More: Romans 5:21 / Ephesians 5:8 / 1 Thessalonians 3:12

LORD GOD OF ISRAEL

Blessed be the Lord God of Israel. LUKE 1:68

Zacharias, the father of John the Baptist, used this name for God. It was part of his song of praise at the news that the Messiah would soon be born. Just as the Lord had blessed His people in the past, He was getting ready to fulfill His promise to send a great Deliverer.

Israel's gift to the world was belief in one universal God—a concept known as monotheism. The pagan peoples of the ancient world believed that many gods existed, with small deities ruling over different dimensions of life such as fire, war, and fertility. But the Israelites affirmed their belief in God and the ethical behavior He demanded in a formula known as the Shema: "Hear, O Israel: The LORD our God is one LORD: And thou shalt love the LORD thy God with all thine heart, and with all thy soul, and with all thy might" (Deuteronomy 6:4–5).

This Messiah from the Lord mentioned in Zacharias's song was more than a gift to Israel alone. Through Jesus the entire world would be blessed by His redemptive sacrifice on the cross.

Learn More: Exodus 32:27 / Psalm 41:13; 106:48

LORD OF HOSTS

Nations shall come to seek the Lord of hosts in Jerusalem. Zechariah 8:22

Zechariah 8 could be called the "Lord of Hosts" chapter of the Bible, because this divine name appears eighteen times within in. Actually, this name is one of the most popular in the entire Bible. It appears about 250 times, particularly in the prophets and the Psalms.

The compound Hebrew word behind this name is Yahweh-sabaoth, "Lord of Hosts." *Sabaoth* means "armies" or "hosts." Thus one meaning of the name is that God is superior to any human army, no matter its number. The Lord often led His people to victory over superior military forces (see, for example, Judges 7:12–25).

Another possible meaning of "Lord of Hosts" is that God exercises control over all the hosts of heaven—the heavenly bodies—including the sun, moon, and stars. The psalmist declared, "Praise ye him, all his hosts. Praise ye him, sun and moon: praise ye him, all ye stars of light" (Psalm 148:2–3).

In the King James Version, the title Lord of Sabaoth appears two times (Romans 9:29; James 5:4). These are rendered as "Lord of Hosts" by some modern translations.

Learn More: 1 Samuel 1:11 / Psalm 46:7 / Isaiah 5:16 / Jeremiah 25:32

LORD OF PEACE

Now the Lord of peace himself give you peace. 2 Thessalonians 3:16

As the apostle Paul ended his second letter to the Thessalonian believers, he blessed them with this beautiful benediction. Paul wanted these Christians, who were going through disagreement and turmoil, to experience the peace that Jesus promises to those who abide in Him.

The dictionary defines *peace* as "freedom from disquieting or oppressive thoughts or emotions." This definition assumes that peace is the *absence* of elements such as conflict or negative feelings. But we as believers know that peace is actually the *presence* of something greater. This presence is Jesus Christ, who brings peace and inner tranquility to those who have placed their trust in Him. With Jesus as the "Lord of peace" in our lives, we can have peace even in the midst of troubling circumstances.

When Jesus was born in Bethlehem, the angels celebrated His arrival by declaring "peace, good will toward men" (Luke 2:14). Jesus would one day tell His disciples, "Let not your heart be troubled: ye believe in God, believe also in me" (John 14:1). We don't have to go around with troubled looks on our faces if the Lord of peace reigns in our hearts.

Learn More: Isaiah 9:6 / Romans 16:20 / Ephesians 2:14 / Hebrews 13:20

LORD OF THE DEAD AND LIVING

. . .that he might be Lord both of the dead and living. Romans 14:9

In this verse from Paul's letter to the believers at Rome, he referred to every individual who knew Christ as Lord and Savior. Jesus is Lord of the millions of Christians who have lived in the past and have now passed on to their heavenly reward. He is also Lord of all believers still living who look forward to eternal life with Him in heaven after their days on earth are over.

Whether we are alive or dead, there is no better place to be than in the hands of our loving Lord. This is the promise Jesus made to all believers just before He purchased our salvation through His redemptive death: "And I give unto them eternal life; and they shall never perish, neither shall any man pluck them out of my hand" (John 10:28).

Learn More: John 3:16 / Romans 6:23 / 2 Corinthians 5:15

LORD OF THE HARVEST

Pray ye therefore the Lord of the harvest. Matthew 9:38

Jesus spoke these words to His disciples regarding the crowds who came to Him for healing and instruction. He was moved with compassion when He saw their need. Jesus longed for more workers to help Him, as the "Lord of the harvest," with the pressing people.

Jesus had unlimited power, so why didn't He just take care of these difficulties Himself? Why tell the disciples to pray for more workers? Perhaps it was because He knew His time on earth was limited. Even if Jesus healed all the sick and taught everyone who followed Him, others in the same condition would take their place after He was gone. He needed committed workers who would carry on His work after His earthly ministry came to an end.

Jesus is still in the harvesting business. His work on earth continues through His church, and He still needs workers to gather the harvest. Our genuine concern for others should cause us to pray for them, and then work to bring them into God's kingdom. As the apostle Paul expressed it, "All things are of God, who hath reconciled us to himself by Jesus Christ, and hath given to us the ministry of reconciliation" (2 Corinthians 5:18).

Learn More: Matthew 13:30 / Luke 10:2 / John 4:35

LORD OF THE SABBATH

The Son of man is Lord also of the sabbath. Mark 2:28

This is how Jesus answered the Pharisees when they criticized Him for picking grain on the sabbath to feed Himself and the hungry disciples. The original law about sabbath observance stated simply, "Remember the sabbath day, to keep it holy" (Exodus 20:8). People were restricted from working on this day.

Over the years the Pharisees had added many human traditions to this simple law. For example, people were not to travel more than half a mile—or a "sabbath's day journey" (Acts 1:12)—on this day. These silly rules had reduced the sabbath from a spiritual principle to a meaningless ritual.

When Jesus claimed to be the "Lord of the Sabbath," He declared that He would not be bound by the human rules that the Pharisees had established. To Him, doing good on the sabbath by healing people was more important than obeying the religious leaders' silly rules (Matthew 12:12).

Jesus' claim to be the Lord of the Sabbath also placed Him on the same level as God the Father. God had established the sabbath, with Jesus as the agent of creation (John 1:1–3). This gave Him authority over the sabbath.

Learn More: Genesis 2:2–3 / Matthew 12:8 / Luke 6:5–11

LORD OUR RIGHTEOUSNESS

The Lord Our Righteousness. Jeremiah 23:6

God the Father delivered this message through the prophet Jeremiah. The Lord would punish His people for their sin by allowing them to be defeated by the Babylonians. But He would preserve a remnant who would remain faithful. God would bless them, eventually allow them to return to their homeland, and give them a special name—"The Lord Our Righteousness."

This name of God emphasizes two of the most important truths of the Bible: The Lord demands righteousness of His people, and we are not able to meet this demand on our own. He as the Lord Our Righteousness must provide righteousness on our behalf.

The ultimate fulfillment of this verse happened several centuries after Jeremiah's time. God sent His own Son into the world to pay the price for our sin so we could become justified, or righteous, in His sight. This is strictly a gift of God's grace, not something that we deserve because we measure up to His demands. The apostle Paul declared that God made Jesus "to be sin for us, who knew no sin; that we might be made the righteousness of God in him" (2 Corinthians 5:21).

Learn More: Psalm 4:1; 96:13 / Isaiah 45:19; 54:17

LORD OVER ALL

The same Lord over all is rich unto all that call upon him. ROMANS 10:12

This name of Jesus may seem to express the same idea as Lord of Lords (Revelation 19:16). But there is an important distinction between these two names.

Lord of Lords refers to Jesus' supreme rule throughout the earth at His second coming. Lord Over All declares that all people are on the same level in relationship to Jesus Christ. Jesus does not have one plan of salvation for the Jewish people and another for Greeks, or non-Jews. Everyone comes to salvation by accepting through faith the price He paid to redeem us from our sin.

The Jews looked upon Greeks, or Gentiles, as pagans who were excluded from God's favor. The learned Greeks, in turn, thought of all people who were not Greek citizens as uncultured barbarians. But Paul declared that Jesus wiped out all such distinctions between people. Everyone stood before God as sinners with no hope except the forgiveness they could experience through Jesus' sacrifice.

Paul also made it clear that something is required of sinners who desire this salvation. They must "call upon" Jesus (Romans 10:13). This involves repenting of their sins, confessing Him as Savior, and committing their lives to His lordship.

Learn More: Acts 10:28 / Romans 3:29 / 1 Corinthians 12:13 / James 3:17

LORD WHO HEALS

I am the Lord that healeth thee. EXODUS 15:26

This is the only place in the Bible where God is called the Lord Who Heals. God used this name to describe Himself after He healed the bitter waters at Marah in the wilderness, making them safe for the Israelites to drink.

The healing power of God is often demonstrated in the Old Testament. For example, He healed Miriam of her leprosy (Numbers 12:10–15). He healed King Hezekiah of Judah of a mysterious illness (2 Kings 20:1–6). And He healed people in the wilderness after they were bitten by poisonous snakes (Numbers 21:5–9).

God is also portrayed in the Old Testament as the healer of the ultimate sickness—sin. The psalmist prayed, "LORD, be merciful unto me: heal my soul; for I have sinned against thee" (Psalm 41:4). In His earthly ministry, Jesus continued this ministry through compassionate healing of the sick and suffering, including those in bondage to sin.

Learn More: 1 Kings 17:22 / 2 Kings 4:34–35 / Mark 2:17; 5:41–42

LORD WHO SANCTIFIES

I am the Lord that doth sanctify you. EXODUS 31:13

God reminded the Israelites through Moses that the Sabbath was a special day that had been set apart, or sanctified, by Him (Genesis 2:3). His people were to honor this day by resting from their labors and praising Him through acts of worship.

Just as God set apart the seventh day of the week as a memorial to Him, so He sanctified the Israelites as a nation devoted to Him. As the Lord Who Sanctifies, He has the right to demand loyalty and commitment from His people. When God sets us apart for His special use, He also empowers us with the strength and ability to serve as His witnesses in the world.

The apostle Paul expressed every believer's commission to service like this: "I beseech you therefore, brethren, by the mercies of God, that ye present your bodies a living sacrifice, holy, acceptable unto God, which is your reasonable service" (Romans 12:1).

Learn More: Leviticus 20:8 / Ezekiel 20:12 / 1 Thessalonians 5:23

MAJESTY ON HIGH

...sat down on the right hand of the Majesty on high. HEBREWS 1:3

This verse from the book of Hebrews refers to the ascension of Jesus. After His resurrection, Jesus spent forty days among His followers. Then He was "taken up" into heaven and "a cloud received him out of their sight" (Acts 1:9). Now in heaven, He is seated at the right hand of God His Father (Ephesians 1:20)—or, as the writer of Hebrews put it, next to the "Majesty on high."

This name of God is a poetic way of referring to His power and glory. He is incomparable in His excellence, magnificence, and splendor. King David expressed this truth in a profound way when He declared, "Thine, O LORD is the greatness, and the power, and the glory, and the victory, and the majesty: for all that is in the heaven and in the earth is thine" (1 Chronicles 29:11).

"Majesty on high" as a divine name appears only here in the Bible. The writer of Hebrews also spoke of God as the "Majesty in the heavens" (Hebrews 8:1).

Learn More: Psalm 29:4; 96:6; 104:1; 145:12 / Colossians 3:1 / 1 Peter 3:22

MAKER

Shall a man be more pure than his maker? JOB 4:17

Eliphaz the Temanite, one of Job's three friends, referred to God by this name. Job had accused God of causing his suffering, even though Job thought himself innocent of any wrongdoing. To Eliphaz, a mere mortal such as Job had no right to question the actions of his Maker, the immortal One who did not have to explain His actions to anyone.

God's role as our Maker is similar to His acts as our Creator and provider. He brought the first man, Adam, into being and breathed into him the breath of life (Genesis 2:7). And God continues to provide the elements needed to sustain life in His universe. We owe our very lives to Him as our Maker.

The psalmist acknowledged this truth when he declared, "Know ye that the LORD he is God: it is he that hath made us, and not we ourselves; we are his people, and the sheep of his pasture" (Psalm 100:3). See also *Creator*.

Learn More: Job 36:3 / Isaiah 45:9 / Hosea 8:14

MAN OF SORROWS

He is despised and rejected of men; a man of sorrows. ISAIAH 53:3–4

The dictionary defines *sorrow* as a state of remorse over a great loss. If we apply this definition to Isaiah's prophecy, perhaps an alternative translation of this name of Jesus is in order. Jesus was a "man of suffering" (as the New Revised Standard Version says) more than a "man of sorrows."

Jesus was not immersed in regret over a loss. He was an overcomer—a victorious person—in spite of the problems He faced during His earthly ministry. Even the suffering that led to His death was swallowed up in victory when He drew His last breath and declared, "It is finished" (John 19:30). He had accomplished the purpose for which He had been sent into the world.

Jesus' suffering on the cross was real. So is the pain that we as believers feel when we are ridiculed for our faith. But this should not drive us to despair. The Man of Suffering has already "borne our griefs, and carried our sorrows" by dying in our place. Jesus invites us to cast our cares on Him and share in the victory He achieved on the cross.

Learn More: Matthew 16:21 / Acts 3:18 / Hebrews 2:10

MASTER

One is your Master, even Christ. MATTHEW 23:9–10

This name that Jesus used of Himself appears in the famous "woe" chapter in which He condemned the Pharisees (Matthew 23). He was particularly critical of their hypocrisy and religious pride. They enjoyed being greeted with titles that recognized them for their standing in the community and their expertise in the Jewish law. But Jesus declared that He as God's Son was the only person who deserved the title of "Master."

The term used in this verse comes from a Greek word that means "commander" or "ruler." Modern translations sometimes render this word as "teacher." But Jesus was claiming to be more than a teacher. He made it clear to His disciples and others who were listening that He had the right to serve as the supreme authority in their lives.

In New Testament times, slave owners were sometimes called "masters" (Colossians 4:1), implying their total control over the lives of their subjects. As believers, we are also subject to the will of our Master, the Lord Jesus, who has redeemed us for His service.

Learn More: Matthew 6:24 / John 13:13 / Ephesians 6:9 / Colossians 4:1

MEDIATOR

. . .one mediator between God and men, the man Christ Jesus. 1 TIMOTHY 2:5–6

A mediator is a "middleman" or "go-between" who brings two opposing parties together. In this verse, according to the apostle Paul, Jesus fills the role of spiritual mediator in the world. He is the in-between agent who reconciles humankind to God.

All people by nature are sinners. We are estranged from a holy God, who will not tolerate anything that is unholy or unclean. But Jesus eliminated this gap between God and humankind by sacrificing Himself for our sins and purchasing our forgiveness. Cleansed of our sin through His blood, we now have fellowship with God the Father. We have been reconciled to God through His work as our Mediator.

Jesus is the perfect Mediator because He had both divine and human attributes. As God, He understood what God the Father demanded of sinners in order to be acceptable in His sight. As a man, He realized the desperate situation of sinful human beings. Jesus was the God-man who was able to bring these two opposites together. Through His sinless life and perfect sacrifice, He glorified God and gave the human race access to God's unlimited blessings.

Learn More: 2 Corinthians 5:18 / Hebrews 8:6; 9:15; 12:24

MESSIAH

I know that Messias cometh, which is called Christ. JOHN 4:25

These two verses are part of Jesus' conversation with the Samaritan woman at the well. He admitted to her that He was the Messiah, the deliverer whom God had been promising to send to His people for hundreds of years.

The only other place in the New Testament where the word *Messiah* appears is also in John's Gospel. After meeting Jesus, Andrew told his brother, Simon Peter, "We have found the Messias" (John 1:41).

It's not surprising that the title Messiah appears rarely in the New Testament, because Jesus discouraged others from referring to Him in this way (Matthew 16:20). The Jewish people expected their messiah to be a political and military deliverer who would throw off the yoke of Rome and restore the fortunes of Israel. Jesus had come into the world as the spiritual Messiah, so He avoided this name because it would lead the people to expect Him to be something He was not.

Though the word *Messiah* is rare in the New Testament, the concept appears often. The Greek term *christos*, rendered as "Christ," means "anointed" or "anointed one"—a word referring to the Messiah or God's Chosen One.

Learn More: Daniel 9:25–26

MIGHTY ONE OF JACOB

. . .the mighty One of Jacob. Isaiah 49:26

This name of God appears only twice in the Bible, both times in the book of Isaiah (see Isaiah 60:16). In these two verses, "Jacob" is a poetic way of referring to the nation of Israel. The descendants of Jacob's twelve sons developed into the twelve tribes that made up the nation of Israel. Jacob himself was also known as "Israel," a name given to him by the Lord after his struggle with God at Peniel (Genesis 32:28; 35:10).

Jacob, the grandson of Abraham, was a schemer who deceived his father, Isaac, into blessing him rather than his twin brother, Esau. But over time he developed into a person who honored the Lord and became heir to the covenant that God had established with Abraham.

Three divine names similar to "mighty One of Jacob" that appear in the Old Testament are "God of Jacob" (2 Samuel 23:1), "Holy One of Jacob" (Isaiah 29:23), and "King of Jacob" (Isaiah 41:21).

Learn More: Genesis 27:1–41; 32:27–28

MINISTER OF THE TRUE TABERNACLE

. . .a minister of the sanctuary, and of the true tabernacle. Hebrews 8:1–2

In this verse the writer of Hebrews claims that the Old Testament priestly system was only a shadow of the eternal priesthood provided by Jesus in heaven. He is the priest of the heavenly sanctuary, or true tabernacle, that God has established for His people.

The most holy place in the Jewish religious system was the "holy of holies" in the tabernacle or temple. This sanctuary represented God's holy and awesome presence. Only the high priest could enter this section of the temple, and he could do so only once a year on the Day of Atonement. On this occasion, he offered sacrifice first for his own sins and then for the sins of the people (Leviticus 16:1–6).

When Jesus died on the cross, the heavy curtain that sealed off this section of the temple was torn from top to bottom (Matthew 27:50–51). This symbolized that all people now had access to God's presence and forgiveness through the sacrificial death of His Son.

Jesus is the perfect priest in heaven, where He conducts His ministry of intercession for all believers (Hebrews 7:25).

Learn More: Exodus 40:12–15 / Matthew 20:28 / Mark 10:43 / Romans 15:8

MOST HIGH

The most High uttered his voice. 2 Samuel 22:14

This name of God appears in a psalm that David wrote after he was delivered from King Saul and others who were trying to kill him (1 Samuel 20:1; Psalm 18 title). David compared God's ability to save to the power unleashed during a severe thunderstorm. The rolling thunder was like God's voice from heaven. Anyone who has ever been caught outside during a sudden storm can testify to the awesome power of nature and its Creator.

The name "most High" appears primarily in the Old Testament. One exception occurs in Stephen's long speech in the book of Acts. This early Christian martyr declared that "the most High dwelleth not in temples made with hands" (Acts 7:48).

There is nothing in this world more powerful than the most High. The only appropriate response to displays of His power in the universe is to bow down and worship. As the psalmist declared, "O worship the LORD in the beauty of holiness: fear before him, all the earth" (Psalm 96:9).

Learn More: Psalm 9:2; 73:11; 107:11 / Isaiah 14:14 / Daniel 4:24; 7:18

NEW SPIRIT

A new spirit will I put within you. Ezekiel 36:26

Just as Jeremiah is known as the prophet of the new covenant (Jeremiah 31:31–34), Ezekiel might be called the prophet of the "new spirit." This name of the Holy Spirit is unique to him, and he uses it three times in his book (see also Ezekiel 11:19; 18:31).

The word *new* does not mean that God would give His people the Holy Spirit for the first time at some point in the future. The Holy Spirit was active with God the Father in the creation and among selected people in Old Testament times, including Joshua, Othniel the judge, Samson, and David. The name "new spirit" refers to the spiritual redemption that God would provide for His people through His love and grace. God's Spirit would bind believers to Him in a new covenant sealed with the blood of Jesus Christ.

Learn More: Numbers 27:18 / Judges 3:9–10; 14:5–6 / 1 Samuel 16:13 / 2 Corinthians 3:6

ONE CHOSEN OUT OF THE PEOPLE

I have exalted one chosen out of the people. Psalm 89:19

Psalm 89 focuses on God's promise to King David that one of his descendants would always occupy the throne of Israel (2 Samuel 7:8–17). Thus the "one chosen out of the people" in this verse refers to David, because he was chosen by the Lord from among the sons of Jesse to replace Saul as king (1 Samuel 16:10–13).

But this psalm also looks beyond David's time to its ultimate fulfillment in Jesus the Messiah. The angel Gabriel made this clear when he told the virgin Mary that she would give birth to God's Chosen One. "He shall be great, and shall be called the Son of the Highest," Gabriel declared, "and the Lord God shall give unto him the throne of his father David" (Luke 1:32).

As the one chosen out of the people, Jesus was not a king in the same sense as David. He did not seek political or military power. His kingship was spiritual in nature. Jesus ushered in the kingdom of God, the dominion over which He reigns with all who have accepted Him as Lord and Savior.

Learn More: Psalm 135:4 / Isaiah 42:1 / 1 Peter 2:4

ONLY BEGOTTEN SON

God so loved the world, that he gave his only begotten Son. John 3:16

Jesus used this name for Himself in His long discussion with Nicodemus about the meaning of the new birth (John 3:1–21). This verse from that discussion is probably the best known passage in the entire Bible. Most believers can quote it from memory. It has been called "the gospel in a nutshell" because its twenty-five words tell so clearly and simply why Jesus came into the world.

The name "only begotten Son" describes Jesus' special relationship with the Father. He is unique—the only one of His kind who has ever existed. The fact that He was God's one and only Son makes His role as our Savior all the more significant. God the Father sent the very best when He sent Jesus to die for our sins.

This name of Jesus appears only in the writings of the apostle John. In his Gospel, John also referred to Jesus as the "only begotten of the Father" (John 1:14).

Learn More: Psalm 2:7 / John 1:18; 3:18 / 1 John 4:9 / Hebrews 1:5

ONLY WISE GOD

. . .to the only wise God our Saviour, be glory. JUDE 25

The writer of the epistle of Jude closed his brief book with this inspiring benediction. He wanted his readers to experience the joy of their salvation and to continue to be faithful to the "only wise God," whom he clearly identified as Jesus their Savior.

This is the only place in the Bible where Jesus is called by this name. The New King James Version translates the phrase as "God our Savior, who alone is wise." Only Jesus Christ has divine wisdom. Worldly wisdom is a poor substitute for the wisdom that God grants those who follow Him as Savior and Lord.

Jesus the Son and God the Father impart wisdom to believers in several ways—through the Holy Spirit, through the counsel of fellow believers, and through the scriptures, the written Word of God. We will never be as wise as God, who is the fount of all wisdom. But we should be growing in this gift of grace every day as we walk with Him.

Learn More: Matthew 11:25 / 1 Corinthians 1:24 / James 1:5

OUR PASSOVER

Christ our passover is sacrificed for us. 1 CORINTHIANS 5:7

The festival of Passover commemorated the "passing over" of the houses of the Israelites when God destroyed all the Egyptian firstborn. This was God's final plague that convinced the pharaoh to release the Jewish people from slavery.

Jesus is "our passover," Paul declared, because He shed His blood to bring deliverance for God's people, just as sacrificial lambs inaugurated the first Passover. We remember Jesus' sacrifice with reverence every time we partake of communion, or the Lord's Supper.

The word *leaven* in this verse refers to yeast, an ingredient used by the Israelites to cause their bread to rise. On the first Passover, they left Egypt in such a hurry that they didn't have time to add leaven to their bread dough (Exodus 12:34). Whenever they observed this holiday from that day on, they were to eat unleavened bread.

Paul referred to believers in this verse as a "new lump" because they were "unleavened." Just as unleavened bread symbolized the Israelites' freedom from Egyptian slavery, so believers are unleavened, or separated from sin and death, by the perfect Passover Lamb, Jesus Christ.

Learn More: 2 Kings 23:21 / Matthew 26:2 / Mark 14:1

PHYSICIAN

They that are whole need not a physician; but they that are sick. LUKE 5:31

Jesus spoke these words soon after He called the tax collector Matthew as His disciple. To celebrate the occasion, Matthew invited his tax collector associates and other friends to a meal for Jesus and the other disciples.

The scribes and Pharisees were horrified that Jesus and His disciples would associate with such "sinful" people. But Jesus made it clear that He had been sent to people such as these. They needed a Savior and Deliverer. He was the Physician who could heal them of their desperate sickness known as sin.

Jesus' role as physician is one of the most prominent in the Gospels. Most of His miracle were performed for people who were suffering from physical ailments. But in many of these miracles, He went beyond healing the body to healing the soul and the spirit through forgiveness of sin (Matthew 9:2).

Jesus the Physician is still in the healing business. He offers hope to the discouraged, His presence to the lonely, comfort to the grieving, and peace to those who are troubled. But most of all, He brings deliverance from the most serious problems of the human race—sin and death.

Learn More: Matthew 4:23 / Mark 2:17 / Luke 5:31

PORTION

Thou art my portion, O Lord. PSALM 119:57

The word *portion* appears often in the Bible in connection with inheritance rights. For example, each of the twelve tribes of Israel received a portion of the land of Canaan as an inheritance that the Lord had promised (Joshua 19:9). By law, the firstborn son in a family received a double portion of his father's estate as an inheritance (Deuteronomy 21:17). In Jesus' parable of the prodigal son, the youngest son asked his father for his portion or share of the estate ahead of time (Luke 15:12).

The psalmist probably had this inheritance imagery in mind when he called God "my portion." The Lord was his spiritual heritage, passed down to him by godly people of past generations. Unlike an earthly inheritance that can be squandered, this is an inheritance that will last forever.

But comparing God to a legacy from the past has its limits. Truths about God can be passed on from generation to generation, but personal faith cannot. Parents can and should teach their offspring about God, but it is up to each child to accept this heritage through his or her own personal choice.

Learn More: Psalm 16:5; 119:57; 142:5 / Lamentations 3:24

POTTER

Lord, thou art our father; we are the clay, and thou our potter. ISAIAH 64:8

The prophet Isaiah longed for the wayward people of Judah to return to the Lord. If they became pliable clay in God's hands, they would be shaped into beautiful vessels who would glorify His name.

God as the master potter is a graphic image that appears often throughout the Bible. For example, while the prophet Jeremiah looked on, a potter ruined a vase he was working on and had to start over again with the same lump of clay. Jeremiah compared the nation of Judah to this pottery reshaping process. Shape up, he declared, or you will be reshaped by the Lord's discipline.

In the New Testament, the apostle Paul observed that believers are nothing but "earthen vessels" (*jars of clay*, NIV), who are filled with the treasure of God's grace (2 Corinthians 4:7). But our unworthiness as recipients of His grace should not prevent us from serving as witnesses of His love to others.

Learn More: Jeremiah 18:2–6 / Revelation 2:27

POWER OF GOD

. . .Christ the power of God. 1 CORINTHIANS 1:24

The apostle Paul admitted that many people were skeptical of a crucified Savior. If Jesus was such a deliverer, they reasoned, why was He executed on a Roman cross like a common criminal? To them, Jesus' death was a sign of weakness.

On the contrary, Paul pointed out, Christ showed great power in His crucifixion. He was the very "power of God" whom the Father sent to atone for the sins of the world. The death of One on behalf of the many showed the extent of this divine power.

Jesus demonstrated His awesome power many times during His earthly ministry. But He refused to come down from the cross and save Himself, although the crowd taunted Him to do so.

This is a good example of power under control. Jesus could have called legions of angels to come to His rescue. But this would have nullified the purpose for which God the Father had sent Him into the world. His divine power was never greater than when He refused to use it.

Learn More: Matthew 26:53; 27:39–43 / 1 Corinthians 2:5 / Ephesians 6:10 / 2 Timothy 1:8

POWER OF THE HIGHEST

The power of the Highest shall overshadow thee. LUKE 1:35

The angel Gabriel spoke these words of assurance to the virgin Mary. She would give birth to the Son of God. Jesus' conception in her womb would occur through the action of the Holy Spirit, whom Gabriel referred to as the "power of the Highest."

No other word describes the work of God's Spirit as well as *power*. In the Old Testament, King Saul experienced this firsthand when he sent several assassins to kill David. But the Spirit of God came upon them, causing them to utter prophecies instead of carrying out the king's orders (1 Samuel 19:20).

In the New Testament, Jesus told His disciples that the Holy Spirit would empower them to continue His mission in the world (Acts 1:8). The outpouring of the Holy Spirit on the day of Pentecost transformed the small group into bold witnesses for Jesus.

But the Holy Spirit's power is not restricted to that time long ago. He is still at work through the church and those who follow Jesus as Lord and Savior. This is possible "not by might, nor by power, but by my spirit, saith the LORD of hosts" (Zechariah 4:6).

Learn More: Acts 1:8; 2:1–11 / Romans 15:13

PRINCE OF THE KINGS OF THE EARTH

. . .the prince of the kings of the earth. REVELATION 1:5

The apostle John addressed the book of Revelation to seven churches of Asia Minor whose members were undergoing persecution by Roman authorities. John wanted these believers to understand that he was not writing under his own authority but under the command and direction of Jesus Christ, the "prince of the kings of the earth."

Rulers like the emperors of the Roman Empire would come and go. But Jesus was an eternal King, not a temporary monarch who would rule for a few years, then be replaced by another. He stands above and beyond all the kings of the earth.

Since Jesus is the world's supreme King, He has the right to reign over His church and in the lives of those who claim Him as Savior and Lord. As the apostle Paul reminded the believers at Ephesus, "We are his workmanship, created in Christ Jesus unto good works, which God hath before ordained that we should walk in them" (Ephesians 2:10).

Learn More: Zechariah 14:9 / Acts 3:15; 5:31 / Revelation 19:16

PROPITIATION FOR OUR SINS

. . .sent his Son to be the propitiation for our sins. 1 JOHN 4:10

The word *propitiation* comes from an old English word that means "to satisfy." Thus, the apostle John declared that God the Father sent His Son, Jesus, to serve as the satisfaction for our sins. This word is the key to one of the classical theories of the atonement, or the sacrificial death of Jesus.

According to this view, God is a holy God who cannot tolerate sin. This puts us as humans in a dilemma because we are not capable of living a sinless life, no matter how hard we try. To make matters worse, God is also a just God who—in order to be true to His nature—must punish sin wherever He finds it. So our sin separates us from God and makes us liable to His punishment. *Hopeless* is the only word that describes the human situation.

But God loved us too much to allow us to continue in this dilemma. He sent Jesus to satisfy His own demand for righteousness in His people. Jesus sacrificed His life, atoned for our sins, and restored the broken relationship between a holy God and sinful humanity.

Learn More: Mark 10:45 / 1 Timothy 2:6 / 1 John 1:7 / Revelation 1:5

RABBI

Rabbi, we know that thou art a teacher come from God. JOHN 3:2

In modern society, *rabbi* is the official title of the leader of a Jewish congregation. It is similar to the title *reverend* for a Protestant minister or *father* for a Catholic priest.

But in Jesus' time, *rabbi* was a term of respect meaning "teacher" or "master." In John 3:2, Nicodemus's use of this title for Jesus probably meant "teacher." Nicodemus wanted to learn more about this Jewish teacher and miracle worker who was impressing the crowds in the region of Galilee.

In John 20:16, Mary Magdalene's recognition of Jesus as "rabboni" paid homage to Him as her master. After Jesus' resurrection, Mary recognized Him as such when He called her by name. *Rabboni* is the Aramaic form of rabbi. Aramaic was the common language spoken in Israel during New Testament times.

Whether we call Jesus *Rabbi* or *Rabboni*, the meaning is the same: He is our Master, Teacher, and Guide who deserves our utmost respect and loyalty.

Learn More: John 1:38, 49; 6:25

REDEEMER

And the Redeemer shall come to Zion. ISAIAH 59:20

This divine name is a reflection of the Old Testament concept of the kinsman-redeemer. In Bible times, a family member in trouble depended on his nearest relative to come to his rescue.

For example, if a person lost his property to a debtor, his kinsman-redeemer was responsible for buying it back and restoring it to this family member. This is what happened in the case of Naomi in the book of Ruth. Boaz, a kinsman of Naomi's deceased husband, bought back the property her husband had lost and restored it to her (Ruth 4:1–11).

The prophet Isaiah declared that God is the ultimate Redeemer who will come to the rescue of His people. The patriarch Job also received a glimpse of this Redeemer of the future. Out of his suffering and despair, Job declared, "I know that my redeemer liveth, and that he shall stand at the latter day upon the earth" (Job 19:25).

What Isaiah and Job only hoped for has now come to pass. We can rest assured that no trouble that we experience is so deep that it is beyond the reach of a loving Lord.

Learn More: Psalm 19:14 / Isaiah 49:7 / Jeremiah 50:34

REFINER'S FIRE

He is like a refiner's fire. MALACHI 3:2

This name of Jesus appears in the final chapter of the Old Testament. The prophet Malachi compared the coming Messiah to the hot fire that metalworkers used to purify ore such as silver. The ore was heated in a pot until it turned to liquid and the dross (waste material) rose to the surface. Then the metalworker used a ladle to skim off the dross, leaving the pure and uncontaminated silver.

This image of the Messiah must have been a surprise to the Jewish people of Malachi's time. They expected the Messiah to come as a conquering hero who would restore Israel to its glory days as a political kingdom. But the prophet informed them that the Messiah would come in judgment against Israel because of its sin and rebellion.

The name "refiner's fire" emphasizes Jesus' role as judge. His second coming will bring judgment against all who have refused to accept Him as Savior and Lord.

Learn More: Proverbs 17:3; 25:4 / Isaiah 1:25 / Ezekiel 22:22 / Malachi 3:3 / 2 Peter 2:9

REFUGE

The eternal God is thy refuge. Deuteronomy 33:27

Moses called God by this name as the Israelites were getting ready to enter the promised land. He reminded the people to follow the Lord as they settled in the land because He alone was a dependable source of refuge and protection.

After they occupied Canaan, the Israelites designated certain population centers as cities of refuge (Joshua 20:7–9). An Israelite who killed another person accidentally could flee to one of these cities to escape the dead man's family who were seeking revenge. The person's safety was guaranteed by the elders of the city while the circumstances surrounding the death were under investigation.

With God as our refuge, we have nothing to fear from those who seek to do us harm. Even in death, there is no safer place to be than in the arms of the everlasting God. The psalmist declared, "I will say of the LORD, He is my refuge and my fortress: my God; in him will I trust" (Psalm 91:2).

Another divine name that emphasizes God's protection of His people is "hiding place" (Psalm 32:7).

Learn More: Numbers 35:12–15 / Psalm 46:1; 61:3; 142:5 / Jeremiah 16:19

RESURRECTION AND THE LIFE

I am the resurrection, and the life. John 11:25

Jesus applied this name to Himself while talking with Martha, sister of Lazarus. She was disappointed that Jesus had not arrived to heal her brother before he died. Jesus' reply made it clear that He was the master of the living and the dead. He had the power to raise Lazarus, as well as any others who had died. At the same time, He could guarantee eternal life for the living.

Then Jesus proceeded to deliver on His promise. He stood before the burial chamber where the body had been placed, and with the simple command, "Lazarus, come forth," brought His friend back to life.

Note that Jesus delivered no incantations over the body; there was no lightning flash from heaven, no magical tricks to dazzle the crowd. Just three simple words from the Master, and Lazarus walked out of the tomb.

Jesus alone has the keys to life and death. Fortunate are those who commit their lives and their eternal destiny into His hands.

Learn More: John 11:26 / Acts 4:33 / Philippians 3:10 / 1 Peter 1:3

RIGHTEOUS SERVANT

My righteous servant justify many. Isaiah 53:11

Several different people in the Bible are referred to as a "servant of God" or "God's servant" because of the loyal work they rendered for the Lord. But Jesus is the only person who deserves to be called God's "righteous servant."

This name for Jesus appears in one of the famous messianic "Servant Songs" of the prophet Isaiah. At the beginning of the Lord's public ministry, Matthew quoted this passage and identified Jesus as this person the prophet had predicted (Isaiah 42:1–4; Matthew 12:15–18). The servant's mission was being fulfilled through Jesus' teaching and healing ministry. He was the holy and righteous agent whom the Father sent on a mission of redemption into a dark and sinful world.

Jesus lived up to this name through His healing and teaching ministry. On one occasion His disciples began to argue over who would occupy the places of honor in His future glory. "Whosoever of you will be the chiefest, shall be servant of all," He gently reminded them. "For even the Son of man came not to be ministered unto, but to minister, and to give his life a ransom for many" (Mark 10:44–45).

Learn More: John 13:16 / Philippians 2:5–8

ROCK

Neither is there any rock like our God. 1 SAMUEL 2:2

Hannah uttered this prayer when she brought her son Samuel to Eli the priest. God had answered her prayer for a son, and she followed through on her promise to devote him to the Lord. She had found the Lord to be the Rock, the strong and dependable One who answers the prayers of His people.

The imagery of God as a rock appears often in the book of Psalms. In a psalm attributed to David, he praised God for serving as his Rock of defense against the murderous schemes of King Saul. "The LORD is my rock, and my fortress, and my deliverer," he declared, "my God, my strength, in whom I will trust" (Psalm 18:2).

The word *rock* when used of God refers not to a small stone but to a massive outcropping of solid rock, such as that on a mountainside. These huge formations are common throughout the land of Israel. They remain from one generation to the next, just as God is the eternal, unmovable One who is not subject to the ravages of time. See also *Spiritual Rock.*

Learn More: 2 Samuel 22:47; 23:3 / Psalm 62:7; 94:22

ROOT AND OFFSPRING OF DAVID

I am the root and the offspring of David. REVELATION 22:16

Jesus used this name for Himself in the closing verses of the final chapter of the last book of the Bible. It's as if He seized the last opportunity to tell the world who He is and what His life and ministry are all about.

Notice the dual focus of this name—the *root* of David and the *offspring* of David. It summarizes His existence as the God-man, the One who is both fully human and fully divine.

Because Jesus is the divine Son who served as the agent of creation, He is David's creator, or root. But because he came to earth in human form, He is also David's descendant, or offspring—the Messiah from the line of David who reigns over the spiritual kingdom that He came to establish. Thus Jesus is both superior to David and the rightful heir to his throne.

During Jesus' earthly ministry, people often addressed Him as the "Son of David" (see, for example, Matthew 20:31). They recognized Him as the spiritual heir to God's promise that a descendant of David would always reign over His people (2 Samuel 7:16). See also *Son of David.*

Learn More: Isaiah 9:7; 11:1; 55:3 / Jeremiah 23:5

SAVIOUR

There is no God else beside me; a just God and a Saviour. ISAIAH 45:21

In the Bible, the name *Saviour* is applied to both God the Father and God the Son. In this verse from the prophet Isaiah, the Lord assured His people that He as their Savior was the only true God. He demanded their loyalty and obedience.

A savior is a person who rescues or delivers others from danger. When this name is used of God in the Old Testament, it usually refers to physical deliverance. The supreme example of this was God's rescue of the Israelites from Egyptian slavery. Acting as deliverer, God sent plagues against the Egyptians until the pharaoh gave in and allowed the people to leave his country.

God's role as a Savior reaches its full flower in the New Testament. An angel told shepherds near Bethlehem when Jesus was born, "I bring you good tidings of great joy, which shall be to all people. For unto you is born this day in the city of David a Saviour, which is Christ the Lord" (Luke 2:10–11). The shepherds were awestruck by the news that this newborn baby was to be a Savior for God's people (Luke 2:8–15).

Learn More: Ephesians 5:23 / 1 Timothy 4:10 / 1 John 4:14

SCEPTRE OUT OF ISRAEL

A Sceptre shall rise out of Israel. NUMBERS 24:17

Balaam, a pagan wizard, was hired by the king of Moab to pronounce a curse against the Israelites. But the Lord led Balaam to *bless* the Israelites instead. In this verse, Balaam even prophesied that a "Sceptre…out of Israel," a strong leader, would rise up to crush the Moabites. This verse is also considered a prophecy with a long-range fulfillment, referring to Jesus as the Savior-Messiah whom God would send to deliver His people.

A scepter was a short staff, similar to a walking stick, that symbolized the power and authority of a king. In the book of Esther, King Ahasuerus of Persia extended his royal scepter for Queen Esther to touch (Esther 5:2). This gave her permission to come into his presence and present her request to the king.

The imagery of a royal scepter as applied to Jesus symbolizes His power, authority, and universal dominion. In the book of Hebrews, God the Father declares to Jesus the Son, "Thy…throne is for ever and ever: a sceptre of righteousness is the sceptre of thy kingdom" (Hebrews 1:8).

Learn More: Genesis 49:10 / Esther 4:11 / Psalm 45:6 / Zechariah 10:11

SEED OF THE WOMAN

I will put enmity…between thy seed and her seed. GENESIS 3:15

God spoke these words to Satan in the garden of Eden after Satan had persuaded Adam and Eve to eat the forbidden fruit. This verse is known as the *protoevangelium*, a Latin word meaning "the first gospel."

It is called the first gospel because it contains the Bible's first prediction of the coming of Christ. Jesus is depicted as the "seed" of the woman, Eve. He will wage war against Satan's forces. Satan will manage to bruise Jesus' heel—a reference to the forces that executed Him on the cross. But Jesus will rise from the dead and deal a crushing blow to Satan's head. In the end time, Jesus will win the final victory over Satan and cast him into the lake of fire (Revelation 20:10).

This name may be a subtle reference to the virgin birth of Jesus. He was conceived in Mary's womb by the Holy Spirit, not by a human father. She was told by the angel Gabriel, "The Holy Ghost shall come upon thee, and the power of the Highest shall overshadow thee: therefore also that holy thing which shall be born of thee shall be called the son of God" (Luke 1:35).

Learn More: Genesis 3:1 / Romans 3:23 / 1 Corinthians 15:45 / 1 Timothy 2:14

SEVEN SPIRITS

…from the seven Spirits which are before his throne. REVELATION 1:4

This reference to the Holy Spirit as "seven Spirits" is puzzling to many Bible students. We know from the apostle Paul's writings that the Holy Spirit is one. He declared to the believers at Corinth, "By one Spirit are we all baptized into one body" (1 Corinthians 12:13). So how could the apostle John in these verses from Revelation claim that the Holy Spirit is seven in number?

The best explanation is that John used the number seven to emphasize the fullness and completeness of the Holy Spirit. Seven was considered the perfect number in Bible times, and it appears often throughout the Bible to symbolize wholeness and perfection (see, for example, Deuteronomy 16:15; Matthew 18:21–22). John used the number in this sense many times throughout Revelation: seven candlesticks (1:12), seven stars (1:16), seven seals (5:1), seven horns and seven eyes (5:6).

Learn More: Genesis 33:3 / Job 2:13 / Psalm 12:6 / John 14:16

SHEPHERD

The Lord is my shepherd. PSALM 23:1

This name of God is one of the favorites of Bible students, perhaps because it occurs in one of the most familiar passages of scripture—the Twenty-third Psalm. This psalm has been called the "Shepherd Psalm" because of its beautiful description of the Lord as the Shepherd of His people.

David apparently wrote this psalm toward the end of his life as he reflected how the Lord had been his never-failing guide. Like a shepherd who leads his sheep to green pastures and quiet streams for food and water, the Lord had supplied David's needs. From his humble beginnings as a shepherd boy, all the way to the throne of Israel, God had blessed David with more than he deserved. David was confident that God would continue to sustain him, even as he walked "through the valley of the shadow of death" (Psalm 23:4).

Like David, all of us need the divine Shepherd, who will guide us throughout this life and beyond. What a blessing it is to count ourselves as "the sheep of his pasture" (Psalm 100:3). See also *Good Shepherd.*

Learn More: Psalm 80:1 / Isaiah 40:11 / John 10:11 / Hebrews 13:20

SHIELD

. . .with favour wilt thou compass him as with a shield. PSALM 5:12

This verse is from a psalm of David in which he prayed for protection from his enemies. He used military terminology to characterize God as his "shield" who would surround him and absorb the blows of those who attacked.

The original Hebrew word in this verse refers to the large, full-body shield that warriors crouched behind. This protected them from soldiers with swords and spears, as well as from archers who were shooting arrows from a distance.

Another type of shield was the buckler. It was strapped to the arm for protection in hand-to-hand combat. The buckler as a metaphor for God's protection also appears in the Bible (Psalm 18:30).

The psalmist described the Lord's salvation as a shield (Psalm 18:35). In the New Testament, the apostle Paul urged believers to take up "the shield of faith, wherewith ye shall be able to quench all the fiery darts of the wicked" (Ephesians 6:16).

As our Shield, God assures our well-being in the midst of earthly trials and conflicts. He literally surrounds us with His watchful care.

Learn More: 2 Samuel 22:3 / Psalm 3:3; 84:9 / Proverbs 30:5

SHILOH

. . .until Shiloh come; and unto him shall the gathering of the people be. GENESIS 49:10

Genesis 49 contains the aging Jacob's blessings on his twelve sons, whose descendants would become the twelve tribes of Israel. This verse is part of his blessing of Judah, the tribe out of which the rulers of Israel would emerge, beginning with King David.

Shiloh is a Hebrew word meaning "the one to whom it belongs." Thus, Jacob was saying that Judah would wield the royal scepter of leadership in Israel until the one to whom the scepter belonged arrived on the scene. This is a veiled reference to the coming Messiah.

All authority and power belong to Jesus because God has delegated His jurisdiction over His people to His Son. Jesus is also deserving of all power because He rules in justice and righteousness. He will never use His power for anything but the good of His church and those who devote their lives to Him and His service.

No matter what happens to us in this life, we can rest safe and secure in the arms of Shiloh—the One who holds the whole world in His hands.

Learn More: Luke 4:36 / Colossians 1:16 / Revelation 5:1–8

SON OF ABRAHAM

Jesus Christ, the son of David, the son of Abraham. MATTHEW 1:1

Abraham was the father of the Jewish people. Many centuries before Jesus' time, God called Abraham to leave his home and family in Mesopotamia and move to the land of Canaan. Here God would begin to build a nation that would be His exclusive possession. He promised Abraham, "I will bless them that bless thee, and curse him that curseth thee: and in thee shall all families of the earth be blessed" (Genesis 12:3).

As the Son of Abraham, Jesus is the ultimate fulfillment of this promise, or covenant, that God made with Abraham. In His human lineage and by His nationality, Jesus was a Jew—the people whom God promised to bless above all the nations of the earth.

But God never intended for His promise of blessing to apply only to the Jewish people. He wanted to bless all nations through the influence of Abraham's offspring. When the Jews forgot this part of the covenant, God sent His Son Jesus to remind them that He had placed no limits on His love and grace. Jesus as the Son of Abraham fulfilled God's redemptive plan by coming as Savior for the entire world.

Learn More: Isaiah 42:6 / Matthew 28:19–20 / Acts 3:13; 13:47

SON OF DAVID

The book of the generation of Jesus Christ, the son of David. MATTHEW 1:1

This name of Jesus appears in the very first verse of the New Testament for good reason. It expresses the truth that Jesus as the Son of David ties together the Old and New Testaments. The genealogies of Jesus in the Gospels of Matthew and Luke declare that Jesus in His human lineage was descended from David (Matthew 1:6; Luke 3:31). Thus, Jesus fulfilled God's promise to David that one of David's descendants would always reign over His people (2 Samuel 7:1–16; Psalm 132:11–12).

During Jesus' earthly ministry, those who sought Him out for healing often called Him by this name. For example, blind Bartimaeus of Jericho shouted to Him, "Jesus, thou son of David, have mercy on me" (Mark 10:47).

But Jesus never referred to Himself by this name. He may have avoided it because it tended to feed the expectation of the Jewish people that the Messiah would come as a political conqueror, not a spiritual Savior.

Learn More: Matthew 9:27; 12:23 / Luke 18:38 / 2 Timothy 2:8

SON OF GOD

Truly this was the Son of God. MATTHEW 27:54

This verse refers to the Roman military officer who presided over the execution of Jesus. He was so impressed with the miraculous signs at Jesus' death (Matthew 27:50–53) that he declared Jesus was none other than the Son of God.

This name emphasizes Jesus' divine nature and shows that He came to earth under the authority of God the Father on a mission of redemption. It also highlights Jesus' close, personal relationship with His heavenly Father. He knew God like no other person has ever known Him. He addressed God often in His prayers as "Father" (John 17:1–26).

Jesus as God's Son was perfectly obedient to His Father. He refused to be sidetracked by Satan's temptations at the beginning of His public ministry. His last words from the cross were "It is finished" (John 19:30). This was not the whimper of a dying man but a declaration of victory over the forces of sin and death. He accomplished the work that His Father commissioned Him to do. See also *Abba, Father.*

Learn More: Matthew 6:9; 14:33 / Luke 4:1–13 / Acts 9:20 / Romans 1:4

SON OF MAN

The Son of man hath not where to lay his head. Luke 9:58

Jesus identified Himself by this name when He responded to a man who promised to become His disciple. He wanted this would-be follower to know that serving Him as the Son of man would require sacrifice.

This name occurs often in the Gospel narratives. Jesus used the title as a substitute for the first-person pronoun "I," as in the verse above. He called Himself the "Son of man" when predicting His suffering and death (Luke 9:22). And He also used it when referring to His authority and power, as in "the Son of man is Lord also of the Sabbath" (Mark 2:28).

Jesus may have borrowed this name from the prophet Ezekiel. It appears many times throughout this Old Testament book. The basic meaning of *Son of man* is "mortal" or "human being." Perhaps Jesus preferred this title because it implied His total identification with humankind. The Son of man came to earth as a man—our brother and fellow sufferer—to deliver us from our bondage to sin. He summed up His mission of redemption in a few simple words: "The Son of man is come to seek and to save that which was lost" (Luke 19:10).

Learn More: Ezekiel 2:1; 11:2; 33:7

SON OF MARY

Is not this the carpenter, the son of Mary? Mark 6:3

The citizens of Nazareth could not believe the boy who had grown up among them was a prophet sent from God. They knew Him only as the carpenter and the "son of Mary."

The virgin Mary knew from the very beginning that her son was God's special gift to the world (Luke 1:26–38). But she apparently brought Him up like any normal Jewish boy (Luke 2:51–52). She had other children who were born by natural means after Jesus' miraculous conception (Mark 6:3). But Jesus as her firstborn son must have had a special place in her heart.

She knew about His special powers because she told the servants at a wedding feast where the wine had run out, "Whatsoever he saith unto you, do it" (John 2:5). Jesus responded by turning water into wine.

Did Mary realize that her son Jesus was destined to be executed like a common criminal No one knows, but she was at the execution site when He was nailed to the cross. One of the last things Jesus did before He died was to make arrangements for the welfare of His mother (John 19:27).

Learn More: Matthew 1:18; 13:55 / Luke 1:26–30; 2:34 / Acts 1:14

SON OVER HIS OWN HOUSE

. . .Christ as a son over his own house. Hebrews 3:6

The writer of Hebrews posed these verses as an argument that Jesus is superior to Moses, the great deliverer of God's people from slavery. Moses was faithful in his house, or the household of God's people of faith. But he was a mere *servant* in this house. By contrast, Jesus was a Son who *ruled over* His own house, or the church that He founded. So it follows logically that Jesus is superior to Moses.

This passage refers to a time in the wilderness when Moses' brother, Aaron, and his sister, Miriam, questioned his leadership. God stopped their rebellion by pointing out that Moses was His true prophet "who is faithful in all mine house" (Numbers 12:7).

But no matter how faithful Moses was to God, Jesus was even more so. He was God's own Son who gave His life to set people free from their bondage to sin. All believers are blessed by the faithfulness He demonstrated to God's redemptive plan.

Learn More: John 1:17; 6:32 / Hebrews 3:3

SPIRIT OF ADOPTION

Ye have received the Spirit of adoption. Romans 8:15

In this verse the apostle Paul contrasts the situation of a person before he becomes a believer to the new status he enjoys after his conversion. The old life is comparable to that of a slave in bondage who has no rights or privileges. But after being converted to new life in Christ, a person has all the advantages of sonship as a child of God the Father.

Paul used the concept of adoption to emphasize our new status with God. We were once children of sin, but God delivered us from our bondage and adopted us as His own. So close is our relationship to God as our adoptive Father that we can call Him *Abba*, an Aramaic word equivalent to our modern "Daddy" or "Papa."

The Holy Spirit has a vital role in this adoption process. His presence in our lives assures us that we belong to God. His Spirit will never let us forget that we enjoy a position of dignity and honor in the family of God the Father and Jesus the Son.

Learn More: Romans 8:23 / Galatians 4:5 / Ephesians 1:5

SPIRIT OF FAITH

We having the same spirit of faith. . . 2 Corinthians 4:13

To understand these words from the apostle Paul, we must consider his famous statement about the centrality of faith: "For by grace are ye saved through faith; and that not of yourselves: it is the gift of God: not of works, lest any man should boast" (Ephesians 2:8–9).

Paul did not say that we are saved *by* faith, but *through* faith. It is Christ's sacrifice on the cross that saves; we claim this truth for ourselves by placing our faith in Him. This is our human response to His sacrifice. Through faith in Christ, we experience forgiveness for our sins and accept Him as the Lord of our lives.

If human faith is an essential element of the salvation process, how do we have such faith? Paul's answer is that saving faith is a work of the Holy Spirit—the "spirit of faith." He alone can convict us of sin and lead us to declare our faith in Jesus Christ. Without the movement of the Holy Spirit to kindle faith in our hearts and minds, we would remain hopelessly lost in our sin.

Learn More: Romans 5:1 / 1 Corinthians 12:9 / Galatians 3:14 / 2 Timothy 4:7

SPIRIT OF GLORY

The spirit of glory and of God resteth upon you. 1 Peter 4:14

The apostle Peter in this verse may have been thinking back to the time when Jesus told the disciples what to do when they were persecuted for following Him. They were to "take no thought how or what ye shall speak: for it shall be given you in that same hour what ye shall speak. For it is not you that speak, but the Spirit of your Father which speaketh in you" (Matthew 10:19–20).

In effect, Jesus told the disciples not to retaliate against or resist their persecutors but to trust the Holy Spirit—the "spirit of glory"—to take care of them and give them the words to say in rebuttal. The same Spirit that guided Jesus throughout His ministry would also abide with them, strengthening them to serve as His bold witnesses.

The spirit of glory does not desert us during our times of persecution. He honors us for our sacrificial suffering in God's service, just as He glorified Jesus by raising Him from the dead (1 Peter 3:18).

Learn More: Ezekiel 43:5 / Ephesians 3:16 / 1 Peter 4:14

SPIRIT OF KNOWLEDGE AND THE FEAR OF THE LORD ———————

. . .the spirit of knowledge and of the fear of the Lord. ISAIAH 11:2

These two names of the Holy Spirit are among six that the prophet Isaiah used in this one verse. The prophet grouped these names together into three sets of two names each. He must have thought of these twin names as closely related to each other.

So how do the "spirit of knowledge" and the "spirit of the fear of the LORD" relate? Isaiah may have had in mind a well-known verse from the book of Proverbs: "The fear of the LORD is the beginning of knowledge" (Proverbs 1:7). "Fear of the Lord" means respect or reverence for God. So this proverb declares that a healthy respect for God is the most important attitude for a person to have as he accumulates the knowledge he needs to be happy and successful in life.

Through His Spirit, God plants in our hearts a reverence that leads us to honor Him in our lives. This is the foundation on which we build knowledge and understanding of Him and His work in the world.

Learn More: Daniel 5:12 / 1 Corinthians 12:8 / Ephesians 1:17

SPIRIT OF LIFE ———————————————————————

The law of the Spirit of life in Christ Jesus hath made me free. ROMANS 8:2

This statement of the apostle Paul reminds us of another of his famous declarations about the Holy Spirit: "Where the Spirit of the Lord is, there is liberty" (2 Corinthians 3:17). By the "law of the Spirit of life" in the verse above, Paul means the principle by which the Holy Spirit operates.

Life in the Spirit gives us the power to live free from the bondage of sin and death. This does not mean that believers will never experience death, because physical death is the lot of every human being. Paul means that those who have accepted Jesus Christ as Savior and Lord are no longer in bondage to our sinful nature. Just as Jesus defeated death, He has promised that all believers will enjoy eternal life with Him.

As the Spirit of "life," the Holy Spirit shares this aspect with Jesus (John 11:25–26). Those who have Jesus and the Holy Spirit in their lives have no reason to fear the grave.

Learn More: Job 10:12; 33:4 / 2 Corinthians 3:6

SPIRIT OF PROPHECY ————————————————————————

The testimony of Jesus is the spirit of prophecy. REVELATION 19:10

The apostle John, author of the book of Revelation, fell in awe before an angel at the throne of God. The angel told John not to worship him but to worship God and His Son, Jesus Christ. The angel went on to identify the Holy Spirit who bore witness of Jesus as the "spirit of prophecy."

The coming Messiah was often spoken of by the prophets of the Old Testament. This insight did not come to them through the power of their intellect but by direct revelation of God through the agency of His Holy Spirit.

These inspired prophecies were not restricted to the Old Testament. When Simeon saw the infant Jesus in the temple, he declared that the baby was the long-awaited Messiah whom God had finally sent to His people. This truth was revealed to Simeon by the Holy Spirit (Luke 2:25–27).

Learn More: Numbers 12:6 / Luke 7:16 / Acts 3:22 / 2 Peter 1:20

SPIRIT OF TRUTH

When he, the Spirit of truth, is come, he will guide you into all truth. JOHN 16:13

Jesus told His disciples He would soon be leaving them to return to the Father. But they would continue to feel His presence through the operation of the "Spirit of truth" in their lives.

The word *truth* can refer to something that is enduring or authentic, in contrast to something that is temporary or of little value. This aspect of truth is what Jesus had in mind. His disciples would discover that the Spirit was enduring and dependable. He would never leave them. When all else disappeared, the Spirit would continue to infuse them with power.

Jesus also told His disciples that the Spirit of truth would help them continue to bear witness of Him (John 15:26). The memory of His physical presence would eventually grow dim in their minds. But the Holy Spirit would help them recall His life and teachings and pass these truths on to others.

All who follow Christ are beneficiaries of the faithful witness of the disciples and other early believers. They eventually wrote down their eyewitness accounts of Jesus' life and ministry. These narratives were passed on to future generations through the inspired writings of the New Testament.

Learn More: John 14:16–17; 15:26 / 1 John 4:6

SPIRIT OF WISDOM AND REVELATION

. . .may give unto you the spirit of wisdom and revelation. EPHESIANS 1:17

This name of the Holy Spirit from the apostle Paul combines three important ingredients of the spiritual life—wisdom, revelation, and knowledge.

Revelation is the process by which God makes Himself known. Our human minds would know nothing about God unless He had chosen to reveal Himself to us. He has done this supremely through the written scriptures.

The writings that make up the Bible were revealed by God. But He inspired human beings through the activity of His Spirit to understand these divine messages and to write them down. Through the inspired scriptures, we gain knowledge about God—His nature as Creator, Sustainer, and Redeemer. But the Spirit teaches us more than factual information about God. We come to know Him in a personal sense as the God who loved us enough to send His own Son to save us from our sins.

Wisdom is the ability to apply what we know to real-life situations. The Holy Spirit gives us the wisdom to honor God in the way we live out our faith in the world.

Learn More: Deuteronomy 34:9 / Isaiah 11:2 / Acts 6:10 / 2 Peter 1:20–21

SPIRITUAL ROCK

They drank of that spiritual Rock that followed them. 1 CORINTHIANS 10:1, 4

These verses from the apostle Paul reminded the Jewish people of their years of wandering in the wilderness after their deliverance from slavery. God guided them with a cloud (Exodus 13:21), and He saved them from the Egyptian army at the Red Sea (Exodus 14:21–27).

In the barren wilderness, God also provided water for His people. It gushed from a rock when Moses struck it with his staff at God's command (Numbers 20:8–11). Paul picked up on this rock imagery and described Jesus as the "spiritual Rock" who meets the needs of God's people. Just as the rock in the desert was the source of water for the Israelites, Christ guides and protects those who place their trust in Him.

Was Jesus actually present with the Israelites in the wilderness? Paul declares that Christ their spiritual Rock "followed them." Or was Paul speaking metaphorically? We can't say for sure. But one thing we know for certain is that Jesus is a modern-day spiritual Rock who quenches our thirst and provides strength and stability for daily living. See also *Rock*.

Learn More: Exodus 17:6 / 1 Samuel 2:2 / Psalm 31:2; 62:6

STAR OUT OF JACOB

There shall come a Star out of Jacob. NUMBERS 24:17

Balaam, a pagan magician, assigned this name to the coming Messiah. He would be a "Star out of Jacob" who would rule over His people with great power and authority.

The nation of Israel is sometimes referred to in the Bible as "Jacob" because it sprang from the twelve sons, or tribes, of the patriarch Jacob. A star was considered the symbol of an exceptional king. When Jesus was born in Bethlehem, a bright star appeared in the sky to mark the occasion. This star guided the wise men from the east to the place in Bethlehem where He was Matthew 2:2–9 (Matthew 2:2–9).

The word *star* is tossed around loosely in our time. We have rock stars, movie stars, and superstars in every sport from baseball to wrestling. But the name of Jesus will live on long after these pseudo-stars have disappeared. He alone has the power to save and bring people into fellowship with God the Father. He reigns over His people as the Star that will never burn out. See also *Bright and Morning Star, Dayspring from on High*.

Learn More: Genesis 26:4 / Daniel 12:3 / 2 Peter 1:19 / Revelation 11:15; 22:16

STRENGTH

The Lord is my strength and song. EXODUS 15:2

This verse is part of the passage of scripture known as the "Song of Moses" (Exodus 15:1–19). Moses led the Israelites to sing this praise to the Lord after He rescued them from the pursuing army of the Egyptian pharaoh at the Red Sea.

The people had witnessed the awesome power of the Lord as He divided the waters of the sea to give them safe passage. Even before this event, He had plagued the Egyptians again and again until Pharaoh allowed the Israelites to leave the country. No wonder Moses referred to this wonder-working God as his "strength."

In later years the Lord also provided a meal for the prophet Elijah that gave him strength to escape the plot of the wicked queen Jezebel (1 Kings 19:8).

There is no shortage of power in the God we serve. And He invites us to partake of His strength in our times of need. The prophet Isaiah declared, "He giveth power to the faint; and to them that have no might he increaseth strength" (Isaiah 40:29).

Learn More: Psalm 18:1–2; 19:14 / Jeremiah 16:19 / Habakkuk 3:19

STRONG TOWER

The name of the Lord is a strong tower. PROVERBS 18:10

Towers were massive stone structures built above the defensive walls of ancient cities. From these elevated positions, defenders could shoot arrows or hurl stones on the enemy forces outside the wall. These towers also served as a final line of defense if the invading army should succeed in breaking through the wall or battering down the city gate.

The author of this proverb compared the Lord to one of these defensive towers. His righteous followers can seek safety and security in Him as the "strong tower." In a prayer of gratitude, King David expressed his praise to the Lord for serving as his "tower of salvation" against his enemies. The Lord "sheweth mercy to his anointed, unto David," he declared, "and to his seed for evermore" (2 Samuel 22:51).

The Lord used the imagery of a tower to assure the prophet Jeremiah that He would strengthen him for the task of delivering His unpopular message to the nation of Judah. "I have set thee for a tower and a fortress among my people," He told the prophet, "that thou mayest know and try their way" (Jeremiah 6:27). See also *Fortress*.

Learn More: 2 Samuel 22:3 / Psalm 18:2; 61:3; 144:2

TEACHER COME FROM GOD

Rabbi, we know that thou art a teacher come from God. JOHN 3:2

Nicodemus was a respected Pharisee who recognized Jesus as a "teacher come from God." He wanted to learn more about Him and His teachings. So he came to talk with Jesus face to face.

In His role as teacher, Jesus communicated God's message to individuals like Nicodemus, as well as large groups of people (see Mark 4:1). He was also a patient teacher with His disciples, who were slow to understand His mission of redemptive suffering (Luke 24:45–47).

Jesus was an effective communicator of divine truth because of His teaching style. He did not focus on abstract theories but on down-to-earth truths that the common people could understand. He used objects from everyday life to connect with His audience.

But the most impressive thing about His teaching is that it was stamped with the power of God the Father. He made it clear that He spoke under authority from God Himself. The people "were astonished at his doctrine: for he taught them as one that had authority, and not as the scribes" (Mark 1:22).

Learn More: Proverbs 23:12 / Matthew 23:34 / Mark 12:37 / Luke 4:32 / 2 Timothy 3:16

TRUTH

I am the way, the truth, and the life. JOHN 14:6

Jesus always spoke the truth to His followers. But beyond saying the truth, He *was* and *is* the Truth—the ultimate reality in the universe. This is the sense in which Jesus referred to Himself as "the truth" in His conversation with the disciple Thomas.

Our world has many different views of truth. Some people think that money and possessions are the ultimate goal of life. Others say learning or knowledge lead to truth. Many believe that each person has to find truth for himself by constructing it from his own life experiences.

These modern theories remind us of Pilate, the Roman governor who pronounced the death sentence against Jesus. When Jesus told him that He had come into the world to "bear witness unto the truth," Pilate asked, "What is truth?" (John 18:37–38). The Truth stood so close to Pilate that he could reach out and touch it, but he missed it because of his unbelief.

What a tragedy! And what an accurate picture of an unbelieving world—the arena into which we as believers are sent to bear witness of Him who is Truth (Mark 16:15).

Learn More: Psalm 25:5; 31:5 / Malachi 2:6 / John 8:32 / Ephesians 4:21

VINE

I am the vine, ye are the branches. JOHN 15:5

Jesus spoke these words to the disciples during the Last Supper, on the night of His arrest. He knew His followers would need to be firmly attached to Him as the vine in order to weather the crisis of His forthcoming execution and death.

The plant that Jesus referred to was a grapevine. It had one main stem with several smaller shoots or runners branching off in all directions. These smaller branches owed their lives to the main stem. With this imagery, Jesus emphasized that His disciples should stay attached to Him as their Lord and Savior. He as "the vine" would sustain and nourish them so they would bear "much fruit" in the days ahead.

The fruit Jesus mentioned probably referred to the witness they would bear for Him after His resurrection and ascension. Most of these disciples—His "branches"—did abandon Him when He was arrested and crucified (Matthew 26:56). But after His resurrection, they regained their courage and continued the work that Jesus had trained them to do (Acts 1:13–14; 2:42–43).

Learn More: Job 15:33 / Isaiah 5:1–2 / Ezekiel 17:8 / Hosea 10:1 / John 15:1–4

WALL OF FIRE

I, saith the Lord, will be unto her a wall of fire round about. ZECHARIAH 2:5

This name of God appears only here in the Bible. The prophet Zechariah used it to describe God's protection of the city of Jerusalem after the exile. The city's defensive walls had been destroyed by the Babylonians several decades before; this meant the Jewish exiles who returned to Jerusalem were in a precarious position. But God promised to protect them by becoming a "wall of fire" around the city.

Fire is often associated in the Bible with God's presence and protection. For example, God appeared in a burning bush to call Moses to deliver the Israelites from slavery in Egypt (Exodus 3:2). During the Exodus, the Lord used a pillar of fire to protect the Israelites from the pursuing Egyptian army while the Israelites crossed the Red Sea (Exodus 14:24–25). Then He sent a pillar of fire at night to guide His people on their journey through the wilderness (Exodus 13:21).

God still serves as the protector of His people. We can declare in confidence with the psalmist, "My help cometh from the LORD, which made heaven and earth" (Psalm 121:2). See also *Consuming Fire; Refiner's Fire.*

Learn More: Exodus 24:17 / Psalm 78:21 / Daniel 3:20–26

WAY

I am the way, the truth, and the life. JOHN 14:6

The disciple Thomas was puzzled by Jesus' statement that He would leave His followers soon after His resurrection (John 14:1–4). Thomas wanted to know how he and the other disciples could find Jesus aHim after He left. Jesus assured Thomas that He was the only "way" to their eternal reward. Thomas didn't need to know every detail about this destination or how to get there.

This conversation has a valuable lesson for modern Christians. Sometimes our curiosity about heaven takes our eyes off the One who has promised to take us there. We wonder where heaven will be and what it will look like.

We don't know the answers to these questions. But we do have a grasp of the most important thing: Jesus is the only way to that wonderful place. He knows the way there, and we know Him as "the way." So we can relax and trust His promise: "There is more than enough room in my Father's home. . . . When everything is ready, I will come and get you, so that you will always be with me where I am" (John 14:2–3 NLT).

Learn More: Psalm 86:11; 119:1; 143:8

WORD

In the beginning was the Word, and the Word was with God, and the Word was God. JOHN 1:1

The prologue of John's Gospel (John 1:1–18), of which this verse is part, focuses on Jesus as the eternal Son who existed with God the Father before the creation of the world. The verse is an obvious reference to the first three words of the first book of the Bible, in Genesis 1:1.

Just as God was "in the beginning," so Jesus existed "in the beginning" (John 1:1) as the eternal Word. This Word, who assumed human form to make His dwelling among human beings (John 1:14), is comparable to the words that God used to speak the universe into being (Genesis 1:3).

Words are the primary units of language that enable humans to communicate with one another. In the same way, Jesus reveals the will and mind of God the Father to earthbound mortals.

The description of Jesus as "the Word" is unique to the apostle John's writings. In his first epistle, John declared, "There are three that bear record in heaven, the Father, the Word, and the Holy Ghost: and these three are one" (1 John 5:7). This leaves little doubt that John thought of Jesus as the Word who was the second person of the Trinity.

Learn More: Psalm 12:6; 33:6 / John 15:3 / Revelation 19:13

THE 1-MINUTE
BIBLE
GUIDE

180 Key People

An alphabetical listing of the 180 most important individuals named in scripture.

Written by George W. Knight
Edited by Paul Kent

AARON

Aaron spoke all the words which the Lord had spoken unto Moses. Exodus 4:30

The Lord chose Aaron as spokesman for Moses during the exodus from Egypt. But Aaron did more than just speak for his brother. Through God's power, he also stretched out his staff to bring some of the ten plagues against the land (Exodus 7:9, 19). In the wilderness, Aaron and Hur helped Moses hold up his hands to bring victory over the forces of Amalek (Exodus 17:12).

But Aaron also had his moments of weakness. While Moses was receiving the Ten Commandments on Mount Sinai, Aaron allowed the people to fashion an idol as an object of worship. Only Moses' intercession on his brother's behalf saved him from God's punishment (Exodus 32:3–10; Deuteronomy 9:20).

When the official priesthood was established in the wilderness, Aaron was set apart as the first high priest of Israel (Exodus 28–29). Upon his death, Aaron's son Eleazar succeeded him in this role. But this human priestly system is inferior to the priesthood of Christ. Jesus' intercession on our behalf never ends, and it offers the promise of eternal life to all believers (Hebrews 5:2–5; 7:11–12).

Learn More: Exodus 7:8–20 / Numbers 20:12, 29

ABEL

The Lord had respect unto Abel and to his offering. Genesis 4:4

Abel was the second son of Adam and Eve, a man whose gift of choice animals from his flock was accepted by the Lord (Genesis 4:1–16). He serves as a good example of sacrificial giving.

Abel's brother Cain brought an offering of harvested fruit and grain to the Lord, but God refused to accept it. This made Cain angry and envious, and he murdered Abel in the first recorded instance of violence in the Bible.

This event is mentioned several times in the New Testament. The writer of Hebrews declared that Abel offered a better sacrifice than his brother. This apparently refers to Abel's faith, his superior character as a righteous person, and the correct motives behind his gift (Hebrews 11:4). The apostle John wrote that Cain murdered Abel because Cain's works were evil, in comparison to the righteous acts of his brother (1 John 3:12).

Jesus spoke of "the blood of righteous Abel" (Matthew 23:35). As the first martyr in the Bible, Abel's shed blood symbolizes God's demand for punishment against sin and unrighteousness. But the blood shed under the new covenant—Jesus' atoning death on the cross—"speaketh better things than that of Abel" (Hebrews 12:24) because it is the agent of salvation for hopeless sinners. See also *Cain.*

Learn More: Genesis 4:1–25

ABIATHAR

. . .named Abiathar, escaped, and fled after David. 1 Samuel 22:20

Abiathar, a priest, was the sole survivor of King Saul's massacre of eighty-five priests in the city of Nob. Saul was enraged because Abiathar's father, the high priest of Nob, came to David's aid while Saul was trying to kill the future king (1 Samuel 22:6–23).

After Abiathar escaped, he lived under David's protection during David's fugitive years. When David became the unchallenged king of Israel, Abiathar emerged as a priest in the royal court (1 Samuel 30:7).

At David's orders Abiathar and another priest named Zadok took care of the ark of the covenant in Jerusalem when David fled the city to escape Absalom's rebellion. These two priests remained in Jerusalem as spies to keep the king informed of Absalom's actions.

Abiathar had another brush with death after David passed from the scene. The priest threw his support behind the king's son Adonijah as successor to the throne. But another son, Solomon, won the power struggle. This was bad news for any subject who was not totally loyal to the new regime, and Solomon promptly banished Abiathar and his family from Jerusalem. Only his previous loyalty to David saved the priest from execution (1 Kings 2:26–27).

Learn More: 2 Samuel 19:11–15

ABIGAIL

David said to Abigail, Blessed be the Lord God of Israel. 1 Samuel 25:32

Abigail's quick thinking and sound advice kept David from making a terrible mistake. It all started when David was on the run from Saul in Abigail's territory. He asked her husband, Nabal, to provide food for his hungry men. Nabal refused and insulted David by calling him a no-good leader of a band of outlaws.

When Abigail learned about this, she gathered the provisions David had asked for and set off toward his camp. She met a man boiling with anger—David had his men armed and ready to settle the score with Abigail's husband.

But she urged David not to return one foolish act with another, reminding David that he was destined to become the next king of Israel. Surely he didn't want a thoughtless act of revenge as a blot on his record. David saw the wisdom in Abigail's reasoning and had his men stand down (1 Samuel 25:1–35).

Several days after Abigail returned home, Nabal died following a drunken orgy. When David heard the news, he took Abigail as his wife. She became the mother of one of David's sons (2 Samuel 3:3).

Learn More: 1 Chronicles 3:1–9

ABNER

And David said. . .mourn before Abner. 2 Samuel 3:31

Abner was a chief military officer under both King Saul and King David. Abner was on the scene when David the shepherd boy defeated the Philistine giant Goliath. When Saul asked about the boy, Abner looked David up and introduced him to the king. Abner led Saul's army during the years when David hid from Saul in the wilderness.

After Saul was killed in a battle with the Philistines, a power struggle broke out between David's supporters and those who favored Ish-bosheth, one of Saul's sons. Abner threw his support behind Ish-bosheth.

Later, Abner changed his mind, shifted his loyalty to David, and convinced other influential leaders to do the same. But just as things were going David's way, he faced another crisis. Joab, commander of David's army, murdered Abner to avenge Abner's killing of Joab's brother.

David realized this would look like an assassination he had plotted. This could undermine the support of Abner's friends. So the king reprimanded Joab publicly and arranged for Abner to be buried with full honors.

Learn More: 1 Samuel 17:55–58; 26:14–15 / 2 Samuel 3:17–38

ABRAHAM

The Lord had said unto Abram, Get thee out of thy country. Genesis 12:1

God's determination to build a special people who would be devoted to Him began with Abraham. The Lord called him to leave his native land for a place that would be revealed to him in due time. Abraham obeyed and moved into Canaan, a land that God promised to give to him and his descendants (Genesis 12:1–5).

The problem was that Abraham had no children, and the prospects of having any were bleak because of his advanced age. The Lord solved this dilemma by allowing his wife Sarah to conceive and give birth to Isaac in their old age (Genesis 21:1–8). Abraham had fathered a previous son through Sarah's servant. But God made it clear that His promise to Abraham was to be fulfilled through Isaac (Genesis 17:20–21).

To test Abraham's faith, the Lord directed him to sacrifice his beloved son Isaac. Then God himself stepped in to save the boy and renewed His promise to bless Abraham because of his great faith (Genesis 22:1–12). Abraham lived to the age of 175 and was buried beside Sarah in a cave he had purchased near the city of Hebron (Genesis 25:7–10).

Learn More: Genesis 20:1–17; 25:1–6 / Psalm 105:6–10 / Romans 4:1–3 / Matthew 1:1–2

ABSALOM

Absalom returned to his own house, and saw not the king's face. 2 SAMUEL 14:24

When David committed adultery with Bathsheba, the prophet Nathan predicted that his family would be struck with tragedy because of this sin (2 Samuel 12:9–12). A chain of family difficulties finally reached its climax when David's own son, Absalom, tried to take the kingship by force.

This all began with another tragedy. Absalom ordered the murder of his half-brother Amnon for molesting their sister Tamar (2 Samuel 13:22–32). Absalom then fled from Jerusalem. Although David loved Absalom dearly, he refused to communicate with him, even after he returned to the city. This shunning may have been one reason why Absalom tried to take down his father (2 Samuel 14:24–28).

During a battle with David's forces, Absalom's long hair got entangled in the branch of a tree. He was killed by Joab, David's commander (2 Samuel 18:9–14).

When David heard the news, he wept with some of the saddest words in the Bible. "O my son Absalom! My son, my son Absalom!" he cried. "If only I had died instead of you— O Absalom, my son, my son!" (2 Samuel 18:33 NIV).

Learn More: 2 Samuel 15:1–12

ACHAN

Achan answered Joshua, and said, Indeed I have sinned against the Lord. JOSHUA 7:20

Before Joshua led an attack on the city of Jericho, God made it clear that no one was to claim the spoils of war for himself. These were to be consecrated to God and placed in "the treasury of the LORD" (Joshua 6:19).

But an Israelite soldier named Achan took several valuable articles from the booty and hid them in his tent. Meanwhile, the Israelites attacked the small town of Ai. Compared to Jericho, Ai should have been an easy target, since it had only a few defenders. But surprisingly, the Israelites suffered a humiliating defeat.

Joshua prayed for an answer to the dilemma, and the Lord revealed that someone had disobeyed His command. A thorough search brought Achan's forbidden cache to light. He had taken a Babylonian garment, two hundred shekels of silver, and a wedge of gold.

Achan and his family were taken to a nearby valley, where they were stoned to death (Joshua 7:1–26). Soon thereafter, the Israelites attacked Ai again and won an easy victory (Joshua 8:21–26).

Learn More: 1 Chronicles 2:7; *Achar:* KJV / Joshua 22:20

ADAM

And the Lord God formed man of the dust of the ground. GENESIS 2:7

Adam was the crowning achievement of the creation (Genesis 1:26). But he was fashioned from the dust of the ground, symbolizing his humble status as an earthbound being who owed his existence to the Lord.

God placed Adam in the garden of Eden and gave him the task of working the ground (Genesis 2:15). The fruit from all the trees in the garden were his for the taking—with one exception. He was not to touch the tree of the knowledge of good and evil (Genesis 2:17).

Eve, Adam's female counterpart, yielded to temptation from Satan and ate the forbidden fruit, then encouraged Adam to do the same. This act of disobedience led God to banish the couple from the garden and to subject them to a life of difficulties (Genesis 3:1–24).

Adam's rebellion against God was the original transgression that infected the entire human race (Romans 3:23). But according to the apostle Paul, God sent another Adam—the Last Adam, Jesus Christ—to solve the problem caused by the original man. Adam's legacy of death has been canceled by the atoning death of Jesus on the cross (1 Corinthians 15:21–22). See also *Eve.*

Learn More: Luke 3:38

ADONIJAH

Then Adonijah the son of Haggith exalted himself. 1 Kings 1:5

Adonijah was a son of King David whose ambition got him into trouble. While his father was still alive, he made a bold move to set himself up as David's successor.

When the king was old and in failing health, Adonijah summoned his supporters, including several of David's other sons, to a meeting near Jerusalem. David's son Solomon was not invited (1 Kings 1:18–19). So Adonijah must have known that Solomon was the king's choice as his successor.

But several people, including Solomon's mother, Bathsheba, hurried to the king to tell him what was going on. They convinced David to have Solomon anointed immediately as the new king. When Adonijah heard the news, he realized his kingly ambitions were over and that Solomon could kill him. He fled to the tabernacle and grabbed the horns of the altar, an act that supposedly guaranteed his safety. Solomon released him with a warning not to cause any more trouble (1 Kings 1:50–52).

Later, Adonijah asked Solomon to let him marry Abishag, the young woman who had served as David's nurse in his old age. Solomon apparently interpreted this as evidence that he still had kingly ambitions, so he had Adonijah executed (1 Kings 2:13–25).

Learn More: 1 Chronicles 3:1–2

AGRIPPA

Agrippa said unto Paul, Thou art permitted to speak for thyself. Acts 26:1

Agrippa was a Roman official before whom the apostle Paul appeared while imprisoned at Caesarea. The apostle made a passionate speech in which he recounted the events of his life, particularly his conversion from persecutor to preacher of the Christian faith (Acts 26:1–27).

Paul ended his speech with a direct appeal to Agrippa to believe the prophecies about Jesus, whom God had raised from the dead. "King Agrippa, do you believe the prophets?" he asked. "I know you do" (verse 27 NIV).

Agrippa responded, "Almost thou persuadest me to be a Christian" (verse 28). Was he on the verge of becoming a believer, or was he being sarcastic? It's impossible to say for sure. One modern translation renders his response like this: "Do you think you can persuade me to become a Christian so quickly?" (NLT).

Either way, Agrippa was impressed with Paul's stirring defense. He declared that the apostle was innocent and could be set free had he not appealed his case to Rome (Acts 26:32).

This Agrippa is often referred to as Agrippa II, to distinguish him from his father, Agrippa I, who persecuted the Christians in Jerusalem (Acts 12:1–23).

Learn More: Acts 25:13–27

AHAB

Ahab the son of Omri did evil in the sight of the Lord. 1 Kings 16:30

Ahab had a lot going for him when he took the throne of the northern kingdom of Israel. His father had built a new capital city, and the country was in good shape financially. Ahab built several new cities throughout the nation (1 Kings 22:39) and established peaceful relations with Judah, the sister nation to the south (1 Kings 22:2–4).

Ahab's problems began with his political marriage to Jezebel, daughter of a Phoenician king. She worshiped the pagan god Baal, and she influenced Ahab to allow Baal worship throughout the nation. The king even built a temple to Baal in the capital city (1 Kings 16:32–33).

Ahab's greed also got him into trouble. He wanted a plot of ground near his summer palace. But the landowner, Naboth, refused to sell. With Jezebel's help, the two had Naboth executed on a false charge of blasphemy. Then the king confiscated the property (1 Kings 21:1–16).

The prophet Elijah predicted that God would punish the king severely for this crime (1 Kings 21:19). Several years later Ahab was killed in a battle with the Syrians. When his blood was flushed from his chariot, dogs lapped up the bloody water (1 Kings 22:38).

Learn More: 1 Kings 20:1–21

AHASUERUS

And the king loved Esther above all the women. ESTHER 2:17

A king of Persia, Ahasuerus is portrayed throughout the book of Esther as a sensual plea-sure-seeker (1:7–8) who was vain (1:4), quick-tempered (1:13–22), and subject to manipulation by others (3:1–15). But he did have the good sense to select the young Jewish woman Esther as his queen.

Ahasuerus deposed his first queen, Vashti, because she refused his command to display her beauty to his drunken guests. Esther eventually succeeded Vashti in the royal court.

Some time later, the king's second-in-command—a man named Haman—convinced Ahasuerus to issue a death order against all Jewish people throughout his kingdom. This act of retaliation against an entire race came about because one Jewish man, Mordecai, refused to bow down and pay homage to Haman (Esther 3:1–11).

When Esther learned about the plot, she used her influence with the king to expose Haman, have him executed, and save her people from genocide. Ahasuerus issued a second proclamation that allowed the Jews to defend themselves against the original death order (Esther 8:11–13).

Learn More: Esther 6:1–10

AMALEK

Joshua discomfited Amalek and his people with the edge of the sword. EXODUS 17:13

Amalek was a grandson of Esau, Jacob's twin brother. Amalek was the ancestor of a tribal group known as the Amalekites, fierce enemies of the Israelites. They lived in southern Canaan, the land promised by the Lord to Abraham and his descendants.

Amalek as a person is cited only three times in the Bible (Genesis 36:12, 16; 1 Chronicles 1:36). But the Amalekites as a tribe are mentioned throughout the Old Testament. In the King James Version, the singular name *Amalek* is often used to refer to this tribe, as in Exodus 17:13.

While wandering in the wilderness, the Israelites were attacked by the Amalekites. Under Joshua's leadership, the Israelites won the battle—but only because Moses held his hands up over the battle scene. Aaron and Hur steadied his hands when Moses grew tired (Exodus 17:8–13).

In later years, campaigns against the Amalekites were conducted by King Saul (1 Samuel 15:1–5) and King David (1 Samuel 27:8–10).

Learn More: Genesis 36:1–12

AMAZIAH

Amaziah. . .brought the gods of the children of Seir. 2 CHRONICLES 25:14

King Amaziah of Judah got off to a good start by following the Lord. But he soon found trouble because of his flawed judgment and poor choices.

The king's problems began when he won a decisive victory over the Edomites. For some strange reason, he adopted their pagan gods as his own and began to worship them in his homeland. It was as if the Edomites lost the battle but won a war for Amaziah's heart.

God was angered by this turn of events, so He sent a prophet to ask the king a sobering question: "Why have you sought a people's gods that could not deliver their own people from your hands?" (2 Chronicles 25:15 HCSB).

Energized by his victory over Edom, Amaziah foolishly renewed hostilities against Israel, Judah's sister Jewish kingdom to the north. This time he suffered a humiliating defeat. The Israelite army attacked Jerusalem and carried away captives as well as treasures from the temple and Amaziah's palace (2 Chronicles 25:20–24).

Learn More: 2 Kings 14:1–6, 17–19

AMNON

Amnon was so vexed, that he fell sick for his sister Tamar. 2 SAMUEL 13:2

Just like his father David before him, Amnon's sexual desires caused a chain reaction of family tragedies. He was so infatuated with his half-sister Tamar that he forced himself upon her (2 Samuel 13:1–20). This caused her great shame and humiliation. It also led Absalom, Tamar's full brother, to avenge this crime by murdering Amnon (2 Samuel 13:22–29).

Another spin-off of this tragic event was the alienation of Absalom from his father, David. The king treated Absalom as an outcast and apparently never spoke to him again (2 Samuel 14:24, 28). This ill will between father and son eventually led Absalom to rebel against David's authority and to try to take the throne by force (2 Samuel 15:1–14).

If not for Amnon's sin that led to his death, he could have been in line to succeed David as king. He was his father's oldest son, born while David ruled southern Judah from the city of Hebron (2 Samuel 3:2).

Learn More: 2 Samuel 13:30–33

AMOS

The words of Amos. . .which he saw concerning Israel. AMOS 1:1

The prophet Amos admitted he was simply a shepherd and a farmer. But God called him to deliver a message of judgment against the northern kingdom of Israel. This was all the authority he needed to speak on behalf of the Lord (Amos 7:15–16). His prophecies appear in the Old Testament book that bears his name.

The prophet condemned the people of Israel because they had rejected the Lord and turned to the worship of false gods. He also criticized the wealthy class for oppressing the poor (Amos 2:6).

Amos insisted that righteous behavior—not observing empty rituals such as feast days and bringing sacrifices to the altar—was what God required of His people. "Let justice roll on like a river," he declared, "righteousness like a never-failing stream" (Amos 5:24 NIV).

The prophet is well known for the visions he received from the Lord. One of the most striking was a basket of ripe fruit. Like these delicacies that would quickly spoil in the summer heat, Israel was overdue for God's judgment because of her disobedience of the Lord (Amos 8:1–2).

Learn More: Amos 7:7–9

ANANIAS

Ananias answered, Lord, I have heard by many of this man. ACTS 9:13

Ananias, a believer in the city of Damascus, could have been persecuted by the man who became the apostle Paul. Instead, Ananias was the instrument God used to help Paul and commission him as a preacher of the gospel (Acts 9:10–20).

The apostle, then known as Saul, was headed to Damascus to persecute its Christians when he was gloriously converted. In the process, he was struck blind for three days, and the Lord called Ananias to put his hands on Paul so his sight could be restored.

Because of Paul's reputation as a fierce enemy of the church, Ananias was reluctant to obey God. But he did after the Lord explained that Paul had been selected as His special witness who would lead many people, including Gentiles, to the Lord.

This Ananias is the second of three men by that name in the book of Acts. The first mentioned was struck dead for lying about the amount of money he had given to the Lord's work (Acts 5:1–11). The third is the high priest in Jerusalem, who was involved in Paul's trial (Acts 23:1–5).

Learn More: Acts 22:11–16

ANDREW

We have found the Messias, which is, being interpreted, the Christ. JOHN 1:41

After becoming one of Jesus' disciples, Andrew always seemed to be introducing other people to the Lord. At first, Andrew was a follower of John the Baptist, but he turned to Jesus after John identified Him as "the Lamb of God." Andrew spent a day at Jesus' home, then went immediately to his brother Peter to introduce him to the Master (John 1:37–42).

Later, Andrew told Jesus about a boy who had brought his lunch to an isolated place where many people had gathered. Jesus multiplied the boy's loaves and fish to feed the hungry crowd (John 6:1–11). This event became known as the miracle of the feeding of the five thousand.

On another occasion, Andrew and Philip—another member of the Twelve—told Jesus about a group of Greeks who wanted to talk with Him (John 12:20–22). Andrew is mentioned a final time in the gospels when he asked Jesus about the events of the end times (Mark 13:3–4).

Learn More: Acts 1:8–14

ANNA

She coming in that instant gave thanks likewise unto the Lord. LUKE 2:38

Jewish custom dictated that all firstborn infants be presented, along with an offering, at the temple in Jerusalem. Mary and Joseph observed this custom when Jesus was eight days old (Luke 2:22–38).

In the building that day was an aged widow named Anna. A prophetess, she was probably a temple attendant, since she "departed not from the temple, but served God with fastings and prayers night and day" (Luke 2:37).

Through divine revelation, Anna recognized this eight-day-old boy as the long-awaited Messiah. She broke out in praise to the Lord for sending Jesus as the agent of redemption for His people.

Anna is a good example of how to grow old gracefully. She remained faithful to the Lord in spite of the loss of her husband at a young age. She communed constantly with her Lord through prayer. And she never lost faith that God would fulfill His promise.

Learn More: 1 Corinthians 4:1–7

APOLLOS

He mightily convinced the Jews, and that publicly. ACTS 18:28

Some time after the apostle Paul founded the church at Ephesus, a zealous and learned believer named Apollos visited the city. He used his knowledge of the Old Testament scriptures to convince the Jews in the local synagogue that Jesus was the Messiah they had been looking for (Acts 18:24–28).

Aquila and Priscilla, two leaders in the church at Ephesus, heard about his powerful preaching. Apollos had been a disciple of John the Baptist, so apparently he had an inadequate understanding of the gospel message. These two leaders befriended Apollos and "explained the way of God even more accurately" (verse 26 NLT).

Apollos went on to become a popular preacher, particularly in Achaia (verse 27) and the church at Corinth. A faction of Corinthian believers favored Apollos over all other human leaders. Paul dealt with this problem by pointing out that Jesus was the true source and foundation of their faith (1 Corinthians 3:3–11).

Apollos may also have served on the island of Crete. Paul encouraged Titus, leader of this church, to send two believers—one of whom was named Apollos—on their way with everything they needed for the journey (Titus 3:13).

Learn More: 1 Corinthians 4:1–7

ASA

Asa did that which was right in the eyes of the Lord. 1 Kings 15:11

Asa, the third king of Judah, presided over many religious reforms in the land. He removed the idols that had been erected during the reign of Abijam, his father and predecessor. He restored the altar in the temple and encouraged the people to renew their covenant with the Lord. He even deposed his own mother from power because she had set up a shrine devoted to a pagan god (1 Kings 15:9–13).

But the king's record was not perfect. After winning a victory over the Ethiopians by relying on the Lord, he hired an army from Syria to turn back an assault by Israel, Judah's sister kingdom to the north. A prophet named Hanani rebuked Asa for relying on foreign soldiers rather than trusting the Lord. Enraged, the king had the prophet thrown into prison (2 Chronicles 16:1–10).

Before his reign ended, Asa developed a foot disease. The recorder of his administration noted that "he did not seek help from the Lord, but only from the physicians" (2 Chronicles 16:12 NIV). Asa is mentioned in the New Testament, in Matthew's genealogy of Jesus (Matthew 1:7).

Learn More: 2 Chronicles 14:1–15; 15:1–16; 16:1–14

ASAPH

The singers, Heman, Asaph, and Ethan. . . 1 Chronicles 15:19

A Levite musician in David's time, Asaph was responsible for sounding cymbals in praise to the Lord when the ark of the covenant was relocated to Jerusalem. This was a joyous occasion for all the people of the city. They joined in the celebration with "shouting, and with sound of the cornet, and with trumpets, and with cymbals, making a noise with psalteries and with harps" (1 Chronicles 15:28). King David himself was so excited that he danced before the ark as it entered the city.

In later years, David organized the priests and Levites of Judah into units and assigned them specific responsibilities to perform. Asaph and his descendants were charged with providing music for worship at the tabernacle. Their work as musicians carried over to the temple after it was built under King Solomon (1 Chronicles 25:1–9).

After the exile, descendants of Asaph returned to Jerusalem and led the singing at the dediation of the foundation of the rebuilt temple (Ezra 2:41; 3:10–11). Twelve psalms (Psalms 50; 73–83) are identified as "psalms of Asaph" or given similar titles.

Learn More: Psalm 73

ATHALIAH

Athaliah. . .arose and destroyed all the seed royal. 2 Kings 11:1

Athaliah grew up in a political family as the daughter of a king of Israel (2 Kings 8:26). So she was ready to make a political move of her own during the chaos that followed the assassination of her son, King Ahaziah of Judah. She promptly executed her own grandsons to eliminate any possible claimants to the throne and took control as queen of Judah.

But the Lord saw to it that the ruthless queen missed one grandson, Joash, who was only a year old at the time. For six years the young prince was hidden in the temple. Then Jehoiada, the high priest, brought the boy out of hiding. The priest rallied the people to execute Athaliah and replace her with Joash as the rightful claimant to the throne (2 Kings 11:1–20).

Athaliah was the only woman and the only non-descendant of David to occupy the throne of Judah. But thanks to Jehoiada and others, she did not destroy the royal Davidic line from which the Messiah eventually emerged.

Learn More: 2 Chronicles 22:10–23:21

AUGUSTUS

There went out a decree from Caesar Augustus that all the world should be taxed. LUKE 2:1

Augustus was a title of honor, meaning "his reverence," that was bestowed on all emperors of the Roman Empire after his death (see, for example, Acts 25:21). He issued the census decree for taxation purposes that brought Mary and Joseph to Bethlehem, where Jesus was born. Augustus's policies, including taxation of all subject nations, led to the extension of the boundaries of the empire and the development of its capital city, Rome.

Augustus has been identified by secular historians as Octavian (ruled 31 BC–AD 14). Thus he was alive during Jesus' boyhood years before, the Lord launched His public ministry.

BALAAM

How shall I curse, whom God hath not cursed? NUMBERS 23:8

Balaam, a pagan wizard, shows that God can use even an evil force to bring about His will.

The king of Moab had hired Balaam to pronounce a curse against the Israelites as they passed through his territory on their way to the Canaan. But God intervened and caused Balaam to bless the Israelites instead. This happened not once but three times (Numbers 24:1–11).

Enraged at this turn of events, the king refused to pay the generous fee he had promised for Balaam's services. Then the wizard predicted, "A star will arise from Jacob, and a scepter will arise from Israel" (Numbers 24:17 HCSB). This has been interpreted as a reference to Jesus the Messiah.

Balaam is best known as the man with a talking donkey. When he set out to find the Israelite camp, his donkey balked because the angel of the Lord blocked their path. The donkey detoured around the angel three times until Balaam finally beat the innocent beast with a stick. At this the donkey told his master, "What have I done unto thee, that thou hast smitten me these three times?" (Numbers 22:28).

The moral of the story is probably Balaam's lack of spiritual sensitivity. A simple donkey saw the angel of the Lord, while Balaam—supposed to have magical powers—was blind to what God was doing.

Learn More: Numbers 23–24 / Joshua 13:22 / Jude 11 / 2 Peter 2:15 / Revelation 2:14

BARABBAS

Away with this man, and release unto us Barabbas. LUKE 23:18

Locked away in prison on the day of Jesus' crucifixion was a notorious criminal named Barabbas. Pilate asked the crowd whether they wanted him or Jesus released from custody. The crowd, agitated by the religious leaders, chose Barabbas.

During the Passover celebration that was going on at the time, Roman authorities apparently released one prisoner as a goodwill gesture to the Jewish people. Barabbas had led a revolt against the authority of Rome. The people hated their Roman overlords, so they naturally clamored for Barabbas rather than Jesus to be set free (Matthew 27:15–22).

The contrast between this criminal and Jesus could not be more dramatic. One was a military leader, the other a spiritual Savior. One called for political deliverance from the power of Rome; the other offered hope for spiritual deliverance from the darkness of sin.

Learn More: Mark 15:6–15 / John 18:39–40

BARNABAS

Barnabas took [Paul], and brought him to the apostles. Acts 9:27

The name of Barnabas, a believer in the early church, means "son of encouragement." He lived up to his name by speaking up for Paul when many Christians did not trust the former persecutor of the church (Acts 9:27–28).

After Barnabas became a leader in the church at Antioch, he enlisted Paul to help him in this ministry (Acts 11:19–26). Later, the church sent Barnabas and Paul to witness in territories that had not been reached by the gospel. Barnabas was in the lead when they left, but Paul had moved to the forefront by the time they returned. This trip eventually became known as the apostle's first missionary journey (Acts 13:1–3; 14:26–28).

Barnabas would have been with Paul on his second journey, if not for a disagreement between them. Barnabas wanted to take his relative John Mark with them as he had done before. But Paul refused because the young man had returned home without completing the first missionary tour. So Barnabas left Paul, took Mark with him, and set off in a different direction (Acts 15:36–41).

Learn More: Acts 4:36–37; 11:29–30; 12:25; 15:1–2

BARTIMAEUS

He began to cry out, and say, Jesus, thou son of David, have mercy on me. Mark 10:47

Bartimaeus, a blind beggar from the city of Jericho, is a study in perseverance. He was sitting by the road begging for handouts when Jesus passed by. He had heard about this miraculous teacher and healer, so he called out above the noise of the crowd for Jesus to make him well.

Some people standing nearby told Bartimaeus to stop yelling, but he shouted even louder to get Jesus' attention (Mark 10:46–52).

Jesus heard the blind man, called him over, and asked him what he wanted. Then the Lord restored the man's sight with the words, "Go thy way; thy faith hath made thee whole" (verse 52). Bartimaeus's faith and determination were richly rewarded.

Accounts of the healing of a blind man at Jericho also appear in the gospels of Matthew and Luke, but only Mark identifies him as Bartimaeus.

Learn More: Matthew 20:29–34 / Luke 18:35–43

BATHSHEBA

Assuredly Solomon thy son shall reign after me. 1 Kings 1:30

Bathsheba was a mother who wanted the best for her son. As a wife of King David and the mother of Solomon, she used her influence with the king to ensure that her son would follow David on the throne.

Bathsheba became David's wife after their adulterous affair resulted in the birth of a son. This child died as an infant. Later, she gave birth to Solomon, one of four children she bore to David (2 Samuel 12:24; 1 Chronicles 3:5).

David had many sons by several different wives (1 Chronicles 3:1–9), so it was not surprising that a dispute erupted over which one would be his successor. The fourth-born, Adonijah, enlisted supporters and declared himself the legitimate successor to the throne. This brought Bathsheba and Nathan the prophet on the run to confront David.

These two insisted that David declare publicly that he wanted Solomon to succeed him. The king not only agreed, but he made arrangements for Solomon to be sworn in immediately as the new king (1 Kings 1:15–30).

Learn More: 2 Samuel 11:1–27; Bathshua: KJV

BELSHAZZAR

Then was king Belshazzar greatly troubled. Daniel 5:9

Belshazzar, king of Babylon, threw a rowdy banquet for his top officials. Their revelry was interrupted when a human hand appeared and wrote a message on the wall of the royal palace: "Mene, Mene, Tekel, Upharsin." The king was so frightened by this ghostly image that "the joints of his loins were loosed, and his knees smote one against another" (Daniel 5:6; see 5:1–31).

None of Belshazzar's court magicians could tell what the writing meant. So his queen urged him to summon Daniel, a Jewish exile in Babylon known for his wisdom.

Daniel chastised the king for his pride and disrespect. He and his guests had been drinking from sacred vessels stolen by the Babylonians from the Jewish temple in Jerusalem. Then the prophet turned to the strange handwriting on the wall. It meant that the king had been measured by the Lord and found wanting. Belshazzar's kingdom was coming to an end; it would fall to a stronger world power.

As it turned out, Belshazzar was the last king of the mighty Babylonian Empire. That very night he was killed when his nation fell to the Persian army (Daniel 5:30–31).

Learn More: Daniel 7:1; 8:1

BENJAMIN

She called his name Benoni: but his father called him Benjamin. Genesis 35:18

Rachel had such difficulty delivering Benjamin that she gave him a name meaning "son of my pain." She died soon after he was born. But Jacob changed his son's name to one that means "son of the right hand" (Genesis 35:16–20).

The name shows that Jacob, who had children by four women, felt a special affection for this son of his favorite wife. He had displayed the same favoritism toward Joseph, Rachel's other son and Benjamin's only full brother (Genesis 43:29–34).

Joseph's jealous half-brothers had sold him into slavery, but God brought him into leadership in Egypt. When all of Jacob's sons were eventually reunited, Joseph welcomed each with a kiss of affection—but he was so glad to see his full brother that he "threw his arms around Benjamin and wept, and Benjamin wept on his shoulder" (Genesis 45:14 HCSB).

Benjamin's descendants grew into the tribe of Benjamin, one of the twelve tribes of Israel. Two notable Benjamites mentioned in the Bible are Saul, the first king of Israel (1 Samuel 10:20–24), and Paul, apostle to the Gentiles (Romans 11:1).

When King Solomon's united kingdom split into two factions following his death, the tribe of Benjamin joined the tribe of Judah in remaining loyal to the house of David. They comprised the nation of Judah, also known as the southern kingdom.

Learn More: Genesis 46:21 / Numbers 26:38–41

BILDAD

Now when Job's three friends heard of all this evil. . . Job 2:11

After Job lost his family and possessions, Bildad was one of the three friends who came to offer sympathy. The other two were Elihu and Zophar. For seven days the men just sat with Job in silence. But when they began to speak, they became accusers rather than friends.

Bildad told Job that his claim to be an innocent sufferer was nothing but a "blustering wind" (Job 8:2 NIV). He was certain that Job had sinned and that this was the reason for his affliction (Job 8:5–6).

In one of his responses to Bildad's accusations, Job basically called him a know-it-all. "How you have enlightened my stupidity!" he exclaimed in a tone dripping with sarcasm. "Where have you gotten all these wise sayings?" (Job 26:3–4 NLT).

Bildad and his friends were eventually reprimanded for their misguided attempts to explain how and why the Lord was dealing with Job. He prayed for them, and God restored Job's fortunes (Job 42:7–10). See also *Job*.

Learn More: Job 18; 25

BOAZ

Then said Boaz unto Ruth, Hearest thou not, my daughter? RUTH 2:8

Boaz, a wealthy landowner of Bethlehem, was kind to Ruth when she came to his fields to glean—that is, to gather leftover grain for herself and her mother-in-law Naomi (Ruth 2:1–23). Both Ruth and Naomi were destitute widows who had to forage in the fields near Bethlehem to support themselves.

Later, Naomi told Ruth that Boaz was a distant relative of her late husband. At Naomi's encouragement, Ruth lay down at Boaz's feet while he slept to signify her willingness to marry him. Under Old Testament law, a man was encouraged to marry the widow of his deceased relative in order to produce children to carry on the family name.

Boaz wanted to marry Ruth, but had to reach an agreement with another relative who was first in line. That done, Boaz took Ruth as his wife. From their union came a son named Obed, grandfather of the great King David of Israel (Ruth 4:21–22).

Boaz is listed in the two genealogies of Jesus in the New Testament (Matthew 1:5; Luke 3:32; *Booz*: KJV). See also *Ruth*.

Learn More: 1 Chronicles 2:11–12

CAIAPHAS

Then the high priest rent his clothes. MATTHEW 26:65

Caiaphas was the high priest who presided over the Sanhedrin, the religious high court of the Jewish people. After Lazarus was raised from the dead, members of this body were disturbed by Jesus' growing popularity among the people. Caiaphas declared that Jesus had to die, and led the plot to have Jesus arrested (John 11:44–54).

The high priest also led the questioning of Jesus at His trial, and probably sanctioned the search for two false witnesses who testified against Jesus. Caiaphas pronounced the court's verdict of capital punishment against Jesus for violating Jewish laws against blasphemy, or assuming authority that belonged only to God (Matthew 26:57–67).

Caiaphas continued his opposition to Jesus even after the resurrection and ascension. He was one of the religious leaders who questioned Peter and John about their healing of a lame man at the temple in Jerusalem (Acts 3:1–8; 4:6–7).

The remains of a "Caiaphas," along with those of his family members, have been discovered by archaeologists in a burial cave in Jerusalem. But it is not known for certain if they belong to this opponent of Jesus.

Learn More: Matthew 26:3–5; Luke 3:2

CAIN

The Lord said unto Cain, Where is Abel thy brother? GENESIS 4:9

The oldest son of Adam and Eve, Cain will always be remembered as the man who committed the first act of violence recorded in the Bible. He murdered his brother Abel out of jealousy because Abel's offering was accepted by the Lord while his was not (Genesis 4:3–16). Cain, a farmer, offered the Lord fruits he had grown, while his brother, a shepherd, presented a sacrificial lamb from his flock.

God punished Cain by sending him into exile. Cain protested that this made him an easy target for anyone who wanted to avenge Abel's murder. So in an act of compassion, God marked Cain to keep this from happening. Cain eventually had a son, and he founded a city known as Enoch that he named for his son (Genesis 4:17).

In the New Testament, the apostle John reminded believers to love one another, unlike Cain, "who belonged to the evil one and murdered his brother" (1 John 3:12 NIV). See also *Abel*.

Learn More: Hebrews 11:4

CALEB

Caleb stilled the people before Moses. NUMBERS 13:30

While the Israelites were in the wilderness, Moses selected a scouting party to investigate the land of Canaan. Caleb was a member of this task force (Numbers 13:1–21).

The scouts returned with good news and bad news: The land was fertile and productive, but it was inhabited by fierce people who would not be easy to defeat. Ten members of the group advised against entering the land. But Caleb—along with Joshua—declared the Israelites should place their faith in the Lord and move on Canaan immediately (Numbers 14:6–9).

God punished the faithless Israelites by sentencing them to forty more years of fruitless wandering in the wilderness. During this time most of the older generation would die. But Caleb and Joshua would live to enter the land that God had promised to Abraham and his descendants (Numbers 14:29–33).

More than two generations later, after Joshua led the Israelites to conquer the land, Caleb received the city of Hebron as a reward for his faithfulness (Joshua 14:6–14).

Learn More: Deuteronomy 1:35–36 / 1 Chronicles 4:15 / Joshua 15:13–19

CANAAN

Cursed be Canaan; a servant of servants shall he be. GENESIS 9:25

Canaan, a grandson of Noah, was born to Ham, one of Noah's three sons. Noah awoke, unclothed, in the presence of Ham after sleeping off an unfortunate episode of drunkenness. He realized that Ham had seen his nude body while he was asleep, so he cursed Ham's son Canaan. Noah declared that Canaan's offspring would serve the descendants of his two other sons—Shem and Japheth—who had covered him without looking at his nakedness (Genesis 9:18–29).

Canaan's descendants were apparently widespread throughout the ancient world, in places including Babylon and Phoenicia (Genesis 10:6–20). But over time, Canaan's name was attached to the Canaanites, pagan inhabitants of the territory that God promised to Abraham and his descendants.

Canaan's descendants and the tribes into which they developed are familiar names to readers of the Old Testament: Jebusites, Amorites, Girgashites, Hivites, Arkites, Sinites, Arvadites, Zemarites, and Hamathites.

Learn More: 1 Chronicles 1:13–16

CLEOPAS

Cleopas, answering said unto him, Art thou only a stranger in Jerusalem? LUKE 24:18

Cleopas and an unnamed friend—both followers of Jesus—were walking from Jerusalem to their home in Emmaus. They were discussing rumors they had heard about Jesus' resurrection that had happened that very day (Luke 24:13–32).

Jesus himself joined the two on the road, but they did not recognize Him. This "stranger" explained that the resurrection was a reality, and that it had happened exactly as foretold in Old Testament prophecies.

When Cleopas and his friend reached their destination, Jesus joined them for a meal. As He offered a blessing, He revealed himself to them and then disappeared. The two believers rushed back to Jerusalem to tell the disciples they had seen the resurrected Lord. Suddenly Jesus appeared among them, and they thought they were seeing a ghost. But Jesus calmed their fears and assured them He was more than a spirit, by inviting them to touch His body

Learn More: Luke 24:33–48

CORNELIUS

Cornelius. . .had called together his kinsmen and near friends. ACTS 10:24

Cornelius, a Roman military officer, was praying for spiritual guidance when an angel appeared to him in a vision. The angel told him to send for the apostle Peter, who could help him find answers to his spiritual questions.

Meanwhile, Peter was having a vision of his own in the coastal city of Joppa, about thirty-five miles away. Through a vision of clean and unclean animals, the Lord revealed to the apostle that all people, Gentiles as well as Jews, were equal in God's sight (Acts 10:1–43).

Peter accompanied the messengers sent by Cornelius back to Caesarea, where the Roman officer lived. Here the apostle preached the gospel to him and other people who had gathered at the centurion's house. Cornelius and many of these people professed their faith in Jesus and were baptized (Acts 10:44–48).

Up to this event, the gospel had been presented mainly to Jews. But the conversion of Cornelius and his Gentile friends showed clearly that everyone was included in the "whosoever will" of the gospel.

Peter may have had Cornelius's conversion in mind in his speech before the Jerusalem Council. This group of church leaders met to decide whether Gentiles could become Christians without going through the Jewish rite of circumcision. Peter declared that God accepted Gentiles "by giving them the Holy Spirit, just as he did to us" (Acts 15:8 NLT).

CYRUS

Let him. . .build the house of the Lord God of Israel. EZRA 1:3

Cyrus was a pagan king whom God used as an instrument of blessing for His people. This ruler over Persia allowed the Jewish exiles to go back to Jerusalem to rebuild their homeland (2 Chronicles 36:22–23).

When Cyrus issued his decree, several decades had gone by since the Babylonians had sacked Jerusalem and taken Israel's most influential people into exile. These captives passed into the hands of Cyrus when Persia defeated Babylon and became the dominant power of the ancient world.

In contrast to the Babylonians, Cyrus treated the Jews and other subject nations with respect. He divided his empire into districts and appointed governors to watch over these territories. His goal was to generate tax revenue from all points of his empire for the Persian treasury.

Cyrus reasoned that allowing his subjects to observe their own religious customs would generate goodwill and prosperity for his government. So he returned the valuables from the temple that the Babylonians had claimed as spoils of war.

Learn More: Ezra 1:7–11; 2:1–2 / Isaiah 44:28; 45:1

DANIEL

Daniel, I am now come forth to give thee skill and understanding. DANIEL 9:22

The prophet Daniel was taken into captivity when the nation of Judah fell to the Babylonian army. He, along with three friends—Shadrach, Meshach, and Abednego—was selected as a trainee for service in the administration of the king of Babylon.

Daniel and his friends refused to eat the rich food provided by the king as part of their training regimen. But they flourished on the food they were accustomed to eating. This showed their commitment to the Lord and the Jewish dietary restrictions He had commanded.

Daniel's faith was also tested when he was thrown into a den of lions for refusing to pay homage to the king of Babylon as a god. The prophet emerged unharmed after spending a night among these savage beasts (Daniel 6:26; see 6:13–28).

Daniel's most famous prediction is his "seventy weeks" prophecy. It refers to a period of 490 years, or seventy times seven (Daniel 9:20–27). Some interpreters see this as a reference to the time in history when Jesus the Messiah would appear. This happened with the birth of Jesus about 490 years after the exile came to an end.

Learn More: Daniel 5:1–31; 7:1–28 / Matthew 24:15

DAVID

Then said David. . .I come to thee in the name of the Lord of hosts. 1 Samuel 17:45

After King Saul disobeyed God, David was anointed as the second king of Israel. His godly character and wise leadership established him as the standard against which all future Jewish kings would be judged (see, for example, 2 Kings 14:1–3).

When just a boy, David killed the giant warrior Goliath of the Philistines, a people at war with Israel (1 Samuel 17:50). King Saul then made David his armor bearer; he eventually became a commander in Saul's army. His popularity in Israel turned Saul against him (1 Samuel 18:5–11), so David fled into the wilderness for several years.

Upon Saul's death, David became king over Israel's southern territory (2 Samuel 2:4). He eventually united the twelve tribes, becoming the undisputed king over all Israel. He captured Jerusalem and turned it into his capital (2 Samuel 5:1–9).

The major blot on David's record was his adulterous affair with Bathsheba and the murder of her husband to cover his crime. Although David confessed his sin and was restored by the Lord, the consequences would break his heart. Still, God had promised David that one of his descendants would always occupy the throne of Israel. The promise was fulfilled in one sense through the offspring who succeeded him. In a spiritual sense, Jesus fulfilled this promise as the Messiah from David's family line (Luke 18:38; see also Matthew 1:1).

Learn More: 2 Samuel 17–18 / 1 Kings 1:1–39 / 1 Chronicles 3:1–9; 11:1–9; 17:1–11 / Acts 13:22

DEBORAH

Deborah, a prophetess, the wife of Lapidoth, she judged Israel. Judges 4:4

Deborah was a unique combination of judge, prophetess, and military deliverer. As a prophetess, she told an Israelite leader named Barak that the time was right for him to defeat their Canaanite oppressors.

Barak answered that he would lead the battle only if Deborah went with him. This shows that she was well-known and highly respected among her people. As a judge or mediator, she heard cases brought by members of her clan at a landmark known as the palm tree of Deborah (Judges 4:5).

Deborah agreed to go with Barak, and this solidified her role as a military deliverer of Israel. She is the only woman among the thirteen deliverers who came to Israel's rescue during the period of the judges. God brought victory to the Israelites by sending a rainstorm that caused the Kishon River to overflow, sweeping away the Canaanite chariots (Judges 5:21).

After Deborah and Barak defeated the Canaanites, she led a song of praise to the Lord for giving them victory over their enemies (Judges 5:1–31).

Learn More: Judges 4:1–10

DORCAS

. . .called Dorcas: this woman was full of good works. Acts 9:36

The apostle Peter was preaching near the city of Joppa on the Mediterranean coast. Several believers approached him with the news that a kind believer named Dorcas had just died. She had been known for helping the poor widows of the area, particularly for making clothing for them. Dorcas was also known by her Aramaic name, Tabitha.

Taking Dorcas by the hand, Peter said simply, "Tabitha, arise" (Acts 9:40; see 9:36–42). This scene is similar to Jesus' raising of the daughter of Jairus. He used almost the same words to bring her back to life: "Little girl, I say to you, get up" (Mark 5:41 niv).

At Peter's command, Dorcas opened her eyes and sat up. Then the apostle presented her to the believers and the widows who had been grieving over her death. News of this miracle spread throughout the region, and many people turned to the Lord.

Dorcas may have been converted under the ministry of Philip the evangelist. He had preached in several cities along the coast of the Mediterranean Sea several years before (Acts 8:40).

ELI

Now the sons of Eli were sons of Belial. 1 SAMUEL 2:12

Samuel's mother, Hannah, took him to live with Eli, high priest of Israel, when Samuel was very young. She had promised to dedicate the boy to the Lord if He would allow her to conceive and give birth to a child (1 Samuel 1:22–28).

As he grew up, Samuel saw what was going on behind the scenes in the high priest's household. Eli's sons were using their authority as priests to take meat from sacrificial offerings before it was fully dedicated to the Lord. Even worse, they were seducing unsuspecting women who gathered at the tabernacle for worship and prayer.

But Eli took no action to discipline his sons, so a prophet warned him that God would judge the entire family severely if the wrongdoing continued. Finally, even the boy Samuel told Eli about a dream he had experienced in which God vowed to judge Eli's family "because of the sin he knew about" (1 Samuel 3:13 NIV).

God's punishment came when Eli's sons were killed in a battle with the Philistines. The news was such a shock that the aged priest fell backward off his chair, and died from a broken neck (1 Samuel 4:18).

Learn More: 1 Kings 2:27

ELIJAH

Elijah. . .said, How long halt ye between two opinions? 1 KINGS 18:21

The prophet Elijah is best known for his dramatic encounter with the prophets of the false god Baal. God proved through this contest that He was the one true God. Then Elijah ordered the execution of these false prophets (1 Kings 18:21–40). This kindled the wrath of Jezebel, wife of King Ahab of Israel, and Elijah had to hide in the wilderness (1 Kings 19:1–4).

Elijah also clashed with King Ahab and his son and successor, Ahaziah, on several occasions. The prophet pronounced God's judgment against Ahab for stealing Naboth's land and having him framed and executed (1 Kings 21:1–24).

As Elijah's ministry wound down, he anointed Elisha as his successor (1 Kings 19:16). Then Elijah was carried bodily into heaven without experiencing physical death. Elisha took Elijah's robe as he ascended to show that his prophetic ministry would continue (2 Kings 2:1–14).

The prophet Malachi predicted that the Lord would send Elijah back to earth before the arrival of the Messiah (Malachi 4:5). This prophecy came to pass in a spiritual sense with the preaching of John the Baptist, forerunner of Jesus. John's lifestyle and preaching were similar to Elijah's (Matthew 17:10–13; *Elias*: KJV).

Learn More: 1 Kings 19:15–16 / 2 Kings 1:2–15 / Matthew 17:1–8 / Luke 9:8

ELISABETH

Elisabeth was filled with the Holy Ghost. LUKE 1:41

Elisabeth was beyond the age when a woman would normally give birth to a child. Imagine her surprise when her husband, Zacharias, told her she would become a mother. This had been revealed to him by an angel while he performed his duties as a priest in the temple in Jerusalem (Luke 1:5–24).

After Elisabeth conceived, she went into seclusion for five months. During this time she was visited by her relative Mary, who was also expecting a child. When Elisabeth greeted Mary, the baby in Elisabeth's womb moved, as if to honor the child whom Mary was carrying (Luke 1:39–45).

This slight move was prophetic. Elisabeth's son grew up to become John the Baptist, forerunner of Mary's son—Jesus the Messiah. (See also *Zacharias*.)

Elisabeth had been carrying her child for six months when Mary came to visit (Luke 1:36). Since Mary stayed on as Elisabeth's guest for three months (Luke 1:56), it's possible Mary had gone to help her relative during the final months of her pregnancy.

Learn More: Luke 1:57–60

ELISHA

Elisha said, I pray thee, let a double portion of thy spirit be upon me. 2 KINGS 2:9

Elisha ministered in the northern kingdom of Israel during the days of the prophet Elijah. When Elisha realized he was destined to succeed this great prophet, he asked for a double portion of Elijah's spirit to be given to him.

God granted this request, and Elisha went on to become the greatest miracle worker in the Old Testament. More than a dozen of these miracles are recorded in the book of 2 Kings. He purified the bad waters of a spring (2 Kings 2:19–22), provided a destitute widow with a supply of oil that never had to be replenished (2 Kings 4:1–7), provided food for one hundred prophets (2 Kings 4:42–44), and healed a Syrian military officer (2 Kings 5:1–27).

Elisha was not as active in political matters as Elijah had been. But he did cause soldiers of the Syrian army to go blind to prevent their attacks against Israel (2 Kings 6:18–23). The prophet also played a role in the miraculous deliverance of the city of Samaria from a siege by the Assyrians (2 Kings 7:1–20).

Learn More: 2 Kings 8:7–15 / Luke 4:27; Eliseus: KJV

ELYMAS

Elymas the sorcerer (for so is his name by interpretation). . . ACTS 13:8

Elymas provides proof that some people will oppose God's plan of salvation—but that God will still reach those He intends to save. On the island of Cyprus, the missionaries Paul and Barnabas were meeting in Paphos with the Roman proconsul, a "prudent" (*intelligent*, NIV) man named Sergius Paulus. He had called for Paul and Barnabas specifically to hear God's word. But the governor's attendant, described as a Jewish sorcerer and false prophet called Bar-Jesus or Elymas, interfered, trying to keep his boss from the faith.

Paul, "filled with the Holy Ghost," gave Elymas a public dressing down, telling him, "thou child of the devil, thou enemy of all righteousness, wilt thou not cease to pervert the right ways of the Lord?" (Acts 13:10). When Paul called a temporary blindness on Elymas, Sergius Paulus, "astonished at the doctrine of the Lord," believed Paul's teaching (verse 12).

Learn more: Acts 13:4–12

ENOCH

By faith Enoch was translated that he should not see death. HEBREWS 11:5

A person who "walked" with God was known for his steady, consistent relationship to the Lord—a daily pattern of faithfulness to His will. This distinction of "walking with God" was applied to Enoch's life (Genesis 5:24). One modern translation renders this phrase as "walking in close fellowship with God" (NLT).

This brief mention of Enoch in Genesis also says that "he was not; for God took him." The writer of Hebrews explains this by saying Enoch transported (or "translated") into God's presence without experiencing physical death.

Enoch lived for 365 years before this translation experience. He was the father of Methuselah, who lived for 969 years—longer than any other person mentioned in the Bible. Enoch is listed in Luke's genealogy of Jesus in the New Testament (Luke 3:37).

The righteous man Noah, who obeyed God and built an ark to escape the great flood, is also said to have walked with God (Genesis 6:9).

Learn More: Jude 14

ESAU

. . .red, all over like a hairy garment; and they called his name Esau. GENESIS 25:25

Esau and his twin brother, Jacob, seemed to be destined for disagreement from the day they were born. Esau emerged first from the womb of his mother, Rebekah. Right behind came Jacob, who was grasping his brother's heel as if he were struggling to be the firstborn (Genesis 25:21–26).

After the boys grew up, Esau traded his birthright—that is, his rights as the firstborn son—to Jacob for a bowl of stew (Genesis 25:29–34). Jacob also plotted with his mother to trick his father, Isaac, into blessing him rather than Esau (Genesis 27:1–41).

Esau vowed to kill his brother for this act of deception, so Jacob fled into exile. Years later, when Jacob decided to return to Canaan, he knew Esau would be waiting with revenge on his mind. But to his surprise, Esau accepted the gifts he offered and welcomed him back with no hard feelings (Genesis 33:1–16).

Esau was also knows as Edom, a name meaning "red," from the red stew for which he traded his birthright (Genesis 25:30). His descendants were the Edomites, a tribal group that lived in an area near the Dead Sea.

Read More: Genesis 35:29; 36:1–19 / Romans 9:12–13

ESTHER

Esther bade them return Mordecai this answer. . .if I perish, I perish. ESTHER 4:15–16

Esther's story begins in Persia, where she lived with her cousin Mordecai. He had adopted her as a child when both her parents died (Esther 2:5–7). Through a combination of miraculous circumstances, Esther became queen of the Persian Empire when King Ahasuerus deposed his original wife and queen for disobeying one of his orders (Esther 2:12–17).

Later, the king's chief aide, Haman, convinced Ahasuerus to issue a decree authorizing the execution of all Jewish subjects throughout his empire. This was Haman's way of venting his wrath against Mordecai, a minor official in the royal palace. Mordecai had refused to bow before Haman and pay him the respect Haman thought he deserved (Esther 3:5–13).

But Mordecai and Esther acted swiftly and created a plan of their own to save their people. Esther used her influence with the king to expose Haman's plot and have him executed (Esther 7:3–10). Then she had Ahasuerus issue another decree giving the Jews permission to defend themselves on the day of their planned mass execution (Esther 8:3–11). See also *Mordecai.*

Learn More: Esther 9:31–32

EUTYCHUS

They brought the young man alive, and were not a little comforted. ACTS 20:12

Anyone who has ever drifted off during a long speech can sympathize with a young man named Eutychus, a believer in the city of Troas.

Eutychus was with other believers on the third floor of a private home. He was listening to a sermon by the apostle Paul that droned on until midnight. Many oil-burning lamps were being used for illumination, and we can guess that this caused the room to become warm and stuffy, since Eutychus was sitting by an open window. He fell fast asleep and apparently tumbled through the opening to his death below. Paul immediately went into action, though, stretching himself over the young man's body and restoring him to life (Acts 20:7–10).

This disturbing event would have caused most preachers to call a halt to the service and send everyone home. But not Paul. He participated with other believers in observance of the Lord's Supper, and did not leave the house until "after talking until daylight" (verse 11 NIV).

EVE

She took of the fruit thereof, and did eat. GENESIS 3:6

God fashioned Eve from one of Adam's ribs to serve as his helpmate and companion. He placed both of them in a beautiful garden with all kinds of delicious fruit for them to eat. But He warned that one particular tree was off limits: "You must not eat it or touch it," He declared, "or you will die" (Genesis 3:3 HCSB).

Satan planted doubt in Eve's mind about God's command. So Eve ate from the tree, and convinced Adam to do the same. Their disobedience resulted in the loss of innocence. God punished the couple by driving them from the idyllic garden, and Eve was destined to experience pain and suffering in the process of childbirth (Genesis 3:16).

In the New Testament, the apostle Paul declared that he feared the believers at Corinth would be led astray "just as Eve was deceived by the cunning ways of the serpent" (2 Corinthians 11:3 NLT). Thus, she is an example of the power of temptation and how easily a person can slip into sin. See also *Adam.*

Learn More: 1 Timothy 2:12–14

EZEKIEL

The word of the Lord came expressly unto Ezekiel the priest. EZEKIEL 1:3

Ezekiel was taken into exile with other Jewish citizens when the Babylonians defeated Judah (Ezekiel 1:1–3). Here he apparently spent the rest of his life. He is often referred to as "the prophet to the exiles."

This spokesman for God is also known for acting out his messages through strange behavior, such as lying on his side for more than a year (4:4–6), eating bread baked over cow dung (4:12–15), and shaving off his hair (5:1–4). These actions symbolized the suffering during and after the Babylonian siege of Jerusalem.

Ezekiel's visions from the Lord are also legendary. His call came through a vision of a storm cloud in which mysterious heavenly creatures known as cherubim appeared. God spoke from a throne in the midst of the cloud, commissioning him to his prophetic ministry (1:4–2:3).

The prophet's most spectacular vision, perhaps, was of a valley filled with dry bones. The bones came to life, signifying God's intention to restore His people after their period of exile came to an end (37:1–14).

Learn More: Ezekiel 24:1 –24

EZRA

Ezra had prepared his heart to seek the law of the Lord. EZRA 7:10

Ezra was a priest and scribe who led religious reforms in Judah after his countrymen returned from exile. One group of people had already returned to Judah under Zerubbabel when Ezra was granted permission to take another party back. Zerubbabel's task was to rebuild the temple, while Ezra was determined to restore the people's commitment to God's law (Ezra 7:6–28).

Ezra's mission received the blessing of the reigning Persian king, Artaxerxes. The king gave Ezra a royal letter that authorized him to carry out reforms. Artaxerxes also provided funds to furnish the temple after it was rebuilt.

When he arrived in Jerusalem, Ezra was shocked to learn that many Israelite men had married foreign women from the surrounding pagan nations. He launched a mass movement that convinced the offenders to divorce these wives (Ezra 10:1–17).

Ezra also led the people of Judah to give attention to the Old Testament law. With help from several priests, he read from the law for seven days to emphasize the Lord's commands During this assembly, the people celebrated the Feast of Tabernacles to commemorate God's provision for His people in the wilderness during their escape from slavery in Egypt (Nehemiah 8:16–18).

Learn More: Nehemiah 8:1–9

GAMALIEL

A Pharisee, named Gamaliel, a doctor of the law. . . ACTS 5:34

Peter and the other apostles were arrested by the Jewish Sanhedrin for preaching that Jesus was the long-awaited Messiah. This religious high court threatened to execute them for blasphemy. Then Gamaliel, an esteemed teacher and member of the court, stepped forward in the apostles' defense (Acts 5:33–41).

Gamaliel's argument was simple: If the Jesus whom they were preaching was a false prophet, the Christian movement would soon fade away. But if they were preaching the truth, he declared, it could not be stopped by human opposition. The full Sanhedrin was convinced by this reasoning, and they released the apostles to continue their preaching.

This Gamaliel is probably the same learned rabbi under whom the apostle Paul studied in his early years as a zealous advocate of the Jewish law (Acts 22:3).

GEHAZI

As the Lord liveth, I will run after him, and take somewhat of him. 2 KINGS 5:20

Gehazi, a servant of the prophet Elisha, acted wisely in some situations. For example, he helped a poor widow get her land restored by pleading her case before the king of Israel (2 Kings 8:1–6). But Gehazi's greed eventually led to his downfall.

After Elisha healed Naaman the Syrian of leprosy, the prophet refused Naaman's offer of a reward. But Gehazi saw this as an opportunity to better himself. He followed the Syrian military officer, who gave him some items that Gehazi claimed would be used to help needy prophets who worked with Elisha. But he actually kept the gifts for himself (2 Kings 5:20–27).

Elisha learned what his servant had done and confronted him about it. Gehazi made matters worse by lying to his master and refusing to own up to his sin. Then the prophet cursed Gehazi with leprosy—the same disease from which Naaman had been cured.

Learn More: 2 Kings 4:12–31

GIDEON

By the three hundred men that lapped will I save you. JUDGES 7:7

Gideon was threshing wheat by a winepress when the angel of the Lord greeted him as a "mighty man of valour" (Judges 6:12; see 6:1–12). Gideon didn't feel like a brave warrior, since he was trying to hide his grain from the Midianites. These raiders were driving the Israelites into poverty by stealing their crops and livestock.

The angel told Gideon that the Lord had selected him to deliver the Israelites from these enemies. Gideon protested that he was not up to the task. Only after the Lord gave Gideon three miraculous signs did he agree to serve as the next judge, or military deliverer, of God's people (Judges 6:19–40).

Gideon raised a huge army, only to have it reduced—at God's command—to an elite force of just three hundred. Armed with pitchers, torches, and trumpets, Gideon's band crept into the enemy camp at night. At his signal, they blew their trumpets and broke their pitchers that masked the torches inside. This flooded the camp with noise and light, creating panic. In their confusion, the Midianites actually killed some of their own comrades. Gideon and the Israelites won a resounding victory (Judges 7:18–25).

Learn More: Judges 6:25–32 / Hebrews 11:32; *Gedeon:* KJV

GOLIATH

When they saw the man [Goliath], fled from him. 1 SAMUEL 17:24

The boy David visited the camp of King Saul to bring provisions for his three brothers. These three older sons of Jesse were fighting with Saul in a campaign against the Philistines.

David quickly learned that a huge Philistine soldier named Goliath had bullied Israel's entire army into inaction. Goliath challenged Saul to send one warrior against him in a winner-take-all contest. But not one man volunteered to take on the Philistine champion—that is, not until David stepped forward to put a stop to the giant's brash talk (1 Samuel 17:1–58).

The contrast between Goliath and David could not have been greater. The Philistine, in full armor with a shield and a sword, stood more than nine feet tall. David was a mere lad with nothing but a sling in his hand. But the shepherd boy put his trust in the Lord and felled the giant with one stone expertly slung into his forehead. Then David used Goliath's own sword to cut off his head.

The Philistine army fled when they learned their champion was dead. The Israelites pursued them and won a great victory.

Learn More: 1 Samuel 21:8–10 / 1 Chronicles 20:5

HAGAR

He went in unto Hagar, and she conceived. GENESIS 16:4

Abraham's wife Sarah was not able to bear children. So she encouraged him to father a child through Hagar, her Egyptian servant. But even before the child was born, Sarah became so resentful that Hagar had to flee into the wilderness. Here the Lord assured her that He would bless her child with many descendants (Genesis 16:1–16).

At God's encouragement, Hagar returned to Abraham's camp. But, several years later after her son Ishmael was born, she was banished again because of Sarah's jealousy. The mother and son almost died in the wilderness before God intervened and renewed His initial promise about Ishmael's future (Genesis 21:9–21).

In the New Testament, the apostle Paul used Hagar's experience as an allegory of the freedom of the gospel. As a slave-wife, Hagar represented bondage to the Old Testament law. But Sarah was a freeborn wife who eventually gave birth to Isaac, the child through whom God's covenant with Abraham was passed on. Thus, Sarah and Isaac symbolized the new covenant instituted by Jesus Christ and the freedom of the gospel. See also *Ishmael*.

Learn More: Galatians 4:22–31; *Agar:* KJV

HAM

Ham, the father of Canaan, saw the nakedness of his father. GENESIS 9:22

The second of Noah's three sons (Genesis 5:32), Ham and the rest of Noah's family survived the great flood by entering the ark. After the flood, Ham discovered his father naked and asleep in a drunken stupor. Ham told his brothers, Japheth and Shem. These two covered Noah without looking at his nude body.

Noah, apparently furious because Ham had seen him naked, pronounced a curse against Ham's son Canaan. This meant that the descendants of Ham and his son would serve the offspring of Noah's other sons, Shem and Japheth (Genesis 9:18–26).

Ham had four sons: Cush, Mizraim, Put, and Canaan (Genesis 10:6). Mizraim's descendants settled in Egypt, while the tribes of Cush and Put apparently lived in other African territories. Canaan's descendants evolved into the Canaanite people of Phoenicia and Palestine (Genesis 10:6–20).

Learn More: 1 Chronicles 1:4, 8

HAMAN

. . .then was Haman full of wrath. Esther 3:5

Haman, chief aide of the king of Persia, had a problem controlling his anger. He burned with rage when Mordecai, a Jew and a minor official in the royal court, refused to bow down and give him the respect he thought he deserved.

So Haman hatched a plot to exterminate all the Jewish people throughout the Persian Empire. Then he convinced his boss, King Ahasuerus, to sanction the plan with a royal decree.

What Haman failed to take into account was Mordecai's influence with Queen Esther, the king's wife. Mordecai was her cousin and guardian. He had adopted Esther when she was orphaned as a little girl (Esther 2:5–7). Mordecai told the queen what was going on, and she stepped in to inform the king and thwart Haman's plan.

In an ironic twist, Haman was hanged on the very gallows he had built for Mordecai's execution, and Mordecai was promoted to a higher position in the king's administration.

Haman's untimely end shows that the Lord is always in control of events, even when evil seems to have the upper hand.

Learn More: Esther 6:1–11

HANNAH

Therefore also I have lent him to the Lord. 1 Samuel 1:28

Hannah was heartbroken because she could not bear children. Her distress was made even worse by the ridicule from her husband's second wife, Peninnah, who had several children.

But when she visited the high priest Eli at the tabernacle in Shiloh, Hannah took her problem to the Lord. She promised that if God would bless her with a son, she would devote him to His service. The Lord heard her prayer, and Hannah did have a son. She named him Samuel, meaning "heard of God," because she had "asked him of the Lord" (1 Samuel 1:20; see 1:1–28).

When Samuel was about two years old, Hannah kept her promise by placing Samuel in the custody of Eli. The boy Samuel eventually became a great priest and prophet who anointed Saul and David as the first two kings of Israel.

Hannah expressed thanks for her good fortune in a beautiful song of praise to the Lord. She was eventually blessed even further for her faithfulness when she gave birth to three additional sons and two daughters (1 Samuel 2:21).

Learn More: 1 Samuel 2:1–10

HEROD

Herod. . .enquired of them diligently what time the star appeared. Matthew 2:7

This Roman ruler over Palestine, also known as King Herod the Great, attempted to put the baby Jesus to death soon after He was born.

When Herod had suspected several members of his own family of plotting to take over his throne, he had executed them. This same paranoid fear of losing power is probably what motivated him to order the slaughter of all male infants in the vicinity of Bethlehem, the village where Jesus was born. The king had learned that a "king of the Jews" had been born in that village when wise men from the east arrived in Jerusalem searching for the young ruler.

But Mary and Joseph were warned in a dream about Herod's plot. They fled to safety in Egypt until the king died. Their sojourn in Egypt fulfilled this messianic prophecy: "Out of Egypt have I called my son" (Matthew 2:15; see Hosea 11:1). Even an evil king's best-laid plans could not turn aside the purpose of God.

Herod was known for his ambitious building projects throughout Israel, particularly the renovation of the Jewish temple in Jerusalem. This was a huge project that dragged on over several decades. It may have been underway during the years of Jesus' public ministry (John 2:18–21).

Learn More: Matthew 2:19–21

HEZEKIAH

He did that which was right in the sight of the Lord. 2 CHRONICLES 29:2

A king of Judah, Hezekiah reversed the trend toward idolatry that infected his country. He destroyed pagan images and altars, reopened the temple in Jerusalem that his father had closed, and renewed the celebration of religious festivals. He even destroyed the bronze serpent that Moses had erected in the wilderness centuries earlier because it had become an object of worship (2 Kings 18:1–6; 2 Chronicles 29:3–15).

During Hezekiah's reign, Assyria became a dominant world power that threatened his nation. The king made extensive military preparations by strengthening Jerusalem's defensive wall. He also built a tunnel that connected the city to a spring outside the wall to provide water in the event of a prolonged Assyrian siege (2 Kings 20:20).

When King Sennacherib of Assyria attacked the city, the Lord intervened by striking the enemy camp with a mysterious illness. With his army decimated, Sennacherib withdrew in humiliation and defeat (2 Kings 19:35–36).

Hezekiah suffered a serious illness toward the end of his reign. He prayed for recovery, and the Lord granted him fifteen additional years of life (Isaiah 38:1–8).

Learn More: Jeremiah 26:18–19 / Matthew 1:9–10; Ezekias: KJV

HOSEA

The Lord said to Hosea, Go, take unto thee a wife of whoredoms. HOSEA 1:2

Hosea was a prophet to the northern Jewish kingdom, the nation of Israel, during the final chaotic years before it fell to the Assyrians. His name in itself, meaning "deliverance," sent a message about the precarious situation of Israel as it teetered on the brink of destruction. Hosea recorded his prophecies in the Old Testament book that bears his name.

The prophet's personal life also sent a dramatic message to his countrymen. At God's command, Hosea married a prostitute named Gomer. This represented the "harlotries" or sin of the nation in rejecting God. Gomer eventually returned to her wayward life, only to have Hosea buy her back from the slave market (Hosea 3:1–5). The prophet's action of redemption sent the message that God had not turned His back on His people. He continued to love them, and He wanted to restore them to His love and favor.

In the New Testament, the apostle Paul cited the prophet's love of his wayward wife as an object lesson of God's redeeming grace (Romans 9:25; *Osee*: KJV). Hosea's own life echoed this truth more effectively than the words he spoke.

Learn More: Hosea 5:1–15

HULDAH

So Hilkiah the priest. . .WENT UNTO HULDAH THE PROPHETESS. 2 KINGS 22:14

While making preparations to repair the temple, the high priest Hilkiah found a copy of the book of the law. This was probably the first five books of the Old Testament. A delegation of religious officials read parts of this document to King Josiah.

The king was disturbed because he realized the people of Judah had turned away from the precepts in this written law and fallen into worship of false gods. So he sent this delegation to ask Huldah the prophetess if God's judgment would fall on the nation because of these sins.

The prophetess had bad news and good news for Josiah. Yes, she told him, the Lord's judgment would be "kindled against this place, and shall not be quenched" (2 Kings 22:17). But the king could rest easy. This disaster wouldn't happen until after he had passed from the scene. Her prophecy was fulfilled about thirty years later when the Babylonian army sacked Jerusalem.

Huldah is one of the few female prophets mentioned in the Bible. Others are Miriam (Exodus 15:20), Deborah (Judges 4:4), Noadiah (Nehemiah 6:14), and the unnamed wife of the prophet Isaiah (Isaiah 8:3).

Learn More: 2 Chronicles 34:22–28

ISAAC

Thou shalt call his name Isaac. GENESIS 17:19

God's promise to Abraham that his descendants would become a great nation began to be fulfilled when Isaac was born to this couple in their old age. Isaac's name, meaning "laughter," reflects their disbelief that Sarah could give birth to a child, as well as their overwhelming joy that she finally did (Genesis 17:17–19; 21:1–7).

When Isaac was young, the Lord tested Abraham's faith by directing him to offer his beloved son as a sacrifice. But just as Abraham raised a knife to take the boy's life, God stopped him and provided a ram as a substitute offering. This proved without a doubt that Isaac was destined to become heir to the covenant that God had established with Abraham (Genesis 17:19).

The Bible describes Isaac as a person devoted to God (Genesis 26:25) who lived a quiet life of simple faith (Hebrews 11:17–20). He had an easygoing nature which led him to seek peace with the Canaanites in whose territory he lived (Genesis 26:17–31).

Isaac fathered twin sons, Jacob and Esau. Jacob's sons in turn became the twelve tribes that developed into the nation of Israel.

Learn More: Genesis 26:1–12; 27:1–40

ISAIAH

The word that Isaiah the son of Amoz saw concerning Judah and Jerusalem. ISAIAH 2:1

The prophet Isaiah was called to his ministry in a dramatic vision of God. This encounter made Isaiah aware of his sinfulness. But at the same time, he answered God's call with enthusiasm and determination: "Here am I; send me" (Isaiah 6:8; see 6:1–13).

Isaiah spoke God's message to several kings of Judah in the capital city of Jerusalem. He warned that the nation faced destruction by Assyria unless the people gave up their worship of false gods and turned back to the Lord (Isaiah 10:1–10).

The prophet's book is often called the "fifth gospel" because of its emphasis on God's spiritual deliverance of His people. At the beginning of Jesus' public ministry, He identified himself as the agent of God's redemption whom the prophet had described about seven centuries before (Isaiah 61:1–3; Luke 4:18–19).

Isaiah made more predictions about the coming Messiah than any other Old Testament prophet. His most famous is probably the one quoted every year to help us remember the true meaning of Christmas: "Therefore the Lord himself shall give you a sign; Behold, a virgin shall conceive, and bear a son, and shall call his name Immanuel" (Isaiah 7:14).

Learn More: 2 Kings 19:2–20; 20:1–19 / Isaiah 11:1–10; 35:5–6; 53:3–12 / Acts 8:27–38; Esaias: KJV

ISHMAEL

Abram called his son's name, which Hagar bare, Ishmael. GENESIS 16:15

Ishmael was the son of Abraham whom he fathered through Hagar, the Egyptian servant of his wife, Sarah. After Ishmael was born, God appeared to Abraham with a special message—this son was not the fulfillment of God's promise to make Abraham's descendants into a great nation. This would come about through a son named Isaac, who would be born to him and Sarah within a year (Genesis 17:15–21).

After Isaac was born, Sarah favored her own son over Ishmael. One day she saw the older boy mocking Isaac. She insisted that Ishmael and his mother be banished into the wilderness. In this barren place without food and water, the two almost died, but God intervened to save them. He promised that Ishmael would also grow up to become the father of a great nation, just as Isaac's descendants were destined to evolve into the nation of Israel (Genesis 21:12–20).

When Abraham died, Ishmael helped Isaac bury their father (Genesis 25:8–9). Ishmael's descendants eventually settled in northern Arabia. Modern-day Arabs claim him as their distant ancestor. See also *Hagar.*

Learn More: Genesis 25:12–18 / 1 Chronicles 1:28–29

JACOB

Jacob took advantage of his twin brother Esau by securing Esau's rights as the oldest son through a shrewd trade. Then Jacob tricked their father, Isaac, into blessing him rather than Esau (Genesis 27:18–41).

Jacob was on the run from Esau when the Lord got the trickster's attention through a dream. He saw angels going up and down a stairway into heaven. At the top stood God Himself, who declared that Jacob and his descendants would inherit the covenant promise He had initially made to Abraham (Genesis 28:13–15).

Later, Jacob had another divine experience that was even more startling—a wrestling match with the Lord. As they struggled, God dislocated Jacob's hip, blessed him, and gave him the new name *Israel*, meaning "prince with God" (Genesis 32:28; see 32:24–30).

Humbled by this experience, Jacob was now ready to fulfill the purpose that God had for his life. He eventually fathered twelve sons whose descendants grew into the twelve tribes of Israel.

In the New Testament, the writer of the book of Hebrews included Jacob as one of the heroes of the faith (Hebrews 11:21). Jacob is also listed in the genealogies of Jesus in the gospels of Matthew (1:2) and Luke (3:34).

Learn More: Genesis 29–31

JAEL

Deborah and Barak, judges of Israel, won a decisive victory over Canaanite forces under the command of a military officer named Sisera. Before the battle, Deborah—who was also a prophetess—had predicted that "the LORD shall sell Sisera into the hand of a woman" (Judges 4:9; see also 4:4–24).

It happened exactly as Deborah predicted. Sisera fled the battle scene after his army was defeated. He approached the tent of Jael, wife of Heber the Kenite, seeing refuge in what he thought was friendly territory. She welcomed Sisera by giving him milk to drink, inviting him to hide in her tent, and even promising to warn him if any enemies approached. But then Jael killed the exhausted Sisera as he slept by driving a tent peg through his temple.

To commemorate Israel's defeat of Sisera's forces, Deborah praised the Lord in song. She honored Jael as "blessed above women" for her role in the victory (Judges 5:24).

Learn More: Judges 5:1–7

JAIRUS

Jairus, an official in the local synagogue, was a desperate man. His beloved twelve-year-old daughter—his only child—was at death's door. So he came to Jesus, fell at His feet, and begged Him to come quickly and make her well (Luke 8:41–55). He obviously had heard about this miracle worker who was healing and teaching in and around the city of Capernaum.

Jesus began to follow Jairus to his house. But then He stopped to heal a woman in the crowd with a serious need of her own. Jairus must have thought, *Hurry up, Jesus, or my little girl will die before you get there.*

Sure enough, messengers arrived at just that moment to confirm Jairus's fears. "Your daughter is dead," they told him. "There's no use troubling the Teacher now" (verse 49 NLT).

Jesus ignored their words, calmed Jairus down, and followed him home. Then He entered the house with the disciples Peter, James, and John and raised Jairus's daughter from the dead with the simple command, "Maid, arise" (verse 54).

Learn More: Mark 5:22–41

JAMES, BROTHER OF JESUS

James answered, saying, Men and brethren, hearken unto me. Acts 15:13

James shows the powerful influence of Jesus' resurrection. As the Lord's brother—more precisely His half-brother—James was skeptical of Jesus during His earthly ministry (John 7:3–5). But he eventually became a believer, perhaps after Jesus appeared to him after rising from the dead (1 Corinthians 15:7).

In the early years of the church, James emerged as leader of the believers in Jerusalem. He presided at the council which met in this city to consider whether Gentiles could be saved without undergoing the Jewish rite of circumcision (Acts 15:1–22). James expressed in a few words the position eventually adopted by the entire council: "It is my judgment. . .that we should not make it difficult for the Gentiles who are turning to God" (Acts 15:19 NIV).

The apostle Paul referred to James as an apostle—or a special messenger of Jesus—although neither of them was a member of Jesus' original twelve disciples (Galatians 1:19). James was probably the author of the New Testament epistle of James.

Learn More: James 1:1 / Jude 1

JAMES, BROTHER OF JOHN

Jesus taketh with him Peter, and James, and John. . . Mark 9:2

James, a fisherman, was busy at his trade on the Sea of Galilee when Jesus arrived on the scene. Working with him were his brother John and two other fishermen brothers, Peter and Andrew. All four accepted Jesus' call to become His disciples after He miraculously produced a huge catch of fish (Luke 5:3–10).

James and John, along with Peter, emerged as the leading three disciples among the Twelve They were with Jesus at several major events in His ministry—the raising of Jairus's daughter from the dead (Mark 5:37), His transfiguration (Matthew 17:1–8), and His prayer of anguish in the garden of Gethsemane over His approaching death (Mark 14:33–42).

While James was totally loyal to Jesus, his pride and quick temper sometimes clouded his judgment. He and his brother John asked Jesus to give them places of honor in His coming kingdom (Mark 10:35–45). On another occasion, they asked Jesus to destroy an unwelcoming Samaritan village (Luke 9:52–54). Perhaps this is why Jesus gave them the nickname, "The Sons of Thunder" (Mark 3:17).

Learn More: Acts 12:1–2

JEHOIACHIN

Jehoiachin the king of Judah went out to the king of Babylon. 2 Kings 24:12

Jehoiachin could not have become king of Judah at a worse time. His father and predecessor, King Jehoiakim, had not done his son any favors by stopping tribute payments to the Babylonians and rebelling against their authority. Now the army of Babylon's King Nebuchadnezzar was preparing to invade the Jewish nation and seize the payments he had been promised.

As it turned out, Jehoiachin ruled only three months before surrendering peacefully to these well-armed enemies. He and the rest of the royal family, along with other leading citizens of Judah, were taken away to Babylon (2 Kings 24:6–15).

The king's peaceful surrender may have worked to his advantage. He was eventually released from prison and treated with respect by the Babylonian king (Jeremiah 52:31–34).

Jehoiachin was also known as Coniah (Jeremiah 37:1) and Jeconiah (1 Chronicles 3:16–17). He is listed in Matthew's genealogy of Jesus in the New Testament (Matthew 1:11–12; *Jechonias*: KJV).

Learn More: 2 Kings 25:27–30 / 2 Chronicles 36:9–10

JEHOSHAPHAT

The Lord was with Jehoshaphat. 2 CHRONICLES 17:3

Jehoshaphat, the fourth king of Judah, continued the godly practices of his father and predecessor, King Asa. Jehoshaphat banned pagan worship and sent teachers throughout the land to instruct the people in God's law (2 Chronicles 17:3–9).

Jehoshaphat also relied on the Lord in military matters. When a huge coalition army of Judah's enemies threatened to overrun the country, the king prayed for the Lord's help. There was no battle to fight when the king's warriors arrived on the scene. A mysterious foe had decimated the enemy forces (2 Chronicles 20:1–25).

During Jehoshaphat's long reign of twenty-five years, the strained relations between Judah and Israel, the sister kingdom to the north, grew more cordial. Jehoshaphat and King Ahab of Israel even joined forces to go to war against the nation of Aram, or Syria. Ahab was killed in a battle for control of the city of Ramoth Gilead (1 Kings 22:29–38).

Jehoshaphat is listed in the genealogy of Jesus in Matthew's gospel (Matthew 1:8; *Josaphat*: KJV).

Learn More: 2 Kings 3:6–14 / 2 Chronicles 18:1–31; 19:4–9

JEHU

Jehu slew all that remained of the house of Ahab in Jezreel. 2 KINGS 10:11

Jehu was anointed as the eleventh king of the northern kingdom by the prophet Elisha. The new king was charged with the task of ending the dynasty of King Ahab, who had led Israel to worship the pagan god Baal (2 Kings 9:1–13). Jehu accomplished this by assassinating King Joram, also known as Jehoram, who had succeeded his father Ahab as king (2 Kings 9:22–24). Next on Jehu's hit list was Jezebel, Ahab's wicked queen, who was behind the nation's slide into idolatry (2 Kings 9:29–37).

Once the killing started, Jehu launched an orgy of executions that went beyond what the Lord desired and what the new king needed to do to establish his authority. These victims included the king of Judah, Israel's sister kingdom to the south, and members of this royal family (2 Kings 9:27; 10:12–14), plus numerous male descendants of King Ahab, as well as Ahab's former court officials and close friends (2 Kings 10:6–11).

Jehu paid for his sins by having a large section of his territory fall to the Arameans, or Syrians (2 Kings 10:30–37).

Learn More: Hosea 1:4

JEPHTHAH

Jephthah said unto the elders of Gilead, Did not ye hate me? Judges 11:7

Making a rash vow is always dangerous. And no one shows this more dramatically than Jephthah, a military leader in Israel during the period of the judges.

Jephthah was driven into exile from his home in the territory of Gilead because he was the son of a prostitute. But when the Gileadites got into trouble, their leaders approached him in a contrite spirit: Would he please come back and deliver them from their enemy, the Ammonites (Judges 11:1–11)?

Jephthah agreed to do so after receiving their assurance that he would be rewarded with a place of leadership in Gilead. Then he proceeded to raise an army and rout the Ammonites—but not before making a thoughtless promise: If the Lord would give him success in battle, he vowed, he would offer as a burnt offering whatever came out of his house to greet him on his return.

To Jephthah's horror, his only child—a daughter—came out to meet him, celebrating with a victory dance. The brave military leader tore his clothes in anguish when he realized what a foolish vow he had made (Judges 11:30–35).

Learn More: Judges 12:1–7 / Hebrews 11:32; *Jephthae*: KJV

JEREMIAH

The Lord said unto me, Behold, I have put my words in thy mouth. JEREMIAH 1:9

Jeremiah was set apart as God's messenger even before he was born (Jeremiah 1:5). His destiny was to preach one uncompromising message—Judah was headed for disaster unless the people renewed their commitment to the Lord.

Five different kings of Judah came and went during the forty years of the prophet's ministry. His message was denied by false prophets. He was imprisoned for saying that defeat at the hands of the Babylonians was inevitable. He was accused of being a traitor because he declared that God would use this pagan nation as an instrument of judgment against His people.

But gloom and doom were not the only themes of Jeremiah's preaching. He also offered hope to the people. While they would be brutalized and carried into captivity, they would eventually return to their homeland and renew their commitment to the Lord.

Jeremiah's prophecies of disaster were fulfilled during his lifetime. The Babylonian army sacked Jerusalem, tore down its temple and defensive wall, and carried the leading citizens into captivity in Babylon (Jeremiah 52:4–16).

Learn More: Daniel 9:2 / Jeremiah 31:31–34 / Matthew 16:14; *Jeremias:* KJV

JEROBOAM

. . .Jeroboam, who did sin, and who made Israel to sin. 1 KINGS 14:16

King Solomon's high taxes and oppressive labor practices led to widespread discontent among the citizens of Judah. When his kingdom split into two factions after he died, Jeroboam emerged as the first king of the ten northern tribes known as Israel. Two tribes, known as the southern kingdom, or Judah, remained loyal to the house of Solomon (1 Kings 12:1–32).

Jeroboam feared that the people in his territory would eventually switch their loyalty to Judah if they continued to go to Jerusalem to worship at the temple. So he designated two cities, Bethel and Dan, at opposite ends of Israel as alternative worship sites. Here he erected two bull statues that looked similar to the pagan god Baal. These shrines led the people away from worship of the one true God—a problem that plagued all the succeeding kings of Israel.

The Lord sent a prophet to tell Jeroboam that his sins would be severely punished. His army was decimated by the forces of King Abijah of Judah, and Jeroboam died soon thereafter (2 Chronicles 13:1–20).

Learn More: 1 Kings 11:26–40; 13:33–34

JESSE

Samuel said unto Jesse. . . SEND AND FETCH HIM. 1 SAMUEL 16:11

After King Saul failed to follow the Lord, God sent the prophet Samuel to anoint one of Jesse's eight sons as the new king of Israel. Beginning with the oldest, Jesse presented seven of his boys to the prophet, only to have each one turned down. Finally, Jesse called his youngest son, David, home from his duties as a shepherd. "Rise and anoint him," the Lord told Samuel. "This is the one" (1 Samuel 16:12 NIV; see 16:1–22).

Later, Saul asked Jesse to permit David to come to his camp and play his harp to calm the king's troubling thoughts. Jesse agreed and sent presents to Saul (1 Samuel 16:16–23). Jesse also sent David to Saul's camp to take food for his sons who were serving in the king's army. While on this mission from his father, David killed the Philistine giant Goliath (1 Samuel 17:12–17, 50–51).

The prophet Isaiah described the coming Messiah as "a rod out of the stem of Jesse" (Isaiah 11:1) and "a root of Jesse" (Isaiah 11:10). This prophecy was fulfilled through Jesus Christ, who emerged from the tribe of Judah through Jesse's family line (Matthew 1:5–6; Luke 3:32).

Learn More: Ruth 4:17, 22 / 1 Samuel 17:12; 25:10 / 1 Chronicles 2:12

JESUS

God. . .hath in these last days spoken unto us by his Son. HEBREWS 1:1

The Jewish people had long expected a Messiah. Finally, Jesus was born in a Bethlehem stable during the reign of Herod the Great (Matthew 2:1–2). Conceived by the Holy Spirit and born to the virgin Mary, He grew up like any Jewish boy (Luke 2:51–52). Yet He had an early consciousness of His divine mission (Luke 2:49).

His baptism by John the Baptist, divinely appointed to pave Jesus' way, launched His public ministry (Matthew 3:1–6). He preached and healed (Mark 1:38–42), taught about the kingdom of God (Luke 12:31–32), and sought the lost (Luke 19:10). He ministered first in Judea, then moved north into Galilee, establishing Capernaum as His home base.

As His three-year ministry drew to a close, Jesus disappointed many with His triumphal entry into Jerusalem on a donkey. This symbolized His humility and commitment to a spiritual rather than earthly kingdom.

Betrayed into the hands of the Jewish Sanhedrin, Jesus was declared guilty of blasphemy. Then the Roman governor, Pilate, crucified Him on a charge of treason. But the grave was not the final word: as predicted, Jesus arose from the dead, conquering sin and death for His followers (1 Corinthians 15:57).

Jesus ascended to heaven where He intercedes for all believers (Hebrews 7:25) and awaits His victorious return when everyone will confess Him as Lord, "to the glory of God the Father."

Learn More: John 1:1–14 / Matthew 4:1–11; 6:1–34 / Colossians 1:12–29

JETHRO

Moses' father in law said unto him, The thing that thou doest is not good. EXODUS 18:17

After killing an Egyptian slave foreman, Moses fled to the territory of Midian. Here in the wilderness area near Mount Sinai, he worked as a shepherd for a priest named Jethro—also known as Hobab—and eventually married his daughter (Exodus 2:15–3:1).

Jethro visited Moses and the Israelites in the wilderness near Midian after they had been released from slavery in Egypt. He quickly noticed that Moses was stretching himself too thin by trying to solve every problem that came up among the people.

This wise priest advised his son-in-law to appoint leaders who would share Moses' burden of leadership. To Moses' credit, he did not shrug off this advice as the idle words of a meddling father-in-law. He did as Jethro suggested and became a more effective leader (Exodus 18:13–27).

Learn More: Exodus 4:18 / Numbers 10:29–30 / Hobab: KJV

JEZEBEL

Jezebel sent a messenger unto Elijah. 1 KINGS 19:2

King Ahab of Israel was bad enough on his own. But he doubled his wrongdoing when he married Jezebel, daughter of a pagan ruler of Sidon. She influenced Ahab to promote worship of the pagan god Baal throughout his kingdom (1 Kings 16:31–32).

When the prophet Elijah killed some of the prophets of Baal, Jezebel determined to kill him. Only intervention by the Lord, who hid and sustained Elijah in the wilderness, prevented her from carrying out her death order (1 Kings 19:3–8).

This evil queen was also responsible for the death of Naboth, who owned a plot of ground that King Ahab wanted. She bribed false witnesses to testify against Naboth on a charge of blasphemy, and then had him executed. For this evil deed, the prophet Elijah predicted she would die a violent death (1 Kings 21:23).

This prediction came true several years later when Jehu seized the kingship from Ahab's successor. Jehu ordered Jezebel thrown from an upper story window, then trampled her with his horse. Later, only a few parts of her body were recovered (2 Kings 9:36).

Learn More: Revelation 2:20

JOAB

Joab. . .thrust them through the heart of Absalom. 2 SAMUEL 18:14

After David was acclaimed king over all Israel, he captured Jerusalem and turned it into his capital city. A soldier named Joab led the assault, and David rewarded him by naming him his chief military officer (1 Chronicles 11:1–6).

Joab led David's forces in several victories over his enemies, including the Edomites (2 Samuel 8:13–16) and the Ammonites (2 Samuel 11:1). In one campaign, Joab placed a brave warrior named Uriah on the front lines so he would be killed. This was done at David's orders to hide the king's adulterous affair with Uriah's wife (2 Samuel 11:14–24). But Joab was not so compliant when it came to David's rebellious son Absalom. He killed Absalom, even though the king had ordered that his life be spared.

Joab's fate was sealed when he threw his support behind Adonijah rather than Solomon as the claimant to David's throne. At David's orders, Solomon had Joab executed (1 Kings 2:5–6, 28–34).

Learn More: 2 Samuel 3:27; 20:9-10; 14:1-22; 19:5-7; 24:2-4

JOB

There was a man in the land of Uz, whose name was Job. JOB 1:1

Job was a righteous man whom God allowed Satan to test. God wanted to prove that Job's faithfulness was heartfelt, not simply due to the physical blessings he had been given.

First, Satan was permitted to take Job's livestock and servants—and then his ten children. Job continued to worship God. Soon, Satan covered Job with sores, and his wife urged him to curse God and die. Even at that, he remained faithful.

Before long, three friends came to share in his misery. For a week they were silent, but when Job began to speak, they accused him of wrongdoing. Each tried to convince Job that he needed to repent. He defended himself but—aware that no one is completely righteous before God—was confused as to why he was suffering so terribly. Job voiced many moving expressions of faith, including one of the Bible's earliest hints of Jesus: "I know that my redeemer lives, and that in the end he will stand on the earth" (Job 19:25 NIV).

Ultimately, God intervened to demonstrate Job's limited understanding, and Job repented of his complaining. God rebuked the three friends and restored all of Job's original blessings. See also *Bildad.*

Learn More: Job 1 / James 5:11

JOEL

The word of the Lord that came to Joel the son of Pethuel. JOEL 1:1

The prophet Joel used the devastation of a plague of locusts to call the people of Israel back to worship of the one true God. As bad as this calamity was, he declared, it was nothing in comparison to the coming day of God's judgment if the people refused to repent (Joel 1:3–15). His prophecies appear in the Old Testament book that bears his name.

On a more positive note, Joel predicted that God's spirit would fill His people if they obeyed the Lord (Joel 2:28–32). In the New Testament, the apostle Peter declared that this prophecy was fulfilled with the outpouring of the Holy Spirit on the early believers on the day of Pentecost (Acts 2:16–21).

Joel's book shows that God can sometimes deliver His message in the form of a natural disaster. Not every calamity should be interpreted in this way. But any natural disturbance—whether flood, storm, or fire—should motivate believers to be more sensitive to His purpose in our lives and the world He has created.

Learn More: Joel 3:9–16

JOHN THE APOSTLE

James the son of Zebedee, and John his brother. . . MATTHEW 10:2

John was one of the first disciples called by Jesus. He and his brother James were tending their fishing nets on the Sea of Galilee when Jesus invited them to follow Him and become "fishers of men" (Matthew 4:19; see 4:19–22).

John refers to himself in the Gospel that he wrote as "that disciple whom Jesus loved" (John 21:7). John was apparently the disciple whom Jesus asked to care for His mother, Mary, while He was dying on the cross (John 19:26–27).

After Jesus ascended to His Father, John worked with the apostle Peter in Jerusalem to call people to faith in Christ (Acts 4:13; 8:14–15). Later, he wrote a significant part of the New Testament—the Gospel that bears his name as well as the three letters of John and the book of Revelation.

John was probably an old man when he was imprisoned by the Roman government on the island of Patmos near the coastal city of Ephesus. Here he received a series of visions from the Lord that he recorded in Revelation (1:9–11).

Learn More: Matthew 17:1–8 / Mark 3:17; 5:37–42; 14:32–42 /
Luke 9:51–56 / John 13:23; 20:2, 20; 21:7; 21:20

JOHN THE BAPTIST

John did baptize in the wilderness. MARK 1:4

John the Baptist reminded people of a prophet like Elijah from the past. John lived in the wilderness and urged people to repent of their sins and be baptized to signify their spiritual renewal and total commitment to God (Matthew 3:1–2).

Jesus launched His public ministry by asking to be baptized by John. This request showed that Jesus identified with John's message and role as the Lord's forerunner. John was the last of the prophets, while Jesus was the proclaimer of the kingdom of God that dawned with His life and ministry.

Some people thought John was the Messiah. But John insisted that Jesus was the Promised One who would baptize with the Holy Spirit and bring salvation to sinners as the sacrificial Lamb of God (John 1:35–36).

John was eventually imprisoned by Herod Antipas for condemning the Roman official's illicit marriage. He would die by beheading. Jesus declared, "Of all who have ever lived, none is greater than John the Baptist" (Matthew 11:11 NLT).

Learn More: Mark 1:1–8 / Luke 3:1–18

JONAH

Jonah was in the belly of the fish three days and three nights. JONAH 1:17

Jonah has been called "the reluctant prophet." God called him to preach a message of judgment to the people of Assyria, an enemy nation that Israel hated. But Jonah wanted no part of God's dealings with these pagans, so he fled on a ship in the opposite direction (Jonah 1:1–2).

As punishment for his disobedience, the Lord sent a great fish to swallow Jonah, then delivered him on dry land with a renewal of His original call. Finally, the prophet set off grudgingly to Nineveh, Assyria's capital city (Jonah 3:1–2).

At the prophet's preaching, the people repented and turned to the Lord, much to Jonah's disappointment. "Didn't I say before I left home that you would do this, LORD?" Jonah complained. "I knew that you are a merciful and compassionate God. . . . You are eager to turn back from destroying people" (Jonah 4:2 NLT). Then God reminded the prophet that His love had no limits; it extended to all peoples and nations of the world.

Learn More: Jonah 4:3–11 / Matthew 12:40 / Jonas: KJV

180 Key People — 103

JONATHAN

Jonathan. . .loved him as he loved his own soul. 1 SAMUEL 20:17

The friendship between Jonathan, King Saul's oldest son, and David is legendary. Jonathan went behind his father's back several times to keep his friend safe from Saul's wrath (1 Samuel 19:1–7). Eventually David fled into the wilderness when Jonathan risked his own life to warn him that Saul was determined to kill him (1 Samuel 20:27–42).

Even though Jonathan was first in line to succeed his father, he gave his friend his royal robe to signify that David would be the next king (1 Samuel 18:1–4). And he secured David's promise that he would deal kindly with Jonathan's family when that day arrived (1 Samuel 20:14–16).

Jonathan and his father were eventually killed in a battle with the Philistines. David poured out his grief for his friend in words of deep sorrow (2 Samuel 1:26). After David became the undisputed king of Israel, he brought Jonathan's handicapped son Mephibosheth to the royal palace and took care of him for the rest of his life (2 Samuel 9:3–7).

Learn More: 2 Samuel 21:12–14

JOSEPH, HUSBAND OF MARY

Joseph. . .took unto him his wife. MATTHEW 1:24

How tongues must have wagged in Nazareth when Mary became pregnant during her engagement. And Joseph, her husband-to-be, was caught right in the middle.

When he heard the news, Joseph decided to break their engagement quietly to spare Mary any more embarrassment. While thinking about how to proceed, he fell asleep and had a dream in which an angel told him that Mary's pregnancy had happened through the supernatural action of the Holy Spirit. So, the angel told him, he should "not be afraid to take Mary as your wife" (Matthew 1:20 NLT).

This startling message must have been hard to believe, but Joseph accepted it in faith. And so it came about that this godly man became the stand-in father for the Son who had no father but God Himself.

Joseph was with Mary when Jesus was born in Bethlehem (Luke 2:16). He took Jesus and Mary to Egypt to escape Herod's wrath (Matthew 2:13). Later, he brought the family to Nazareth, where Jesus grew up and probably worked with Joseph in his trade as a carpenter (Matthew 13:55; Luke 2:51).

Learn More: Matthew 1:16 / John 1:45; 6:42

JOSEPH, SON OF JACOB

God. . .hath made me a father to Pharaoh. GENESIS 45:8

Joseph had the good fortune of being born to Jacob's favorite wife, Rachel. Joseph was also conceived when his father was an old man, so Jacob favored him above all his other sons. The jealousy that grew out of his situation led the older brothers to sell Joseph to a caravan of traveling merchants. They covered their evil deed by telling Jacob that his favorite son had been killed by a wild animal (Genesis 37:24–34).

Joseph wound up in Egypt, where he developed a reputation as an interpreter of dreams. He was brought before the pharaoh to tell him the meaning of one of his strange dreams—seven productive years for Egyptian grain, followed by seven years of crop failure. Joseph recommended that grain be stored during the good years to feed the nation during the famine. Pharaoh responded by naming Joseph as his chief aide to supervise the storage plan.

During the lean years, Joseph's brothers came to Egypt to buy grain. Some time had passed since they had seen him, so they did not recognize Joseph at first. After subjecting them to several character tests, he told them who he was and forgave their wrongdoing. Joseph considered the circumstances that brought him to Egypt a series of divine actions that saved the lives of Jacob's family. He made arrangements for his father and all his descendants to move to Egypt to escape the famine.

Learn More: Genesis 37:5–8; 41:50–52 / Joshua 24:32 / Psalm 105:17 / Hebrews 11:22

JOSEPH OF ARIMATHEA

Joseph of Arimathaea. . .went in boldly unto Pilate. MARK 15:43

Joseph of Arimathea was a follower of Jesus. But he was also a member of the Sanhedrin, the Jewish high court that sentenced Jesus to death. So Joseph lingered in the shadows as a secret follower until the day Jesus died.

Then, in a bold act that left no doubt about his commitment to Jesus, Joseph claimed the Lord's body and placed it in his own new tomb (Mark 15:42–46). Nicodemus, another secret follower, helped Joseph anoint the body with spices before it was entombed.

According to Matthew's gospel, Joseph was a wealthy man (Matthew 27:57–60). So Jesus' burial in his tomb was a fulfillment of an Old Testament prophecy: "They made His grave with the wicked and with a rich man at His death, although He had done no violence and had not spoken deceitfully" (Isaiah 53:9 HCSB).

Arimathea was a small town about twenty miles northwest of Jerusalem.

Learn More: Luke 23:50–53 / John 19:38–42

JOSHUA

As I was with Moses, so I will be with thee. JOSHUA 1:5

Great leaders are hard to follow, and this was particularly true in the case of Moses. He had led the people out of Egypt and brought them through the wilderness for more than forty years. The task of leading the people in conquering Canaan fell to Moses' servant and associate, Joshua. He began with assurance from the Lord that He would give strength for the task, just as He had walked with Moses. Joshua encouraged the people with the same message (Joshua 1:16).

The first city to fall to Joshua's army was Jericho (Joshua 6:1–27). Then he defeated Canaanite strongholds throughout the entire territory. When the days of fighting were over, Joshua convened representatives of the twelve tribes and supervised the assignment of land allotments to each tribe (Joshua 13–19).

Near the end of his life, Joshua called the Israelite leaders together and led them to renew the covenant with the Lord. He reminded them of how God had blessed them by giving them this land. He also cautioned them against worshiping the gods of the pagan Canaanites whom they had defeated (Joshua 24:1–28).

Learn More: Exodus 17:9–13; 24:13 / Deuteronomy 31:7

JOSIAH

He. . .walked in all the way of David his father. 2 KINGS 22:2

Josiah was only eight years old when he succeeded his father as king of Judah (2 Kings 22:1). In his first few years on the throne, he probably had trusted advisors to help him govern the country.

In contrast to his evil father, Amon, Josiah was committed to the Lord. He soon began a series of reforms to turn the nation back to God. He tore down pagan altars and launched a campaign to purify the temple from defilement and to make needed repairs (2 Chronicles 34:1–9).

During the construction project, a copy of the Book of the Law was found. This was probably a portion of the book of Deuteronomy. When Josiah listened to passages from the book, he was shocked at how far the nation had drifted from God's commands.

This book gave new momentum to the reform movement the king had already authorized. Soon afterward, he assembled the people and led them in a public renewal of their commitment to the Lord (2 Chronicles 34:29–32).

Learn More: 2 Kings 22:1–20; 23:1–29 / Matthew 1:10–11; Josias: KJV

JUDAH

The sceptre shall not depart from Judah. Genesis 49:10

Judah was the fourth son of Jacob by his wife Leah. Judah became one of the most prominent of Jacob's twelve sons. The tribe that descended from him became the messianic line through which Jesus's ancestry is traced (Matthew 1:2–3; *Judas*: kjv; Luke 3:30; *Juda*: kjv).

When Joseph's brothers conspired to kill him, Judah stepped forward to plead for the boy's life. They decided to sell Joseph into slavery in Egypt instead (Genesis 37:26–28). Later, when dealing with Joseph as a high Egyptian official, Judah volunteered to be held as a hostage rather than his younger brother Benjamin (Genesis 44:18–34). In response to Judah's eloquent speech, Joseph wept openly and finally identified himself as their long-lost brother (Genesis 45:1–8).

When Jacob blessed his sons near the end of his life, it was Judah rather than the three older sons who received the patriarch's blessing. Jacob predicted that Judah's descendants would become the dominant tribe of the nation of Israel (Genesis 49:8–11).

Learn More: Genesis 38 / 1 Chronicles 2:3–4 / Revelation 5:5

JUDAS ISCARIOT

Jesus. . .gave it to Judas Iscariot, the son of Simon. John 13:26

Judas Iscariot will always be remembered as the disciple who betrayed Jesus. Toward the end of Jesus' ministry, Judas realized that His enemies were determined to have Him put to death. So he decided to profit from the situation by turning Jesus over to the Sanhedrin, the Jewish high court. For thirty pieces of silver, Judas led them to Jesus and identified Him with the infamous "Judas kiss" (Matthew 26:47–50).

Jesus knew that Judas was plotting to betray Him. On the night before His arrest, Jesus told His disciples that one of them would turn against Him. Then He clearly identified Judas as the one by giving him a piece of bread while quoting these words from the Old Testament: "The one who eats My bread has raised his heel against me" (John 13:18 hcsb; see Psalm 41:9).

Judas was from the town of Kerioth in southern Judea; thus his name, as Judas of Iscariot, was a veiled reference to the place. He was the only member of the Twelve who was not a native of the region of Galilee in northern Palestine.

Learn More: Matthew 27:3–10 / John 12:2–8 / Acts 1:16–20

KETURAH

Then again Abraham took a wife, and her name was Keturah. Genesis 25:1

Keturah was the second wife of Abraham; he apparently married her after the death of Sarah. Keturah gave birth to six sons, who became the ancestors of six Arabian tribes in Palestine and surrounding territories (Genesis 23:1–2; 25:1–6).

God's covenant with Abraham, to make his descendants into a great nation, was continued through Isaac, the son whom he fathered through Sarah. So before he died, Abraham presented gifts to Keturah's sons and sent them "away from his son Isaac, to the land of the East" (Genesis 25:6 hcsb).

One of Keturah's sons was Midian, apparently the ancestor of the tribe known as the Midianites. Jethro, Moses' father-in-law, was from Midian. Joseph's brothers sold him to Midianite traders, who sold him into slavery in Egypt.

Keturah is also referred to as Abraham's concubine. She may have been Abraham's second wife, even before Sarah died.

Learn More: 1 Chronicles 1:32–33

KORAH

The earth opened her mouth, and swallowed them up. NUMBERS 16:32

While wandering in the wilderness, the Israelites often complained about Moses and his leadership. But a Levite named Korah took this grumbling to a new level with an organized challenge to Moses' authority. Korah gathered a following of 250 disgruntled clan leaders and confronted Moses and Aaron. These rebels were jealous of Aaron's position as high priest and of Moses' authority in general. The group apparently thought that all Levites, not just Aaron's priestly family, should be able to perform priestly duties (Numbers 16:1–32).

Moses put the dispute in God's hands. The Korah coalition was instructed to bring containers of incense to the altar of the tabernacle as offerings to the Lord. When they did, the ground on which they were standing suddenly split apart, taking them to their death.

Moses then ordered their bronze incense containers to be collected and hammered into a covering for the altar. This would serve as a warning that "no unauthorized person—no one who was not a descendant of Aaron—should ever enter the LORD's presence to burn incense."

Learn More: Jude 8–11

LABAN

God came to Laban the Syrian in a dream by night. GENESIS 31:24

We could think of Laban as a matchmaker. He was involved in the marriages of two of the famous patriarchs of the Bible, Isaac and Jacob. Laban gave permission for his sister Rebekah to marry Isaac (Genesis 24:55–67). In later years, he provided sanctuary for his sister's son Jacob, who eventually married two of Laban's daughters (Genesis 29:16–30).

After tricking his father into giving him his blessing, Jacob fled to Laban's home to escape the wrath of his brother Esau. While lodging with Laban, Jacob found himself on the receiving end of the kind of trickery he had pulled on others.

Jacob was promised his uncle's daughter Rachel if he would work for Laban for seven years. But Laban tricked Jacob into marrying Leah, Rachel's older sister, instead. Jacob had to work seven more years for Rachel's hand. Then Laban persuaded his nephew to work for him a while longer, but apparently didn't pay him what he promised (Genesis 31:7).

Fed up with Laban's trickery, Jacob finally left with his wives and possessions to return to his homeland. But Laban pursued him, convinced that Jacob had taken some livestock that belonged to him. They eventually parted ways on peaceful terms, with an agreement that neither would take advantage of the other in their future dealings (Genesis 31:45–55).

Learn More: Genesis 31:1–16

LAZARUS

Jesus saith unto her, Thy brother shall rise again. JOHN 11:23

Jesus and His disciples were teaching not far from Jerusalem when word came that His friend Lazarus was very sick. Jesus waited two days before setting off toward Bethany, the village where Lazarus lived with his two sisters, Mary and Martha. Jesus often stayed in their home when preaching and healing near Jerusalem.

When Jesus arrived, Martha met Him with the news that Lazarus had died. Her words amounted to a gentle reprimand that Jesus had not come sooner. "If you had been here," she told Him, "my brother would not have died" (John 11:21 NIV; see 11:1–44).

Jesus assured Martha that her brother would live again because He had the divine power to bring the dead back to life. Then He called Lazarus out of the tomb with three simple words: "Lazarus, come forth" (verse 43).

According to the Gospel of John, this miracle was the last performed by Jesus before His crucifixion. Because it was so spectacular and so close to Jerusalem, the Jewish Sanhedrin stepped up their plans to arrest Jesus and have Him executed (John 11:45–57). Their murderous plans even included Lazarus because his miraculous emergence from the grave had caused many people to believe in Jesus.

Learn More: Luke 10:38–41 / John 12:1–11

LEAH

He took Leah his daughter, and brought her to [Jacob]. GENESIS 29:23

Imagine how surprised Jacob must have been: he thought he had taken Rachel as his wife, but he ended up married to her sister Leah instead (Genesis 29:16–28).

Jacob's father-in-law, Laban, was the man behind the scam. He promised Jacob he could marry Rachel in exchange for seven years of Jacob's work. But Laban substituted his older daughter Leah for Rachel on Jacob's wedding night. Jacob didn't realize he had been tricked until the next morning, after their marriage had been consummated. So the cunning Laban got seven more years of labor out of Jacob for the privilege of marrying his true love.

Leah was always the less-favored of Jacob's two sister wives. But Leah bore six of his twelve sons—Reuben, Simeon, Levi, Judah, Issachar, and Zebulun (Genesis 29:31–35; 30:17–20). These sons were ancestors of six of the twelve tribes that developed into the nation of Israel

Learn More: Ruth 4:11

LEVI

. . .therefore was his name called Levi. GENESIS 29:34

Levi, third son of Jacob and Leah, grew angry when a Canaanite man named Shechem forced himself upon Levi's sister Dinah. In an act of revenge, Levi and his brother Simeon killed all the male members of Shechem's clan, stole their possessions, and took Dinah back to their camp (Genesis 34:1–31).

Levi's three sons grew into the three main divisions of the Levitical priesthood—the Gershonites, the Kohathites, and the Merarites (Genesis 46:11). These Levites served as assistants to the priests in the sacrificial worship system of the Israelites. They performed such duties as preparing the sacred bread known as showbread for the altar, slaughtering and skinning animals for sacrifice, and leading music during worship.

At the end of his life, Jacob condemned Levi and Simeon for their act of violence against the men of Shechem for violating their sister Dinah. "Cursed be their anger, for it was fierce," he declared, "and their wrath, for it was cruel: I will divide them in Jacob, and scatter them in Israel" (Genesis 49:7).

Learn More: Exodus 6:16 / Numbers 3:17

LOIS

. . .faith that is in thee, which dwelt first in thy grandmother Lois. 2 TIMOTHY 1:5

Lois was the grandmother of Timothy, a missionary associate of the apostle Paul. She probably played a key role in bringing her grandson to faith in the Lord. The apostle Paul commended Lois for her contribution to Timothy's spiritual development.

Paul also recognized Timothy's mother, Eunice, for the same thing. Perhaps Lois had taught her daughter about the Lord, and Eunice in turn had passed her Christian values on to young Timothy.

Lois shows that the Christian faith, while it cannot be inherited from one's family, is a powerful influence in the lives of many people who turn to the Lord.

LOT

Lot also, which went with Abram, had flocks, and herds, and tents. GENESIS 13:5

When Abraham left his homeland at God's call to settle in Canaan, his nephew Lot went with him. Lot was also with his uncle when Abraham lived for a time in Egypt to escape a famine in Canaan (Genesis 12:1–3; 13:1).

Later, back in Canaan, Abraham and Lot accumulated herds of livestock that competed for the same pasturelands. Given first choice of the available land, Lot chose the fertile plains in the Jordan River valley. He failed to consider the consequences of living close to the pagan cities of Sodom and Gomorrah (Genesis 13:6–12).

When God destroyed these two cities because of their wickedness, He sent two angels to rescue Lot and his family. But Lot's wife was turned to a pillar of salt when she looked back at the burning city of Sodom (Genesis 19:26).

After the rest of the family escaped, Lot's two daughters tricked him into sleeping with them in order to bear children to preserve his family line. From their incestuous union came two sons, who became the ancestors of the Moabite and Ammonite peoples (Genesis 19:30–38).

In the New Testament, the apostle Peter used Lot's experience as an example of God's power "to rescue the godly from trials and to hold the unrighteous for punishment on the day of judgment" (2 Peter 2:9 NIV).

Learn More: Genesis 11:27–32

LUKE

Only Luke is with me. 2 TIMOTHY 4:11

Luke was a traveling companion and missionary associate of the apostle Paul. Although Luke wrote the entire book of Acts, he does not refer to himself by name anywhere in the book. Instead, most scholars believe he used the personal pronouns "we" and "us" to refer to events in which he was involved.

If this is true, Luke was with Paul on at least part of the apostle's first missionary journey (Acts 16:10–17), as well as his second journey (Acts 20:5–21:18). He also accompanied Paul on his trip by ship to Rome (Acts 27:1–28:16). Once in Rome, Luke apparently remained with Paul or somewhere nearby while the apostle was in prison, as Paul indicated in his second epistle to Timothy.

According to Paul, Luke was a physician by profession (Colossians 4:14). In addition to the book of Acts, Luke also wrote the Gospel that bears his name. These two books together make up about one-fourth of the entire New Testament. Both are noted for their historical accuracy and careful attention to detail. Luke addressed both books to a person whom he called Theophilus (Luke 1:1–3; Acts 1:1). See also *Theophilus*.

Learn More: Philemon 24; *Lucas:* KJV

LYDIA

Lydia, a seller of purple, of the city of Thyatira. . . ACTS 16:14

The apostle Paul was on his second missionary journey with Timothy and Silas when they stopped at the city of Philippi. On the Sabbath they went to a nearby river, seeking people who might be open to the gospel.

Here they found several women who had apparently gathered to pray. Among them was a woman named Lydia, a seller of cloth colored with a purple dye. She paid careful attention to Paul's presentation of the gospel, turned to the Lord, and was baptized. Members of her household followed her in placing their faith in Jesus (Acts 16:13–15).

Lydia was probably the first convert to Christianity in Philippi, and thus a member of the church that Paul founded here. At her invitation, he and his missionary associates stayed at her house while ministering in the city (Acts 16:40).

MALACHI

The burden of the word of the Lord to Israel by Malachi. MALACHI 1:1

The prophet Malachi was one of God's messenger to His people after they returned to Judah from their exile in Babylon and Persia.

At first the people of Judah were enthusiastic about rebuilding their homeland and restoring their religious heritage. But their zeal soon cooled and turned to indifference. They began to withhold tithes and offerings and to bring defective animals as sacrifices. Even the priests became negligent in their duties. Malachi addressed these abuses and called the people to renew their faith in the Lord (Malachi 2:1–8; 3:8–10).

The most familiar passage from Malachi's book is his encouragement to test the Lord in the matter of tithing: "'Bring the whole tithe into the storehouse, that there may be food in my house. Test me in this,' says the LORD Almighty, 'and see if I will not throw open the floodgates of heaven and pour out so much blessing that there will not be room enough to store it'" (Malachi 3:10 NIV).

Malachi closed his book, the last in the Old Testament, with a word of hope about the future Messiah. God would send a messenger similar to the prophet Elijah, who would announce the arrival of the day of the Lord (Malachi 4:5–6). Many interpreters see this as a reference to John the Baptist, forerunner of Jesus.

Learn More: Malachi 1:6–14

MALCHUS

The servant's name was Malchus. JOHN 18:10

Malchus, a servant of the high priest, accompanied the religious leaders who came to arrest Jesus. In an attempt to protect his Master, Peter lashed out with his sword and cut off Malchus's ear. Jesus told Peter to stand down and put his weapon away—because His arrest and forthcoming death were a part of God's redemptive plan (John 18:3–11).

This incident appears in all four Gospels. But only John identifies the servant as Malchus, and only Luke reports that Jesus restored the man's severed ear (Luke 22:51).

Learn More: Matthew 26:51–52 / Mark 14:47

MANASSEH

Manasseh made Judah and the inhabitants of Jerusalem to err. 2 CHRONICLES 33:9

Unlike his godly father and predecessor Hezekiah, King Manasseh of Judah led the nation into a dark age of rebellion against God. Manasseh brought back all the idols his father had destroyed and even erected an image of the pagan goddess Asherah in the temple. He practiced black magic and worshiped the sun, moon, and stars. He paid homage to Molech and sacrificed one of his own sons to this pagan god of the Ammonites (2 Kings 21:1–9).

God punished the king for these evil acts by sending him into captivity in Babylon. Here he repented and turned to the Lord. His captors eventually allowed Manasseh to return to Judah, where he tried to make amends for his mistakes. But he died soon afterwards, and his reforms were reversed by Amon, his evil son and successor (2 Chronicles 33:13–33).

Manasseh's reign of fifty-five years planted seeds of unfaithfulness to the Lord from which Judah never recovered. When the nation fell to the Babylonians in later years, the biblical writer blamed this king for its downfall (2 Kings 24:3).

Learn More: Jeremiah 15:4

MARK

Barnabas and Saul. . .took with them John, whose surname was Mark. ACTS 12:25

Because of God's grace, failure is never the final word. This is the clear message that comes from a young believer known as John Mark.

Mark went with the apostle Paul and his associate Barnabas on their first missionary journey. But for some unknown reason, Mark left them midway through the trip and returned to Jerusalem (Acts 13:13). Because of this, Paul refused to take the young man on his second journey. So Barnabas took Mark and set off in a different direction (Acts 15:37–39).

This novice believer eventually recovered from his initial failure and became a faithful church leader. Even Paul spoke of him with kindness and affection.

Mark went on to write the Gospel of Mark, probably the first account of Jesus' ministry to be written. He may have based his narrative on eyewitness testimony from the apostle Peter. Mark was apparently Peter's missionary associate, since the apostle referred to him as "my son."

Learn More: Mark 14:43–52

MARTHA

She saith unto him, Yea, Lord: I believe that thou art the Christ. JOHN 11:27

Martha teaches a valuable lesson about what is really important in life. Jesus was a guest in her home in Bethany, where she lived with her sister Mary and her brother Lazarus. Martha was busy in the kitchen, probably fixing a meal for Jesus. But Mary was sitting at Jesus' feet, listening to His teachings.

Martha expressed her frustration that Mary was not lifting a finger to help with the meal. "Lord, dost thou not care that my sister hath left me alone?" she asked Jesus. "Bid her therefore that she help me" (Luke 10:40; see 10:39–42).

Jesus replied that Martha was busy with secondary matters while Mary had chosen to do what was most important at that particular time—spending time with Him.

Martha had another encounter with Jesus near the end of His public ministry. She sent word that His friend Lazarus was very sick. But Jesus didn't arrive at their home until after Lazarus had died. Martha met Him with words of disappointment that He had not come sooner.

Jesus assured her that Lazarus would live again because He was the master over life and death. Then He raised her brother from the grave with the simple words, "Lazarus, come forth" (John 11:43; see 11:17–44). See also *Mary, Sister of Martha.*

MARY, MOTHER OF JESUS

His mother kept all these sayings in her heart. LUKE 2:51

Mary, a peasant girl from the village of Nazareth, was engaged to be married to Joseph. Imagine her shock when the angel Gabriel told her she would give birth to the Son of God. How could this be, she wondered, since she had never slept with a man? But the angel quieted Mary's anxiety by explaining that this was all part of God's plan (Luke 1:26–35).

Mary accepted this news as a divine miracle. Then she visited her relative Elizabeth, who was also carrying a child. The unborn baby stirred in Elizabeth's womb when Mary entered her house. This signified that Elizabeth's child—John the Baptist—recognized Mary's son as the long-awaited Messiah.

When Jesus was twelve years old, He accompanied his parents to Jerusalem to observe a Jewish festival. He lagged behind in the Holy City to discuss religious matters with the learned teachers of the day. When Mary found Him, she scolded Him for causing anxiety, but Jesus explained that she and Joseph should not be worried—because He had been called to do the work of God the Father (Luke 2:42–49).

Mary was present when Jesus turned water into wine at a wedding feast (John 2:3–11). She also looked on as He was crucified. Jesus commended His mother to the care of His disciple John (John 19:26–27).

Learn More: Luke 1:39–55 / Acts 1:14

MARY, SISTER OF MARTHA

Mary...anointed the feet of Jesus, and wiped his feet with her hair. John 12:3

Mary lived with her sister Martha and her brother Lazarus in the village of Bethany near Jerusalem. During one of Jesus' visits in their home, He commended Mary for sitting at His feet and listening to His teachings (Luke 10:39–42).

When her brother Lazarus died, Mary grieved in her own quiet way inside the house while her sister went out to meet Jesus. When Martha called Mary to come outside, she fell at Jesus' feet, weeping. Then, like Martha, she declared, "Lord, if thou hadst been here, my brother had not died" (John 11:32).

After Jesus brought Lazarus back to life, Mary showed her gratitude by pouring an expensive ointment on His feet and wiping them with her hair. The disciple Judas objected to this lavish and wasteful display. But Jesus interpreted this unselfish act as an anointing for His forthcoming death. "Leave her alone," He declared. "It was intended that she should save this perfume for the day of my burial" (John 12:7 NIV). See also *Martha*.

The account of Jesus' anointing by a woman also appears in the Gospels of Matthew and Mark. But only John's gospel identifies her as Mary of Bethany.

Learn More: Matthew 26:6–13 / Mark 14:3–9

MARY MAGDALENE

Mary Magdalene came and told the disciples that she had seen the Lord. John 20:18

Mary apparently was a native of Magdala, a village on the shore of the Sea of Galilee, so she was known as Mary Magdalene. Jesus healed her of demon possession, and she became one of His most loyal followers. She, along with other women, provided food for Him and His disciples (Luke 8:1–3).

Mary was one of the women who looked on as Jesus was crucified (Mark 15:40). She came to His tomb on resurrection morning to finish anointing His body, only to find that the tomb was empty (Mark 16:1–8).

According to the Gospel of John, Mary was the first person to whom Jesus appeared after He rose from the dead. At Jesus' command, she told the disciples that she had seen Him alive. To prove that Mary's report was true, Jesus appeared to them in His resurrection body that same day (John 20:11–20).

Some interpreters suggest that Mary was the sinful woman who anointed Jesus' feet with expensive perfume (Mark 14:3), or the woman accused of adultery whom Jesus forgave (John 8:1–11). But there is no evidence to support either of these theories.

Learn More: Matthew 27:57–61 / Mark 16:9–14

MATTHEW

And Levi made him a great feast in his own house. Luke 5:29

Matthew was busy at his job of collecting taxes when Jesus stopped at his station. Matthew knew that tax collectors, as agents of the Roman government, were hated by their Jewish countrymen. So he must have been shocked when Jesus called him to become one of His disciples. But without hesitation, Matthew got up and followed Jesus (Matthew 9:9–13).

What happened next was even more shocking to the religious elite of the town. Matthew, also known as Levi, hosted a big meal for Jesus and His disciples. He also invited many of his tax collector friends. The scribes and Pharisees heard about this gathering of outcasts, and asked Jesus' disciples why they were eating with such sinful and unworthy people. Jesus answered that He had come into the world to minister to people just like Matthew and his friends (Luke 5:31–32).

Matthew was a loyal follower of Jesus for the rest of His earthly ministry and beyond. Several years after Jesus ascended into heaven, Matthew wrote a narrative about the Lord's life that we know as the Gospel of Matthew. This writing focuses on Jesus as the fulfillment of Old Testament prophecy. It serves as the perfect bridge between the Old and New Testaments.

Learn More: Matthew 10:2–4 / Luke 6:13–16 / Acts 1:13–14

MATTHIAS

The lot fell upon Matthias; and he was numbered with the eleven apostles. ACTS 1:26

Soon after Jesus' ascension, a group of His followers, including the eleven disciples, gathered in Jerusalem. Peter led them to see that the logical next step was to select a person to replace Judas, the disciple who had betrayed Jesus.

Peter pointed to Psalm 69 as a passage that had predicted Judas's act. Psalm 109, a similar section of scripture, left no doubt in the apostle's mind that a replacement was necessary. He quoted a verse from this psalm: "Let his [the betrayer's] days be few; and let another take his office" (verse 8).

The group agreed that whoever took Judas's place should have been an eyewitness of Jesus' life and teachings during His entire public ministry. The names of two believers who met this qualification were put forward. Then Matthias was chosen through the casting of lots as the newest member of the Twelve (Acts 1:15–26).

Nothing else is known about Matthias. While he was obviously a loyal follower of Jesus, he is never mentioned in the Gospels. And after he joined the other apostles, his name never appears again.

MELCHIZEDEK

Thou art a priest for ever after the order of Melchizedek. PSALM 110:4

Abraham once battled several tribal leaders who had captured his nephew Lot along with Lot's family and possessions. On his way home from the victory, Abraham was greeted and blessed by a mysterious man known as Melchizedek, whose name means "king of righteousness."

Abraham gave Melchizedek a tenth of all the spoils he had collected. This showed that he honored this man's role as a priest and a fellow worshiper of the one true God (Genesis 14:18–20).

The writer of the book of Hebrews described both Jesus and Melchizedek as kings of peace and righteousness. This New Testament author pointed out that the formal priesthood of Israel was temporary in nature. Priests would serve for a while, then die and be replaced by others in the priestly lineage. But Melchizedek was a priest long before the formal priesthood was established through the tribe of Levi and the descendants of Aaron. In the same way, Jesus' priesthood was eternal and non-inherited.

The psalmist David also described Melchizedek as a type of the coming Messiah (Psalm 110:4).

Learn More: Hebrews 7:1–12

MEPHIBOSHETH

I will surely shew thee kindness for Jonathan thy father's sake. 2 SAMUEL 9:7

Although King Saul hated and tried to kill David, Saul's son Jonathan was a close friend. Their bond was so strong that David, after he became king, honored Jonathan in a special way. David brought his friend's son Mephibosheth into the royal palace and took care of him for the rest of his life (2 Samuel 9:6–13).

Mephibosheth needed this helping hand. He was lame from a freak accident that happened when he was only five years old. The child's caretaker heard that Jonathan had been killed in a battle with the Philistines. Fearing for Mephibosheth's life, she fled with him in her arms and dropped him. He had been crippled ever since (2 Samuel 4:4).

King David also granted to Mephibosheth the estate of his grandfather Saul. The king also arranged for a former servant of Saul to manage the property on Mephibosheth's behalf.

Learn More: 2 Samuel 19:24–30

METHUSELAH

All the days of Methuselah were nine hundred sixty and nine years. GENESIS 5:27

Methuselah was a descendant of Seth, a family line known for its godliness. Beginning with Seth's son Enos, members of this lineage began to "call on the name of the LORD" (Genesis 4:26). Methuselah fathered Lamech, who in turn was the father of Noah, the righteous man who survived the flood by obeying the Lord.

After the birth of Lamech, Methuselah lived for 782 years and died at the age of 969. This life span is longer than that of any other person mentioned in the Bible. He is listed in the genealogy of Jesus in the New Testament (Luke 3:37; *Mathusala*: KJV).

Many years after Methuselah had passed on, Abraham died at the age of 175 (Genesis 25:7). The Bible observes that Abraham at his death was an "old man" who was "full of years" (Genesis 25:8). But he came in a distant second to Methuselah.

Learn More: Genesis 5:21–27

MICAH

Micah the Morasthite prophesied. . . Zion shall be plowed like a field. JEREMIAH 26:18

The prophet Micah is best known for his prediction that the Messiah would be born in Bethlehem. This look into the future appears in the Old Testament book that bears his name: "But you, Bethlehem Ephrathah, though you are small among the clans of Judah, out of you will come for me one who will be ruler over Israel" (Micah 5:2 NIV).

Micah's ministry occurred during the reigns of three kings of Judah—Jotham, Ahaz, and Hezekiah (Micah 1:1). Thus, he issued his messianic prediction about seven centuries before Jesus was born.

The prophet addressed the moral decline of both Judah and Israel, declaring that God would judge His people because of their sin and rebellion (Micah 3:1–4). He also condemned the social injustices of his time (Micah 2:1–3).

Learn More: Micah 1:8–16

MIRIAM

Miriam the prophetess, the sister of Aaron, took a timbrel in her hand. EXODUS 15:20

Miriam, sister of Moses and Aaron, played a key role in several major events in the life of Moses, beginning with his days as a baby. She was probably the unnamed sister who arranged for her mother to care for Moses after he was hidden in a basket on the river to escape the Egyptian pharaoh's death order (Exodus 2:1–8).

Later, Miriam led a celebration after the Egyptian army was wiped out at the Red Sea. She assumed the role of a prophetess and led the Israelite women in a song of praise to the Lord (Exodus 15:20–21).

In the wilderness, after Moses had married an Ethiopian woman, Miriam and Aaron questioned his authority. God punished their rebellious spirit by striking Miriam with leprosy. But Moses prayed for her, and she was healed after seven days (Numbers 12:1–15).

Learn More: Deuteronomy 24:9 / 1 Chronicles 6:3

MOAB

Moses the servant of the Lord died there in the land of Moab. DEUTERONOMY 34:5

Moab was fathered by Lot through an incestuous relationship with his daughter. Moab's descendants grew into a tribal group known as the Moabites, who lived in a rugged territory along the Dead Sea.

Moab as a person is mentioned only once in the Bible (Genesis 19:37). But the Moabites as a tribe are cited numerous times throughout the Old Testament. Moses died after getting a glimpse of Canaan from one of the land of Moab's high peaks.

The Israelites enjoyed peaceful relationships with Moab throughout most of their history. But when they passed through Moab on their way to Canaan, the king of Moab tried to pronounce a curse on the people through a pagan magician named Balaam (Numbers 22:1–6). The attempt failed when God intervened to cause Balaam to bless the Israelites instead (Numbers 24:1–10).

Learn More: Ruth 1:1–4

MORDECAI

Haman saw that Mordecai bowed not, nor did him reverence. ESTHER 3:5

Mordecai was the guardian of his orphaned cousin Hadassah (Esther 2:5–7), who rose from humble beginnings to become known as Esther, queen of Persia.

This quiet man of deep religious convictions was a minor servant in the court of the Persian king. Mordecai refused to bow down and honor a man named Haman, the king's second in command. Enraged, Haman persuaded his boss to issue a decree for the slaughter of all Jewish people throughout his kingdom (Esther 3:8–12).

Through Queen Esther, Mordecai worked quietly behind the scenes to counteract the threat to his people (Esther 4:1–17). A previous action Mordecai had taken to save the king from assassination worked in his favor (Esther 2:21–22). Haman was hanged on the very gallows he had erected for Mordecai's execution (Esther 7:10), and the king promoted Mordecai to a higher position in his court (Esther 10:2–3). See also *Esther.*

Learn More: Esther 6:1–12

MOSES

The Lord spake unto Moses, Go unto Pharaoh. EXODUS 8:1

God spoke face-to-face with Moses, "as a man speaketh unto his friend" (Exodus 33:11). Perhaps this is because of Moses' faithfulness and his status as a leader of God's people. With the help of his brother Aaron, Moses led the Israelites out of slavery in Egypt and brought them to the border of the promised land. He is the central character in the books of Exodus, Leviticus, Numbers, and Deuteronomy.

Moses had grown up in Egypt, so he knew its customs and traditions. From shepherding in the land of Midian, he knew the wilderness territory the Israelites would have to cross on their way to Canaan. Still, Moses made excuses to try to avoid God's call. The Lord finally quieted his objections with a guarantee he couldn't ignore: "Certainly I will be with thee" (Exodus 3:12).

Strengthened by this promise, Moses presided over ten plagues against Egypt that finally convinced Pharaoh to free the Israelites (Exodus 7–11). Moses led the people through the wilderness for more than forty years. Along the way, he tapped the Lord's power to provide food and water (Exodus 16:14–16; 17:6); weathered complaints and even rebellion against his leadership (Exodus 17:3–4); received the Ten Commandments that provided guidelines for the people's behavior (Exodus 20:1–17); and supervised the building of the tabernacle to bring order and energy to their religious life (Exodus 40:1–8). Moses died at age 120 (Deuteronomy 34:7).

In the New Testament, he is listed as one of the great heroes of the faith (Hebrews 11:23–26).

Learn More: Numbers 20:1–13 / Matthew 17:1–3 / 2 Corinthians 3:12–16

NAAMAN

Then went he down, and dipped himself seven times in Jordan. 2 KINGS 5:14

Naaman was an officer in the Syrian army, but he had a problem that couldn't be solved with swords and spears. He had leprosy, a dreaded skin disease.

Through his wife's Israelite servant girl, Naaman learned there was a prophet in Israel named Elisha who could heal his disease. But he was not prepared for the cure that Elisha prescribed—to wash seven times in the Jordan River. Enraged, the military man declared that the rivers of his home country were better than all the rivers of Israel. "Why shouldn't I wash in them and be healed?" he asked (2 Kings 5:12 NLT; see 5:1–14). His pride threatened to rob him of a cure.

Fortunately, Naaman's servants were smarter than their boss—they persuaded him to obey the prophet, and he was cured.

Learn More: Luke 4:27

NABOTH

Naboth said to Ahab, The Lord forbid it me. 1 KINGS 21:3

Naboth owned a fine vineyard, but it couldn't have been in a more unlucky place: it was located near the summer palace of Ahab, evil ruler of the northern kingdom of Israel.

Ahab wanted to turn his neighbor's property into a garden. But Naboth refused to sell because it was part of a family inheritance that he planned to pass on to his own descendants (1 Kings 21:1–19).

Ahab's queen, the wicked Jezebel, plotted to take the land by bribing witnesses to accuse Naboth of blasphemy against God and the king. After Naboth and his sons were stoned to death, Ahab seized the property.

God sent Elijah the prophet with a disturbing message of judgment against Ahab: "In the place where dogs licked the blood of Naboth shall dogs lick thy blood, even thine" (verse 19). This prophecy was fulfilled when Ahab was killed in a battle with the Syrians. Dogs lapped up the water when the king's blood was flushed from his chariot (1 Kings 22:34–38).

Learn More: 2 Kings 9:21–37

NADAB

There went out fire from the Lord, and devoured them. LEVITICUS 10:2

Nadab, a son of Aaron, was part of the elite group allowed to accompany Moses, Aaron, and seventy elders when they ascended Mount Sinai to commune with the Lord (Exodus 24:1–10). Along with his father and brothers, Nadab was part of the priestly lineage established when his father was consecrated as the first high priest of Israel (Numbers 3:32).

But Nadab committed a profane act that the Lord punished with his sudden death, as well as that of his brother Abihu. Their sin was burning an incense offering with "strange fire" (Leviticus 10:1). Incense used in worship was to be carefully prepared to exact standards (Exodus 30:34–38). But exactly why Nadab and Abihu's incense offering was unacceptable is unknown.

Learn More: Numbers 3:4; 26:60–61

NATHAN

And Nathan said to David, Thou art the man. 2 SAMUEL 12:7

Nathan was a courageous prophet who condemned King David for his infamous double sin—his adulterous affair with Bathsheba and the murder of her husband, Uriah. Nathan told the king a clever story about a rich man who had many flocks of sheep. But he took the only little lamb that a poor man owned to provide a meal for a guest.

David was outraged at this selfish act. He declared that the rich man should be put to death. Then Nathan pointed out that David was actually the man in the story. He had everything a man could ever want, yet he had Uriah killed and took his wife as his own (2 Samuel 12:1–14).

Deeply convicted, David confessed his sin. Later he wrote Psalm 51 about this occasion when "Nathan the prophet came to him" (psalm title). In this psalm he admitted his wrong-doing and pleaded for God's forgiveness.

Nathan was probably attached to David's administration as a court prophet. He wrote accounts of the reigns of both David (1 Chronicles 29:29) and Solomon (2 Chronicles 9:29). This makes his confrontation of David even more daring—David could have refused to heed his message and had him executed.

Learn More: 1 Kings 1:22–40 / 1 Chronicles 17:1–14

NEBUCHADNEZZAR

Nebuchadnezzar king of Babylon came. . .against Jerusalem. 2 KINGS 25:1

As king of Babylon, Nebuchadnezzar was responsible for destroying Jerusalem and its temple and carrying the leading citizens of the nation into exile (2 Kings 25:1–12).

Nebuchadnezzar's resettlement of subject peoples in Babylon provided slave labor for his building projects. But he also trained intelligent Jewish exiles for minor roles in his adminis-tration. The prophet Daniel is a notable example of this policy (Daniel 1:3–6).

One night Nebuchadnezzar had a disturbing dream that none of his court wizards could interpret. So he called on Daniel to tell him what it meant. The flourishing tree in the dream that was cut down, Daniel told him, meant the king would be humiliated and dishonored as the result of God's judgment.

About a year later Nebuchadnezzar was driven from office. He apparently went mad and lived for a time among animals, eating grass like an ox (Daniel 4:33). Later he recovered his sanity and served as a witness to God's power and authority. Nebuchadnezzar praised the Lord and declared, "Those who walk in pride he is able to humble" (Daniel 4:37 NIV).

Learn More: Ezra 5:12 / Ezekiel 29:18–20; *Nebuchadrezzar:* KJV; Daniel 3:1–30

NEHEMIAH

I sat down and wept, and mourned certain days. NEHEMIAH 1:4

Nehemiah was a man of prayer as well as a strong leader who knew how to get things done. A descendant of Jewish exiles in Persia, he served as cupbearer to the Persian king.

Word came to Nehemiah that Judah, his ancestral homeland, was in dire straits. Even though the Jewish exiles had been allowed to return to Judah almost one hundred years before, the defensive wall of its capital city had not been rebuilt. This left Jerusalem exposed to its enemies.

Nehemiah prayed earnestly about the problem. Then he secured the king's permission to go to Jerusalem to lead a rebuilding effort (Nehemiah 2:1–6). He inspired the people to commit to the project, enlisted and organized a work force, and led them to rebuild the wall in fifty-two days (Nehemiah 6:15).

Religious reform was next on Nehemiah's agenda. Along with Ezra the priest, he led the people to renew their commitment to God's law (Nehemiah 8:1–10). Nehemiah also restored the sanctity of the temple and put a stop to buying and selling on the Sabbath (Nehemiah 13:1–22).

Learn More: Nehemiah 4:1–9; 5:1–13

NICODEMUS

How can a man be born when he is old? John 3:4

Nicodemus was the very first person to hear the words of Jesus that we now know as John 3:16—"For God so loved the world, that he gave his only begotten Son, that whosoever believeth in him should not perish, but have everlasting life." That quote was part of a conversation in which Jesus told the man he needed to be "born again."

A member of the Jewish ruling council called the Sanhedrin, Nicodemus bucked the tide of hatred that the national and religious leaders showed toward Jesus. Nicodemus seemed genuinely interested in the Lord, but chose to visit him under cover of darkness. Later, when the Pharisees wanted to arrest Jesus, Nicodemus stood up for Him, saying, "Does our law condemn a man without first hearing him to find out what he has been doing?" (John 7:51 NIV). In his last appearance in the Bible, Nicodemus provided the spices with which Jesus' body was wrapped after His death.

But the man's greatest legacy is undoubtedly the nighttime visit that prompted Jesus' discussion of salvation recorded in John 3, words that have led millions to Christ over the centuries.

Learn more: John 3:1–21; 7:45–52; 19:38–40

NOAH

And Noah did all that the Lord commanded him. Genesis 7:5

Noah was a righteous man in a time when the entire world had become hopelessly corrupt. The Lord told Noah that He intended to destroy all living things with a great flood. But Noah and his clan—his sons, Shem, Ham and Japheth and their wives—would be spared if he would build a giant ark, or boat, in which they could ride out the catastrophe (Genesis 6:11–18).

Noah obeyed the Lord, built the vessel, and entered it with his family and different species of animals before it began to rain. The downpour lasted forty days, and water covered the surface of the earth. But just as God had promised, Noah and his family were safe in the ark (Genesis 7:11–24).

After the flood was over, Noah built an altar and offered a sacrifice of thanksgiving to the Lord (Genesis 8:20–21). Then God told Noah that He would never judge the world again with floodwaters. The Lord sealed this promise by placing a rainbow in the sky (Genesis 9:8–17).

Jesus compared the great flood of Noah's time to His second coming. Just like those who did not expect God's judgment by water in Old Testament times, many people will be unprepared for Jesus' return (Luke 17:22–27; *Noe:* KJV).

Learn More: Genesis 9:20–25 / Hebrews 11:7 / 1 Peter 3:20 / 2 Peter 2:5

ONESIMUS

I beseech thee for my son Onesimus. Philemon 10

Onesimus, a runaway slave, had the good fortune to flee to Rome, where he met the apostle Paul and became a Christian under Paul's influence. The apostle eventually sent Onesimus back to his master, Philemon, a wealthy believer in the city of Colosse. Onesimus carried a letter from Paul which is now known as his epistle to Philemon.

In this letter Paul encouraged Philemon to treat Onesimus with brotherly love because he had been so helpful to Paul's ministry (Philemon 11). The apostle reminded Philemon that Onesimus was now more than a slave—he was a fellow believer in the Lord. These words from Paul amounted to a strong hint that this Christian slave should be granted his freedom (verse 16).

Whether Onesimus was ever set free is not known. But Paul did mention him, along with the apostle's missionary associate Tychicus, in his letter to the Colossian believers (Colossians 4:7–9).

Learn More: Philemon 13–14

PAUL

Saul, Saul, why persecutest thou me? ACTS 9:4

Paul, also known as Saul, was a strict Pharisee who developed a hatred for the Christian movement in its early years in Jerusalem. He looked on while Jewish religious leaders stoned Stephen to death (Acts 7:59–60; 8:1).

Later, Paul traveled north of Jerusalem to persecute believers in Damascus. He was converted to Christianity in his famous encounter with Jesus known as his "Damascus road" experience (Acts 9:1–8). From then on he was a loyal follower of Jesus who became known as the "apostle to the Gentiles" (see Acts 9:15).

Under the sponsorship of the church in Antioch, Syria, Paul traveled with various missionary partners throughout the Roman world for several years. He founded churches in several major cities of the Roman Empire, including Philippi, Thessalonica, Corinth, and Ephesus. His witness for Christ came to an end in the city of Rome, where he was detained by the Roman authorities (Acts 28:30–31). Most scholars believe he was eventually released but finally executed during a second Roman imprisonment.

During his ministry, Paul wrote thirteen letters, or epistles, to encourage the churches he founded as well as individuals associated with him in his missionary work. These letters—Romans, 1 and 2 Corinthians, Galatians, Ephesians, Philippians, Colossians, 1 and 2 Thessalonians, 1 and 2 Timothy, Titus, and Philemon—make up about one-fourth of the New Testament.

Learn More: Acts 9–28

PETER

Simon Peter answered and said, Thou art the Christ. MATTHEW 16:16

Peter, one of the first disciples called by Jesus, is often stereotyped as a blundering fisherman who spoke before he thought. But this doesn't do him justice.

The most prominent of the disciples, Peter was part of the trio often described as Jesus' "inner circle"—Peter, James, and John. They were with Jesus during some of the most important events of His ministry—the transfiguration (Matthew 17:1–8), the raising of Jairus's daughter from the dead (Mark 5:37–42), and Jesus' struggle with God's will in the garden of Gethsemane (Mark 14:32–42).

Peter was the first disciple to recognize Jesus as the Messiah—God's Son, sent into the world to redeem sinful humankind. Jesus told Peter that His church would be established through believers who accepted the truth that Peter had declared (Matthew 16:13–19).

Peter swore he would always be faithful to his Master. But then he denied Jesus three times on the night He was arrested. After being forgiven and restored by Jesus, Peter went on to become a bold witness in the early years of the church. On the day of Pentecost, he preached the famous sermon that led three thousand people to declare their faith in Jesus (Acts 2:14–41).

Peter also played a key role in one of the turning points of early Christianity. Through a vision of clean and unclean animals, he realized that God included all people, not just Jews, in His invitation to salvation. This insight opened the door for acceptance of Gentiles into the church (Acts 10:9–15). In later years, Peter wrote the New Testament epistles of 1 and 2 Peter.

Learn More: Matthew 14:24–36 / Luke 4:38–39

PHILIP, THE DISCIPLE

Philip findeth Nathanael, and saith unto him, We have found him. JOHN 1:45

Philip demonstrates one of the basic principles of discipleship—that believers are ideal witnesses to their family and friends.

As soon as Philip answered Jesus' call to become a disciple, he found his friend Nathanael, also known as Bartholomew. Philip told Nathanael he had met the prophet whom Moses had foretold many centuries before. To Nathanael's skepticism, Philip had the perfect answer: "Come and see for yourself" (John 1:46 NLT; see 1:43–46).

Learn More: John 14:8–9 / Acts 1:13

PHILIP, THE EVANGELIST

Philip went down to the city of Samaria, and preached Christ unto them. Acts 8:5

Philip is called "the evangelist" for good reason. He was the first believer in the early church to preach the gospel to people who were not full-blooded Jews.

Philip fled from Jerusalem to Samaria when persecution of Christians heated up after the martyrdom of Stephen (Acts 8:1–5). Under his ministry, many Samaritans turned to the Lord. These people were despised by most Jews because their Jewish bloodline had been diluted through intermarriage with foreigners.

After his Samaritan ministry, Philip was directed by an angel to go to the road that led from Jerusalem to the city of Gaza. Here he met an official from the queen of Ethiopia's court. Philip explained the scriptures about Jesus to the man and led him to accept Christ (Acts 8:26–38).

Philip was then caught up by the Holy Spirit and transported to the city of Azotus, where he continued his evangelistic work. He eventually settled in the coastal city of Caesarea (Acts 8:39–40). He was still here about twenty years later when the apostle Paul passed through this city on his way to Jerusalem (Acts 21:8–9).

Learn More: Acts 6:1–5

PILATE

Pilate. . .saith unto them, I find in him no fault at all. John 18:38

The Jewish Sanhedrin did not have authority to execute a prisoner. So they brought Jesus to Pilate, the Roman governor of Judea, to be tried and sentenced. After questioning Jesus, Pilate sensed that He did not deserve the death penalty. The governor tried to dodge responsibility for Jesus' fate by sending Him to Herod at the next judicial level (Luke 23:6–7).

When this ploy failed, Pilate proposed that Jesus be set free to satisfy the Roman custom of releasing one Jewish prisoner during the Passover festival. But the crowd refused, crying out instead for the freedom of a notorious criminal named Barabbas (John 18:39–40). Pilate finally bowed to public pressure and sentenced Jesus to death. He washed his hands in view of the crowd, to signify that he was "innocent of the blood of this just person" (Matthew 27:24).

Over the cross Pilate posted a sign that identified Jesus as the king of the Jews. When the religious leaders objected, he refused to change it. This was a deliberate insult to his Jewish subjects. *Is this the best king you can produce,* he seemed to say, *a man you hate dying on a Roman cross?*

As it turned out, Jesus *was* a king on a cross, and He held the salvation of the whole world in His hands. "When he was hung on the cross," the apostle Paul declared, "he took upon himself the curse for our wrongdoing" (Galatians 3:13 NLT).

Learn More: Mark 15:1–15 / Luke 23:1–25 / John 18:29–38

PRISCILLA

Greet Priscilla and Aquila. Romans 16:3

Priscilla was a believer who, with her husband, Aquila, put her life on the line for the apostle Paul and helped him in several of the churches he founded. No details about their risk for Paul are known, but it may have happened in Ephesus during the riot incited by Demetrius the silversmith (Acts 19:23–41).

What is clear is that the couple was associated with the apostle in his work with the Ephesian believers. After Paul left Ephesus, they stayed on and instructed an eloquent preacher named Apollos more thoroughly in the Christian faith (Acts 18:18–28).

Priscilla and Aquila also apparently helped Paul in his work at Corinth. They were already in the city when the apostle arrived. He lived with them for a time, and they practiced their mutual craft of tentmaking while presenting the gospel to citizens of the area (Acts 18:1–3).

The couple joined Paul in sending greetings to the believers at Corinth. He wrote this letter from Ephesus, noting that a house church was meeting at that time in Priscilla and Aquila's home (1 Corinthians 16:19).

Learn More: 2 Timothy 4:19; *Prisca:* KJV

RACHEL

*Rachel died, and was buried in the way to. . .*BETHLEHEM. GENESIS 35:19

Rachel first caught Jacob's eye when he arrived in Haran while fleeing from his brother Esau. He learned that Rachel was his cousin, the daughter of his uncle Laban (Genesis 29:9–12). Jacob stayed with Laban and worked out an agreement to pay for the privilege of marrying Rachel. But Laban tricked Jacob into marrying her older sister Leah instead. Then Jacob had to work seven additional years to take Rachel as his wife (Genesis 29:16–28).

Although Rachel was Jacob's favorite wife, she was not able to bear children. She envied her sister, who presented Jacob with several sons. Finally, Rachel allowed Jacob to father two sons through her servant Bilhah (Genesis 30:1–8).

Rachel did eventually have two sons—Joseph (Genesis 30:22–24) and Benjamin (Genesis 35:16–20). But she died giving birth to Benjamin. Jacob buried her in a tomb near Bethlehem. This tomb was still visible several centuries later during the period of the judges (1 Samuel 10:2).

Learn More: Genesis 30:14–15 / Ruth 4:11 / Jeremiah 31:15; Rahel: KJV / Matthew 2:16–18

RAHAB

Joshua saved Rahab the harlot alive. JOSHUA 6:25

Soon after the Israelites entered the promised land, Joshua sent spies to determine the strength of Jericho, a major Canaanite city. The spies went to the home of a prostitute named Rahab, probably to avoid arousing suspicion. But they were detected, and a force was sent to arrest them.

The spies persuaded Rahab to hide them on the roof of her house. In return, they promised to spare her and her family when Joshua and his forces destroyed the city. Rahab's conversation with the spies shows she was a believer in the one true God (Joshua 2:1–21). She helped them escape to safety by letting them down over the city wall through a window in her house.

After Jericho fell, Rahab and her family apparently joined the Israelite community (Joshua 6:25). From her family line emerged King David, and eventually the long-awaited Messiah. She is listed in Matthew's genealogy of Jesus (Matthew 1:5; *Rachab*: KJV).

Rahab was also cited for her great faith by the writer of the New Testament book of Hebrews (Hebrews 11:30–31).

Learn More: James 2:25

REBEKAH

Isaac. . .took Rebekah, and she became his wife; and he loved her. GENESIS 24:67

Rebekah may be the only wife ever selected by thirsty camels. Abraham's servant chose her because she allowed him and his weary camels to drink from the well where she was drawing water. Abraham had sent his servant into Rebekah's territory—Abraham's ancestral home in Haran—to find a wife for his son Isaac (Genesis 24:1–28).

Isaac was pleased with the servant's choice from the moment he saw Rebekah. She apparently was his one and only wife for the rest of his life.

Rebekah eventually gave birth to twin boys, Esau and Jacob. She showed favoritism toward Jacob (Genesis 25:28). She conspired with Jacob to fool Isaac into blessing Jacob rather than the oldest son, Esau. When Esau threatened to kill his brother, Rebekah sent Jacob to live with her brother Laban in Haran (Genesis 27:41–45).

After Rebekah died, she was buried in the family tomb at Machpelah. This is where Abraham and his wife Sarah, Jacob and his wife Leah, and Rebekah's husband Isaac were also laid to rest (Genesis 49:29–31).

Learn More: Genesis 26:1–11 / Romans 9:10; *Rebecca:* KJV

REHOBOAM

Rehoboam. . .forsook the law of the Lord, and all Israel with him. 2 Chronicles 12:1

Rehoboam was the foolish son who succeeded his father Solomon as king of Judah. Rather than relaxing Solomon's oppressive policies as some of his subjects requested, Rehoboam vowed to make them even worse (1 Kings 12:11).

This out-of-touch attitude drove the ten northern tribes in Solomon's kingdom to rebel and establish their own country. So from the time of Rehoboam on, the Jewish people were divided into two factions: the southern kingdom known as Judah and the northern kingdom that was called Israel.

Refusing to listen to his subjects was not the last of Rehoboam's foolish acts. He also deployed his army to force Israel back under his authority. Not until the Lord sent a prophet to tell the king to stand down did he stop these senseless campaigns (1 Kings 12:21–24).

Like his father before him, Rehoboam also built up a huge harem. Many of these wives were foreigners whom he catered to by setting up shrines for their worship of false gods. The Lord punished this sin by sending the pharaoh of Egypt to plunder the temple and Rehoboam's royal palace (1 Kings 14:22–26).

Learn More: 2 Chronicles 11:1–22; 12:1–16

REUBEN

Reuben said unto them, Shed no blood. Genesis 37:22

Reuben was the oldest of the twelve sons of Jacob. As the firstborn son, he would have received a double share of his father's estate and become leader of the clan. But he foolishly committed incest with Jacob's concubine and forfeited his birthright (Genesis 35:22; 49:3–4).

In spite of this poor judgment, Reuben fared better when it came to his half brother Joseph. Reuben saved Joseph's life by convincing the other jealous brothers not to kill their younger sibling. When a caravan of traders happened by, Joseph's brothers sold him as a slave (Genesis 37:19–29).

Later, Reuben and his brothers dealt with Joseph face-to-face when they came to Egypt to buy grain during a famine in Canaan. When Joseph insisted that one of them be held as a hostage, Reuben reminded his siblings that they were being repaid for the way they had treated Joseph years before (Genesis 42:21–22).

Reuben was the father of four sons. His descendants developed into one of the twelve tribes of the nation of Israel (1 Chronicles 5:1–3).

Learn More: Genesis 29:32; 30:14; 46:9

RHODA

When she knew Peter's voice, she opened not the gate for gladness. Acts 12:14

Have you ever been so surprised by something that it caused you to act irrationally? That happened to Rhoda, a servant girl in the home of Mary, mother of John Mark. Several believers were gathered inside this Jerusalem house for a prayer meeting. They were probably praying for the apostle Peter, who had just been imprisoned by the local Roman ruler, Herod Agrippa I (Acts 12:1).

Someone knocked at the door, and Rhoda went to answer. She recognized the voice of Peter, but she was so shocked that she rushed back inside to tell the others without letting him in. This left Peter standing outside, still knocking.

These believers knew Peter was locked away, so they thought Rhoda was out of her mind. When they opened the door and saw the apostle, they were just as shocked as she was (Acts 12:11–16).

The irony is that the believers were so surprised that their pleas for Peter's safety were answered so dramatically and so quickly. Sometimes God overwhelms us with His answer to our earnest prayers.

RUTH

Ruth said. . .whither thou goest, I will go. RUTH 1:16

Although Ruth was a Gentile, her story played out in Jewish territory. It is recorded in the Old Testament book that bears her name. A severe famine in Bethlehem forced a Jewish family—Naomi, her husband, and her two sons—to move to Ruth's home country of Moab. But tragedy followed them there: Naomi's husband died, followed by the death of her sons, who had married Moabite women.

One of Naomi's daughters-in-law was Ruth. When Naomi decided to return to Bethlehem, Ruth insisted on going with her, although that meant leaving her own people. Ruth's words to Naomi, "Intreat me not to leave thee," are often used in modern wedding ceremonies to dramatize the unconditional commitment the husband and wife are making to each other (see Ruth 1:1–17).

Once settled in Bethlehem, Ruth went to the fields to glean—that is, to gather grain left behind by harvesters to feed the poor. Here she met the landowner, a man named Boaz, who was a distant relative of Naomi and her deceased husband.

Naomi encouraged Ruth to follow up on this brief introduction by cultivating a closer relationship with Boaz. This led to their marriage and the birth of a son named Obed, the grandfather of King David (Ruth 4:13–22). See also *Boaz*.

Learn More: Matthew 1:5

SALOME

There were also women looking on afar off: among whom was. . .Salome. MARK 15:40

A follower of Jesus, Salome was one of the women who looked on as Jesus was crucified. Along with other women, she also brought spices to anoint His body on the morning when He arose from the grave (Mark 16:1).

Salome may be the same woman identified in a parallel passage as "the mother of Zebedee's children" (Matthew 27:56). Jesus' disciples James and John were the sons of a man named Zebedee (Matthew 4:21–22); if this is the same Salome, she asked Jesus to grant special favors to her sons in His coming kingdom.

Jesus told the three that the real honor they would receive would flow from the sacrifices they made to follow Him. This was more honorable than prestigious positions in His coming kingdom (Matthew 20:20–23).

SAMSON

The Spirit of the Lord began to move him at times in the camp of Dan. JUDGES 13:25

Samson's parents had great hopes for their son. Even before he was born, they set him apart as a Nazarite, a person who would be totally devoted to the Lord. To show this commitment, he was not to partake of strong drink (Judges 13:7). This vow also stipulated that a Nazarite should never cut his hair (Numbers 6:5).

Samson grew up to become the last of the judges, or military heroes, who delivered Israel from its enemies. In his case, he clashed with the Philistines. His superhuman strength from the Lord enabled him to burn their crops (Judges 15:4–5), kill a thousand warriors with nothing but a bone as a weapon (Judges 15:15), and rip the gate from one of their walled cities (Judges 16:3).

But Samson's physical strength was offset by his weak moral character. His lust led to several encounters with pagan Philistine women, the worst of which was Delilah. She betrayed him to his enemies while he slept. They cut his hair, causing Samson's strength to leave him. He was captured and imprisoned by his enemies.

Samson performed one final heroic act after his strength returned. He toppled a pagan Philistine temple and wiped out many of his enemies. This was also an act of suicide, since he too was killed by the falling stones (Judges 16:28–30).

Samson is listed as a hero of the faith in the New Testament book of Hebrews (Hebrews 11:32).

Learn More: Judges 14:1–20

SAMUEL

Samuel answered, Speak; for thy servant heareth. 1 SAMUEL 3:10

The prophet Samuel was born in answer to the prayer of his mother, Hannah, who had not been able to have children. In gratitude to the Lord, she dedicated Samuel to God's service and placed him in the custody of Eli, the high priest of Israel (1 Samuel 1:24–28).

Samuel followed the Lord, and he was faithful to speak God's message to others. Even as a boy, he predicted God's judgment against Eli and his family (1 Samuel 3:11–18). Samuel also served in a priestly role by offering sacrifices on behalf of the people and leading them to commit themselves to the Lord (1 Samuel 7:3–17).

At God's command, Samuel also anointed Saul as the first king of Israel (1 Samuel 10:1). When Saul failed to obey the Lord, Samuel selected a new king from among the sons of Jesse. God made it clear to Samuel that David, the youngest son of this family, was His choice as Saul's replacement and successor (1 Samuel 16:11–13).

Samuel is listed in the New Testament as one of the Old Testament heroes of the faith (Hebrews 11:32).

Learn More: 1 Samuel 12:1–19; 28:11–19 / 1 Chronicles 6:33; *Shemuel:* KJV

SAPPHIRA

How is it that ye have agreed together to tempt the Spirit of the Lord? ACTS 5:9

In the early days of the Christian movement, the believers looked out for one another by pooling their possessions. When a member of the group needed financial help, this need was met from the common treasury.

Two believers, Sapphira and her husband, Ananias, placed money into this fund from a sale of their property. But then the apostles discovered they had kept back part of the money for themselves while claiming they had dedicated all of it to help the needy.

The apostle Peter first confronted Ananias about what he had done. Peter explained that Ananias was not required to give all he had gained from the sale. It was his money to use as he wished. But lying about what he had done was an attempt to deceive the Holy Spirit.

Ananias was so shocked by this revelation that he fell down and died. Later, the same thing happened to Sapphira when she repeated the same lie. This event sent shock waves through the church and everyone else who heard about it. God's supernatural power was alive and active in the movement known as the early Christian church (Acts 5:1–11).

SARAH

And God said, Sarah thy wife shall bear thee a son indeed. GENESIS 17:19

The wife of Abraham, Sarah was not able to bear children. This presented a dilemma, since God had promised to bless Abraham and make him the ancestor of a people who would bring honor and glory to the Lord (Genesis 12:2; 15:1–2).

In desperation, Sarah persuaded Abraham to father a child through her servant, Hagar. But God revealed to the couple that the son of this secondary union was not the child who would fulfill God's covenant promise (Genesis 16:1–2; 17:19–21).

Finally, when Sarah was ninety years old, she and Abraham had a son who was God's chosen one. They called him Isaac, a name meaning "laughter," because Sarah had laughed when the Lord told her she would bear a son in her old age (Genesis 18:11–15).

The writer of the New Testament book of Hebrews included Sarah among those commended for their great faith in the Lord (Hebrews 11:11; *Sara:* KJV).

Learn More: Isaiah 51:2

SAUL

Samuel said to all the people, See ye him whom the Lord hath chosen? 1 SAMUEL 10:24

Saul had a lot going for him when he was anointed as the first king of Israel. He showed genuine humility and surprise that he'd been selected (1 Samuel 9:21; 10:22), and he looked like a royal figure—tall and commanding in appearance (1 Samuel 9:2). He also developed into a capable military commander, leading the Israelites to victory over many of their enemies, including the powerful Philistines (1 Samuel 14:47).

But not long into his kingship, Saul's true character came to light. He performed a ritual sacrifice, a duty reserved for priests (1 Samuel 13:9–14). Then he disobeyed the Lord by keeping some of the spoils of war after defeating the Amalekites (1 Samuel 15:21–23). Because of these serious violation, God withdrew His spirit from Saul, rejected him as king, and had David anointed as his replacement (1 Samuel 16:11–14).

Saul did not relinquish power without a fight. For several years he tried to kill David. He even slaughtered eighty-five priests whom he suspected of aiding and befriending the man who was destined to replace him (1 Samuel 22:13–18).

Facing a crucial battle with the Philistines, Saul called up the spirit of the deceased Samuel to ask about the outcome. The prophet told Saul that Israel would be defeated and the king and his sons would be killed. As predicted, Saul was seriously wounded during the battle. He committed suicide by falling on a sword to keep from being captured by the enemy.

Learn More: 1 Samuel 28:11–20

SENNACHERIB

Sennacherib king of Assyria [came] up against all the fenced cities of Judah. 2 KINGS 18:13

Judah's King Hezekiah had the misfortune of ruling when the Assyrians were on a mission of world conquest. King Sennacherib of Assyria captured several fortified cities of Judah. But the capital city, Jerusalem, was the coveted prize that he really wanted.

Hezekiah kept the Assyrian king at bay for a while by paying protection money (2 Kings 18:13–16). But Hezekiah eventually quit paying. Sennacherib sent messengers to threaten the king, who prayed for divine guidance. Hezekiah stood his ground after the prophet Isaiah assured him that God would not allow Jerusalem to fall into Sennacherib's hands.

When the Assyrian army camped outside Jerusalem, it was devastated by a mysterious plague that killed thousands of soldiers. Sennacherib was forced to withdraw in humiliation and defeat. Later, this powerful king was assassinated by two of his own sons while worshiping at a pagan temple in his capital city (2 Kings 19:35–37).

Learn More: 2 Chronicles 32:1–22 / Isaiah 36:1–37:38

SHADRACH

Shadrach. . .fell down bound into the midst of the burning fiery furnace. DANIEL 3:23

Shadrach was a Jewish exile in Babylon whose faith in the one true God remained unshaken, although it was tested by fire—literally.

Nebuchadnezzar, the Babylonian king, set up a huge statue of himself that he ordered all his subjects to worship. Shadrach, along with his friends Meshach and Abednego, refused to do so. They declared that only the one true God of their native land was worthy of worship.

Enraged, the king had them thrown into a "fiery furnace," perhaps an ore smelter or brick kiln. But when the king checked to see how the execution was proceeding, he was astonished to see them walking around, untouched by the flames. Even more amazing, he saw a fourth man, an angel, among them.

Nebuchadnezzar was impressed with the power of this divine Being who delivered Shadrach and his friends. He decreed that anyone who spoke against God would be severely punished.

Although they were Jewish exiles, Shadrach and his friends had been trained to serve in the royal palace of Babylon. After their miraculous deliverance, the king promoted them to higher positions.

Learn More: Daniel 1:3–20

SHEM

And [Noah] said, Blessed be the Lord God of Shem. GENESIS 9:26

Shem was the oldest of Noah's three sons who survived the great flood by entering the ark. After the flood, Shem and his brother Japheth covered their father's nudity while he was sleeping off a drunken stupor. They did so by walking backwards toward Noah so they would not see his naked body (Genesis 9:18–27).

After Noah woke up, he was pleased with Shem's actions to cover him up. He blessed Shem and declared that the descendants of Noah's third son, Ham, would be servants of Shem and his offspring. Noah was angry with Ham because he had seen his father's nakedness before notifying his two brothers.

Shem was the father of several sons whose descendants gave rise to peoples of the ancient world (Genesis 10:22). He is listed in the genealogy of Jesus in the New Testament (Luke 3:36; *Sem*: KJV).

Learn More: 1 Chronicles 1:17

SHIPHRAH

The midwives feared God, and. . .saved the men children alive. EXODUS 1:17

Shiphrah and her associate, Puah, were midwives in Egypt who assisted Israelite women during the process of childbirth. Since they are named in the Bible, they were probably in charge of other midwives who attended Hebrew mothers-to-be (Exodus 1:15).

The Egyptian pharaoh was alarmed at the dramatic increase of his Israelite slaves, particularly the males, who could grow up to stage a revolution. So he ordered Shiphrah and Puah to see to it that all male Israelite babies were killed as soon as they were born (Exodus 1:15–22).

When these midwives refused to obey his command, the king demanded an explanation. They came up with a creative answer: these babies were born so quickly to the strong Israelite mothers, they told him, that the midwives could not get there in time to carry out the death order.

Foiled by the brave, clever midwives, the pharaoh then ordered his own people to enforce his decree.

SILAS

Paul chose Silas, and departed. ACTS 15:40

Silas was a believer in the early church who worked with the apostle Paul as an evangelist and church planter. The two probably first met at a gathering of church leaders in Jerusalem. This body decided that Gentiles could be saved without going through certain Jewish rituals such as circumcision.

This group sent its decision in a letter to the church at Antioch through Paul and Barnabas. Two delegates from Jerusalem, one of whom was Silas, were also appointed to go with the two missionaries. After helping deliver the good news, Silas stayed on in Antioch to help Paul and Barnabas encourage and strengthen the new believers in the city (Acts 15:22–34).

Paul enlisted Silas to accompany him on his second missionary journey. In the city of Philippi, they were beaten and imprisoned for causing a disturbance. They were praying and singing to the Lord at midnight when an earthquake shook the building, setting them free. This led to the conversion of the jailer and his family (Acts 16:25–33).

In later years, Silas apparently worked with Paul in the churches at Thessalonica (1 Thessalonians 1:1; 2 Thessalonians 1:1; *Silvanus*: KJV) and Corinth (Acts 18:5).

Learn More: 2 Corinthians 1:19

SIMEON, SON OF JACOB

Simeon and Levi. . .came upon the city boldly, and slew all the males. GENESIS 34:25

Simeon was a son of Jacob through his wife Leah. Simeon and his full brother Levi burned with anger when a Canaanite man named Shechem violated the virginity of their sister Dinah. Pretending to invite Shechem into Jacob's family, they talked all the male inhabitants of Shechem's clan into being circumcised—the physical ritual God demanded of all His males. But when the Shechemites were recovering from the painful procedure, Simeon and Levi killed them all, plundered their possessions, and returned Dinah to their own camp (Genesis 34:1–29).

Later, Simeon traveled with all his brothers except Benjamin to Egypt to buy grain. Their half-brother Joseph held Simeon as a hostage to make sure Joseph's younger brother Benjamin came with them when they returned (Genesis 42:23–24).

When Jacob blessed his twelve sons at the end of his life, he condemned Simeon and Levi for their act of revenge against Shechem and the other Canaanites (Genesis 49:5–7). Simeon's descendants grew into one of the twelve tribes of the nation of Israel.

Learn More: Genesis 34:30–31

SIMEON. THE PROPHET

He should not see death, before he had seen the Lord's Christ. LUKE 2:26

When Jesus was eight days old, Mary and Joseph brought Him to the temple in Jerusalem with an offering to present Him to the Lord. They must have been surprised when a prophet named Simeon arrived at that very moment, took the baby in his arms, and blessed the entire family.

The Holy Spirit had revealed to Simeon that he would live to see the long-awaited Messiah. Now that he had held Jesus in his arms, he was ready to die in peace (Luke 2:21–35).

But then the prophet interjected a sobering prophecy into this joyous occasion. He told Mary that this child, while He would be God's agent of redemption for many people, would cause great anguish for her. Perhaps she thought about Simeon's words more than thirty years later when she watched her firstborn Son suffer and die on the cross (John 19:25–27).

SIMON OF CYRENE

Simon, a Cyrenian. . .on him they laid the cross, that he might bear it after Jesus. LUKE 23:26

Simon has been immortalized as the man who carried Jesus' cross to the crucifixion site. Apparently he was just passing by when he was pressed into service for this task (Matthew 27:32).

Simon was from Cyrene, a city on the northern coast of Africa. Cyrene had a large Jewish population, so he may have been a Greek-speaking Jew who was in Jerusalem for the Passover celebration when Jesus was crucified.

Mark's gospel adds the additional detail that Simon was the father of Alexander and Rufus (Mark 15:21). This may have been the same Rufus greeted by the apostle Paul in his letter to the Christians at Rome (Romans 16:13).

After Jesus' ascension, residents of Cyrene were in Jerusalem on the day of Pentecost (Acts 2:10). Some of them became believers and were later scatted in the persecution that broke out after the martyrdom of Stephen (Acts 11:19–29).

Learn More: Mark 15:21

SIMON THE PHARISEE

Simon answered and said, I suppose that he, to whom he forgave most. Luke 7:43

A Pharisee named Simon invited Jesus to his house for a meal. While they were eating, a woman who was a known sinner approached Jesus, washed His feet, and wiped them dry with her hair.

Simon was thinking that no true prophet would allow himself to be touched and contaminated by such a sinner. But Jesus read his thoughts and told him a parable to challenge his attitude. If two debtors had their debts canceled, which would love his creditor most, Jesus asked, the person who owed little or the one who owed a greater sum? Simon admitted that it was the person with the largest debt (Luke 7:36–47).

Jesus then drove home His point: Simon had not shown Jesus the customary hospitality extended to a guest, but this sinful woman had gone above and beyond what was expected. She had been forgiven abundantly. But Simon—a self-righteous Pharisee who thought he had no need for forgiveness—remained in his sin.

SOLOMON

Give therefore thy servant an understanding heart to judge thy people. 1 Kings 3:9

As King David's successor, Solomon got an impressive start by asking the Lord to grant him wisdom to govern the nation. He went on to complete many building projects, the most impressive of which was the temple in the capital city of Jerusalem (1 Kings 6:1–38).

Solomon was an effective administrator. He divided the nation into districts that funneled goods into Jerusalem to support the central government. The king's system of trade with surrounding countries also brought unprecedented wealth to Judah as well as the king himself (1 Kings 9:26–28; 10:26–29).

Solomon also wrote many proverbs and other wise sayings (1 Kings 4:32). The wisdom books of Proverbs, Ecclesiastes, and Song of Solomon in the Old Testament are attributed to him, either in part or in full.

Despite his wisdom, though, Solomon's lapses in judgment are well known. He built a harem of hundreds of wives and concubines. Many of these marriages were political unions to seal alliances with foreign nations. He allowed these women to pay homage to their national deities and eventually fell under the influence of these pagan gods himself (1 Kings 11:1–5).

The king's expensive projects and lavish lifestyle required high taxes from his subjects. When he died, the disgruntled ten northern tribes of the nation rebelled and formed their own nation known as Israel, or the northern kingdom. The two tribes that remained loyal to Solomon and his successors continued as the nation of Judah, the southern kingdom.

Learn More: 1 Kings 1–3; 10:1–10 / 2 Chronicles 1–9

STEPHEN

They stoned Stephen, calling upon God, and saying, Lord Jesus, receive my spirit. Acts 7:59

Stephen was a believer from a Greek-speaking background in the early church in Jerusalem. He, along with six other trustworthy followers of Christ, was appointed to a task force to oversee distribution of food to needy believers (Acts 6:1–7).

This zealous disciple quickly became a defender of the gospel against the Jewish religious leaders. In one of the longest speeches in the book of Acts, Stephen accused his opponents of killing Jesus the Messiah, just as their ancestors had murdered the prophets sent by the Lord in Old Testament times. He ended his remarks by declaring that he had seen a vision of God in heaven, with Jesus at His side (Acts 6:8–7:58). Enraged, the Jewish leaders accused Stephen of blasphemy, dragged him outside the city, and stoned him to death. Stephen's martyrdom set off a wave of persecution that drove believers out of Jerusalem. This brought more people to the Lord as "they that were scattered abroad went every where preaching the word" (Acts 8:4).

Learn More: Acts 22:20

THEOPHILUS

. . .to write unto thee in order, most excellent Theophilus. LUKE 1:3

All of us are indebted to people we know very little about. This is certainly true in the case of Theophilus, the person for whom Luke wrote his Gospel and the book of Acts (Luke 1:1–3; Acts 1:1).

The name Theophilus means "friend of God," and this is the only fact about him that is known for sure. Luke could have used the name in a generic sense—that is, his Gospel was meant for anyone who was a "friend of God." Or, Luke's description of Theophilus as "most excellent" could mean he was a high Roman official. Or Theophilus could have been a novice believer who needed to be assured of "the certainty of the things about which you have been instructed" regarding the life and ministry of Jesus (Luke 1:4 HCSB).

No matter who he was, Theophilus was at least partially responsible for Luke's writing of his Gospel and the book of Acts. If not for him, many acts of Jesus and the early church might never have been recorded and passed on to future generations. See also *Luke.*

THOMAS

Thomas, because thou hast seen me, thou hast believed. JOHN 20:29

All twelve of Jesus' disciples had a hard time believing He had been raised from the dead. But Thomas was the biggest doubter of all.

Thomas was not with the rest of the group when Jesus appeared to them on the day of His resurrection. The others told Thomas they had seen Him alive, but he was not convinced. "Unless I see the nail marks in his hands and put my finger where the nails were, and put my hand into his side," he declared, "I will not believe" (John 20:25 NIV).

Eight days later, Jesus appeared again to His disciples, and personally invited Thomas to touch His wounds. This time Thomas believed and professed Jesus as his Lord and Master.

On another occasion, Jesus told the disciples He was going away to prepare a place for them. Thomas asked, "Lord, we don't know where you are going, so how can we know the way?" Jesus responded with His famous answer, "I am the way and the truth and the life. No one comes to the Father except through me" (John 14:5–6 NIV).

Learn More: John 11:11–16

TIMOTHY

I sent unto you Timotheus, who is my beloved son. 1 CORINTHIANS 4:17

During his visit to Lystra on his second missionary journey, the apostle Paul met a young believer named Timothy, or Timotheus. Impressed with his faith and commitment, the apostle invited him to join his missionary party (Acts 16:1). Timothy traveled and worked with Paul for several years, eventually becoming perhaps his most trusted and dependable missionary associate.

Timothy was apparently associated with Paul in his work at churches in several cities, including Corinth, Philippi, Colosse, and Thessalonica. Several of the apostle's letters to these congregations—as well as his epistle to Philemon—open with greetings from Paul as well as Timothy.

Paul's important work in Ephesus also had a Timothy connection. After the apostle worked in this city for more than two years, he apparently left Timothy in charge and moved on to plant churches in other locations (1 Timothy 1:3).

Paul addressed two of his pastoral epistles to Timothy as a church leader. The apostle encouraged his associate to act with integrity in spite of his young age (1 Timothy 4:12) and to base his actions on the teachings of the Bible.

Learn More: Acts 17:5; 19:22 / Philippians 2:19

TITUS

God. . .comforted us by the coming of Titus. 2 Corinthians 7:6

An associate of the apostle Paul, Titus performed several important tasks in the churches founded by the apostle. Titus carried letters from Paul to the troubled church at Corinth and reported back to the apostle on how the congregation was dealing with these problems (2 Corinthians 2:13; 7:5–16).

This dependable missionary appears in another important role in the church on the island of Crete. Paul sent him there to deal with false teachings and to strengthen the new believers in their faith. The apostle addressed one of his pastoral epistles to Titus, encouraging him to teach sound doctrine (Titus 2:1) and to appoint elders to lead the church (Titus 1:5–9).

Titus was also associated with evangelistic work in the province of Dalmatia (2 Timothy 4:10). Paul referred to him as "mine own son after the common faith" (Titus 1:4).

Learn More: Galatians 2:1–3

URIAH

But Uriah slept at the door of the king's house. 2 Samuel 11:9

Uriah was a brave warrior whose death was arranged by King David to cover up his adulterous relationship with Uriah's wife, Bathsheba. How it all came about shows a serious abuse of power by one of the Bible's most admirable characters.

The affair occurred while Uriah was away from Jerusalem on a military campaign. When Bathsheba got pregnant, the king had Uriah sent home on leave so he would sleep with his wife and thus make it seem that the unborn child had been fathered by her soldier husband.

But Uriah refused to enjoy himself at home while his fellow soldiers were on the battlefield. So David got Uriah drunk in a desperate attempt to get him to change his mind. But still the soldier refused.

Finally, David sent Uriah back to the front lines. He didn't realize he was carrying his own death sentence—a letter from the king to his commander to station Uriah in the thick of battle with limited support (2 Samuel 11:14–17).

This plot succeeded, and Uriah was killed. David waited until Bathsheba's period of mourning for her husband was over. Then he brought her to the royal palace as one of his wives (2 Samuel 11:26–27).

Learn More: 2 Samuel 23:8–39

UZZA

The anger of the Lord was kindled against Uzza, and he smote him. 1 Chronicles 13:10

Shortly after David was made king of all Israel, he decided to restore the nearly-forgotten ark of the covenant to its proper prominence. So he ordered men, including Uzza, to bring it from Kirjath-Jearim to Jerusalem. These men were not Levites, the tribe assigned to such holy duties, and they unwisely put the ark on an oxcart rather than carrying it on poles as God had instructed Moses.

When the oxen stumbled, Uzza reached out to steady the ark, and was immediately struck dead for "his error" (2 Samuel 6:7). The incident frightened David, who asked himself, "How shall I bring the ark of God home to me?" (1 Chronicles 13:12). Three months later, though, having set up a tent for the ark in Jerusalem, David tried again, this time calling on the Levites and demanding that they follow God's instructions to the letter.

Learn more: 2 Samuel 6:1–11 / 1 Chronicles 13

UZZIAH

He. . .went into the temple of the Lord to burn incense. 2 CHRONICLES 26:16

King Uzziah of Judah—also known as Azariah and Ozias—obeyed God and governed wisely during a time of great prosperity for his country. A good military strategist, he defeated the Philistines and the Ammonites, fortified key cities, and built up his army to protect Judah from enemy attacks.

The king also improved living conditions for his people by digging wells to provide water for their crops and livestock. His progressive policies were admired by the surrounding peoples of the region (2 Chronicles 26:1–15).

But Uzziah's success brought out his dark side. Proud of his achievements, he decided to try his hand at offering a sacrifice in the temple—a role reserved for priests. When he prepared to burn incense, the priests stopped him. He lashed out in anger, and was struck with leprosy that sidelined him for the rest of his life (2 Chronicles 26:16–21).

Uzziah's reign of fifty-two years was one of the longest in Judah's history. Isaiah was called to the prophetic ministry through a stirring vision of God "in the year that King Uzziah died" (Isaiah 6:1).

Learn More: 2 Kings 15:1–7; [*Azariah:* KJV] / Amos 1:1 / Matthew 1:8–10; *Ozias:* KJV

ZACCHAEUS

He ran before, and climbed up into a sycomore tree to see him. LUKE 19:4

As a chief tax collector, Zacchaeus probably had other agents for the Roman government working under his supervision. This coveted position in the city of Jericho had made him a rich man.

Zacchaeus was anxious to get a glimpse of Jesus as He passed through Jericho on His way to Jerusalem. Since Zacchaeus was not very tall, he climbed a tree to get a better view. The tax collector must have been shocked when Jesus called him down. Then Jesus invited Himself to Zacchaeus's house for a visit (Luke 19:1–10)!

As he talked with Jesus, Zacchaeus faced up to some of the less-than-ethical things he had done in his profession. He promised to repay the people he had cheated four times more than what he had taken. He also vowed to give half of what he owned to the poor.

Jesus welcomed Zacchaeus into God's kingdom and added that "he also is a son of Abraham" (verse 9). The Jewish people hated tax collectors. But Jesus declared that Zacchaeus's profession had nothing to do with his status as a Jewish citizen. Even a despised agent of the Roman government could respond to the grace of God.

ZACHARIAS

I am an old man, and my wife well stricken in years. LUKE 1:18

The priest Zacharias and his wife, Elisabeth, had not been able to have children. And the possibility of that happening was slim, since both were in their senior years.

But God had other plans for this good couple. While Zacharias was going about his priestly duties in the temple, an angel told him that Elisabeth would give birth to a son. They should call him John, a name meaning "God has been gracious." This miracle child would become God's special messenger who would "make ready a people prepared for the Lord" (Luke 1:17; see 1:5–25).

Because Zacharias expressed doubt that this would happen, the angel took away his ability to speak. Imagine what anguish he must have felt at not being able to tell others that he was going to be a father in his old age.

After John was born, the speech of Zacharias returned. In a beautiful song known as the Benedictus, he praised the Lord for sending this son who would prepare the way for the coming Messiah. His son grew up to become John the Baptist, forerunner of Jesus the Messiah (Luke 1:67–80). See also *Elisabeth.*

Learn More: Luke 1:57–64

ZECHARIAH

. . .Zechariah, the son of Berechiah, the son of Iddo the prophet. ZECHARIAH 1:1

The prophet Zechariah delivered his messages to the people of Judah during the years after they returned from exile. Perhaps the most famous passage from his book is his prediction that the future Messiah would enter the city of Jerusalem "riding on a donkey, on a colt, the foal of a donkey" (Zechariah 9:9 HCSB). Matthew quoted this verse in his Gospel to show that Jesus fulfilled Zechariah's prophecy in His triumphal entry into the Holy City (Matthew 21:5).

Zechariah is also known for his symbolic language about the end times—a literary form similar to the visions in the books of Daniel and Revelation. In one of Zechariah's visions, God appeared as a lampstand beside two olive trees. These trees symbolized Zerubbabel and Joshua, two people whom God had charged with the task of rebuilding the temple in Jerusalem (Zechariah 4:1–14).

Zechariah ministered in Judah at about the same time as the priest Ezra. Zechariah's prophecies occur in the Old Testament book that bears his name.

Learn More: Ezra 5:1; 6:14

ZELOPHEHAD

The Lord spake unto Moses, saying, The daughters of Zelophehad speak right. NUMBERS 27:7

Zelophehad, a member of the tribe of Manasseh, died in the wilderness during the exodus from Egypt. He had no sons who would inherit his property after he settled in Canaan. But he did have five intelligent and far-sighted daughters—Mahlah, Noah, Hoglah, Milcah, and Tirzah.

These daughters approached Moses with a request: they wanted to inherit their father's property in the distribution of land that was coming to him when the people entered Canaan. Moses agreed, but he made it clear that each of them must marry within their father's tribe. This would assure that the land allotted to each of the twelve tribes would always be owned by members of the tribal group to which it was first granted (Numbers 36:7; see 27:1–7).

Their request was granted years later when the Israelites conquered Canaan and settled on the land (Joshua 17:3–6).

Learn More: Numbers 26:33

ZERUBBABEL

The hands of Zerubbabel have laid the foundation of this house. ZECHARIAH 4:9

Zerubbabel faced a difficult task—rebuilding the temple in Jerusalem after the Jewish exiles returned to their homeland (Ezra 1:1–3; 2:1–2). This building had been in ruins for several decades since its destruction by the Babylonians. Enemies of the Jews opposed the rebuilding effort and even succeeded in getting it stopped for several years (Ezra 4:1–24). The Jewish people themselves waxed hot and cold in their commitment to the project.

With prodding from two Old Testament prophets (Haggai 2:1–3; Zechariah 4:6–10), Zerubbabel finally completed the task. It was dedicated with great fanfare, but mysteriously Zerubbabel is not mentioned in connection with the celebration (Ezra 6:14–22).

This building—often referred to as "Zerubbabel's Temple"—was not as ornate as the original structure built by King Solomon several centuries before. The exiles who returned to Judah sometimes used this as an excuse for not working diligently on the project. But the prophet Haggai kept the pressure on with these encouraging words: "'The final glory of this house will be greater than the first,' says the LORD of Hosts. 'I will provide peace in this place'—this is the declaration of the LORD of Hosts" (Haggai 2:9 HCSB).

Learn More: Ezra 3:8; 5:2

THE 1-MINUTE
BIBLE
GUIDE

180 Key Places

An alphabetical listing of the 180 most
important locales named in scripture.

Written by George W. Knight
Edited by Paul Kent

ACCHO

Neither did Asher drive out the inhabitants of Accho. Judges 1:31

This city on the coast of the Mediterranean Sea is mentioned only once in the Bible—and that in connection with a failure. After the conquest of Canaan, Accho was granted to the tribe of Asher. But this tribe failed to drive the Canaanites out of the city.

Accho was an important port city long before Joshua's time. A river flowed into the sea at this site, giving it a natural landing place for ships that sailed the Mediterranean Sea. In New Testament times, the city was known as Ptolemais, named for the king of Egypt, Ptolemy, who captured it and rebuilt it about 100 BC.

The apostle Paul visited Christian believers in Ptolemais at the end of his third missionary journey while his ship was anchored in the nearby harbor (Acts 21:7).

In the Middle Ages, Accho/Ptolemais was known as Acre. This city became one of the last strongholds of the Crusaders, Christian militants who battled the Muslims for control of the Holy Land. Acre eventually fell to the Muslims, but remains of its massive crusader fortress are still visible today.

ACELDAMA

Aceldama, that is to say, The field of blood. Acts 1:19

This is the name of a field in the Hinnom Valley outside the walls of the Old City of Jerusalem. The word means "Field of Blood," so named because of the blood money paid to Judas to betray Jesus. Here Judas committed suicide because of his remorse over this heinous act.

Matthew's account of Judas's change of heart states that he returned the betrayal money to the Jewish religious leaders. They used the money to buy this plot and then turned it into a cemetery for the burial of strangers (Matthew 27:3–10).

Recent discoveries at the site of Aceldama reveal that it was, indeed, a burial site for many years, beginning in the first Christian century. Excavations were conducted when construction workers on the site uncovered several huge caves that had been used as burial chambers.

Learn More: Matthew 26:14–16 / Mark 14:10–11 / Luke 22:3–6 / John 18:2–5

ACHAIA

It hath pleased them of Macedonia and Achaia to make a certain contribution. Romans 15:26

In his letter to the Christians at Rome, the apostle Paul commended believers in Macedonia and Achaia for contributing to an offering for suffering Christians in Jerusalem. These two Roman provinces were located in Greece—Macedonia in the north and Achaia in the south.

The major city of Achaia was Corinth, where Paul established a church and spent about eighteen months ministering to these new believers. While in Corinth, he was accused of blasphemy by zealous Jews. But Gallio, the Roman proconsul of Achaia, refused to rule in the case and the apostle was released.

According to an inscription discovered at another Grecian city, Gallio was an official in Achaia in AD 51–52. This date is an important clue for establishing a chronology of Paul's life and missionary work throughout the Roman world of the first Christian century.

In his letters, Paul referred to two different believers in Achaia: Epaenetus (Romans 16:5) and Stephanas (1 Corinthians 16:15). These may have been members of the church at Corinth.

Learn More: Acts 18:12–17; 19:21 / 2 Corinthians 1:1 / 1 Thessalonians 1:7–8

ADULLAM, CAVE OF

David therefore departed thence, and escaped to the cave Adullam. 1 SAMUEL 22:1

While on the run from King Saul, David and his men took refuge in this cave. This site has never been identified with certainty, but it was probably somewhere near the Dead Sea. This desolate area contains many caves, including the ones where the Dead Sea Scrolls were discovered in the 1940s.

At this site, David's forces increased from a handful of warriors to about four hundred—those who were "in distress, and every one that was in debt, and every one that was discontented" (1 Samuel 22:2). This shows that at this early point in his career, David was already attracting a following of loyalists who supported him in opposition to King Saul.

David also hid from Saul in two other places in the region around the Dead Sea: the oasis of Engedi (1 Samuel 24:1) and the city of Ziklag (1 Chronicles 12:1).

Learn More: 2 Samuel 23:13 / 1 Chronicles 11:15

AI

They fled before the men of Ai. JOSHUA 7:4

At this small town about ten miles west of Jericho, the Israelites learned a valuable lesson about the perils of overconfidence and disobedience of the Lord.

After their easy victory over the city of Jericho, Joshua and the invading Israelites expected the smaller city of Ai to be a pushover. But the defenders of Ai put up a strong resistance, killed some of Israel's warriors, and even chased them from the field of battle. This humiliated Joshua's troops and paralyzed them with fear. Why had the Lord seemingly abandoned them when they advanced against this weak little place?

The problem was Israel's disobedience. An Israelite man named Achan had confiscated some of the spoils of war from Jericho and hidden them in his tent. This was a flagrant violation of God's command that all the booty was to be destroyed. Achan and his family were put to death for their deception. After this, God gave the Israelites victory over Ai.

Learn More: Genesis 12:8: Hai; 13:3: Hai / Joshua 7:1–3; 8:1–28 /
Nehemiah 11:31: Aija / Isaiah 10:28: Aiath

AJALON

Sun, stand thou still upon Gibeon; and thou, Moon, in the valley of Ajalon. JOSHUA 10:12

Soon after entering the land of Canaan, Joshua and the Israelites faced a coalition army gathered by five different Amorite kings. The battle scene turned into one of the most spectacular miracles of the Bible. The Lord caused the sun and moon to stand still for an entire day "until the people had avenged themselves upon their enemies" (Joshua 10:13).

Ajalon, also spelled Aijalon, was a town and a nearby valley located about twenty miles west of Jerusalem. After Joshua's victory over its Amorite inhabitants, the area was allotted to the tribe of Dan.

In later years, Saul, first king of the Israelites, won a great victory over the Philistines at Ajalon. Still later, King Rehoboam of the southern kingdom fortified the city to defend Jerusalem from an attack along its western side. The Philistines succeeded in retaking the city during the reign of King Ahaz of Judah.

Learn More: Joshua 19:40–42 / Judges 12:12 / 1 Samuel 14:31 / 1 Chronicles 8:13 /
2 Chronicles 11:5–10; 28:18

ALEXANDRIA

A certain Jew named Apollos, born at Alexandria. Acts 18:24

This city, named for Alexander the Great, was the capital as well as the cultural center of Egypt in New Testament times. Apollos, a native of this city, was well known for his knowledge of the Old Testament when he arrived in Ephesus, where the apostle Paul had established a church. After patient instruction from Aquila and Priscilla, Apollos developed into an influential leader in the early church (Acts 18:25–28).

Several years before Apollos arrived in Ephesus, other Jewish natives of Alexandria were in Jerusalem for a religious celebration. Here they listened to Stephen's claim that Jewish religious leaders were responsible for the death of Jesus. These Alexandrian Jews were probably among the mob that stoned Stephen to death (Acts 6:9; 7:54–60).

In later years, the apostle Paul was shipwrecked while on his way to the city of Rome. After ministering on the island of Melita for some time, he continued his voyage on a ship from Alexandria.

Learn More: Acts 27:6; 28:11

ANATHOTH

I bought the field of Hanameel my uncle's son, that was in Anathoth. JEREMIAH 32:9

The prophet Jeremiah was from the village of Anathoth not far from Jerusalem. He had been preaching a message of God's judgment against the nation of Judah for many years when his cousin Hanameel from his hometown showed up.

Hanameel wanted to know if Jeremiah was interested in buying a field he had for sale. The prophet knew this property, along with all of Judah, would soon be confiscated by the conquering Babylonians, just as he had been predicting. But he agreed to the deal, had the deed recorded and authenticated by witnesses, sealed the papers in an airtight jar, and placed them in a safe place for protection (Jeremiah 32:10–14).

This was Jeremiah's expression of confidence in the Lord's promise of ultimate redemption for His people. He would bring them back to their homeland in about seventy years after their time of discipline and punishment was over (Jeremiah 29:10–14).

The modern Arab village of Anata, not far from Jerusalem, probably preserves the name of Anathoth. But most scholars agree the ruins known as Ras el-Kharrubeh, less than a mile from Anata, is the site of the city where Jeremiah grew up.

Learn More: Joshua 21:18 / Jeremiah 1:1; 11:21–23

ANTIOCH OF PISIDIA

They came to Antioch in Pisidia, and went into the synagogue. ACTS 13:14

During Paul's first missionary journey, he spoke in the Jewish synagogue in this important commercial city in southern Asia Minor (modern Turkey). This place is referred to as Antioch in the province of Pisidia to distingish it from the Antioch of Syria from which Paul and Barnabas launched their evangelistic campaign (Acts 13:1–3).

At Antioch of Pisidia, Paul delivered his first long sermon recorded in the book of Acts (Acts 13:16–41). Many Gentiles of the city listened eagerly and turned to the Lord. But zealous Jews accused Paul and Barnabas of blasphemy and expelled them from the city. This led Paul to begin to focus his ministry on a non-Jewish audience, so that he eventually became known as the "apostle to the Gentiles" (Acts 13:46–47).

Antioch's influence in this region of the Roman world made it an important hub for the spread of the Gospel. After Paul and Barnabas planted the seed, "the word of the Lord was published throughout all the region" (Acts 13:49).

Learn More: Acts 14:19 / 2 Timothy 3:11

ANTIOCH OF SYRIA

The disciples were called Christians first in Antioch. ACTS 11:26

Ministering to new believers in the growing church in this city was more than one person could handle. So Barnabas recruited Saul, later known as the apostle Paul, to help him in this ministry.

Antioch, capital of the Roman province of Syria, was about three hundred miles north of Jerusalem. It was one of the largest cities in the Roman Empire during New Testament times. Believers had fled to Antioch when persecution of the church broke out after the martyrdom of Stephen in the Holy City.

Under the leadership of Barnabas and Saul, the church at Antioch reached both Jews and Gentiles with the Gospel. These zealous early believers developed a reputation throughout the city as "Christ-ones" or Christians. This was probably a term of reproach at the time, but early believers gladly embraced the name.

Barnabas and Saul launched their missionary journeys into the Roman provinces west of Antioch under the sponsorship of this church. Controversy over conversion of Gentiles at Antioch led the early church to decide that the Gospel was meant for all people.

Learn More: Acts 6:5; 11:19, 22; 14:26; 15:35 / Galatians 2:11

APHEK

Joshua and the children of Israel smote. . . THE KING OF APHEK. JOSHUA 12:7, 18

The city of Aphek, not far from the Mediterranean Sea, was conquered by the Israelites when they entered the land of Canaan. By that time this city was already several centuries old. Later it fell into the hands of the Philistines and was one of the cities on their northern border.

In a battle at Aphek, the Philistines captured the ark of the covenant from the Israelites (1 Samuel 4:1–11). Centuries later, Herod the Great—Roman ruler over Palestine—rebuilt and enlarged Aphek and renamed it Antipatris in honor of his father, Antipater. The apostle Paul passed through Antipatris when he was transported under Roman guard from Jerusalem to Caesarea (Acts 23:31).

The ruins of Aphek/Antipatris are off the beaten path today, but the city was strategically located in ancient times. It stood on the road known as the Way of the Sea that ran from Egypt into Syria. Along this route passed trading caravans, carrying goods to these two major markets.

In modern times, springs flowing from the nearby mountains converge at Aphek, providing the perfect setting for a tranquil park along the Yarkon River.

Learn More: 1 Samuel 29:1 / 1 Kings 20:30

ARABIA

Geshem the Arabian. . .said, What is this thing that ye do? NEHEMIAH 2:19

Arabia was a hot, dry, desert region south and east of Canaan. When the Israelites fell to foreign invaders, people from Arabia apparently settled in their territory. Geshem was one of these Arabians who opposed the Israelites when they returned to their homeland and set out to rebuild Jerusalem and the temple.

The most famous Arabian in the Bible is the queen of Sheba, who brought gifts to King Solomon of Israel. She was impressed with his wisdom, riches, and skills as an administrator. She told the king, "Thy wisdom and prosperity exceedeth the fame which I heard" (1 Kings 10:7).

Solomon and other Israelite kings traded extensively with Arabia. The Arabian cities of Ophir, Raamah, and Sheba were known for their exports of gold, silver, and precious stones (1 Kings 9:28; Ezekiel 27:22).

The "Arabia" to which the apostle Paul retreated after his conversion (Galatians 1:17) was probably the territory of the Nabateans, an Arabic tribe that lived south of the city of Damascus.

Learn More: 2 Chronicles 9:14; 17:11; 22:1 / Isaiah 13:20 / Acts 2:11

ARARAT, MOUNT

The ark rested. . .upon the mountains of Ararat. GENESIS 8:4

When the waters of the flood in Noah's time finally went down, the ark came to rest in this rugged mountain range. The site is uncertain, but most scholars place the Ararat mountains somewhere in the isolated territory where the borders of Turkey, Iran, and Armenia come together. In this region several small streams converge to form the headwaters of the Tigris and the Euphrates Rivers.

Before emerging from the ark, Noah "tested the waters" by releasing a raven, followed by two doves that he sent out several days apart. When the second dove returned with an olive leaf in its mouth, he knew the water had gone down enough for him and his family to leave the ship (Genesis 8:7–11).

Several expeditions to find Noah's ark have been undertaken but without success. The first hurdle is getting official permission to conduct a search. But this problem pales in comparison to the hazards of navigating the deep snow, sudden storms, and hidden crevices of the mountains themselves. Locals refer to the peak on which searches have focused as the "Painful Mountain."

Learn More: Jeremiah 51:27

AREOPAGUS

They took him, and brought him unto Areopagus. ACTS 17:19

The Areopagus in ancient Athens was the site of the apostle Paul's speech before the philosophers of the city. These learned teachers spent their time debating about "some new thing" (Acts 17:21), so they were naturally curious about the strange doctrine being preached by the apostle. This meeting place was apparently on Mars' Hill, a prominent hill that overlooked the city (Acts 17:22).

These philosophers were apparently not bothered by Paul's discussion of God or His relationship to His creation. But most of them mocked Paul's claim that God had raised Jesus from the dead. The resurrection was a central doctrine of Christian theology to Paul, but it was unbelievable and unacceptable to the learned men of Athens—just like it is for many people today.

Paul's witness before the Areopagus was not totally fruitless. Some people wanted to hear more, and several became believers. These included "Dionysius the Areopagite, and a woman named Damaris, and others with them" (Acts 17:34).

ASHDOD

When they of Ashdod arose. . .Dagon was fallen upon his face. 1 SAMUEL 5:3

The Israelites carried the ark of the covenant into a battle with their Philistine enemies, thinking it would bring them good luck. Instead, the Philistines won the battle and captured the ark.

These pagan worshippers carried the ark to Ashdod, one of their major cities. Here they put it on display before an image of their god Dagon. This signified to them that Dagon was superior to this religious icon of the Israelites. But instead their idol toppled before the ark during the night.

This happened a second time, and then the Philistines began to suffer from a mysterious illness. Finally, fearing for their lives, they convinced the unsuspecting citizens of Gath, another Philistine city, to take the ark off their hands.

During New Testament times, Ashdod was known as Azotus. Philip the evangelist was miraculously transported by the Spirit of God to Azotus after the conversion of a man from Ethiopia near Gaza. From Azotus Philip launched a preaching tour that took him all the way up the coast of the Mediterranean Sea to Caesarea.

Learn More: Joshua 15:46–47 / 1 Samuel 5:6–7 / 2 Chronicles 26:6 / Zephaniah 2:4 / Acts 8:39–40

ASHKELON

He went down to Ashkelon, and slew thirty men of them. JUDGES 14:19

Samson, a military champion of the Israelites, killed thirty Philistines at Ashkelon, one of their major cities. Then he took their clothes to pay off a debt he owed to thirty of his friends. Samson had lost a bet he made with these companions that they couldn't solve a silly riddle about a dead lion he had killed (Judges 14:12–18).

Even before Samson's time, Ashkelon was an important city. Its location on the main road between Egypt in the south and Mesopotamia to the north made it an important trade center. Excavations show that it was inhabited successively by the Canaanites, Philistines, Israelites, Persians, and Romans. At one point in its long history, it was surrounded by a huge defensive wall with a massive gate.

Several Old Testament prophets predicted that Ashkelon would be punished by the Lord, probably because of the worship of pagan gods among its citizens. The excavated ruins of ancient Ashkelon are preserved today in a national park on the shore of the Mediterranean Sea.

Learn More: 2 Samuel 1:20: Askelon / Jeremiah 25:20 / Amos 1:8 / Zephaniah 2:4 / Zechariah 9:5

ASIA

John to the seven churches which are in Asia. REVELATION 1:4

This large Roman province north of Greece contained the seven churches which the apostle John addressed in the book of Revelation. These several churches attested to the fact that the Gospel had received a favorable hearing in this part of the Roman world. As the book of Acts expressed it, "All they which dwelt in Asia heard the word of the Lord Jesus, both Jews and Greeks" (Acts 19:10).

During his second missionary journey, the apostle Paul was prevented by the Holy Spirit from entering Asia (Acts 16:6). Instead, he and Silas were directed to the province of Macedonia, where Paul established a church at the city of Philippi. But on his third evangelistic tour, Paul ministered for about two years at Ephesus, Asia's major city. The Gospel spread from Ephesus to other cities in this part of the Roman Empire.

The apostle Peter addressed his first letter to believers in Asia. These early believers had probably responded to the Gospel as a result of Paul's ministry in this region.

Learn More: Acts 2:9; 6:9; 19:26–27; 20:18; 21:27 / 1 Corinthians 16:19 / 1 Peter 1:1

ASSYRIA

The king of Assyria took Samaria, and carried Israel away. 2 KINGS 17:6

The Jewish nation known as the northern kingdom of Israel fell to this pagan empire in 722 BC. This happened within a century after the Assyrians began to conquer surrounding countries. Thousands of Israelites were carried away to Assyria as slaves—a humiliation that brought the northern kingdom to an end.

Assyria was situated between the Tigris and Euphrates Rivers in Mesopotamia. This territory was originally settled by the hunter Nimrod, a descendant of Noah. An early name for Assyria was *Asshur*, after a son of Shem who was connected with its early history (Genesis 10:8–12).

The Assyrians were known for their cruelty. They often cut off their victims' hands and impaled them on stakes. For this violence and their pagan worship, they were condemned by the Old Testament prophets.

Several years after conquering Israel, Assyria invaded the southern kingdom of Judah. But the Lord's miraculous intervention caused the death of thousands of Assyrian soldiers, and the army withdrew in defeat (2 Kings 19:35–36).

Learn More: 2 Kings 15:19; 18:14–16 / Isaiah 10:5–12; 37:33–37 / Micah 5:6 / Zephaniah 2:13

ATHENS

Now while Paul waited for them at Athens, his spirit was stirred in him. Acts 17:16

While on his way from Berea to Corinth during his second missionary journey, the apostle Paul stopped in Athens. This city was the center of Greek culture during the golden age of Grecian history about five centuries before Paul arrived. Here the apostle waited for his missionary associates, Silas and Timothy, to join him. He noticed the numerous shrines to false gods that stood throughout the city.

After the apostle preached in the local synagogue, a group of Greek philosophers wanted to hear more about these "strange things" he was teaching. Paul began by noting that one of their religious shrines was devoted to "the unknown god" (Acts 17:23). He declared that this God was none other than the one true God who had sent Jesus into the world as His righteous judge.

Most of these philosophers mocked Paul's claim that this God had raised Jesus from the dead. But a few were eager to hear more, and at least two became believers: "Dionysius the Areopagite, and a woman named Damaris" (Acts 17:34).

Learn More: Acts 17:22; 18:1 / 1 Thessalonians 3:1

BABYLON

Those carried [Nebuchadnezzar] into captivity from Jerusalem to Babylon. 2 Kings 24:15

This powerful nation between the Tigris and Euphrates Rivers in Mesopotamia carried the nation of Judah into exile about 587 BC. The prophet Jeremiah had been warning for years that this would happen unless the people gave up their worship of false gods and turned back to the one true God (Jeremiah 20:4).

The Babylonian Empire reached the height of its power under King Nebuchadnezzar, who conquered many surrounding nations, including Judah. He used spoils that he captured from other nations to fund the construction of his magnificent capital city, also known as Babylon. The famous hanging gardens of this city became known as one of the seven wonders of the ancient world.

After holding the Jewish people captive for many years, the Babylonians were defeated by the Persians about 539 BC, fulfilling the prophecies of Isaiah and Jeremiah. Other names for Babylon are Sheshach (Jeremiah 25:26), Shinar (Isaiah 11:11), and the land of the Chaldeans (Ezekiel 12:13).

Learn More: 2 Kings 20:14; 25:1–21 / 2 Chronicles 36:6–10 /
Psalm 137:1 / Isaiah 14:22 / Jeremiah 50:9

BAHURIM

Shimei. . .a Benjamite of Bahurim, which cursed me with a grievous curse. 1 Kings 2:8

King David passed through this little town near Jerusalem while fleeing from his son Absalom. The king was already in a sorrowful mood because of Absalom's attempt to kill him and take over the kingship. But a man named Shimei added insult to injury by cursing and insulting David and his officials.

The king's aides wanted to kill Shimei because of his disrespect. But David ignored the insults. "Let him alone, and let him curse; for the LORD hath bidden him," he replied. "It may be that the LORD will look on mine affliction, and that the LORD will requite me good for his cursing this day" (2 Samuel 16:11–12).

The village of Bahurim had a huge well. Two of David's officials hid in this shaft when Absalom sent out a search party to take them into custody. Some people identify this water source with a modern site known as Job's Well. This shaft sits at the junction of the Kidron and Hinnom Valleys not far from the walls of Jerusalem's Old City.

Learn More: 2 Samuel 3:16; 17:18; 19:16 / 1 Kings 2:8

BASHAN

Hear this word, ye kine [cows, NIV] of Bashan. Amos 4:1

The prophet Amos delivered this message from the Lord to the rich women of Bashan, a region in the northern kingdom of Israel. They would be punished for encouraging their husbands to exploit the poor, which fed their lavish lifestyle.

Bashan, on the eastern side of the Jordan River, was known for its productivity (Ezekiel 39:18). Its rich, fertile soil produced abundant crops of grain and grass. After the invading Israelites captured this territory, the tribe of Manasseh asked to settle here because it was ideal for their herds of livestock.

The psalmist prayed to be delivered from the "strong bulls of Bashan" (Psalm 22:12). This has been interpreted as a messianic psalm, in which Christ prayed to be delivered from His enemies, who were threatening His life. The psalmist also referred to a "hill of Bashan" (Psalm 68:15). This was probably Mount Hermon, the highest peak in Israel, which stood nearby.

Learn More: Deuteronomy 3:3 / Joshua 17:5; 22:7 / 1 Chronicles 5:23 / Jeremiah 50:19

BEERSHEBA

Wherefore he called that place Beersheba. Genesis 21:31

Deep wells were essential in the dry section of southern Canaan, where Abraham lived for a time. Soon after arriving here, Abraham dug a well to provide water for his livestock. Then he complained to Abimelech, the Philistine ruler of the area, that Abimelech's servants had taken over the well.

Abimelech promised to return the well. Then he pledged that both of them would live together as friends and share the water supply. To seal the agreement, Abraham gave Abimelech seven lambs. Then Abraham named the site Beersheba, meaning "well of an oath" or "well of the seven." Here Abraham also built an altar and worshipped the Lord.

The site of this well developed into a city in later years. A modern city with the same name still exists near the place the original well and the Old Testament city are thought to have been. Visitors are shown an ancient well at this site, but whether this is the well that Abraham dug is uncertain.

Beersheba was the southernmost city in Israel. So the phrase "from Beersheba even to Dan" (1 Chronicles 21:2) was a poetic way of referring to the entire nation.

Learn More: Genesis 22:19 / 1 Samuel 3:20 / 2 Samuel 24:2 / 1 Kings 19:1–3 / Amos 5:5

BEREA

The brethren immediately sent away Paul and Silas by night unto Berea. Acts 17:10

Under threat from Jews in Thessalonica, the apostle Paul and his two missionary associates, Silas and Timothy, fled to this nearby city. Here they found fruitful soil for the Gospel. The Jews of Berea were openminded and eager to learn.

The book of Acts describes these Bereans as "more noble than those in Thessalonica" because "they received the word with all readiness of mind, and searched the scriptures daily" to determine whether Paul's preaching was true (Acts 17:11). Several of these citizens of Berea accepted the Gospel and became believers.

But the Jews of Thessalonica followed the apostle and his party to Berea and "stirred up the people" (Acts 17:13). Paul hit the road again, but only after leaving Silas and Timothy in Berea to minister to these new converts.

One of Paul's converts at Berea, Sopater, became a missionary associate and a fellow traveler with the apostle in later years. This may be the Sosipater who joined Paul in sending greetings to the believers in Rome (Romans 16:21).

Learn More: Acts 20:4

BETHABARA

These things were done in Bethabara beyond Jordan, where John was baptizing. JOHN 1:28

Bethabara is the place where John the Baptist was preaching east of the Jordan River or "beyond Jordan." Jesus arrived on the scene and asked John to baptize Him. John protested that the sinless Jesus didn't need to be baptized. But Jesus insisted, and John did as Jesus requested.

Many scholars claim that the site of this Bethabara has never been identified with certainty. But the nation of Jordan insists that it is on their side of the Jordan River about six miles north of the Dead Sea. Jordanian officials have conducted extensive archaeological excavations in the area to develop it into a major tourism destination for Holy Land visitors.

The fact is that the exact location of Jesus' baptism is uncertain. The lower Jordan has changed its course several times over the centuries, so any supposed site is a matter of speculation.

After John baptized Jesus in the lower Jordan, he apparently also baptized along its upper reaches. Just before he was arrested by Herod Antipas, John was baptizing "in Aenon near to Salim, because there was much water there" (John 3:23). Neither of these places has been precisely identified, although they were probably somewhere near the city of Shechem in central Israel.

BETHANY

Now a certain man was sick, named Lazarus, of Bethany. JOHN 11:1

Bethany was a village on the Mount of Olives about two miles east of Jerusalem. It will always be remembered as the town where a man named Lazarus walked out of his tomb at a simple command from his friend, Jesus (John 11:43–44).

Jesus withdrew often to the home of Lazarus where He spent many relaxing hours with him and his sisters, Mary and Martha. Here Jesus delivered a gentle rebuke to Martha when she complained that her sister was talking to Him rather than helping her in the kitchen. Jesus made it clear that Martha should listen to His teachings like her sister rather than rushing around in her domestic duties (Luke 10:38–42).

The raising of Lazarus at Bethany is commemorated by a church known as the Church of Saint Lazarus, built on the site in 1955. Inside are mosaics depicting this miracle. Just up the hill from the church, visitors walk down several crude stone steps into an underground chamber that is reputed to be the tomb of Lazarus. This may not be the actual burial site, but it is typical of tombs from the time of Jesus.

Learn More: Mark 11:1; 14:3 / Luke 24:50 / John 12:1–3

BETHEL

And he called the name of that place Bethel. GENESIS 28:19

Bethel got its name because of Jacob's disturbing dream on this site. While camped here, he dreamed of angels going up and down a stairway. At the top stood God, who renewed the promise He had made to Jacob's grandfather, Abraham, many years before.

Jacob set up the stone he'd been using as a pillow to form a makeshift altar. Then he named the place Bethel, meaning "house of God," to show that God had blessed him in this hallowed place.

For centuries after this event, Bethel was considered a sacred site. In the time of the judges, the ark of the covenant was kept here for a time (Judges 20:26–28). But this changed when the united kingdom split into two factions. King Jeroboam I of the northern kingdom set up calf idols at Bethel and Dan in his territory as worship sites for his people (1 Kings 12:28–29).

The prophets were quick to denounce Jeroboam for encouraging his people to worship these false gods. Hosea used a play on words to show how far Bethel had fallen from its exalted position. Bethel ("house of God") had degenerated into Bethaven ("house of wickedness") (Hosea 10:5).

Learn More: Genesis 12:8 / Joshua 7:2 / Judges 4:5 / 2 Kings 23:15 / Amos 7:13

BETHESDA, POOL OF

A pool, which is called in the Hebrew tongue Bethesda. JOHN 5:2

Jesus was in Jerusalem to observe a Jewish holy day when He noticed several sick and disabled people gathered around this pool. They believed an angel came periodically to stir the waters, and whoever entered the pool first would be healed.

One man in the group, because he had been lame for many years, could not get in the water ahead of the others. Jesus had compassion on the man, healing him with the command, "Rise, take up thy bed, and walk" (John 5:8).

Jesus' words were more powerful than the mysterious bubbling of the pool by an angel. This showed that the false gods and superstitious beliefs of His time were weak and ineffective in comparison to His God-given authority and power.

Archaeologists have uncovered two ancient pools, or water reservoirs, in the Old City of Jerusalem. Each was about sixty feet long and several feet deep. They were fed by an ingenious system of channels that diverted runoff water from the nearby Kidron Valley. Around one pool were five separate sheltered areas, perhaps the "five porches" mentioned in John's Gospel.

BETH HORON

Chased them along the way that goeth up to Bethhoron. JOSHUA 10:10

At this city about eight miles northwest of Jerusalem, Joshua and the Israelites won a decisive battle against the Amorites during their invasion of the land of Canaan. The Lord assured victory by sending a severe hailstorm against the Amorites. As a result, "they were more which died with hailstones than they whom the children of Israel slew with the sword" (Joshua 10:11).

"Beth Horon" was actually twin cities with the same name. They sat on opposite sides of a deep valley on the ancient road between Jerusalem and the Mediterranean Sea. Called Upper Beth Horon and Lower Beth Horon, the first named sat about eight hundred feet higher in elevation than the second.

Several centuries after Joshua's time, King Solomon fortified both these cities to protect Jerusalem from invading armies.

Learn More: Joshua 16:3, 5 / 1 Samuel 13:18 / 2 Chronicles 8:5; 25:13

BETHLEHEM

Out of thee shall he come forth unto me that is to be ruler in Israel. MICAH 5:2

About seven centuries before Jesus came into the world, the prophet Micah predicted He would be born in Bethlehem. This little village was in the hill country of Judah about six miles south of Jerusalem.

According to Luke's Gospel, Jesus' earthly parents traveled about seventy miles from their home in Nazareth to Bethlehem. Here Joseph registered in a census that had been ordered for taxation purposes by the Roman emperor. Jesus was born in a stable, with an animal's feeding trough for His crib, because "there was no room for them in the inn" (Luke 2:7).

The traditional place of Jesus' birth is visited every year by thousands of Holy Land pilgrims. In a cave beneath an ancient church, they view a spot marked by a star that is reputed to be the very place where He was born.

Bethlehem was called the "city of David" because King David tended sheep in this area when he was just a boy. A few generations earlier, Ruth gleaned grain from the fields of Boaz near Bethlehem.

Learn More: Genesis 48:7 / Ruth 2:4–6 / 1 Samuel 17:15 /
2 Samuel 23:15–16 / Matthew 2:5 / Luke 2:4–5

BETHPHAGE

When he was come nigh to Bethphage. . .he sent two of his disciples. LUKE 19:29

Jesus sent two of His disciples into this village to find a donkey on which He could make His triumphal entry into Jerusalem. Apparently the Lord had made prior arrangements to borrow the animal from someone in this little town—perhaps one of His followers.

The actual site of Bethphage is unknown. But tradition places it on the Mount of Olives near the town of Bethany. This traditional site is marked by a church known as the Church of Bethphage. Inside the building is a painting depicting Jesus riding a donkey into Jerusalem while the crowds place palm leaves on the ground to welcome Him as a king.

Jesus' entry into Jerusalem in this fashion fulfilled biblical prophecy. The prophet Zechariah had declared many centuries before: "Rejoice greatly, O daughter of Zion; shout, O daughter of Jerusalem: behold, thy King cometh unto thee: he is just, and having salvation; lowly, and riding upon an ass, and upon a colt the foal of an ass" (Zechariah 9:9).

Learn More: Matthew 21:1 / Luke 19:29

BETHSAIDA

He cometh to Bethsaida; and they bring a blind man unto him. MARK 8:22

This fishing village on the shore of the Sea of Galilee was the site of one of Jesus' healing miracles. Here He rubbed saliva on the eyes of a blind man to restore his sight. At first the man could not see clearly. Then Jesus touched his eyes a second time to complete the healing process. This is the only two-stage miracle of Jesus recorded in the Gospels.

Bethsaida was the hometown of three of Jesus' disciples—Peter, Andrew, and Philip. Peter and Andrew probably made their living as fishermen in the nearby Sea of Galilee. Excavations at the town have uncovered the remains of a fisherman's residence, along with a fishhook, an anchor, stone net weights, and a needle for repairing fishing nets.

The tragedy of Bethsaida was its spiritual apathy in spite of Jesus' healing and teaching among its residents. He condemned the village, along with its sister towns of Corazin and Capernaum, for its unbelief.

Learn More: Matthew 11:21 / Mark 6:45 / Luke 9:10; 10:13–14 / John 1:44; 12:21

BETH SHAN

They fastened his body to the wall of Bethshan. 1 SAMUEL 31:10

Here is where the Philistines hung the body of King Saul and his sons on the city wall after overrunning the Israelite army on nearby Mount Gilboa. This primitive "billboard" declared that the Philistines were powerful enough to bully the Israelites and seize large portions of their territory.

Residents of nearby Jabesh Gilead retrieved the bodies of Saul and his sons and buried them at their city. King David eventually paid honor to Saul and his sons by having their remains unearthed and buried in Saul's family tomb in the territory of Benjamin (2 Samuel 21:12–14).

David's son and successor, Solomon, turned Beth Shan into one of his administrative cities. It was responsible for collecting taxes and providing food from its surrounding territory for the royal court in Jerusalem.

In later centuries, Beth Shan grew into a major Roman city known as Scythopolis. Archaeologists have uncovered the remains of this city, as well as several others that preceded it on this site. Scythopolis is not mentioned in the New Testament.

Learn More: 1 Samuel 31:12 / Beth Shean in Joshua 17:16 / Judges 1:27 / 1 Chronicles 7:29

BETH SHEMESH

The kine took the straight way to the way of Bethshemesh. 1 SAMUEL 6:12

This ancient town lay on the border between the territory of Israel and the region occupied by the Philistines. It is best known as the town where Israel's ark of the covenant was kept for a time.

The Philistines captured the ark in a battle but sent it back to the Israelites after it caused confusion and disease among them (1 Samuel 5:1–12). They put the ark on a cart, hitched two kine—or cows—to it, and sent the cart away with no human driver. The cows pulled the ark straight to Beth Shemesh.

The ark brought trouble even to the Israelites at Beth Shemesh, when the people examined it inappropriately. They sent it to Kirjath Jearim, where it remained for several years until being relocated permanently to Jerusalem (1 Chronicles 15:25–28).

Excavations at the site of Beth Shemesh have uncovered the ruins of an ancient city from the time of the judges, possibly a Canaanite settlement captured by Joshua. It had a huge underground reservoir that provided water for the residents of the town. An impressive system of pipes from the streets above channeled water into this huge cistern.

Learn More: Joshua 15:10 / Judges 1:33 / 1 Samuel 6:9, 19–20 / 2 Chronicles 28:18

CAESAREA

They came to Caesarea and delivered the epistle to the governor. ACTS 23:33

At this major seaport city on the Mediterranean Sea, the apostle Paul was imprisoned for two years. This was the headquarters city of the Roman governor of the province of Judaea at the time. Paul was brought here for his protection after Jewish zealots threatened to kill him on a false charge of blasphemy (Acts 21:27–33).

Here at Caesarea the apostle also made a speech in his own defense before several Roman officials and appealed his case to a higher court at the capital city of the Roman Empire (Acts 26:32). He sailed from Caesarea to Rome, where he continued his witness for Christ from another prison cell.

Before Paul was imprisoned at Caesarea, a Roman military officer named Cornelius was converted here under the ministry of the apostle Peter (Acts 10:1–8, 44–48). This opened the doors for the reception of Gentiles into the church.

Caesarea was built by Herod the Great, Roman ruler over Palestine, and named for the Roman emperor, Caesar Augustus. Impressive ruins of this ancient city still visible today include an outdoor theater and an aqueduct that brought water to the city from Mount Carmel about thirteen miles away.

Learn More: Acts 8:40; 9:29–30; 18:22; 21:8, 16

CAESAREA PHILIPPI

Jesus came into the coasts of Caesarea Philippi. MATTHEW 16:13

This isolated place has been immortalized because of the pointed question that Jesus asked His disciples here. Here at the foot of Mount Hermon in northern Israel, He wanted to know if they really believed He was the Messiah He claimed to be. Jesus knew they had heard the rumors about His identity that were circulating among the people.

Peter spoke for all the disciples when he answered, "Thou art the Christ [the Messiah, the anointed one], the Son of the living God" (Matthew 16:16).

This confession is significant because of the background of Caesarea Philippi. It had been associated for many years with worship of pagan gods, extending back to its occupation by the Canaanites before the Israelites occupied the territory. The village that occupies the site today—Banyas—is derived from the name of the ancient Greek deity Pan, the god of nature.

In contrast to these dead, impotent gods of the past, Peter declared that Jesus was the Son of the *living* God. He was alive and active on behalf of His people, as Jesus demonstrated through His healing and teaching ministry.

Learn More: Mark 8:27

CALVARY

The place, which is called Calvary, there they crucified him. LUKE 23:33

Calvary is a hill just outside the walls of Jerusalem where Jesus was crucified. The word comes from a Latin word meaning "skull," thus "the place of a skull" (John 19:17). The Aramaic form of this word is *Golgotha* (Mark 15:22).

In 1863 British general Charles Gordon identified a hill he believed could be "the skull" described in scripture—a rocky cliff with deep crevices resembling eye sockets and a nose. He popularized the site through his writings and lectures. Known as Gordon's Calvary, it has been venerated ever since by generations of evangelical Christians who visit the Holy Land.

A site closely associated with Calvary is the Garden Tomb, the reputed site of Jesus' burial and resurrection. It was discovered by archaeologists soon after Gordon's Calvary was identified.

Not all believers accept this hill as the site of the crucifixion. Many think the more likely spot is inside an ancient church known as the Church of the Holy Sepulchre. Located within the walls of Jerusalem's Old City, the church is the successor to several other houses of worship that have been built here since the site was first identified in AD 335.

Learn More: Matthew 27:33

CANA

This beginning of miracles did Jesus in Cana of Galilee. JOHN 2:11

Jesus performed His first miracle at this village about thirteen miles west of the Sea of Galilee. It happened at a wedding where Jesus, His disciples, and His mother, Mary, were guests. Jesus' mother informed Him of a problem that threatened to turn the occasion into a disaster: the host had miscalculated and was about to run out of wine.

At first Jesus hesitated to do anything about this dilemma. He had just launched His public ministry, and He apparently thought this was not the right time to reveal His supernatural powers as the Messiah. But then He took action by producing wine from common water (John 2:6–10). This saved the host from embarrassment and prolonged the joyful celebration.

The Gospel of John cites this miracle as the first of seven "signs" that Jesus performed to show His unique mission as the Son of God. These signs increase in intensity throughout this Gospel, concluding with Jesus' raising of Lazarus from the dead (John 11:38–44).

The traditional site of Cana is marked today by a place of worship known as the Wedding Church, a popular place for weddings and the renewal of marriage vows.

Learn More: John 4:46; 21:2

CANAAN

Abram passed through the land. . . . And the Canaanite was then in the land. GENESIS 12:6

The land known as Canaan, or the promised land, consisted of the strip of land between the Mediterranean Sea and the Jordan River that God promised to Abraham and his descendants (Genesis 13:15–17). When Abraham arrived, he must have wondered about this promise because the territory was inhabited by a tribal people who had claimed it as their own for many centuries.

Long after Abraham's time, the Lord renewed this promise. Moses was called to lead God's people, the Israelites, out of Egyptian slavery and to make their way to Canaan. After years of wandering in the wilderness, they finally arrived at their destination.

The task of conquering Canaan fell to Joshua, who succeeded Moses as leader of the people. Joshua also presided over the process of dividing the territory among the tribes of Israel (Joshua 14:1).

Although small in size, Canaan was strategically located between the two great civilizations of Egypt to the south and Mesopotamia to the north. Under King Solomon, the nation developed a lucrative network of trade with other nations along Canaan's ancient caravan routes.

Learn More: Genesis 28:6; 42:5; 50:13 / Exodus 23:23 / Leviticus 25:38 / Psalm 105:11

CAPERNAUM

And leaving Nazareth, he came and dwelt in Capernaum. Matthew 4:13

Jesus grew up at Nazareth, a town not far from the Sea of Galilee. But after His rejection at Nazareth, He moved to Capernaum and made it the center of His Galilean ministry. He lived at this village for about two years.

Capernaum was the hometown of at least four of Jesus' disciples: Peter, Andrew, James, and John (Matthew 4:18–22). A fifth disciple, Matthew, was apparently a tax collector in the town (Luke 5:27–32).

Some of Jesus' most important miracles and teachings occurred in or near this little town on the shore of Lake Galilee. But in spite of all these good works, the people were generally unresponsive to His message. He condemned Capernaum for its unbelief.

About two miles southwest of Capernaum is a site known as Tabgha, the traditional site where Jesus multiplied a boy's lunch to feed a crowd of more than five thousand people (John 6:1–15). A church on the site, known as the Church of the Multiplication, commemorates this event. Capernaum is also the place where Jesus healed a lame man carried on a mat by his four friends.

Learn More: Mark 2:1–5 / Luke 4:31; 10:15 / John 6:59

CARMEL, MOUNT

Gather to me all Israel unto mount Carmel, and the prophets of Baal. 1 Kings 18:19

On a high peak in this mountain range near the Mediterranean Sea, the prophet Elijah proved that the Lord was superior to a pagan god known as Baal.

Baal's worshippers placed a sacrificial animal on an altar. Nothing happened after they implored their god to set the wood on fire to complete the sacrifice (1 Kings 18:20–29). Then Elijah built an altar and piled on wood with a sacrificial animal. Next he dug a trench around the altar and soaked the wood with water. Finally, the prophet uttered a simple prayer to the Lord.

What happened next was one of the most dramatic events in the Bible: "Then the fire of the Lord fell, and consumed the burnt sacrifice, and the wood, and the stones, and the dust, and licked up the water that was in the trench" (1 Kings 18:38).

The reputed site of this dramatic event is marked today by a monastery with an adjoining church. In the courtyard stands a statue of Elijah with upraised sword. This symbolizes the mass execution of these false prophets at his command (1 Kings 18:40).

Learn More: 2 Kings 2:25; 4:25 / Song of Solomon 7:5 / Isaiah 35:2 / Jeremiah 46:18 / Amos 9:3

CARMEL, TOWN OF

Get you up to Carmel, and go to Nabal, and greet him in my name. 1 Samuel 25:5

David was in hiding from King Saul when he approached this town in southern Judah about seven miles south of Hebron. Desperate for food for his hungry warriors, he sent a unit to Carmel to ask a rich man named Nabal for provisions.

Nabal's refusal sent David into a rage. He set out to kill Nabal and his servants. But Nabal's wife, Abigail, pacified the future king by bringing food for him and his men. She told him that more reasonable behavior was expected of a person who would someday rule over others as the king. David relented and praised the beautiful Abigail for her wisdom (1 Samuel 25:23–35).

Shortly afterward, when Abigail told him how close he had come to being killed by David, Nabal had a stroke and died within a few days. The future king then took Nabal's widow as his wife. She eventually became the mother of one of David's sons.

One of David's brave warriors, Hezrai, was a native of Carmel.

Learn More: 1 Samuel 15:12; 25:40; 30:5 / 2 Samuel 3:3; 23:35

CHEBAR RIVER

I was among the captives by the river of Chebar. Ezekiel 1:1

Jewish exiles were apparently settled along this river after they were carried into captivity by the Babylonians. Here the prophet Ezekiel received several visions from the Lord to encourage His captive people and to show that God was in control of world history.

Ezekiel's most famous vision by the Chebar River was of four creatures. Each of these beings had the faces of a lion, a man, an eagle, and an ox. Above these creatures was a throne symbolizing the glory of God. This vision depicted God in His awesome power coming in judgment against the sins of His people (Ezekiel 1:4–28).

The prophet's later vision of dry bones coming to life represented hope for God's people. Although they were under the thumb of a foreign power at the present time, they would eventually be restored to their homeland (Ezekiel 37:1–14).

The river beside which Ezekiel received his visions has been identified with one of several rivers in ancient Babylon. But many people believe this stream was actually the famous Royal Canal built by King Nebuchadnezzar to connect the Tigris and Euphrates Rivers.

Learn More: Ezekiel 3:15, 23; 10:15, 20, 22; 43:3

CHERITH BROOK

Hide thyself by the brook Cherith, that is before Jordan. 1 Kings 17:3

This little stream that runs into the Jordan River was the site of God's miraculous provision for one of His faithful prophets. It happened when God sent Elijah into hiding here to escape the wrath of King Ahab of the northern kingdom and his scheming wife, Jezebel.

The king and Jezebel had promoted worship of the false god Baal throughout the country. God sent Elijah to tell Ahab that the country would suffer from lack of rain for several years because of these sinful acts. Elijah then fled to the rugged country beside this stream, where he was sustained by its water and the food brought to him by ravens.

When the brook dried up because of the drought, God stepped in again to preserve His faithful prophet. Elijah lodged with a poor widow, who agreed to feed him with the last bit of meal and oil in her house. When she did so, these ingredients were miraculously restored. This happened day after day so that she and her son and Elijah had enough to eat as long as the drought lasted.

Learn More: 1 Kings 17:5

CHORAZIN

Woe unto thee, Chorazin! Matthew 11:21

This city not far from the northern shore of the Sea of Galilee is mentioned only twice in the New Testament. These two passages are actually parallels that record the same event—Jesus' condemnation of the city because of its unbelief. Yet, the Gospels do not record that Jesus ever visited this place. Why would He condemn a city in which He had never taught?

The Gospel of John has a possible answer to this puzzle. John declared that if everything that Jesus did was written down, "even the world itself could not contain the books that should be written" (John 21:25).

Not all the actions and words of Jesus were recorded by the Gospel writers. He must have visited Chorazin several times, since it was near Capernaum, the headquarters of His Galilean ministry. But for some reason, nothing He said or did at Chorazin made it into the New Testament.

Two other nearby towns condemned by Jesus were Bethsaida and Capernaum (Matthew 11:20–24). Much of His Galilean ministry must have occurred in these three towns. This is why He had such strong words for their unbelief.

Learn More: Luke 10:13

CILICIA

And he went through Syria and Cilicia, confirming the churches. ACTS 15:41

This coastal province in southeastern Asia Minor (modern Turkey) fronted the Mediterranean Sea. One of its major cities was Tarsus, hometown of the apostle Paul. Soon after his conversion, Paul returned to this territory for protection from a group of zealous Jews who threatened his life (Acts 9:29–30).

In later years, Paul visited Cilicia during his first missionary journey. He apparently returned here several times on other evangelistic tours. The apostle often identified himself to others as a native of Cilicia.

The western section of Cilicia was dominated by the Taurus Mountains. Through a pass in these mountains ran one of the great Roman roads. This international trade route linked the city of Rome to its eastern provinces and ultimately to Egypt in the south and to other ancient nations in Mesopotamia.

This was only one of a network of roads built by the Roman government throughout its provinces. These well-traveled highways helped Christianity spread rapidly throughout the Mediterranean world in Paul's time.

Learn More: Acts 15:23; 21:39; 22:3; 23:34; 27:5 / Galatians 1:21

CITIES OF REFUGE

They shall be unto you cities for refuge from the avenger. NUMBERS 35:12

In Old Testament times, the closest relative of a person who had been killed was expected to avenge the death by taking the life of the guilty party. The law of Moses set aside six cities throughout Israel as places to which persons guilty of an accidental homicide could flee. This guaranteed safety while the circumstances of the death were under review.

These six cities were scattered throughout the country—three on each side of the Jordan River—for convenient access. The three eastern cities were Bezer, Ramoth Gilead, and Golan. On Jordan's western side were Kedesh, Shechem, and Hebron, also known as Kiriath Arba.

A person who sought asylum in one of these cities was given a fair trial. If found innocent of the charges, he could stay on without fear of retaliation from the dead person's relatives.

The law of Moses makes a clear distinction between murder and manslaughter. Murder is committed out of enmity, or the malicious intent to harm a person, while manslaughter is an accidental or unintentional act that causes the death of another (Numbers 35:20–24).

Learn More: Numbers 35:6–7 / Deuteronomy 19:3 / Joshua 20:1–5

COLOSSE

To the saints and faithful brethren in Christ which are at Colosse. . . COLOSSIANS 1:2

This letter from the apostle Paul to the church at Colosse is the only mention of the city in the New Testament. Paul apparently never visited the town. If he did, the book of Acts does not report it. Colosse was about one hundred miles east of Ephesus in modern Turkey. It formed a triangle with two other neaby towns, Laodicea and Hierapolis, which are mentioned in this letter (Colossians 4:13).

Paul's missionary associate, Epaphras, may have founded churches and ministered to believers in all three of these cities. The apostle described him as "one of you" and "a servant of Christ" who was "labouring fervently for you in prayers, that ye may stand perfect and complete in all the will of God" (Colossians 4:12).

This faithful believer may have been the same Epaphras who was imprisoned for a time with Paul in Rome (Philemon 23). He may have asked the apostle to write this encouraging letter to the Colossian church (Colossians 1:4, 7).

CORINTH

Many of the Corinthians hearing believed, and were baptized. ACTS 18:8

The apostle Paul spent about eighteen months at this city in Greece. Under his ministry, converts like Crispus became witnesses to the power of the Gospel in a major commercial center of the Roman Empire.

Corinth was known for its secularism and diversity. Sailors, gamblers, merchants, athletes, and prostitutes migrated here, drawn by its reputation for loose living and its business opportunities. Developing converts from such different backgrounds into a harmonious church demanded Paul's best efforts.

In his letters to the church, Paul cautioned them against divisions, reprimanded them for not dealing with sin in their midst, and corrected their misunderstanding about spiritual gifts.

At Corinth Paul worked with a Christian couple named Aquila and Priscilla. This trio supported themselves in their occupation as tentmakers (Acts 18:1–3). They may have worked out of a shop in the city's busy commercial center.

One of the most interesting recent discoveries from ancient Corinth is an inscription with the name Erastus. This has led to speculation that it refers to the Erastus who sent greetings through Paul to the church at Rome (Romans 16:23).

Learn More: Acts 18:1 / 2 Timothy 4:20 / 1 Corinthians 1:2 / 2 Corinthians 1:23

CRETE

I thee in Crete, that thou shouldest set in order the things that are wanting. TITUS 1:5

Crete is a large island near the middle of the Mediterranean Sea. The circumstances that led to the development of a church on this island are not known, but the apostle Paul knew about this congregation and its need. So he assigned to Titus, his missionary associate, the responsibility of working with the Cretan believers.

Several churches may have existed on the island, because Paul directed Titus to ordain elders, or church leaders, "in every city." Some secular sources indicate that Crete had as many as one hundred cities at one time.

No matter the number of churches, working with the believers on this island would not be easy. Paul reminded Titus that one of the islanders had said about his fellow citizens, "The Cretians are alway liars, evil beasts, slow bellies" (Titus 1:12). The apostle wanted Titus to be mentally prepared for the task at hand.

The ship on which Paul was traveling to Rome was blown off course near Crete and eventually wrecked. The prophets Jeremiah and Amos identified Crete, or Caphtor, as the original home of the Philistines.

Learn More: Jeremiah 47:4 / Amos 9:7 / Acts 2:11; 27:12–14, 21

CYPRUS

So they, being sent forth by the Holy Ghost. . .sailed to Cyprus. ACTS 13:4

From Seleucia, a coastal town near Antioch of Syria, Paul, Barnabas, and John Mark launched their first missionary tour. Their destination was Cyprus, a large island about sixty miles off the Syrian coast. They may have selected this island because Barnabas was a native of Cyprus and thus familiar with its culture and traditions.

At the city of Salamis on the island's eastern tip, they preached at the Jewish synagogue before traveling west across Cyprus to Paphos, the capital city. Here Paul confronted a sorcerer who tried to stop their witnessing efforts. Paul called him a "child of the devil" who was hindering the work of the Holy Spirit (Acts 13:10).

After striking the magician blind, Paul witnessed to Sergius Paulus, the island's chief official. He turned to the Lord, becoming the first convert on the apostle's first evangelistic tour.

Later, Paul and Barnabas disagreed over whether to take John Mark on their second journey. Barnabas took John and revisited the island while Paul and Silas set off in a different direction. Several Old Testament prophets referred to Cyprus as Chittim.

Learn More: Isaiah 23:1 / Jeremiah 2:10 / Ezekiel 27:6 / Acts 4:36; 15:39; 21:16

DAMASCUS

He came near Damascus: and suddenly there shined round about him a light. Acts 9:3

Saul (later known as Paul) was traveling to Damascus north of Israel to persecute Christians in that Syrian city. On the Damascus road, he was converted through a dramatic encounter with Jesus (Acts 9:1–8). Blinded in the experience, he continued on to Damascus, where a believer named Ananias was sent by the Lord to restore Saul's sight.

Saul spent several days at Damascus, preaching the Gospel in Jewish synagogues. Here he was threatened by radical Jews for proclaiming that Jesus was the Messiah, and he had to escape over the city wall. This pattern of Jewish persecution would continue for the rest of his life.

Several centuries earlier, King David captured Damascus from the Syrians and stationed his troops in the city (2 Samuel 8:5–6). David's son and successor, Solomon, lost control over the city, and other Israelite kings battled with Syria, also known as Aram (1 Kings 15:18–20).

Damascus, one of the oldest continually inhabited cities in the world, is the capital of the modern nation of Syria.

Learn More: Genesis 15:2 / 1 Kings 19:15 / 2 Kings 5:12; 14:28 / 2 Chronicles 24:23 / Isaiah 7:8

DAN

Go now through all the tribes of Israel, from Dan even to Beersheba. 2 Samuel 24:2

These words of King David to his aide Joab give an important clue about the location of the city of Dan. It was in the extreme northern section of Israel during David's time. The phrase "from Dan to Beersheba"—Israel's southernmost city—was a figurative way of referring to the entire country.

Dan was inhabited by the Canaanites until it was captured by members of Israel's tribe of Dan and named for their famous ancestor (Judges 18:29). The city's original name was Leshem or Laish (Judges 18:29; Joshua 19:47).

Archaeologists have discovered a massive gate at Dan that dates back to about 1750 BC. It has been dubbed "Abraham's Gate" because Abraham lived about this time, and he rescued his nephew Lot from a raiding party near this ancient Canaanite city (Genesis 14:14–15).

After the united kingdom split into two factions following Solomon's death, King Jeroboam of the northern kingdom (still called "Israel") placed a calf idol in a shrine at Dan. He hoped his subjects would forget about the temple in Jerusalem and come to worship at this substitute site. This led to widespread idol worship among Jeroboam's subjects.

Learn More: Judges 20:1 / 1 Kings 4:25; 12:30 / 2 Kings 10:29

DEAD SEA

The outgoings of the border were at the north bay of the salt sea. Joshua 18:19

The name *Dead Sea* does not appear in the King James Version. It is referred to instead as the "salt sea" because of its high mineral content. After the Israelites conquered Canaan, this body of water was considered the southern boundary of their territory.

The Dead Sea lies about 1,300 feet below sea level at the lowest point on earth. It receives inflow from the Jordan River and other smaller streams, but the water is released only through evaporation. The salts and minerals left behind have turned the lake into a stagnant pool in which few living things can survive—thus the name "Dead Sea."

The Jewish historian Josephus called this body of water the Sea of Sodom. Some scholars believe the wicked cities of Sodom and Gomorrah were located nearby, but no evidence of their existence has ever been found.

In the 1940s and 1950s, several ancient manuscripts known as the Dead Sea Scrolls were discovered in nearby caves. These included a copy of the book of Isaiah.

Learn More: Numbers 34:3 / Deuteronomy 3:17 / Joshua 3:16; 15:2 / 2 Kings 14:25: sea of the plain / Joel 2:20: east sea

DECAPOLIS

He departed, and began to publish in Decapolis how great things Jesus had done. MARK 5:20

In this region east of the Sea of Galilee, Jesus healed a demon-possessed man who lived among the tombs. The man was so thrilled at being restored to his right mind that he wanted to go with the Lord. But Jesus told him, "Go home to thy friends, and tell them how great things the Lord hath done for thee" (Mark 5:19). The man obeyed and became a great witness for Jesus throughout this Gentile territory.

The name *Decapolis* means "ten cities." The towns of this area, including Gadara (Luke 8:26) or Gerasa (Matthew 8:28), had been influenced by Greek culture and tradition. It was populated mainly by people of pagan background.

Besides healing this man, Jesus performed two other miracles in the Decapolis. He restored the hearing of a deaf man with a speech impediment, amazing the people and causing news of His power to spread throughout the territory (Mark 7:31–37). And Jesus fed four thousand people in this area by multiplying a few pieces of fish and bread (Mark 8:1–10). So here, He provided for non-Jews just as He had previously met the needs of five thousand Jews (Mark 6:30–44). This points to Jesus as a universal Savior.

Learn More: Matthew 4:25

DERBE

Then came [Paul] to Derbe and Lystra. ACTS 16:1

This verse records the apostle Paul's visit to Derbe during his second missionary journey. This city in the region of Pamphylia (modern Turkey) must have been of strategic importance to Paul, since he also visited Derbe during his two other evangelistic tours.

Derbe was near the city of Lystra. During the first missionary journey, Paul and Barnabas retreated to these two cities after unbelieving Jews from nearby Iconium drove them out of their town. Paul probably visited Derbe again during his third missionary tour while he "went over all the country of Galatia and Phrygia in order, strengthening all the disciples" (Acts 18:23). One of the apostle's missionary associates, Gaius, was a native of Derbe.

Archaeologists have conducted excavations at the site of Derbe. One of the most significant discoveries was an inscription that marked the grave of a bishop of Derbe. This shows that Christianity flourished here for several centuries after Paul's visits to the city.

Learn More: Acts 14:6, 20; 20:4

DOTHAN

I heard them say, Let us go to Dothan. GENESIS 37:17

This town about eleven miles north of Samaria in northern Israel is where Joseph found his brothers taking care of their father's sheep. The older siblings, envious of Joseph's position as their father's favorite, decided to get rid of their younger brother. They sold him to a passing caravan, and Joseph ended up a slave in Egypt.

But God was with Joseph, and he eventually became a high official in the Egyptian government (Genesis 41:37–44). In later years Joseph used his political pull to save his family from a severe famine by moving them to Egypt (Genesis 46:28–34).

Several centuries after Joseph's time, Dothan was the scene of another example of God's provision and protection. Enemy soldiers were sent to arrest the prophet Elisha at this city. But God struck them with blindness, allowing the prophet to escape.

A large mound known as Tell Dotha marks the site of this ancient city today. Here archaeologists have unearthed the remains of several cities from the past. At the base of the mound is a spring, perhaps the water source that brought Joseph's brothers to this area to pasture their father's flocks.

Learn More: 2 Kings 6:12–18

EBAL, MOUNT

Thou shalt put. . .the curse upon mount Ebal. DEUTERONOMY 11:29

Shortly before he died, Moses gave these instructions to the Israelites. After they entered the land of Canaan, they were to stand on northern Israel's twin mountains, Gerizim and Ebal, to renew their dedication to the Lord.

After entering the land, Joshua did as Moses had directed. He stationed some of the people on Gerizim and others on Ebal. After building an altar and presenting offerings to the Lord, he led the people to renew the covenant that God had established with His people.

Next Joshua read the blessings promised in the law if the people remained faithful to God. People stationed on Mount Gerizim responded with "Amen." Then He read the curses that would happen if they disobeyed the Lord. People on Mount Ebal also shouted "Amen." From then on, Mount Ebal was known as the "mount of cursing."

These twin mountains are only about two miles apart. Thus, the shouts of the people from these two peaks would have been heard by each party.

Learn More: Deuteronomy 27:4 / Joshua 8:33

EDEN, GARDEN OF

And the Lord God planted a garden eastward in Eden. GENESIS 2:8

Eden was the beautiful garden that God created as home for Adam and Eve, the first man and woman. It was a place of joy and delight, containing everything they needed for a happy life.

A major unnamed river flowed out of Eden and divided into four smaller rivers, including the Tigris (NIV) and the Euphrates. This suggests that Eden was somewhere in Mesopotamia—"the land between the rivers"—the area where many ancient civilizations thrived in Bible times. The modern nation of Iraq covers most of this region today.

In the garden of Eden, Adam and Eve rebelled against God's clear command and introduced the blight of sin into the world. The Lord banished them from the garden as part of His punishment for their disobedience.

After Israel was taken into captivity by foreigners, the prophets often compared the coming restoration of God's people to the idyllic condition that existed in Eden.

Learn More: Genesis 2:10–11; 3:23 / Isaiah 51:3 / Ezekiel 28:13 / Revelation 22:1

EDOM

Thus Edom refused to give Israel passage through his border. NUMBERS 20:21

During the Exodus, while traveling through the wilderness toward Canaan, the Israelites stopped at the border of Edom. Here, on the eastern side of the Jordan River, they were refused permission to pass through Edomite territory.

This refusal shows the bad blood that had existed between the Israelites and the Edomites for many centuries. It began in the time of Jacob and his older twin brother, Esau. In a fit of hunger, Esau traded his birthright as the oldest son of Isaac to his younger brother for a pot of stew. Esau's descendants eventually developed into the tribal group known as the Edomites. Jacob's offspring grew into the twelve tribes that made up the nation of Israel.

The territory of Edom was eventually conquered by King David of Israel, but later wavered back and forth between independence and captivity for several centuries. The end finally came with the Assyrian onslaught against the nations of the region.

Edom's territory was eventually resettled by an Arabic people known as the Nabateans. Among the limestone cliffs of ancient Edom, these newcomers carved a city known as Petra, an awe-inspiring site to modern tourists.

Learn More: Genesis 25:30 / Numbers 20:18–21 / 2 Samuel 8:14 /
2 Kings 8:20 / Psalm 60:8 / Jeremiah 49:17

EGYPT

Now there arose up a new king over Egypt, which knew not Joseph. EXODUS 1:8

As a high official of the Egyptian government, Joseph brought his family to Egypt to escape a famine in his home country. For a while the Israelites lived peacefully with their Egyptian neighbors.

After Joseph passed from the scene, government officials grew alarmed when the Israelite population increased dramatically. They responded by enslaving the people. Only after the Lord afflicted the Egyptians with a series of plagues under the leadership of Moses did the Egyptian pharaoh set the people free.

Centuries after the exodus, King Solomon of Israel married an Egyptian princess to seal an alliance with her country. In later years the two countries faced off against each other in minor skirmishes. When the nation of Judah fell to the Babylonians in 587 BC, several Israelite citizens, including the prophet Jeremiah, escaped into Egypt.

Egypt also figures prominently in biblical prophecy. After Jesus was born, His parents took Him into Egypt to escape a death threat from Herod the Great. When they returned to their own country, Hosea's prophecy was fulfilled: "Out of Egypt I called my son" (Hosea 11:1 NIV).

Learn More: Genesis 12:10; 37:36; 46:3 / Exodus 3:7–9; 12:27–30 / 1 Kings 3:1; 14:25

EKRON

The ark of God came to Ekron. 1 SAMUEL 5:10

Ekron was a Philistine city about midway between Jerusalem and the Mediterranean Sea where Israel's ark of the covenant was kept for a time. This sacred object had been captured by the Philistines. The ark's reputation as a troublemaker in another Philistine town had preceded it, and the people of Ekron wanted nothing to do with it.

Their fears were well founded. Many citizens of Ekron were struck by a mysterious sickness as long as the ark remained there. They eventually sent it back to the Israelites.

In later biblical history, Ekron was a place where the pagan god Baalzebub was worshiped. King Ahaziah of Israel sent messengers to Ekron to ask priests of this false god whether he would recover from a fall. The prophet Elijah declared that the king would soon die because he had consulted a false god rather than the Lord (2 Kings 1:2–3).

Iron tools have been discovered at the site of ancient Ekron. The Philistines were known for their production of this metal (1 Samuel 13:19–22).

Learn More: 1 Samuel 7:14; 17:52 / Jeremiah 25:20 / Amos 1:8 / Zechariah 9:5

ELAH VALLEY

And Saul and the men of Israel. . .pitched by the valley of Elah. 1 SAMUEL 17:2

King Saul and his army were camped near this valley not far from the territory of the Philistines when the shepherd boy David arrived on the scene. The Israelites were being taunted by a Philistine giant named Goliath, who dared a single Israelite warrior to face him in battle.

David stepped forward to answer the challenge. While the lad trusted God to give him the victory, he was also smart in his battle tactics. He didn't let Goliath lure him into hand-to-hand combat; instead he felled him from a distance with a stone from his sling (1 Samuel 17:40–50).

This courageous act inspired Saul's army to win a decisive victory over the Philistines. It also added to David's reputation as a leader and paved the way for his succession to the throne after Saul's death several years later.

The brook that provided David's sling stones still meanders today through the valley of Elah. It is actually a wadi that dries up during the summertime. Tourists can't resist picking up small stones from this stream bed to take home as souvenirs.

Learn More: 1 Samuel 17:19; 21:9

EMMAUS

Two of them went that same day to a village called Emmaus. LUKE 24:13

This village is where Jesus revealed Himself to two of His followers on the day He arose from the grave. They were walking to their home in Emmaus about seven miles from Jerusalem. Suddenly a stranger joined their discussion about the rumors of Jesus' death and resurrection.

The stranger was Jesus, but they didn't recognize Him. He accompanied them all the way to their home, where He revealed His identity when they sat down for a meal (Luke 24:14–31).

The site of this village has never been identified. In his Gospel, Luke says it was threescore furlongs—or about seven miles—from the Holy City, but he didn't specify in which direction. Several places have been suggested as the site, but none offers any scientific evidence to support these claims.

While Emmaus's location is a question mark, believers know what is really important—that we serve a living Lord whose presence gives meaning to our lives. We can feel what these followers experienced as they walked with Jesus: "Did not our heart burn within us, while he talked with us by the way, and while he opened to us the scriptures?" (Luke 24:32).

ENDOR

Behold, there is a woman that hath a familiar spirit at Endor. 1 SAMUEL 28:7

King Saul of Israel was facing a major battle with the Philistines, and he needed some advice. Since the prophet Samuel was dead, the king decided to call up Samuel's spirit through a well-known medium at the village of Endor in northern Israel.

The problem was that Saul had banned from Israel all black-magic practitioners like this woman (1 Samuel 28:3). If she recognized him, she would refuse to call up the prophet. So he went to Endor in the clothes of a common man rather than his royal robes.

Here was the most powerful man in Israel hiding his identity, seeking the services of a banned psychic, and asking advice from a dead man. This was certainly the darkest moment in the tragic career of the first king of Israel.

The woman did agree to call up Samuel's spirit. But the prophet's message was not what Saul wanted to hear—the king and his sons would die in the forthcoming battle (1 Samuel 28:19). This is exactly what happened some time later on nearby Mount Gilboa (1 Samuel 31:6).

Learn More: Joshua 17:11 / Psalm 83:9–10

EN GEDI

Behold, David is in the wilderness of Engedi. 1 SAMUEL 24:1

En Gedi was an oasis with a freshwater spring on the western shore of the Dead Sea. The name came to be applied to the entire region, which contained many caves. David hid in one of these caves while on the run from King Saul.

Saul and his troops followed David to this site. By chance, the king went into the very cave in which David was hiding. David crept up to Saul and cut off a piece of his robe. When Saul came out of the cave, David confronted him from the safety of a nearby cliff. He showed the piece of cloth to indicate that he meant the king no harm, although Saul was trying to kill him.

The spring at En Gedi issues from beneath a rock more than four hundred feet above the Dead Sea and rushes into a pool before continuing on to the salty lake. The site is surrounded by the Ein Gedi Nature Reserve. This green oasis is a pleasant contrast to the drab desert that surrounds the Dead Sea.

Learn More: Joshua 15:62 / Song of Solomon 1:14 / Ezekiel 47:10

EPHESUS

Paul having passed through the upper coasts came to Ephesus. ACTS 19:1

The apostle Paul arrived at this major city of Asia Minor (modern Turkey) during his third missionary journey. He worked here for almost three years. This was longer than he stayed at any one place as a traveling evangelist.

A huge statue of a pagan goddess known as Diana stood in the city. Paul's teachings about Jesus and the one true God began to cut into sales of images of this false god. This led to a riot incited by the silversmiths who crafted these trinkets. But Paul continued his ministry after a city official intervened on his behalf (Acts 19:35–41).

Remains of the statue of Diana, also known as Artemis, have been uncovered by archaeologists. It stood about sixty feet high and was considered one of the wonders of the ancient world. A large outdoor theater has also been discovered at Ephesus. This may be the very theater where rioters gathered to protest Paul's teachings.

The church at Ephesus is one of the seven addressed in the book of Revelation. Sadly, since Paul's time, this group of believers had lost their initial zeal for Jesus and the Gospel (Revelation 2:1–4).

Learn More: Acts 18:21, 24; 20:16–17 / 1 Corinthians 15:32; 16:8 / Ephesians 1:1

EPHRAIM

Jesus. . .went thence unto a country near to the wilderness, into a city called Ephraim. JOHN 11:54

This village is mentioned only once in the Bible. All we know about it is that it was a safe haven for Jesus during the closing days of His earthly ministry. Here He withdrew with His disciples after raising Lazarus from the dead when His enemies began to plot His death.

How long did Jesus stay in Ephraim before emerging with His disciples to face His enemies? Apparently not very long, since John's Gospel tells us in the very next verse that it was almost time for the Jewish Passover celebration to begin (John 11:55). It was during that Passover celebration that Jesus was crucified, becoming the sacrificial Lamb of God to deliver people from the curse of sin. Perhaps Jesus retreated to Ephraim to await the beginning of this Passover event in nearby Jerusalem.

The exact location of Ephraim is unknown. Some people believe the modern Israeli town of Taiyibeh marks the site today. If so, this would place Jesus' withdrawal from Jerusalem about a day's walk away, since Taiyibeh is about fourteen miles northeast of the Holy City.

ESHCOL BROOK AND VALLEY

The place was called the brook Eshcol. NUMBERS 13:24

This little stream is famous because of a bunch of grapes. Here is where the scouts sent into Canaan by Moses cut down a large cluster of the fruit. They carried it back to Moses in the wilderness to show the fertility of the land. This cluster was so large and heavy that it had to be carried on a pole by two of the scouts.

This brook has never been identified with certainty. But according to Numbers 13:21–24, it was somewhere in the vicinity of Hebron. A later passage refers to a valley through which this brook apparently flowed (Numbers 32:9).

The soil and climate of Israel were ideal for growing grapes, and vineyards abounded here in Bible times. Grape vineyards still grow today in this section of modern Israel. To the people of Israel, for every person to sit "under his vine and under his fig tree" (Micah 4:4) was a symbol of peace and prosperity.

Learn More: Deuteronomy 1:24–26

ETHIOPIA

So the Lord smote the Ethiopians before Asa, and before Judah. 2 CHRONICLES 14:12

Ethiopia was an ancient African nation south of Egypt. During the days of King Asa of Judah, the Ethiopians went on the attack with an army of more than one million soldiers. Seriously outnumbered, the godly king turned to the Lord for help.

"In thy name we go against this multitude," Asa prayed. "O LORD, thou art our God; let not man prevail against thee" (2 Chronicles 14:11). The Lord honored Asa's prayer and brought victory to His people.

Across much of its history, Ethiopia was controlled by Egypt. For this reason, they are often mentioned together in the Bible (see Ezekiel 30:4). In some circumstances, Ethiopians even served as hired soldiers in the Egyptian army (2 Chronicles 12:3). Another name for Ethiopia in the Bible is Cush (Isaiah 11:11).

Perhaps the most famous Ethiopian in the Bible is the eunuch who was baptized by Philip the evangelist. He served as royal treasurer under Candace, queen of Ethiopia.

Learn More: Numbers 12:1 / Esther 1:1 / Job 28:19 / Isaiah 20:4 / Jeremiah 13:23 / Nahum 3:9 / Acts 8:27

EZION GEBER

King Solomon made a navy of ships in Eziongeber. 1 KINGS 9:26

This port city on the Red Sea was the southernmost city in the land of Israel during King Solomon's administration. From this thriving urban center, ships in the king's navy conducted trade with many nations of the ancient world, including Africa, Arabia, and the Far East. These commercial activities contributed to Israel's prosperity and made Solomon the wealthiest ruler of his time (1 Kings 10:23).

Archaeological exploration at this site reveals that Ezion Geber was also the center of a thriving smelting industry during Solomon's reign. Scholars believe the wind patterns of the area made it an ideal location for the mining and processing of copper.

Near Ezion Geber was the Israelite city of Eloth. These two cities have evolved into a modern resort city known as Eilat. Tourists from Israel and throughout the world travel here to enjoy its abundant sunshine and pristine beaches and to scuba dive in its clear waters.

Learn More: Numbers 33:35–36: Ezion-Gaber / 1 Kings 22:48 / 2 Chronicles 8:17

GADARA

They arrived at the country of the Gadarenes, which is over against Galilee. LUKE 8:26

This verse describes one of Jesus' rare visits to Gentile territory in the region east of the Jordan River. Gadara was one of the cities of the Decapolis, a territory with ten cities populated by people of non-Jewish background.

At this city Jesus encountered a demon-possessed man who lived among the tombs. The townspeople apparently had exiled him to this lonely place because they feared his erratic behavior. But Jesus was not afraid of this unfortunate outcast, who claimed to be inhabited by legions of evil spirits.

When Jesus cast out these demons, He allowed them to enter a herd of pigs on a nearby mountain. They rushed into the Sea of Galilee and were drowned. This chaotic scene caused great fear among the residents of the town, and they begged Jesus and His disciples to leave their territory (Luke 8:37).

Excavations at this site have uncovered two outdoor theaters and a street lined with massive columns. These show that Gadara was a major Roman city during New Testament times.

Learn More: Matthew 8:28: Gergesenes / Luke 8:26, 37

GALATIA

He. . .went over all the country of Galatia and Phrygia in order. ACTS 18:23

Galatia was a region in central Asia Minor (modern Turkey) that contained several cities visited by the apostle Paul and Barnabas on the first missionary journey. These cities were Antioch of Pisidia, Iconium, Lystra, and Derbe (Acts 13–14). Paul visited these cities again in his later evangelistic tours (Acts 16:1).

Several years after Paul founded churches throughout Galatia, he received disturbing news that these believers were wavering in their commitment to the truths of the Gospel he had taught them. False teachers were trying to convince them that Gentiles had to undergo the Jewish ritual of circumcision before they could be saved. Paul declared in his letter to the Galatians that faith alone in Jesus Christ was necessary for salvation.

Galatians is often called the "epistle of Christian liberty" because law-keeping is no longer the basis of salvation. In one of its most famous passages, the apostle declared: "Stand fast therefore in the liberty wherewith Christ hath made us free, and be not entangled again with the yoke of bondage" (Galatians 5:1).

Learn More: 1 Corinthians 16:1 / Galatians 1:2 / 2 Timothy 4:10 / 1 Peter 1:1

GALILEE

Jesus went about all Galilee, teaching in their synagogues. MATTHEW 4:23

Most people associate the word *Galilee* with the Sea of Galilee, the lake in northern Israel around which so much of Jesus' ministry took place. But Galilee is also a distinct *region* of the Holy Land.

In New Testament times, Galilee was one of three provinces into which Israel was divided for administrative purposes by the Roman government (the other two were Judaea and Samaria). The region of Galilee ranged from high mountains in the northern section to gently sloping hills and fertile valleys in the southern part of the territory. Important towns in this territory during Jesus' earthly ministry included Cana, Bethsaida, Capernaum, Nazareth, Magdala, and Tiberias.

Many people of Gentile, or non-Jewish, descent lived in this Roman province, so it was often referred to as "Galilee of the Gentiles" (Matthew 4:15). Thus, Jesus' years in this territory signified that His ministry was intended for all people and all nations, not just the Jewish people of His native land.

Learn More: 1 Kings 9:11 / Matthew 21:11 / Mark 1:28 / Luke 4:44 / John 2:11 / Acts 1:11

GATH

A champion out of the camp of the Philistines, named Goliath, of Gath. 1 SAMUEL 17:4

This city was one of the five major cities of the Philistines, a tribal people who were fierce enemies of Israel. Most people know it as the home of Goliath, the nine-foot-tall giant felled by David.

This against-all-odds victory proved that the Lord didn't need weapons to rescue His people. A shepherd boy with a sling succeeded because he faced the giant in the name of "the LORD of hosts, the God of the armies of Israel" (1 Samuel 17:45).

This city is thought to be one of the places where the descendants of a giant named Anak lived during Old Testament times. The size of these people struck fear into the hearts of ten of the spies who were sent by Moses to explore the land of Canaan (Numbers 13:32–33).

On the site of this ancient city, archaeologists have discovered a piece of pottery inscribed with a name similar to "Goliath." This has been dubbed the "Goliath Shard." It doesn't prove the giant's existence, but it does give evidence of the culture of the Philistines who lived here during David's time.

Learn More: 1 Samuel 21:10; 27:3 / 2 Samuel 21:22 / 1 Kings 2:40 / 1 Chronicles 20:6 / Micah 1:10

GAZA

And it was told the Gazites, saying, Samson is come hither. JUDGES 16:2

Gaza was a Philistine city where the judge Samson demonstrated his superhuman strength. His enemies thought they had him trapped inside the city. But Samson ripped the gate out of the city wall and carried it all the way to Hebron, about fifty miles away (Judges 16:1–3).

Later, the Philistines managed to capture Samson when Delilah revealed the secret of his strength—his long hair. They cut his hair while he was asleep and imprisoned him at the city of Gaza. When Samson's hair grew back and his strength returned, he took revenge against his enemies and committed suicide by toppling the temple of their pagan god (Judges 16:30).

Gaza was also associated with the evangelist Philip in New Testament times. Commanded by the Lord to travel toward Gaza, Philip met a man who was reading from a scroll of the book of Isaiah. Philip led him to understand that he was reading about the long-expected Messiah. The man professed faith in Christ, and Philip baptized him in a nearby pool (Acts 8:26–38).

Learn More: Genesis 10:19 / Judges 1:18 / 2 Kings 18:8 / Jeremiah 47:5 / Zechariah 9:5

GERAR

Abraham. . .sojourned in Gerar. GENESIS 20:1

Since Abraham was a stranger in the land of Canaan, he probably moved from place to place to find grass and water for his herds of livestock. The place in southern Canaan known as Gerar was only one of several places where he "sojourned," or lived temporarily, while in this land that God had promised to him and his descendants.

While in Gerar, Abraham told the king of this territory that his wife, Sarah, was his sister. Abraham feared the king might kill him and take Sarah into his harem because of her beauty. This did not happen, and when the king eventually discovered the truth, he scolded Abraham for his deceit.

After Abraham died, his son Isaac grazed his flocks in the area around Gerar. He and the Philistine residents squabbled over the rights to several local wells. Because Isaac was a foreigner with no property rights, he had to settle for a well in an undisputed plot of land (Genesis 26:12–33).

Gerar may have been little more than a crossroads settlement when Abraham and Isaac lived here. Later, it developed into a larger city that has been excavated in recent years by archaeologists.

Learn More: Genesis 10:19; 20:2 / 2 Chronicles 14:13–14

GETHSEMANE, GARDEN OF

Then cometh Jesus with them unto a place called Gethsemane. MATTHEW 26:36

This garden on the Mount of Olives outside Jerusalem is where Jesus prayed on the night of His betrayal and arrest. Here He faced the temptation to reject His divine mission as Savior of the world and avoid the suffering of the cross. But He was strengthened through prayer to God the Father to declare, "Not my will, but thine, be done" (Luke 22:42).

To modern visitors, the most striking features of this little garden are its ancient olive trees. These are probably not the actual trees that grew here in Jesus' time. But they could have sprung from the roots of old trees from that era. Whether or not they can be traced to the first century, their gnarled and weathered trunks remind visitors of the agony that Jesus experienced when He prayed here almost two thousand years ago.

A church known as the Church of All Nations occupies the site of Gethsemane today. This name recognizes the contributions from people in sixteen different countries that enabled the church to be built in 1924. Inside the building hangs a painting of Jesus in prayer, flanked by giant olive trees.

Learn More: Mark 14:32

GEZER

And Solomon built Gezer. 1 KINGS 9:17

This city sat on the main road between Jerusalem and Joppa. Gezer changed hands several times before King Solomon of Israel turned it into a heavily fortified outpost to provide protection from enemy attacks.

The Canaanites held the city until Joshua drove them out (Joshua 12:12). Then Gezer apparently fell to Philistia, only to be taken by King David in his campaign against the Philistines some years later (1 Chronicles 20:4).

Then the Egyptians apparently controlled the city for a time. Finally, King Solomon came into possession of Gezer when he married the daughter of the pharaoh of Egypt to seal a political alliance (1 Kings 9:16).

Excavations at the site reveal that Solomon turned Gezer into one of the most heavily fortified cities in the ancient world. It featured a massive gate complex with a double wall. Huge stone partitions and tons of rubble were piled between these walls for extra strength. This complex would have presented a challenge to any besieging army.

Learn More: Joshua 10:33 / 1 Chronicles 6:67; 20:4

GIBEAH

And Saul also went home to Gibeah. 1 SAMUEL 10:26

This city is notable because of its association with Saul, first king of Israel. Here he was born in the territory of the tribe of Benjamin, and here he established his headquarters after he was anointed as leader of the nation by the prophet Samuel.

Before Saul's time, the city of Gibeah was destroyed during a civil war between the tribe of Benjamin and the other tribes of the nation. They were outraged because the Benjaminites took no action against a tribal member who had brutalized, murdered, and dismembered a prostitute.

King Saul apparently later rebuilt and fortified Gibeah and made it his capital city. Excavations at the site have identified the remains of both the city destroyed before Saul's time and the king's rebuilt fortified outpost.

When modern Holy Land visitors see the ruins of Gibeah, they understand the meaning behind its name—"hill." The city's hilltop location made it easy to defend, and it gave its defenders a panoramic view of the surrounding countryside.

Learn More: Judges 19–20 / 1 Samuel 14:16; 15:34 / 2 Samuel 6:3 / Isaiah 10:29 / Hosea 9:9

GIBEON

Joshua made peace with them [residents of Gibeon]. JOSHUA 9:15

This ancient Canaanite city is a case study in trickery and self-preservation. Other Canaanite towns were falling to the invading Israelites. The leaders of Gibeon realized this would happen to them unless they acted quickly. So they made a treaty with the Israelites by convincing Joshua they were not Canaanites but were residents of a distant land.

This agreement kept Gibeon from being destroyed by Joshua's forces. Even when the truth came out, the Israelites were bound by the terms of the treaty. Joshua did save face to some degree by pressing the Gibeonites into service as woodcutters and water carriers for the Israelites (Joshua 9:26–27).

Excavations at ancient Gibeon have uncovered a huge well that descends through solid rock to a depth of eighty-two feet. At the bottom of the shaft is a tunnel that leads to an underground spring. This well provided water for a wine-making industry, and the tunnel may have provided access to a water source in the event of a prolonged siege by an enemy army.

This huge well may be the same as "the great waters. . .in Gibeon" mentioned by the prophet Jeremiah (Jeremiah 41:12).

Learn More: 2 Samuel 2:12–16; 21:1–9 / 1 Kings 3:3–15 / Nehemiah 3:6–7

GILBOA, MOUNT

They found Saul and his three sons fallen in mount Gilboa. 1 SAMUEL 31:8

This mountain range in northern Israel is where King Saul and his sons lost their lives in a fierce battle with the Philistines. Severely wounded, the king feared he would be tortured if he fell into the hands of his enemies. So he committed suicide by falling on his own sword (1 Samuel 31:3–6).

This was a tragic conclusion to the reign of the first king of Israel. He began with great promise but let his pride and jealousy cloud his judgment until they brought him to this shameful end.

David, who succeeded Saul as king, mourned these deaths in a lament known as the Song of the Bow. "Ye mountains of Gilboa," he cried, "let there be no dew, neither let there be rain, upon you. . .for there the shield of the mighty is vilely cast away" (2 Samuel 1:21).

This tragic event contrasts sharply with the mountains themselves. They are serenely beautiful, offering breathtaking views of the surrounding valleys. Visitors enjoy the cool, tranquil setting, with its hiking trails, forests, and picnic areas.

Learn More: 2 Samuel 1:6 / 1 Chronicles 10:1–6

GILEAD

Let this land be given unto thy servants for a possession. NUMBERS 32:5

The region of Gilead contained many fertile valleys with lush grasslands. This impressed the tribes of Reuben and Gad when the Israelites explored this area of the promised land. These grasslands were ideal for their livestock, so they asked Moses to allow them to settle here rather than in Canaan on the western side of the Jordan River.

Moses agreed to their request. But he made them promise to support the other ten tribes militarily when they went to war with the Canaanites. Eventually, half the tribe of Manasseh also settled in Gilead alongside Reuben and Gad.

The region of Gilead was also noted for its spices and perfumes that it exported to other countries. A popular ointment for the treatment of wounds was known as the balm of Gilead. The prophet Jeremiah asked, "Is there no balm in Gilead; is there no physician there?" (Jeremiah 8:22). This rhetorical question implied that nothing—not even Gilead's famous medicine—could heal God's people unless they gave up their idolatry and turned back to the one true God.

Learn More: Genesis 37:25 / Numbers 32:1 / Deuteronomy 3:16 / Judges 11:1 / Psalm 108:8

GILGAL

Those twelve stones, which they took out of Jordan, did Joshua pitch in Gilgal. JOSHUA 4:20

When the Israelites entered Canaan, they set up camp at a place called Gilgal. God had enabled them to cross the Jordan River at this point by stopping the flow of the water. From the river they selected twelve stones to represent the twelve tribes of Israel. At Gilgal they set up these stones to memorialize God's promise to give this land to His people.

Gilgal became the base of operations for the Israelites for several generations while the people fanned out to settle the land. Also at Gilgal, Joshua circumcised all male Israelites to signify their covenant with the Lord. Apparently this ritual had not been practiced during their wilderness-wandering years. The first Passover observed in their new homeland also occurred at Gilgal.

In later years, when the people of Israel asked for a king to rule over them, Gilgal was closely associated with the reign of Saul, their first king. Gilgal was the site of Saul's coronation.

Learn More: Joshua 5:8–10; 10:6–9 / 1 Samuel 7:16; 11:15; 13:7–14 / 2 Samuel 19:15–18 / 2 Kings 2:1 / Amos 5:5

GOSHEN

Israel dwelt in the land of Egypt, in the country of Goshen. GENESIS 47:27

This territory in southern Egypt between the Nile River and the Red Sea is where the Israelites lived during their time in Egypt. The leaders of Israel requested permission from the pharaoh of Egypt to settle here. Goshen's extensive grasslands provided adequate food for their large herds (Genesis 47:1–6). The pharaoh had no objection to their living in this territory because the Egyptians considered taking care of livestock an abominable vocation (Genesis 46:34).

Happily settled in Goshen, the Israelites increased dramatically in numbers until they became a threat to Egypt's national security. Then they were enslaved and forced to work on the pharaoh's construction projects. When the Lord sent plagues against the Egyptians to convince the pharaoh to release the Israelite captives, Goshen was miraculously spared from these calamities.

The storage cities of Pithom and Rameses, built by Israelite slave labor, were located in Goshen. Rameses was the starting point for the Exodus when the Israelites finally left Egypt under the leadership of Moses.

Learn More: Genesis 45:10; 50:8 / Exodus 1:11; 8:22 / Numbers 33:3

GREECE

He came into Greece, and there abode three months. ACTS 20:2-3

This is the only place in the New Testament where Greece is mentioned by name, although the apostle Paul had a fruitful ministry in this sophisticated nation of the ancient world. He made a brief visit to Athens, where he addressed the learned men of this Greek city. While few people responded positively to this initial visit, he later returned to Greece for an extended ministry in the city of Corinth. This time he established a thriving church that shed the light of the Gospel throughout Greece and beyond.

Before Paul's time the Greek general Alexander the Great had spread Greek customs and culture throughout the nations he conquered. This resulted in the adoption of Greek as the universal language of the time. So wherever Paul traveled throughout the Mediterranean world, his hearers could understand his preaching of the central truths of the Gospel.

Another name for Greece in the Old Testament was *Javan*. In the New Testament, the word *Greeks* may refers to citizens of Greece and to Greek-speaking Jews, as well as to Gentiles, or non-Jews (Mark 7:26).

Learn More: Isaiah 66:19 / Ezekiel 27:13 / Zechariah 9:13 / Joel 3:6 / Acts 19:17 / 1 Corinthians 1:23

HARAN

They came unto Haran, and dwelt there. GENESIS 11:31

This city in Mesopotamia is where Abram (later to be called Abraham) lived with his family, along with his father, Terah, for several years. Terah eventually died in Haran, and Abram left the city, at God's call, to settle in a distant place that God promised to show him (Genesis 12:1). This place turned out to be Canaan, several hundred miles south of Haran, which God promised to Abram and his descendants (Genesis 12:2–7).

In later years, Abraham's grandson Jacob plotted to gain his father's blessing, although it belonged to his older twin, Esau. When Esau threatened to kill him, Jacob fled from Canaan to live with his mother's brother Laban in Haran. Here Jacob spent several years working for Laban, eventually marrying two of his daughters before returning to Canaan.

During its campaign of world conquest, the Assyrians captured Haran (2 Kings 19:12). This ancient site is occupied today by a small Arab village known as Charran.

Learn More: Genesis 27:43; 28:10; 29:4 / Acts 7:2, 4: Charran

HAZOR

He burnt Hazor with fire. Joshua 11:11

This city about ten miles north of the Sea of Galilee was an important fortress of the Canaanites. Under Joshua's leadership, the Israelites burned it and killed all its inhabitants.

Later, during the period of the judges, the Canaanites managed to rebuild and repopulate the city. From this command post, they waged war against the Israelites. But again the Canaanites under Jabin, king of Hazor, and his general, Sisera, were defeated—this time by Israelite forces under Deborah and Barak (Judges 4:1–16).

In later centuries King Solomon built Hazor into a heavily fortified military outpost to protect his kingdom from attack from the north. Excavations at Hazor have uncovered the remains of a massive city gate from Solomon's time—a feature similar to his other fortified cities of Megiddo in central Israel and Gezer in the south.

The site of ancient Hazor is one of the largest and most important archaeological projects in the Holy Land. The dig and the surrounding area are part of Israel's national park system.

Learn More: 1 Samuel 12:9 / 1 Kings 9:15 / 2 Kings 15:29 / Jeremiah 49:30, 33

HEBRON

Abraham buried Sarah his wife in. . .Hebron in the land of Canaan. Genesis 23:19

This city about twenty miles west of the Dead Sea is known as the place where Abraham was buried. Near here he bought a plot of ground with a cave that became the final resting place for himself and other members of his family.

This burial place is known as the cave of Machpelah. Here Abraham and his wife, Sarah, were buried; followed later by his son, Isaac, and Isaac's wife, Rebekah; and Abraham's grandson, Jacob, and Jacob's wife, Leah (Genesis 49:29–33).

Hebron is associated with several other important events in the Bible. David made this his capital city for the first seven and one-half years of his reign. Here all the tribal leaders met and proclaimed David king of all Israel. From Hebron, Absalom plotted his rebellion against his father, David. And even before David's time, Caleb received Hebron as part of his share of the land of Canaan.

Today a modern Muslim city has been built up around the cave of Machpelah. It is such a revered site in Muslim tradition that entrance to the cave is forbidden.

Learn More: Genesis 13:18; 37:14 / Numbers 13:22 / Joshua 10:39; 14:13–15 / 2 Samuel 2:11; 5:1–5; 15:10

HERMON, MOUNT

As the dew of Hermon. . . Psalm 133:3

The peak of Mount Hermon on the northern border of Israel was so noticeable that it inspired this stirring tribute from the psalmist. He had seen the heavy dews that fell on the mountain and the surrounding area. He compared these dews to the harmony that should exist among God's people: "How wonderful and pleasant it is when brothers live together in harmony! . . . Harmony is as refreshing as the dew from Mount Hermon that falls on the mountains of Zion" (Psalm 133:1, 3 NLT).

The highest point in Israel, Mount Hermon can be seen on a clear day from the Dead Sea, about 120 miles away. It is the only mountain in Israel that has snow on its summit during the winter and spring months. The snow lingers even into the summer in some of its shaded ravines.

In Old Testament times, this mountain was considered the northern limits of the land promised to the Israelites. Today, Israel occupies part of the territory on its slopes, but the highest peaks are within the borders of Syria and Lebanon.

Learn More: Deuteronomy 3:8 / Joshua 11:16–17 / 1 Chronicles 5:23 / Psalm 89:12 / Song of Solomon 4:8

HINNOM VALLEY

Moreover [Ahaz] burnt incense in the valley of the son of Hinnom. 2 Chronicles 28:3

This king of Judah committed one of the worst atrocities possible when he sacrificed his children to the pagan god Molech in the Hinnom Valley outside Jerusalem. In later years Ahaz's grandson, King Manasseh, continued the same heinous sin.

The ritual of sacrificing one's children to a pagan god had been practiced centuries before by the Canaanites when they inhabited the land. But this ghastly practice was expressly forbidden by the Lord, and was not to be practiced among His people (Leviticus 20:1–5).

The Hinnom Valley was a garbage dump for the city of Jerusalem. Sometimes the piles of waste caught fire and gave off foul odors and clouds of smoke. The valley became an image of hell, the place of eternal punishment for the wicked. The Greek word for Hinnom is *Gehenna*, the word Jesus used when He declared that the scribes and Pharisees would not escape "the damnation of hell" (Matthew 23:33).

Another word for the valley of Hinnom is Topheth or Tophet, a term meaning "inferno" and derived from the burning garbage piles on this site.

Learn More: 2 Chronicles 33:6 / Joshua 18:16 / Nehemiah 11:30 / Jeremiah 7:32

HOR, MOUNT

Aaron the priest went up into mount Hor. . .and died there. Numbers 33:38

Aaron, the first high priest of Israel, helped his brother, Moses, lead the Israelites out of slavery in Egypt. While traveling toward Canaan, Aaron died on Mount Hor, a mountain peak in the wilderness that has never been identified with certainty.

Some scholars believe Mount Hor was on the eastern side of the Dead Sea near Mount Nebo, the place where Moses later died (Deuteronomy 34:1, 5). But a site southwest of the Dead Sea is more likely. The Bible indicates that the entire community of Israel "journeyed from Kadesh, and came unto Mount Hor" (Numbers 20:22) before Aaron's death. This suggests that Hor was just a short distance from Kadesh.

Muslims accept the first suggested location for Mount Hor—the eastern side of the Dead Sea, in the territory of the modern state of Jordan. For centuries they have trekked to a shrine dedicated to Aaron on a mountain that they call Jebel Haroun ("Mountain of Aaron"). This mountain towers more than six thousand feet above the Dead Sea. At its summit is a little shrine with a white dome said to mark the site of Aaron's tomb.

Learn More: Numbers 33:37–41; 34:7–8 / Deuteronomy 32:50

ISRAEL

So Israel rebelled against the house of David unto this day. 1 Kings 12:19

After the nation of Israel divided into two factions following the death of King Solomon, the northern kingdom retained the name *Israel* (1 Kings 12:16–17). The southern kingdom was referred to after this event as Judah. Israel had by far the largest territory of the two nations, since it encompassed the region allotted originally to ten northern tribes. Judah included the area in and around Jerusalem held by the two southern tribes, Judah and Benjamin.

Israel got off to a poor start when King Jeroboam I established calf idols at opposite ends of his country. He hoped these sites would pull his people away from loyalty to the temple in Jerusalem. This led to widespread idolatry among the people of Israel throughout their history. This tragedy is best exemplified by King Ahab, who, with his wife, Jezebel, encouraged worship of the pagan god Baal among his subjects (1 Kings 16:30–33).

After stumbling from one bad king to another for about two centuries, the nation of Israel fell to the Assyrian army. The writer of 2 Kings placed the blame for Israel's downfall right where it belonged: because of their sin and rebellion against God, "the Lord was very angry with Israel, and removed them out of his sight" (2 Kings 17:18).

Learn More: 1 Kings 14:14; 15:16; 19:18 / 2 Kings 3:6; 10:32

JABBOK RIVER

And he. . .passed over the ford Jabbok. GENESIS 32:22

Jacob crossed this small river soon after a reunion with his estranged brother, Esau. While camped along its banks during the night, Jacob wrestled with an angel until dawn.

During this struggle the angel knocked Jacob's hip out of joint. Then the angel changed Jacob's name to *Israel*, meaning "prince of God" or "he who strives with God." The angel declared, "As a prince hast thou power with God and with men, and hast prevailed" (Genesis 32:28).

To commemorate this spiritual event, Jacob named the site *Peniel*, meaning "face of God." He had survived this struggle because of the Lord's favor. This event signified that the covenant between God and His special people, the Israelites, was still in effect. From that point on, the nation that sprang from the twelve sons of Jacob was known as Israel.

The Jabbok River runs through a deep ravine for about sixty-five miles before emptying into the Jordan River from the east. In later years, it served as the boundary between the tribe of Gad and the half tribe of Manasseh.

Learn More: Numbers 21:24 / Deuteronomy 3:16 / Judges 11:22

JABESH GILEAD

The valiant men. . .came to Jabesh, and burnt them there. 1 SAMUEL 31:12

The town of Jabesh, also known as Jabesh Gilead, was located near the Sea of Galilee just east of the Jordan River. When King Saul of Israel and his sons were killed in a battle with the Philistines, the citizens of Jabesh retrieved their bodies and brought them to their town for cremation and burial. The Philistines had insulted the king and all of Israel by hanging their bodies on the wall of a nearby city.

Through this act of respect, the residents of Jabesh Gilead returned the favor that Saul had extended to them several years before. When the Ammonites besieged Jabesh Gilead, the king raised an army and came to their rescue. At that time Saul had just been selected by Samuel as the first king of Israel. This decisive action solidified his role as the ruler over all the tribes of Israel (1 Samuel 11:1–15).

After David became king of Israel, he expressed his thanks to the people of Jabesh Gilead for giving Saul and his sons a decent burial.

Learn More: Judges 21:12 / 2 Samuel 2:4–5; 21:12 / 1 Chronicles 10:11–12

JEHOSHAPHAT, VALLEY OF

Let the heathen be wakened, and come up to the valley of Jehoshaphat. JOEL 3:12

The prophet Joel declared that God would judge the nations in the end time at this valley near Jerusalem. The name *Jehoshaphat*, meaning "God shall judge," emphasizes this theme. The site is believed to be part of the Kidron Valley that runs along Jerusalem's eastern side between the walls of the Old City and the Mount of Olives.

In the past many people were buried in tombs on the slopes of this valley. This gives the site a feeling of gloom to modern tourists, adding to its reputation as a place of judgment. One of the tombs in the area is that of Absalom, the son of King David. Absalom was killed when he tried to take the kingship from his father in an armed rebellion (2 Samuel 18:14). This valley may also have been known as the king's dale, where Absalom had previously selected a plot for his own burial (2 Samuel 18:18).

The prophet Joel also appears to refer to this place as the "valley of decision" (Joel 3:14). Some interpreters believe Joel was not referring to a literal place but was speaking symbolically of God's worldwide judgment at the end of time.

Learn More: Joel 3:2

JERICHO

The Lord said unto Joshua, See, I have given into thine hand Jericho. JOSHUA 6:2

This city not far from the Jordan River will always be known as the first Canaanite stronghold to fall to the Israelites when they entered the promised land. The battle strategy for its defeat came straight from the Lord Himself.

Joshua's forces marched around the city for six consecutive days. Then, on the seventh day, they made a loud noise by shouting and blowing trumpets. The walls of this heavily fortified city collapsed, making its defenders easy prey for the Israelites. Joshua then pronounced a curse against the city, directing that it should never be rebuilt (Joshua 6:26).

Archaeological digs at Jericho have revealed that it was one of the oldest cities in the world. Debris from successive settlements on the site reached a depth of seventy feet.

Over time a new city known as New Testament Jericho was built about two miles from the city that Joshua destroyed. This newer town is where Jesus healed blind Bartimaeus and confronted the unscrupulous tax collector Zacchaeus.

Learn More: 2 Kings 2:5 / Mark 10:46 / Luke 19:1 / Hebrews 11:30

JERUSALEM

If I prefer not Jerusalem above my chief joy. PSALM 137:6

These words from the psalmist show how the people of Israel loved Jerusalem, their religious and political capital. The city is still revered today by three world religions—Christianity, Judaism, and Islam—so it deserves its reputation as the "Holy City."

King David captured the city from the Jebusites about 1000 BC and turned it into his capital. His son Solomon built the temple in Jerusalem as the center of worship for the Jewish people about 950 BC. About five centuries later, the city fell to the Babylonians, and its leading citizens were taken into exile.

After the Persians defeated Babylon, Jewish exiles were allowed to return to their homeland and rebuild Jerusalem. Centuries later, in New Testament times, Christ wept over the city because of its spiritual indifference. He entered Jerusalem as a victorious spiritual leader and was crucified on a hill just outside the city wall.

After Jesus ascended into heaven, the church was launched in Jerusalem, where it experienced spectacular growth. The apostle John described the future heavenly city as "new Jerusalem" (Revelation 21:2).

Learn More: 2 Samuel 5:6–9 / Jeremiah 39:1–8 / Nehemiah 12:27–28 / Matthew 21:9–10

JEZREEL, CITY OF

The dogs shall eat Jezebel by the wall of Jezreel. 1 KINGS 21:23

Jezebel was the wicked wife of Ahab, king of the northern kingdom of Israel. She plotted to have an innocent man killed so the king could confiscate his property (1 Kings 21:1–16). The Lord declared through the prophet Elijah that this city in northern Israel would be the place where Jezebel would die for this crime as well as other evil acts she had committed.

It's ironic that *Jezreel*, name of the site of Ahab's summer palace, sounds a lot like *Jezebel*. She was thrown to her death over the city wall, where dogs ate her body. The instrument of God's judgment was a man named Jehu, who took the throne after assassinating Ahab's son and successor, Joram (2 Kings 9:1–24). In later years the prophet Hosea named his son Jezreel to symbolize God's judgment against Jehu for his murder of members of Joram's family.

During Ahab's reign, Samaria was his capital city, but Jezreel, about thirty miles away, was the site of his summer palace. The city's name was applied to a large nearby plain, the valley of Jezreel (Joshua 17:16).

Learn More: 1 Samuel 29:11 / 1 Kings 18:46 / 2 Kings 9:10, 30; 10:11 / Hosea 1:4

JEZREEL, VALLEY OF

Then all the Midianites. . .pitched in the valley of Jezreel. JUDGES 6:33

This valley south of the Sea of Galilee is where an army allied against the Israelites camped in Gideon's time. Here he defeated this superior military force with only three hundred warriors, thanks to the Lord's intervention (Judges 7:15–23).

This large plain is a striking contrast to Israel's mostly hilly terrain. The different names by which it is known also make the Jezreel Valley a biblical anomaly. It is referred to as the Plain of Tabor (1 Samuel 10:3) because Mount Tabor is the only mountain that rises up from its otherwise flat landscape. The prophet Zechariah called it the valley of Megiddon because the city of Megiddo overlooked the valley (Zechariah 12:11).

Jezreel is also known as the Plain of Esdraelon—the Greek equivalent of the Hebrew word. But no matter what it's called, this valley has always served as the natural dividing line between the regions of Samaria and Galilee in northern Israel.

A major trade route passed through the valley of Jezreel. Many nations have battled over control of this commercial highway between Egypt in the south and Mesopotamia to the north.

Learn More: 2 Chronicles 35:22 / Hosea 1:5

JOPPA

I was in the city of Joppa praying: and in a trance I saw a vision. ACTS 11:5

At this city on the shore of the Mediterranean Sea, the apostle Peter had a revolutionary vision. The Lord revealed that the Jewish food laws Peter had always observed were no longer in effect. This meant that Gentiles were not second-class citizens, as the Jews believed, but people whom God loved and accepted.

A few days later, Peter acted on this insight by baptizing a Gentile named Cornelius along with several members of his household (Acts 10:44–48). From that point on, the church was no longer restricted to Jews. It was open to all people.

Joppa was the only Israelite port on the Mediterranean Sea. In Old Testament times, cedar logs from Lebanon north of Israel were shipped by sea to Joppa, then hauled to Jerusalem and used in construction of the Jewish temple (2 Chronicles 2:11–12, 16).

This ancient city is also associated with one of the most famous runaways in history. Here the prophet Jonah caught a ship to escape God's command to preach in the pagan city of Nineveh, Assyria.

Learn More: Joshua 19:46: Japho / Jonah 1:3 / Acts 9:36–38, 43; 10:5; 11:13

JORDAN RIVER

Jesus came from Nazareth of Galilee, and was baptized of John in Jordan. MARK 1:9

When Jesus launched His public ministry, He asked to be baptized by John the Baptist in the Jordan River. Through this act, Jesus identified with John's message about the kingdom of God and set an example for all believers.

The Jordan runs the entire length of Israel, descending from about 1,500 feet above sea level to the lowest point on earth at the Dead Sea. This sharp fall has given the river its name, which means "the descender."

The Jordan is tiny in comparison to the major rivers of the world. This is why Naaman the Syrian protested against dipping himself in its waters in order to be cured of his leprosy. But he finally agreed to do so and was miraculously healed.

Long before Naaman's time, the Jordan played a central role in the entrance of God's people into Canaan. God miraculously stopped the river's flow, and they crossed safely into the land that God had promised to Abraham and his descendants (Joshua 3:14–16). This crossing was similar to the Israelites' miraculous escape across the Red Sea from the pursuing Egyptian army (Exodus 14:15–28).

Learn More: Genesis 13:10 / Numbers 32:29 / Deuteronomy 31:2 / Judges 8:4 / 2 Kings 5:14

JUDAEA

Ye shall be witnesses unto me both in Jerusalem, and in all Judaea. ACTS 1:8

Jesus spoke these words to His disciples after His resurrection, just before He ascended into heaven. His charge, often referred to as the Great Commission, left no doubt that He expected them to continue His work.

Judaea, in the southern part of Israel, was one of three provinces into which the Roman authorities had divided the land for administrative purposes. The other two districts were Samaria and Galilee. Jesus made it clear that their witness for Him should begin close to home—in Judaea in and around Jerusalem—then spread northward into Samaria, and finally to the rest of the world.

This is exactly what happened when the church was born in Jerusalem on the day of Pentecost (Acts 2:1–8). Next the Gospel spread into Samaria, then to Antioch in Gentile territory, and finally to both Jews and Gentiles throughout the Roman Empire.

Judaea and its city of Jerusalem stood at the center of the Jewish religious establishment during Jesus' ministry. The opposition of these leaders to His teaching and healing ministry eventually led to Jesus' execution on a Roman cross.

Learn More: Matthew 2:1 / Luke 1:65 / John 11:7 / Acts 15:1 / 1 Thessalonians 2:14

JUDAH

Rehoboam. . .assembled all the house of Judah. 1 KINGS 12:21

Judah is the name by which the southern Jewish kingdom was known after the united kingdom split into factions after King Solomon's death. The nation of Judah was composed largely of the tribes of Judah and Benjamin, while the rebellious ten northern tribes retained the name of Israel. Judah took its name from Jacob's son, Judah, whose descendants developed into one of the most numerous and influential of the twelve Israelite tribes.

Solomon's son, Rehoboam, was the first king of Judah, and he continued to reign from the capital at Jerusalem (1 Kings 14:21). The most notable and godly kings of Judah were Asa, Josiah, and Hezekiah.

The nation of Judah eventually drifted into idolatry, turning a deaf ear to great prophets such as Isaiah and Jeremiah, who tried to bring them back to worship of the one true God. Judah was overrun and taken into exile by the Babylonians about 587 BC. A remnant returned to rebuild Jerusalem about 530 BC (2 Chronicles 36:20–23).

Learn More: 1 Kings 14:22; 19:3 / 2 Kings 8:19 / 2 Chronicles 14:4–5 / Ezra 1:5 / Isaiah 1:1 / Jeremiah 7:30

KADESH

And they went and came to Moses. . .to Kadesh. NUMBERS 13:26

This site in the wilderness south of the Dead Sea is where Moses sent scouts into Canaan (Numbers 13:1–16, 25). Their mission was to gather facts about the land, its crops, and the people who lived there. The scouts returned with a good news/bad news report. The land was fertile enough to support the people. But it would have to be taken from powerful tribes who were entrenched behind their walled cities (Numbers 13:28–29).

At this report the people lost faith in God's promise to give them the land of Canaan. They cried out against the Lord for leading them to what they perceived to be a dead end. God punished them for their disobedience by forcing them to wander for forty years in the wilderness until all the doubters were dead (Numbers 14:31–34).

Kadesh is also referred to as Kadesh Barnea. Excavations at the site have uncovered fragments of pottery engraved with Hebrew writing. These link Kadesh with the wilderness wandering period of Israel's history. In later centuries cities were built on this site.

Learn More: Genesis 20:1 / Deuteronomy 1:46 / Joshua 14:6–7 / Psalm 29:8 / Ezekiel 47:19

KIDRON VALLEY AND BROOK

The king also himself passed over the brook Kidron. 2 SAMUEL 15:23

David and members of his court crossed this little stream and its surrounding valley while fleeing Jerusalem to escape the rebellion of the king's son Absalom. This valley runs along the eastern edge of Jerusalem's Old City. Its name means "gloomy" or "dusky place," perhaps because of the many burial sites in the area.

In addition to its function as a burial site, parts of the Kidron Valley were also used as a dumping ground. Priests during the time of King Hezekiah removed pagan objects from the temple. Then the Levites "carted it all out to the Kidron Valley" (2 Chronicles 29:16 NLT).

This dumping continued across the centuries until the debris piled up to an estimated fifty to one hundred feet. Tourists today marvel at the depth of the Kidron gorge, but how much more impressive it would be if they could see all the way to the original valley floor.

The Kidron Brook was actually a wadi, a dry stream bed that drained water after a rain. It has been replaced with an underground culvert beneath a modern road.

Learn More: 1 Kings 2:37 / 2 Kings 23:4 / 2 Chronicles 15:16 / Jeremiah 31:40

KING'S HIGHWAY

We will go by the king's high way. NUMBERS 20:17

The King's Highway was a well-traveled primitive road that passed through Canaan, linking several nations and tribal groups of the ancient world. While traveling through the wilderness toward Canaan, the Israelites asked permission to use this road in the territory of the Edomites but were denied (Numbers 20:18–21).

Later, Moses asked the Amorites to use the same road when the Israelites passed through their territory. When they also refused, he launched an attack and captured several Amorite kings and their fortified cities (Numbers 21:21–35).

This ancient road had existed for several centuries before the Israelites passed through this area. Caravans of merchants carried their goods from Egypt in the south to Syria in the north along this major commercial route. It ran through the territories of the Ammonites, Amorites, Edomites, and Moabites and connected with other ancient roads in southern Canaan that led into Egypt.

Learn More: Numbers 21:22

KIRJATH JEARIM

The men of Kirjathjearim came, and fetched up the ark of the Lord. 1 SAMUEL 7:1

This city's claim to fame is that the ark of the covenant was kept here for twenty years. Kirjath Jearim, it seems, won this honor by default because no other town seemed willing to keep it.

The Philistines had captured the ark from Israel but sent it back after it caused sickness among them (1 Samuel 6:1–12). The residents of the Israelite town of Beth Shemesh agreed to take it, only to send it to Kirjath Jearim after seventy of their citizens were killed when they looked into the ark (1 Samuel 6:13–21).

At Kirjath Jearim the ark was lodged in the home of Abinadab. His son, Eleazar, was charged with its safekeeping. Finally, after twenty years, King David moved the ark to his new capital city, Jerusalem, where it was placed in the tabernacle (2 Samuel 6:1–15).

No one was killed for treating the ark disrespectfully while it was under Eleazar's care. But he was probably relieved when he bid it good-bye on its way to Jerusalem.

Learn More: Judges 18:12 / 1 Chronicles 13:5–6 / 2 Chronicles 1:4

KISHON RIVER

I will draw unto thee to the river Kishon Sisera, the captain of Jabin's army. JUDGES 4:7

The Lord made this promise of victory to Deborah and Barak, two Israelite military champions who faced oppression from the Canaanites. God made it clear that the Kishon River, a stream in northern Israel, would play a crucial role in their success.

These leaders gathered their forces on higher ground near Mount Tabor and waited for the right time to attack. When the Kishon overflowed in a sudden rainstorm, they swooped down on the enemy in the valley along the river. The Canaanite chariots got stuck in the mud, making them an easy target for the Israelite warriors (Judges 4:4–16).

In a hymn known as the Song of Deborah, this courageous leader gave credit to the Lord and the river for this decisive victory: "The stars in their courses fought against Sisera," she sang. "The river of Kishon swept them away, that ancient river, the river Kishon" (Judges 5:20–21).

Several centuries later, this river was associated with the ministry of the prophet Elijah. Here he executed worshippers of Baal after showing the Lord's superiority over this pagan god on Mount Carmel.

Learn More: Judges 4:13 / 1 Kings 18:40

LACHISH

[Sennacherib] himself laid siege against Lachish. 2 CHRONICLES 32:9

King Hezekiah of Judah faced a dire situation. The Assyrian army under King Sennacherib was laying siege to the heavily fortified city of Lachish about thirty miles southwest of Jerusalem. If Lachish fell, Jerusalem would be next on the Assyrian hit list. So the king decided to pay protection money if Sennacherib would leave Jerusalem alone.

The Assyrian ruler took the money and prepared to advance against Jerusalem anyway. Then the Lord stepped in and struck the Assyrian army with a mysterious illness that killed thousands of their number, causing Sennacherib to withdraw (2 Kings 19:35–36).

Lachish was inhabited by the Canaanites at least three centuries before it fell to Joshua and the Israelites (Joshua 10:31–33). Over the centuries it was heavily fortified to provide protection against enemy attacks along Israel's southern border.

This ancient city is one of the most significant archaeological sites in Israel. Discoveries here include early Hebrew writings, known as the Lachish Letters, that shed light on biblical history and culture from about 600 BC.

Learn More: 2 Kings 14:19 / 2 Chronicles 25:27 / Isaiah 36:2 / Jeremiah 34:7

LAODICEA

Unto the angel of the church of the Laodiceans write. . . REVELATION 3:14

The city of Laodicea was about eighty miles east of Ephesus in western Asia Minor (modern Turkey). The risen Christ, in the apostle John's book of Revelation, expressed concerns about the spiritual condition of the church in this city.

Jesus charged the believers at Laodicea with being lukewarm—spiritually tepid, neither hot nor cold—in their devotion to Him. This laxity was so sickening to Jesus that He determined to "spue thee out of my mouth" (Revelation 3:16).

Laodicea was apparently a wealthy city. The members of this church took pride in their economic prosperity. But Jesus told them they were actually poor when it came to spiritual matters. They should invest in gold "tried in the fire" (Revelation 3:18). This probably refers to righteous behavior or authentic faith that leads to deeds that bring honor and glory to the Lord.

In spite of these sharp reprimands, Jesus' love for these believers is unquestionable. In a tone of tenderness, He called on this apathetic church to "be zealous. . .and repent" (Revelation 3:19).

Learn More: Colossians 2:1; 4:13–16

LEBANON

We will cut wood out of Lebanon, as much as thou shalt need. 2 CHRONICLES 2:16

This verse reflects an agreement between King Solomon of Judah and King Huram of Tyre about timber needed to build the temple in Jerusalem. Huram would float logs from Mount Lebanon in his country of Phoenicia to the Israelite port at Joppa. From there they would be transported overland to the construction site in Jerusalem.

The Lebanon mountain range along the coast of ancient Phoenicia formed the northwestern border of the land that God promised to His people. Israel enjoyed peaceful relations with the Phoenicians during their history. King Solomon even formed an alliance with King Huram in which the Phoenicians built and operated the ships needed for Israel's international trade with other nations (2 Chronicles 8:18; 9:21).

Mount Lebanon was known for its magnificent cedar trees that Phoenicia exported to many nations of the ancient world. Extensive cutting eventually reduced these forests to a fraction of their former size. But the modern state of Lebanon has reversed this trend in recent years with ambitious reforestation projects.

Learn More: Deuteronomy 3:25 / Judges 9:15 / 1 Kings 5:6 / 2 Kings 19:23 / Psalm 29:5 / Isaiah 14:8 / Ezekiel 17:3

LYDDA

All that dwelt at Lydda and Saron saw him, and turned to the Lord. ACTS 9:35

The major event for which this city is known is this miraculous healing of a paralyzed man by the apostle Peter. He arrived at Lydda while visiting believers along the coast of the Mediterranean Sea near Joppa (Acts 9:32). The healing amazed the people of the area, and many turned to the Lord.

In Old Testament times, this city was known as Lod (1 Chronicles 8:12). Its location on two major roads made it an important prize for nations that wanted to monopolize international trade. It was repopulated by Jews who returned here after the Babylonian exile.

Today the city is still known as Lod. It is one of the largest cities in the coastal region of Israel. The nation's major airport, Ben Gurion International, is located in Lod. Most pilgrims to the Holy Land arrive and depart through this airport.

Learn More: Ezra 2:33: Lod / Nehemiah 11:35: Lod

LYSTRA

There sat a certain man at Lystra, impotent in his feet. ACTS 14:8

At this city in Asia Minor (modern Turkey), while on his first missionary journey, the apostle Paul experienced the highs and lows that every preacher of the Gospel knows all too well. He healed this lame man, only to have the crowds assume that he was one of their pagan gods in human form. He corrected their ignorance by declaring that he was an ordinary person just like them who had been commissioned to preach the Gospel of Jesus Christ.

No sooner had Paul uttered these words than radical Jews from previous towns he had visited showed up. They convinced the citizens of Lystra to stone Paul as a troublemaker. So the apostle was demoted from a divine being to a worthless vagabond in the span of one brief visit.

The good news is that Paul lived to preach another day, and he never lost his courage. He came back through Lystra heading home after his first preaching tour. During this visit he met and enlisted a young man named Timothy, who eventually became one of his most beloved missionary associates.

Learn More: Acts 14:21; 16:1–2 / 2 Timothy 3:11

MACEDONIA

Come over into Macedonia, and help us. ACTS 16:9

At this Roman province north of Greece, the apostle Paul had a vision that changed his travel. During his second missionary journey, he and his associate Silas traveled through several territories where they planned to preach the Gospel. But at each place, the Holy Spirit told them to keep moving.

Finally, at the city of Troas just off the coast of Greece, Paul had his vision of a man from Macedonia urging them to bring the Gospel to this section of the Roman world. They crossed over by ship into Macedonia, where they visited several cities that were responsive to the message.

These cities included Thessalonica and Philippi, where Paul founded churches to which he later sent letters of encouragement and instruction. At Berea he encountered people who listened eagerly to his teachings and "searched the scriptures daily, whether those things were so" (Acts 17:11).

Paul's visit to Macedonia brought the Gospel to the territory now occupied by modern Europe.

Learn More: Acts 20:1 / Romans 15:26 / 2 Corinthians 2:13 / Philippians 4:15 / 1 Thessalonians 1:8

MAGDALA

He. . .took ship, and came into the coasts of Magdala. MATTHEW 15:39

Magdala was a fishing village near the Sea of Galilee during the time of Jesus. Here fish taken from the lake were probably processed for shipment to all parts of Israel. The village was either the birthplace or the home of Mary Magdalene, a follower of Jesus. While she is mentioned several times in the Gospels, this verse from Matthew is the only specific New Testament reference to the village itself.

We know several things about this Mary, including the fact that Jesus cast seven demons out of her. She was present at His crucifixion, and Jesus appeared to Mary Magdalene when she visited His tomb on the day of His resurrection. She also provided eyewitness testimony to the disciples that Jesus was alive.

On display in a museum near what is believed to be the site of this fishing village is a vessel dubbed the "Jesus Boat." This wooden craft that once sailed the Sea of Galilee was pulled from the mud not far from shore in 1986. Scientific testing has dated it to the first century AD, the time when Jesus taught and healed along the shores of this lake.

Learn More: Matthew 27:55–56 / Luke 8:2 / John 20:11–18

MAHANAIM

Jacob. . .called the name of that place Mahanaim. GENESIS 32:2

Jacob was returning to Canaan when he arrived at this place on the Jabbok River. He had fled several years earlier after cheating his brother, Esau, of their father's blessing. Now, Jacob feared, his brother was waiting to settle the score.

But God sent angels to assure Jacob of His divine protection. Jacob named the place Mahanaim, meaning "two camps." This apparently referred to Jacob's party of wives and servants, as well as this host of angels. To Jacob's relief, Esau welcomed him and assured him that all had been forgiven (Genesis 33:1–4).

In later centuries this campsite developed into a city. Mahanaim was the place from which King Saul's son, Ishbosheth, reigned for two years as king over parts of northern Israel, while David ruled in the south (2 Samuel 2:8–11). After Ishbosheth was assassinated, David became the undisputed king over all Israel (2 Samuel 4:5–7; 5:1–4).

Mahanaim is the city to which David fled after his son Absalom tried to take the kingship by force. Here the king received the sad news that Absalom had been killed in a battle with David's army (2 Samuel 18:31–33).

Learn More: Joshua 13:30 / 2 Samuel 2:29; 17:24 / 1 Kings 2:8

MAMRE

Abram removed his tent, and came and dwelt in the plain of Mamre. GENESIS 13:18

Abram (later known as Abraham) lived at many different places while sojourning in the land of Canaan, but Mamre must have been his favorite. Here he was sitting at the entrance of his tent when he was assured that Sarah would give birth to a son. This good news came from three strangers to whom Abraham served a meal after they appeared mysteriously at his door. This son and his descendants would become a people known as the Israelites, whom God would bless and make a blessing to the rest of the world (Genesis 18:1–19).

At Mamre, Abraham also learned that the Lord planned to destroy the cities of Sodom and Gomorrah because of their wickedness. Abraham tried without success to get God to spare these cities (Genesis 18:23–33).

Abraham bought a cave near Mamre to serve as a burial site for his family. Here he and Sarah were buried, along with his son Isaac, his grandson Jacob, and their wives (Genesis 49:31; 50:13).

Learn More: Genesis 14:13; 23:19; 25:9; 35:27

MEDIA

Two horns are the kings of Media and Persia. DANIEL 8:20

In this vision, the prophet Daniel saw a ram with two horns being defeated by a male goat. The two horns represented the Medes and Persians. They had been the dominant world powers for a time, but they were destined to be conquered by the Greek nation, represented by the aggressive goat in this vision.

Before Daniel's time, the Medes and Persians had battled one another for supremacy for several decades. Persia eventually prevailed and brought the Medes into a coalition that made up the Persian Empire.

Although they lost their independence, the Medes continued to hold a place of honor in the territory ruled by Persia. They are often mentioned together to emphasize this unique relationship. During the incident of the handwriting on the wall, for example, Daniel told Belshazzar, the Babylonian king, it meant that his kingdom would be divided and "given to the Medes and Persians" (Daniel 5:28).

That very night Belshazzar was killed, and he was replaced by "Darius the Median" (Daniel 5:31). This is the Darius who ordered the reconstruction of the temple in Jerusalem to continue after it had been halted for several years (Ezra 6:1–12).

Learn More: Esther 1:14 / 2 Kings 18:11 / Jeremiah 51:11 / Daniel 9:1 / Acts 2:9

MEDITERRANEAN SEA

And the west border was to the great sea, and the coast thereof. JOSHUA 15:12

When the land of Canaan was divided among the Israelites, the tribe of Judah received land that extended westward to the Mediterranean Sea, referred to in this verse as the "great sea." This large body of water was the western boundary of the entire nation of Israel throughout its history. The Mediterranean stretched from Israel's coast for about 2,200 miles all the way to the Atlantic Ocean. Other nations touched by this ocean included Egypt, Syria, Greece, Lebanon, and Italy.

In Old Testament times, King Solomon traded goods with other nations across these waters through an alliance with Hiram, king of Tyre (1 Kings 10:22). These commercial activities brought unparalleled prosperity to Israel.

In New Testament times, the apostle Paul visited many places in the territory around this body of water. While sailing toward Rome, his ship was wrecked in a storm. But he survived and went on to share his faith with others in this Roman capital city.

The Mediterranean Sea is referred to in the King James Version variously as "the sea," "Sea of Joppa," "utmost sea," and "sea of the Philistines."

Learn More: Genesis 49:13 / Ezra 3:7 / Deuteronomy 34:2 / Exodus 23:31

MEGIDDO

A place called in the Hebrew tongue Armageddon. REVELATION 16:16

This Greek word refers to the valley between Mount Carmel and the city of Jezreel in northern Israel. According to the apostle John in this verse, Armageddon will be the site of the final conflict between God and the forces of evil. The site is named for the ancient fortress city of Megiddo, which overlooked the Jezreel Valley.

A major trade route linking Egypt in the south to Syria in the north passed through this valley. Thus, the country that occupied Megiddo had a distinct commercial and military advantage over other nations of the ancient world. Many important battles have been fought for control of this city and the territory through which this ancient highway passed. King Josiah of Judah was killed at Megiddo in a battle with the Egyptians.

Megiddo's association with many decisive battles may explain why John spoke of the final conflict of the end time at Armageddon. He predicted that "the cup of the wine of the fierceness of [God's] wrath" (Revelation 16:19) would be poured out, and the Lord would overthrow the forces of evil.

Learn More: Judges 5:19 / 1 Kings 9:15 / 2 Kings 23:29–30 / 2 Chronicles 35:22 / Zechariah 12:11

MELITA

Then they knew that the island was called Melita. ACTS 28:1

Melita, now known as Malta, was an island in the Mediterranean Sea about sixty miles south of modern Sicily. This little island is where the apostle Paul escaped to shore when his ship was wrecked while on his voyage to Rome.

The account of this event is one of the most riveting in the book of Acts. After drifting for several days in the grip of a ferocious storm, the crew lost all hope of saving the ship. But Paul was calm after an angel appeared to him in a dream. "Fear not, Paul," the angel told him, "thou must be brought before Caesar: and, lo, God hath given thee all them that sail with thee" (Acts 27:24).

It happened exactly as God promised when all the people on board escaped to the island as the ship ran aground. Paul and the other passengers remained on Melita for three months until another ship arrived to take them on to Rome. The apostle made good use of the time by healing several people, including the father of Publius, the local island official.

A parish church known as the Church of St. Paul's Shipwreck in a town on modern Malta commemorates this biblical event.

Learn More: Acts 28:2–10

MESOPOTAMIA

He arose, and went to Mesopotamia, unto the city of Nahor. GENESIS 24:10

Abraham sent his servant to Mesopotamia on an important mission—to find a wife for his son, Isaac. This region between the Tigris and Euphrates Rivers is where Abraham had lived before migrating to Canaan. He wanted Isaac to marry from among his own people rather than to take a Canaanite woman as his bride.

Mesopotamia, situated about five hundred miles north of Canaan, is mentioned several times in the Bible. The pagan prophet Balaam came from the city of Pethor in this region. In the time of the judges, the Israelites were harassed by Chushan Rishathaim, a king of Mesopotamia. In New Testament times, Jews who had settled in this region were in Jerusalem on the day of Pentecost.

The Babylonian Empire flourished in Mesopotamia during Old Testament times. Most of the region today is in modern Iraq.

Learn More: Genesis 28:2: Padam Aram / Deuteronomy 23:4 /
1 Chronicles 19:6 / Judges 3:8–10 / Acts 2:9; 7:2

MIDIAN

Moses fled from the face of Pharaoh, and dwelt in the land of Midian. EXODUS 2:15

The Midianites occupied a desert region along the eastern side of the Dead Sea. Moses fled here to escape threats from the pharaoh after killing an Egyptian slave supervisor. Here Moses married the daughter of a Midianite priest and spent forty years as a shepherd. He was living a quiet, uneventful life in Midian until the Lord called Moses to return to Egypt and lead His people out of slavery.

Midian and its people were not always friendly to the Israelites. During the period of the judges, they conducted periodic raids into Israel, stealing crops and livestock. To deliver His people from this menace, the Lord raised up a champion named Gideon. With an elite force of only three hundred warriors and by following the Lord's battle plan, Gideon won a decisive victory over the Midianites.

Abraham's son Midian, who was born to his concubine, Keturah, was apparently the ancestor of the Midianites. Their settlement east of Canaan may have led to their alliance with other Arabic tribes known as the "children of the east" (Judges 6:3).

Learn More: Genesis 37:28, 36 / Exodus 3:1 / Numbers 31:8 / Judges 7:25 / Habakkuk 3:7

MIZPEH

Samuel took a stone, and set it between Mizpeh and Shen. 1 SAMUEL 7:12

This city just north of Jerusalem was the site of a battle with the Philistines during the time of the prophet Samuel. To commemorate the Israelite victory, Samuel erected a memorial to declare that the Lord had been their Ebenezer, or "stone of help."

Some time before this battle, Samuel presented Saul as the first king of Israel to the people at this city. Mizpeh was also one of the sites visited by Samuel on his circuit throughout the nation as a judge and prophet.

In later years, Mizpeh's closeness to Jerusalem made it an important site for the protection of the Holy City. King Asa of Judah fortified it as a defense outpost against invasion from the north (1 Kings 15:22: *Mizpah*). When the Babylonians destroyed Jerusalem, they apparently selected nearby Mizpeh as their administrative center over the surrounding territory (Jeremiah 40:6: *Mizpah*).

Learn More: Judges 10:17; 11:34 / 1 Samuel 7:5–6, 16–17; 22:3

MOAB

Moses the servant of the Lord died there in the land of Moab. DEUTERONOMY 34:5

The Moabites lived in the area east of the Jordan River and the Dead Sea. This is the territory where Moses died after climbing a peak known as Mount Nebo and looking into the promised land.

While traveling toward Canaan, the Israelites camped near Moabite territory. The king of Moab was so frightened by their numbers that he hired a pagan magician named Balaam to curse the Israelites. But through God's intervention, Balaam blessed the Israelites instead.

The strength of the Moabites varied across several centuries of Israel's history. The tribes of Reuben and Gad settled in northern Moab before the conquest of Canaan (Numbers 32:1–37). The Israelite judge Ehud won a significant victory over their forces after assassinating their leader (Judges 3:15–30). Once he came into power, David also fought and conquered the Moabites.

One Moabite known for her kindness was Ruth, daughter-in-law of Naomi. She left her home country to live with Naomi in Bethlehem and eventually gave birth to Obed, an ancestor of King David (Ruth 4:17) and Jesus.

Learn More: Genesis 19:37 / Numbers 21:13 / Deuteronomy 2:9 / 2 Samuel 8:2 / Ruth 1:22

NAIN

He went into a city called Nain. LUKE 7:11–12

Only one event in this village not far from Jesus' hometown is recorded—and Luke's Gospel alone tells about it. Jesus and His disciples encountered a funeral procession coming out of the village. In a spirit of compassion, He reached out, touched the coffin, and brought back to life the only son of a grieving widow.

The residents of the town were amazed. "A great prophet is risen up among us," they declared (Luke 7:16). Perhaps they were comparing Jesus to the prophet Elisha, who had brought another widow's son back to life in Old Testament times. Elisha's miracle had occurred at Shunem, a town only about three miles north of Nain (2 Kings 4:32–37).

Elisha stretched out over the dead boy's body to bring him back to life. But Jesus raised the son of this widow with a simple command. This was indisputable evidence of the work of God the Father through Jesus.

A small church built on the site of Nain in the 1800s commemorates this event. Two paintings inside the church depict this miracle of Jesus.

NAZARETH

The angel Gabriel was sent from God unto a city of Galilee, named Nazareth. LUKE 1:26–27

This obscure town in the region of Galilee is where an angel announced to the virgin Mary that she would give birth to the Messiah. Here is where Jesus lived until He launched His public ministry. But the people in the town refused to believe that a hometown boy could be the long-expected Messiah (Luke 4:16–30).

A man named Nathanael was also skeptical about Jesus' humble beginnings. When his friend Philip told him he had found the Messiah, Nathanael responded, "Can there any good thing come out of Nazareth?" (John 1:46). To Nathanael's credit, he overcame his initial doubt and became a disciple of Jesus.

During Jesus' public ministry, many people identified Him by His hometown, calling Him "Jesus of Nazareth" (Luke 4:34). Even the sign over His cross used this phrase. Thus Nazareth was transformed into a famous place because of its association with the Savior of the world.

Nazareth has grown from an insignificant village into a thriving population center today. Its main attraction for Holy Land visitors is the Basilica of the Annunciation, a church built over the reputed site of the angel's announcement to Mary.

Learn More: Matthew 2:23 / Luke 2:39, 51 / John 19:19 / Acts 3:6

NEBO, MOUNT

Moses went up from the plains of Moab unto the mountain of Nebo. DEUTERONOMY 34:1

Just east of the northern tip of the Dead Sea in modern Jordan is a peak of the Pisgah mountains known as Mount Nebo, where Moses died. He looked west across the Dead Sea into the land that God had promised Abraham and his descendants several centuries before.

Moses' helper and coleader, his brother, Aaron, had already died. Now it was Moses' turn to step aside as leader of God's people. The Lord had promised Moses that he would see the land of Canaan, but he would not live to enter and take possession of the land (Numbers 20:6–12).

Mount Nebo rises to an elevation of about 2,700 feet, giving a spectacular view of the surrounding area. This site has been recognized for centuries by Christians and Jews as the place of Moses' death and burial. A church was built here as early as AD 394. On the site today is a modern place of worship known as the Memorial Church of Moses that pays tribute to this great leader.

Learn More: Numbers 33:47 / Deuteronomy 3:27; 32:49

NILE RIVER

The waters which are in the river, and they shall be turned to blood. EXODUS 7:17

The Nile is a major river that begins in Africa and runs for more than 4,000 miles across Africa and Egypt, emptying finally into the Mediterranean Sea. The actual name *Nile* does not appear in the Bible; it is referred to simply as "the river." But it is without doubt the body of water that the Lord turned to blood at the hand of Moses.

This river was also associated with Moses as a baby when his mother hid him in a basket along its bank (Exodus 2:1–3). Discovered by the pharaoh's daughter, he grew up in the royal family. This first-hand experience of Egyptian culture prepared Moses to lead God's people out of slavery.

The annual overflow of the Nile built up rich soil ideal for growing grain. From irrigation canals radiating out from the main channel, the Egyptians also watered these crops. The river was so essential to the people's livelihood that they revered it as a god. So when the Nile's waters ran red with blood, God proved He was superior to the pagan religious system of this ancient nation.

Learn More: Exodus 1:22; 7:20 / Isaiah 19:1–5 / Zechariah 10:11

NINEVEH

Arise, go to Nineveh, that great city, and cry against it. JONAH 1:2

Nineveh was the capital city of the Assyrian Empire. The Lord called Jonah to proclaim His judgment against its residents. But the prophet fled in the opposite direction. These enemies of the Israelites were known for their wickedness and violence, and Jonah was determined not to go near Nineveh.

Jonah eventually did preach God's judgment against the city. And to his horror, many of the people repented of their misdeeds. When God decided not to destroy Nineveh, Jonah sulked like a spoiled child. Then the Lord reminded Him that He was a compassionate God who could show mercy to whomever He pleased, even ungodly pagans. So Nineveh is a case study in God's love for all people.

Excavations at Nineveh have revealed that it was, indeed, the "great city" described in the book of Jonah (Jonah 3:2). Its massive defensive wall was eight miles long. Archaeologists also uncovered the ornate palace of King Sennacherib that covered about five acres. Carvings in the palace depicted his capture of several cities of the ancient world. These included Lachish in Judah, which fell during King Hezekiah's administration (2 Chronicles 32:9).

Learn More: Genesis 10:11 / Isaiah 37:37 / Jonah 4:11 / Nahum 3:7 / Zephaniah 2:13 / Matthew 12:41

NOB

And Nob, the city of the priests, smote he with the edge of the sword. 1 SAMUEL 22:19

This town just outside Jerusalem shows King Saul, the first king of Israel, at his worst. He ordered the slaughter of eighty-five priests who lived here because one of them had assisted David and his men. The king was insanely jealous because David had been selected by the Lord to replace him as Israel's leader.

But Saul didn't stop with this senseless slaughter. He wanted to send the message that anyone who assisted David would be dealt with as a traitor. So he sent his assassins to wipe out the families of these priests as well as their livestock.

Ahimelech, a priest at Nob, had provided food for David and his hungry warriors. Ahimelech also gave David Goliath's sword, which the young man had used to kill the Philistine giant (1 Samuel 21:6–9). Freshly provisioned and armed, David and his men slipped away and went into hiding.

The prophet Isaiah mentioned Nob as a place where a foreign army would gather for an assault on Jerusalem (Isaiah 10:32).

Learn More: 1 Samuel 22:9–18 / Nehemiah 11:31–32

OLIVES, MOUNT OF

At the mount called the mount of Olives, he sent two of his disciples. LUKE 19:29

This "mountain" is actually a hill about two hundred feet high that towers over the city of Jerusalem. It took its name from the olive trees that grew on the site. From this location Jesus sent two of His disciples into the Holy City to locate a room where they could observe the Passover meal together. He turned this meal into a memorial of His approaching death, now referred to as the Last Supper or the Lord's Supper.

On the night of this meal, Jesus went into the garden of Gethsemane on the Mount of Olives. Here, as His enemies were plotting His death, He prayed in agony for God's will to be done (Matthew 26:36–42). After His death and resurrection, Jesus ascended to God the Father, apparently from a site on the Mount of Olives (Acts 1:12: *Olivet*).

Several centuries before Jesus' time, King David and his aides climbed the Mount of Olives as they fled Jerusalem to escape Absalom's rebellion.

Learn More: 2 Samuel 15:30 / Zechariah 14:4 / Matthew 21:1; 24:3 / Mark 14:26 / Luke 22:39 / John 8:1

OPHRAH

There came an angel of the Lord, and sat under an oak which was in Ophrah. JUDGES 6:11

At Ophrah, God transformed a frightened farmer into a courageous military leader. It happened when Midianite raiders began to strip the Israelites of their crops and livestock. God's people were cowed into inaction by these camel-riding enemies. Gideon, a man from Ophrah, was frightened like everyone else, threshing wheat in a winepress to keep it from being stolen when an angel greeted him as a brave hero (Judges 6:12).

Through a series of miraculous signs, the angel convinced Gideon that he had been chosen to battle the Midianites. Gideon responded by gathering a huge army. But the Lord thinned it down from several thousand to just three hundred warriors. With this handful of men and by relying on the Lord, Gideon defeated the enemy and drove them from the land (Judges 6:36–7:22).

The location of Ophrah is a mystery. But Holy Land visitors are shown another site that is traditionally associated with him and his victory. It's Harod Spring on Mount Gilboa—reputed to be the place where the Israelite warriors quenched their thirst before they went into battle (Judges 7:1).

Learn More: Judges 6:24; 8:27, 32; 9:5

PARAN, WILDERNESS OF

The cloud rested in the wilderness of Paran. NUMBERS 10:12

The wilderness of Paran was a barren and mountainous area south of the Dead Sea. Here the Israelites camped for a time during their exodus from Egypt while traveling to the land of Canaan.

Paran was the area where Ishmael lived. The first son of Abraham, he was born to Sarah's Egyptian servant, Hagar. She and her son were driven into the wilderness because of Sarah's resentment of the boy after her own son, Isaac, was born (Genesis 21:1–21).

From the Paran wilderness, Moses sent spies into Canaan to find out about the land and its people (Numbers 13:1–3). Several centuries later, David and his supporters entered Paran, apparently to escape King Saul's death threats. The prophet Habakkuk mentioned a "Mount Paran," perhaps a distinct mountain peak in this desolate region.

This wilderness territory is only one of several through which the Israelites traveled during the Exodus. Others were Shur (Exodus 15:22), Sin (Exodus 16:1), Sinai (Numbers 9:5), Zin (Numbers 27:14), Etham (Numbers 33:8), and Moab (Deuteronomy 2:8).

Learn More: Numbers 10:12; 12:16 / Deuteronomy 1:1 / 1 Samuel 25:1 / Habakkuk 3:3

PATMOS

I John. . .was in the isle that is called Patmos. REVELATION 1:9

The apostle John wrote the book of Revelation while in exile on this small island off the coast of Asia Minor (modern Turkey). He had probably been imprisoned here during the persecution of believers that broke out during the reign of the Roman emperor Domitian.

Patmos was a rocky, desolate place only about ten miles long and six miles wide. The Romans were known to send prisoners to other isolated specks of land in the Mediterranean Sea. Was John alone or surrounded by other prisoners? No one knows. What we do know is that God used this place and time to give John a series of visions that told about the future—the end of the present age and the arrival of the kingdom of God in its fullness.

The island of Patmos today is a part of Greece. Several quaint little towns on Patmos draw tourists to enjoy its pristine blue waters and beaches on the Mediterranean Sea. Another popular attraction is the fortress-like Monastery of St. John the Theologian, built almost a thousand years ago on the ruins of a previous church.

PENIEL

Jacob called the name of the place Peniel. GENESIS 32:30

This is the only place in the Bible made famous by a wrestling match. Jacob was camped at this site on the Jabbok River while waiting for the arrival of his estranged brother, Esau. During the night, a man—apparently an angel—came and wrestled with Jacob.

When neither could gain an advantage over the other, the angel knocked Jacob's hip out of joint. Then the angel changed the man's name from *Jacob* to *Israel*, meaning "prince of God" or "he who strives with God."

To commemorate this event, Jacob gave the site the name *Peniel*, meaning "face of God." He had survived this struggle because of the Lord's favor. This event signified that the covenant between God and His special people was still in effect. From that point on, the nation that sprang from the twelve sons of Jacob was known as Israel.

In later centuries, Peniel developed into a city that served as an important defense outpost for the nation of Israel. Jeroboam I, first king of the northern Jewish kingdom, fortified it to protect his nation from attack along its eastern border (1 Kings 12:25: *Penuel*).

Learn More: Genesis 32:24–32

PERGAMOS

And to the angel of the church in Pergamos write. . . REVELATION 2:12

This city in western Asia Minor (modern Turkey) was located about fifteen miles inland from the Aegean Sea. In the book of Revelation, Jesus identified Pergamos as the place "where Satan's seat is" (Revelation 2:13).

This probably refers to the practice of emperor worship. Remains of a temple devoted to worship of the Roman emperor Trajan have been uncovered at Pergamos. This supports the theory that Pergamos was a center where this pagan cult was practiced.

Some members of the church at Pergamos had succumbed to the false doctrine of a group known as the Nicolaitans. Jesus compared their teachings to those of the Old Testament magician Balaam, who taught Israel "to eat things sacrificed unto idols, and to commit fornication" (Revelation 2:14).

The Nicolaitans may have been guilty of immoral sexual behavior, based on a false interpretation of the doctrine of Christian liberty. Jesus called on these people to repent, or He would confront them personally and "fight against them with the sword of my mouth" (Revelation 2:16).

On a positive note, Jesus commended one of their number, Antipas, as a faithful martyr for the Christian faith (Revelation 2:13).

Learn More: Revelation 1:11

PERSIA

Thus saith Cyrus king of Persia. . . 2 CHRONICLES 36:23

Persia was the ancient world empire that conquered Babylon, paving the way for Jewish exiles to return to their homeland. Second Chronicles 36:23 refers to the decree from King Cyrus that authorized this return. The edict also called for the rebuilding of Jerusalem after its destruction by the Babylonians several decades before.

Several Persian kings in addition to Cyrus are mentioned in the Old Testament. Under Darius the Great, the Persian kingdom developed into an empire that controlled a large portion of the ancient world. He ordered the work on the temple in Jerusalem to continue after it had been stopped for several years (Ezra 4:21; 6:1–3).

Ahasuerus, also known as Xerxes, selected a Jewish girl named Esther as his queen (Esther 2:16–17). Later, another Persian king, Artaxerxes, authorized other parties of Jewish exiles to return to Jerusalem. He even sent materials with Nehemiah to be used in construction of Jerusalem's defensive wall (Nehemiah 2:1–8).

Persia's capital city was Shushan, where the prophet Daniel had visions of great world empires and the future Messiah (Daniel 8:2).

Learn More: 2 Chronicles 36:22 / Ezra 1:1–2; 4:24 / Daniel 6:28; 11:2

PHILADELPHIA

And to the angel of the church in Philadelphia write. . . REVELATION 3:7

This church in Asia Minor (modern Turkey) is one of the seven addressed by Jesus in the book of Revelation. Its name means "city of brotherly love," and it had lived up to its name by doing unselfish works of service to others. Jesus commended these believers for taking advantage of the opportunity He had given them. "I have set before thee an open door," Jesus declared, "and no man can shut it" (Revelation 3:8).

Philadelphia sat on one of the main roads the Romans had built to foster travel and trade between the city of Rome and its provinces around the Mediterranean Sea. This was an "open door" for the spread of the Gospel. The apostle Paul and his missionary associates traveled these roads as they witnessed for Christ from city to city throughout the Roman Empire.

Jesus reminded these believers of the certainty of His second coming. Keeping their eyes on this promise should enable them to remain faithful until they received the crown of eternal life (Revelation 3:11).

Learn More: Revelation 1:11

PHILIPPI

Philippi, which is the chief city of that part of Macedonia. ACTS 16:12

Paul and his associate Silas visited this city in Macedonia during his second missionary journey. The apostle departed from his normal custom of preaching in the local Jewish synagogue. Instead he witnessed outside the city beside a river where a group of Jews had gathered for prayer. He baptized a businesswoman named Lydia, along with her servants, when they placed their faith in Christ.

After Paul healed a demented slave girl, he and Silas were imprisoned for disturbing the peace. During the night they were miraculously freed from their chains by an earthquake. This led to the conversion of the prison keeper, who asked them, "What must I do to be saved?" (Acts 16:30).

This jailer and his family may have been the nucleus of the church that Paul established in Philippi. After the apostle left the city, these Christians continued to support him with their gifts and prayers. In a letter that he wrote to them several years later, Paul remembered the Philippians fondly with thanksgiving. Of all the believers whom the apostle gathered into a church, these Christians at Philippi were his "joy and crown" (Philippians 4:1).

Learn More: Acts 20:6 / Philippians 1:1; 4:15 / 1 Thessalonians 2:2

PHILISTIA

Over Philistia will I triumph. Psalm 108:9

This mention of Philistia in the book of Psalms refers to the coastal plain along the Mediterranean Sea adjacent to the territory of the Israelites. Philistia is where the Philistines, enemies of Israel, lived during Old Testament times.

The Philistines are first mentioned in connection with the patriarch Abraham. He grazed his herds in the region of Gerar, where he dealt with the local Philistine leader, Abimelech (Genesis 20:15; 21:34). In later centuries, the Philistines tried to enlarge their territory into the region occupied by Israel. Saul, the first Israelite king, was killed in a battle with the Philistines.

As a shepherd boy, David defeated a Philistine champion named Goliath. After he became king of Israel, David won victories against the Philistines and neutralized their threat to the nation of Israel.

According to the prophets Jeremiah and Amos, the Philistines migrated to Canaan from Caphtor, probably the island of Crete in the Mediterranean Sea. The five major Philistine cities along the Mediterranean coast were Ashdod, Ashkelon, Ekron, Gath, and Gaza.

Learn More: Genesis 26:15 / Exodus 23:31 / Judges 10:7; 16:21 / 1 Samuel 17:51; 31:2 / 2 Samuel 8:1 / Jeremiah 47:4 / Amos 9:7

POOLS OF SOLOMON

I made me pools of water. Ecclesiastes 2:6

In the book of Ecclesiastes, Solomon listed "pools of water" among the many achievements of his administration as king of Israel. Some people identify these pools as a water storage system built by the king, parts of which are still visible today in the land of Israel. But others believe this project was completed several centuries after Solomon's time, perhaps by Herod the Great. This Roman ruler was known for his massive building projects throughout Israel.

No matter when or by whom it was built, the Pools of Solomon complex was an ingenious system for bringing water into the city of Jerusalem. The complex consists of several large water reservoirs fed by several springs near the city of Bethlehem. The pools were connected by aqueducts that used gravity to carry water all the way to the Holy City about five miles away.

Some of these reservoirs were about four hundred feet long by more than two hundred feet wide by about thirty feet deep. They would have been capable of holding millions of gallons of water. This was a precious commodity in a land known for its hot, dry climate and scarcity of water.

RABBAH

They destroyed the children of Ammon, and besieged Rabbah. 2 Samuel 11:1

King David sent his army off to besiege this capital city of the Ammonites while he stayed behind in Jerusalem. He should have gone with his army. While "tarrying" in the Holy City, he yielded to temptation and committed adultery with Bathsheba (2 Samuel 11:3–4).

Rabbah was about thirty-five miles northeast of Jerusalem on the eastern side of the Jordan River. Joab, the commander of David's army, brought the city to its knees. Then he brought David to the battle scene to spearhead the final assault so the king could take credit for the victory (2 Samuel 12:26–29).

Rabbah will always be associated with one of the low moments in the life of David. To cover up his adulterous affair with Bathsheba, he sent her husband, Uriah, to the front lines of the assault on the city. This resulted in Uriah's death (2 Samuel 11:14–17). David suffered the effects of this sin for the rest of his life through the scandalous behavior of members of his own family.

Several Old Testament prophets predicted the total destruction of the city of Rabbah.

Learn More: Deuteronomy 3:11: Rabbath / Joshua 13:25 / 2 Samuel 12:26–27 / 1 Chronicles 20:1 / Jeremiah 49:2 / Ezekiel 25:5 / Amos 1:14

RAMAH

And buried [Samuel] in his house at Ramah. 1 Samuel 25:1

Several cities with this name existed in Bible times. But the most famous was the Ramah where the prophet Samuel was born and where he was buried. It is also called Ramathaim Zophim (1 Samuel 1:1).

Before Samuel was born, his mother dedicated him to the Lord. When he was just a child, she took him to live with the priest Eli at Shiloh. Samuel became one of the most beloved leaders of Israel in his roles as prophet, priest, and judge. He served during the time when the Israelites were moving away from a loose tribal confederacy to centralized rule under a king.

At Ramah, the elders of Israel asked Samuel to appoint a king to rule the nation (1 Samuel 8:4–5). He anointed Saul as the first leader, then later selected David to replace him when Saul proved unworthy (1 Samuel 16:13).

The site of Ramah has never been identified. But it must have been north of Jerusalem near the cities of Bethel and Gilgal. Samuel traveled between his hometown and these two cities, performing his duties as a judge (1 Samuel 7:15–17).

Learn More: Judges 4:5 / 1 Samuel 1:19; 7:17; 15:34; 16:13; 19:18; 28:3

RAMOTH GILEAD

Know ye that Ramoth in Gilead is ours? 1 Kings 22:3

Ramoth Gilead was a city in northern Israel where King Ahab met his Waterloo. Here he died because of his evil reign over the northern kingdom and his confidence in the advice of false prophets.

Ahab enlisted the help of the king of Judah in an attempt to take the city from the Syrians. He thought this massive military force, coupled with assurances from false prophets in his own country, would bring victory.

But the Lord had other plans. The battle ended with the city still in Syrian hands and the king mortally wounded by a stray arrow. This brought an end to Ahab's evil reign. Among other atrocities, he had led his nation to worship false gods and had authorized the murder of an innocent man in order to seize his property (1 Kings 21:15–16).

Ramoth Gilead was so named because it was located in Gilead, a territory of fertile pastureland on the eastern side of the Jordan River. This region was a part of Israel in Old Testament times, but it lies in the nation of Jordan today.

Learn More: Joshua 21:38 / 1 Kings 22:12 / 2 Kings 8:28 / 2 Chronicles 18:3–11

RED SEA

Pharaoh's. . .chosen captains also are drowned in the Red sea. Exodus 15:4

This verse is part of a passage known as the Song of Moses (Exodus 15:1–19). It celebrates the safe passage of the Israelites over the Red Sea after leaving Egypt. The Lord divided this body of water so they could cross on dry land. When the pursuing Egyptians followed, the waters closed, destroying Pharaoh's army (Exodus 14:22–23).

Several theories about the identity of this body of water have been suggested. These range from the Gulf of Suez to the Gulf of Aqaba to one of the shallow lakes in the marshlands south of the Gulf of Aqaba.

Some scholars insist that the Hebrew term for Red Sea, *Yam Suph*, should be translated as "Reed Sea." They believe this term can refer to any marshy area near the coast of the Mediterranean Sea that provided a crossing point from Egypt into the Sinai wilderness.

No matter its location, the crossing of the Red Sea was clearly a miracle that God provided to deliver His people. As Moses declared of the Egyptians in his song, "Thou didst blow with thy wind, the sea covered them: they sank as lead in the mighty waters" (Exodus 15:10).

Learn More: Exodus 13:18; 23:31 / Numbers 21:14 / Deuteronomy 1:40 / Joshua 4:23 / Psalm 136:13

ROME, CITY OF

As thou hast testified of me in Jerusalem, so must thou bear witness also at Rome. ACTS 23:11

The apostle Paul was assured in a vision that he would eventually make his way to Rome, capital city of the Roman Empire. This vision occurred after the Jewish Sanhedrin in Jerusalem had accused him of blasphemy. When Paul realized he would never receive a fair trial at their hands, he appealed his case to Rome. From that moment on, his visit to this pagan city was inevitable.

In Paul's time, Rome was a city of more than a million people. Its ornate public buildings gave it the appearance of a city of modern times. The massive Coliseum, similar to a football stadium, drew thousands to watch the sporting events sponsored by the Roman government.

When Paul arrived in Rome, Christianity had already been planted here (Acts 28:14–15). He was placed under house arrest and allowed to continue his witnessing efforts. From prison he wrote letters—Ephesians, Philippians, and Colossians—to three of the churches he had founded.

Most scholars believe the apostle was released, then imprisoned a second time and eventually executed at Rome during the reign of the cruel emperor Nero.

Learn More: Acts 2:10; 19:21; 28:16 / 2 Timothy 1:17

SAMARIA

And he bought the hill Samaria of Shemer. 1 KINGS 16:24

King Omri of the northern kingdom had one notable accomplishment: he built Samaria from the ground up as his new capital city. Before then, Israel's kings had reigned from Shechem and Tirzah.

Samaria sat atop a high hill that gave it good protection from enemy attacks. The Assyrian army finally overran Samaria in 722 BC, but it took a three-year siege to bring the city to its knees (2 Kings 17:5–6).

The Assyrians repopulated the city with foreigners who worshiped pagan gods (2 Kings 17:24–33). Over the centuries, intermarriage with these Gentiles produced a half-breed race that pure-blooded Jews despised. The names *Samaritans* and *Samaria* were eventually applied to these people and the territory where they lived.

In excavations at the city of Samaria, archaeologists have discovered pieces of ivory apparently used as furniture inlays and as decorative wall panels. These may have been used in the infamous "ivory house" built here by King Ahab, Omri's son and successor (1 Kings 22:39).

Learn More: 1 Kings 16:29; 22:37–38 / 2 Kings 1:3 / Ezekiel 23:4 / Hosea 13:16 / Acts 8:5

SARDIS

And unto the angel of the church in Sardis write. . . REVELATION 3:1

The believers at Sardis in western Asia Minor (modern Turkey) received this severe rebuke from Jesus. Of the seven churches mentioned in the book of Revelation, only Sardis was characterized as a "dead" church. It claimed to be a Christian assembly but apparently gave little evidence of this through its actions. Some of its members may have been in danger of slipping back into their former pagan way of life.

The antidote prescribed for their spiritual weakness was to renew their commitment to Christ. If they did not repent and turn back to the Lord, Jesus promised to visit them quickly and exercise appropriate judgment.

In spite of the shortcomings of this church, Jesus recognized that a few members were His loyal and committed followers. They would be dressed in "white raiment" (Revelation 3:5), a symbol of their eternal fellowship with the Lord in heaven.

Learn More: Revelation 1:11

SEA OF GALILEE

By the sea of Galilee, he saw Simon and Andrew his brother casting a net. Mark 1:16

This small freshwater lake in northern Israel is where Jesus called the fisherman brothers Peter and Andrew to become His disciples (Mark 1:16–18). Two other brothers who were fishing nearby—James and John—also agreed to follow Him and join His cause as "fishers of men" (Matthew 4:19–22).

During His ministry in the region of Galilee, this lake was associated with many of Jesus' miracles and teachings. Here He walked on the water to meet His disciples, calmed a storm that threatened to swamp their boat on another occasion, and taught the crowds from a little vessel anchored just offshore.

Lake Galilee is fed by the Jordan River, the main source of water for the nation of Israel. Its beaches and striking blue water are a favorite recreation spot for the nation's citizens. The part of the lake near the modern city of Tiberias features such amenities as water slides, campgrounds, mineral springs, restaurants, and hotels.

The Sea of Galilee is also called the sea of Chinnereth (Numbers 34:11), the lake of Gennesaret (Luke 5:1), and the Sea of Tiberias (John 21:1).

Learn More: Joshua 13:27 / Matthew 4:18; 15:29 / Mark 3:7; 7:31 / John 6:1

SHARON, PLAIN OF

I am the rose of Sharon, and the lily of the valleys. Song of Solomon 2:1

The bride of King Solomon in this verse compared herself to a wildflower that grew in the fertile soil of the plain of Sharon. This name is applied to the coastal plain of Israel that runs about forty miles along the Mediterranean Sea from Joppa all the way up Mount Carmel.

Only a few other references to this fertile strip of land appear in the Bible. The prophet Isaiah spoke of a future time when the Lord would display His glory with the arrival of the Messiah. When this happened, the deserts of the land of Israel would be "as lovely as. . .the plain of Sharon" (Isaiah 35:2 NLT).

The apostle Peter was ministering along the southern section of this plain near Joppa when he healed a paralyzed man named Aeneas. This impressed the people, and many turned to the Lord (Acts 9:33–36: *Saron*).

Large sections of the plain of Sharon were once covered with sand dunes and marshland. But drainage projects by the Israeli government have turned it into rich farmland where citrus orchards flourish. Sharon is also referred to as *Lasharon* (Joshua 12:18).

Learn More: 1 Chronicles 5:16; 27:29 / Isaiah 33:9; 65:10

SHECHEM

And Abram passed through the land unto the place of Sichem. Genesis 12:6-7

Although this place is called Sichem in this verse, it later became known as Shechem. It was probably nothing more than a camping spot when Abraham built an altar here after arriving in Canaan. But over time the site grew into a village, then a town, and finally a city.

Centuries after Abraham's time, Joshua gave his farewell address to the tribes of Israel at Shechem after the Israelites conquered the Canaanites (Joshua 24:1–15). Shechem eventually developed into a major city with a defensive wall. When the united kingdom of Solomon split into two factions, King Jeroboam I turned the city into the capital of the northern kingdom (1 Kings 12:25).

Shechem sat in a narrow valley between the twin peaks of Gerizim and Ebal in central Israel. Nearby was the village of Sychar, where Jesus talked with a woman at the well (John 4:5).

This ancient city is reputed to be the site of Joseph's tomb. His bones were eventually brought from Egypt and buried here on the property bought by his father, Jacob, several years before (Genesis 33:19; Joshua 24:32).

Learn More: Genesis 35:4; 37:13–14 / Joshua 21:21 / 1 Kings 12:1 / Jeremiah 41:5

SHILOH

And Joshua cast lots for them in Shiloh before the Lord. JOSHUA 18:10

Shiloh was an important place of worship about twenty miles north of Jerusalem. Here the Israelites set up the tabernacle where they paid homage to the Lord soon after entering the land of Canaan. A few years later, the people gathered at Shiloh to receive their share of the land.

The city of Shiloh also played an important role in the early life of the prophet Samuel. His mother, Hannah, had been unable to have children. So she traveled to the tabernacle at Shiloh to pray for a son. After giving birth to Samuel, she took the boy to live with Eli the priest at Shiloh, where he devoted his life to service at the tabernacle.

At Shiloh the ark of the covenant was captured by the Philistines, and it was never returned to the city. All that remains of this site today is a shapeless mass of rocks. Excavations reveal that Shiloh was destroyed about three centuries after Joshua's time. The prophet Jeremiah cited this event as a call for Israel to remain faithful to the Lord (Jeremiah 7:12).

Learn More: Joshua 22:12 / Judges 21:21 / 1 Samuel 3:21 / 1 Kings 14:2 / Jeremiah 26:6

SHUNEM

Elisha passed to Shunem, where was a great woman. 2 KINGS 4:8

This village was in the northern section of Israel south of the Sea of Galilee. It was the home of a kind woman who provided food and lodging for the prophet Elisha and his servant. In return for her kindness, the prophet promised her that she would give birth to a son.

Later on, when this son died, she traveled all the way across the Jezreel Valley to Mount Carmel to ask for Elisha's help. He returned with her to Shunem, where he brought the boy back to life (2 Kings 4:18–37).

This town was also the home of a young woman named Abishag, who was brought to Jerusalem to serve as a nurse and companion for the aging King David. She is referred to in the King James Version as a "Shunammite," or a person from Shunem (1 Kings 1:3).

A minor village in Bible times, Shunem never developed into much of a town in later centuries. An Arab village known as Sulem or Solam occupies the site today.

Learn More: 1 Samuel 28:4 / 1 Kings 1:15; 2:22

SHUSHAN

Ahasuerus sat on the throne of his kingdom, which was in Shushan. ESTHER 1:2

Most of the events recorded in the book of Esther happened in this royal city of the Persian Empire. At Shushan stood the palace of King Ahasuerus, also known as Xerxes I, who selected the Jewish girl Esther as his new queen.

The prophet Daniel had a vision in which he was "at Shushan. . .in the province of Elam" (Daniel 8:2). This suggests that Shushan was originally a city of the Elamites, an ancient kingdom near the Tigris and Euphrates Rivers. The Persians may have captured this city from the Elamites and turned it into a royal residence for their king.

Excavations at Shushan have uncovered the remains of this palace. Thirty-six huge columns stood in a large open room—perhaps the very place where Ahasuerus sponsored raucous drinking parties for his court officials (Esther 1:7).

Several pieces of art were also found, bringing to mind the Bible's descriptions of its opulent furnishings: "Where were white, green, and blue, hangings, fastened with cords of fine linen and purple to silver rings and pillars of marble: the beds were of gold and silver, upon a pavement of red, and blue, and white, and black, marble" (Esther 1:6).

Learn More: Nehemiah 1:1 / Esther 4:16; 9:15

SIDON

The next day we touched at Sidon. ACTS 27:3

The apostle Paul's journey to Rome began when he boarded a ship at this port city on the coast of Phoenicia. He may have preached in the city previously, since he visited friends at Sidon before setting sail on this trip of more than a thousand miles.

Sidon was a major city long before Paul's time. During Israel's conquest of Canaan, the tribe of Asher settled nearby but was not able to conquer the Sidonians. Centuries later, Sidon's pagan culture infected Israel when Jezebel, wife of King Ahab, promoted the worship of Baal and Ashtoreth among God's people. She was the daughter of Ethbaal, the king of Sidon.

Sidon was only about twenty miles north of Tyre, another major Phoenician city. These two cities are often mentioned together in the Bible. Jesus made one visit to the area, where He honored the faith of a Gentile woman by healing her demon-possessed daughter.

Several Old Testament prophets predicted the destruction of Sidon because of its idolatry. The city eventually fell to the Assyrians.

Learn More: Genesis 10:19 / Joshua 13:6 / Judges 1:31: Zidon; 3:3 / 1 Kings 16:31: Zidonians / Mark 3:8 / Luke 10:13

SILOAM, POOL OF

[Jesus] said unto him, Go, wash in the pool of Siloam. JOHN 9:7

While walking in Jerusalem, Jesus met a man who had been blind his entire life. Jesus mixed mud with His own saliva, then covered the man's eyes and sent him to wash in this pool. The man obeyed and was miraculously healed.

Skeptical Pharisees tried to discredit Jesus by calling Him a sinner and casting doubt on the man's account of what had happened. But the man replied, "Whether he be a sinner or no, I know not: one thing I know, that, whereas I was blind, now I see" (John 9:25).

The Pool of Siloam and the tunnel through which it receives its water still exist today in the city of Jerusalem. Also known as Hezekiah's Pool, it was constructed by King Hezekiah of Judah about 650 BC. He built it to store water for Jerusalem in case of a prolonged siege by the Assyrian army.

The water tunnel runs for more than 1,700 feet through solid rock to a spring that was then outside the city wall. This project is considered one of the most remarkable engineering achievements of Bible times.

Learn More: 2 Chronicles 32:30

SINAI, MOUNT

The Lord came down upon mount Sinai, on the top of the mount. EXODUS 19:20

On this mountain peak in the wilderness, God delivered to Moses the Ten Commandments, the law intended as a moral compass for the lives of His people. Also known as Horeb (Exodus 3:1), this was also the place where God called Moses through a burning bush to lead the Israelites out of slavery in Egypt.

At Sinai the Lord also ordered the people to keep the covenant He had established with their ancestor, Abraham. God showed His power by causing the mountain to shake and covering it with smoke (Exodus 19:16).

The mountain most widely accepted as Mount Sinai is known today by its Arabic name, *Jebel Musa* ("mountain of Moses"). This peak rises above the surrounding plain to an elevation of more than seven thousand feet above sea level. At the foot of this mountain sits the monastery of Saint Catherine, which memorializes God's encounter with Moses and the Israelites at this sacred site.

Mount Sinai, or Horeb, was also the secluded place to which the prophet Elijah fled to escape the wrath of Queen Jezebel.

Learn More: Exodus 16:1 / Leviticus 7:38 / Deuteronomy 1:6 / 1 Kings 19:8 / Nehemiah 9:13

SMYRNA

And unto the angel of the church in Smyrna write... REVELATION 2:8–9

Smyrna was a city in the Roman province of Asia (modern Turkey) that fronted the Aegean Sea. Its natural harbor and location on a major Roman road contributed to its prosperity.

The church at Smyrna was being persecuted, apparently by radical Jews. Jesus encouraged these believers through the book of Revelation to remain faithful to Him in spite of these difficulties. Although they were poor in the world's goods, He reminded them that they were rich in what really mattered. They had the great privilege of belonging to Jesus, the first and the last—the One who transcended time and eternity.

Jesus promised these believers a crown of life if they were willing to die rather than renounce their faith in Him (Revelation 2:10). About sixty years later, a church official in Smyrna named Polycarp claimed this promise when he was burned at the stake for refusing to worship the Roman emperor.

Smyrna is known today as Izmir, a major Turkish city.

Learn More: Revelation 1:11

SODOM AND GOMORRAH

The Lord rained upon Sodom and upon Gomorrah brimstone and fire. GENESIS 19:24

These twin cities near the Dead Sea were destroyed because of their wickedness. Only Abraham's nephew Lot and Lot's family escaped when the cities were burned (Genesis 19:29).

The exact location of these cities has been debated for centuries. Some scholars argue for a location along the northern section of the Dead Sea, while others think they were somewhere near its eastern shore. But the most widely accepted sites for Sodom and Gomorrah are on the western shore of the Dead Sea's southern tip. This area matches the biblical description of how the cities were destroyed with brimstone [*sulphur*: NIV] and fire that fell from the sky. Large deposits of sulfur and asphalt still exist in this area today.

God promised Abraham that He would not destroy Sodom if it contained just ten righteous people. But He proceeded with His plan when only Lot and his wife and two daughters met this qualification (Genesis 18:23–33; 19:14–15).

Sodom and Gomorrah are cited often throughout the Bible as examples of human wickedness and rebellion against God.

Learn More: Genesis 13:12; 14:22 / Deuteronomy 29:23 / Isaiah 3:9 /
Jeremiah 23:14 / Matthew 11:23–24 / Jude 7

SYCHAR

Then cometh [Jesus] to a city of Samaria, which is called Sychar. JOHN 4:5

A woman from this little town in the region of Samaria went out one day to draw water from the local well. Here she met Jesus, who surprised her by asking her to give Him a drink of water from her jar. Jews normally had nothing to do with Samaritans. Then Jesus surprised her even more by offering her a different kind of water in return—living water that would fill the spiritual emptiness in her life.

This is the only place in the Bible where Sychar is mentioned. The site is now occupied by an Arab village known as Askar. This village is about a ten-minute walk from Jacob's Well, reputed to be the very water source where Jesus talked with this Samaritan woman.

Over the centuries several churches have been built on this site to commemorate this event in Jesus' ministry. Today the deep well is preserved within the complex of an Eastern Orthodox monastery.

This woman was so impressed with Jesus that she urged her villagers, "Come, see a man, which told me all things that ever I did: Is not this the Christ?" (John 4:29).

Learn More: John 4:6–30

SYRIA

When they were come to. . .the camp of Syria, behold, there was no man there. 2 KINGS 7:5

Syria was a nation north of Israel that often battled God's people for control of its northern territory. It had no connection to Assyria, the pagan nation much farther to the north in the region known as Mesopotamia. Another name for Syria in the Old Testament is *Aram.*

During one of its campaigns against the Israelites, the Syrians besieged Samaria, Israel's capital city. Just as the Israelites were about to run out of food and water, two lepers ventured into the Syrian camp. To their surprise, the entire army had fled. The Lord had sent a great noise to convince the Syrians an army allied with Israel was coming to wipe them out.

The Syrians were particularly hostile toward the Israelites during the ministry of the prophet Elisha. On one occasion he healed a Syrian military officer of leprosy in an act of goodwill. At God's instructions, the prophet also anointed Hazael as king of Syria. He was apparently selected to serve as an instrument of judgment against God's people because of their idolatry (2 Kings 10:32).

Learn More: Numbers 23:7 / Judges 10:6 / 2 Samuel 8:5–6 / 1 Kings 11:25; 15:18–20 /
2 Kings 5:1 / Amos 1:5 / Luke 2:2

TAANACH

Joshua and the children of Israel smote. . .the king of Taanach. JOSHUA 12:7, 21

Taanach developed into an important royal city of the Canaanites long before the Israelites swept into their territory. Even though it was well defended with a massive wall, Taanach's Canaanite king was one of many defeated by the Israelites. In later years, during the period of the judges, the Canaanites again became a threat to Israel. But their power was broken by Deborah and Barak, who were victorious over Sisera and his Canaanite army near Taanach (Judges 5:19).

Taanach and nearby Megiddo sat on opposite sides of an ancient trade route that ran from Egypt in the south to Mesopotamia in the north. Control of these two cities was important for commercial and military reasons. King Solomon turned them both into administrative centers. His representatives at Taanach and Megiddo were responsible for collecting taxes and supplies throughout the surrounding territory to support the king's central government in Jerusalem.

The ruins of ancient Taanach are known today as Tell Taanek. At this site, remains of the city from its Canaanite origins more than forty-five hundred years ago have been discovered.

Learn More: 1 Kings 4:12 / 1 Chronicles 7:29

TABOR, MOUNT

Jesus. . .leadeth them up into an high mountain apart by themselves. MARK 9:2

According to an early Christian tradition, this mountain about ten miles south of the Sea of Galilee is where Jesus was transfigured before three of His disciples. The slopes of this high peak are covered with trees and wildflowers, providing a colorful contrast to the drab landscape of the surrounding area.

Jesus had told His disciples several times that He would eventually be glorified by the Father, received into heaven, and then would return to earth one day. In His glorified appearance on Tabor, He was giving them a glimpse of His future glory to prepare them for His death.

Over the centuries, several churches have been built on Mount Tabor to commemorate this important event. Two modern monasteries stand on the ruins of these ancient buildings. Not everyone agrees that Tabor is the site of the transfiguration. Some scholars believe that Mount Hermon north of the Sea of Galilee is the more likely site.

In Old Testament times, the judge Barak gathered an army at Mount Tabor and attacked his Canaanite enemies at nearby Megiddo (Judges 4:6–12).

Learn More: Judges 4:6–12; 8:18 / Psalm 89:12 / Jeremiah 46:18 / Hosea 5:1

TARSHISH

But Jonah rose up to flee unto Tarshish from the presence of the Lord. JONAH 1:3

The prophet Jonah was determined not to obey God's call to preach to Israel's Assyrian enemies at Nineveh. So he boarded a ship headed for the city of Tarshish in the opposite direction. Tarshish was a city in the western reaches of the Mediterranean Sea, several hundred miles from Israel. The Phoenicians to the north of Israel engaged in trade with this far-flung city.

In an alliance with the Phoenician ruler Hiram, king of Tyre, King Solomon also imported goods into Israel by ships stationed at Tarshish. These goods included "gold, and silver, ivory, and apes, and peacocks" (1 Kings 10:22: *Tharshish*).

Jonah's journey toward Tarshish did not go well. Tossed overboard in the midst of a great storm, he was swallowed by a great fish, then miraculously delivered by the Lord. He finally made it to Nineveh, where many Assyrian citizens were spared from God's judgment when convicted of their sins by his reluctant preaching (Jonah 4:2–3).

Learn More: 2 Chronicles 9:21; 20:36–37 / Psalm 48:7; 72:10 / Isaiah 23:14 / Jeremiah 10:9 / Ezekiel 38:13

TARSUS

But Paul said, I am a man which am a Jew of Tarsus, a city in Cilicia. ACTS 21:39

The apostle Paul was detained by Roman soldiers to protect him from a crowd of angry Jews. Paul identified himself as a Jew, just like his accusers, who was a native of the city of Tarsus.

Tarsus was the major city of the province of Cilicia in modern Turkey. Situated about ten miles north of the shore of the Mediterranean Sea, it was flanked on the north by the Taurus Mountains. Through these mountains ran a trade route that connected this section of the Roman world with Syria. This prime location had led to its prosperity and reputation as "no ordinary city" (Acts 21:39 NIV). Paul's trade of tentmaking may have been influenced by one of the products for which Tarsus was famous—a rough fabric woven from the hair of black goats.

When and why Paul left Tarsus is unknown. But he showed up in Jerusalem as a persecutor of the church before his conversion to Christianity. When he began to preach the Gospel in Jerusalem, zealous Jews threatened to kill him. His fellow believers sent him off to Tarsus for his own protection.

Learn More: Acts 9:30; 11:25; 22:3

TEKOA

Blow the trumpet in Tekoa. . .for evil appeareth out of the north. JEREMIAH 6:1

This city sat on top of a mountain about ten miles south of Jerusalem. From this high plateau, the Mount of Olives just outside Jerusalem could be seen. Thus, Tekoa could warn officials at the Holy City about an enemy attack. Trumpets were often sounded to rally warriors to their battle stations—thus the meaning of Tekoa's name, "trumpet blast."

The prophet Jeremiah was called by the Lord to sound a trumpet of warning for a different reason. He was concerned about the nation's worship of false gods. Unless the people turned back to the Lord, He would send a foreign nation to take them into exile.

Tekoa is also mentioned during the time of David. Joab, one of David's military officers, summoned a wise woman from Tekoa to Jerusalem. With a story about her own family's broken relationships, she tried to convince the king to make amends with his own son, Absalom.

But this woman's efforts were only partially successful. The bad blood between father and son continued (2 Samuel 14:2–24). Absalom eventually tried to take over David's kingship by force (2 Samuel 15:14).

Learn More: 2 Chronicles 11:5-6; 20:20 / Amos 1:1

THESSALONICA

They came to Thessalonica, where was a synagogue of the Jews. ACTS 17:1

During his second missionary journey, Paul and his associate Silas visited this major port city in Greece. Their evangelistic efforts in the local synagogue were well received. A church consisting of Jews and Gentiles from a pagan background soon sprang up. But radical Jews enlisted the rabble of the city, incited a riot, and forced the two missionaries to move on to the nearby city of Berea.

Paul later wrote two letters to the believers at Thessalonica. The major theme of these epistles was the certainty of the second coming of Christ. But the apostle also commended them for their faithfulness and encouraged idlers to earn their own living rather than live off the generosity of others.

By the time Paul wrote to the Thessalonians, this church had apparently heeded the apostle's plea to serve as a witness to unbelievers of the area. He noted their Christian influence had blossomed "not only in Macedonia and Achaia, but also in every place your faith to God-ward is spread abroad" (1 Thessalonians 1:8).

In later years, two believers from Thessalonica—Aristarchus and Secundus—traveled with the apostle on his evangelistic tours.

Learn More: Acts 17:13; 20:4; 27:2 / Philippians 4:16 / 2 Timothy 4:10

THYATIRA

And unto the angel of the church in Thyatira write. . . REVELATION 2:18

Thyatira, a city with one of the seven churches addressed in the book of Revelation, was located in Asia Minor (modern Turkey). Jesus commended this church for several things. Its works of faith, love, service, and patient endurance were increasing day by day, unlike the decline of these virtues that were evident in several of the other six churches.

But the church at Thyatira had permitted a false prophetess named Jezebel to lead some of its members astray. She was encouraging them to engage in illicit sexual acts and to "eat things sacrificed unto idols" (Revelation 2:20).

Because Jezebel refused to repent of these actions, Jesus promised to cast her into a bed of tribulation instead of the bed of sin that she was promoting. He encouraged those not influenced by her teachings to continue to uphold the true principles of the Gospel.

Thyatira was the home of Lydia, a seller of purple cloth, who was converted during the apostle Paul's ministry at Philippi. She may have been one of the believers who formed the nucleus of the church at Thyatira.

Learn More: Acts 16:14 / Revelation 2:19–29

TIBERIAS

There came other boats from Tiberias nigh unto the place where they did eat bread. JOHN 6:23

People from this city on the western shore of the Sea of Galilee apparently looked for Jesus in this area after the miracle of the feeding of the five thousand. This is the only mention of Tiberias in the Bible.

Herod Antipas, a son of Herod the Great, built Tiberias in AD 20 to serve as his administrative capital for the province of Galilee. He named the city for the Roman emperor, Tiberius Caesar.

Tiberias must have been an important city in New Testament times, since its name was attached to the well-known body of water along which it stood. Another name for the Sea of Galilee in Jesus' time was the Sea of Tiberias (John 6:1). The Gospels do not record a single visit of Jesus to this city, although Tiberias was only about eight miles from Capernaum, the headquarters of His Galilean ministry.

A modern resort city of the same name still stands at the site of New Testament Tiberias. One nearby site of interest to visitors is the Anchor Church, named for a huge rock that looks like an ancient anchor. This may have been part of a place of worship that was built here several centuries ago.

TIMNATH SERAH

They gave [Joshua] the city which he asked, even Timnathserah. JOSHUA 19:50

Joshua received this city in the mountains north of Jerusalem as a reward for his faithful leadership of the tribes of Israel. No leader was ever more deserving of such an inheritance. He took over when Moses died, brought the people into Canaan, and then led them in their military campaigns to make the land their own. Joshua left a legacy of courageous leadership for future generations (Joshua 24:15).

When Joshua died, he was buried at Timnath Serah. This town is identified today with the Arab village of Kefel Hares. Here, according to Muslim tradition, are the tombs of Joshua, Caleb, and Joshua's father.

Another name for Timnath Serah is Timnath Heres (Judges 2:9), meaning "portion of the sun." In its distant past, this may have been a pagan site devoted to worship of the sun. *Heres* may be a deliberate backward spelling of *Serah* to emphasize the city's pagan past.

Learn More: Joshua 24:30

TIRZAH

Began Baasha the son of Ahijah to reign over all Israel in Tirzah. 1 KINGS 15:33

A city in northern Israel, Tirzah served for a time as the capital city of the northern kingdom of Israel. King Baasha's twenty-four-year rule was the longest period any king reigned from this location. Tirzah was Israel's second capital, preceded by Shechem (1 Kings 12:1) and followed by Samaria (1 Kings 16:24).

After reigning at Tirzah for six years, King Omri built a brand-new capital city at Samaria just a few miles away. Excavations at Tirzah's ruins have uncovered buildings that were started but never finished. These were probably abandoned when Omri decided to move to Samaria's higher ground—a more defensible site.

Tirzah was also the site of one of the few suicides recorded in the Bible. This happened when Omri took the city from King Zimri. Realizing that he would be assassinated, Zimri set his palace ablaze and died in the flames (1 Kings 16:18).

Several centuries before Omri's time, the Israelites under Joshua's leadership captured Tirzah from the Canaanites. It was apparently known for its beauty, since King Solomon declared that his bride was as beautiful as Tirzah (Song of Solomon 6:4).

Learn More: 1 Kings 16:16–23 / 2 Kings 15:14–16

TYRE

Jesus went thence, and departed into the coasts of Tyre and Sidon. MATTHEW 15:21

Jesus' journey from Galilee to this city on the coast of the Mediterranean Sea was the longest trip He took during His three-year ministry. Like the territory known as the Decapolis, Tyre was in Gentile territory.

When He arrived, Jesus was approached by a desperate woman. Her daughter was possessed by a demon, and she begged Him to make her well. Jesus told her, "It isn't right to take food from the children and throw it to the dogs" (Matthew 15:26 NLT). This implied that His mission was to minister to His own people, the Jews.

But Jesus was moved to act and heal the sick girl when the mother responded in faith: "Truth, Lord: yet the dogs eat of the crumbs which fall from their masters' table" (Matthew 15:27). This healing of a Gentile girl leaves no doubt that Jesus was sent as a Savior for all the world.

In Old Testament times, Tyre was ruled by King Hiram, who provided timber for the construction of the temple in Jerusalem during King Solomon's reign. The apostle Paul stopped at Tyre on his return trip by ship from his third missionary journey.

Learn More: 1 Kings 9:11 / Ezra 3:7 / Isaiah 23:1 / Amos 1:10: Tyrus / Luke 10:13 / Acts 21:3, 7

UR OF THE CHALDEES

And Terah. . .went forth with them from Ur of the Chaldees. GENESIS 11:31

This ancient city between the Tigris and Euphrates Rivers is where Abraham grew up. His father, Terah, eventually moved Abraham and other family members to Haran, another Mesopotamian city. Abraham lived in Haran for a time before God called him to travel to a land that He promised to Abraham and his descendants (Genesis 12:1–3).

Excavations have revealed that Ur was a center for worship of the pagan moon god known as Sin. How did Abraham resist this pagan culture and come to worship the one true God? The only explanation seems to be that God revealed this truth to him through divine revelation.

The most striking evidence of Ur's pagan culture is its famous pyramid-like structure known as a ziggurat. This terraced tower, capped with pagan shrines, rose about seventy feet above the surrounding plain. It was probably similar to the tower of Babel, a symbol of human pride and rebellion against God (Genesis 11:4–9).

Ur is referred to as Ur of the Chaldees because the Babylonians, also known as Chaldeans, occupied this territory for a time.

Learn More: Genesis 11:28; 15:7 / Nehemiah 9:7

WATERS OF MEROM

Joshua came. . .against them by the waters of Merom. JOSHUA 11:7

This body of water in northern Israel marks the site where Joshua and the Israelites fought one of the last battles in their campaign to claim the land of promise. Several Canaanite kings combined their forces into a large army under the command of Jabin. But Joshua seized the initiative and attacked first, and the Israelites were victorious over their enemies.

The exact location of the Waters of Merom is unknown, although some scholars think Lake Huleh in northern Israel is the most likely site. It is a small body of water about three miles wide by five miles long that is fed by the Jordan River. Lake Huleh is shaped like a harp, much like the Sea of Galilee, its larger sister lake to the south.

Today the lake is part of the Hula Nature Reserve, a place set aside for the protection of wildlife and aquatic plants. Its swampy terrain was drained at one time, but part of it has been restored to marshland in recent years. Lake Huleh is home to large flocks of waterfowl of several different species.

ZAREPHATH

Arise, get thee to Zarephath. . .and dwell there. 1 KINGS 17:9

The Lord spoke these words to the prophet Elijah after he predicted a severe famine would strike the land of Israel. Food would be scarce. But God promised to sustain His prophet through the kindness of this woman at Zarephath, a town on the coast of the Mediterranean Sea near Tyre and Sidon.

When Elijah found the woman and her son, they were on the verge of starvation. But she fed the prophet from her last bit of meal and cooking oil. God blessed the woman's generosity by replenishing this meager supply so that it never ran out (1 Kings 17:16).

This woman also provided lodging for Elijah. Some time after the prophet performed this feeding miracle, her son died. Elijah brought him back to life. At this miracle she declared, "Now by this I know that thou art a man of God, and that the word of the LORD in thy mouth is truth" (1 Kings 17:24).

Zarephath was a Phoenician coastal city long before Elijah's time. More than twenty pottery kilns have been discovered on this ancient site, showing that it was probably a center for manufacturing at one time.

Learn More: 1 Kings 17:10 / Obadiah 20 / Luke 4:26: Sarepta

ZELAH

*The bones of Saul. . .*BURIED THEY IN THE COUNTRY OF BENJAMIN IN ZELAH. 2 SAMUEL 21:14

This unidentified town not far from Jerusalem is where the remains of King Saul, the first king of Israel, were buried. But it took a while for his body to make it to this final resting place.

After Saul was killed with his sons in a battle in northern Israel, the Philistines hung their bodies on the wall of the city of Beth Shan as an insult and as a public example to the Israelites. But several brave men from the city of Jabesh Gilead east of the Jordan River rescued the bodies and gave them a decent burial in their city (1 Samuel 31:11–12).

Finally, King David retrieved the bones of Saul and his sons from Jabesh Gilead. Then he brought them to Zelah for their final entombment with Saul's ancestors. Even though David and Saul were enemies, David respected the kingly office and was grateful for Saul's service to his country.

Learn More: Joshua 18:25–28

ZIKLAG

These are they that came to David to Ziklag. 1 CHRONICLES 12:1

This city in southern Israel is associated with David during his fugitive years. Here David hid from King Saul and began to pull together a unit of brave warriors and other supporters. They would help him transition to the kingship after Saul had passed from the scene.

At Ziklag, David proved that he was a person of godly character as well as an effective leader. When a party of Amalekites raided Ziklag and carried off all the women and children, he sought the Lord's will before he acted.

After the captives were rescued, David insisted that the spoils of war should be shared with everyone—even those who couldn't finish the campaign because they were exhausted (1 Samuel 30:22–25). This reflected David's solid character and generous spirit.

The ruins of Ziklag have never been identified, although several sites have been suggested. The Bible says that the raiding Amalekites had "smitten Ziklag, and burned it with fire" (1 Samuel 30:1). None of these possible locations show any evidence of destruction during David's time.

Learn More: Joshua 19:1–5 / 1 Samuel 30:26 / 1 Chronicles 12:20

ZOAR

Therefore the name of the city was called Zoar. GENESIS 19:22

An angel spoke these words to Abraham's nephew Lot as he and his family fled the city of Sodom. Zoar was the only one of the five cities of the plain that was not destroyed by the Lord because of its wickedness. God apparently spared Zoar because Lot requested that he and his family be allowed to seek refuge in this city rather than the nearby mountains (Genesis 19:17–22).

Zoar is also associated with another significant time in the history of Israel. Moses led the Israelites right up to the borders of Canaan. He could almost reach out and touch this territory that he had dreamed about for more than forty years. He looked out over the land from the top of Mount Nebo. It must have been a clear day because Moses could see most of the territory of Israel, including the village of Zoar off to the south of the Dead Sea. But God would not allow him to set foot on this sacred soil (Deuteronomy 34:1–5).

The site of ancient Zoar has never been identified. Another name for the city is Bela (Genesis 14:2).

Learn More: Genesis 13:10; 14:2, 8; 19:23, 30 / Deuteronomy 34:3 / Isaiah 15:5

THE 1-MINUTE
BIBLE
GUIDE

180 Key Events

A chronological listing of the 180
most important occurrences of scripture.

Written by Ed Strauss
Edited by Jill Jones

CREATION OF LIGHT

God said, Let there be light: and there was light. GENESIS 1:3

Light isn't the first thing God created—"the heaven and the earth" predate it—but the Bible places light within the first day of Creation.

"Let there be light" are God's first recorded words (Genesis 1:3), and they immediately brought definition to the primordial world. Until light appeared, the earth was "without form, and void" and "darkness was upon the face of the deep" (verse 2).

Suddenly, though, half of creation was bathed in a glowing energy that God called "day." Though darkness would remain (as "night"), everything that God would later bring into existence could now interact differently, more effectively, with the rest of Creation. That's undoubtedly why God "saw the light, that it was good" (Genesis 1:4).

Light travels at an incredible speed (more than 186,000 miles per second in the vacuum of space), and it takes sunlight between eight and nine minutes to reach the earth. But it's interesting to note that there was light before the sun existed—God made the sun on Creation's fourth day.

Light allows us to see and understand the world around us.

Learn More: Genesis 1:1–5

CREATION OF THE EARTH

In the beginning God created the heaven and the earth. GENESIS 1:1

The Bible opens with these sweeping words: "In the beginning God created the heaven and the earth. And the earth was without form, and void" (Genesis 1:1–2). Not only was the earth initially formless and empty, but the entire universe was a chaotic mass of unformed energy and matter. Even the stars hadn't coalesced yet!

We live in what is called "a fine-tuned universe." Even secular scientists are forced to admit that the laws of the universe seem deliberately designed to make life possible and are therefore proof of an intelligent Creator.

But at this early stage, only the raw stuff of creation existed—from which all of God's order and structure and beauty would spring. No place in the universe was yet fit for life. But God had a plan to create a habitable world for mankind.

"For the LORD is God, and he created the heavens and earth and put everything in place. He made the world to be lived in, not to be a place of empty chaos" (Isaiah 45:18 NLT).

Learn More: Genesis 1:1–2, 6–10

CREATION OF PLANTS

God said, Let the earth bring forth grass. GENESIS 1:11

By the third morning of creation, the earth was fully formed. That's when God caused the entire planet to burst forth with a dizzying profusion of plant life.

The Lord created all plants, from delicate orchids in the sun-dappled jungles to mighty redwoods towering along fog-shrouded coasts. You get the impression that the almighty God had a great deal of fun being creative. But He had immensely practical purposes in mind as well.

"The living God, which made heaven, and earth, and the sea, and all things that are therein. . .filling our hearts with food and gladness" (Acts 14:15, 17). God created plants not only to awe us into silence with their beauty, but to serve as food. They nourish our bodies and give us energy.

But underlying this basic human need and woven throughout the fabric of God's plan was His desire to fill our hearts with joy.

Learn More: Genesis 1:11–13

CREATION OF ANIMALS

God created great whales, and every living creature that moveth. GENESIS 1:21

On the fifth and sixth days of creation, God designed every imaginable kind of animal—from colorful clownfish nestling among sea anemones to jaguars lurking in steaming rain forests; from pterodactyls soaring above windswept cliffs to monarch butterflies fluttering over delicate flowers; from thundering herds of shaggy bison to reclusive mountain gorillas.

Animals filled the rivers and the seas, the forests and the plains. In fact, every gram of soil on earth swarmed with millions of microscopic life forms. Even heat vents at the bottoms of the oceans and rocks far beneath the earth's surface were not forgotten. The entire planet teemed with an astonishing variety of life.

After God had created all these myriad species, He stamped every single one of them with His personal blessing—a blessing He intended to endure until the end of time: "And God blessed them, saying, Be fruitful, and multiply" (Genesis 1:22).

Learn More: Genesis 1:20–25

CREATION OF MAN

God created man in his own image. GENESIS 1:27

When God finished creating all animal life, the pale blue globe called Earth was overflowing with an unbelievably rich diversity of flora and fauna. The planet's entire interdependent ecosystem was up and running. Everything seemed complete. But it wasn't.

The triune God already enjoyed eternal communion. And God had created millions of angels before the first star came into being. When He "laid the earth's foundation. . .all the angels shouted for joy" (Job 38:4, 7 NIV). But even communion with angels wasn't enough. God longed for sentient physical beings to share His creation with.

"God said, Let us make man in our image, after our likeness. . . . And the LORD God formed man of the dust of the ground, and breathed into his nostrils the breath of life; and man became a living soul" (Genesis 1:26; 2:7).

Adam was created on the same day as the land animals, but though he had a physical body like them, he also had an eternal spirit. And this spirit was made in the image of God—literally designed for communion with the Father.

Learn More: Genesis 1:26–28; 2:7

CREATION OF WOMAN

So God created. . .male and female. GENESIS 1:27

God created Adam and Eve on the sixth day, and like man, woman is also a spiritual being—made in the image of God.

However, Eve was created differently than any other living being. Every male and female animal was made from the earth. God said, "Let the earth bring forth the living creature after his kind" (Genesis 1:24). And man was created from "the dust of the ground" (2:7). In contrast, the first woman was formed from a rib taken from the man's side.

Why did God create Eve in such a unique way? Because men and women are not simply animals, creatures of the earth, and God intended their relationship to be more than a physical union driven by sexual instincts.

Very likely, the female was taken from the male because human beings were not only created to have a relationship with—and spiritual union to—God but with each other. Men and women become "one flesh" (Genesis 2:24), but they are also to experience intimate spiritual union.

Learn More: Genesis 1:27; 2:18–24 / 1 Corinthians 6:17

FALL OF SATAN

How art thou fallen from heaven, O Lucifer! Isaiah 14:12

Angels, archangels, and other mighty heavenly beings called cherubim and seraphim were created before the physical universe came into existence—and they rejoiced at creation. They worshipped God and gave Him great joy. But some of them weren't content with their places in His kingdom.

A highly exalted cherub named Lucifer ("Light bearer") had a position of great majesty and authority. But he was envious of God and aspired to be worshipped in His place.

Ezekiel describes his rebellion, saying, "Thou art the anointed cherub. . . . Thou wast perfect in thy ways from the day that thou wast created, till iniquity was found in thee. . . . Therefore I will cast thee as profane out of the mountain of God" (Ezekiel 28:14–16).

Satan didn't rebel alone, and he didn't fall alone. He led one third of the angels of heaven in his great rebellion, and they were cast out with him.

When Lucifer fell, he became known as the devil or Satan, and when his angels fell, they became known as evil spirits or demons.

Learn More: Isaiah 14:12–15 / Ezekiel 28:11–17 / Revelation 12:3–4, 7–9

TEMPTATION OF EVE

The woman. . .took of the fruit thereof, and did eat. Genesis 3:6

Adam and Eve lived in the garden of Eden, a breathtakingly beautiful paradise. They simply picked their food off the trees. They should have been content—and they were until they were deceived and became dissatisfied.

God had told Adam that he was free to eat the fruit of any tree in the garden but one. Even the Tree of Life was available to him, but he was not to eat fruit from the Tree of the Knowledge of Good and Evil. Eve also knew this command, and she knew that the punishment for disobeying was death.

But one day Satan, disguised as a serpent, tricked the woman. He told her that God was withholding the best from them, that if she would eat the fruit of this certain tree, she would know good and evil just like God. He convinced her to disbelieve God.

Eve was deceived. She not only ate the forbidden fruit herself, but gave some to Adam. And their disobedience brought physical and spiritual death upon humanity.

Learn More: Genesis 2:15–17; 3:1–7 / Revelation 12:9

GOD CURSES THE EARTH

Cursed is the ground for thy sake. Genesis 3:17

Because Adam and Eve sinned, several curses overwhelmed the world. First, their once-perfect physical bodies became mortal. God informed Adam that he would "return unto the ground . . .for dust thou art, and unto dust shalt thou return" (Genesis 3:19). This would fulfill God's warning that eating the forbidden fruit brought death.

Their disobedience also brought a curse upon the entire natural world. God said, "Cursed is the ground. . .thorns also and thistles shall it bring forth for thee" (Genesis 3:17–18). The apostle Paul said that as a result, all creation came under "the bondage of corruption" (Romans 8:21).

Up till then, Adam and Eve had an easy life. But God told Eve that now she would only give birth by "painful labor," and He told Adam that now he would only produce food by "painful toil" (Genesis 3:16–17 NIV).

Amazingly, a promise of redemption was made when God cursed the serpent. God told the devil that there would be war between him and a descendent of the woman—the Messiah. "Thou shalt bruise his heel [seek to kill Jesus]" but Jesus will "bruise thy head [deliver a mortal blow]" (Genesis 3:15).

Learn More: Genesis 3:8–24 / 1 John 3:8

CAIN MURDERS ABEL

Cain rose up against Abel his brother, and slew him. Genesis 4:8

When God refused to accept his offering, "Cain was very wroth," or angry (Genesis 4:5). Knowing where such anger could lead, God warned him: "If thou doest well, shalt thou not be accepted? and if thou doest not well, sin lieth at the door. And unto thee shall be his desire, and thou shalt rule over him" (Genesis 4:7).

Peter warned that "your adversary the devil, as a roaring lion, walketh about, seeking whom he may devour" (1 Peter 5:8). In Cain's case, the devil was no longer prowling around. Thoughts of violence were even now crouching at the door of Cain's heart.

Rage desired to overcome Cain; the solution was for him to exercise self-control. But he failed to do so, and the result was the world's first crime. Cain murdered his brother then buried him to cover his evil deed. But God had seen everything.

Cain was banished from the very thing that had given him his sense of worth. From then on, he would no longer till the soil but be a restless wanderer on earth.

Learn More: Genesis 4:5–16 / Isaiah 48:22

NOAH BUILDS THE ARK

Make thee an ark of gopher wood. Genesis 6:14

God told Noah to construct a ship "450 feet long, 75 feet wide, and 45 feet high" (Genesis 6:15 NLT). It needed to be that huge to hold pairs of every land animal on earth, as well as food to last for over a year. Noah was likely living beside a forest, because such an ambitious project required untold tons of cypress wood.

Many people believe it took 120 years to build the ark because Genesis 6:3 says that mankind's "days shall be an hundred and twenty years." Finally, the day came when Noah was finished, so he took the animals on board. Then he and his family boarded.

"By faith Noah, being warned of God of things not seen as yet, moved with fear, prepared an ark to the saving of his house; by the which he condemned the world, and became heir of the righteousness which is by faith" (Hebrews 11:7).

How did Noah's actions condemn the world? Because, besides his family, not one other person on earth was moved with godly fear. No one helped him prepare the ark, and no one got on board.

Learn More: Genesis 6:13–22; 7:1–9

THE FLOOD

The waters prevailed, and were increased greatly upon the earth. Genesis 7:18

The ark was built. The food was loaded. The animals were on board. Then Noah and his family sat inside the ship for seven days, waiting for the end.

Suddenly powerful quakes ruptured the crust of the earth, and vast subterranean oceans burst out with tremendous force. A monstrous rainstorm engulfed the entire planet for forty days.

The floodwaters rose swiftly, sweeping away everything in their path. Those who survived the initial cataclysm sought refuge on hilltops—but these too were soon engulfed by the churning, rising waters.

"All in whose nostrils was the breath of life, of all that was in the dry land, died. And every living substance was destroyed which was upon the face of the ground. . .they were destroyed from the earth: and Noah only remained alive, and they that were with him in the ark" (Genesis 7:22–23).

The waters finally receded, and the ark came to rest on the mountains of Ararat. Then Noah and every living creature on the ark stepped forth into a new world. Humanity had been given a second chance.

Learn More: Genesis 7:10–24; 8:1–19

THE TOWER OF BABEL

The Lord scattered them. . .and they left off to build the city. GENESIS 11:8

After Noah's family emerged from the ark, the population of the earth increased rapidly. At that time, all people lived together and spoke the same language. They all traveled to what is now southern Iraq, at the junction of the Tigris and Euphrates Rivers. There they found a warm climate and fertile land, so they settled down.

Now, God's first command to mankind had been, "Be fruitful, and multiply, and replenish the earth" (Genesis 1:28). This command was still in force. They were to populate the entire earth.

But Noah's descendants decided to stay together and build a great city with a tower that stood high over the plains. They reasoned that they needed a focal point "lest we be scattered abroad upon the face of the whole earth" (Genesis 11:4). So they began to build the tower.

When God saw what the people were doing, He caused them to speak different languages. One group of people couldn't understand what the next group was saying. Unable to work together or even to live together, they scattered. . .as God always intended.

Learn More: Genesis 11:1–9

GOD CALLS ABRAM

Get thee out of thy country. . .unto a land that I will shew thee. GENESIS 12:1

Terah and his family lived in Ur, in southern Mesopotamia. One day, he took his son Abram (later called Abraham), Abram's wife Sarai, and Abram's nephew Lot and traveled north to Haran. There they lived many years and prospered. But after Terah's death, God called Abram to leave this comfortable life and go to the land He would show him. Abram obeyed. He packed up and headed south to Canaan.

It was not the first time God had spoken to this man. "The God of glory appeared unto our father Abraham, when he was in Mesopotamia, before he dwelt in [Haran], and said unto him, Get thee out of thy country, and from thy kindred, and come into the land which I shall show thee" (Acts 7:2–3).

Terah had apparently moved north at his son's request, but when they got as far as Haran, he decided to settle there. Going to Canaan was Abram's call, not Terah's. Abram had to step out from his father's shadow to fulfill his own destiny.

Learn More: Genesis 11:31–32; 12:1–5

GOD PROMISES ABRAHAM A SON

He said unto him, So shall thy seed be. GENESIS 15:5

The sun had set, and darkness settled over Canaan. Abram was in his tent, but he wasn't exactly sleeping. . .he was having a vision from God. Abram was troubled by the fact that he was now old but still had no son. God had promised him Canaan, but Abram had no children to inherit the land. God said to him, "Fear not, Abram: I am thy shield, and thy exceeding great reward" (Genesis 15:1).

It was wonderful that God was a shield protecting Abram. It was deeply rewarding knowing God personally. But Abram was concerned over his childlessness. When he died, Abram figured, his servant Eliezer would inherit everything. God told Abram that this wasn't so. His own descendants would inherit the promise.

God led Abram out of his tent, telling him to look up at the immense vault of heaven and try to count all the stars. Then God said this was how many descendants Abram would have. "And he believed in the LORD; and he counted it to him for righteousness" (Genesis 15:6).

Learn More: Genesis 15:1–7

DESTRUCTION OF SODOM AND GOMORRAH

The Lord rained upon Sodom and upon Gomorrah brimstone and fire. GENESIS 19:24

One day three visitors—God and two angels in human form—visited Abram, now called Abraham. God warned Abraham that Sodom and Gomorrah were in imminent danger of being destroyed.

Later, the angels entered Sodom, where Abraham's nephew Lot took them into his home. Soon, a mob surrounded Lot's house, demanding that he bring the strangers out for their sexual pleasure. In blazing power, the angels blinded the crowd.

Just after sunrise, the angels led Lot and his family out the city gates and warned them, "Escape for thy life; look not behind thee, neither stay thou in all the plain; escape to the mountain, lest thou be consumed" (Genesis 19:17).

No sooner had they reached the city of Zoar than a burning rain fell on Sodom and Gomorrah, utterly destroying them. Perhaps God had caused the valley's vast bitumen deposits to erupt in a tremendous explosion, sending sulfur and salt over the cities. . .or perhaps He simply dropped His fire from the sky.

Lot and his daughters retreated behind the city walls, but Lot's wife stopped and gave a last longing look at her home—and became a "pillar of salt" (Genesis 19:26).

Learn More: Genesis 18:1-2, 16-22; 19:1-28

BIRTH OF ISAAC

Sarah conceived, and bare Abraham a son in his old age. GENESIS 21:2

When God had visited Abraham, He'd shared some astonishing news: within a year Abraham's wife would bear a son. This was no small miracle. Sarah (formerly Sarai) was nearly ninety.

Abraham believed God. Being strong in faith, he overlooked the fact that he and Sarah were elderly. "He staggered not at the promise of God through unbelief; but was strong in faith . . .fully persuaded that, what he had promised, he was able also to perform" (Romans 4:20–21).

When Sarah heard the news, however, she laughed—so God asked, "Wherefore did Sarah laugh, saying, Shall I of a surety bear a child, which am old? Is any thing too hard for the LORD?" But Sarah lied, "I laughed not." God replied, "Nay; but thou didst laugh" (Genesis 18:13–15).

Sure enough, the following year Sarah gave birth to a son and called him Isaac, which means "laughter." The amazing miracle constantly made her laugh with joy, and others who heard about it couldn't keep from laughing as well.

Learn More: Genesis 18:1-15; 21:1-7

ISAAC IS NEARLY SACRIFICED

Thou hast not withheld thy son, thine only son from me. GENESIS 22:12

One day God called, "Abraham!" He replied, "Here I am" (Genesis 22:1). God then shocked the old man by telling him to take his son, Isaac—the boy who was to inherit the promises God had made to Abraham—and sacrifice him on Mount Moriah. You have to think that Abraham was stunned, but early next morning he set out.

Abraham left his servants a distance away, promising, "I and the lad will go yonder and worship, and come again to you" (Genesis 22:5). Then he and Isaac walked on. Once on the mount, Abraham built an altar, bound Isaac, and raised the knife.

Suddenly God called, "Abraham, Abraham." Again Abraham answered, "Here am I" (Genesis 22:11). God then told him *not* to sacrifice Isaac—stating that because he had been willing to sacrifice his beloved son, God would bless him beyond measure.

How could Abraham believe that God's promises would be fulfilled if he sacrificed Isaac? The Bible explains: "Abraham reasoned that if Isaac died, God was able to bring him back to life again" (Hebrews 11:19 NLT).

Learn More: Genesis 22:1-19

JACOB ACQUIRES ESAU'S BLESSING

Yea, and he shall be blessed. GENESIS 27:3

When Isaac's wife, Rebecca, was pregnant with Jacob and Esau, God told her, "Two nations are in thy womb. . .and the elder shall serve the younger" (Genesis 25:23). This reversed the typical custom, by which the firstborn child was accorded special status within a family.

To Jacob it was obvious that he was destined to rule over his brother. For that, however, he needed the birthright. One day when Isaac felt he'd soon die, he sent Esau out hunting for game. He told him to cook it the way he liked it, promising that after he'd eaten, he would pronounce the oldest son's blessing upon him.

However, Rebekah overheard and quickly had two young goats prepared. She then sent Jacob into blind Isaac's tent pretending to be Esau. By wearing goatskins on his arms—to feel like his hairy brother—Jacob convinced his father that he was Esau.

After he had eaten, Isaac blessed Jacob. When it later became obvious that deception was involved, Isaac recognized that the blessing he'd given was final.

Learn More: Genesis 27:1–37; 28:1–4

JACOB WRESTLES WITH GOD

As a prince hast thou power with God and with men, and hast prevailed. GENESIS 32:28

Jacob fled from his angry, vengeful brother and spent a number of years in Haran before returning to Canaan. God had blessed him, but he knew that he'd now have to face Esau—and he was fearful. What if his brother still wanted to kill him?

Jacob sent his family and flocks on ahead, staying behind to pray. But as he was alone, battling his fears and desperately seeking God, a man approached from the gathering gloom to attack him.

From his years of hard, physical work, Jacob was likely in excellent shape, so for hours he and the stranger battled. At some point, Jacob realized that his opponent was no mere man but a divine being. This was a test! So Jacob absolutely refused to stop fighting.

Suddenly the man dislocated Jacob's hip. Unable to continue wrestling, Jacob simply locked his arms around the stranger and held on. The man said, "Let me go, for the day breaketh." Jacob answered, "I will not let thee go, except thou bless me!" (Genesis 32:26).

So the Lord blessed Jacob, adding, "As a prince hast thou power with God and with men, and hast prevailed" (Genesis 32:28).

Learn More: Genesis 32:3–32

JOSEPH IS SOLD AS A SLAVE

And sold Joseph to the Ishmeelites for twenty pieces of silver. GENESIS 37:28

Jacob had a son by his beloved wife, Rachel, and named him Joseph. Jacob loved him more than his ten older sons and showered him with favors. One day he gave him "a coat of many colours" (Genesis 37:3) but apparently gave nothing to the others.

Joseph, in turn, was loyal to his father, and whenever his older brothers did something wrong, "brought unto his father their evil report" (Genesis 37:2).

All of this was already enough to make Joseph's older brothers hate him. But then Joseph started having vivid dreams in which he saw all his brothers bowing down to him. These dreams were from God, but Joseph's mistake was to boast about them to his brothers. They were furious.

One day when Joseph was checking up on his brothers, far from their father's camp, they ripped his colorful tunic from him, threw him into an empty water pit, and sold him to some Midianite merchants. The merchants took Joseph to Egypt, where he became a slave.

Learn More: Genesis 37:1–36

JOSEPH INTERPRETS PHARAOH'S DREAMS

Joseph said unto them, Do not interpretations belong to God? Genesis 40:8

When Joseph arrived in prison "they bruised his feet with shackles, his neck was put in irons" (Psalm 105:18 NIV). But God favored him, and soon Joseph was running the entire prison.

One night, two of Pharaoh's prisoners had dreams, and Joseph correctly interpreted them. Just as Joseph said, one man was restored to his position as royal cupbearer. The other man was executed.

Then one night Pharaoh himself had troubling dreams. Seven starving cows came out of the Nile River and devoured seven well-fed cattle. Then seven shriveled, scorched heads of grain consumed seven full heads of grain.

Pharaoh asked his wise men and magicians to interpret his dreams, but they couldn't. Then the cupbearer remembered Joseph, and he was quickly brought from prison. When asked if he could explain the dreams, Joseph replied, "It is not in me: God shall give Pharaoh an answer of peace" (Genesis 41:16).

God gave Joseph the interpretation: seven years of abundant harvests would be followed by seven years of unprecedented famine. Pharaoh promptly placed Joseph in charge of Egypt to prepare for the coming disaster.

Learn More: Genesis 40:1–23; 41:1–43

JOSEPH FORGIVES HIS BROTHERS

But as for you, ye thought evil against me; but God meant it unto good. Genesis 50:20

As Joseph had predicted, seven years of bountiful harvests came to Egypt, and he stored up vast quantities of grain. Then the famine began, devastating not only Egypt but also Canaan.

One day Joseph's brothers came to Egypt to buy grain. Joseph was now grown, so they didn't recognize him—but he knew them, and he decided to test them. Joseph accused his older brothers of being spies, threw Simeon in prison, and said that he'd only release him if the others brought back their youngest brother, Benjamin, to Egypt.

Joseph's brothers began talking together in Hebrew, lamenting that God was paying them back for what they'd done to Joseph. Joseph understood their words and was moved to tears.

Sometime later the brothers returned with Benjamin. When Joseph accused Benjamin of theft, announcing that he'd keep him as a slave, the fourth oldest brother, Judah, made an impassioned plea. He argued that losing this son would kill their aged father, Jacob. As a result, Joseph revealed to them that he was their long-lost brother. Then he "kissed all his brethren, and wept upon them" (Genesis 45:15). In that moment, Joseph forgave them.

Learn More: Genesis 42:1–24; 43:15–16; 45:1–15

THE ISRAELITES MOVE TO EGYPT

Fear not to go down into Egypt; for I will there make of thee a great nation. Genesis 46:3

When news reached Pharaoh's palace that Joseph's brothers had come, Pharaoh and all his officials were pleased. Pharaoh told Joseph to tell his brothers, "Do this. . .get your father and come. Never mind about your belongings, because the best of all Egypt will be yours" (Genesis 45:119–20 NIV).

When the eleven brothers informed their father that Joseph was not only alive but was governor of the kingdom of Egypt, Jacob couldn't believe it. But after they shared the details, and he saw the carts full of costly goods Joseph had sent, he was convinced. So Jacob and all his extended family—sons, daughters, and grandchildren—left drought-stricken Canaan behind and trekked to Egypt. True to his word, Pharaoh gave them the well-watered, fertile land of Goshen to dwell in.

When he heard that they had arrived, Joseph mounted his chariot and went to meet them, especially his father, Jacob. "And he fell on his neck, and wept on his neck a good while" (Genesis 46:29).

Learn More: Genesis 45:16–28; 46:26–30

SATAN ATTACKS JOB

Though he slay me, yet will I trust in him. JOB 13:1

Shortly after Jacob and his family moved to Egypt, an amazing story took place in the land of Uz, to the southeast of Canaan.

A man there named Job was the wealthiest of all the men of the East, and he believed in the God of Abraham. His closest friends came from Edom and were descended from Esau.

Job was a righteous man who constantly communed with God. As a result, God put a hedge of protection around Job and everything he owned.

One day, the devil appeared before God and asked, "Doth Job fear God for nought?" He challenged God, "Put forth thine hand now, and touch all that he hath, and he will curse thee to thy face" (Job 1:9, 11).

God allowed Satan to take away all of Job's material possessions—even to kill his sons and daughters—but still Job worshipped God. Then Satan received permission to strike Job with disgusting, painful boils from head to toe, but still Job refused to curse God. Job's sufferings, both physical and psychological, lasted for months.

Learn More: Job 1:1–22; 2:1–8; 7:3–5

JOB IS RESTORED

The Lord blessed the latter end of Job more than his beginning. JOB 42:12

When Job's friends heard about his troubles, they came to comfort him. And at first they did. When they saw how great his grief was, they sat for seven days saying nothing.

But, eventually, the friends convinced themselves that Job was guilty of secret sin—in fact, God wasn't even judging him as much as he deserved. One friend, Zophar, urged Job to repent. From then on, he continued to protest his innocence, and his three friends continued to insist that he must be guilty.

They argued from every possible angle that God always judges wickedness—and even though they couldn't think of any sin Job had committed, they were convinced that he must have sinned. Why? Because he was suffering.

In the end, God rebuked Job's friends and restored the suffering man's fortunes. A New Testament writer said, centuries later, "Ye have heard of the patience of Job, and have seen the end of the Lord; that the Lord is very pitiful, and of tender mercy" (James 5:11).

Learn More: Job 2:11–13; 4:3–8; 8:6, 21; 11:6, 10–17; 15:1–6

ABANDONED BABY ADOPTED

She called his name Moses: and she said, Because I drew him out of the water. EXODUS 2:10

After the deaths of Joseph and the pharaoh he served, with the Hebrews increasing in number in Egypt, new leaders worried that the people would rise up and take over. So the Egyptians reduced the Hebrews to slavery. Soon the oppression became so bad that the pharaoh commanded the Israelites to kill their newborn males, letting only the females live.

One Hebrew couple already had a daughter and a son when the murderous order came down. But when their second son was born, they just couldn't obey. Amram and Jochebed hid the boy for three months. But when they could no longer do that, his mother placed him in a papyrus basket and nestled it among the reeds at the edge of the Nile.

By chance (really, divine intervention), Pharaoh's daughter came to that spot to bathe in the river. She saw the basket and had one of her slave girls bring it to her. When she saw the beautiful child and heard him cry, her heart went out, and she decided to adopt him. She named him Moses, which means "drawn from the water."

Learn More: Exodus 2:1–10 / Numbers 26:59 / Hebrews 11:23

MOSES FLEES AS A FUGITIVE

Moses fled from the face of Pharaoh, and dwelt in the land of Midian. Exodus 2:15

Moses "was learned in all the wisdom of the Egyptians" (Acts 7:22), and when he discovered that he himself was Hebrew, he studied their wisdom too. He came across an ancient prophecy that Abraham's descendants would spend four hundred years in Egypt before leaving, and it had been almost four hundred years! "But when the time of the promise drew nigh, which God had sworn to Abraham. . .he supposed his brethren would have understood how that God by his hand would deliver them" (Acts 7:17, 25).

Convinced that he was the mighty deliverer, Moses set about to fulfill his destiny. But in one rash act, he killed an Egyptian taskmaster. Instead of setting all the slaves free, he was forced to flee Egypt. . .alone.

He spent the next forty years in exile, learning patience and dependence upon God. When God was ready, He did use Moses to deliver His people—but it took 430 years. It turns out that "four hundred years" had been a general time frame, not a precise figure.

Learn More: Genesis 15:13–14 / Exodus 2:11–15; 12:40–41

ENCOUNTER AT THE BURNING BUSH

He looked, and, behold, the bush burned with fire, and the bush was not consumed. Exodus 3:2

Moses spent forty years as a shepherd. One day when he was watching flocks near Mount Horeb, he saw a strange sight: a bush was aflame, but it wasn't consumed. Curious, he moved in for a closer look.

That's when God spoke out of the bush! The Lord said that He was the God of Moses' forefathers and that He was sending Moses to Egypt to deliver His people.

It seems Moses had once prided himself in his training and abilities, but now he asked, "Who am I, that I should go unto Pharaoh, and that I should bring forth the children of Israel out of Egypt?" (Exodus 3:11). God told Moses not to worry: He would go with him. God then gave Moses miraculous signs to perform.

However, Moses had lost self-confidence to the point where he didn't believe God could use him. He begged, "Please send someone else" (Exodus 4:13 niv). God was angry, but He agreed to provide help to Moses. The Lord would also send Moses' brother, Aaron, to assist.

Learn More: Exodus 3:1–17; 4:10–15

MOSES CONFRONTS PHARAOH

Thus saith the Lord God of Israel, Let my people go. Exodus 5:1

Moses was already suffering a lack of confidence. What happened after he arrived in Egypt tested him severely. When he asked Pharaoh to let the Israelites go into the wilderness to worship God, Pharaoh increased their workload instead. From then on, the people had to gather their own straw to make bricks.

The Israelites became angry with Moses, so he complained, "Lord, wherefore hast thou so evil entreated this people? why is it that thou hast sent me? For since I came to Pharaoh to speak in thy name, he hath done evil to this people; neither hast thou delivered thy people at all" (Exodus 5:22–23).

God sent Moses back to Pharaoh to do a miracle. But God warned Moses that even this wouldn't change the Egyptian leader's mind. Aaron threw down Moses' staff, and right before Pharaoh's eyes, it morphed into a snake.

Pharaoh summoned his magicians who cast down their staffs—which also changed into snakes. The fact that Moses' serpent consumed theirs didn't impress Pharaoh. He hardened his heart and refused to let the Israelites go.

Learn More: Exodus 5:1–23; 7:1–13

TEN PLAGUES DEVASTATE EGYPT

I will harden Pharaoh's heart, and multiply my signs and my wonders. Exodus 7:3

When Pharaoh hardened his heart, God began to do astonishing wonders in Egypt. He sent a plague of blood upon the Nile River. But Pharaoh refused to relent. This was followed by a grotesque plague of frogs, a plague of gnats, and a plague of flies. Still Pharaoh resisted. So far, the plagues had merely caused discomfort.

God then sent a plague that killed the Egyptians' livestock. This was followed by a plague of painful boils that afflicted both man and beast. Still Pharaoh resisted.

So God sent an unprecedented hailstorm that flattened all the Egyptians' crops, stripped trees bare, and killed anyone who was out in the open. Pharaoh persisted in his stubborn resistance.

Then as new crops began springing up, God sent the largest locust swarm in Egypt's history to devour every plant in sight. This was followed by three days of utter darkness.

Some Bible scholars suggest that each of these plagues were natural yearly occurrences in Egypt, albeit greatly amplified by God in this case. That may partly explain why Pharaoh refused to believe that they were divine miracles.

Learn More: Exodus 7:14–10:29

THE LORD PASSES OVER

All the firstborn in the land of Egypt shall die. Exodus 11:4-5

God was about to bring one final plague. Moses told Pharaoh, "Thus saith the LORD, About midnight will I go out into the midst of Egypt: and all the firstborn in the land of Egypt shall die" (Exodus 11:4–5).

God instructed the Israelites to kill a lamb and to smear its blood on their doorposts. He promised, "When I see the blood, I will pass over you, and the plague shall not be upon you to destroy you" (Exodus 12:13). This is where the term *Passover* originates.

While the plague was striking the land, the Israelites were eating the lambs they'd killed. And they were dressed and ready to leave.

At midnight the Lord struck the firstborn of every family in Egypt—from the firstborn of Pharaoh to the firstborn of the prisoners in their dungeons.

This final mighty plague shook Pharaoh to his core. He sent for Moses and Aaron during the night and ordered, "Get out! Leave my people—and take the rest of the Israelites with you!" (Exodus 12:31 NLT).

Learn More: Exodus 11:1–12:31

GOD PARTS THE RED SEA

The Lord shall fight for you. Exodus 14:14

When the Israelites came to the Red Sea, they learned that Pharaoh had changed his mind and had sent his chariots after them. They were trapped.

Then God did an astonishing miracle by parting the waters before them. "The floods stood upright as an heap, and the depths were congealed in the heart of the sea" (Exodus 15:8). *Congealed* means "hardened," so it appears that God performed a completely supernatural miracle.

God could also have amplified natural phenomenon. Genesis 14:21 specifies, "The LORD caused the sea to go back by a strong east wind all that night. . .and the waters were divided." Even today, a phenomenon called "wind setdown" (sustained east-west winds) at the Bitter Lakes, north of the Red Sea, pushes the waters aside, exposing the bottom.

God then stopped the wind abruptly, causing the waters to rush back with punishing force, drowning Pharaoh's chariots.

However God performed this miracle, He did it. The Israelites escaped their slavery, and Egypt's chariot armies were destroyed. For centuries, this miracle was referred to as the greatest of God's wonders of old—the defining event in the Hebrews' history.

Learn More: Exodus 14:1–31

GOD PROVIDES MANNA, AND WATER FROM A ROCK

Behold, I will rain bread from heaven for you. Exodus 16:4

Soon after the Israelites journeyed into the Sinai desert, they ran out of food. Then they complained that Moses had brought them into the wilderness to starve them to death.

That, of course, was not the plan—but they were in a barren desert. So God said, "I will rain bread from heaven for you" (Exodus 16:4). And He did. The next morning thin flakes like frost covered the desert floor for miles around. The Israelites asked, "Manna?" which is Hebrew for "What is it?"

A miraculous pillar of cloud and fire led the Israelites in all their travels. Now it guided them southward, finally stopping at a place near Mount Sinai. There was a new problem, however: there was no water. The Israelites whined and complained. Some were so mad they began plotting to stone Moses to death.

Moses cried out to God, "What shall I do unto this people? they be almost ready to stone me." The Lord answered, "Go on before the people, and take with thee of the elders of Israel; and thy rod. . .and thou shalt smite the rock, and there shall come water out of it, that the people may drink" (Exodus 17:4–6). So Moses believed God, struck the rock, and water flowed.

Learn More: Exodus 13:21–22; 16:1–35; 17:1–7; 40:36–37

RECEIVING THE TEN COMMANDMENTS

He gave unto Moses. . .two tables of testimony. Exodus 31:18

God called Moses to the top of the mountain, and for forty days, the Lord gave him laws to govern the Israelites.

"And when He had made an end of speaking with him on Mount Sinai, He gave Moses two. . .tablets of stone, written with the finger of God" (Exodus 31:18 NKJV). These tablets contained the Ten Commandments. Moses then carried them down the mountain.

But he arrived to find people dancing around a golden calf idol. It had been made by Moses' brother, Aaron, at the request of the people, who didn't think Moses was coming back. He did, though, and his "anger become hot, and he cast the tablets out of his hands and broke them at the foot of the mountain" (Exodus 32:19).

Then God told Moses, "Cut two tablets of stone like the first ones, and I will write on these tablets the words that were on the first tablets which you broke" (Exodus 34:1). The first time, God Himself had carved the stone tablets. This time Moses had to carve them. And he had to carry them to the top of the mountain and spend another forty days there.

Learn More: Exodus 20:1–17; 34:1–4, 27–28

THE GOLDEN CALF

These be thy gods, O Israel, which brought thee up out of the land of Egypt. Exodus 32:4

The first time Moses went up the mountain, he was gone many days and the people became restless. They told Aaron. "Come on, make us some gods who can lead us. We don't know what happened to this fellow Moses" (Exodus 32:1 NLT).

This was wrong on several levels.

First of all, God had led the people to this mountain and was on it with Moses at this very moment—and they weren't to go anywhere until He said so. Secondly, they didn't actually want to be led anywhere, they just wanted to have a party. Thirdly, Aaron was their human leader while Moses was absent. But he wasn't up to the task, so he yielded to their pressure and made an idol of a golden calf. "Moses saw that the people were running wild and that Aaron had let them get out of control" (Exodus 32:25 NIV).

God was prepared to wipe out everyone for their rebellion, but Moses pleaded with God, who decided to spare them. Nevertheless, three thousand of the worst offenders died.

When Moses returned to the mountain for another forty-day visit with God, there wasn't a repeat incident. The people had learned their lesson.

Learn More: Exodus 32:1–35

TWELVE SPIES REPORT ON CANAAN

Send thou men, that they may search the land of Canaan. NUMBERS 13:2

When the Israelites finally left Mount Sinai, they traveled until they came to the oasis of Kadesh, just south of Canaan. From there Moses sent twelve men to spy out the land promised to Abraham's descendants.

After forty days, the spies returned. Ten of them conceded it was a good land but focused on the negatives: the people living there were strong, and their cities were large and fortified. There were even giants!

When the Israelites heard this, they were greatly discouraged. But a spy named Caleb shouted, "Let us go up at once, and possess it; for we are well able to overcome it." The other spies argued, "We be not able to go up against the people; for they are stronger than we" (Numbers 13:30–31).

Caleb argued that there was no need to fear giants or any Canaanites, because their strength would crumble. God was for Israel. The people, however, were too discouraged to trust God. And their unbelief caused them years of needless privation and hardship.

Learn More: Numbers 13:1–33; 14:1–10

WANDERING FORTY YEARS

The children of Israel walked forty years in the wilderness. JOSHUA 5:6

From the day they left Egypt, it took the Israelites two years to reach Kadesh. Their spies then spent forty days sneaking around Canaan.

But when the spies brought back a negative report, the people wept and wailed, "Would God that we had died in the land of Egypt! or would God we had died in this wilderness! And wherefore hath the LORD brought us unto this land, to fall by the sword?" (Numbers 14:2–3).

God told the people that He would give them exactly what they requested: the entire older generation who refused to enter the promised land would die in the wilderness. They would wander a year for each of the spies' forty days in Canaan. Since the Israelites had already spent two years in the desert; there were thirty-eight to go.

The older generation had complained that if they attempted an invasion, the Canaanites would kill them and enslave their children. God said the opposite would happen: their children would go in and conquer the Canaanites. When that entire older generation of doubters finally died, God told Moses it was time for the younger generation to enter Canaan.

Learn More: Numbers 14:11–38 / Deuteronomy 2:14–15

JOSHUA BECOMES LEADER

Moses my servant is dead; now therefore arise, go over this Jordan. JOSHUA 1:2

Joshua had been commander of Israel's armies ever since they left Egypt and had repeatedly proved himself to be a godly, courageous leader. He had also been Moses' personal aide for years. So when Moses' time came to die, God told him to commission Joshua as his successor.

After Moses died, God told Joshua, "As I was with Moses, so I will be with thee: I will not fail thee, nor forsake thee. Be strong and of a good courage: for unto this people shalt thou divide for an inheritance the land" (Joshua 1:5–6).

Then God told Joshua two more times, "Be strong and courageous." He would need to be . . .he had a huge, dangerous job ahead of him.

God then gave Joshua the secret to ongoing power and success, saying, "This book of the law shall not depart out of thy mouth; but thou shalt meditate therein day and night. . .for then thou shalt make thy way prosperous, and then thou shalt have good success" (Joshua 1:8).

Learn More: Exodus 17:9, 24:13 / Deuteronomy 31:1–8; 34:9 / Joshua 1:1–11

CROSSING THE JORDAN RIVER

All the Israelites passed over on dry ground. JOSHUA 3:17

The Israelites were ready to cross the Jordan River into the promised land of Canaan. Normally, the Jordan isn't very wide, but it was springtime and the river was swollen with rain and melted snow. It overflowed its banks onto the floodplains.

But the instant the priests stepped into the river carrying the ark, the water dropped and the riverbed emptied. Only after all the Israelites crossed did the river flow again.

How did God do this? Joshua 3:16 (NIV) tells us that the water "piled up in a heap a great distance away, at a town called Adam." The river gorge is narrow at that spot and in 1927 cliffs collapsed there, damming the Jordan for twenty hours.

Perhaps God caused a similar landslide in Joshua's day. Psalm 114 indicates that He once used an earthquake to "drive back" the Jordan.

Even though God may have used natural means, the exact timing of the river drying up was a huge miracle. Speaking of timing, the instant the last priest walked out of the riverbed, the Jordan flooded back again.

Learn More: Joshua 3:1–17; 4:1–18; 5:1

RAHAB SPARES THE ISRAELITE SPIES

They. . .came into an harlot's house, named Rahab, and lodged there. JOSHUA 2:1

Joshua sent two men out as spies, and they entered Jericho and rented a room from a harlot named Rahab. But someone apparently reported them.

When Rahab realized this, she quickly led the men up to her flat roof, where she had laid out stalks of flax to dry. She declared that the Lord God of the Hebrews was the true God and that she knew He had given them the land of Canaan.

Then she said, "Now therefore, I pray you, swear unto me by the LORD, since I have shewed you kindness, that ye will also. . .deliver our lives from death" (Joshua 2:12–13). The spies promised, so she concealed them under the flax.

Soldiers arrived to search her house, but Rahab said the spies had already slipped out the city gates. The soldiers rushed off, and Rahab let the spies down the city wall on a rope.

When Jericho was taken, Joshua spared Rahab and her family because she believed in God and had acted on her faith.

Learn More: Joshua 2:1–24; 6:22–25 / Hebrews 11:31

JERICHO'S WALLS COLLAPSE

The wall fell down flat. . .and they took the city. JOSHUA 6:20

Jericho was the gateway to Canaan, just across the Jordan River. It had high, thick walls and was virtually impregnable. And now that the Israelites surrounded the city, the residents barred their gates and settled in for a siege.

God then gave Joshua odd instructions: for six days his army was to escort the ark of the covenant around Jericho, once a day. On the seventh day, they were to circle the city seven times. When the priests sounded a long blast on the trumpets, the army was to shout. And the city walls would simply collapse.

It took tremendous faith to believe such a tactic would work—but Joshua believed. So he and the Israelites obeyed God's instructions to the letter, and the mighty walls of Jericho came crashing down. Then they conquered the defenseless city.

We don't know how God did this miracle. Maybe He sent an earthquake at the exact second the army shouted. However He did it, the surrounding Canaanites heard of Jericho's fall and were absolutely terrified.

Learn More: Joshua 6:1–21

GOD STRETCHES OUT DAYLIGHT

The sun stood still, and the moon stayed. JOSHUA 10:13

As the Israelites spread into Canaan, the people of Gibeon escaped death by tricking Joshua and his men. Other people of the land were outraged and decided to annihilate the Gibeonites for making peace with the enemy. Soon the armies of five Amorite kings were besieging the city.

Gibeon begged Israel to come to their defense, and Joshua lived up to his commitment, even though it was obtained falsely. After an all-night march, the Israelites struck the Amorite armies at dawn. The fighting was fierce and lasted all day. It continued to rage even as the sun was setting in the west.

Joshua wanted to finish the battle, so he prayed, "Sun, stand thou still upon Gibeon; and thou, Moon, in the valley of Ajalon" (Joshua 10:12). And that is exactly what happened: "The sun stood still, and the moon stayed, until the people had avenged themselves upon their enemies" (verse 13).

As this bizarre day simply refused to end, the Amorites finally broke ranks and fled—but the Lord destroyed them with a terrific hailstorm that pounded the soldiers. The hail killed more men than the Israelites had.

Learn More: Joshua 10:1–15

DEBORAH GOES TO BATTLE

Deborah, a prophetess, the wife of Lapidoth, she judged Israel. JUDGES 4:4

A Canaanite king named Jabin built an army of nine hundred chariots, then conquered all the Israelites of the north. He oppressed them for twenty years.

God raised up a woman named Deborah to judge Israel. One day she summoned the warrior Barak, telling him that if he gathered an army on Mount Tabor near the Kishon River, God would lure the Canaanites and deliver them into his hands.

Barak knew that God's presence was with Deborah, so he said, "If thou wilt go with me, then I will go: but if thou wilt not go with me, then I will not go" (Judges 4:8). So Deborah went.

Apparently, God sent a sudden, heavy downpour, causing the Kishon River to overflow its banks, and most of the nine hundred chariots were swept away. Barak then attacked those who survived.

This battle broke the back of the Canaanite army. "And the hand of the children of Israel prospered, and prevailed against Jabin the king of Canaan, until they had destroyed Jabin king of Canaan" (Judges 4:24).

Learn More: Judges 4:1–24; 5:4, 21

GIDEON ROUTS THE MIDIANITES

The Lord said unto Gideon, By the three hundred men. . .will I save you. JUDGES 7:7

For seven years, whenever it was harvest time, hordes of Midianites swept into Canaan from the desert, and their massive flocks and herds devoured the Israelites' crops.

One day an angel appeared to Gideon saying, "The LORD is with thee, thou mighty man of valour" (Judges 6:12). Gideon replied, "Oh my Lord, if the LORD be with us, why then is all this befallen us? and where be all his miracles which our fathers told us of?" (verse 13). Gideon would get his answer.

Gideon had faltering faith and had to be reassured repeatedly—but in the end, he gathered an army of thirty-two thousand men. Then God said, "If I let all of you fight the Midianites, the Israelites will boast to me that they saved themselves by their own strength" (Judges 7:2 NLT). So God had Gideon send everyone home except for three hundred men.

Gideon positioned these men on the hills around the vast enemy camp by night. Then every man smashed a clay pot, held up a torch, and blew on a trumpet. The Midianites panicked, began killing one another, and fled. Then all Israel helped defeat them.

Learn More: Judges 6:1–7:25

SAMSON BATTLES THE PHILISTINES

The Spirit of the Lord came mightily upon [Samson]. Judges 15:14

Philistines overran the land and ruled Israel for forty years. At this time Samson was born, and when he grew up, he fell in love with a Philistine woman. At his wedding feast, he presented a riddle to his guests, promising them that if they answered it, he'd give them sixty garments. Otherwise, they had to give him sixty garments. The Philistines, however, forced Samson's wife to divulge the answer.

Samson was furious. With the Spirit of God empowering him, Samson went out, killed thirty Philistines, took their garments, and gave them to his guests. And the uprising began.

After Samson stormed out of his wedding feast, his father-in-law gave his bride to another man. That made Samson so mad he set the Philistines' grain fields on fire. Soon half of Philistia was burning.

In retaliation, the Philistines burned down the house of Samson's wife, killing her and her father. Infuriated, Samson slaughtered many more Philistines. Then, with the entire country stirred up, he retreated to Judah.

The Philistine army tracked him down and captured him. Then the Spirit of the Lord came mightily on Samson, and he snapped the ropes binding his wrists as if they were burned threads. Then he killed a thousand men with a donkey's jawbone.

Learn More: Judges 13:1–14:20; 15:1–20

THE DOWNFALL OF SAMSON

The dead which he slew at his death were more than they which he slew in his life. Judges 16:30

After several years of Samson's leadership, things seemed to be settling down with the Philistines. Samson went to the Valley of Sorek near the Philistine city of Gath. There he fell in love with a woman named Delilah. We don't know if she was Hebrew or Philistine, but she had her price.

The Philistines offered Delilah a great reward if she could discover the secret to Samson's strength and tell it to them. At first, Samson refused to divulge the truth, but Delilah "pressed him daily with her words, and urged him, so that his soul was vexed unto death" (Judges 16:16).

Samson finally revealed that his strength was due to his long hair. So while he slept, Delilah cut it off. Samson's strength immediately departed, and the Philistines captured and blinded him. They threw him in prison, forcing him to grind grain.

One day, however, during a huge public feast, the Philistines brought Samson out to mock him. But his hair had grown back, and in one final, mighty act, he pushed apart the two main pillars supporting the temple roof. The entire temple collapsed—killing thousands of enemies.

Learn More: Judges 16:1–31

GOD GIVES HANNAH A SON

For this child I prayed; and the Lord hath given me my petition. 1 Samuel 1:27

Hannah was an ordinary woman with a painful dilemma. Her husband loved her dearly, but although she had persistently tried to get pregnant, she hadn't been able to.

To make matters worse, her husband's other wife was blessed with several children. She taunted Hannah, making her life miserable. Hannah wept and refused to eat.

When the family went to the Lord's house to worship, Hannah prayed desperately. She promised God that if He gave her a child, she would dedicate that child to Him. The priest thought her passionate silent prayer was drunkenness. But Hannah answered respectfully, and Eli responded, "Go in peace: and the God of Israel grant thee thy petition that thou hast asked of him" (verse 17).

Hannah believed that God would answer her prayer. She stopped grieving, began to eat, and was no longer sad. Not long after, she had a child—and no ordinary child: Samuel would be Israel's greatest prophet since Moses.

Learn More: 1 Samuel 1:1–28

GOD SPEAKS TO YOUNG SAMUEL

Samuel grew on, and was in favour both with the Lord, and also with men. 1 SAMUEL 2:26

Eli, the high priest, was very old and overweight, so his two sons handled the day-to-day duties at the tabernacle. Sadly, they were godless men, and their abuses greatly offended many Israelites. Eli heard about their bad behavior, but he didn't stop them.

Samuel was still a child, living at the house of God and helping Eli. One night when he was lying down to sleep, he heard a voice call, "Samuel!" He ran to Eli to see what he wanted, but the old man assured him that he hadn't called.

This happened two more times, and the last time, Eli realized the Lord was calling the boy. When God called again Eli said, Samuel should respond, "Speak; for thy servant heareth" (1 Samuel 3:10).

God then gave Samuel a prophecy: the Lord was going to judge Eli and his house for their sins. Fortunately, Eli accepted the message. "And all Israel. . .knew that Samuel was established to be a prophet of the LORD" (1 Samuel 3:20).

Learn More: 1 Samuel 2:12-17, 22-36; 3:1-21

THE ARK OF GOD IS CAPTURED

The Philistines fought. . . . And the ark of God was taken. 1 SAMUEL 4:10-11

For hundreds of years, ever since the ark of the covenant had been crafted, it had symbolized the presence of the Lord. God sometimes descended and appeared between the two golden cherubim on its cover.

Now, with the Philistines oppressing Israel, God's people went out to battle. The Philistines were victorious, killing four thousand men. Shaken, the Israelites decided to bring the ark of God out to the battlefield.

They weren't desperately begging God to help them. In fact, they had a very limited relationship with God at that point. They were treating the ark almost as a good luck charm.

The Philistines were initially terrified by the ark's arrival. But their commanders realized that if they gave in to fear, they were done for. . .so they ordered their troops to stand up like men and to fight as never before.

They did, and as a result, there was a very great slaughter of Israelites. Even worse, the ark itself was captured. The Philistines would send it back after many harrowing experiences.

Learn More: 1 Samuel 4:1-22; 5:1-6:17

ISRAEL INSISTS ON A KING

Now make us a king to judge us like all the nations. 1 SAMUEL 8:4-5

God had prophesied that the Israelites would one day have a king, but for centuries they'd been satisfied to be ruled by God through human judges.

But one day the Israelites demanded a king. When Samuel prayed about it, God told him, "Hearken unto the voice of the people in all that they say unto thee: for they have not rejected thee, but they have rejected me, that I should not reign over them" (1 Samuel 8:7). Nevertheless, God told Samuel to warn them of the downsides of having a king.

But the people didn't listen. "Nay; but we will have a king over us; That we also may be like all the nations; and that our king may judge us, and go out before us, and fight our battle" (1 Samuel 8:19-20).

Samuel anointed Saul as king during the wheat harvest. The prophet called out to God, who sent thunder and heavy rain that made reaping impossible, "and all the people greatly feared the LORD and Samuel" (1 Samuel 12:18).

Learn More: Deuteronomy 17:14-20 / 1 Samuel 8:1-22; 12:13-25

SAUL DISOBEYS GOD

Samuel said to Saul, Thou hast done foolishly. 1 SAMUEL 13:13

At this time the Philistines dominated Israel, so when King Saul's son Jonathan attacked their garrison in Geba, the Philistines marshaled to crush the revolt.

Saul had a mere three thousand men, but the Philistines arrived with an innumerable army. In addition, only Saul and Jonathan had iron swords, but all the Philistines were heavily armed with these state-of-the-art weapons. The Israelites were in terrible danger, and thousands fled or hid. Even Saul's small army "followed him trembling" (1 Samuel 13:7).

Samuel had said he'd come to Gilgal to sacrifice and pray for God's help, but when the prophet didn't show up on time, Saul impulsively offered the sacrifice himself. No sooner had he finished, however, than Samuel arrived.

Samuel informed Saul that his kingdom wouldn't continue. Due to Saul's disobedience, God had chosen "a man after his own heart" as king (1 Samuel 13:14).

Learn More: 1 Samuel 13:1–23

SAMUEL ANOINTS DAVID KING

Samuel took the horn of oil, and anointed him in the midst of his brethren. 1 SAMUEL 16:13

Saul disobeyed God again by refusing to completely destroy the Amalekites—he left the king, Agag, alive and kept the enemy's best livestock. Samuel mourned greatly that Saul wasn't the king he could have been, but one day God told the aged prophet to stop mourning. Samuel was to go to Bethlehem, where God had chosen one of Jesse's sons as king.

Samuel asked, "How can I go? if Saul hear it, he will kill me" (1 Samuel 16:2). . .another indication that Saul was no longer fit to be king.

God told Samuel to take a heifer as if he were merely going to sacrifice. When Jesse and his sons came to the sacrifice, Samuel took one look at Eliab, Jesse's oldest son, a tall, handsome man, and thought that he was God's choice.

But God told Samuel, "Look not on his countenance, or on the height of his stature; because I have refused him: for the LORD seeth not as man seeth; for man looketh on the outward appearance, but the LORD looketh on the heart" (1 Samuel 16:7).

David, Jesse's youngest and least esteemed son, was finally summoned. When he arrived, God instructed Samuel to anoint him as king.

Learn More: 1 Samuel 15:34–35; 16:1–13

DAVID SLAYS A PHILISTINE GIANT

David to the Philistine. . .I come to thee in the name of the Lord of hosts. 1 SAMUEL 17:45

One day when the Philistines were arrayed in battle against the Israelites, Goliath, their champion—one of the last of a race of giants called Anakim—strode forward and bellowed out a challenge.

Goliath dared any Israelite soldier to face him in one-on-one combat. The people of whichever champion lost would become slaves of the other side. For forty days, Goliath repeated his challenge, but no Israelite dared step forward.

One day, David visited the battle lines with food for his brothers. When he heard the challenge, he asked for permission to fight. . .and King Saul granted it. As David advanced, he proclaimed, "I come to thee in the name of the LORD of hosts, the God of the armies of Israel, whom thou hast defied" (1 Samuel 17:45).

Goliath was not only huge (upward of ten feet tall), he was covered in protective armor. David rushed forward without armor, and as he ran, he swung his sling and sent a stone slamming into the giant's forehead. Goliath dropped like a rock. The Philistine army fled, and God gave the Israelites a great victory.

Learn More: Joshua 11:21–22 / 1 Samuel 17:1–54

DAVID RUNS FROM SAUL

Saul became David's enemy continually. 1 SAMUEL 18:28–29

After killing Goliath, David served in King Saul's army. He made a great name for himself, so that "all Israel and Judah loved David because he was so successful at leading his troops into battle" (1 Samuel 18:16 NLT).

David also spent time as Saul's court musician, playing tunes to soothe the king's troubled spirit. In addition, David married Saul's youngest daughter, Michal. This gave him a claim to the throne—though that wasn't David's motive for marrying her.

Saul became insanely jealous of David, seeing him as a threat to his rule. The king even tried to kill David with a javelin. After the second attempt, David fled the palace and stayed in the wilderness. There a group of valiant warriors gathered around him.

Saul repeatedly led his army out to hunt David down, obsessed with trying to kill the young man. But God protected him and eventually made him king, just as He had promised.

Learn More: 1 Samuel 18:5–16; 19:1–18; 22:1–2; 23:7–8, 14

JONATHAN GIVES DAVID THE KINGDOM

[Jonathan] said unto him. . .thou shalt be king over Israel. 1 SAMUEL 23:17

Saul was determined to destroy David, but Jonathan remained his loyal friend and constantly spoke up to defend him. When Saul insisted that David must die, Jonathan asked, "Wherefore shall he be slain? what hath he done?" (1 Samuel 20:32).

Saul tried to appeal to Jonathan's desire to rule, saying, "For as long as the son of Jesse liveth upon the ground, thou shalt not be established, nor thy kingdom" (1 Samuel 20:31).

But Jonathan refused to betray his friend. Instead, he warned David about his father's intentions and made an eternal covenant of friendship with David.

When Saul was pursuing David in the wilderness, Jonathan slipped away from the army, met David secretly, and encouraged him. "Don't be afraid," he said. "My father Saul will not lay a hand on you. You will be king over Israel, and I will be second to you. Even my father Saul knows this" (1 Samuel 23:17 NIV).

Saul did know this, but he couldn't bring himself to accept the fact.

Learn More: 1 Samuel 20:1–42; 23:14–18

SAUL CONSULTS A MEDIUM

Then said Saul unto his servants, Seek me a woman that hath a familiar spirit. 1 SAMUEL 28:7

Israel's great prophet Samuel had died. The Philistine army continued to harass Israel. King Saul gathered his fighting men, but when he saw what he faced, he was terrified.

"When Saul saw the host of the Philistines, he was afraid, and his heart greatly trembled. And when Saul enquired of the LORD, the LORD answered him not" (1 Samuel 28:5–6). Saul had not listened to God for many years, so God had stopped speaking to him.

Desperate to know what to do, Saul went to a medium, though he himself had earlier banned such people from Israel. He ordered her to summon the spirit of Samuel, and it appears the woman was prepared to fake it. But to her amazement, Samuel's spirit actually appeared, telling the king that Israel would be defeated in battle and that Saul would die.

In the terrific battle that followed, Saul and many Israelites were slain. The disaster was so great that countless Israelites abandoned their cities and fled.

"Saul died because he was unfaithful to the LORD; he did not keep the word of the LORD and even consulted a medium for guidance" (1 Chronicles 10:13 NIV).

Learn More: 1 Samuel 28:3–25; 31:1–10

CIVIL WAR IN ISRAEL

There was long war between the house of Saul and the house of David. 2 Samuel 3:1

After their disastrous defeat and the Philistine invasion of the land, Israel was broken. Their king had been killed. However, Saul's son Ish-Bosheth had survived, so Abner, commander of Saul's army, brought him to a city across the Jordan River and made him king. However, Ish-Bosheth was a weak ruler. Abner was the real power.

Meanwhile, David went to Hebron in Judah. The men of Judah, knowing the prophecies about David, anointed him king over their tribe. The stage was now set for a protracted struggle for the throne of all Israel.

"The war between the house of Saul and the house of David lasted a long time. David grew stronger and stronger, while the house of Saul grew weaker and weaker" (2 Samuel 3:1 NIV). This simmering civil war lasted seven years.

David could have mounted a major assault, but this would have resulted in many Israelite deaths. So he settled for a slow, steady campaign. He had the faith to wait for God to act.

Learn More: 2 Samuel 2:1–3:1

DAVID CAPTURES JERUSALEM

David took the strong hold of Zion. 2 Samuel 5:7

During the time of war between David and the family of Saul, Abner had a falling-out with Ish-Bosheth. The military commander decided to give his allegiance to David. But when Joab, David's commander, found out, he was furious because Abner had killed his brother Asahel. Joab took Abner aside as if to speak to him and fatally stabbed him.

With the death of Abner, Ish-Bosheth was greatly weakened and not long afterward was assassinated by his own servants. Soon all Israel accepted David as king.

David now needed a centralized capital, so he chose the Canaanite stronghold of Jebus, formerly called Jerusalem. Jebus had high walls, and its inhabitants mocked David, saying he wouldn't be able to take their city.

But David had grown up nearby and knew a detail the Canaanites didn't consider important: the city's water supply was just outside the walls, and a small opening led underneath—and from there a water shaft went straight up.

David sent his men through the opening, and they scaled the vertical water shaft. Once inside, they fought their way to a gate and opened it for the army. David then took the city—and renamed it Jerusalem, which became known as "the city of David."

Learn More: 2 Samuel 2:17–23; 3:6–39; 5:6–8 / 1 Chronicles 11:4–6

THE ARK COMES TO JERUSALEM

David went and brought up the ark of God. . .into the city of David. 2 Samuel 6:12

Now king over all Israel, David decided to bring the ark of God to Jerusalem. It was a wonderful idea, but he failed to heed the scriptures that specified how to transport the ark. So some men simply placed it on an oxcart and headed down the road.

David had gathered priests and Levites from all over Israel, and they were singing and rejoicing with all their might when suddenly the oxen stumbled. A man reached out to steady the ark and keep it from falling, and he was immediately struck dead.

So David was afraid to bring the ark into his city. It stayed where it had stopped, and all the Levites went home. Years passed and David had built his own palace before he attempted to move the ark again. By then he knew that Levites had to carry it in a very specific way.

Once again David gathered Levites from all over Israel, and once again they sang and rejoiced as they moved the ark. This time they did things right, and they brought it safely into Jerusalem.

Learn More: Exodus 25:10–14 / Numbers 4:5–6, 15 / 2 Samuel 6:1–19 / 1 Chronicles 13:1–14; 15:1–28

GOD MAKES A COVENANT WITH DAVID

Thine house and thy kingdom shall be established for ever before thee. 2 Samuel 7:16

After David had finished his wars and was settled in his palace, he said to the prophet Nathan, "That the king said unto Nathan the prophet, See now, I dwell in an house of cedar, but the ark of God dwelleth within curtains. And Nathan said to the king, Go, do all that is in thine heart; for the Lord is with thee" (2 Samuel 7:2–3).

God indeed was with David, but Nathan had spoken hastily. That night, God told the prophet that because David had fought many wars and shed much blood, the task of building Him a house was reserved for David's son.

However, God vowed that He would build David's house: "The Lord telleth thee that he will make thee an house. . . . Thine house and thy kingdom shall be established for ever before thee: thy throne shall be established for ever" (2 Samuel 7:11, 16). This promise would be ultimately fulfilled in Jesus Christ, the Son of David, who would live and reign forever.

Although David couldn't build a temple himself, he made extensive preparations for Solomon.

Learn More: 2 Samuel 7:1–29 / 1 Chronicles 22:1–19 / Luke 1:31–33

DAVID STEALS URIAH'S WIFE

Is not this Bathsheba, the daughter of Eliam, the wife of Uriah? 2 Samuel 11:3

Considering all of his great, God-given victories, you'd think David would have been keenly aware of the Lord's presence and power. But he had been so highly honored, it seems he began to think he was entitled to whatever he desired.

One evening when he was on his palace roof, he glanced down into a neighboring courtyard and saw a beautiful woman bathing. David immediately had Bathsheba brought to him and committed adultery with her.

When she became pregnant, David summoned Bathsheba's husband home from the war, hoping that he'd sleep with her and think that the child was his own.

But when the honorable Uriah refused to enjoy the pleasures of home while his comrades were still on the battlefield, David plotted his death. He ordered Uriah to be placed in the area of heaviest fighting, then had the army withdraw from him, leaving him to die. Immediately, David took Bathsheba as his own wife.

This affair was a blot on his life. "David had done what was right in the eyes of the Lord and had not failed to keep any of the Lord's commands all the days of his life—except in the case of Uriah the Hittite" (1 Kings 15:5 NIV).

Learn More: 2 Samuel 11:1–12:15

ABSALOM'S CONSPIRACY

Absalom said moreover, Oh that I were made judge in the land! 2 Samuel 15:4

David had a son named Amnon, who lusted so much for his half-sister Tamar that one day he violated her, and "when king David heard of all these things, he was very wroth" (2 Samuel 13:21). Amnon was David's firstborn, destined to be king. But his sin derailed any such plans.

Two years later, Absalom, Tamar's full brother, had Amnon murdered, then fled to a place called Geshur.

After three more years, David's temper cooled, and he invited Absalom back to Jerusalem. Soon, David fully reinstated him.

But Absalom rewarded his father by plotting to murder him too. Absalom thought he would make a great king, probably meting out better justice than his father. And wasn't he strikingly handsome with five pounds of long, beautiful hair?

Absalom began to flatter all the Israelites who came seeking justice. He would tell them there was no one to hear their complaints but that he would help them if only he had the authority. "So Absalom stole the hearts of the men of Israel" (2 Samuel 15:6).

Learn More: 2 Samuel 13:1–15:12

A CENSUS CAUSES A PLAGUE IN ISRAEL

Satan stood up against Israel, and provoked David to number Israel. 1 Chronicles 21:1

Many years into his kingship, David decided to number all Israel to know how strong he was. Now, there was technically nothing wrong with a census: in the very last battle David had numbered the fighters who were with him, and God had twice told Moses to c,ount Israel's warriors. But in this case, the idea of a census was a direct temptation by Satan.

Even Joab, David's military commander, knew the king's motives were wrong. He protested, "Why then doth my lord require this thing? why will he be a cause of trespass to Israel?" (1 Chronicles 21:3).

David insisted, though, so it was done. But "God was displeased with this thing; therefore he smote Israel" (1 Chronicles 21:7).

God sent a plague on Israel, and seventy thousand people died. Soon the angel causing the plague arrived at Jerusalem. When David saw him, he prayed for God to spare the people because he—not they—had sinned. God listened to David's prayer and halted the judgment.

Learn More: Numbers 1:1–3; 26:1–2 / 2 Samuel 18:1; 24:1–25 / 1 Chronicles 21:1–30

SOLOMON PRAYS FOR WISDOM

Give therefore thy servant an understanding heart to judge thy people. 1 Kings 3:9

King Solomon started out on a terrific note, for "Solomon loved the Lord" (1 Kings 3:3) and obeyed all His commandments. At this time, although the ark was in Jerusalem, the altar of sacrifice was in Gibeon, so Solomon went there to sacrifice to the Lord.

That night while he was sleeping, God appeared to Solomon in a dream and told him, "Ask what I shall give thee" (1 Kings 3:5).

Solomon could have asked for great wealth or victory over his enemies. Instead he unselfishly asked for the wisdom to rule and judge God's people. The Lord replied, "I will do what you have asked. I will give you a wise and discerning heart, so that there will never have been anyone like you, nor will there ever be" (1 Kings 3:12 niv).

God also gave Solomon what he had not asked for—tremendous riches, honor, and peace in his kingdom.

Learn More: 1 Kings 3:1–15

SOLOMON BUILDS GOD'S TEMPLE

So Solomon built the house, and finished it. 1 Kings 6:14

David had made extensive preparations for God's temple, and once Solomon became king, he requested King Hiram of Tyre to send the necessary cedar.

In his fourth year, Solomon began building. Hiram sent skilled architects and stonemasons to help him.

Solomon needed artisans to create pillars, statues of oxen, carts, a great basin, and other articles of bronze—as well as objects of gold and silver. A skilled bronze worker named Huram (an Israelite) was living in Tyre, so King Hiram sent him as well.

Seven years later, the temple was complete, paneled inside with cedar boards and covered with gold. And all the articles for the temple were finished.

The priests placed the ark of God in the holy place inside the temple. Then Solomon dedicated God's house. When he finished praying, fire fell from heaven and consumed the sacrifices! And the cloud of the Lord's presence completely filled the temple.

Learn More: 1 Kings 5:1–6:9, 37–38; 7:13–14; 8:1–11 / 1 Chronicles 22:2–5 / 2 Chronicles 7:1–3

SOLOMON FALLS INTO IDOLATRY

When Solomon was old. . .his wives turned away his heart after other gods. 1 KINGS 11:4

After the temple was complete, God appeared to Solomon again. He promised that if Solomon loved and obeyed Him, He would bless him; but if Solomon or his sons turned to worship other gods, God would abandon the temple the king had built.

For most of his life, Solomon was faithful, so God fulfilled His promise to make him wealthier, wiser, and more glorious than all other kings on earth.

Solomon, however, "loved many strange [foreign] women.... He had seven hundred wives, princesses, and three hundred concubines: and his wives turned away his heart" (1 Kings 11:1, 3).

Solomon compromised to please his many pagan wives. As a result, the Spirit of God departed from his life, taking Solomon's wisdom with Him. God determined to remove most of Solomon's kingdom, leaving only Judah to David's line. Worst of all, Solomon led all Israel into great sin.

Solomon himself had written, "The fear of the LORD is the beginning of wisdom; and the knowledge of the holy is understanding" (Proverbs 9:10). When Solomon ceased to fear the Lord, he lost true wisdom.

Learn More: 1 Kings 9:1–9; 11:1–13

ISRAEL DIVIDES

To your tents, O Israel: now see to thine own house, David. 1 KINGS 12:16

Due to Solomon's sin, God had vowed to tear most of the kingdom away from David's descendants. So while Solomon was still king, God sent the prophet Ahijah to anoint one of Solomon's officers, Jeroboam, as king over the ten northern tribes.

After Solomon died, all Israel gathered to make his son Rehoboam king. But first they complained that Solomon had imposed heavy taxes and labor requirements on them; if Rehoboam would lighten their load, they would serve him faithfully.

When Rehoboam asked his older advisors what to do, they urged him to listen to the people. But when Rehoboam asked his young companions for advice, they convinced him to make a show of strength by declaring that he'd make their load even heavier. When the northern tribes heard this answer, they revolted. Then Jeroboam stepped up and became their king.

Rehoboam was preparing for war, but the prophet Shemaiah gave him a message from God: "Ye shall not go up, nor fight against your brethren. . . for this thing is from me" (1 Kings 12:24). God had used even Rehoboam's foolish boast to accomplish His will.

Learn More: 1 Kings 11:26–12:24

ELIJAH CALLS DOWN A DROUGHT

There shall not be dew nor rain these years, but according to my word. 1 KINGS 17:1

At one point in Israel's history, only seven thousand people remained faithful to God and refused to worship Baal. But God still loved His people and sent them a powerful prophet—Elijah.

One day Elijah stormed in and declared to Ahab: "As the LORD, the God of Israel, lives, whom I serve, there will be neither dew nor rain in the next few years except at my word" (1 Kings 17:1 NIV). This drought was more than just a punishment for sin. For forty-two months, it was a daily reminder of the power of God.

It also showed the effectiveness of prayer. "The effectual fervent prayer of a righteous man availeth much. Elijah. . .prayed earnestly that it might not rain: and it rained not on the earth by the space of three years and six months. And he prayed again, and the heaven gave rain" (James 5:16–18).

The entire nation suffered during this drought because almost the entire nation was guilty and needed to return to God.

Learn More: 1 Kings 17:1–7; 18:41–45; 19:18

A WIDOW RECEIVES MIRACLE FOOD

The barrel of meal shall not waste, neither shall the cruse of oil fail. 1 KINGS 17:14

After warning of the coming drought, Elijah hid. Israel's King Ahab sent men to every nation looking for him but without success. He never dreamed Elijah was in Zarephath, just eight miles south of Queen Jezebel's hometown of Sidon.

When he arrived in Zarephath, Elijah asked a Canaanite widow for bread. She answered, "As the LORD thy God liveth, I have not a cake, but an handful of meal in a barrel, and a little oil in a cruse" (1 Kings 17:12).

Elijah told the woman not to fear, promising that if she shared the last of her food with him, God would perform a miracle: He would make her meager supply of flour and oil last for years. And He did.

The widow believed the word of the Lord and "she, and he, and her house, did eat many days. And the barrel of meal wasted not, neither did the cruse of oil fail" (1 Kings 17:15–16).

Centuries later, Jesus Himself spoke of God's tender care for this Canaanite woman.

Learn More: 1 Kings 17:8–24; 18:10–11; Luke 4:25–26

CONFRONTATION ON MOUNT CARMEL

If the Lord be God, follow him: but if Baal, then follow him. 1 KINGS 18:21

At God's command, Elijah sent a message to Israel's King Ahab, telling him to gather the Israelites—and all the prophets of Baal and Asherah—on Mount Carmel.

Both Elijah and the false prophets built an altar, piled up wood, and put a sacrifice on top. Elijah then stated: "Call ye on the name of your gods, and I will call on the name of the LORD: and the God that answereth by fire, let him be God" (1 Kings 18:24). All the people agreed.

Now, Baal was a storm god. Lightning was supposedly his forte. But though Baal's prophets prayed from morning till evening, there was no answer. Finally they gave up.

Then Elijah soaked the wood of his altar with water three times and prayed to God. Immediately fire blazed down from heaven and burned up the sacrifice, the wood, the stones, and the dust. It even vaporized the water on the ground.

Then all the people cried out, "The LORD, he is the God; The LORD, he is the God" (1 Kings 18:39).

Learn More: 1 Kings 18:1–39

ELIJAH IS SWEPT UP TO HEAVEN

Elijah went up by a whirlwind into heaven. 2 KINGS 2:11

As the Lord prepared to take Elijah up to heaven, the prophet's successor, Elisha, refused to leave Elijah's side.

When they came to the Jordan River, Elijah rolled up his cloak, striking the waters to make them part so that the two prophets could cross over.

Elijah asked Elisha what he wanted, and the younger man asked for a double anointing of his spirit. Moments later, "a chariot of fire and horses of fire appeared and separated the two of them, and Elijah went up to heaven in a whirlwind" (2 Kings 2:11 NIV).

Elisha picked up Elijah's cloak that had fallen, walked back to the river, and struck the waters with it. They immediately parted again. Other prophets who witnessed this said, "The spirit of Elijah is resting on Elisha" (2 Kings 2:15).

Only one other time in the Old Testament did God transport a living man to heaven: "Enoch walked with God: and he was not; for God took him" (Genesis 5:24). In the New Testament, after His resurrection, Jesus Himself ascended into the sky on His way back to heaven.

Learn More: 2 Kings 2:1–18 / Luke 24:50–51 / Acts 1:9

A WIDOW'S OIL IS MIRACULOUSLY MULTIPLIED

He said unto her, There is not a vessel more. And the oil stayed. 2 KINGS 4:6

A group of prophets had followed Elijah—and was now following Elisha—to learn. There were fifty of these prophets living in Jericho alone.

Then one of them died, and his sudden passing left his wife and two children deeply in debt. The widow came to Elisha and said, "Thy servant my husband is dead; and thou knowest that thy servant did fear the LORD: and the creditor is come to take unto him my two sons to be bondmen" (2 Kings 4:1).

Elisha asked what she had in her house. The poor lady was down to just one jar of oil. Elisha said, "Go, borrow thee vessels abroad of all thy neighbours, even empty vessels; borrow not a few" (2 Kings 4:3). Elisha told her to then pour oil into the jars. She obeyed.

The oil miraculously kept flowing until all the empty jars were filled. Elisha then told her to sell the oil, pay off her debt, and live on the money that remained.

Learn More: 2 Kings 2:7; 4:1–7

ELISHA REVIVES A DEAD BOY

She. . .took up her son, and went out. 2 KINGS 4:37

A wealthy woman of the town of Shunem was very hospitable to Elisha, so in return God miraculously gave her a son, even though her husband was old.

But one day the boy was out in the sun watching his father's men harvesting, when he was overcome, possibly by sunstroke. The father had the boy taken to the house, where he died in his grief-stricken mother's arms.

Quickly, the woman mounted a donkey and rode to Mount Carmel, twenty-five miles away. There she told Elisha the news. Elisha sent his servant Gehazi ahead with his staff, telling him to lay it on the boy to raise him up. But this was unsuccessful.

Late in the day Elisha and the woman arrived. The boy's corpse was now cold, so Elisha prayed fervently and then stretched himself out on the body until it became warm. Then Elisha paced back and forth. He stretched himself out again. Suddenly the boy sneezed seven times and opened his eyes. He was alive again!

Learn More: 1 Kings 17:17–24 / 2 Kings 4:8–37

NAAMAN'S LEPROSY IS HEALED

And his flesh came again like unto the flesh of a little child. 2 KINGS 5:14

Arameans had fought several pitched battles with Israel. For a while, though, there was a cessation of hostilities.

Naaman, commander of the Aramean army, was mighty and honorable. But he was a leper. One day his wife's Hebrew slave girl said, "Would God my lord were with the prophet that is in Samaria! for he would recover him of his leprosy" (2 Kings 5:3). Soon Naaman was outside Elisha's house.

Elisha sent a man out to tell Naaman to wash himself seven times in the Jordan River to be healed of his leprosy.

Naaman was enraged. "'I thought, He will surely come out to me, and stand, and call on the name of the LORD his God, and strike his hand over the place, and recover the leper" (2 Kings 5:10–11).

Naaman was about to leave, but his servants pointed out that, after all, he'd been told to do something easy. It was worth trying. So Naaman washed. . .and was healed.

Learn More: 2 Kings 5:1–19

PROPHET JONAH RUNS AWAY

But Jonah rose up to flee unto Tarshish from the presence of the Lord. JONAH 1:3

Jonah had prophesied that Israel's King Jeroboam II would defeat Aram, and he did. Israel was now larger, stronger, and more prosperous than it had ever been.

But a mighty warring empire to the north was an imminent threat. The Assyrians were the most violent, cruel empire the world had ever seen, and Jonah knew it. You would think he'd be delighted to preach God's message: "Yet forty days, and Nineveh shall be overthrown" (Jonah 3:4).

But Jonah wanted nothing at all to do with Assyria or its capital city. He jumped aboard a ship going in the opposite direction to avoid his task entirely.

We all know the rest of the story, though. God sent a storm, the sailors threw Jonah overboard, he was swallowed by a great sea creature, was finally vomited on the shore. . .and once again ordered to go warn Nineveh. This time he obeyed.

Amazingly, Nineveh repented. God delayed His judgment. And the prejudiced Jonah was angry.

Learn More: Jonah 1:1–4:11

ISAIAH PROPHESIES THE VIRGIN BIRTH

Behold, a virgin shall conceive, and bear a son. ISAIAH 7:14

Judah's King Ahaz was an especially idolatrous leader, so you'd think that God wouldn't have cared for him. But the fact that Ahaz believed in signs and the supernatural meant that he was also open to appreciating the power of the true God—if he saw it.

One day Ahaz heard that Aram and Israel would invade Judah again, "so the hearts of Ahaz and his people were shaken, as the trees of the forest are shaken by the wind" (Isaiah 7:2 NIV). But the prophet Isaiah assured him, "It shall not stand, neither shall it come to pass" (Isaiah 7:7).

Isaiah challenged Ahaz to ask God for a sign of confirmation. The sign could be as difficult as he wished. But Ahaz refused to ask.

God wanted to give a sign. He wanted to demonstrate His power. But when Ahaz wasn't interested, God gave a sign that was fulfilled in the distant future: "Behold, a virgin shall conceive, and bear a son, and shall call his name Immanuel" (Isaiah 7:14). Immanuel means "God with us."

Ahaz didn't see this sign, but it has encouraged millions of people since then to believe that Jesus is God's Son. . .and God with us.

Learn More: Isaiah 7:1–14 / Matthew 1:21–23

THE NORTHERN KINGDOM FALLS

Assyria took Samaria, and carried Israel away into Assyria. 2 KINGS 17:6

A prophet had told Israel that "the fierce wrath of the LORD is upon you" (2 Chronicles 28:11). It had finally come time to pay for centuries of sin and idol worship.

Therefore, during King Pekah's reign, Tiglath-Pileser of Assyria attacked Israel and sacked many cities. He also conquered the regions of Gilead, Galilee, and the north, taking many captives. Then there was a brief reprieve.

After Hoshea became king of Israel, however, the Assyrians returned—this time to stay—and Hoshea was forced to pay heavy tribute for several years.

Then Hoshea tried to break free with Egypt's help. The Assyrians discovered his plot and invaded the entire country. After a three-year siege, the capital city of Samaria fell. The Assyrians took all Israel captive. . .and that was the end of the northern kingdom.

"This disaster came upon the people of Israel because they. . .had done many evil things, arousing the LORD's anger. Yes, they worshiped idols, despite the LORD's specific and repeated warnings" (2 Kings 17:7, 11–12 NLT).

Learn More: 2 Kings 15:27–30; 17:1–23

JOSIAH FINDS THE LOST LAW

When the king had heard the words of the book of the law. . .he rent his clothes. 2 KINGS 22:11

God's temple in Jerusalem had been neglected for many decades and had fallen into disrepair. When Josiah, grandson of Judah's evil King Manasseh, had been king for eighteen years, he ordered workmen to repair it.

At this time the high priest found the long-lost law of Moses. A scribe took it to Josiah, saying, "Hilkiah the priest hath delivered me a book" (2 Kings 22:10). The scribe then read it out loud.

The law had been lost for many decades, and Josiah had never even heard it. So when the scribe began reading God's warnings from Deuteronomy 28:15–68, Josiah became afraid. Israel had disobeyed God greatly, and judgment was imminent.

Josiah asked the prophetess Huldah for insight, and she quoted God as saying, "I will bring evil upon this place, and upon the inhabitants thereof, even all the curses that are written in the book" (2 Chronicles 34:24). But God promised that because of Josiah's tender heart, the disaster wouldn't happen in his day.

Learn More: 2 Kings 22:1–20 / 2 Chronicles 34:1–28

TWO EMPIRES CONQUER JUDAH

The Lord shall cause thee to be smitten before thine enemies. DEUTERONOMY 28:15, 25

After King Josiah's death in Judah, Jehoahaz took the throne—but reigned only three months before the Egyptians deposed him and set up Jehoiakim as puppet king. Pharaoh demanded tribute payments, so Jehoiakim taxed everyone to raise the money.

Jehoiakim didn't love God as Josiah had, and, during his reign, worship of Baal and Asherah flourished once more.

Meanwhile, in 606 BC, Egypt's Pharaoh Necho attacked the other world power, the Babylonians. At first he was winning, but at the Battle of Carchemish in 605 BC, Necho's army was badly mauled. That same year, Nebuchadnezzar became king of Babylon.

Following this battle, Pharaoh Necho lost control of Syria, Phoenicia, and Israel. After that, Necho stayed in Egypt. Judah was still in trouble, though, ruled by an idolatrous king, Jehoiakim, and ultimately under Babylonian control.

Learn More: 2 Kings 23:28–37; 24:7 / 2 Chronicles 36:1–4 / Jeremiah 46:2 / Daniel 1:1–2

DANIEL TAKES A STAND IN BABYLON

I beseech thee, ten days; and let them give us pulse to eat, and water to drink. DANIEL 1:12

When Nebuchadnezzar conquered Judah in 605 BC, he took several members of the royal house and noble families back to Babylon. Among them were four youths—Daniel and his friends, whose Babylonian names were Shadrach, Meshach, and Abednego.

In a three-year crash course, Daniel and friends were taught the language and literature of the Babylonians. Fortunately, they were quick learners.

However, there was a serious challenge: they were given provision from the king's table, yet this included food forbidden to the Jews. So "Daniel purposed in his heart that he would not defile himself with the portion of the king's meat, nor with the wine which he drank" (Daniel 1:8).

His supervisor was afraid to change the king's orders and have the Israelites look sickly, but Daniel suggested that he and his friends have only vegetables and water for ten days. . . after that the supervisor could judge the results. Sure enough, after ten days, the four Israelite youths were in excellent health, and every other young man was put on that diet.

Learn More: Leviticus 11 / Daniel 1:1–20

NEBUCHADNEZZAR HAS A FANTASTIC DREAM

God. . .maketh known to the king Nebuchadnezzar what shall be. DANIEL 2:28

One night King Nebuchadnezzar had a mysterious dream—and to make matters worse, when he woke up, he couldn't remember it. So he called his wise men, demanding that they tell him what he had dreamed and what it meant.

They protested that he was asking an impossible thing. But this only made the king so mad that he ordered all the wise men to be killed! Daniel, however, asked Nebuchadnezzar for time and promised that he would do what was asked.

Then Daniel prayed desperately—because this truly was an impossible task. And that night God miraculously revealed the king's dream to him.

The next day, Nebuchadnezzar asked, "Art thou able to make known unto me the dream which I have seen, and the interpretation thereof?" (Daniel 2:26). Daniel answered that this mystery was beyond his ability to solve, then added, "But there is a God in heaven that revealeth secrets" (verse 28).

When Daniel shared what God had showed him, Nebuchadnezzar was astonished. He exclaimed, "Of a truth it is, that your God is a God of gods" (Daniel 2:47).

Learn More: Daniel 2:1–49

ISRAELITES ARE HURLED INTO A FURNACE

Our God whom we serve is able to deliver us from the burning fiery furnace. DANIEL 3:17

King Nebuchadnezzar had a ninety-foot-high golden idol erected in Babylon. Then he commanded everyone to bow down and worship it. Shadrach, Meshach, and Abednego refused.

Nebuchadnezzar summoned them, offering one last chance to obey. If they didn't, they'd be hurled into a burning furnace. He assured the three men that no god would be able to deliver them.

But they answered, "Our God whom we serve is able to deliver us. . . . But if not, be it known unto thee, O king, that we will not serve thy gods, nor worship the golden image which thou hast set up" (Daniel 3:17–18).

Nebuchadnezzar's face contorted with rage, and he ordered the furnace to be heated seven times hotter than usual. Shadrach, Meshach, and Abednego were hurled into the flames, but moments later, to the king's astonishment, the three men were walking around inside the furnace. And a fourth man appeared with them!

Shadrach, Meshach, and Abednego came out of the furnace completely unharmed.

Learn More: Daniel 3:1–30

EZEKIEL SEES GOD'S MAJESTY

The word of the Lord came expressly unto Ezekiel the priest. EZEKIEL 1:3

In Judah, King Jehoiakim rebelled against the Babylonians, so Nebuchadnezzar captured Jerusalem and took his vassal to Babylon. Jehoiakim's son Jehoiachin then reigned. But only three months later, Jehoiachin was also taken to Babylon.

Several other Jews went to Babylon with him; among them was a Levite named Ezekiel. Soon Ezekiel was living with other Jews along the Chebar Canal. There, five years later, he had an astonishing vision.

The heavens opened, and Ezekiel saw "a whirlwind was coming out of the north, a great cloud with raging fire engulfing itself; and brightness was all around it and radiating out of its midst like the color of amber" (Ezekiel 1:4 NKJV).

Ezekiel then saw four heavenly creatures called cherubim. Each one had four faces, and "their appearance was like burning coals of fire. . .and out of the fire went forth lightning" (Ezekiel 1:13).

Above the four creatures was a throne where God sat, gleaming brilliantly like fire with a rainbow around Him. God then called Ezekiel to be a prophet to the Israelites.

Learn More: 2 Kings 24:1–17 / Ezekiel 1:1–28; 2:2–3

JERUSALEM'S FALL

The city was broken up, and all the men of war fled by night. 2 KINGS 25:4

For years the Babylonian army besieged Jerusalem. When soldiers finally broke through the wall, they rushed into the city. Judah's King Zedekiah then put his plan into operation: he and his army burst out from a secret gate, fought their way through the enemy lines, and fled toward Jericho.

It might have seemed like a clever plan, but God made sure the Babylonians caught Zedekiah. His army was scattered, his sons were killed, and he was blinded and taken to Babylon.

Meanwhile, the Babylonians looted God's temple. One month later Nebuzaradan, the Babylonian general, burned the temple, the king's palace, and all the houses of Jerusalem. His army then broke down all the city's walls to discourage future rebellion. And he took most of the surviving Jews as prisoners to Babylon.

The judgments that had been threatened in Deuteronomy 28:15–68 had finally arrived. God's punishment had been mercifully delayed time and again. But Judah's time was up.

Learn More: 2 Kings 25:1–12 / 2 Chronicles 36:11–20

BABYLON FALLS SUDDENLY

In that night was Belshazzar the king of the Chaldeans slain. DANIEL 5:30

Years after Nebuchadnezzar ruled Babylon, Belshazzar was king. He reigned poorly and lost most of his empire to the Medes and Persians.

Armies of this new empire were camped around Babylon itself. But Belshazzar was confident that the capital was impregnable, so one evening he threw a drunken party. He even used golden goblets that had been taken from God's temple in Jerusalem.

Suddenly a disembodied hand appeared in the hall, writing ominous words on the palace wall. Belshazzar shook with fear, quickly summoning the elderly Daniel to interpret the handwriting.

Daniel first reminded Belshazzar of his predecessor, Nebuchadnezzar: "When his heart was lifted up, and his mind hardened in pride, he was deposed from his kingly throne. . . . And thou his son, O Belshazzar, hast not humbled thine heart, though thou knewest all this" (Daniel 5:20, 22).

Daniel then informed the king that the handwriting declared that God had brought Belshazzar's reign to an end. His kingdom would be given to the Medes and Persians. That very night their armies broke through the city's defenses, and Belshazzar was killed.

Learn More: Daniel 5:1–31

DANIEL IS DROPPED INTO A DEN OF LIONS

Daniel was taken up out of the den, and no manner of hurt was found upon him. DANIEL 6:23

Darius the Mede was now in charge of the conquered Babylonian territories. Darius favored Daniel and appointed him as one of the three top rulers of the kingdom.

This made many governors and satraps jealous, and they plotted against Daniel. They "sought to occasion against Daniel. . .but they could find none occasion nor fault; forasmuch as he was faithful" (Daniel 6:4).

Then the plotter had an idea: they told Darius that he should enact a law that no one could pray to any god for thirty days—only to Darius. All offenders should be thrown to the lions. Darius foolishly agreed.

Daniel, of course, continued praying faithfully to God. When the governors and satraps told Darius about it, he tried to rescue Daniel—but the law couldn't be broken. So, with a heavy heart, he ordered Daniel thrown into the lions' den.

Early the next morning, after a sleepless night, Darius called to Daniel, asking if he was still alive. Daniel answered that, yes, God had sent an angel to shut the lions' mouths. Darius then threw Daniel's accusers to the lions.

Learn More: Daniel 6:1–28

CYRUS LETS THE EXILES RETURN

The Lord God. . .hath charged me to build him an house at Jerusalem. Ezra 1:2

Around 680 BC, about 130 years before the Medes and Persians conquered Babylon, Isaiah prophesied "to his anointed, to Cyrus" (Isaiah 45:1), saying, "I have raised him up. . .he shall build my city, and he shall let go my captives" (Isaiah 45:13).

God also declared, "I am the Lord. . .that saith of Cyrus, He is my shepherd, and shall perform all my pleasure, even saying to Jerusalem, Thou shalt be built; and to the temple, Thy foundation shall be laid" (Isaiah 44:24, 28).

Amazingly, at the time of these prophecies, Jerusalem was still intact, the temple was still standing, and the Jews hadn't yet gone into captivity. That all changed in 586 BC, when the Babylonians burned the temple, destroyed Jerusalem, and took many Jewish people to Babylon. For decades the Jews were captives in a foreign land.

In 538 BC the Persian king, Cyrus, made a decree allowing the Jews to return home. This decree also fulfilled a prophecy by Jeremiah. Cyrus accepted his divine mandate.

Learn More: 2 Chronicles 36:22–23 / Isaiah 44:24–28; 45:1–13 / Ezra 1:1–11

TEMPLE BUILDING RECOMMENCES

Then rose up Zerubbabel. . .and began to build the house of God. Ezra 5:2

Cyrus had written an edict telling the Jews to rebuild their temple, so they had a right to build. But the present ruler was against them. So the people postponed things for a more favorable season, saying, "The time is not come, the time that the Lord's house should be built" (Haggai 1:2).

But God spoke through the prophet Haggai: "Why are you living in luxurious houses while my house lies in ruins?" (Haggai 1:4 NLT). God then judged them to get their attention: "You have planted much but harvest little. . . . Your wages disappear as though you were putting them in pockets filled with holes!" (verse 6).

God was withholding His blessing because His people were putting their needs first. They were taking the easy way out, afraid to stand up for the Lord. But God ordered them to boldly start building once again.

The prophet Zechariah echoed this message. Then Zerubbabel and Jeshua took courage and started to rebuild, "and with them were the prophets of God helping them" (Ezra 5:2).

Learn More: Ezra 5:1–2 / Haggai 1:1–15

JEWESS BECOMES QUEEN OF PERSIA

The king loved Esther above all the women. . .and made her queen. Esther 2:17

Just before King Xerxes (also known as Ahasuerus) launched an invasion of Greece (482–479 BC), he hosted an extravagant banquet for 180 days. This assembly was also to plan his war.

One evening he commanded Queen Vashti to appear before his guests to display her beauty, but Vashti refused to come. As a result, she was deposed as queen. Xerxes then busied himself with preparations for war.

The campaign was a disaster, so when Xerxes returned, history tells us that he consoled himself by indulging in pleasures. One of the things he did was to search for beautiful young virgins. The woman who pleased him would be his queen instead of Vashti.

Now, in the capital lived a Jew named Mordecai, who had a beautiful young cousin named Hadassah (Esther). When her parents died, Mordecai had taken her in as his own daughter. Esther was brought to the king's palace with the other women.

"Now the king was attracted to Esther more than to any of the other women" (Esther 2:17 NIV), so he made her queen.

Learn More: Esther 1:1–22; 2:1–18

ESTHER SAVES THE JEWS

Who knoweth whether thou art come to the kingdom for such a time as this? ESTHER 4:14

A Persian official named Haman hatched a plan to kill all the Jews in the kingdom. He was angry because Esther's cousin Mordecai had refused to bow before him.

When Mordecai learned of the plot, he urged Esther to implore King Xerxes for help. But not even the queen could approach the king without an invitation, so she risked her own life by entering his presence.

Xerxes was pleased to see her, though, and offered Esther anything she wanted. She invited the king and Haman to a banquet, where she revealed the peril of her Jewish people.

Haman had set up a great pole to impale Mordecai on, so the king commanded Haman to be executed on it instead. He then gave Haman's position and ring of authority to Mordecai.

When Esther asked Xerxes to countermand Haman's edict, he explained that no law of the Medes and Persians could be annulled. But there was something he could do: he immediately sent out a new message giving the Jews the right to defend themselves.

Mordecai became the king's new right-hand man, and Esther continued to enjoy great influence in the kingdom. This day of the Jews' deliverance was established as a new feast day called Purim.

Learn More: Esther 7:1–10; 8:1–17

NEHEMIAH REBUILDS JERUSALEM'S WALLS

So built we the wall. . .for the people had a mind to work. NEHEMIAH 4:6

Nehemiah, a Jewish exile and close advisor to the Persian king Artaxerxes, longed to repair the walls of Jerusalem. Having returned to his homeland with the kings' blessing, Nehemiah gathered the Jews together and told them his vision. So they began to build.

It was no easy task. They had nothing to build with other than the burned stones buried under tons of rubble. So they dug them out and began setting them in place.

When the laborers nearly gave up because there was so much rubble, Nehemiah urged them on. And they kept working. "So we rebuilt the wall. . .for the people worked with all their heart" (Nehemiah 4:6 NIV).

Their enemies, meanwhile, were determined to stop them. They threatened to attack, and they sent other Jews, ten times, to tell the workers that an attack was imminent. They threatened to report them to the king. But Nehemiah refused to give in to fear and kept building.

Day after day, they "laboured in the work. . .from the rising of the morning till the stars came appeared" (Nehemiah 4:21). In a miraculous fifty-two days, the wall was completed, and the Jews had tremendous joy.

Learn More: Nehemiah 2:11–20; 4:1–23; 6:15–16

AN ANGEL DELIVERS WORLD-CHANGING NEWS

Hail, thou that art highly favoured. . .blessed art thou among women. LUKE 1:28

With the Jewish people now under the control of Rome, a man from Nazareth named Joseph became engaged to a young woman named Mary.

One day the angel Gabriel appeared and greeted Mary, saying, "Thou shalt conceive in thy womb, and bring forth a son, and shalt call his name JESUS. He shall be great, and shall be called the Son of the Highest" (Luke 1:31–32). Mary was a virgin, so she asked how this was possible. The angel told her that the Spirit of God would come upon her and cause her to conceive.

When Mary became pregnant, Joseph was deeply troubled. Thinking that she had been unfaithful to him, he decided to call off the marriage.

But an angel appeared to him in a dream, saying, "Fear not to take unto thee Mary thy wife: for that which is conceived in her is of the Holy Ghost And she shall bring forth a son, and thou shalt call His name JESUS, for he shall save his people from their sins" (Matthew 1:20–21).

Isaiah's 730-year-old prophecy about a virgin bearing a son was about to be fulfilled.

Learn More: Isaiah 7:14 / Matthew 1:18–25 / Luke 1:26–38

JOHN THE BAPTIST IS BORN

Thy wife Elisabeth shall bear thee a son, and thou shalt call his name John. LUKE 1:13

The angel Gabriel told Mary that her cousin Elizabeth, well past childbearing years, was also pregnant. Here's what had happened:

One day while the elderly priest Zacharias was burning incense in the temple, Gabriel appeared to him and said, "Your wife, Elizabeth, will give you a son, and you are to name him John. . . . He will prepare the people for the coming of the Lord" (Luke 1:13, 17 NLT).

Zacharias doubted that his elderly wife could get pregnant, so the angel struck him mute.

In Elizabeth's sixth month, Mary arrived for a visit and stayed until the baby was born. Now, everyone wondered what the child would be named. Zacharias was mute, so they handed him a writing tablet, and he wrote, "His name is John" (Luke 1:63). Immediately Zacharias could speak again and prophesied: "thou, child, shalt be called the prophet of the Highest: for thou shalt go before the face of the Lord to prepare his ways; to give knowledge of salvation unto his people by the remission of their sins" (Luke 1:76–77).

God's great plan for the salvation of mankind was now beginning to unfold.

Learn More: Luke 1:5–25, 36–45, 57–66

JESUS IS BORN IN BETHLEHEM

[Mary] brought forth her firstborn son, and wrapped him in swaddling clothes. LUKE 2:7

After John's birth, Mary returned to Nazareth. A few months later, just as her due date neared, Caesar Augustus had decreed that the entire Roman world would be taxed. Everyone had to return to the town of their birth to register.

Both Joseph and Mary were descended from King David of Bethlehem, which is where they needed to appear. So Joseph and his very pregnant wife made the journey south.

When they arrived, Bethlehem was overflowing with people who had also come to register, so there was no room for them with relatives or at the inn. Mary and Joseph were forced to take shelter in a space that served as an animal stable. There Jesus was born.

In the nearby hills, shepherds were watching their flocks when an angel appeared exclaiming: "I bring you good tidings of great joy, which shall be to all people. For unto you is born this day in the city of David a Saviour, which is Christ the Lord" (Luke 2:10–11).

Suddenly a great multitude of angels appeared, praising God. The astonished shepherds immediately left their flocks, went to Bethlehem, and worshipped Jesus.

Learn More: Luke 2:1–20

WISE MEN VISIT YOUNG JESUS

Now when Jesus was born. . .there came wise men from the east to Jerusalem. MATTHEW 2:1

Back in Moses' day, a Mesopotamian prophet named Balaam prophesied, "I shall behold him, but not nigh: there shall come a Star out of Jacob, and a Sceptre shall rise out of Israel" (Numbers 24:17).

Some fourteen hundred years later, wise men known as Magi, living in Persia, saw a bright star in the skies over Israel. There were many Jews living in Persia in those days, and Jewish scholars likely told the wise men the star meant a great king had been born in Israel.

When the Magi arrived in Jerusalem, they went to King Herod's palace and asked, "Where is he that is born King of the Jews? for we have seen his star in the east, and are come to worship him" (Matthew 2:2).

Herod was greatly disturbed. He summoned the Jewish priests and scribes and asked where the Messiah was supposed to be born. They told him in Bethlehem of Judah (see Micah 5:2).

Herod then told the wise men to go to Bethlehem and find the child, then tell him where He was. The Magi did find Jesus and worshipped Him. But they returned to their own country by another route, for God had warned them against returning to Herod, since in his jealousy he wanted to kill the child.

Learn More: Matthew 2:1–12

NIGHTTIME FLIGHT FROM A MASSACRE

[Joseph] took the young child and his mother by night, and departed into Egypt. MATTHEW 2:14

After the wise men left Mary, Joseph, and young Jesus, an angel appeared in a dream to Joseph. The angel said, "Arise, and take the young child and his mother, and flee into Egypt, and be thou there until I bring thee word: for Herod will seek the young child to destroy him" (Matthew 2:13).

Joseph immediately got to work. He and Mary hastily packed their belongings, bundled up baby Jesus, and abandoned their house in the middle of the night. They were already far to the south in the Sinai desert when Herod's soldiers rode into Bethlehem.

There were nearly a million Jews living in Egypt in those days, so one more small Jewish family melted into the crowd without anyone noticing.

About two years later, Herod died. The angel again appeared to Joseph and told him that it was now safe to return to Israel. But when Joseph arrived and heard that Herod's son Archelaus was king in Judea, he didn't know what to do.

So God warned him in another dream, and Joseph turned north to Galilee and settled there. So Jesus was raised in Nazareth.

Learn More: Matthew 2:13–23

YOUNG JESUS ASTONISHES THE TEACHERS

All that heard him were astonished at his understanding and answers. LUKE 2:47

In Nazareth, as in all the towns of Galilee and Judea, boys were taught the scriptures from an early age.

At age five, they attended a *bet ha-sefer* ("house of the book") where they studied God's Word from dawn until noon. At age ten, boys entered the *bet talmud* ("house of learning") where they studied the scriptures and the "oral law" in depth. This second level required some reasoning but still mostly meant memorizing rote answers.

This was the state of Jesus' education when He went to Jerusalem with His parents at age twelve to attend the Passover.

When Joseph and Mary departed with a crowd of fellow villagers, Jesus stayed at the temple. Realizing sometime later that Jesus wasn't with them, they hurried back to Jerusalem and searched for Him for three days.

They finally found Him in the temple, talking with the teachers. "All that heard him were astonished at his understanding and answers" (Luke 2:47). Jesus had outstanding wisdom, even as a preteen.

Learn More: Luke 2:41–50

JOHN BAPTIZES JESUS

Then cometh Jesus from Galilee to Jordan unto John, to be baptized of him. MATTHEW 3:13

One day when Jesus was about thirty, He came from Galilee to where John was baptizing in the Jordan. Jesus asked John to baptize Him.

Why? Jesus had no sins to confess. As He stated of His Father, "I always do those things that please him" (John 8:29). John was astonished by the request, since he knew that this man was the "Lamb of God, which taketh away the sin of the world" (John 1:29).

John protested that he couldn't baptize Jesus—he needed Jesus to baptize him. But Jesus insisted, so John proceeded.

As soon as Jesus emerged from the water, heaven opened and the Spirit of God descended like a dove, lighting on Him. And God declared, "This is my beloved Son, in whom I am well pleased" (Matthew 3:17).

John, of course, witnessed all this. God had told him, "Upon whom thou shalt see the Spirit descending, and remaining on him, the same is he which baptizeth with the Holy Ghost" (John 1:33). So John said, "I saw, and bare record that this is the Son of God" (verse 34).

Learn More: Matthew 3:13–17 / John 1:29–34

THE DEVIL TEMPTS JESUS

Then was Jesus led up of the Spirit into the wilderness to be tempted of the devil. MATTHEW 4:1

When He took on a human body, Jesus emptied Himself of His divine power. Now, at His baptism, the Father anointed Him with the Holy Spirit to perform miracles.

Then the Spirit led Jesus into the desert, where He fasted for forty days. Afterward the devil tempted Him, saying, "If thou be the Son of God, command that these stones be made bread" (Matthew 4:3). Then, at the top of the temple, Satan demanded, "If thou be the Son of God, cast thyself down" (verse 6).

Satan was tempting Jesus to use His power for His own self-serving ends. But that's not why Jesus had come. He declared later that He had come down from heaven not to do His own will but the will of the Father who sent Him.

Quoting the scripture, Jesus resisted all of Satan's deceitful temptations.

Learn More: Matthew 4:1–11 / Luke 4:1–13 / John 6:38 / Acts 10:38

JESUS PERFORMS HIS FIRST MIRACLE

This beginning of miracles did Jesus in Cana of Galilee. JOHN 2:11

With His first four followers, Jesus headed off to a town called Cana in Galilee. Apparently, sometime before His forty-day fast, He'd been invited to a wedding, and He hadn't forgotten about it.

The groom, however, wasn't as organized as Jesus. He had greatly miscalculated the amount of wine needed. Not far into the wedding, it was all gone.

Jesus' mother and brothers were present, and Mary was aware that her son was the Son of God. So she told Him, "They have no wine" (John 2:3).

Jesus replied, "Woman, what have I to do with thee? mine hour is not yet come" (John 2:4). Undeterred, Mary turned to the servants and ordered, "Whatsoever he saith unto you, do it" (verse 5). Mary truly believed in her son. Jesus then told the servants, "Fill the waterpots with water" (verse 7).

Six stone jars were filled with about 150 gallons of water, and Jesus promptly turned it all into high-quality wine. Only a few days previously, when starving, He'd refused to turn stones into ordinary bread. Jesus refused to do a miracle unless it glorified God.

After He did this astonishing wonder, His new disciples "believed on him" (John 2:11).

Learn More: Luke 1:35 / John 2:1–12

JESUS DRIVES GREEDY MERCHANTS FROM THE TEMPLE

Make not my Father's house an house of merchandise. JOHN 2:16

Several months after the wedding at Cana, just before Passover, Jesus and His disciples went to Jerusalem. There He saw merchants selling cattle, sheep, and doves in the temple courts. Moneychangers had also set up their tables there.

Furious, Jesus braided a whip from some cords and beat them all out of the courts. He drove out the sheep and cattle, violently overturned the moneychangers' tables, and scattered their coins across the paving stones.

He turned to those who sold doves and shouted, "Take these things away! Do not make My Father's house a house of merchandise!" (John 2:16 NKJV).

The high priests were getting kickback from allowing merchants to be on the temple grounds, so they protested. Since Jesus was acting as if He had the right to drive them out, they wanted to see a miraculous sign as proof of that authority.

Jesus' authority rested in the fact that He was the Son of God with the power to rise from the dead, so He replied, "Destroy this temple, and in three days I will raise it up" (John 2:19).

Jesus made some bitter enemies that day. The priests remembered His statement and quoted it three years later, just before He was crucified.

Learn More: Matthew 26:60–61 / John 2:13–22

NICODEMUS SECRETLY MEETS JESUS

Nicodemus, a ruler of the Jews: the same came to Jesus by night. JOHN 3:1–2

While Jesus was in Jerusalem, a wealthy man named Nicodemus visited with Him secretly one night. Jesus was controversial, and Nicodemus was a respected member of the Sanhedrin, the ruling Jewish council.

When Nicodemus declared that he knew Jesus was from God, Jesus abruptly told him, "Verily, verily, I say unto thee, Except a man be born again, he cannot see the kingdom of God" (John 3:3).

Nicodemus thought Jesus was referring to a second physical birth, but He clarified that He meant being "born of the Spirit" (John 3:8).

Jesus then described the heart of His message, explaining how a person could be born again: "For God so loved the world, that he gave his only begotten Son, that whosoever believeth in him should not perish, but have everlasting life" (John 3:16).

Nicodemus thought deeply about this simple truth—and evidently accepted it, because he later repeatedly stood up for Jesus. And, together with Joseph of Arimathea, became a secret disciple.

Learn More: John 3:1–21; 7:47–51; 19:38–42

JESUS TALKS WITH A SAMARITAN WOMAN

How is it that thou, being a Jew, askest drink of me, which am a woman of Samaria? JOHN 4:9

As Jesus and His handful of disciples were traveling north to Galilee, they stopped on the way in Samaria. Jesus rested at Jacob's well while His disciples went into Sychar to buy food.

As He rested, a woman came to draw water, so Jesus asked her to give Him a drink. The woman was surprised, since Jews and Samaritans typically despised one another. She bluntly asked why He, a Jew, asked her, a Samaritan woman, for water.

Jesus answered, "If thou knewest the gift of God, and who it is that saith to thee, Give me to drink; thou wouldest have asked of him, and he would have given thee living water" (John 4:10). What is the "gift of God"? The apostle Paul wrote that "the gift of God is eternal life through Jesus Christ our Lord" (Romans 6:23).

The woman thought Jesus was talking about a perpetual supply of cool fresh water, but He explained that He was referring to "a fresh, bubbling spring within them, giving them eternal life" (John 4:14 NLT).

Jesus ended up staying with the Samaritans for two days, and many of them believed in Him.

Learn More: John 4:1–42

JESUS IS REJECTED AT NAZARETH

Verily I say unto you, No prophet is accepted in his own country. LUKE 4:24

One Sabbath in His hometown of Nazareth, Jesus entered the synagogue and was handed the scroll of Isaiah. Unrolling it, He read Isaiah 61:1–2 and 58:6. Then He said that this very day the scripture had been fulfilled.

The people were amazed. How could an ordinary local boy fulfill prophecy? They grumbled, "Is not this Joseph's son?" (Luke 4:22). They were thinking, *Do miracles here like the healing You did in Capernaum. Then we'll believe!*

Jesus responded that no prophet is ever accepted in his own hometown. He pointed out that though there were many starving widows in Israel during a famine, Elijah was only sent to provide for a Canaanite widow. And though there were many lepers in Israel in Elisha's day, only a foreign enemy, Naaman, was healed.

When the people grasped that God was rejecting them, they were furious. They seized Jesus, dragged Him to the cliff that their town was built on, and tried to hurl Him down. But He escaped and moved on to Capernaum.

Learn More: Luke 4:16–31

JESUS CALLS FOUR FISHERMEN

Jesus said unto them. . .I will make you to become fishers of men. MARK 1:17

Jesus found Simon Peter and Andrew on the outskirts of Capernaum. They were fishermen, and although they'd followed Him for a while, they were now back at their jobs.

Peter and Andrew were partners with Zebedee and his sons, John and James—to whom they had described Jesus the Messiah.

The four men determined to follow Jesus. They had apparently talked about this to Zebedee and his wife, Salome, who agreed to help support Jesus' ministry. Historians tell us that fishermen were wealthier than most Galileans, so they had the means.

And now the day had come.

As Jesus walked beside the Sea of Galilee, he saw Peter and Andrew casting a net into the water. Jesus said, "Come, follow me, and I will send you out to fish for people" (Mark 1:17 NIV). They immediately dropped their nets and followed.

James and John were in a boat nearby, preparing their nets. Jesus called them, and they immediately left Zebedee in the boat with the hired men.

Learn More: Matthew 4:18–22, 27:55–56 / Mark 1:16–20, 15:40–41

JESUS CHOOSES TWELVE APOSTLES

He called unto him his disciples: and of them he chose twelve. LUKE 6:13

Jesus had been traveling around Israel, teaching and healing, for well over a year. He now had a large crowd of disciples following Him everywhere, learning from Him daily.

One evening around the beginning of AD 28, as His disciples camped out in the open, Jesus climbed a high hill and spent the entire night alone, praying to God.

When morning came, "He called unto him his disciples: and of them he chose twelve, whom also he named apostles" (Luke 6:13). Jesus had about eighty full-time disciples in total, but from this number He chose twelve as apostles.

The other seventy men were also disciples, but Jesus appointed twelve to be His closest followers, His primary ambassadors whom He would send out to preach the Gospel, perform healings, and drive out demons. In fact, *apostle* means "one sent out."

These men were: Simon Peter and Andrew, James and John, Philip, Bartholomew, Matthew, Thomas, James son of Alphaeus, Simon the Zealot, Judas son of James, and Judas Iscariot.

Learn More: Mark 3:13–19 / Luke 6:12–16, 10:1

THE SERMON ON THE MOUNT

Seeing the multitudes, he went up into a mountain. . .and taught them. MATTHEW 5:1–2

Jesus' "Sermon on the Mount" (Matthew 5–7) contains some of His best-known teachings and quotations. "Now when Jesus saw the crowds, he went up on a mountainside and sat down. His disciples came to him, and he began to teach them. He said: 'Blessed are the poor in spirit, for theirs is the kingdom of heaven. . . .' " (Matthew 5:1–3 NIV).

Luke 6 describes a similar sermon: "And he came down with them, and stood in the plain" (Luke 6:17). Jesus taught, "Blessed be ye poor: for yours is the kingdom of God" (verse 20). Matthew says Jesus sat on a mountainside, while Luke says He stood on a plain. Also, Jesus' sayings in each, though similar, have striking differences. There's a reason for this.

The Sermon on the Mount contains the heart of Christ's teaching—on love, forgiveness, prayer, and obedience—so He repeated these important thoughts in different towns, villages, and open-air settings during the years of His public ministry. The slightly different sermon in Luke was given in a different setting on another date.

Learn More: Matthew 5:1–12 / Luke 6:17–26

A SINFUL WOMAN ANOINTS JESUS

A woman in the city. . .kissed his feet, and anointed them with the ointment. LUKE 7:37-38

A Pharisee named Simon invited Jesus to dinner, so Jesus reclined at the man's table.

When a prostitute heard that Jesus was there, she slipped into the house, knelt behind Him, wept over His feet, and wiped them with her hair. She kept kissing Jesus' feet and pouring expensive perfume on them.

Simon thought, "This man, if he were a prophet, would have known who and what manner of woman this is that toucheth him: for she is a sinner" (Luke 7:39).

Jesus, however, pointed out that when He'd entered this home, Simon hadn't washed the dust from His feet, though this woman had washed them with tears. Simon had failed to greet Jesus with a customary kiss, but the woman hadn't stopped kissing His feet and anointing them with perfume.

Jesus concluded, "I say unto thee, Her sins, which are many, are forgiven; for she loved much: but to whom little is forgiven, the same loveth little. . . . Thy faith hath saved thee; go in peace" (Luke 7:47, 50).

Learn More: Luke 7:36–50

JESUS CALMS AN INTENSE STORM

He. . .rebuked the wind, and said unto the sea, Peace, be still. MARK 4:39

After a day of teaching on the shores of the Sea of Galilee, Jesus said to His twelve apostles that they should cross over to the other side of the lake. As they sailed, Jesus fell asleep on a cushion in the stern of the boat.

Suddenly a furious storm swept down on the lake, and powerful waves broke over the boat so that it began to fill with water.

Jesus was so exhausted that He slept through the chaos. The disciples frantically woke Him, shouting, "Lord, save us: we perish" (Matthew 8:25). Jesus didn't seem concerned, so they cried out, "Master, carest thou not that we perish?" (Mark 4:38).

Finally getting up, Jesus commanded the winds and raging waters: "Peace, be still" (Mark 4:39). Instantly, the wind died down and it was calm. Looking at the disciples, Jesus asked, "How is it that ye have no faith?" (Mark 4:40).

In amazement they asked one another, "What manner of man is this! for he commandeth even the winds and water, and they obey him" (Luke 8:25).

Learn More: Matthew 8:23–27 / Mark 4:35–41 / Luke 8:22–25

HEROD BEHEADS JOHN THE BAPTIST

He sent, and beheaded John in the prison. MATTHEW 14:10

When his birthday came, the ruler Herod hosted a banquet for his officials and commanders. And Salome, the daughter of Herod's wife, Herodias, danced before everyone. Herod, his judgment perhaps befuddled by wine, was so taken by her dance that he swore, "Whatsoever thou shalt ask of me, I will give it thee, unto the half of my kingdom."

The girl could have asked for many things to benefit herself, but decided she should check with her mother first. So she hurried out of the chamber and asked, "What shall I ask?" Herodias was consumed with hatred for John the Baptist, who had publicly denounced her marriage to Herod—he had taken her from his own brother, Philip.

So the girl went back into the banquet hall and announced, "Give me here on a platter the head of John the Baptist" (Matthew 14:8 NIV).

Herod had sworn an oath, and now all his party guests were watching. So, in distress, he sent an executioner who beheaded John and returned carrying his head on a platter. He presented it to the girl, and she gave it to her mother.

Learn More: Matthew 14:6–12 / Mark 6:19–29

MIRACLE FEEDS A MULTITUDE

And they did all eat, and were filled. MATTHEW 14:20

John the Baptist's disciples came to Jesus, bringing news of their teacher's execution.

So Jesus left Galilee and entered the province of Gaulanitis, which was not under Herod's rule. He was going to a deserted region, but people saw Him leave and flocked to Him even there.

As it became late, because they were in such a desolate place, Jesus' disciples urged Him to send the people away to buy food in the nearby villages.

Jesus replied, "They need not depart; give ye them to eat. And they say unto him, We have here but five loaves, and two fishes" (Matthew 14:16–17).

Jesus took the bread and fish, gave thanks, began breaking the food into pieces, and had His disciples distribute it. Some five thousand men (not counting women and children) ate until they were full.

The devil had once tempted Jesus to create a couple loaves, but Jesus refused. Now He did a similar work, on a vast scale, to feed a multitude and bring glory to God.

Learn More: Matthew 4:3, 14:13–21 / Mark 6:30–44 / Luke 9:10–17

A CROWD ATTEMPTS TO CROWN JESUS KING

They would come and take him by force, to make him a king. JOHN 6:15

With the shock of John the Baptist's execution still fresh, speculation swirling around Jesus intensified: "Could it be that Jesus is the Son of David, the Messiah?" (Matthew 12:23 NLT).

When the crowds became aware of Jesus' tremendous miracle of feeding over five thousand people in a desolate region, they needed no further sign.

Some fourteen hundred years earlier, in Moses' day, God had fed the Israelites with manna—"bread from heaven"—in the desert (Exodus 16:4, 14–15). Moses had prophesied, "The LORD thy God will raise up unto thee a Prophet from the midst of thee, of thy brethren, like unto me" (Deuteronomy 18:15). Now Jesus had miraculously provided bread—just as Moses had done! The crowds exclaimed, "This is of a truth the prophet that should come into the world" (John 6:14).

This Prophet was the Messiah, so the crowds prepared to proclaim Jesus king. But when He "perceived that they would come and take him by force, to make him a king, he departed again into a mountain himself alone" (John 6:15).

Learn More: John 6:1–15

JESUS WALKS ON WATER

Jesus spake unto them, saying, Be of good cheer; it is I; be not afraid. MATTHEW 14:27

After feeding the five thousand and then dispersing the crowd, Jesus sent His disciples across the sea of Galilee. He Himself stayed to pray. After a while, a strong wind rose, and the disciples were soon fighting heavy waves far from land.

About three o'clock in the morning, in the dark and storm, Jesus came walking on the water! When the disciples saw Him, they shouted out in terror, "It's a ghost!" (Matthew 14:26 NLT). But Jesus assured them that it was He Himself, so not to fear.

Peter, impetuous as always, said that if it was really Jesus, he wanted to walk out on the water to Him. So Jesus said, "Come."

Peter stepped out of the boat and to his utter amazement walked on the waves. But when he had gone a certain distance on the surging water, he lost faith and started to sink and "immediately Jesus stretched forth his hand, and caught him" (Matthew 14:31).

When the two men climbed into the boat, the wind stopped. The disciples, amazed by what they had seen, worshipped Jesus: "Of a truth thou art the Son of God" (Matthew 14:32–33).

Learn More: Matthew 14:23–33 / Mark 6:47–52 / John 6:16–21

PETER DECLARES JESUS IS THE MESSIAH

Simon Peter answered and said, Thou art the Christ, the Son of the living God. MATTHEW 16:16

Jesus was heading to the region of Caesarea Philippi. He had previously moved freely throughout Galilee with over eighty disciples, but He was now traveling everywhere but Galilee with just the twelve apostles. While there, Jesus asked them who the crowds said that He was.

They answered, "Some say John the Baptist; others say Elijah; and still others, that one of the prophets of long ago has come back to life" (Luke 9:19 NIV).

Then Jesus asked, "But whom say ye that I am?" (Luke 9:20). Peter answered, 'You are the Messiah, the Son of the living God'" (Matthew 16:16 NLT).

Jesus replied, "Blessed art thou, Simon Bar-Jona: for flesh and blood hath not revealed it unto thee, but my Father which is in heaven" (Matthew 16:17). Now, the disciples had declared that Jesus was the Messiah, the Son of God, from the beginning—but many had since lost faith because Jesus wasn't acting as they expected the Messiah to. It took a revelation, the light of God continually burning in their hearts, to still believe that Jesus was God's Son.

Learn More: Matthew 16:13–20 / Luke 9:18–21 / John 1:41, 49

JESUS PREDICTS HIS DEATH

Jesus. . .must go unto Jerusalem. . .and be killed. MATTHEW 16:21

After Peter confessed that Jesus was the Messiah, the Lord commanded His apostles to tell this to no one. These were dangerous times, and though it was God's will for Jesus to be crucified, this had to happen in Jerusalem and at a set time—during the Passover.

It was at this point that Jesus began to explain to His disciples what would happen in less than a year. He told them plainly that it was God's will that He go to Jerusalem, where He'd suffer many things at the hands of the elders, the chief priests, and the scribes.

Jesus then shocked His disciples by announcing that He would then be killed. . .but on the third day rise from the dead.

All Peter seemed to hear was the "killed" part. He abruptly took Jesus aside and reprimanded Him. "Heaven forbid, Lord," he said. "This will never happen to you!" (Matthew 16:22 NLT).

Jesus responded, "Get thee behind me, Satan. . . . Thou savourest not the things that be of God, but those that be of men" (Matthew 16:23).

Learn More: Matthew 16:21–26 / Mark 8:31–37

JESUS IS TRANSFIGURED

Jesus. . .was transfigured before them. MATTHEW 17:1–2

About a week after Jesus described His upcoming death and resurrection, He climbed a high mountain with Peter, James, and John. This was likely Mount Hermon, towering over nearby Caesarea Philippi.

There, Jesus was transfigured. His face blazed like the sun, and his clothes became dazzling white, as bright as lightning. Then two men—Moses and Elijah—also appeared and began talking with Jesus about the events to come.

The Feast of Booths was nearing, so Peter—apparently overwhelmed by what he was seeing—offered to build three booths, one for each man.

Suddenly a bright cloud engulfed the summit, and God spoke: "This is my beloved Son, in whom I am well pleased; hear ye him" (Matthew 17:5). Terrified, the three disciples fell to the ground.

Later, as they returned down the mountain, Jesus warned them not to talk about what they'd seen until after He was resurrected. Some thirty-five years later, Peter still marveled at the day that he and his fellow apostles were "eyewitnesses of his majesty" (2 Peter 1:16).

Learn More: Matthew 17:1–9 / Mark 9:2–10 / Luke 9:28–36

JESUS FORGIVES AN ADULTERESS

He that is without sin among you, let him first cast a stone at her. JOHN 8:7

One day as Jesus was teaching, scribes and Pharisees brought a woman who had been caught committing adultery. They first reminded Jesus that Moses, in the Law, commanded such people to be stoned. They then asked Jesus to give His ruling.

If Jesus had answered, "Stone her," He'd have been arrested for breaking Roman law, which didn't allow Jews to execute criminals. If He'd said, "Let her go," He'd be breaking Jewish law. Jesus stooped down and wrote on the ground with His finger. When the accusers kept insisting He answer, He replied that whoever was without sin among them should throw the first stone.

Again He stooped and wrote. Then the scribes and Pharisees, overcome by their own guilty consciences, left. Finally, only the woman remained. Jesus looked up and asked, "Woman, where are those thine accusers? Hath no man condemned thee?" (John 8:10).

She answered, "No man, Lord" (John 8:11). So Jesus said, "Neither do I condemn thee; go, and sin no more" (John 8:10–11). He had gently but firmly told the woman to repent.

This story illustrates a very important point: "The law was given by Moses, but grace and truth came by Jesus Christ" (John 1:17).

Learn More: John 8:1–11

LAZARUS RISES FROM THE DEAD

He that was dead came forth, bound hand and foot with graveclothes. JOHN 11:44

Jesus was across the Jordan River in Perea when a messenger arrived from Mary and Martha, telling Him that their brother Lazarus was deathly sick. The sisters, personal friends of Jesus, asked Him to come heal "he whom thou lovest." However, Jesus stayed where He was two more days before going to Judea.

When He arrived, Lazarus was already dead and buried. Martha and Mary went out to meet Jesus. Their town of Bethany was near Jerusalem, so many leading Jews had come to comfort the sisters. They now followed Mary, thinking she was going out to mourn.

When Jesus arrived at the tomb, He told them to move the stone. Martha replied, "Lord, by this time he stinketh: for he hath been dead four days" (John 11:39).

Jesus reminded her to believe. Then He shouted, "Lazarus, come forth" (John 11:43). And Lazarus, bound with grave wrappings, walked out. The crowd witnessing this was shocked.

As one of Jesus' greatest miracles, the raising of Lazarus caused many to believe in Him. John, who committed this event to paper, said, "These are written that ye might believe that Jesus is. . .the Son of God; and that believing ye might have life through his name" (John 20:31).

Learn More: John 11:1–44

THE SANHEDRIN PASSES A DEATH SENTENCE ON JESUS

From that day forth they took counsel together for to put him to death. JOHN 11:53

After Jesus raised Lazarus, several stunned witnesses hurried to report to the authorities.

Jesus' enemies called an emergency council and asked, "What do we? For this man doeth many miracles. If we let him thus alone, all men will believe on him: and the Romans shall come and take away both our place and nation" (John 11:47–48).

Caiaphas, the high priest, observed that it was expedient that one man should die for the people rather than that the whole nation perish. He was unwittingly prophesying that Jesus would die for the Jewish nation. "Then, from that day forth they took counsel together for to put him to death" (John 11:53). Jesus was no longer able to move publicly in Judea because they "had given a commandment, that, if anyone knew where he were, he should shew it, that they might take him" (John 11:53, 57).

Jesus was now in danger in both Galilee and Judah, so He and His disciples withdrew quietly to a city in northern Judah, on the Samarian border, and stayed there.

Learn More: John 11:45–57; 12:9–11

TEN LEPERS ARE HEALED

And it came to pass, that, as they went, they were cleansed. Luke 17:14

One time, as Jesus crossed north through Samaria and entered Galilee, He was warned, "Get thee out, and depart hence: for Herod will kill thee" (Luke 13:31). Knowing that He must die in Jerusalem, not Galilee, Jesus returned south.

At the Galilee-Samaria border, He passed ten lepers, both Jews and Samaritans, standing a great distance away. Recognizing Jesus, they began yelling, "Jesus, Master, have mercy on us" (Luke 17:13). Jesus answered, "Go, shew yourselves unto the priests" (verse 14). According to the law, those healed from leprosy were to do this. And as they went, they were cleansed.

One of them, a Samaritan, realizing that his leprosy had been cured, ran back, loudly praising God. He flung himself at Jesus' feet and profusely thanked Him.

Jesus asked, "Were there not ten cleansed? but where are the nine? There are not found that returned to give glory to God, save this stranger" (Luke 17:17–18).

Learn More: Leviticus 14:2–32 / Luke 13:31–33; 17:11–19

ZACCHAEUS THE TAX COLLECTOR MEETS JESUS

Zacchaeus, make haste, and come down; for to day I must abide at thy house. Luke 19:5

From Perea, Jesus and His disciples crossed the Jordan River and came to Jericho. A large crowd of Jews, mostly Galileans, arriving for the Passover, began traveling with them.

Many Galileans accepted Jesus as a great prophet. Surrounded by so many supporters, He was safe from being arrested. . .for now.

As Jesus walked through Jericho, a tax collector was eager to see Him. Being short, he couldn't see over the crowds, so he ran ahead, scaled a tree, and waited for Jesus to pass under. Jesus looked up and said, "Zacchaeus, come down immediately. I must stay at your house today" (Luke 19:5 NIV).

The crowd grumbled that Jesus was consorting with a disreputable tax collector, but Zacchaeus announced that he'd give half his possessions to the poor, and if he'd cheated anybody, he'd pay back four times as much. Therefore Jesus said, "This day is salvation come to this house. . . . For the Son of man is come to seek and to save that which was lost" (Luke 19:9–10).

Learn More: Luke 19:1–10

BLIND BARTIMAEUS IS HEALED

Jesus said unto him, Go thy way; thy faith hath made thee whole. Mark 10:52

As Jesus and His disciples left Jericho, a large crowd followed them. A blind man named Bartimaeus was sitting at the roadside, begging. Matthew 20:30 specifies that there were two men, but Bartimaeus was the outspoken one, so Luke and Mark's Gospels focus on him.

When Bartimaeus heard that Jesus was passing by, he began shouting, "Jesus, thou son of David, have mercy on me!" ("Son of David" meant "Messiah.") The crowd ordered Bartimaeus to be quiet, but he only shouted louder, "Thou son of David, have mercy on me!" (Mark 10:47–48).

Jesus heard Bartimaeus, so He stopped and said to call the blind man. Moments later, he approached Jesus, followed by his friend. Jesus asked, "What wilt thou that I should do unto thee?" Bartimaeus answered, "Lord, that I might receive my sight!" (Mark 10:50–51).

Jesus responded, "Go thy way; thy faith hath made thee whole" (Mark 10:52). Instantly he and the other beggar could see. Bartimaeus then followed Jesus down the road.

Learn More: Mark 10:46–52 / Luke 18:35–43 / Matthew 20:29–34

MARY ANOINTS JESUS AT BETHANY

Then said Jesus. . .against the day of my burying hath she kept this. John 12:7

When Jesus arrived at Bethany, a dinner was held in His honor, and Mary, Martha, and Lazarus were present. During the meal, Mary broke open a one-pint alabaster vase of nard (a rare, costly perfume) and poured it on Jesus' head and feet. It was customary to anoint the heads of guests—but not to this extent!

Jesus' disciples grumbled, "Why was this waste of the ointment made?" (Mark 14:4). Judas Iscariot rebuked Mary harshly: "Why wasn't this perfume sold and the money given to the poor? It was worth a year's wages" (John 12:5 NIV).

Jesus responded, "Why trouble ye the woman? . . . For in that she hath poured this ointment on my body, she did it for my burial" (Matthew 26:10, 12).

Indeed, although Nicodemus placed spices (myrrh and aloes) in Jesus' burial linens, there wasn't time to anoint His body. This is what the women wanted to accomplish the Sunday morning after the crucifixion.

Jesus said that Mary's good deed would be forever told in honor of her. And it has been.

Learn More: Matthew 26:6–13 / Mark 14:3–9 / Luke 23:56; 24:1–3 / John 12:2–8; 19:39–40

THE MESSIAH ENTERS JERUSALEM

The multitudes that went before, and that followed, cried, saying, Hosanna. Matthew 21:9

News of Jesus raising Lazarus had spread among the thousands of pilgrims camped on the Mount of Olives. So in the morning, when Jesus headed to Jerusalem, the crowds rushed out to meet Him.

Then Jesus sent two disciples to the village ahead and had them bring a donkey and her colt. This fulfilled an ancient prophecy: "Behold, thy King cometh unto thee: he is just, and having salvation; lowly, and riding upon an ass, and upon a colt the foal of an ass" (Zechariah 9:9).

Then the multitudes spread their cloaks and branches from the trees on the road for Jesus to ride over. They began jubilantly shouting, "Hosanna to the son of David!" (Matthew 21:9). "Hosanna" means "God save us!"

As Jesus rode down the western slope and entered Jerusalem, the entire city was caught up in the excitement. Yet Jesus wept over unrepentant Jerusalem for the destruction that was coming upon her.

Learn More: Matthew 21:1–11 / Luke 19:29–44 / John 12:12–18

JESUS PROPHESIES ABOUT THE END TIME

Watch therefore: for ye know not what hour your Lord doth come. Matthew 24:42

When Jesus told His disciples that the temple would be destroyed, they asked, "Tell us, when shall these things be? and what shall be the sign of thy coming, and of the end of the world?" (Matthew 24:3). The temple was destroyed in AD 70, but the world would obviously end much later.

Jesus said that there would be many wars, famines, earthquakes, and false messiahs—but these would be just the beginning of trouble.

He warned, "Ye shall be hated of all nations for my name's sake" (Matthew 24:9). Despite intense persecution, Christians would preach the Gospel in the entire world, "and then shall the end come" (verse 19).

When the "abomination of desolation" is set up in God's temple, believers must flee—for then the Great Tribulation begins, the greatest time of trouble the world has ever known.

Then, immediately after those days, "they will see the Son of man coming in the clouds of heaven with power and great glory" (Matthew 24:30). He will gather all believers to Himself and, shortly after, set up His kingdom on the earth.

Learn More: Matthew 24:1–31 / Mark 13:1–27

THE LAST SUPPER

This do in remembrance of me. 1 CORINTHIANS 11:24

When Passover arrived, Jesus sent two disciples into Jerusalem to a certain man's house to make preparations. That evening, Jesus and the other disciples arrived.

Judas was present for only the first portion of the meal. Immediately after Jesus dipped some bread into the dish and handed it to him, Judas hurried out to betray the Lord. Jesus and His remaining disciples then celebrated the full Passover.

After the meal, Jesus infused the bread and the cup of wine with new meaning.

Jeremiah had prophesied six hundred years earlier, "Behold, days come, declares the LORD, that I will make a new covenant with the house of Israel. . .and I will remember their sin no more" (Jeremiah 31:31, 34).

Jesus therefore broke the bread and gave it to His disciples, saying, "Take, eat; this is my body" (Matthew 26:26). Then He passed the cup, saying, "Drink ye all of it; for this is my blood of the new testament, which is shed for many for the remission of sins" (verses 27–28).

The following day, Jesus' body was broken with scourging, and His blood was poured out so that our sins could be forgiven.

Learn More: Matthew 26:17–29 / Mark 14:12–25 / Luke 22:7–20

JESUS PRAYS IN GETHSEMANE

And being in an agony he prayed more earnestly. LUKE 22:44

Jesus and His disciples came to the garden of Gethsemane on the Mount of Olives. He told most of them to wait in the lower garden but took Peter, James, and John higher up. After telling the three, "Tarry ye here, and watch" (Mark 14:34), He went some distance farther and began to pray fervently.

Jesus knew how greatly He would suffer, so He prayed that if possible He might avoid the agony. But He added, "Nevertheless not what I will, but what thou wilt" (Mark 14:36).

After praying, Jesus went to the three disciples, who were asleep. He woke Peter up and asked if he was unable to watch with Him even one hour.

Again Jesus went away and prayed, repeating the same desperate words. Then He returned and found the three asleep once more. They were embarrassed and didn't know what to say. Heavy at heart, Jesus left to pray again.

Finally He came and woke them a third time, informing them that the hour had come—He was about to be arrested.

Learn More: Matthew 26:30–46 / Mark 14:26–42

JESUS IS ARRESTED AND ABANDONED

They that had laid hold on Jesus led him away to Caiaphas the high priest. MATTHEW 26:57

In the garden of Gethsemane, Jesus' heavy-eyed disciples were suddenly shocked awake. Judas Iscariot had arrived, leading a large crowd armed with swords and clubs and brandishing torches.

Heading straight to Jesus, Judas said, "Greetings, Rabbi!" and kissed Him (Matthew 26:49 NIV). Judas anticipated that it would be difficult to identify Jesus in the dark, so this signaled who to arrest.

Jesus asked, "Whom seek ye?" (John 18:4). The mob replied, "Jesus of Nazareth." When Jesus said, "I am he," the entire crowd suddenly surged backward and fell to the ground (verses 5–6). When they arose, Jesus said, "If therefore ye seek me, let these go their way" (verse 8).

The order was given to seize Jesus. Peter, realizing what was happening, drew his sword and swung at Malchus, the high priest's servant.

Jesus ordered Peter to stop. He had just demonstrated that if He didn't want to be arrested, He could prevent it. Plus, God could easily send seventy-two thousand angels to defend Him. Peter's actions were well-meaning but futile.

Then all the disciples abandoned Jesus, and He was arrested.

Learn More: Matthew 26:47–56 / Mark 14:43–52 / John 18:2–12

PETER DENIES JESUS

Peter remembered the word of Jesus. . . . And he went out, and wept bitterly. MATTHEW 26:75

After Jesus was arrested, Peter made his way into the high priest's courtyard. He was taking a huge risk. Some of the crowd might recognize him from the garden. But he had vowed he'd never desert Jesus.

Peter was sitting around the fire when a servant girl said, "Thou also wast with Jesus of Galilee" (Matthew 26:69). One of the men took a closer look. "Did I not see thee in the garden with him?" (John 18:26). But Peter denied it.

Peter retreated to the gateway, but there another woman announced that he was a follower of Jesus. Peter swore an oath that he didn't know what she was talking about.

Soon, however, some men argued that Peter must be Jesus' disciple because, after all, he was from Galilee. His accent gave him away.

Then Peter called down curses on himself if he knew Jesus—and immediately a rooster crowed. Peter had done what he'd boasted he would never do.

Learn More: Matthew 26:33–35, 58, 69–75 / Mark 14:54, 66–72

PILATE GIVES IN TO THE JEWISH RELIGIOUS LEADERS

Pilate. . .took water, and washed his hands before the multitude. MATTHEW 27:24

Pilate, the Roman governor over Judea, had a custom: every Passover feast, to show his "mercy," he released a prisoner. At this time, there was a notorious prisoner called Barabbas who had committed murder in an armed insurrection.

Pilate reasoned that if the chief priests were concerned about Jesus stirring up rebellion, they wouldn't choose Barabbas. So he asked, "Whom will ye that I release unto you? Barabbas, or Jesus which is called Christ?" (Matthew 27:17).

To Pilate's dismay, they requested Barabbas. When the governor asked what he should do with Jesus, the crowd shouted for Him to be crucified.

Pilate asked what evil Jesus had done, but this made the mob angrier. When Pilate saw that he was getting nowhere and that a riot was starting, he released Barabbas. Although he'd repeatedly declared that Jesus was innocent, he still sentenced Him to be crucified.

Pilate wasn't actually being merciful by releasing a prisoner every year—it was simply a public relations move. Nor was he merciful in trying to get Jesus released. He probably just disliked the religious leaders coercing him into doing their dirty work.

Learn More: Matthew 27:15–26 / Luke 23:13–25

JESUS IS NAILED TO A CROSS

When they were come to. . .Calvary, there they crucified him. LUKE 23:33

The Romans forced a passerby to carry Jesus' crossbeam to Golgotha. Once there, Jesus was crucified between two criminals.

The goal of crucifixion was to bring about death in the most painful way possible. Iron nails were driven between the doomed man's wrist bones, causing excruciating pain as they severed the median nerve. After that, a nail was driven through his feet.

For the next six hours, Jesus could inhale while hanging in a slumped position, but to exhale He had to raise himself up. To do so, He had to push against the nail in His feet and pull against the nails through His wrists, causing unbelievable agony.

Not only did Jesus suffer severe muscle cramps, but His back, laid wide open by scourging, constantly scraped against the rough wood of the cross as He pulled Himself up then slumped down to breathe. Jesus was wracked with torment at every moment.

On top of all of this, His enemies mocked Him as He suffered.

Learn More: Matthew 27:32–44 / Luke 23:32–43

JESUS DIES IN DARKNESS

Jesus. . .said, It is finished: and he bowed his head, and gave up the ghost. JOHN 19:30

Jesus was crucified at nine in the morning, and at noon, a terrifying darkness came over the whole land until three in the afternoon. The historian Thallus, writing some twenty years after the crucifixion, referred to this darkness, though he tried to explain it naturally.

When Jesus had finished paying the price for our sins, He gasped, "It is finished" (John 19:30). Then He gave up His spirit.

Heavy blood loss and asphyxiation were the chief causes of His death. But doctors point out the fact that "Jesus cried with a loud voice, and gave up the ghost" (Mark 15:37) suggests that He suffered a sudden cardiac rupture, induced by the severe physical and emotional trauma He had suffered.

Jesus suffered the agony of heartbreak because He had taken the sin of the world upon Himself and was, for the first time, separated from His Father. This is why, earlier, He had groaned, "My God, my God, why hast thou forsaken me?" (Matthew 27:46).

Learn More: Matthew 27:45-50 / Mark 15:33-37 / John 19:28-30

THE SON OF GOD IS BURIED

He. . .took him down, and wrapped him in the linen, and laid him in a sepulchre. MARK 15:46

Sundown was approaching and the Sabbath was about to begin, so to avoid having bodies on crosses on the Sabbath, the Jewish leaders requested that Pilate have the condemned men killed and taken down. So Pilate gave the order.

Moments later, Joseph of Arimathea, a secret disciple of Jesus, arrived at Pilate's fortress, asking for Jesus' body. He had just seen the Lord die. Pilate was surprised to hear that Jesus was already dead, as he'd barely given the order to end His life. So he sent a second messenger to summon the centurion and ascertain Jesus' death.

In the meantime, Pilate's first messenger arrived at Golgotha and gave his order, so the criminals' legs were broken and a spear was thrust through Jesus' heart.

Then when the centurion came and confirmed that Jesus was dead, Pilate gave Joseph permission to bury the corpse. So Joseph took down Jesus' body, wrapped it in linen cloth, and placed it in his own nearby tomb. Then he rolled a great stone in front of it, sealing the entrance.

Learn More: Matthew 27:57-66 / Mark 15:42-47 / John 19:31-37

JESUS RISES FROM THE DEAD

Ye seek Jesus of Nazareth, which was crucified: he is risen; he is not here. MARK 16:6

Glimmers of predawn light tinged the skies early Sunday morning. Suddenly there was a jarring earthquake and a mighty angel descended and rolled the stone away from Jesus' tomb. Seeing this supernatural being, the guards collapsed in terror.

Then the Spirit of God raised Jesus' corpse to life, transforming it into a glorious eternal body. And Jesus walked out of the tomb alive!

Meanwhile, as it was still dark, two groups of women set out, intent on anointing Jesus' body. The first group was led by Mary Magdalene and came from a house close to the tomb, just inside the city gate.

The second group was likely led by Joanna, the wife of King Herod's steward, and came from the palace, farther away from the tomb.

Both groups, arriving at different times, saw the angels in the tomb. They announced, "Fear not ye: for I know that ye seek Jesus, which was crucified. He is not here: for he is risen, as he said" (Matthew 28:5–6).

Learn More: Matthew 28:1-8 / Mark 16:1-8 / Luke 8:2-3, 23:7, 24:1-8, 10

JESUS APPEARS TO MARY MAGDALENE

She turned herself back, and saw Jesus standing, and knew not that it was Jesus. JOHN 20:14

Mary Magdalene had followed Peter and John back to Jesus' tomb, and after they left, she stayed to mourn. As she stood there weeping, she turned and saw a man, not realizing it was Jesus. Jesus asked, "Woman, why weepest thou? whom seekest thou?"

Mary assumed the man was the gardener, so she said, "Sir, if thou have borne him hence, tell me where thou hast laid him, and I will take him away" (John 20:15).

Jesus simply said, "Mary." Crying out in joy, she raced over and threw her arms around Jesus, but He said, "Touch me not, for I am not yet ascended to the Father" (John 20:16–17).

Mary ran back to the house to tell Peter and John, but they'd left for Bethany to discuss events with the other disciples.

Mary Magdalene then returned with the other Mary, and both women saw Jesus. Then they hurried out to Bethany and told the gathered disciples.

Learn More: Matthew 28:1, 5–10 / Mark 16:9–11 / John 20:11–18

JESUS APPEARS TO HIS DISCIPLES

Jesus. . .stood in the midst, and saith unto them, Peace be unto you. JOHN 20:19

The disciples were afraid that their enemies might try to kill them too, so they closed and locked their doors.

Then, as they shared their own recent experiences, Jesus appeared in their midst, saying, "Peace be unto you" (John 20:19). The apostles were frightened, thinking it was Jesus' ghost. He had come right through a locked door, after all.

Jesus asked, "Why are ye troubled? and why do thoughts arise in your hearts? Behold my hands and my feet, that it is I myself: handle me, and see; for a spirit hath not flesh and bones, as ye see me have" (Luke 24:38–39).

Then He showed them His nail-pierced hands and feet and let them touch Him. The disciples were still unsure whether they should believe their senses, so Jesus asked them for some food. Then while they watched, He ate a piece of broiled fish.

They were finally convinced that He wasn't a ghost—and had tremendous joy.

Learn More: Mark 16:14 / Luke 24:36–43 / John 20:19–23

DOUBTING THOMAS IS CHALLENGED

Reach hither thy hand, and thrust it into my side: and be not faithless, but believing. JOHN 20:27

Thomas hadn't been with the other disciples when Jesus had visited the group. When the apostles told him that they'd seen Jesus, even touched Him, Thomas demanded more proof: "Except I shall see in his hands the print of the nails, and put my finger into the print of the nails, and thrust my hand into his side, I will not believe" (John 20:25).

Jesus had instructed His disciples to go to Galilee, so the apostles told everyone, and they all headed north. Thomas went too, even though he didn't believe.

One week later—probably in Peter's house at Capernaum—the apostles were together, and the doors were locked. Once again, Jesus appeared among them and announced, "Peace be unto you" (John 20:26).

Turning to Thomas, Jesus held out a nail-pierced hand. He opened His tunic and showed the spear wound above His heart. Then He said, "Thomas, Reach hither thy finger, and behold my hands; and reach hither thy hand, and thrust it into my side: and be not faithless, but believing" (John 20:27).

Thomas blurted out, "My Lord and my God!" (John 20:28).

Learn More: Matthew 28:7, 16 / John 20:24–31

JESUS APPEARS TO A MULTITUDE

When they saw him, they worshipped him: but some doubted. Matthew 28:17

This is one of Jesus' least-known appearances, but it's almost the most important because of the many people it affected.

Jesus had told His disciples to meet Him on a mountain in Galilee. But He had already appeared to His apostles on three separate occasions. So why did He wish to meet on a mountain?

Very likely this was when He was seen by over five hundred disciples at once, an event the apostle Paul described. Most of Jesus' followers hadn't yet seen Him after His resurrection, and this was an opportunity to encourage many disciples' faith at once.

It wasn't God's will for Jesus to be seen by the public, so they had to meet at an isolated location. Often even going to deserted regions didn't work, as the crowds found out and followed.

So they went to "a mountain where Jesus had appointed them. And when they saw him, they worshipped him: but some doubted" (Matthew 28:16–17). Jesus then proved to them that He was risen from the dead, just as he had done for doubting Thomas.

Learn More: Matthew 28:16–20 / Acts 10:41 / 1 Corinthians 15:6

JESUS ASCENDS TO HEAVEN

While he blessed them, he was parted from them, and carried up into heaven. Luke 24:51

From the mountain, Jesus instructed His disciples to return to Jerusalem. Most of the five hundred couldn't go—they had jobs and obligations in their home villages. But the eleven, the seventy, and Jesus' closest female disciples made the journey.

Later, as this smaller group ate together, Jesus commanded, "Do not leave Jerusalem until the Father sends you the gift he promised. . .in just a few days you will be baptized with the Holy Spirit" (Acts 1:4–5 NLT).

Finally, Jesus led His disciples out to Bethany, lifted up His hands, and blessed them. In that moment He was carried up into heaven and vanished into a cloud. From there "he was received up into heaven, and sat on the right hand of God" (Mark 16:19).

While the disciples continued looking, two angels appeared and said, "Ye men of Galilee, why stand ye gazing up into heaven? this same Jesus, which is taken up from you into heaven, shall so come in like manner as ye have seen him go into heaven" (Acts 1:11). Then the disciples worshipped Jesus and went to Jerusalem with great joy.

Learn More: Mark 16:19–20 / Luke 24:50–53 / Acts 1:4–12

THE HOLY SPIRIT DESCENDS

They were all filled with the Holy Ghost, and began to speak with other tongues. Acts 2:4

It was the Feast of Pentecost, fifty days after Passover, and all 120 disciples were crowded into the large house of a wealthy disciple, when suddenly the sound of a mighty rushing wind filled the place where they were sitting.

"And there appeared unto them cloven tongues like as of fire, and it sat upon each of them" (Acts 2:3). Everyone was filled to overflowing with the Holy Spirit and began to praise God in unknown languages.

Multitudes of Jews had come from foreign lands to attend the Feast of Pentecost, and as the disciples rushed out of the house praising God, the pilgrims were astonished. They could see that these were Galileans, yet they were speaking the various languages the visiting pilgrims spoke.

Peter then declared that this miracle was the fulfillment of a prophecy (Joel 2:28–32) and that, according to the prophecy, it was time to call on the name of the Lord and be saved. As a result, about three thousand people received salvation.

Learn More: Acts 2:1–41

PETER AND JOHN HEAL A LAME MAN

And he leaping up stood, and walked. Acts 3:8

The apostles had healed in Galilee over a year earlier, when Jesus "gave them power and authority. . .to cure diseases" (Luke 9:1). But they hadn't done miracles since then—at least none that are recorded. That was about to change.

One day Peter and John were going to the temple when they saw a lame man. He begged for money, but Peter replied, "Silver and gold have I none; but such as I have I give thee: In the name of Jesus Christ of Nazareth rise up and walk" (Acts 3:6).

Immediately the man was healed. He ran, leaped in the air, and praised God with a loud voice. The crowds, recognizing the formerly lame man, were astonished.

Peter then declared that the man had been healed by the power of Jesus Christ. He preached a powerful sermon, and many people were saved. The religious rulers arrested Peter and John, but when they appeared before them, Peter boldly witnessed that Jesus was the only way to salvation.

Learn More: Acts 3:1–16; 4:1–14

DISCIPLES COMMANDED NOT TO PREACH

They. . .commanded them not to speak at all nor teach in the name of Jesus. Acts 4:18

The people of Jerusalem were praising God for the lame man's healing, and the religious rulers themselves couldn't deny that it had happened. After all, the formerly lame man was standing there with Peter and John.

The rulers also realized that no one would believe the argument that such a wonderful miracle had been done by the power of the devil.

Sending Peter and John out of the chamber, the Sanhedrin discussed what they could do. Unable to think of any way to punish them, they called Peter and John back in and ordered them not to speak any more in the name of Jesus Christ.

However, Jesus had commanded His disciples, "Go ye into all the world, and preach the gospel to every creature" (Mark 16:15).

So Peter and John responded, "Whether it be right in the sight of God to hearken unto you more than unto God, judge ye. For we cannot but speak the things which we have seen and heard" (Acts 4:19–20). The chief priests threatened them again then released them.

Learn More: Acts 4:14–31

ANANIAS AND SAPPHIRA LIE AND DIE

How is it that ye have agreed together to tempt the Spirit of the Lord? Acts 5:9

The temple ran a relief program for widows, orphans, and the destitute. However, when these people became disciples of Jesus, they found themselves excommunicated and in even greater need.

The Christian believers quickly took action: wealthy disciples with extra houses and lands sold them and brought the money to the apostles—who distributed to those in need. These generous donors were highly esteemed, though that wasn't the reason they gave.

A couple named Ananias and Sapphira wanted praise and prestige, so they sold their land and gave a sum to the apostles, claiming it was the full price. But they were lying, keeping back a portion for their personal use.

As Peter pointed out, the land was theirs, and after they'd sold it, the money was still theirs to do with as they wished. Their sin was to lie that they'd sacrificially given everything. So God judged them—and they both fell down dead.

Learn More: Acts 2:44–45; 4:32–37; 5:1–11

STEPHEN IS MARTYRED

They. . .cast him out of the city, and stoned him. ACTS 7:57-58

The apostles had specified that deacons be full of the Holy Spirit, and a man named Stephen was so "full of faith and power" that he "did great wonders and miracles among the people" (Acts 6:8).

Stephen was Greek speaking, so he witnessed his faith to other Greek-speaking Jews. One day, several of them began to debate with him. They soon realized that they couldn't stand against his wisdom and power.

Bitter, they dragged Stephen before the Sanhedrin and had men lie that he had blasphemed both God and Moses.

Suddenly, everyone stopped talking and stared at Stephen, because his face was glowing as brightly as the face of an angel. Stunned, they listened as he gave an impassioned sermon about God's history of dealing with His disobedient people.

But when Stephen ended up by telling the crowd that they themselves disobeyed the law and resisted God's Spirit, they became enraged. They dragged him outside the city and stoned him to death. He became the Christian church's first martyr.

Learn More: Acts 6:8-15; 7:1-60

SAUL PERSECUTES THE CHURCH

I punished them oft in every synagogue, and compelled them to blaspheme. ACTS 26:11

When the mob stoned Stephen, they took off their cloaks and gave them to a young man named Saul. He watched over their clothing, fully agreeing with killing Stephen.

That day, a great persecution broke out against the disciples in Jerusalem. Saul quickly became a leader in the inquisition. He went from one synagogue to another to find secret believers. He had them savagely beaten in the synagogues "to get them to curse Jesus" (Acts 26:11 NLT).

People reported on Christians, and Saul raided home after home. He dragged off both men and women and cast them in prison. If they refused to blaspheme Jesus, Saul voted to kill them.

The believers in Jerusalem fled for their lives and were soon scattered throughout Judea and Samaria, but Saul, being "extremely enraged at them. . .kept pursuing them even to foreign cities" (Acts 26:11 NASB). Having received authority from the chief priests, Saul went far afield, arresting Christians and bringing them back to Jerusalem.

Jesus had warned that such persecution would come—and now it had.

Learn More: Matthew 10:16-23; 23:34-36 / Acts 7:58; 8:1-4; 26:9-11

THE GOSPEL IS PREACHED IN SAMARIA

Philip went down to the city of Samaria, and preached Christ unto them. ACTS 8:5

Saul's persecution, devastating as it was, had an immediate positive effect: it resulted in the Gospel finally being preached to the Samaritans.

Around AD 27, Jesus and His disciples had stayed two days in the Samaritan village of Sychar, and many people there believed that He was the Messiah.

Later, about AD 30, Jesus specifically commanded His disciples to preach the Gospel in Samaria. But five years had passed, and they were still witnessing only to fellow Jews. They knew what Jesus had said, but apparently nobody really wanted the job.

During Saul's persecution, though, many disciples fled to Samaria—and they did preach the Gospel. The Samaritans, who believed in Moses, were receptive.

Philip, one of the seven deacons of the Jerusalem church, went to the city of Samaria and preached that Jesus was the Messiah. Having heard his message and seen his miracles, "there was great joy in that city" (Acts 8:8). The people "believed Philip preaching the things concerning the kingdom of God, and the name of Jesus Christ, they were baptized, both men and women" (verse 12).

Learn More: John 4:39-42 / Acts 1:8; 8:4-8

PHILIP WITNESSES TO AN ETHIOPIAN

Philip opened his mouth. . .and preached unto him Jesus. ACTS 8:35

After Philip preached in Samaria, an angel told him to go south to the road that ran between Jerusalem and Gaza. So Philip went and met the treasurer for Candace, queen of the Ethiopians. The treasurer was returning from Jerusalem and, as he rode in his chariot, was reading aloud from Isaiah. He was at Isaiah 53:7, which says, "He is brought as a lamb to the slaughter, and as a sheep before her shearers is dumb, so he openeth not his mouth."

Philip ran up to the man and asked if he understood what he was reading. The Ethiopian admitted that he didn't, so he invited Philip to ride with him and explain.

Philip then told the man how Jesus had fulfilled these prophecies by refusing to defend Himself from accusations at His trial. Philip also explained that Isaiah 53 went on to describe how Jesus died for people's sin.

They came to some water, stopped the chariot, and Philip baptized the man. Then the Spirit suddenly transported Philip away, and he reappeared at Azotus, miles to the north. Meanwhile, the treasurer returned to Ethiopia rejoicing.

Learn More: Acts 8:26–40

SAUL IS CONVERTED ON THE DAMASCUS ROAD

He. . .heard a voice saying unto him, Saul, Saul, why persecutest thou me? ACTS 9:4

Saul, the great persecutor of the church, was on the road to Damascus. He intended to enter all the synagogues there, arrest Jesus' followers, and bring them back to Jerusalem.

As he and his escort approached the city, though, a light blazed around him. Saul fell to the ground and a voice said, "Saul, Saul, why persecutest thou me?" (Acts 9:4). He asked, "Who art thou, Lord?" The voice answered, "I am Jesus whom thou persecutest. . . . Arise, and go into the city, and it shall be told thee what thou must do" (verse 5–6).

Trembling, Saul rose. Then he realized. . .he was blind!

Saul's guards had no idea what had just happened, but they took him into Damascus, where for three days he ate and drank nothing. The news of this baffling event swept through all the synagogues.

Then the Lord told a disciple named Ananias to go to the house where Saul was staying. Ananias went, laid his hands on Saul, and prayed for him. Instantly scales fell from Saul's eyes. He regained his sight and was filled with the Holy Spirit. Then Ananias baptized him.

Learn More: Acts 9:1–18

SAUL ESCAPES FROM DAMASCUS

The disciples took him by night, and let him down by the wall in a basket. ACTS 9:25

The newly converted Saul spent several days learning from the disciples at Damascus. He then began going from synagogue to synagogue, describing how he had persecuted believers in Jerusalem and had come to Damascus to arrest them. . .but now knew that Jesus was the Son of God.

Saul was knowledgeable in the scriptures, and as the Holy Spirit showed him the prophecies Jesus had fulfilled, Saul astonished the Jews by proving that Jesus was their promised Messiah.

Eventually they plotted to kill him. By the time Saul realized that, it was too late to escape. His enemies had enlisted the help of the city governor, and guards watched the gates both day and night.

So the disciples came up with a daring plan: placing Saul in a large basket, they lowered him down the city walls by rope—and he escaped. He laid low in Arabia for two or three years before finally returning to Damascus.

The Christians then heard, "He which persecuted us in times past now preacheth the faith which once he destroyed" (Galatians 1:23). And they praised God.

Learn More: Acts 9:19–30 / Galatians 1:15–24 / 2 Corinthians 11:32–33

PETER RAISES TABITHA TO LIFE

Peter. . .kneeled down, and prayed; and turning him to the body said, Tabitha, arise. ACTS 9:40

After Saul's persecution, things quieted down; the church had a time of peace, and the number of believers increased.

As Peter traveled about, he visited the disciples in a place called Lydda. A man named Aeneas had been paralyzed for eight years, so Peter told him, "Jesus Christ maketh thee whole" (Acts 9:34). Immediately Aeneas got up! As a result, everyone in Lydda became believers.

Nearby in Joppa was a disciple named Tabitha who always made clothing for other believers and helped the poor. Then she fell sick and died. Two men rushed to Lydda, urging Peter to come.

When Peter arrived, he was taken to the upper room where her body lay. All the widows stood around, weeping and showing him the clothing that Tabitha had sewed.

After sending them all from the room, Peter knelt and prayed. Then looking at the unmoving corpse, he said, "Tabitha, arise." She opened her eyes and sat up. Peter then called the disciples back into the room.

News of this great miracle filled Joppa, and many people believed in Jesus.

Learn More: Acts 9:31–43

PETER HAS A ROOFTOP VISION

What God hath cleansed, that call not thou common. ACTS 10:15

Caesarea, the Roman administrative center of Israel, was thirty miles up the coast from Joppa. A centurion named Cornelius was stationed there, and he and all his family believed in God.

One afternoon while Cornelius was praying, an angel appeared and told him to send men to Joppa to bring back a man called Peter, who was staying with Simon, a tanner. Cornelius obeyed.

The next day, while the noon meal was cooking, Peter went up on Simon's roof to pray. There he had a vision of a large sheet filled with "unclean" animals, reptiles, and birds that Jews were forbidden to eat.

A voice commanded, "Rise, Peter; kill, and eat" (Acts 10:13). Peter protested that he'd never eaten anything impure, but the voice said, "What God hath cleansed, that call not thou common" (verse 15). This vision was repeated three times.

While Peter was wondering what the vision meant, the three men Cornelius sent arrived at the door. God told Peter to go with them, even though Jews were forbidden to keep company with Gentiles.

Learn More: Leviticus 11 / Acts 10:1–23, 28

PETER PREACHES TO GENTILES

Of a truth I perceive that God is no respecter of persons. ACTS 10:34

In visiting Cornelius, Peter broke a major Jewish taboo when he and several other Jews entered the house of a Gentile (non-Jew). It was packed with Gentiles, as Cornelius had invited his relatives and close friends.

The centurion explained that an angel had appeared to him, telling him to send for Peter. The people had therefore all gathered to hear what he had to say.

Peter then gave a brief history of how Jesus had gone throughout Galilee and Judea, doing good and healing the sick—and though the religious rulers had crucified their Messiah, three days later God raised Him from the dead.

Peter had no sooner finished saying, "Whosoever believeth in him shall receive remission of sins" (Acts 10:43), than the Holy Spirit entered everyone's receptive hearts. Peter then baptized the first Gentile believers.

When Peter explained all these things to the church in Jerusalem, they "glorified God, saying, Then hath God also to the Gentiles granted repentance unto life" (Acts 11:18).

Learn More: Acts 10:24–48; 11:1–18

HEROD PERSECUTES THE CHURCH. . .AND DIES

He was eaten of worms, and gave up the ghost. ACTS 12:23

Around AD 44, nearly ten years after Saul's persecution had ended, Herod Agrippa (grandson of Herod the Great) was king of Judea. The Romans normally had governors rule Judea but were allowing Jewish self-rule for a time.

Now, Herod arrested James, the brother of John, and had him executed with a sword. When he realized how much this pleased their enemies, he arrested Peter also. But Peter escaped, and Herod returned to Caesarea in a very bad mood.

Herod had a dispute with the people of Tyre and Sidon, and this was bad news for those cities, since Israel supplied most of their food. So their citizens, wishing for peace, arranged a meeting.

On the appointed day, Herod put on a shimmering silver robe and delivered an oration. The crowd exclaimed, "It is the voice of a god, and not of a man" (Acts 12:22).

Herod claimed to believe in God but didn't rebuke the people. So an angel immediately afflicted him with a terrible infestation of worms that killed him.

Learn More: Acts 12:1–4, 19–23

AN ANGEL FREES PETER FROM PRISON

The angel of the Lord. . .RAISED HIM UP, SAYING, ARISE UP QUICKLY. ACTS 12:7

Before his gruesome death, Herod had arrested Peter during Passover but decided to wait until after the festivities to bring him out for a public trial. So he locked the apostle in prison, commanding "four squads of four soldiers each" to guard him (Acts 12:4 NIV). But many Christians prayed unceasingly for God to do a miracle.

The night before his trial, Peter was sleeping between two soldiers. Suddenly a brilliant light filled the dungeon, and an angel ordered, "Arise up quickly" (Acts 12:7). At once his chains snapped open. Then the angel commanded Peter to get dressed and follow.

They left the cell, passed the first and second set of guards, and came to the outer gate, which opened of its own accord. All the time Peter thought this was a vision. But as they walked down the street, the angel vanished. Then Peter realized that he really was experiencing an escape. He quickly informed the believers then went into hiding.

At daybreak, the guards were in an uproar, unable to find Peter. Herod was so upset that he had them all executed.

Learn More: Acts 12:1–19

BARNABAS AND SAUL BECOME MISSIONARIES

Then the disciples. . .sent it to the elders by the hands of Barnabas and Saul. ACTS 11:29-30

A prophet named Agabus had warned that a great famine was coming. The poor disciples in Judea would be especially hard hit, so the disciples in Antioch sent Barnabas and Saul to Jerusalem with relief money.

When the pair returned to Antioch, they brought a young man named John Mark (commonly called Mark) back with them. Mark was Barnabas's cousin, so Barnabas had a special affection for him.

Christians had been evangelizing Antioch since about AD 35. It was now AD 46. After eleven years, the church had grown large and was strong in the faith—yet the rest of the Roman world had never even heard the Gospel.

So a group of prophets and teachers—Barnabas, Saul, Simeon, Lucius, and Manaen—fasted and prayed for guidance. Then God said, "Separate me Barnabas and Saul for the work whereunto I have called them" (Acts 13:2).

So the other three prayed over Barnabas and Saul and sent them off. "They also had John [Mark] as their assistant" (Acts 13:5 NKJV).

Learn More: Acts 11:27–30 / 12:25; 13:1–5 / Colossians 4:10

A SORCERER IS STRUCK BLIND

The hand of the Lord is upon thee, and thou shalt be blind. ACTS 13:11

The first place Barnabas and Saul traveled to was Cyprus. The island had been briefly evangelized eleven years earlier, but Barnabas was from there and had a strong desire to see his countrymen saved.

Saul's Greek name was Paul, and he now began using this name.

The two began proclaiming the Gospel in the synagogues and traveled throughout the entire island to the capital, Paphos. The governor, Sergius Paulus, was an intelligent, inquisitive man, so he summoned Barnabas and Paul to hear the Word of God.

Previously the governor had consulted a Jewish magician named Elymas, and Elymas now began contradicting Barnabas and Paul to keep the governor from the faith.

Filled with the Holy Spirit, Paul stared at Elymas and said, "You who are full of all deceit and fraud, you son of the devil. . .behold, the hand of the Lord is upon you, and you will be blind and not see the sun for a time" (Acts 13:10–11 NASB).

Instantly, darkness descended on Elymas, and he had to be led out of the chamber. Astonished, Sergius Paulus believed.

Learn More: Acts 4:36; 11:19; 13:4–1

PAUL CONFRONTS PETER IN ANTIOCH

When Peter was come to Antioch, I withstood him to the face. GALATIANS 2:11

Peter was at the top of the "wanted list" in Judea, so it was a good time for him to visit distant cities.

When he visited Antioch, he accepted the Gentile believers and ate with them, although it was against Jewish customs. He had, after all, eaten with Cornelius.

But when disciples came from James, the Lord's brother, Peter began to separate himself from the Greeks. These Jews were zealous for the law, and Peter feared upsetting them.

Unfortunately, the other Jewish Christians followed Peter's example; even Barnabas withdrew from the Greeks' company. This was hypocrisy, so Paul opposed Peter to his face, saying in front of everyone: "If thou, being a Jew, livest after the manner of Gentiles, and not as do the Jews, why compellest thou the Gentiles to live as do the Jews?" (Galatians 2:14).

Paul reminded Peter that they all knew that they weren't made righteous by keeping the law but by faith in Jesus Christ. He argued that "if righteousness come by the law, then Christ is dead in vain" (Galatians 2:21).

Learn More: Galatians 2:11–21

MISSIONARIES GO TO MACEDONIA

We endeavoured to go into Macedonia. . .to preach the gospel unto them. ACTS 16:10

After strengthening the churches of Syria and Cilicia, Paul, Silas, and Timothy headed into new territory. They prayed and asked God to lead them.

The Roman province of Asia seemed like a logical choice, but the Holy Spirit forbade them to preach the Gospel there. They then tried to go into Bithynia, but the Spirit didn't permit that either. Wondering what to do, they came to the port city of Troas.

Around this time, they were joined by a Greek believer named Luke, who was a doctor.

Then one night Paul had a vision. A man appeared and pled: "Come over to Macedonia, and help us" (Acts 16:9). The four men then sailed to Philippi, a leading city of Macedonia (northern Greece).

There was no synagogue in Philippi, and the Jews there met beside the river, so Paul spoke to the women who gathered there to pray. A well-to-do woman named Lydia believed the Gospel and invited Paul and his companions to stay at her house. And so the adventure began.

Learn More: Acts 16:6–15

A DEMON IS CAST OUT OF A PSYCHIC

Paul, being grieved, turned and said to the spirit. . .come out of her. Acts 16:18

Every Greek city had an agora, a market square, where merchants sold goods and people met to talk, and Paul and his companions often witnessed there.

Philippi's market had a fortune-teller, a demon-possessed slave girl who earned a great deal of money for her masters because of her predictions. One day she began following Paul and Silas around, shouting, "These men are the servants of the most high God, which shew unto us the way of salvation" (Acts 16:17).

She continued doing this for several days until Paul, exasperated, turned and commanded the spirit to come out of her. The girl was instantly delivered.

When her masters realized that she could no longer predict fortunes and their livelihood was gone, they dragged Paul and Silas before the authorities, saying they "teach customs, which are not lawful for us to receive, neither to observe, being Romans" (Acts 16:21).

The mob began shouting in anger, so the officials ordered the apostles stripped and beaten with wooden rods. Afterward, they were thrown into prison.

Learn More: Acts 16:16–24

AN EARTHQUAKE FREES PAUL FROM PRISON

There was a great earthquake, so that the foundations of the prison were shaken. Acts 16:26

Paul and Silas were in terrible pain from their beating, but about midnight they were praying and singing praises to God. The other prisoners were undoubtedly impressed.

Then a great earthquake struck, violently shaking the prison. Every jail door broke open and all the prisoners' manacles snapped free. The jailer awoke and, seeing the gaping prison doors, feared that all the prisoners had escaped. This would cost him his life, so he drew his sword to kill himself. But Paul cried out for him to stop, saying all the prisoners were still there.

Trembling with fear, knowing that God had revealed His power, the jailer fell down before Paul and Silas and asked, "Sirs, what must I do to be saved?" (Acts 16:30). They answered, "Believe on the Lord Jesus Christ, and thou shalt be saved" (verse 31).

The jailer took them to his nearby house and washed their wounds. There Paul and Silas witnessed to him, and he and his entire household believed. The next morning, the officials personally escorted them from the prison, realizing that they had made a serious mistake.

Learn More: Acts 16:25–40

PAUL PREACHES ON MARS HILL

Then Paul stood in the midst of Mars' hill, and said. . . Acts 17:22

In Athens, Paul was struck by how many idols and pagan temples there were. Towering over Athens was the Acropolis, filled with temples to the Greek gods.

Paul was preaching in the marketplace when some philosophers heard him. He taught how Jesus had risen from the dead, and this was a strange idea to Greeks. So they brought him to Mars Hill to speak to the Areopagus, Athens' ruling religious council.

Paul established common ground by pointing out that there was an altar in their city with the inscription To the Unknown God. He said, "Whom therefore ye ignorantly worship, him declare I unto you" (Acts 17:23).

Paul was familiar with Greek poets and quoted the verse where Epimenides said, "For in him we live, and move, and have our being" (Acts 17:28). He went on to declare that the true God wasn't worshipped by idols or in temples but had revealed Himself in Jesus Christ. Paul was able to witness to both commoners and intellectuals.

Learn More: Acts 17:16–34

A RIOT BREAKS OUT IN CORINTH

The Jews made insurrection with one accord against Paul. Acts 18:12

From Athens, Paul went on to Corinth, a leading commercial center. He had great success there preaching to both Jews and Greeks. The synagogue leader and his entire household believed in Jesus, as did many Corinthians.

After his previous troubles, Paul wondered if trouble would arise here, but God told him, "Be not afraid, but speak, and hold not thy peace: For I am with thee, and no man shall set on thee to hurt thee: for I have much people in this city" (Acts 18:9–10).

So Paul preached and taught for a year and a half. Then one day the Jews who had rejected the Gospel made an attack on Paul and brought him to the judgment seat of Governor Gallio. They accused him of teaching people to worship God contrary to the law.

Before Paul could speak to defend himself, Gallio impatiently dismissed them, saying, "I will be no judge of such matters" (Acts 18:15). And he sent them away.

They attacked Paul, yes, but as God had promised, they were unable to harm him.

Learn More: Acts 18:1–17

EPHESUS ERUPTS IN AN UPROAR

The whole city was filled with confusion. Acts 19:29

The goddess Diana (Artemis) was worshipped in a renowned temple in Ephesus, and the silversmiths there earned a lucrative income making silver shrines and idols.

Then a man named Demetrius called the silversmiths together, alarmed by Paul's success in convincing people that idols weren't real gods. Not only were they losing money, but Diana and her temple were being discredited.

When they heard this, the tradesmen cried out, "Great is Diana of the Ephesians" (Acts 19:28). Soon the entire city was in a confused uproar. Seizing Paul's travel companions, the mob rushed into the amphitheater and shouted for about two hours, "Great is Diana of the Ephesians!"

Paul wanted to try to speak to the crowd, but the disciples wouldn't let him.

Finally, the city clerk calmed the people down by assuring them that, yes, Diana was great, but that the Christians hadn't robbed temples or blasphemed her—and that if Demetrius had a legitimate grievance, he should bring it to court, not start a riot. Then he dismissed them.

Learn More: Acts 19:21–41

PAUL WRITES TO THE ROMANS

To all that be in Rome, beloved of God, called to be saints. . . Romans 1:7

For over a year, Paul instructed churches to gather donations for the poor believers in Jerusalem and Judea. He now decided to go to Jerusalem with those who would be carrying the donations.

It took three months to finish visiting the churches in Macedonia and Achaia (Greece) and gather the money. In the port city of Cenchrea or in nearby Corinth, Paul sat down and wrote the Christians in Rome, promising to visit them after he'd been to Jerusalem.

What seems to have spurred him to write was that a lady named Phoebe, a deaconess of the church in Cenchrea, was heading to Rome on business. Since there was no postal system, Paul took the opportunity to send a letter with her (Romans 16:1–2).

Paul may have intended to write just a brief epistle, but God inspired him to share profound thoughts that have benefited millions of Christians for the last two thousand years. Repeatedly, Paul described faith in Jesus Christ and the grace and mercy of God that save us.

Learn More: Acts 19:21–22 / Romans 1:11–15 / 2 Corinthians 9:1–5

PAUL IS ARRESTED AT THE TEMPLE

*The chief captain came. . .*AND COMMANDED HIM TO BE BOUND WITH TWO CHAINS. ACTS 21:33

When Paul and company arrived in Jerusalem, James and the church leaders told him that there were many thousands of believers "and they are all zealous of the law" (Acts 21:20).

These believers had heard that Paul taught Jews not to follow the law. So the leaders advised Paul to go through a purification ceremony so that "all may know that those things, whereof they were informed concerning thee, are nothing; but that thou thyself also walkest orderly, and keepest the law" (Acts 21:24).

Paul had just gone through such a Jewish ceremony in Cenchrea. And though he didn't always follow the old rituals, he went along with the church leaders' advice. But when the ceremony was nearly over, some unbelieving Jews recognized him and stirred up the crowd.

They dragged Paul away and tried to kill him, but news reached the commander of the Roman troops, and he immediately took soldiers into the crowd. He then arrested Paul and bound him with chains.

Learn More: Acts 18:18; 21:17–36 / 1 Corinthians 9:19–21

PAUL IS IMPRISONED IN CAESAREA

[Felix] commanded [Paul] to be kept in Herod's judgment hall. ACTS 23:35

Governor Felix ordered Paul kept in the prison, and for the next five years, from about AD 57 to 62, Paul would be under Roman arrest.

Five days after Paul's arrival, the Jewish high priest Ananias, together with elders and an attorney named Tertullus, came, bringing charges against Paul. Tertullus stated: "We have found this man a pestilent fellow, and a mover of sedition among all the Jews throughout the world, and a ringleader of the sect of the Nazarenes: Who also hath gone about to profane the temple" (Acts 24:5–6).

Paul, however, denied that he had been causing any trouble.

Felix realized that Paul had committed no crimes but that this was only a religious quarrel. He nevertheless kept Paul in prison, wanting a large bribe to set him free. But Paul refused. He had, after all, been preaching to Felix about living righteously.

After two years passed, Festus became the new governor, and desiring to do the Jews a favor, Felix left Paul imprisoned.

Learn More: Acts 23:34–35; 24:1–27

PAUL APPEALS TO CAESAR

I appeal unto Caesar. ACTS 25:11

Three days after arriving at Caesarea, the new governor went to Jerusalem. There the priests and elders requested him to transfer Paul to Jerusalem. They planned to ambush him on the way. Festus, however, told them to come to Caesarea and to press charges there. After returning, he had Paul brought in.

Once again the religious rulers brought accusations against him, and once again Paul declared that he hadn't done anything against the Jewish law, the temple, or Caesar.

Festus, eager to establish good relations with the Jews, asked Paul if he was willing to go to Jerusalem and stand trial before him there. Paul, however, knew his rights. He answered: "I have not done any wrong to the Jews, as you yourself know very well. . .no one has the right to hand me over to them. I appeal to Caesar!" (Acts 25:11 NIV).

Roman citizens had the right to be tried by Caesar himself, so Festus said: "Hast thou appealed unto Caesar? unto Caesar shalt thou go" (Acts 25:11–12).

Learn More: Acts 25:1–12

FESTUS AND HEROD JUDGE PAUL

Festus declared Paul's cause unto the king. Acts 25:14

King Herod Agrippa came to Caesarea to greet the new governor, and Festus told him about Paul. He was being sent to Rome, but Festus thought it unreasonable to send a prisoner to Caesar and not to specify the charges against him.

Herod desired to hear Paul, so Festus arranged an audience.

Paul was glad to present his case before Agrippa, since the king was well-versed in Jewish customs. Paul told his life story, and as he was discussing the resurrection, Festus said loudly, "Paul, thou art beside thyself; much learning doth make thee mad" (Acts 26:24).

Paul assured Festus that he wasn't insane but was speaking reasonable things that Agrippa was familiar with. He then asked Agrippa if he believed the prophets. Agrippa answered, "Do you think that in such a short time you can persuade me to be a Christian?" (Acts 26:28 NIV).

The two rulers then ended the audience and agreed that Paul was innocent.

God had promised years earlier that Paul would witness "to the Gentiles and their kings" (Acts 9:15 NIV). Paul was now doing so—and would soon witness to Caesar himself.

Learn More: Acts 25:13–27; 26:1–32

PAUL SURVIVES SHIPWRECK

So it came to pass, that they escaped all safe to land. Acts 27:44

Paul was on his way to Rome when a huge storm struck his ship in the Mediterranean. The seas were so violent that the ship was in danger of breaking apart.

Some of the sailors lowered the lifeboat to escape, "pretending" that "they were going to lower some anchors from the bow" (Acts 27:30 NIV). But Paul warned Julius, the centurion in charge, that unless they stayed with the ship, no one would survive. So Julius had the ropes cut and the lifeboat drifted away. Now they listened to Paul!

In the morning they saw a sandy beach ahead and threw all the ship's grain overboard to lighten the vessel so it would ride higher in the water. They then cut the anchor ropes and hoisted the foresail, hoping to be driven up on the beach.

But they got stuck on a sandbar some ways out, and the stern began breaking to pieces in the heavy surf. The soldiers wanted to kill the prisoners lest they swim away, but Julius determined to spare Paul—so they didn't.

Instead, Julius ordered everyone who could swim to make it to the beach. Those who couldn't swim hung onto planks and were washed ashore. And all 276 people made it to land safely.

Learn More: Acts 27:27–44

PAUL DOES MIRACLES ON MALTA

Others also, which had diseases in the island, came, and were healed. Acts 28:9

The shipwreck survivors found themselves on the island of Malta. And the hospitable islanders hurried to the beach and built a great bonfire to warm their visitors.

As Paul was helping put wood on the fire, a viper, hiding in the brushwood, bit him. The Maltese saw it and exclaimed, "No doubt this man is a murderer, whom, though he hath escaped the sea, yet vengeance suffereth not to live" (Acts 28:4).

Paul, however, simply shook the viper into the fire. The people waited and waited, expecting him to fall down dead. But Paul trusted God and suffered no ill effects.

Publius, the leading Roman official of the island, invited the company into his home for several days. Now, Publius's father was bedridden with dysentery and fever. Paul therefore went into his room, prayed over him, and healed him.

Word of this miracle quickly spread. Soon every sick person on the island came and was healed. Then, for three months, Paul most likely preached the Gospel to the people.

Learn More: Acts 28:1–11

PAUL WITNESSES IN ROME

He expounded and testified the kingdom of God. ACTS 28:23

When Paul's company finally arrived at Rome, the centurion Julius delivered the prisoners to the imperial prison. But Paul was permitted to dwell in his own rented house with a soldier guarding him. After he'd been there only three days, Paul invited the Jewish leaders to visit. They would soon hear that he'd arrived, so he wanted to share the Gospel with them before they were influenced by negative reports.

They had heard bad reports—though not about him personally. They had heard negative opinions about the Christian faith in general. Nevertheless, they took a very open-minded approach, saying, "But we desire to hear of thee what thou thinkest: for as concerning this sect, we know that every where it is spoken against" (Acts 28:22). So for one entire day, Paul taught from the scriptures that Jesus was the Jewish Messiah. Several people believed.

Paul then continued living two years in his own house, freely sharing the Gospel with everyone who came to visit him and strengthening believers. Paul had long dreamed of evangelizing in Rome, and now he was doing it!

Learn More: Acts 28:11–31 / Romans 1:9–15

PAUL MEETS ONESIMUS

I beseech thee for my son Onesimus, whom I have begotten in my bonds. PHILEMON 10

Paul had many visitors in Rome, but one of his most unusual was a runaway slave.

Onesimus belonged to a wealthy Christian master named Philemon, a leader of the church of Colossae. The believers met in Philemon's home.

One day Onesimus fled Colossae, apparently having taken some of his master's money, and sailed for Rome. We surmise that he intended to start a new life as a free man but soon ran out of money and realized his mistake. So he went to Paul and confessed what he'd done.

Paul led the young man to faith in Jesus, and Onesimus was a huge help to the aged apostle. Paul wanted to keep Onesimus with him but decided to send him back to Colossae with Tychicus, bearing the letter to Philemon and an epistle to the church.

Paul called Onesimus "a faithful and beloved brother" (Colossians 4:9) and urged Philemon to treat him "not now as a servant, but above a servant, a brother beloved" (Philemon 16). As for the money, Paul offered to personally repay it.

Learn More: Philemon 1–24 / Colossians 4:7–9

JERUSALEM IS DESTROYED

When ye shall see Jerusalem compassed with armies. . . LUKE 21:20

In AD 30 Jesus prophesied over Jerusalem: "The days shall come upon thee, that thine enemies shall cast a trench about thee, and compass thee round, and keep thee in on every side" (Luke 19:43).

In AD 66 the Jews revolted against Rome, but the Romans struck back and were soon besieging Jerusalem itself. They dug a trench around the city and built a high wall around that. The city was captured in AD 70.

Jesus had also prophesied: "They shall fall by the edge of the sword, and shall be led away captive into all nations" (Luke 21:24). Some 1.1 million Jews were killed during the siege, and 97,000 were sold as slaves throughout the Roman Empire.

Jesus predicted that the temple would be utterly destroyed: "Verily I say unto you, There shall not be left here one stone upon another, that shall not be thrown down" (Matthew 24:2). And it was. The cedar paneling in the temple was set ablaze, and the heat melted the gold covering the temple. The Romans then took apart the temple to get at the gold.

God fulfilled Jesus' prophecies in great detail—proof that He is the Messiah.

Learn More: Luke 19:41–44; 21:5–24

JOHN WRITES HIS GOSPEL

He that saw it bare record, and his record is true. JOHN 19:35

The Gospels of Matthew, Mark, and Luke were written between AD 50 and 60, but the fourth Gospel was not written till AD 85–90.

According to the church fathers, John was living in Ephesus when he was old. Then the bishops of the province of Asia asked him to compose a Gospel that would oppose the heresies of Cerinthus (an early Gnostic) and the Ebionites (Hebrews who believed that Jesus was the Messiah but not the divine Son of God).

Therefore John, more than any other Gospel writer, related stories that stressed the deity of Christ. His opening words, in fact, declare clearly that Jesus is God (John 1:1–3, 14).

The Gospel of John is written in correct, polished Greek, even though Greek wasn't John's mother tongue. The reason for this is that, as the Muratorian Canon states, John had help composing his Gospel. Internal evidence supports this idea (see John 19:35, 21:24).

John also told many stories that the other three Gospels never mentioned.

Learn More: John 1:1–3, 14; 19:35; 21:24

JOHN HAS A VISION ON PATMOS

The Revelation of Jesus Christ, which God gave unto him. . . REVELATION 1:1

In AD 95, Emperor Domitian violently persecuted Christians, and thousands died. Others were banished. The apostle John was imprisoned on the island of Patmos.

One day John heard a loud voice. He turned to see who was speaking, and there, in all His glory, was Jesus Christ, the Son of God.

"His head and his hairs were white like wool, as white as snow; and his eyes as a flame of fire; and his feet were like unto fine brass, as if they burned in a furnace; and his voice as the sound of many waters. . .and his countenance was as the sun shineth in his strength" (Revelation 1:14–16).

When John saw Jesus, he collapsed at His feet like a dead man. But Jesus placed His hand on John and said, "Fear not; I am the first and the last: I am he that liveth, and was dead; and, behold, I am alive for evermore" (Revelation 1:17–18).

He then gave John tremendous visions of the future to encourage generations of believers in their sufferings—from John's day to the present.

Learn More: Revelation 1:9–19

JOHN SEES GOD'S THRONE ROOM

Behold, a throne was set in heaven, and one sat on the throne. REVELATION 4:2

Jesus gave John messages for seven churches of Asia Minor (Revelation 2–3). Then John heard a voice say, "Come up hither, and I will shew thee things which must be hereafter" (Revelation 4:1).

Immediately John saw a throne in heaven, and God sat on it. There was an emerald rainbow glowing around Him. Seven lamps were blazing, reflecting off a sea of crystal glass.

John saw fearsome cherubim, full of eyes. The first one was like a lion, the second like a calf, the third like a man, and the fourth like an eagle. They praised God continually. Sitting on thrones around God were twenty-four elders, clothed in white robes and wearing golden crowns.

John saw God holding a scroll. Then Jesus, "the Lion of the tribe of Judah" (Revelation 5:5), opened the scroll. Jesus appeared as a lamb with seven horns and seven eyes.

This was the beginning of a series of fantastic, mysterious visions of heaven, which not only show us the future but the glory and the power of God.

Learn More: Revelation 4:1–11; 5:1–7

JESUS RETURNS TO EARTH

Behold, he cometh with clouds; and every eye shall see him. REVELATION 1:7

One of the greatest messages of the book of Revelation is that Jesus is coming back. It states in the opening chapter, "Behold, he cometh with clouds; and every eye shall see him, and they also which pierced him" (Revelation 1:7).

Christians have different opinions about exactly when Jesus will return. But one thing is very clear: Jesus *is* coming back! And "they shall see the Son of man coming in the clouds of heaven with power and great glory" (Matthew 24:30). Then the angels "shall gather together his elect from the four winds, from one end of heaven to the other" (verse 31).

Later, John had a vision of Jesus sitting on a cloud, holding a great sickle. He reaped the harvest of the earth—all those who believe in Him (Revelation 14:14–16). Jesus then took the believers to heaven. As the Gospels say, He will "gather his wheat into the garner; but he will burn up the chaff with unquenchable fire" (Matthew 3:12).

We can be comforted knowing that despite the trials and tribulations we suffer here, Jesus cares deeply for us and will one day take us to heaven to be with Him.

Learn More: Matthew 24:29–31 / Revelation 1:4–8

THE BATTLE OF ARMAGEDDON

He gathered them together into a place called. . .Armageddon. REVELATION 16:16

After the rapture of believers, an angel will swing his sickle, harvest the clusters from the grapevine of the earth, and throw them into the winepress of the wrath of God—the Valley of Megiddo in Israel.

The judgments of God will be poured out on the wicked who persecuted His children—and will culminate in a conflict called the Battle of Armageddon. Here's how it happens:

The Euphrates River will be dried up so that an army of 200 million men, led by "the kings of the east" (Revelation 16:12), can cross over. Then "the demonic spirits gathered all the rulers and their armies to a place with the Hebrew name *Armageddon*" (verse 16 NLT).

The battle will stretch south to the walls of Jerusalem, and blood will come "out of the winepress, even unto the horse bridles, by the space of a thousand and six hundred furlongs" (Revelation 14:20). That's almost two hundred miles.

Jesus and the armies of heaven will then decisively defeat these evil armies. After the Battle of Armageddon, the Lord will set up His kingdom on earth.

There are fearful things coming in the future, but Jesus will defeat all His enemies—and then there will be peace at last.

Learn More: Revelation 9:16; 14:18–20; 16:12–16; 19:11–21

HEAVEN COMES TO EARTH

I saw a new heaven and a new earth. REVELATION 21:1

It will be wonderful after Jesus sets up His kingdom on the earth—but the unregenerate humans who survive the Battle of Armageddon won't be satisfied or live peaceably even with Jesus Christ ruling in justice and love over them.

At the end of the thousand-year period called the millennium, the nations of the world will rebel and attack Christ's capital, Jerusalem. God will then wipe out the entire earth with fire.

He will remold the surface of the earth and create new heavens (or atmosphere). There will be "no more sea" (Revelation 21:1). This likely means that there will be plenty land for people to live in.

Then the resplendent city of light, the New Jerusalem, will come down out of the heavenly dimension, and will reside on Earth. God Himself lives in that city, so He will then be personally living on this beautiful new planet with us.

This will be the final, glorious ending to the long history of God's interaction with mankind. And it will be the beginning of His wonderful eternal plan.

Learn More: Revelation 20:1–9; 21:1–11, 22–27

THE 1-MINUTE
BIBLE
GUIDE

180 Key Ideas

An alphabetical listing of the 180 most
important theological concepts of scripture.

Written by George W. Knight
Edited by Paul Kent

ABIDING

He that abideth in me, and I in him, the same bringeth forth much fruit. JOHN 15:5

This verse is part of Jesus' final instructions to His disciples before His arrest and crucifixion. He used the imagery of a grapevine and its branches to emphasize that they should remain committed to Him as their Lord and master in the perilous days ahead.

The fruit that Jesus mentioned probably refers to the testimony the disciples would bear as they continued His work in the world. They should tell others about His life and death, even after His ascension to God the Father. This is exactly what happened in the book of Acts as they preached the good news about a Savior who died to set people free from their bondage to sin.

Those who abide in Christ are assured of eternal life with Him in the world to come. The apostle John declared, "The world passeth away, and the lust thereof: but he that doeth the will of God abideth for ever" (1 John 2:17).

Learn More: Psalm 15:1; 91:1 / Micah 5:4 / John 12:46; 14:16; 15:6, 7, 10

ABOMINATION

Turn away your faces from all your abominations. EZEKIEL 14:6

The Lord expressed through the prophet Ezekiel just how much He detested idol worship by calling it an abomination. The Hebrew word refers to something that is impure and disgusting—that which is foul-smelling and repulsive to a holy God. The concept of abomination appears throughout the Old Testament to register God's extreme disapproval when His people gave in to temptation and began to worship false gods.

Other things that God considered an abomination were the offering of blemished animals as sacrifices, degraded sexual sins, child sacrifice, eating the meat of unclean animals, using false balances in buying and selling, lying, and the practice of witchcraft and magic. Even pretending to worship while remaining disobedient to the Lord was considered an abominable act (Isaiah 1:13).

Learn More: Deuteronomy 7:25–26; 12:31; 17:1; 18:9–12 / Leviticus 11:11–13; 18:26 / 2 Kings 16:3 / Proverbs 11:1; 12:22 / Ezekiel 22:11 / Revelation 21:27

ADOPTION

God sent forth his Son. . .that we might receive the adoption of sons. GALATIANS 4:4–5

Adoption is the act of God's grace by which sinful people are justified by grace and brought into the family of God. The apostle Paul mentions this idea several times in his letters.

Paul was probably influenced by the practice of familial adoption in the Roman culture of his time. The person adopted by a Roman family was usually an adult who had to agree to accept this new relationship. Legally, the adoptee was transformed by the adoption into a new person—an apt illustration of the Christian believer's conversion.

The process of spiritual adoption emphasizes our new status as believers. We were once prisoners of sin, but God delivered us from bondage and adopted us as His own. So close is our relationship to God as our adoptive Father that we can call Him "Abba," an Aramaic word equivalent to our modern "Daddy" or "Papa" (Romans 8:15).

Our spiritual adoption also assures our bodily resurrection in the end times and eternal life with God the Father and Jesus the Son (Romans 8:23).

Learn More: Luke 20:36 / Galatians 3:26 / Ephesians 1:5 / 1 John 3:1

ADULTERY

Thou shalt not commit adultery. EXODUS 20:14

To commit adultery is to have a sexual relationship with a person other than one's husband or wife. This flagrant sin is strictly prohibited in the Ten Commandments, the laws regulating the behavior of God's people revealed to Moses by the Lord on Mount Sinai (Exodus 20:1–17).

The adulterous relationship of King David and Bathsheba dramatizes the problems that can follow this serious sin. Their encounter led to Bathsheba's pregnancy, and the king had her husband murdered to try to cover up his deed. David sought and received God's forgiveness, but a series of disasters struck his family as a consequence of his moral failure.

Jesus taught that lustful thoughts toward members of the opposite sex are also a serious matter. He declared, "Whosoever looketh on a woman to lust after her hath committed adultery with her already in his heart" (Matthew 5:28). Perhaps He meant that giving free rein to such impulses is just a step away from the physical act of adultery itself.

Learn More: 2 Samuel 11:1–4 / Mark 10:11 / John 8:3 / 1 Corinthians 6:9 / Galatians 5:19 / 2 Peter 2:14

ADVENT

But is now made manifest by the appearing of our Saviour Jesus Christ. . . 2 TIMOTHY 1:10

The word *advent* comes from a Latin term meaning "arrival." As used by Christians, it generally refers to the arrival of God's Son in the world. Jesus left the glories of heaven and took on the form of a man in order to reconcile the world to His heavenly Father.

The season known as Advent is celebrated in many churches during the four successive Sundays before Christmas. It is a time of prayer, fasting, and quiet contemplation about the meaning and significance of Jesus' birth.

The phrase "second Advent" is often used to refer to the second coming of Jesus. Just as He came to earth the first time, He will return to bring the world to its appointed end and fulfill His promises to those who belong to Him.

Learn More: Isaiah 7:14; 11:1–2 / John 14:2–3 / Acts 1:10–11

AFFLICTION

Be thou partaker of the afflictions of the gospel according to the power of God. 2 TIMOTHY 1:8

The apostle Paul wrote these words while he was a prisoner in Rome. He wanted his young missionary associate Timothy to know that he considered his own suffering a badge of honor. Paul's affliction was a result of his commitment to Christ. He wanted Timothy to be prepared to endure the same ridicule and persecution that might result from his preaching of the Gospel.

Paul also knew that people sometimes suffer affliction because of personal sin in their lives. "Whatsoever a man soweth," he declared, "that shall he also reap" (Galatians 6:7). But God can use even suffering from our own failures to make us more dependent on Him and help us grow in our understanding of others.

The Bible also affirms that afflictions are a natural part of life (Job 5:7). But the Lord has promised His peace that "passeth all understanding" (Philippians 4:7) to sustain us through our troubles.

Learn More: Job 34:28 / Psalm 119:71 / Isaiah 49:13 / Romans 5:3–5; 8:18 / 2 Corinthians 4:17 / 2 Thessalonians 1:4–5 / James 4:9

ANOINTING

Samuel took the horn of oil, and anointed him in the midst of his brethren. 1 SAMUEL 16:13

When King Saul of Israel disobeyed God, the prophet Samuel anointed his replacement David by pouring oil on his head. This ritual was performed for kings and priests in biblical times. It indicated that they had been especially chosen or set apart to perform the responsibilities of their office.

Sometimes Old Testament prophets were also anointed (1 Kings 19:16). In the New Testament, anointing for healing was practiced with the application of oil (Mark 6:13).

Jesus the Messiah was anointed by God the Father for the special mission of bringing redemption to a sinful world. The Greek term *christos,* translated as "Christ," means "anointed" or "anointed one." The word always refers to the Messiah, God's Chosen One.

The concept of anointing also refers to the action of the Holy Spirit. The third person of the Trinity enables believers to understand God's will. He also empowers us to serve as proclaimers of His love and grace in an unbelieving world (1 John 2:20, 27).

Learn More: Exodus 30:30 / Psalm 23:5 / Isaiah 61:1 / Matthew 26:12 / Luke 4:18 / Acts 10:38 / James 5:14

APOSTASY

An evil heart of unbelief, in departing from the living God. HEBREWS 3:12

The word *apostasy* does not appear in the King James Version, but the concept is evident throughout the Bible. The term comes from a Greek word that means "to stand away from." So to commit apostasy is to renounce one's faith in the Lord.

God's special people, the Israelites, had a bad habit of falling away from their commitment to Him and worshipping false gods. The prophet Jeremiah sometimes referred to these moral lapses as "backsliding" (14:7) and "rebellion" (28:16).

Can a person lose his salvation through deliberate acts of apostasy? Some people say this can't happen. While believers may stray from the faith, they will never totally fall away because of God's sovereignty and His holding power over His children. Others affirm that the Bible's warnings against apostasy are real. They think believers may actually lose their salvation through a deliberate and willful rejection of the Lord and His influence in their lives.

Another point of view between these two extremes is that people who fall away from their faith were never really saved. Although they "believed" for a while, they never experienced true regeneration.

Learn More: Deuteronomy 32:18 / Ephesians 4:13–16 / 2 Timothy 4:10

ASCENSION

He was parted from them, and carried up into heaven. LUKE 24:51

Luke, the author of both the Gospel of Luke and the book of Acts, gives an account of the ascension of Jesus in both of these writings (see also Acts 1:9–11). This event occurred forty days after Jesus' resurrection. He spent this time with His disciples, preparing them for carrying on His work after His return to God the Father.

Jesus made it clear that He was not leaving His followers alone; the Holy Spirit would come upon them in great power, strengthening them for the task of proclaiming the Gospel "in Jerusalem, and in all Judaea, and Samaria, and to the ends of the earth" (Acts 1:8 NIV).

Jesus' ascension marked the beginning of His intercession at the right hand of God for all believers (Romans 8:34). His physical departure was also the occasion for a renewal of His promise that we will see Him again at His return. We can rest assured that just as Jesus ascended into heaven in bodily form, so He will return to earth at His second coming.

Learn More: Psalm 68:18 / Luke 24:50–51 / 1 Corinthians 15:20–28 / Ephesians 4:10

ATONEMENT

Through our Lord Jesus Christ, by whom we have now received the atonement. ROMANS 5:11

Atonement is the process by which God takes the initiative to restore a harmonious relationship between Himself and sinful human beings. This unity may be expressed by dividing this long word into three little words. We find "at-one-ment" with God, in spite of our sin, because of His grace and forgiveness.

This reconciliation came about in Old Testament times through animal sacrifices that symbolized the people's repentance. The Jewish holy day on which atonement was made for all Israel was known as the day of atonement (Leviticus 16:29–30). The Jewish high priest first made atonement for himself and then for the sins of the people by sprinkling the blood of a sacrificial animal on the altar. The scapegoat, representing the sins of the people, was released into the wilderness to symbolize their pardon.

With the advent of Christ, reconciliation now occurs through the sacrificial death of God's Son on the cross (Romans 5:10). God's righteousness is imparted to those who receive Jesus as Savior and Lord.

Learn More: Leviticus 16:21–22 / Romans 3:25; 5:8 / Hebrews 9:12; 10:4

BACKSLIDING

Why then is this people of Jerusalem slidden back by a perpetual backsliding? JEREMIAH 8:5

The prophet Jeremiah could be called "the backsliding preacher of the Bible"—not because he strayed from the Lord himself but because he condemned the nation of Judah for its spiritual apathy. The word appears many times throughout Jeremiah's book. The prophet pulled no punches in declaring that God's people had turned away from the Lord by living immoral lives and serving false gods.

In our time the word *backslider* describes a believer who grows negligent in his devotion to God. The Bible describes many causes of this decline in spiritual vitality: failure to cultivate the fruits of conversion (2 Peter 1:6–9), persecution because of one's faith (Matthew 13:20–21), and love of material things (1 Timothy 6:10). This sin separates the offender from God's blessings, but confession and repentance bring His forgiveness.

After his sin of adultery, David prayed, "Create in me a clean heart, O God; and renew a right spirit within me" (Psalm 51:10). Although the consequences of his sin followed him for the rest of his life, David was restored to a right relationship with the Lord.

Learn More: Proverbs 14:14 / Hosea 4:16; 11:7; 14:4 / 1 John 1:9

BAPTISM

Buried with him in baptism. . . COLOSSIANS 2:12

Baptism is a rite that signifies a believer's conversion to new life through Jesus Christ's atoning death. The practice is rooted in the ministry of John the Baptist, forerunner of Jesus. John called on people to repent and be baptized to show they had been cleansed of their sin. Even Jesus requested baptism by John at the beginning of His public ministry. By doing so, He apparently identified with John's work and set an example for all future believers who would be baptized in His name.

All Christian groups continue to practice this ritual. But they differ widely on who should be baptized and the exact way in which baptism should be administered. All agree, though, that baptism memorializes the death, burial, and resurrection of Jesus Christ and the new life that He confers on those who accept Him as Lord and Savior.

Here is how the apostle Paul expressed this truth: "We are buried with him by baptism into death: that like as Christ was raised up from the dead by the glory of the Father, even so we also should walk in newness of life" (Romans 6:4).

Learn More: Matthew 3:1–6, 13–17 / Acts 2:38 / Romans 6:3–11 / Ephesians 4:5–6

BELIEF

Whosoever believeth in him should not perish, but have everlasting life. JOHN 3:16

Belief and *believed* are two of the most important words in the Bible. A classic case study is that of Abraham. God promised to make his descendants into a great nation at a time when Abraham had no children and little prospect of ever having any. But in spite of this, Abraham took the Lord at His word (Genesis 15:5–6). God honored that belief by allowing Abraham in his old age to father a son, Isaac, who carried on his father's legacy of trust and confidence in the divine promise (Genesis 21:2–3).

In New Testament terms, belief is not an emotion but an act of the will. It comes about when people deliberately place their trust in Christ. Through belief or faith, we place our confidence in God's ability to deliver us from sin and shape us into new beings who bring honor and glory to Him.

In the early church, Christians were often called "believers" (Acts 5:14). This name is often used for followers of Christ even today.

Learn More: John 11:26; 20:29 / Acts 8:36–38 / 1 Corinthians 1:21 / 1 John 5:1

BIRTHRIGHT

And [Esau] sold his birthright unto Jacob. GENESIS 25:33

During Bible times the firstborn son received special rights because of his status as the oldest male offspring of the family. These benefits were known as his birthright. The most famous biblical incident involving a birthright was the bargain struck by the twin brothers Esau and Jacob. In a fit of hunger, Esau traded his birthright to Jacob for a bowl of stew (Genesis 25:29–34).

What Esau gave up was the right to receive a double portion of the inheritance from his father, Isaac. He also forfeited to his brother the authority to take over leadership of the family after his father's death.

In the New Testament, the concept of the birthright is also applied spiritually to Jesus, the "firstborn among many brethren" (Romans 8:29). He holds the supreme place of honor in all creation. And all believers are His brothers and sisters, sharing in His spiritual inheritance from God the Father.

Learn More: Genesis 27:36; 43:33; Deuteronomy 21:15–17 / 1 Chronicles 5:1–2 / Luke 2:7 / Colossians 1:18 / Hebrews 12:16

BLASPHEMY

That the name of God and his doctrine be not blasphemed. 1 TIMOTHY 6:1

Disrespectful acts—such as cursing or slandering—that showed lack of reverence for God were considered blasphemous. In Old Testament times, blaspheming God was a serious crime punishable by death (Leviticus 24:15–16).

Queen Jezebel of Israel used this law for her own evil purposes. She had a landowner named Naboth executed under a charge of blasphemy. Then she claimed his choice vineyard for her husband, King Ahab (1 Kings 21:10–13). God could not overlook this criminal act; Jezebel was tossed to her death from her palace window when Ahab's reign came to an end (2 Kings 9:33).

Jesus was arrested by the Jewish religious leaders on a charge of blasphemy for declaring that He was God's Son. In spite of His miracles, they thought of Him only as a man whose statement amounted to a serious crime. Early in His ministry, He had accused them of this same offense because they claimed His miracles were the work of Satan (Matthew 12:31–32).

Learn More: Matthew 26:65 / John 10:33 / Acts 18:6 / Romans 2:24 / Revelation 13:6

BLESSING

Knowing that ye are thereunto called, that ye should inherit a blessing. 1 Peter 3:9

A blessing is a formal declaration of God's favor upon others. One of the best examples of this in the Bible is the long blessing that the patriarch Jacob invoked upon his twelve sons (Genesis 49:1–28).

A blessing was apparently thought to carry great power. Jacob schemed to have his father, Isaac, bless him instead of his older brother, Esau. Once this blessing was given, it could not be changed or transferred to someone else (Genesis 27:30–35).

God is the source of all blessing, and He desires to bless all people. His blessing in Old Testament times was dependent on a person's obedience to His commands (Deuteronomy 11:26–28). Since the coming of His Son, Jesus, into the world, His most abundant blessing is granted to those who confess Christ as Savior and Lord. God blesses us continually as His people by forgiving our sins and giving us eternal life.

Learn More: Genesis 12:2 / Deuteronomy 33:1–29 / Luke 24:50 / Romans 4:7–8

BODY OF CHRIST

We being many, are one body in Christ, and every one members one of another. Romans 12:5

This symbolic expression for the church appears exclusively in the writings of the apostle Paul. Just as Christ is the head of the church, Paul declared, those who belong to Him are members of His body, the organization that continues His work in the world.

The apostle emphasized that all members of the body are granted spiritual gifts by the Lord. Many different spiritual gifts existed, but all were equal in value. They were given for the benefit of the entire body, and they should be used to build up the church and make it a more effective witness in an unbelieving world.

In his writings Paul also declared that unity in the body of Christ was essential to its work. He reminded the divided church at Corinth that it should come together to serve the One who was founder and head of the church. "Is Christ divided?" he asked. "Was Paul crucified for you? or were ye baptized in the name of Paul?" (1 Corinthians 1:13).

Learn More: Romans 7:4 / 1 Corinthians 12:25–28 / Ephesians 4:11–13; 5:23 / Colossians 1:24

BOOK OF LIFE

With other my fellowlabourers, whose names are in the book of life. Philippians 4:3

The apostle Paul used "the book of life" in a symbolic sense to refer to those people who will enjoy fellowship with the Lord in heaven in the end time.

The concept of a book of life may have originated with Moses. He prayed for his own name to be erased from God's book instead of wiping out the Israelites because of their worship of the golden calf in the wilderness (Exodus 32:32–33).

Those whose names appear in this book have been born into the family of God through the sacrificial death of Jesus Christ. Like those mentioned by Paul in Philippians 4:3, they are fellow workers in the kingdom of God.

The phrase appears several times in the book of Revelation. At the final judgment, those whose names are not written in this book will be "cast into the lake of fire" (Revelation 20:15). But those who are listed will be admitted to the heavenly city known as New Jerusalem.

Learn More: Hebrews 12:23 / Revelation 3:5; 13:8; 17:8; 20:12, 15; 21:27; 22:19

BORN AGAIN

Except a man be born again, he cannot see the kingdom of God. John 3:3

To be born again is to be redeemed from spiritual darkness through the atoning death of Jesus Christ. The phrase comes from Jesus' conversation with Nicodemus, a Pharisee who approached Jesus to learn more about this teacher and miracle worker.

Nicodemus interpreted Jesus' words in a physical sense. He wondered how it was possible for a person to enter his mother's womb and be born a second time. Jesus patiently explained that He was talking about a spiritual rebirth.

The apostle Paul in later years elaborated on the meaning of being born again. "If any man be in Christ," he declared, "he is a new creature: old things are passed away; behold, all things are become new" (2 Corinthians 5:17).

This new state of being comes about when people place their faith in Jesus Christ. This results in forgiveness of their sin through the power of the Holy Spirit, enabling them to have fellowship with God.

Learn More: John 3:1–16 / Romans 6:4–8 / 2 Corinthians 4:16 / Ephesians 2:8–9 / Titus 3:5 / 1 John 5:4–5

CALLING

Not many mighty, not many noble, are called. 1 Corinthians 1:26

Does God call people to special service in His kingdom? If we take the Bible seriously, the answer is a definite yes. Scripture contains several examples of God's call of specific individuals to kingdom ministry.

Perhaps the best example of His special calling is the prophet Jeremiah. Even before the prophet was born, God's hand was on him. The Lord selected Jeremiah to serve as His spokesman to the nation of Judah (Jeremiah 1:4–5). Jeremiah labored at this task for more than forty years, calling on the people to turn away from idolatry and back to worship of the one true God.

But God's call is not just to those who serve Him in vocational ministry. Every believer is called to service in His kingdom. This is sometimes referred to as God's universal call. He calls us first to salvation (1 Thessalonians 2:12). This leads to our involvement in His ministry to others. Our purpose as believers is to "declare the praises of him who called [us] out of darkness into his wonderful light" (1 Peter 2:9 NIV).

Learn More: Genesis 12:1 / 1 Corinthians 7:20 / 2 Thessalonians 1:11 / 2 Peter 1:10

CARNALITY

Abstain from fleshly lusts, which war against the soul. 1 Peter 2:11

The word *carnality* refers to worldly appetites and desires. The apostle Peter in this verse appealed to early believers to refrain from such cravings because they were deadly to the godly mind-set that God desires in His children.

In its natural state, human nature is oriented toward carnality, or a worldly lifestyle. Carnal people are opposed to God and every good motive and behavior He represents. In this state, they are unable to please God and to have fellowship with Him. But Jesus Christ came to earth in a physical body to replace fleshly human weakness with a more satisfying way of living in His Spirit.

Even after conversion, believers can succumb to the ways of the world, give in to temptation, and fall into sin. The apostle Paul admitted this often happened to new Christians who failed to grow in their faith (1 Corinthians 3:2).

Paul was especially disappointed in the novice believers of Galatia. They were tempted to revert to Jewish law as the basis of salvation rather than the grace of Jesus Christ. He called on them to "walk in the Spirit, and ye shall not fulfill the lust of the flesh" (Galatians 5:16).

Learn More: Romans 8:5–7, 13 / 1 Corinthians 3:3 / 1 Peter 4:2 / 1 John 2:16

CHOSEN PEOPLE

The Lord hath chosen thee to be a peculiar people unto himself. DEUTERONOMY 14:2

This phrase refers to the Israelites, the people selected by the Lord to receive His special blessings. Their mission was to represent the one true God to the rest of the world. God promised to bless His people, but they in turn were to be a blessing to "all families of the earth" (Genesis 12:3).

God's promise was first issued to Abraham, then renewed through Abraham's son Isaac and Isaac's son Jacob. This promise also included God's provision of a land of their own. This came to pass several centuries after Abraham's time, when the Israelites occupied the land of Canaan.

The Israelites often repaid God's goodness by rebelling against Him and worshipping false gods. The Lord punished their sin by sending calamities to convince them to turn back to Him.

In the New Testament, the apostle Peter referred to the church founded by Jesus Christ as the new people chosen by the Lord. Its mission is to glorify God through good works and positive witness for Jesus Christ (1 Peter 2:12).

Learn More: Genesis 12:1–3; 22:15–18; 28:14 / Deuteronomy 7:6 / 1 Kings 3:8 / Psalm 33:12

CHURCH, THE

Thou art Peter, and upon this rock I will build my church. MATTHEW 16:18

The church is a local body of believers assembled for Christian worship (Acts 15:4), as well as all the redeemed of the ages who belong to Christ (Ephesians 5:27). The mission of the church is to continue the work of Jesus in the world.

Jesus anticipated the church when He commended His disciple Peter for confessing Him as the Messiah and God's Son. But the church did not begin in a formal way until the dramatic outpouring of the Holy Spirit on Jesus' followers on the day of Pentecost (Acts 2:1–6).

At the close of His earthly ministry, Jesus commissioned His followers to spread the good news about His life, death, and resurrection throughout the world (Matthew 28:18–20). The book of Acts tells how the early church was empowered by the Holy Spirit to carry out this Great Commission. People of Jewish background were the first to claim the promises of the Gospel, but Gentiles eventually were added to the church in great numbers.

Learn More: Acts 2:47 / Ephesians 5:25 / Colossians 1:18 / 1 Timothy 3:15

CIRCUMCISION

Neither circumcision availeth any thing, nor uncircumcision; but faith. GALATIANS 5:6

Circumcision was a ritual that signified the covenant between God and His people, the Israelites. It was performed by removing the loose foreskin of the male sex organ. This practice probably began with Abraham, who was instructed by the Lord to circumcise every male child in his household (Genesis 17:11–12).

Over time, the Jewish people came to think of circumcision as a sign of their racial superiority. They referred to the Gentiles, or non-Jews, as "the uncircumcised" (Ezekiel 32:27). This insult implied that people of other nationalities were not worthy of God's love.

This prideful attitude caused a problem in the early church. Many believers in the years after the ascension of Jesus were converts from Judaism. Some of them believed Gentiles had to undergo the rite of circumcision before they were genuinely converted and worthy of acceptance by other believers (Acts 15:1).

In a meeting called to discuss this issue, church leaders decided that this ritual was not a requirement for salvation. This opened the door for full acceptance of Gentiles into the fellowship of the church. From that point on, missionary work among non-Jews resulted in explosive growth in the church.

Learn More: Acts 15:22–29 / 1 Corinthians 7:19 / Galatians 6:15 / Colossians 3:11

CITIZENSHIP

For our conversation is in heaven. Philippians 3:20

The Greek word behind *conversation* in this verse means "citizenship." This is how it is translated by most modern versions of the Bible (see the New International Version or New American Standard Bible). While this is the only place in the Bible where this Greek word appears, the concept of citizenship in the Lord's spiritual kingdom appears throughout the New Testament.

Jesus came to usher in the kingdom of heaven, or God's rule in the hearts of those who accept Him as Savior and Lord. Jesus urged believers to lay up treasures in heaven that will last forever not to focus on the frivolous, earth-centered things that have no lasting value. While He is no longer present in His physical body, believers are comforted by the thought that He is preparing a place for them in His Father's house in heaven.

In Hebrews 11, often called the "faith chapter" of the New Testament, the author cited the example of Abraham. He was a wanderer or stranger on earth, but he looked for a city "whose builder and maker is God" (Hebrews 11:10). That ultimate destination is assured for those who follow the Lord.

Learn More: Matthew 6:19–21; 25:34 / John 14:1–4 / Hebrews 12:28 / James 2:5

COMMUNION

The bread which we break, is it not the communion of the body of Christ? 1 Corinthians 10:16

People who participate in a common act or event are said to be in "communion." In this verse the apostle Paul applied the word to the ritual of the Lord's Supper in the church at Corinth.

On the night before He was arrested and crucified, Jesus instituted the Lord's Supper with His disciples. They gathered in Jerusalem to eat a meal in observance of the Jewish Passover. Jesus turned this event into a supper of remembrance to signify His approaching death. He made it clear to them that the bread and wine they ate and drank together symbolized His broken and bleeding body. He also charged them to remember His sacrificial death whenever they celebrated this memorial meal in the future.

The Lord's Supper is still observed as a remembrance of Jesus by all church groups, although in forms ranging from very informal to highly ritualistic. Some other names by which it is known are Holy Communion, the Eucharist, and the Lord's Table.

Learn More: Matthew 26:26–29; Mark 14:22–25; Luke 22:19–20; John 13:1–17

CONDEMNATION

There is therefore now no condemnation to them which are in Christ Jesus. Romans 8:1

To condemn someone, according to the dictionary, is to declare him guilty of a crime and deserving of punishment. In a spiritual sense, condemnation is what all people deserve because of their sin against God and their failure to live up to His standards.

But God the Father had a plan to help us avoid His condemnation. He sent His own Son, Jesus Christ, to bear the penalty of our sin through His death on the cross. This brought our justification—the very opposite of condemnation. Jesus Himself said, "God sent not his Son into the world to condemn the world; but that the world through him might be saved" (John 3:17).

In addition to paying the penalty for our sin, Jesus also destroyed—or condemned—sin to release believers from its power (Romans 8:1–3). Because we have been graciously pardoned, He expects us to practice forgiveness toward others.

Those who refuse to accept Jesus as Lord and Savior will experience condemnation at the final judgment. Jesus declared, "These shall go away into everlasting punishment: but the righteous into life eternal" (Matthew 25:46).

Learn More: Psalm 37:33 / Luke 6:37 / John 3:18–19; 5:24 / James 3:1

CONFESSION

Whoso confesseth and forsaketh [their sins] shall have mercy. PROVERBS 28:13

The word *confess* appears many times throughout the Bible. It means to admit, own up to, or take responsibility for one's sin and to turn to God for healing and forgiveness.

One of the strongest confessions in the Bible is David's admission to God of his adulterous relationship with Bathsheba. "Against thee, thee only, have I sinned, and done this evil in thy sight," David prayed (Psalm 51:4). He did not blame any person or circumstance for his wrongdoing. This honesty and openness before the Lord led to David's forgiveness and restoration.

Another form of confession is the forthright declaration of one's faith in Christ. The apostle Paul connected saving faith with the willingness of believers to confess publicly and boldly that Jesus was the new center of influence in their lives. In a long, profound thought, the apostle declared, "If thou shalt confess with thy mouth the Lord Jesus, and shalt believe in thine heart that God hath raised him from the dead, thou shalt be saved. For with the heart man believeth unto righteousness; and with the mouth confession is made unto salvation" (Romans 10:9–10).

Learn More: Psalm 32:5 / Mark 1:5 / Luke 12:8 / James 5:16 / 1 John 1:9

CONSCIENCE

I thank God, whom I serve from my forefathers with pure conscience. . . 2 TIMOTHY 1:3

When making moral decisions, many people use the principle "Let your conscience be your guide." They believe their intuitive sense of right and wrong will always lead them to do the right thing.

But the apostle Paul had a different view on this matter. He warned Titus, his associate in ministry, against false teachers, pointing out that even the conscience can be overwhelmed by sin. "To those who are corrupted and do not believe, nothing is pure," he told Titus. "In fact, both their minds and consciences are corrupted" (Titus 1:15 NIV). Paul knew that the conscience is a poor guide for moral behavior. As a part of man's fallen sinful nature, it has been infected and hopelessly flawed by sin.

Like every other part of human nature, the conscience needs to be redeemed from its fallen condition. This comes about only through the saving power of Jesus Christ (2 Corinthians 5:17–18). But after conversion, a believer should work to maintain a pure conscience before the Lord in all matters.

Learn More: 1 Corinthians 4:4 / 1 Timothy 3:9 / Hebrews 10:22; 13:18

CONSECRATION

The Son, who is consecrated for evermore. HEBREWS 7:28

Consecration is the act of dedicating or setting apart someone or something for God's exclusive use. In the Old Testament, Aaron and his sons were set apart to serve as priests for the rest of the Israelites (Leviticus 8:12–13). The firstborn of livestock and the firstfruits of the agricultural harvest were also dedicated to the Lord (Exodus 23:19).

In the New Testament, Jesus Christ Himself is the best example of the concept of consecration. He was set apart by the heavenly Father to become the agent of salvation for a sinful world. The writer of Hebrews declared, "He sacrificed for [our] sins once for all when he offered himself" (Hebrews 7:27 NIV).

Believers are also sanctified by Christ as His treasured possession. Just as He gave His life for us, we should dedicate ourselves to witness for Him and bring others into His kingdom.

Learn More: Exodus 13:2 / John 17:19 / Romans 12:1 / Hebrews 10:10 / 1 Peter 2:9

CONSOLATION

As ye are partakers of the sufferings, so shall ye be also of the consolation. 2 CORINTHIANS 1:7

Consolation is another word for comfort, specifically the encouragement offered to a person in sorrow. But human consolation has its limits. Job's three friends came to offer their sympathy, but they proved to be "miserable comforters" because they only made his suffering worse by accusing him of wrongdoing (Job 16:2).

The only source of genuine comfort is the Lord. This is the sense in which Paul used the word in the verse above. He admitted the faith of the Corinthian believers had caused them to suffer ridicule and rejection. But he assured them they would feel the comforting hand of their Savior, Jesus Christ, in the midst of their troubles.

When the infant Jesus was dedicated in the temple, a godly man named Simeon recognized Him as the "consolation of Israel" (Luke 2:25). This phrase referred to the Messiah whom God had promised to send into the world. Several centuries before, the prophet Isaiah had predicted that this special servant of the Lord would bring everlasting comfort to His people. "Break forth into joy, sing together, ye waste places of Jerusalem," he declared, "for the LORD hath comforted his people" (Isaiah 52:9).

Learn More: Isaiah 40:1–2; 49:13 / Acts 4:36 / Romans 5:5 / Philippians 2:1–2

CONVERSATION

Be thou an example of the believers, in word, in conversation, in charity. 1 TIMOTHY 4:12

The word *conversation* today refers to talk or speech. But in the King James Version, it generally refers to a person's behavior or way of life. In this verse from the apostle Paul to his missionary associate Timothy, the word is translated as "conduct" in the New International Version. Thus, the apostle Paul wanted this young church leader to set a good example for believers in how he lived among them.

In his letter to the believers in Galatia, Paul contrasted his previous conversation, or way of life, with his current lifestyle. In his zeal as a Jewish Pharisee, he had persecuted followers of Jesus. But all that changed when he had a dramatic vision of Christ on the Damascus road. Now he lived and breathed the Gospel, calling on others to place their faith in the living Lord.

The apostle Peter affirmed that righteous behavior is expected of those who follow Jesus Christ. "As he which hath called you is holy," he declared, "so be ye holy in all manner of conversation" (1 Peter 1:15).

Learn More: Psalm 37:14 / Galatians 1:13 / Philippians 1:27; 3:20 / Hebrews 13:5 / James 3:13 / 2 Peter 3:11

CORRUPTION

The creature itself also shall be delivered from the bondage of corruption. ROMANS 8:21

The word *corruption* in this verse refers to the decay of the physical body in the grave. The apostle Paul contrasts this process with the resurrection hope. Jesus conquered death, and He offers this same victory to His followers. Believers can look forward to a glorious liberation, a new spiritual body fit for eternal fellowship with God the Father and Jesus the Son in heaven.

Paul also used the word *corruption* to refer to the world's tendency toward change and decay because of the prevalence of sin. He told the believers at Corinth, "Flesh and blood cannot inherit the kingdom of God; neither doth corruption inherit incorruption" (1 Corinthians 15:50). He wanted them to live up to the standards of righteousness to which they had committed their lives as followers of Christ.

In the Old Testament, the grave itself is referred to as the pit or the pit of corruption (Isaiah 38:17).

Learn More: Luke 6:43 / 1 Corinthians 15:42, 50 / Galatians 6:8 / Ephesians 4:29 / 2 Peter 1:4

COUNSEL

The counsel of the Lord standeth for ever. PSALM 33:11

The word *counsel* refers to guidance, advice, or instruction. The Bible is filled with models of both wise and foolish counsel.

For example, Joseph gave sound advice to the pharaoh of Egypt about how to prepare for a famine that would strike the land (Genesis 41:34–36). But in later years, King Rehoboam of Judah took some bad advice; he decided to continue the oppressive tactics of his father Solomon. This led to rebellion and the division of his kingdom into two separate nations (1 Kings 12:8–19).

The phrase "inquire of the Lord" often appears in the Old Testament to indicate the seeking of divine counsel. King David often did this before going into battle. God honored his requests with victories over his enemies (1 Chronicles 14:10, 14).

The prophet Isaiah referred to the coming Messiah as a "Wonderful Counselor" (Isaiah 9:6 NIV, HCSB). We can depend on Him to provide us with good instruction for every circumstance of life. He guides us with grace and righteousness. He will never give us bad advice that would cause us to go astray.

Learn More: Exodus 18:19 / Job 12:13 / Proverbs 12:15; 19:21 / Isaiah 9:6; 11:2 / Acts 20:27 / Hebrews 6:17

COURAGE

Be strong and of a good courage. JOSHUA 1:6

God spoke these words to Joshua when he was selected as the new leader of the Israelites after the death of Moses. Joshua needed this "pep talk" to bolster his confidence as the people prepared to enter the promised land.

The Lord assured the young leader He would be with him, just as He had strengthened Moses in previous years. Joshua rose to the occasion and led the Israelites on a successful campaign to conquer the Canaanites and settle in their territory.

Another good example of courage is the prophet Jeremiah. For forty years He warned the people of Judah they would be overrun by a foreign power unless they turned back to the one true God. He was ridiculed and rejected, even imprisoned as a traitor. But he never backed away from His message because God surrounded him with His love and protection.

Some people think of courage as lack of fear in the face of danger. But courage is actually the control of fear, which enables a person to stay true to the Lord.

Learn More: Deuteronomy 31:7–8 / 1 Chronicles 28:20 / Psalm 27:14 / Jeremiah 1:17–18 / Acts 28:15

COVENANT

Behold, my covenant is with thee [Abraham]. GENESIS 17:4

A covenant is an agreement or contract between two people or two groups. In the Bible, the word refers to the agreement between God and His people, the Israelites. God promised to bless the nation of Israel and to make them a blessing to others if they would honor Him and obey His commands. This promise began with Abraham and His descendants (Genesis 12:1–3), and it was renewed by the Lord on several occasions. Representatives of the nation with whom God restated His promise included Isaac, Jacob, and Moses.

But the Israelites broke their part of the agreement again and again. They gave in to the temptation to worship false gods. They failed to follow God's demand for honesty and justice in their dealings with others. Their failure brought on the need for a new covenant. This agreement was based on God's mercy and grace rather than keeping the law (Jeremiah 31:31–33).

Through His sacrificial death, Jesus became the mediator of this new covenant, bringing salvation and eternal life to all who trust in Him (Hebrews 10:12–17).

Learn More: Genesis 9:9; 17:21 / Exodus 2:24 / Deuteronomy 4:23

COVETOUSNESS

Take heed, and beware of covetousness. LUKE 12:15

Covetousness is another word for greed, or excessive desire for material things. Jesus warned against falling into this sin, which is also prohibited by the Ten Commandments of the Old Testament (Exodus 20:17).

The Bible contains many examples of people whose greed led to their downfall. King Ahab of Israel even plotted to have an innocent man killed so he could take possession of his choice plot of land. But God was not blind to the king's greed. He declared through the prophet Elijah that Ahab would pay for his crime (1 Kings 21:7–22). Ahab was eventually killed by a stray arrow in a battle with the Syrians (1 Kings 22:33–40).

To the apostle Paul, covetousness was nothing less than idolatry, or making material things more important than dedication to God (Colossians 3:5).

Learn More: Exodus 20:17 / Psalm 119:36 / Proverbs 21:25–26 / Isaiah 56:11 / 1 Timothy 6:10

CREATION

Thou hast created all things, and for thy pleasure they are and were created. REVELATION 4:11

The Bible declares that God existed before the physical world began and that He produced the universe from nothing (Genesis 1:1–2). This insight was opposed to the typical view of the pagan peoples of Old Testament times. They thought that matter was eternal and that it had no beginning at a specific point in time. But God is eternal, and the physical world owes its existence to Him.

Other insights about the creation from the first chapter of the Bible: it was accomplished in orderly fashion, in six successive days; humankind is the crown of God's creation; the Lord has given humans the responsibility to take care of His world.

Perhaps the most comforting thought about God's creation is that He is still involved in it. He has placed within the universe certain natural laws that keep it running in orderly fashion. The prophet Jeremiah observed, "When he thunders, the waters in the heavens roar; he makes clouds rise from the ends of the earth. He sends lightning with the rain and brings out the wind from his storehouses" (Jeremiah 10:13 NIV).

Learn More: Genesis 1:1–31 / Psalm 8:3–4; 148:5 / Isaiah 45:12

CRUCIFIXION

Then delivered he him therefore unto them to be crucified. JOHN 19:16

Crucifixion was a form of capital punishment inflicted on Jesus by the Roman government. The victim's wrists were nailed to a crossbeam, which was raised into position and attached to a stake in the ground. Sometimes the feet were nailed to the stake. Without any support for the body except the nails through the feet and wrists, the victim slumped forward. This put pressure on the heart and lungs, making breathing difficult. A slow, painful death usually occurred after two or three days from a combination of shock, fatigue, suffocation, and loss of blood.

Sometimes the victim's legs were broken with a club as an act of mercy to hasten death. This was not necessary in Jesus' case because He died after only a few hours (Matthew 27:45–50). The Gospel of John declares that this fulfilled the Old Testament prophecy, "A bone of him shall not be broken" (John 19:36; see Psalm 34:20).

To the Jewish people, crucifixion was a dishonorable way to die. But by His self-sacrifice, Jesus turned the cross into a badge of honor (Philippians 2:5–8).

Learn More: Matthew 27:42 / 1 Corinthians 1:18 / Galatians 3:13; 6:14 / Hebrews 12:2

CURSE

Curse me this people; for they are too mighty for me. NUMBERS 22:6

Balak, the king of Moab, spoke these words to a pagan magician named Balaam. The king wanted Balaam to curse the Israelites to nullify their threat as they passed through his territory.

In Bible times a curse was a call for misfortune to fall upon a person or group. Such a declaration was considered powerful enough to bring about the trouble it invoked. Before he died, Moses told the Israelites they faced the choice of honoring God and receiving His blessing or disobedience that would result in His curse (Deuteronomy 11:26–28).

The apostle Paul spoke of the Old Testament law as a curse because it required a person to obey it to be justified in God's sight. But this was impossible for humans because of their natural bent toward sin and rebellion against the Lord.

But God provided a way out of this dilemma through His Son, Jesus Christ, who "hath redeemed us from the curse of the law, being made a curse for us" (Galatians 3:13). Death by crucifixion was considered a curse, but Jesus turned the cross into a blessing for humankind.

Learn More: Genesis 4:11 / Numbers 22–24 / Deuteronomy 27:15 / Romans 12:14 / Galatians 3:10 / James 3:10

DARKNESS

Whosoever believeth on me should not abide in darkness. JOHN 12:46

Darkness is literally the absence of light. In the Old Testament, *sheol*, or the realm of the dead, was a place of darkness (Job 38:17). But the word is usually used in a symbolic way in the Bible. For example, sin is a form of darkness that causes people to defy God's will (Job 24:13–17).

The worst form of darkness is unbelief. Those who refuse to acknowledge Jesus as God's Son and accept Him in faith are groping in the darkness. Turning away from Jesus, as "the light," leaves a person in a permanent state of darkness (John 3:19–20).

Jesus referred to the Pharisees as "blind guides" (Matthew 23:24). Not only were they in the dark about the truth themselves, through their influence they led other people to remain in their sinful state. This form of spiritual blindness was criticized severely by Jesus. He accused them of shutting people out of the kingdom of God, saying, "You yourselves do not enter, nor will you let those enter who are trying to" (Matthew 23:13 NIV).

The image of darkness also summarizes the condition of those who have not turned to the Lord before the final judgment in the end time (Revelation 16:10).

Learn More: Isaiah 9:2 / John 3:19; 12:35 / 1 Peter 2:9

DEATH

For the wages of sin is death. ROMANS 6:23

The Bible speaks of three different forms of death: physical death, spiritual death, and the "second death." Both physical and spiritual death were the result of Adam and Eve's sin in the garden of Eden (Genesis 2:17).

The Bible says a lot about spiritual death. The statement by the apostle Paul in the verse above makes it clear that all people are spiritually dead because they are separated from God, who is the source of spiritual life. Sin causes people to break His laws and ignore His demand for righteousness.

The second death is the fate of those who reject God. This leads to eternal death, or consignment to the lake of fire in the afterlife (Revelation 21:8).

But God has provided a way for people to avoid this form of death. He sent His Son, Jesus, as an atoning sacrifice to pay the penalty for our sin. All who accept Him as Lord and Savior will enjoy eternal fellowship with Him in heaven after their days on earth come to an end.

Learn More: Job 34:15 / Psalm 116:3 / Isaiah 25:8 / John 5:24 / 1 Corinthians 15:26, 55–57 / Colossians 2:13 / Revelation 1:18

DECEIT

Thy brother came with subtilty, and hath taken away thy blessing. GENESIS 27:35

These verses refer to one of the best-known cases of deceit in the Bible—Jacob's trickery of his father, Isaac, into blessing him rather than his twin brother, Esau. This act of treachery caused bad feelings in the family that lasted for many years.

Deceit is the exact opposite of openness and honesty. It consists of using trickery and behind-the-back methods to take advantage of the unsuspecting. This is the major weapon used by Satan to lure people into temptation. In the garden of Eden, he planted doubt in Eve's mind about God's reason for placing the fruit from one particular tree on the forbidden list. Her act of disobedience of the Lord's clear command brought sin and rebellion into the world (Genesis 3).

In the Bible, another word for deceit is *guile*. The apostle Peter described Jesus as a person who was totally free of this character defect. Not only was He without sin, Peter declared, "Neither was guile found in his mouth" (1 Peter 2:22).

Learn More: Genesis 27:1–33 / Psalm 55:11 / Proverbs 24:28 / Galatians 6:3 / Ephesians 5:6

DISCIPLESHIP

The disciple is not above his master, nor the servant above his lord. MATTHEW 10:24

The first disciples of Jesus set the standard for discipleship when they answered His call to follow Him and learn from His teachings. The basic meaning of the word *disciple* is "learner" or "pupil." So discipleship involves accepting Jesus as Savior and Lord and honoring Him by the way we live.

Salvation and discipleship are two related parts of the one process of conversion. There's nothing we can do to earn our salvation. But genuine saving faith automatically launches a believer on a lifetime of growth and learning under the Lord's leadership. To truly follow Jesus, we have to deny our natural inclinations and the standards of the world.

One interesting metaphor for discipleship in the Bible is "walking" or "walking with God." In the Old Testament, Enoch—an ancestor of Noah—is described as a righteous man who "walked with God" (Genesis 5:24). The apostle Paul called on Christians to "walk in the Spirit" (Galatians 5:16).

Walking is something that most of us do every day. Thus, to walk with the Lord under the banner of discipleship is to honor Him in the routine activities of everyday life.

Learn More: Luke 9:23 / Romans 6:4 / Ephesians 5:8 / 1 Timothy 4:12

DIVORCE

What therefore God hath joined together, let not man put asunder. MATTHEW 19:6

These two verses contain Jesus' reply to the Pharisees on the question of divorce. They wanted to know on what grounds a marriage could be ended. Some people of that time thought only unfaithfulness to the marriage vows was just cause for divorce, while others believed a man could end a marriage for any reason.

Jesus surprised the Pharisees by referring them to the account of the garden of Eden in the Old Testament. God created Adam and Eve for each other, He noted, and brought them together in a one-flesh relationship. God's ideal was for this sacred union not to be broken for any reason. But He went on to state that marital unfaithfulness by one of the marriage partners was the one exception to this no-divorce ideal (Matthew 19:9).

Jesus' teaching on this subject should be compared to His love and forgiveness toward those whose marital situations were less than ideal, particularly the Samaritan woman at the well (John 4:13–26) and the woman accused of adultery (John 8:1–11).

Learn More: Genesis 2:21–24 / Deuteronomy 24:1–4 / Matthew 5:31–32; 19:9 / Luke 16:18

DOCTRINE

Till I come, give attendance to reading, to exhortation, to doctrine. 1 TIMOTHY 4:13

The term *doctrine* refers to a system of religious beliefs—key principles of faith that are considered authoritative and thus worthy of passing on to others. The major doctrines of the Christian faith are those about God the Father, God the Son, and God the Holy Spirit. Other doctrines that fit under these main headings include the doctrines of man, salvation, and the church. These doctrinal insights have been revealed to human authors by the Lord and recorded in the Bible for our edification and instruction.

People were amazed at the teachings of Jesus because they were fresh and new and they issued from His authority as the Son of God (Mark 11:18). After His resurrection and ascension, the apostles declared three major truths about Him that continue to serve as foundational doctrines for His followers: (1) Jesus was the Messiah, or God's anointed one; (2) God had raised Him from the dead; and (3) salvation was available only through faith in Him.

The writings of the apostle Paul show that these principles were sometimes twisted or denied by false teachers in the early church. He encouraged believers to stay true to the authentic teachings of Jesus and the Bible.

Learn More: Acts 2:42 / Ephesians 4:14 / 1 Timothy 6:3–4 / 2 John 9

DOUBT

Lord, I believe; help thou mine unbelief. MARK 9:24

Jesus' disciples had tried and failed to heal a demon-possessed boy. When Jesus arrived on the scene, He asked the boy's father if he thought his son could be made well. The man believed it was possible, but he was not convinced it *would* actually happen. The father asked Jesus to turn his doubt into unwavering faith. Jesus immediately healed the boy, apparently honoring the man's request for stronger faith.

The concept of doubt in the Bible usually refers to weak faith. The apostle Peter's faith was strong when he decided to go out to meet Jesus, who was walking on the water toward His disciples' boat. As Peter too walked on the water, the wind and the waves distracted him and his faith wavered. Peter began to sink, but Jesus pulled him up, declaring, "O thou of little faith, wherefore didst thou doubt?" (Matthew 14:31).

Doubt is sometimes portrayed in the Bible as the very opposite of faith. Jesus called on His followers to exercise the faith—with no hint of doubt or unbelief—that would bring about wondrous spiritual miracles in His name through the medium of prayer (Matthew 21:21).

Learn More: Daniel 5:12 / Matthew 28:17 / Luke 12:29 / John 20:24–29 / 1 Timothy 2:8

ELECTION

Give diligence to make your calling and election sure. 2 PETER 1:10

God's selection of specific people on whom He confers His favor is known as election. In the Old Testament, He chose the Israelites as His special people. He did so not because they deserved this honor but because of His abundant love and the covenant He had made with Abraham (Deuteronomy 7:6–8).

In the New Testament, the apostle Paul enlarged this concept of election to include all people who are included in God's plan of salvation. He gave thanks for the believers at Thessalonica because God had chosen them "to be saved through the sanctifying work of the Spirit and through belief in the truth" (2 Thessalonians 2:13 NIV).

Paul did not mean that God chooses certain people to be saved regardless of their response to His grace. People have the freedom to make their own choice whether to accept or reject His love and grace.

In another of his New Testament letters, Paul declared, "God our Savior. . .wants all people to be saved and to come to a knowledge of the truth" (1 Timothy 2:3–4 NIV). The elect are those who accept the Lord's generous offer of salvation.

Learn More: Isaiah 42:1 / John 3:16 / Colossians 3:12 / Titus 1:1 / 1 Peter 2:6

ENVY

And the patriarchs, moved with envy, sold Joseph into Egypt. Acts 7:9

This verse comes from Stephen's long speech before the Jewish Sanhedrin in Jerusalem. The word *patriarchs* refers to Joseph's brothers in the Old Testament. They grew envious of their younger brother because their father favored him above all his other sons. They plotted to kill Joseph but eventually changed their mind and sold him into slavery in Egypt (Genesis 37:26–28).

Extreme envy or jealousy is bad enough on its own. But it can lead to other serious sins. To cover their crime, Joseph's brothers had to deceive and dishonor their father, Jacob, by lying to him about what had happened to his favorite son. The writer of Proverbs may have had this characteristic of envy in mind when he declared, "Wrath is cruel, and anger is outrageous; but who is able to stand before envy?" (Proverbs 27:4).

The apostle Paul listed envy as one of the works of the flesh in contrast to the fruit of the spirit—traits that should characterize the lives of believers (Galatians 5:19–23).

Learn More: Mark 15:10 / Romans 13:13 / Acts 17:5 / Titus 3:3 / James 3:16

ETERNITY

But thou, O Lord, shall endure for ever. Psalm 102:12

The psalmist sensed that God is the only reality that stands outside time itself. Not only has God existed forever—before time began—but He will also be around for all generations to come. He is the eternal One who has no beginning and no end.

It's difficult for humans to grasp the concept of eternity because we are earth-bound beings with a limited view of time. To us, a life span of seventy or eighty years is a long time, but this amounts to no more than the blink of an eye from God's perspective.

Since God is eternal, so are His laws (Psalm 119:89), His ways (Habakkuk 3:6), His kingdom (Daniel 4:34), and His salvation (Hebrews 5:9). Above all, His love and mercy last forever. References to these attributes of His character occur many times throughout the book of Psalms (see, for example, 136:1).

The God who lives forever also shares this blessing with those who profess faith in His Son. The apostle Paul put it like this: "The gift of God is eternal life through Jesus Christ our Lord" (Romans 6:23).

Learn More: Deuteronomy 33:27 / Ecclesiastes 3:11 / 2 Corinthians 4:18 / 1 Timothy 1:17

EVIL

The eyes of the Lord are in every place, beholding the evil and the good. Proverbs 15:3

Skeptics often pose the problem of evil to deny the existence of God. Their reasoning goes like this: (1) If God is kind and loving, He would not allow evil to exist. (2) But we see evil everywhere. (3) Therefore, God either doesn't exist or is not all-powerful.

This argument fails to consider one important part of the equation—human free will. The Lord did not create people as robots who have no choice but to follow His commands. God gave us the ability to reason, make decisions, and choose our own path—even if these choices are wrong and harmful.

Sin and evil entered the world when Adam and Eve disobeyed God's direct order and ate the forbidden fruit in the garden of Eden (Genesis 3:6). The pattern of sin and rebellion that they set in motion is behind most of the evil and suffering in the world today.

But what about natural disasters such as floods and hurricanes that kill thousands of people? The Lord could prevent these happenings, so why doesn't He?

This question doesn't have a simple answer. But we can declare in faith that nothing on earth escapes the notice of the Lord. He has the ability to shape what seems to be a tragic and meaningless event into an essential part of His divine purpose.

Learn More: Numbers 32:13 / Job 2:10 / Psalm 23:4 / Isaiah 5:20 / Romans 7:19

FAITH

Faith is the substance of things hoped for, the evidence of things not seen. HEBREWS 11:1

Hebrews 11 is known as the great "faith chapter" of the New Testament. The writer introduces the chapter with a definition of faith—trust in God, who we cannot see but who is nevertheless a living and active force in human affairs.

The writer then moves on to list several people from Old Testament times who were known for their great faith in the Lord, including Noah, Abraham, Isaac, Jacob, Joseph, Moses, Rahab, and Gideon.

In the New Testament, faith is one part of God's plan that leads to redemption of sinners. Salvation is possible only because of God's grace. And good works mark the lives of those who are saved. But this process is not complete without human faith—willing acceptance of Jesus Christ as Savior and Lord. As the apostle Paul expressed it, "For by grace are ye saved through faith; and that not of yourselves: it is the gift of God: Not of works, lest any man should boast" (Ephesians 2:8–9).

Paul listed faith as one of the nine results of the Holy Spirit at work in the lives of believers (Galatians 5:22).

Learn More: Proverbs 3:5 / Habakkuk 2:4 / Matthew 17:20 / Galatians 3:24 / Ephesians 2:8–9 / 1 John 5:4

FAITHFULNESS

Great is thy faithfulness. LAMENTATIONS 3:23

The prophet Jeremiah, author of Lamentations, is known for his sorrowful expressions over the sins of the people of Judah and the destruction of Jerusalem. But in this passage, he struck a positive note by recalling God's faithfulness to His people. The Lord had promised to bless the Israelites, and He never gave up on them, in spite of their disloyalty.

God's faithfulness is evident throughout the Bible. *Dependability* is another word that comes to mind when we think about His provision for those who follow Him. The psalmist referred to God as his "rock," a solid, immovable place of safety in an unpredictable world (Psalm 62:2).

Just as the Lord is faithful to His followers, we are called to be loyal to Him. The Bible contains many examples of people who stayed true to Him in spite of severe persecution. The prophet Daniel was thrown to the lions for refusing to stop praying to the one true God. The Lord honored Daniel's faithfulness by delivering him from these beasts without a single scratch (Daniel 6:22).

Learn More: Psalm 36:5; 89:1–2 / Matthew 25:21–23 / 2 Thessalonians 3:3 / Revelation 2:10

FALL, THE

The woman. . .took of the fruit thereof, and did eat. GENESIS 3:6

After creating Adam and Eve, God put them in a perfect place known as the garden of Eden. He provided everything they needed to sustain life in this paradise. But He told them clearly not to eat from one specific tree—the tree of the knowledge of good and evil. This forbidden tree represented God's sovereignty and His authority to place limits on human behavior.

Because of their disobedience, the couple was expelled from the perfect environment they had enjoyed. Other consequences of their sin were the introductions of pain and death into the world.

This original rebellion of Adam and Eve reflects the sin that affects the entire human race. As the apostle Paul put it, "All have sinned, and come short of the glory of God" (Romans 3:23). But God has not left us without hope in our sinful condition. He has provided for our redemption through the atoning sacrifice of His Son, Jesus Christ. He is known as the Last Adam, who corrected the sin problem caused by the first Adam.

Learn More: Genesis 3:1–24 / Romans 5:14 / 1 Corinthians 15:22, 45 / 2 Corinthians 11:3

FEAR OF THE LORD

The people feared the Lord, and believed the Lord. Exodus 14:31

This verse describes the response of the Israelites when they witnessed the destruction of Pharaoh's pursuing army in the Red Sea. Their fear was actually a sense of awe and respect for the all-powerful God who had delivered them from slavery in Egypt.

A healthy respect for the Lord is an important element of biblical faith. It leads to worship of the one true God and obedience to His commands. In the book of Deuteronomy, Moses repeated this truth like the chorus of a hymn in his speech to the Israelites. "Thou shalt fear the LORD thy God," Moses told them. "Him shalt thou serve, and to him shalt thou cleave, and swear by his name" (Deuteronomy 10:20).

True wisdom, according to the writer of Proverbs, begins with the fear of the Lord (Proverbs 9:10). A classic passage on reverence for God comes from the little-known prophet Habakkuk: "The LORD is in his holy temple," he declared. "Let all the earth keep silence before him" (Habakkuk 2:20).

Learn More: Exodus 14:31 / Deuteronomy 10:12 / Psalm 22:23 / Proverbs 10:27

FIRSTFRUITS

Honour the Lord with. . .the firstfruits of all thine increase. Proverbs 3:9

The Jewish people thought of the firstfruits, or the first of their crops to be gathered, as God's harvest. These were presented as offerings to God during the celebration of the harvest festival known as Pentecost.

The apostle Paul picked up on this imagery in his famous passage about the resurrection of Jesus and His promise of a similar resurrection for all believers: "Now is Christ risen from the dead," he declared, "and become the firstfruits of them that slept" (1 Corinthians 15:20).

To Paul, Jesus' victory over death was the first of a spiritual harvest known as eternal life. Believers were the rest of the harvest that would be gathered in at the appointed time. Just as Jesus had been raised from the dead to reign with His Father in glory, so Christians' bodies would be raised at Jesus' second coming, and they would live with Him forever in heaven.

Paul's missionary work resulted in conversions that he considered the "firstfruits" of an unreached area. One of these was Epenaetus, whom he considered "the firstfruits of Achaia unto Christ" (Romans 16:5). Achaia was the Roman name for ancient Greece.

Learn More: Numbers 28:26 / Ezekiel 48:14 / Romans 8:23 /
1 Corinthians 15:23 / James 1:18 / Revelation 14:4

FLESH, THE

The flesh lusteth against the Spirit, and the Spirit against the flesh. Galatians 5:17

In this verse, the apostle Paul drew a contrast between the flesh and God's Spirit. The flesh represents humankind's sinful nature that conflicts with God's standard of righteousness.

Even after conversion, the desires of the flesh can lead to sin. Paul admitted that temptation sometimes wins the battle for control of a Christian's mind and behavior. In his most famous passage on this constant struggle, Paul declared, "I do not do the good I want to do, but the evil I do not want to do—this I keep on doing" (Romans 7:19 NIV).

The antidote for the temptations of the flesh is total reliance on the power of the Holy Spirit. Paul made this clear by contrasting the works of the flesh with the fruit of the Spirit. Yielding to the flesh results in such actions as hatred, envy, and strife, but life under the Holy Spirit's control brings love, joy, and peace (Galatians 5:19–23).

Learn More: John 6:63; Romans 7:5, 18, 25; 8:1–9; 13:14 / Galatians 3:3; 5:16 / 1 Peter 2:11

FOLLY

Shall be likened unto a foolish man, which built his house upon the sand. MATTHEW 7:26

In His parable of the two foundations, Jesus talked about the right and wrong way to build a house. One man built on rock, and the forces of nature couldn't shake his building. But a second man built on sandy soil, and his house collapsed in a thunderstorm. Jesus then compared this foolish builder to those people who refused to live by the principles He taught.

In the Bible the words *folly* and *foolishness* describe senseless and thoughtless human behavior. The book of Proverbs is filled with admonitions to avoid the pitfalls that foolish people are susceptible to. Among other things, they refuse to listen to good advice (12:15), fail to control their temper (14:16), get into heated arguments (18:6), and speak without thinking (29:11).

In a nutshell, foolishness is the exact opposite of wisdom, which results from divine guidance. Perhaps the ultimate folly is denying the reality of God and His influence in the world. The psalmist declared, "The fool hath said in his heart, There is no God" (Psalm 14:1).

Learn More: Psalm 5:5 / Proverbs 26:11 / Matthew 25:1–13 / 1 Corinthians 1:27; 3:19

FORGIVENESS

Forgiving one another, even as God for Christ's sake hath forgiven you. EPHESIANS 4:32

To be forgiven is to be excused by other persons for the wrongs we have committed against them. Forgiveness among people is possible because of God's gracious pardon of our sin and rebellion against Him.

Human sin deserves the Lord's punishment because it violates His holiness and His high moral standards (Romans 1:18–23). In Old Testament times, God accepted an animal sacrifice as a way for people to pay for their sins and receive His forgiveness. But in the New Testament, Christ became the Mediator between God and man. God the Father delegated to Him the authority to forgive sins (Matthew 1:21). Through His death on the cross, He became the once-for-all sacrifice that is the basis for our forgiveness.

Since believers have been forgiven freely through Christ's sacrifice, we are expected to be generous in our forgiveness of others. This was a major theme of Jesus' teachings.

Learn More: Psalm 86:5 / Matthew 18:21–22 / Mark 11:25–26 / Luke 6:37 / 1 John 1:9

FRUIT, SPIRITUAL

But the fruit of the Spirit is love, joy, peace, longsuffering. . . GALATIANS 5:22

In this famous passage, the apostle Paul listed nine attitudes and actions that characterize the believer whose life is under the control of the Holy Spirit. These qualities are known as the "fruit of the Spirit." Jesus also declared that His followers would produce fruit that is appropriate for citizens of the kingdom of God (Matthew 7:19–20).

Heading Paul's list is love, an unselfish quality that leads believers to place the needs of others ahead of their own. Joy and peace in the Lord produce a quiet sense of contentment, no matter the circumstances of life. Longsuffering, or patience, is the ability to remain faithful to the Lord and to others for a lifetime. Temperance, or moderation, is the realization that life is a blend of many different elements rather than a single-minded devotion to one or two.

The qualities of gentleness, goodness, and meekness—in combination with deep faith—produce believers who are effective witnesses for the Lord. Unbelievers are naturally curious about the light they radiate in a dark world.

Learn More: Luke 6:44 / John 15:16 / Ephesians 5:9 / Philippians 1:11 / Colossians 1:10 / James 3:17

GENTILE

Is he the God of the Jews only? is he not also of the Gentiles? Romans 3:29

God chose the Israelites as His special people. Along with this privilege went the responsibility to serve as a light to the other nations of the world (Genesis 12:1–3). But over time the Jews grew proud of their ethnic heritage, viewing any who were not part of their race as inferior Gentiles. This word meant simply "non-Jew."

Jesus struck a blow at this prideful attitude by ministering to Gentiles. He also made it clear in His Great Commission that the Gospel was to be proclaimed to "all nations" (Matthew 28:19–20).

In spite of Jesus' instructions, the church struggled in its early years to accept Gentiles as worthy of the Gospel. Then God sent the apostle Peter a vision of clean and unclean animals to show him that no race was impure in the Lord's eyes. Peter later baptized the Gentile Cornelius after admitting his change of heart: "I now realize," he declared, "that God does not show favoritism but accepts from every nation the one who fears him and does what is right" (Acts 10:34–35 niv).

From that point on, the Gospel broke out of the narrow confines of Judaism and spread throughout the Roman world.

Learn More: Mark 7:25–30 / Luke 8:26–39 / Romans 15:16 / 1 Corinthians 12:13 / Galatians 3:28

GENTLENESS

Be gentle unto all men, apt to teach, patient. 2 Timothy 2:24

As he approached the end of his life, the apostle Paul passed on to Timothy, his young missionary associate, some things he had learned about being a Christian leader (2 Timothy 2:22–26). He advised Timothy to pursue righteousness, avoid foolish controversies, cultivate patience, and deal gently with those under his charge.

A gentle person is known for kindness, consideration for others, fairness, and compassion. What gentleness is definitely *not* is putting others down, disrespecting their opinions, picking a fight over minor issues, and speaking without thinking.

A gentle spirit, according to Isaiah, would characterize the coming Messiah. The prophet compared the Messiah to a shepherd who would tend the most vulnerable sheep among his flock with special care. He would "gather the lambs with his arm, and carry them in his bosom, and shall gently lead those that are with young" (Isaiah 40:11). This prophecy was fulfilled when Jesus exercised His power in a spirit of compassion to heal the sick and raise the dead.

Learn More: Psalm 18:35 / 2 Corinthians 10:1 / Galatians 5:22 / Titus 3:2 / James 3:17

GIFTS, SPIRITUAL

But covet earnestly the best gifts. 1 Corinthians 12:31

Spiritual gifts are talents and abilities bestowed by the Holy Spirit upon believers for the growth and edification of one another and the church. In his first letter to the Corinthians Paul addressed the issue of spiritual gifts because it was causing controversy among these believers.

Some members of the church considered their gifts superior to those of fellow believers. But Paul reminded them that all gifts, no matter how minor, were important in the body of Christ.

To make his point, he wrote the beautiful chapter of 1 Corinthians known as the "love chapter." Unless believers exercised their spiritual gifts in the spirit of love, they were nothing more than "a resounding gong or a clanging cymbal" (1 Corinthians 13:1 niv)—without meaning or purpose.

Paul listed several spiritual gifts in his letters to the believers at Rome and Corinth. They include preaching, serving, teaching, encouraging, giving, leading, helping others, wisdom, knowledge, faith, healing, miracles, and prophecy.

No matter what our spiritual gifts, they should be used to minister to others and expand the kingdom of God.

Learn More: Romans 1:11; 12:6–8 / 1 Corinthians 12:6–12 / 1 Timothy 4:14

GIVING

God loveth a cheerful giver. 2 CORINTHIANS 9:7

This verse is part of the apostle Paul's appeal to the Corinthian Christians to contribute to an offering for suffering believers in Jerusalem. He did not dictate the amount that each believer should give. He wanted these to be voluntary contributions. Beyond that, he wanted the people to give from the right motivation—not with a frown on their face ("grudgingly") or because they were forced into it ("of necessity").

The apostle declared that these contributions should be made "cheerfully." The Greek word he used here is *hilarion*, from which our English word *hilarious* is derived. Joy fills the heart of hilarious givers. They give out of a spirit of love because God has showered His love on them through His Son, Jesus Christ. They show through their lives that true love is always giving itself away.

Paul ended his appeal by reminding the Corinthian believers of this divine gift that none of them deserved: "Thanks be unto God for his unspeakable gift" (2 Corinthians 9:15).

Learn More: 1 Chronicles 29:14 / Psalm 50:10–12 / Matthew 10:8 / James 1:17

GODHEAD

In him [Jesus Christ] dwelleth all the fulness of the Godhead bodily. COLOSSIANS 2:9

The apostle Paul wanted believers at Colossae to understand the unique nature of Jesus Christ. Although He came to earth in the form of a man, He also was fully God. In His divine essence and character, Jesus was the exact likeness of His heavenly Father. The New International Version states this truth like this: "In Christ all the fullness of the Deity lives in bodily form."

The term *godhead* has essentially the same meaning as "godhood." Just as manhood is that quality that makes a man a man, so godhead or godhood refers to those qualities that make God, God. These characteristics are referred to as the "attributes" of God. They are many in number, but here are a few of the most important.

He has always existed, and He always will. He is holy, morally pure, and totally separate from humankind in His essential character. He is all-powerful as well as all-knowing and all-seeing. He is just and merciful in His dealings with humankind. He is the sovereign ruler of the universe who demands our unquestioning loyalty and fervent praise.

Learn More: Acts 17:29 / Romans 1:20

GOODNESS

Oh that men would praise the Lord for his goodness! PSALM 107:8

We don't hear the word *goodness* very often today, except as an expression of shock or surprise: "Oh my goodness!" But the word appears often in the Bible, mostly in reference to the kind and loving deeds of the Lord. God is good and He showers good things upon His people. Goodness is the Lord's overflowing benevolence toward His people.

Psalm 107 refers to God's goodness so many times that it might be called the "Goodness Psalm" of the Bible. This expression appears four times as a refrain throughout the psalm: "Oh that men would praise the LORD for his goodness" (verses 8, 15, 21, 31). The New International Version renders the Hebrew word for goodness in this passage as God's "unfailing love."

Just as God showers goodness upon His people, believers should show goodness and kindness to others. The apostle Paul lists this Christian virtue as one of the nine "fruits" granted by the Holy Spirit (Galatians 5:22–23).

The call to praise issued by the psalmist in the verse above is well taken. We should not allow a day to pass without taking the time to thank the Lord for His goodness.

Learn More: Exodus 18:9 / Psalm 31:19; 33:5 / Jeremiah 31:12 / 2 Thessalonians 1:11

GOSPEL

I am not ashamed of the gospel of Christ: for it is the power of God. ROMANS 1:16

The Greek word behind *Gospel* in the New Testament means "good news." That's exactly what the Gospel is—the glorious good news of salvation that God the Father has provided through His Son, Jesus Christ.

Jesus is more than a *messenger* of the good news. He *is* the good news. God's good news to all people existed in Jesus' life, His teachings, His atoning death, and His resurrection.

The word *gospel* is also applied to the first four books of the New Testament—Matthew, Mark, Luke, and John. These books record the life and teachings of Jesus during His earthly ministry. These accounts are not biographies in the traditional sense; they are selective accounts of Jesus' life and work, written by those who knew Him in the flesh to call people to place their faith in Him as Savior and Lord.

The good news of the Gospel continues to impact the world today through the work of the Holy Spirit in the church. All believers are called to share this good news with other people.

Learn More: Matthew 4:23 / Mark 16:15 / 1 Corinthians 1:17 / Ephesians 3:6 / 1 Peter 4:17

GRACE

And the grace of our Lord was exceeding abundant. 1 TIMOTHY 1:14

Grace is God's unmerited favor shown to sinful and undeserving human beings. *Lovingkindness* is a distinct term for the concept of grace in the Old Testament. It's as if the Old Testament writers had to put two words together to show the depth of God's love and kindness toward His people.

This doubled word appears more than twenty times throughout the psalms. The psalmist prayed, "O continue thy lovingkindness unto them that know thee; and thy righteousness to the upright in heart" (Psalm 36:10).

The ultimate expression of God's grace was His gift of His Son, Jesus, to the world. Christ was the beneficiary of the grace of His Father (Luke 2:40). But He was also the ultimate model of grace, bringing it to sinful people for their salvation (Titus 2:11).

God's grace is one of the major themes in the writings of the apostle Paul. At first a persecutor of the church, Paul was transformed by God's grace into a zealous missionary for the Gospel. In all his writings, he made it clear that God's grace is at the heart of the Christian life.

Learn More: John 1:17 / Romans 5:20 / 1 Corinthians 15:9–10 / Ephesians 2:8–9

GUIDANCE

And the Lord shall guide thee continually. ISAIAH 58:11

The prophet Isaiah declared that God will abide with us and guide us throughout every experience of life. He compared those who followed the Lord's guidance to a productive garden and the refreshing water that comes from a bubbling spring.

The world is filled with counterfeit guides—those who claim to have our best interests at heart but who are actually hoping to better themselves at our expense. Jesus called the Pharisees "blind guides" (Matthew 23:16) because they were more concerned about keeping the law than bringing people into closer fellowship with the Lord.

Before He ascended to God the Father, Jesus told His disciples that after He had ascended into heaven, the Holy Spirit would become their guide. This third person of the Trinity was a leader they could trust because He would guide the disciples "into all truth" (John 16:13).

The prophet Jeremiah spoke of God as "the guide of my youth" (Jeremiah 3:4). Whether our life is just beginning or coming to an end, we can trust the Lord as our never-failing guide.

Learn More: Exodus 15:13 / Psalm 48:14; 78:72 / John 16:13

GUILT

We are verily guilty concerning our brother. GENESIS 42:21

The dictionary defines *guilt* as "remorse at having committed an offense." In a spiritual sense, guilt is a feeling of shame and regret over sin and wrongdoing against the Lord and other people.

The statement of Joseph's brothers in the verse above is a classic example of guilt over sin in human relationships. Their hatred of their younger sibling drove them to sell Joseph into slavery in Egypt. Their guilt must have simmered under the surface for many years. It erupted openly when they were subjected to a series of tests by an Egypt official whom they finally recognized as their missing brother.

We as human beings suffer from guilt because of our sinful nature. God dealt with this problem by sending His own Son as a sacrifice for our sins. Those who accept Jesus as Savior and Lord are delivered from the guilt and condemnation caused by sin. As the apostle Paul expressed it, "Being justified by faith, we have peace with God through our Lord Jesus Christ" (Romans 5:1).

Learn More: Leviticus 6:4 / Ezekiel 22:4 / Matthew 27:3–5 / Romans 3:19/ James 2:10

HADES

The rich man also died, and was buried; and in hell he lift up his eyes. LUKE 16:22-23

The term *hades* does not appear in the Bible. But it is the Greek word behind the English word *hell* in Jesus' parable of the rich man and Lazarus.

This parable makes it clear that Jesus considered hades, or hell, an actual place where the unrighteous suffered punishment for their wicked deeds. A chasm that could not be crossed kept the wicked rich man from receiving relief from his suffering. But the righteous Lazarus was resting peacefully in the bosom of Abraham, a reference to heaven. In the afterlife, the status each man had enjoyed on earth was exactly reversed.

Sometimes the Greek word *hades* does not refer to a literal hell but simply to the grave or the final destiny for both the righteous and the wicked. This is the sense in which the apostle Peter used the word in his famous sermon on the day of Pentecost. In Acts 2:31, he declared that Jesus' body "was not left in hell"—or the grave—but was gloriously resurrected by God the Father.

Learn More: Matthew 11:23 / Revelation 1:18

HATRED

If a man say, I love God, and hateth his brother, he is a liar. 1 JOHN 4:20

The Bible speaks of hatred in both negative and positive terms. The apostle John in this verse focused on the negative, declaring it impossible for a person to hate his brother while claiming to love God. Love for the Lord will automatically lead to love and respect for other people.

But there is also a positive side to hate. For example, the Bible lists several things that God hates, including hypocrisy (Zechariah 8:17), violence (Psalm 11:5), wickedness (Psalm 45:7), lying (Proverb 6:16–17), and empty religious rituals (Amos 5:21).

It's okay to hate the things that God despises, but it's out of character for a Christian to harbor hatred toward other *people*—even those who want to do us harm. "Love your enemies," Jesus declared, "bless them that curse you, do good to them that hate you, and pray for them which despitefully use you, and persecute you" (Matthew 5:44). This is not easy to do, but the world notices when we put this teaching into practice.

Learn More: Psalm 5:5 / Proverbs 8:13 / Matthew 5:44 / Titus 3:3

HEALING

And Jesus went about all Galilee. . .healing all manner of sickness. MATTHEW 4:23

Jesus came into the world on a spiritual mission—to deliver humankind from the bondage of sin. But He was also concerned about those who suffered from physical problems. He restored many people to health and wholeness during His earthly ministry.

Jesus also empowered His disciples to heal (Luke 9:2). They continued this work of compassion after Jesus ascended to God the Father. For example, Peter and John healed a lame beggar at the temple in Jerusalem by calling on the name of Jesus and commanding him to "rise up and walk" (Acts 3:6).

The bystanders who witnessed this miracle were amazed. Peter told them this was an example of the healing power of Jesus, who was the long-expected Messiah. Then He invited them to turn to Him as the agent of healing for their spiritual sickness. "Repent ye therefore, and be converted," he declared, "that your sins may be blotted out" (Acts 3:19).

Learn More: Psalm 147:3 / Malachi 4:2 / Mark 3:10 / Luke 4:18 / Acts 5:16

HEATHEN, THE

Have done after the manners of the heathen that are round about you. EZEKIEL 11:12

In this verse from the prophet Ezekiel, the Lord condemned the Israelites for behaving like "the heathen," the pagan nations that surrounded His special people. The Israelites were probably guilty of worshipping the false gods of their pagan neighbors.

This was a serious matter because the Lord had established a special relationship with the Israelites. He had entered into covenant with them, delivered them from slavery in Egypt, and given them a land of their own.

But these special privileges also involved a great responsibility. They were expected to serve as a witness of the one true God to the other nations of the world (Genesis 12:3). This meant they had to shun such customs as worshipping idols, practicing child sacrifice, and seeking guidance from fortune tellers, mediums, and witches.

In spite of these divine expectations, Israel came under the influence of the heathen surrounding nations many times throughout its checkered history. The Lord often raised up prophets such as Ezekiel to call the nation back to its mission as God's righteous servant in a wicked world.

Learn More: Joel 3:12 / Habakkuk 3:12 / Malachi 1:11 / Galatians 1:16; 3:8

HEAVEN

But lay up for yourselves treasures in heaven. MATTHEW 6:20

Heaven is such a glorious place that words are inadequate to describe it. So biblical writers reverted to symbolic language to tell us what heaven is like. We must probe behind these figures of speech to get a glimpse of its realities.

The first affirmation of the Bible is that heaven is a place where we will enjoy everlasting fellowship with God (Revelation 21:3). While the surroundings will be beautiful, our greatest joy will come from being in the Lord's presence.

The Bible also declares that our heavenly existence will take on the qualities or attributes of God's nature: holiness (Revelation 21:27), love (1 Corinthians 13:13), joy (Revelation 19:6–7), and moral perfection (1 John 3:2).

In heaven, believers will be reunited with their born-again relatives and friends who have preceded them in death. "The dead in Christ will rise first," the apostle Paul declared. "After that, we who are still alive and are left will be caught up together with them in the clouds to meet the Lord in the air" (1 Thessalonians 4:16–17 NIV).

Finally, believers will not be idle in heaven. The apostle John affirmed that God's people would serve Him in that wonderful place (Revelation 22:3).

Learn More: Matthew 6:19–21 / Ephesians 1:20 / Hebrews 9:11 / Revelation 21:18–21

HELL

Fear him which is able to destroy both soul and body in hell. MATTHEW 10:28

The idea of hell developed across a period of many centuries. The closest thing to the concept in the Old Testament was a place known as *sheol*, a Hebrew word translated as "grave" or "hell" (Psalm 16:10). Sheol was the shadowy underworld where people went when they died. And suffering and punishment are never mentioned in connection with sheol.

But the New Testament contains graphic descriptions of the lost who will be consigned to hell. Their suffering is summed up in such phrases as "the fire is not quenched," "weeping and gnashing of teeth," and "outer darkness."

Some people think of hell in a figurative sense—as separation from God in a state of meaningless existence. But Jesus warned that the body (a physical reality) as well as the soul (a spiritual entity) can be cast into hell. This seems to argue that hell is more than a metaphor for endless separation from the Lord.

Whether hell is defined literally or figuratively, it makes sense to avoid it at all costs. Those who accept Jesus Christ as Savior and Lord don't have to worry about their eternal destiny.

Learn More: Matthew 5:22; 8:12; 22:13 / Mark 9:46, 48 / Luke 13:28

HERESY

There shall be false teachers. . .who privily shall bring in damnable heresies. 2 PETER 2:1

Heresy is the denial of one or more of the foundational doctrines of the Christian faith. The apostle Peter in this verse condemned teachers who were spreading heretical beliefs among early believers. These false prophets were probably teaching that salvation came about through special knowledge rather than placing one's faith in Jesus Christ. This belief system was known as gnosticism, a word derived from *gnosis*—a Greek word for "knowledge."

During His earthly ministry, Jesus warned about the rise of false teachers. He characterized them as people who dressed in "sheep's clothing" but were actually "ravening wolves." They would fool believers with their subtle approach, lead them into error, and plant seeds of discord among His followers.

Another heresy that infected the early church was denial of the humanity of Jesus. The apostle John attacked the false teachers who spread this doctrine. He called them "deceivers" because they opposed everything that Christ represented (2 John 7).

Learn More: Matthew 7:15 / 1 Corinthians 11:19 / 2 Corinthians 11:13 / Galatians 5:20 / Colossians 2:8 / 1 John 4:1

HOLINESS

God hath not called us unto uncleanness, but unto holiness. 1 THESSALONIANS 4:7

Holiness is one of the key attributes, or qualities, of God's character. Over and over again throughout the Bible, He reminds His people, "I the LORD your God am holy" (see, for example, Leviticus 19:2).

Holiness means "separation" or "set apart." Thus, God's holiness indicates that He is totally unlike humans or any other part of His creation. As the very essence of righteousness, He is incapable of any wrongdoing. He is on a different plane than anything that is impure, sinful, or morally imperfect.

God's Son, Jesus, was the perfect example of holiness. As the "Holy One of God" (Mark 1:24), he emphasized God's demand for holiness. He made it clear that His followers must have a higher form of righteousness than the hypocritical scribes and Pharisees (Matthew 5:20).

It's not possible in this life for weak and sinful human beings to attain the level of holiness that belongs to the three persons of the Trinity—Father, Son, and Holy Spirit. But the Bible does affirm that believers should be growing toward this ideal (1 Peter 1:15–16).

Learn More: Psalm 99:5 / Isaiah 6:3 / Ephesians 5:27 / 1 Thessalonians 3:12–13 / 1 Peter 2:5

HOPE

Happy is he. . .whose hope is in the Lord his God. Psalm 146:5

Most people think of hope as a feeling that what they want to happen will come to pass. But in the biblical sense, hope is a sure and steady faith in God's promises. Hope does not arise from our desires but from Him, who is the source of our expectations. The psalmist based his confidence in the Lord, who had built a nation from Jacob's descendants. He had led His people in the past, and they could depend on Him as they looked to the future.

The Bible warns about placing hope in things that have no eternal value. These include riches (Proverbs 11:28), military might (Isaiah 31:1–3), earthly rulers (Psalm 146:3), even the temple in Jerusalem (Jeremiah 7:1–7). Only the Lord is an immovable force in whom we can seek refuge. He provides the ultimate security in life (Deuteronomy 33:27).

Jesus is the source of the believer's hope because He brought salvation through His sacrificial death and glorious resurrection. With confident hope, Christians look forward to His return and His promise of eternal fellowship with Him in heaven.

Learn More: Jeremiah 17:7 / Lamentations 3:24 / Colossians 1:23, 27 / Hebrews 6:19 / 1 Peter 3:15

HOSPITALITY

The stranger that dwelleth with you shall be unto you as one born among you. Leviticus 19:34

Early in the Old Testament, the patriarch Abraham set a good example of gracious hospitality. He received two strangers into his camp, washed their feet, and fed them a meal from one of the choice animals of his flock (Genesis 18:2–8).

Later, the exodus from Egypt pictured God as the gracious host of His alienated people. He delivered them from slavery, fed them in the wilderness, and brought them into a land of their own. Because He had shown kindness toward His people, they were expected to practice hospitality toward others.

Jesus came into a world as the model of a perfect host. He ministered to poor and alienated people, those who were considered hopeless sinners by the religious elite of Jewish society. With His death on the cross, he made it possible for all humankind—those who were "strangers from the covenant of promise" (Ephesians 2:12)—to become members of God's family.

Early Christians were encouraged to provide food and lodging for fellow believers who were traveling. This provided safety and security in a time when commercial lodging places were rare.

Learn More: Romans 12:10–13 / Hebrews 13:2 / 1 Timothy 3:2 / Titus 1:8 / 1 Peter 4:9

HUMILITY

Humble yourselves in the sight of the Lord, and he shall lift you up. James 4:10

Humility is an attitude that grows out of the recognition that all we are and everything we own are gifts from God. This attribute is the very opposite of arrogance and pride. Humility motivates a follower of Christ to focus more on God and others than he does on himself.

To have a humble spirit also means that we recognize our sin before a holy God and that we submit ourselves to Him and His will for our lives. The prophet Micah declared that God prefers a spirit of humility in the worshiper more than any outward sacrifice that he might present to the Lord (Micah 6:8).

The best example of humility in the Bible is the life of Jesus (Matthew 11:29). He urged believers to practice this Christian grace in all their relationships (Matthew 23:12).

Learn More: 2 Chronicles 7:14 / Proverbs 16:19 / Matthew 18:4 / Philippians 2:8 / 1 Peter 5:5

HYPOCRISY

Do not sound a trumpet before thee, as the hypocrites do. MATTHEW 6:2

Jesus had no patience with hypocrisy—the sin of pretending to be what one is not. He was particularly critical of the scribes and Pharisees. An entire chapter of Matthew's Gospel, known as the "woe chapter of the Bible," records Jesus' withering criticism of their two-faced behavior (Matthew 23).

These religious leaders made a big show of doing good deeds in order to gain the praise of others. They pretended to be godly and righteous but were actually blind and insensitive to God's truth. They were critical of the faults of others while ignoring their own.

The opposite of hypocrisy is sincerity and purity of motive. One mark of a true believer is doing the right thing for the right reason and not expecting others to praise him for his actions. "Love must be sincere," the apostle Paul told the Christians at Rome. "Hate what is evil; cling to what is good" (Romans 12:9 NIV).

Learn More: Matthew 7:1–5 / Luke 12:1 / James 3:17

IDOLATRY

Repent, and turn yourselves from your idols. EZEKIEL 14:6

The nation of Israel was surrounded by pagan peoples who worshipped gods other than the one true God. Throughout their history the Israelites often fell into the trap of worshipping these pagan deities.

The pagan god mentioned most often in the Bible is Baal, seen as the provider of fertility for livestock and crops. While in the wilderness after their escape from Egypt, the Israelites fashioned a golden calf as an object of worship (Exodus 32:1–4). This was probably an image of the pagan Egyptian fertility god known as Apis.

Most of us never bow down before an idol or a statue that represents a false god. But idolatry is still a problem for people today, just as it was for God's people in Bible times. Any person or thing that we consider more important than God—whether family, career, money, sex, or fame—is a form of idolatry. The first of God's Ten Commandments still speaks to our time: "Thou shalt have no other gods before me" (Exodus 20:3).

Learn More: Leviticus 19:4 / Psalm 135:15 / Isaiah 45:20 / 2 Corinthians 6:16

IGNORANCE

With well doing ye may put to silence the ignorance of foolish men. 1 PETER 2:15

The dictionary defines *ignorance* as "lack of knowledge and intelligence." But the Bible speaks of ignorance in a spiritual sense. The apostle Paul addressed the lack of spiritual knowledge in Athens, Greece, when he addressed the learned men of the city about their worship of many false gods. "In the past God overlooked such ignorance," he told these philosophers, "but now he commands all people everywhere to repent" (Acts 17:30 NIV).

Paul wanted these learned men to know the truth about the supreme God of the universe who had sent His Son, Jesus, to save them from their sins.

The worst form of spiritual ignorance is callous rejection of the truth—refusing to acknowledge God and the evidence about Himself that He has planted in nature and revealed through His Word, the Bible. Paul described people who did this as darkened in their understanding because of their deliberate "blindness of...heart" (Ephesians 4:18). This is life's ultimate tragedy.

Learn More: Psalm 73:22 / Acts 17:23 / Romans 10:3 / 1 Timothy 1:3–4

IMMORTALITY

This mortal must put on immortality. 1 CORINTHIANS 15:53

The apostle Paul declared that believers will receive new bodies as their inheritance in the end time. He used the word *immortality* to express the idea of "not subject to death." Only God, of course, is truly immortal. He does not experience decline, death, and decay like human beings.

But the Bible makes it clear that humans were created with the potential for immortality. God placed Adam and Eve in a beautiful garden and provided everything they needed for an eternal existence. But all that changed when they ate the forbidden fruit and brought sin into the world. The certainty of physical death has haunted the human race ever since.

Then God sent His Son, Jesus, into the world to reverse this situation. In Jesus' prayer near the end of His public ministry, He declared, "This is life eternal, that they might know thee. . .and Jesus Christ, whom thou hast sent" (John 17:3). Thus He promised immortality, or a life that never ends, to those who accept Him as Savior and Lord.

Learn More: John 3:15 / Romans 2:7; 6:23 / 1 Corinthians 9:25 / Philippians 1:20–21 / 1 Timothy 6:19 / Titus 3:7 / 1 John 2:17

IMMUTABILITY

For I am the Lord, I change not. MALACHI 3:6

This big word refers to God's unchangeable nature. He does not "mutate" from one type of being into another. He is constant and dependable—the same yesterday, today, and forever. As the author of the epistle of James put it, He "does not change like shifting shadows" (James 1:17 NIV).

While God is unchanging in His basic nature, this does not mean that He is a static being, frozen and unable to act. When the Israelites failed to serve as a witness to the nations as God desired, He sent His Son, Jesus, to serve as a light to the world. This was a departure from the way He had acted up to that point. But this change grew out of the essence of what He had always been—a loving, benevolent, and merciful God.

The Lord's immutability brings hope to all believers. In a world that is always changing, His grace gives us the strength to overcome every challenge of life.

Learn More: Psalm 90:2 / Hebrews 1:10–12; 6:17–19; 13:8

IMPUTATION

Not having mine own righteousness. . .but that which is through the faith of Christ. PHILIPPIANS 3:9

The Bible declares that not one of us is worthy to have fellowship with God because of our sin. Only righteous people—those of high moral character—can enter His presence. And the only way to become people like this is to have righteousness transferred to us from some source outside ourselves. This in a nutshell is the concept of imputation.

God, who is wholly righteous, enabled His Son, Jesus, to avoid all sin and live a righteous and holy life. Through His death on the cross, Jesus paid the penalty for our sin. When we accept Jesus as our Lord and Savior, he "imputes" (or transfers) His righteousness to us, thus bridging the gap that separates us from God.

The apostle Paul explained it like this: "God made him who had no sin to be sin for us, so that in him we might become the righteousness of God" (2 Corinthians 5:21 NIV).

Learn More: Isaiah 53:5–6 / John 1:29 / Romans 5:19 / Hebrews 4:15

INCARNATION

And the Word was made flesh, and dwelt among us. JOHN 1:14

This statement by the apostle John is the strongest New Testament declaration about the incarnation of Jesus. The word *incarnation* comes from a Latin term, *incarnatio,* meaning "taking flesh." This doctrine affirms that Jesus was born into the world in a human body, although He was also the Son of God.

John knew that Jesus existed in the flesh, because he had lived and worked with the Lord during His public ministry. While Jesus' miracles proved He was the divine Son of God, John was also convinced that Jesus was fully human.

Later, when he wrote his first letter in the New Testament, John made the acceptance of the incarnation a test of authentic faith. "Every spirit that confesseth not that Jesus Christ is come in the flesh is not of God," he declared (1 John 4:3).

The Gospel of Mark also attests to the reality of the incarnation. Like any man, Jesus grew tired (4:38), and He also expressed a wide range of human emotions, including amazement (6:6), disappointment (8:12), and sorrow (14:34).

Learn More: Romans 1:3–4 / Galatians 4:4 / 1 Timothy 3:16 / 1 Peter 4:1 / 2 John 7

INHERITANCE

If children, then heirs; heirs of God, and joint-heirs with Christ. ROMANS 8:16–17

The word *inheritance* refers to property or goods passed on to others after a person's death. But the Bible transforms this concept into *spiritual* blessings granted by the Lord to those who belong to Him. The apostle Paul in this verse declares that this inheritance belongs to believers in this life as well as the life to come.

The New Testament concept of a spiritual inheritance reflects God's promise to Abraham in the Old Testament. Abraham and his descendants would receive the land of Canaan as an eternal possession (Genesis 12:7), not because they deserved it but because God loved the Israelites and adopted them as His special people.

But the central figure in God's provision of a spiritual inheritance is Jesus Christ. As God's one and only Son, He is uniquely qualified to become the heir of His heavenly Father. Not only is He the "heir of all things" (Hebrews 1:2), He shares this inheritance with all believers— salvation through His atoning death as well as the joy of eternal fellowship with Him in heaven.

Learn More: Galatians 4:5–7 / Ephesians 1:13–14 / Titus 3:7 / Hebrews 1:1–2 / Revelation 21:7

INIQUITY

Our iniquities, like the wind, have taken us away. ISAIAH 64:6

Sin is such a serious matter that it takes many biblical words to describe it—*wickedness, lawlessness, transgression, evil,* and *unrighteousness.* But the most dramatic term that describes humankind's deviation from God's standard of righteousness is probably *iniquity.* The prophet Isaiah in this verse declared that our iniquities separate us from fellowship with God.

Iniquity allied with hypocrisy is sin at its worse, as illustrated by the two sons of the priest Eli. They mishandled the offerings at the tabernacle and even seduced unsuspecting women who came to the altar to pray. The Lord declared, "The iniquity of Eli's house shall not be purged with sacrifice nor offering for ever" (1 Samuel 3:14). Divine judgment fell when they were killed in a battle with the Philistines, and their father died upon hearing the news (1 Samuel 4:17–18).

The only cure for human iniquity is the redemptive death of Jesus Christ. As the prophet Isaiah affirmed, "The LORD hath laid on him the iniquity of us all" (Isaiah 53:6).

Learn More: Job 15:16 / Psalm 25:11; 103:10 / Isaiah 53:5–6 / Jeremiah 31:30 /
Romans 4:7 / James 3:6

INSPIRATION

All scripture is given by inspiration of God. 2 TIMOTHY 3:16

Inspiration is the process by which God produced His written Word, the Bible. His Holy Spirit provided supernatural guidance to the people who wrote the scriptures. Although human agents recorded God's words, the Bible is just as authoritative and trustworthy as if He had written them down Himself.

The Bible contains many different types of writing—narrative, history, biography, and poetry. This suggests that the writers of scripture wrote out of their distinctive backgrounds, using words, methods, and styles that were uniquely their own.

The Gospels of the New Testament are a good example of the interplay between the human and divine that God used to produce the Bible. All four of these books focus on the life and ministry of Jesus, but each Gospel writer approached his subject from a little different perspective.

Just as God inspired the Bible, He also works through the Holy Spirit to help us understand the divine instructions in His holy Word.

Learn More: Job 32:8 / Psalm 119:27 / Hebrews 11:3 / 2 Peter 1:20–21

INTERCESSION

Pray one for another, that ye may be healed. JAMES 5:16

James made it clear in this verse that believers should pray for one another. This form of prayer is known as intercession. To pray for others is to intercede—or stand between—the Lord and them on their behalf. Many examples of this type of prayer occur in the Bible.

In the Old Testament, Abraham prayed for God to spare the wicked city of Sodom (Genesis 18). His compassionate prayer was for the welfare of others rather than his own needs. Unselfish concern like this is a trait of genuine intercession.

In the New Testament, Jesus is the greatest example of intercessory prayer. He prayed to God the Father to protect the disciples after His ascension. Jesus also prayed for all future believers. Then, in the most unselfish petition imaginable, He prayed for those who were putting Him to death on the cross.

Now in heaven "at the right hand of God," Jesus continues His intercessory work for all believers (Romans 8:34).

Learn More: John 17 / Romans 8:26–27; 10:1 / Colossians 1:9–12 / 1 Timothy 2:1–2 / Hebrews 7:25

JEALOUSY

They were filled with envy [jealousy: NIV], and spake against those things. ACTS 13:45

This scene of intense jealousy occurred in the city of Antioch of Pisidia during the apostle Paul's first missionary journey. Paul was preaching for the second time in the city synagogue. The large crowd that gathered included many Gentiles. This caused such resentment among the local Jews that they accused Paul of blasphemy and expelled him from the city.

But God used this fit of jealousy to further the Gospel. Paul realized that many Jews were hardened in their traditional beliefs while Gentiles were eager to hear about Jesus and His redemptive death. So he declared, "We turn to the Gentiles" (Acts 13:46). From then on, Paul witnessed mainly to the non-Jewish people of the Mediterranean world.

Many people are puzzled by the biblical statements that the Lord is a "jealous" God (Exodus 34:14). Since He is holy and perfect, how can He be associated with such a negative emotion? This is just another way of expressing God's supremacy. He is jealous in the sense that He tolerates no rivals for our worship and devotion.

Learn More: Genesis 37:11 / Deuteronomy 4:24 / Song of Solomon 8:6 / Romans 11:11; 13:13

JEWS

The Jews. . .raised persecution against Paul and Barnabas. ACTS 13:50

Jews is another word for the Israelites, God's chosen people, also referred to throughout the Old Testament as the "children of Israel." Their God-given mission was to proclaim the truths about the one true God to the rest of the world. God promised to bless them and make their name great. But they in turn were to be a blessing to the nations of the world.

God issued this promise first to Abraham, then passed it on through Abraham's son Isaac and Isaac's son Jacob. He also provided a land for His people by enabling them to settle in Canaan.

In the New Testament, the apostle John referred to the religious leaders who opposed Jesus as "the Jews" (John 18:12). Jewish opposition to Jesus continued in the book of Acts by zealous Jews who considered Him a false Messiah. But many Jews placed their faith in the Lord through the preaching of the apostles. Eventually non-Jews in great numbers also turned to Jesus through the ministry of the apostle Paul, known as the "apostle to the Gentiles."

Learn More: Ezra 5:1 / Esther 3:6 / Jeremiah 44:1 / John 1:19 / Acts 18:5 / 1 Corinthians 9:20

JOY

Behold, I bring you good tidings of great joy, which shall be to all people. LUKE 2:10

The angel who appeared to shepherds in the fields outside Bethlehem brought wonderful news: the birth of Jesus was a moment of joy for the entire world.

Joy is often defined as "a feeling of well-being or pleasure." This meaning of the word may be applied to God Himself. He is portrayed in the Bible as rejoicing over His creation (Psalm 104:31) and His redeemed people (Isaiah 65:18). Those who serve and follow God share this same positive feeling of delight. As the psalmist expressed it, "In thy presence is fulness of joy" (Psalm 16:11).

Some people think of joy as a feeling of happiness. But there's an important difference between the two. A person is happy when everything is going well. But joy is not dependent on circumstances. It never changes because it is based on one's relationship to Jesus Christ and His rock-solid promises.

The apostle Paul listed joy as one of the nine fruits of the spirit (Galatians 5:22–23). This feeling of well-being is possible for believers even when undergoing persecution (James 1:2–3).

Learn More: Psalm 95:1 / Habakkuk 3:18 / Luke 15:10 / John 15:11 / 2 Corinthians 6:10 / Philippians 4:4

JUDGMENT

God shall bring every work into judgment. ECCLESIASTES 12:14

This verse is one of many throughout the Bible that recognize God is the ultimate judge of the world. He alone has the wisdom and power to judge with righteousness and truth. He has delegated this right and authority to His Son, Jesus (John 5:22).

The Bible speaks clearly about a time in the future when God will intervene in history to judge the wicked, reward the righteous, and bring the universe to its appointed conclusion. He alone knows when this will happen. Jesus declared that even He did not know the exact time for the last judgment (Matthew 24:36).

The final judgment is sometimes referred to as the "great white throne" judgment. This term comes from the book of Revelation, where God is depicted as judging the earth while seated on a great white throne.

The last judgment will be universal in scope. All people and nations of the earth—from the beginning to the end of history—will be judged. Unbelievers will be condemned to eternal punishment, while believers will enter into eternal life.

Learn More: Jeremiah 33:15 / Romans 14:10–12 / Hebrews 10:30 / Revelation 14:7; 20:11–15

JUSTICE

A God of truth and without iniquity, just and right is he. Deuteronomy 32:4

The word *justice* today has a legal meaning—we speak of justice being rendered through the courts. But the Bible speaks of "doing justice," or being fair and impartial in our treatment of others. This sense of justice is rooted in the divine nature. The Lord is a God of truth who always does what is just and fair.

In the Old Testament, God is portrayed as the defender of the helpless people of society, including widows, orphans, the poor, and people who were aliens and strangers in the land of Israel. He often raised up prophets to remind His people that He expected them to treat these powerless people the same way. The prophet Amos condemned the wealthy class for their exploitation of the poor. "Let judgment [*justice*, NIV] run down as waters," he declared, "and righteousness as a mighty stream" (Amos 5:24).

In the New Testament, Jesus criticized the Pharisees for majoring on minor matters while ignoring such essentials as mercy, faithfulness, and justice (Matthew 23:23).

Learn More: Job 8:3 / Psalm 82:1–3 / Proverbs 21:3 / Jeremiah 23:5 / Micah 6:8

JUSTIFICATION

Man is not justified by the works of the law, but by the faith of Jesus Christ. Galatians 2:16

Justification is at the heart of the apostle Paul's writings in his epistles to the Romans and Galatians. In this verse he declared that people are made acceptable to the Lord not by keeping a set of rules but by placing their faith in Jesus Christ. In effect, Paul answers life's most important question: How can sinners possibly enter into fellowship with a God who is perfectly holy?

Jesus Christ provides the answer to this question. He fulfilled God's demand for righteousness in those who stand in His presence. Through Jesus' death on the cross, God the Father charged the sin of humans to Christ and credited the godliness of His Son to hopeless sinners.

Although Jesus has paid the price for the justification of believers, they must receive Him through faith by confessing their sin and throwing themselves upon His mercy and grace. Our justification cannot be earned through good works. As Paul expressed it, through Jesus "we have access by faith into this grace wherein we stand, and rejoice in hope of the glory of God" (Romans 5:2).

Learn More: Acts 13:39 / Romans 3:24, 28; 5:1, 9, 18; 8:33 / Titus 3:7

KINDNESS

That I may shew him kindness for Jonathan's sake? 2 Samuel 9:1

One of the most notable acts of kindness in the Bible is King David's treatment of Mephibosheth. He was the handicapped son of the king's deceased friend, Jonathan. David brought Mephibosheth to the royal palace and took care of him for the rest of his life (2 Samuel 9:6–10).

Acts of kindness like this are a reflection of the divine nature. God is benevolent and kin toward His people. In the Old Testament, it takes two words—love allied with kindness—to express this attribute of the Lord. The psalmist expressed it like this: "Withhold not thou thy tender mercies from me, O Lord: let thy lovingkindness and thy truth continually preserve me" (Psalm 40:11).

The ultimate expression of divine kindness was God's gift of Jesus to the world. Christ was the beneficiary of the kindness of His Father. But He was also the ultimate model of kindness, delivering humankind from bondage to sin.

The apostle Paul listed kindness as one of the traits of those who follow Jesus (Colossians 3:12).

Learn More: Ruth 2:20 / Psalm 117:2 / Joel 2:13 / Ephesians 4:32 / Titus 3:3–5

KINGDOM OF GOD

The time is fulfilled, and the kingdom of God is at hand. Mark 1:15

With these words, Jesus declared that God's rule of grace in the world had begun. The kingdom of God would be fully revealed through Jesus' miracles, teaching, and atoning death for the sins of the world.

Jesus taught about the kingdom of God in many of His parables. For example, He compared the kingdom to seed scattered on the ground. Some seed would sprout and grow in good soil. But other seed would fall on rocky ground and fail to take root. This shows that the kingdom will flourish in the hearts of some people but be rejected by others (Matthew 13:3–8).

The kingdom of God is a present reality for those who accept Jesus as their Savior. But this kingdom will not be fully established until His return to earth. Then He will bring the present age to an end and establish a new heaven and new earth under His universal rule.

Another phrase for this kingdom that appears often in the Gospels is "kingdom of heaven" (Matthew 13:44). The apostle Paul also referred to it as the "kingdom of Christ" (Ephesians 5:5).

Learn More: Matthew 6:33 / Luke 4:43 / John 3:5 / Acts 19:8 / Romans 14:17 / Galatians 5:21

LAW, CEREMONIAL

Ye shall offer a burnt offering, a sacrifice made by fire. Numbers 29:13

This verse is a good example of the ceremonial laws that appear throughout the Old Testament books of Exodus, Leviticus, Numbers, and Deuteronomy. These regulations dealt with the distinctive worship rituals of God's chosen people, the Israelites.

A burnt offering consisted of an animal—such as a bull or lamb—that was roasted before being offered to the Lord as a sacrifice on the altar in the tabernacle or temple. Such offerings were thought to atone for sin and to restore fellowship with a holy God.

The ceremonial law also included regulations about the priesthood, religious holidays or festivals, foods that could or could not be eaten, and purification rituals.

In the New Testament, Jesus often ignored these stringent laws, to the horror of the scribes and Pharisees. When they criticized Him for not properly purifying Himself—Jesus didn't wash His hands before eating—He declared, "Nothing outside a person can defile them by going into them. Rather, it is what comes out of a person that defiles them" (Mark 7:15 niv).

Learn More: Exodus 29 / Leviticus 4 / Numbers 8

LAW, CIVIL

Thou shalt make a battlement for thy roof. . .if any man fall from thence. Deuteronomy 22:8

Civil or judicial laws of the Bible were intended to promote a spirit of fairness and justice among God's people. This verse from the book of Deuteronomy addressed a public safety issue. A new house had to be constructed with a rooftop guardrail. This prevented accidental falls because people of that time used their flat roofs much as people today gather on outdoor patios.

Other civil laws in the Bible regulated compensation for personal injuries and damaged property, how slaves were to be treated, and the circumstances that exempted certain people from going to war.

An important judicial precaution for people accused of murder was guaranteed asylum in a "city of refuge." The accused person could stay there in safety until it was determined through due process what punishment, if any, should be levied against him. This protected the accused from any relative of the deceased who was bent on revenge.

Learn More: Exodus 21:2–36; 22:5–6 / Leviticus 20:27 / Deuteronomy 13:6–16; 20:5–9; 22:22

LAW, MORAL

Thou shalt love the Lord thy God, and keep his charge, and his statutes. DEUTERONOMY 11:1

The Lord is the source of truth, righteousness, and holiness. He has the right to set the standards by which people should live. His moral law consists of standards for human behavior that are summarized in the Ten Commandments and other ethical passages in the Bible. Perhaps the most important of these is the command to worship God alone and not to bow down to false gods—the demand of the first commandment.

God's moral law also specifies that we honor God's name, show respect to parents, observe the Sabbath appropriately, refrain from adulterous relationships, deal truthfully with others, avoid excessive desire for material things that leads to greed, practice honesty in business, and show kindness and generosity toward the poor.

Many people have a strictly negative view of God's laws. They think of them only in binding and restrictive terms. But these laws are actually given for our benefit. Following the Lord's directives and commands is the key to finding joy and contentment in life. The psalmist focused on this positive side of God's laws when he declared, "Thou art good, and doest good; teach me thy statutes" (Psalm 119:68).

Learn More: Exodus 20:1–17 / Leviticus 19:9–10 / Deuteronomy 25:13

LAZINESS

Yet a little sleep, a little slumber, a little folding of the hands to sleep. . . PROVERBS 6:10

These verses from Proverbs are a classic passage about laziness. Their rendering by a modern translation shows the biblical writer's subtle sense of humor. Idleness, he declared, would cause poverty to "pounce on you like a bandit" and scarcity to "attack you like an armed robber" (NLT).

The book of Proverbs contains many strong statements about laziness and the people who practice this vice. It refers to them as "sluggards." A related term for laziness is *slothfulness* (Proverbs 19:15). The words conjure up images of a person so listless that he will barely lift a hand to eat. The writer of Proverbs invited such a person to take a lesson from the lowly ant, which provided for its needs without being ordered to get to work.

The apostle Paul was disappointed with certain believers in the church at Thessalonica because they were sitting around doing nothing while waiting for the return of the Lord. "If any would not work," he declared, "neither should he eat" (2 Thessalonians 3:10).

Learn More: Proverbs 6:6–8; 19:24; 22:13; 24:30–31 / Ecclesiastes 10:18 / 1 Timothy 5:13 / Hebrews 6:12

LEAVEN

It was not leavened; because they were thrust out of Egypt. EXODUS 12:39

Leaven was an ingredient mixed with bread dough to cause it to rise. It is first mentioned in connection with the Exodus of the Israelite slaves. They left Egypt in such a hurry that they didn't have time to add leaven to the bread they were baking. Most modern translations render the term as "yeast."

From that point on, the people ate bread with no leaven in a ritual known as the Days of Unleavened Bread. These were observed in connection with the yearly Passover festival, which memorialized their deliverance.

Leaven is also used as a figure of speech for something that has influence out of all proportion to its size. Jesus told a parable about a woman who added a small amount of leaven to a large batch of dough "till the whole was leavened" (Matthew 13:33). He explained this was like God's spiritual rule, which—though small at first—was destined to spread throughout the entire world.

Learn More: Deuteronomy 16:3 / Matthew 16:6–12 / Luke 12:1–2 / 1 Corinthians 5:6–8 / Galatians 5:9

LIBERTY

Stand fast therefore in the liberty wherewith Christ hath made us free. GALATIANS 5:1

The apostle Paul's letter to the Christians of Galatia has been described as the greatest treatise on Christian liberty in the Bible. He stood firm for the truth that grace alone through faith alone is the only requirement for salvation.

Paul was disturbed by certain teachers who had visited the church after his departure. They were spreading false doctrine among the Galatian believers by insisting that salvation depended on observing certain Old Testament customs. These included consenting to circumcision and observing the Sabbath and other Jewish holy days.

Paul reminded these believers that the Gospel he had preached to them in the past was not something he had made up. It came "by the revelation of Jesus Christ" (Galatians 1:12). Those who were trying to change it were opposing the plan of God Himself.

But the apostle went on to say that freedom in Christ does not mean believers can do as they please. "Use not liberty for an occasion to the flesh," he declared, "but by love serve one another" (Galatians 5:13).

Learn More: Psalm 119:45 / Isaiah 61:1 / Luke 4:18 / John 8:36 / Romans 8:21 / 2 Corinthians 3:17

LIFE

God. . .breathed into his nostrils the breath of life. GENESIS 2:7

This verse traces life back to God, who placed this animating force in Adam, the first man. Our existence as living beings is a gift of the Creator, who brought the universe and life itself into being.

But the word *life* is also used in the Bible in a spiritual sense. While the Israelites were wandering in the wilderness, Moses exhorted them to "choose life" to be assured of a future in the land God had promised to give them (Deuteronomy 30:19). Fellowship with the Lord was essential for their well-being. They should continue to follow Him rather than worship the false gods of the people of Canaan.

The concept of life in harmony with the Lord's purpose reached its ultimate fulfillment in the ministry of Jesus. He restored sick people to wholeness. He brought salvation to sinners whose lives were mired in sin.

And best of all, He offers eternal life to those who accept Him as Savior and Lord. He Himself declared, "I am come that they might have life, and that they might have it more abundantly" (John 10:10).

Learn More: Jeremiah 21:8 / John 1:4; 6:35; 10:10 / Philippians 2:16 / 1 John 5:12

LIGHT

The Lord is my light and my salvation; whom shall I fear? PSALM 27:1

The psalmist compared God's guiding presence to the light. The writer was probably familiar with the creation account in the book of Genesis in which God brought light into being. This illumination pushed back the darkness and revealed the earth in its initial form before God began to mold and shape it.

Light often appears in the Bible as an image of the Lord's presence. It also represents truth and goodness and God's redemptive work. The prophet Micah found security in this divine protective light. "When I sit in darkness," he declared, "the LORD shall be a light unto me" (Micah 7:8).

The prophet Isaiah compared the promised Messiah to a great light who would bring salvation to people trapped in the darkness of sin. Jesus fulfilled this prophecy when He declared He had been sent on a redemptive mission by God the Father as the "light of the world" (John 8:12).

In His Sermon on the Mount, Jesus referred to believers as "the light of the world" (Matthew 5:14). He expects us to reflect His light to others.

Learn More: Genesis 1:3–5 / Psalm 89:15; 104:1–2 / Isaiah 2:5; 60:1 / Matthew 4:16 / 1 John 1:5

LORDSHIP

As ye have therefore received Christ Jesus the Lord, so walk ye in him. Colossians 2:6

These verses from the apostle Paul affirm a central truth of the Christian faith: the journey of faith begins with declaring Jesus as Lord, and it continues as believers live out their faith day by day under His lordship.

The term *rooted* in this passage expresses the idea of an event from the past that has a significant influence on the present. Once we experience Christ as Lord in the salvation experience, we will honor Him as Lord and Master—the supreme influence in how we live—for the rest of our earthly journey.

The concept of lordship also means that believers should continue to grow deeper in their commitment to Christ. The apostle Peter encouraged novice Christians to "grow in grace, and in the knowledge of our Lord and Saviour Jesus Christ" (2 Peter 3:18). This involves studying the Bible, praying for others through the ministry of intercession, serving others in the body of Christ, and declaring the good news of the Gospel to unbelievers.

Learn More: Acts 2:36 / 1 Corinthians 15:31 / Ephesians 5:8 / Colossians 1:10

LOVE, BROTHERLY

A new commandment I give unto you, That ye love one another. John 13:34

These words of Jesus to His disciples are a perfect example of the concept of brotherly love, or love for others. Jesus knew their love for one another would have to be strong to carry them through the turbulent days leading up to and following His death, resurrection, and ascension.

During His earthly ministry, Jesus declared that the second greatest commandment in the law was to love one's neighbor as oneself. He also cited the Golden Rule as a guide for positive human relationships. He even declared that citizens of the kingdom of God must resist the urge to hate their enemies and to love them instead.

Later, the apostle Paul wrote the beautiful tribute to love in what has become known as the "love chapter" of the New Testament. True brotherly love, he affirmed, is unselfish concern for the well-being of others. Paul also listed love for others as one of the nine fruits of the spirit (Galatians 5:22–23).

Learn More: Proverbs 17:17 / Matthew 22:39 / Mark 12:31 / 1 Corinthians 13 / Ephesians 5:2 / Philippians 1:9 / 1 Thessalonians 3:12 / James 2:8 / 1 John 4:7

LOVE, GOD'S

God commendeth his love toward us, in that. . .Christ died for us. Romans 5:8

God's love was first revealed in the Old Testament when He showed special favor to His people, the Israelites. He redeemed them from slavery, provided food and water for them in the wilderness, and gave them a land of their own. Moses reminded the people of God's gracious love when they were getting ready to take the promised land (Deuteronomy 7:7–8).

God's love assumed human personality in the person of His own Son, Jesus Christ. The supreme demonstration of God's love was Jesus' death on the cross on our behalf. The apostle John declared, "This is love: not that we loved God, but that he loved us and sent his Son as an atoning sacrifice for our sins" (1 John 4:10 niv).

Since God is eternal and His very nature is love, there has never been a time when He did not love His own. He declared this truth through the prophet Jeremiah: "I have loved thee with an everlasting love" (Jeremiah 31:3). We can rest assured that His love will abide with us throughout this earthly life and beyond.

Learn More: John 3:16; 15:9 / Romans 8:39 / 2 Corinthians 13:11 / Ephesians 2:4–5 / 1 John 3:1; 4:8

LUST

Whosoever looketh on a woman to lust after her hath committed adultery. Matthew 5:28

Lust is a strong desire for what is forbidden. The word usually refers to the temptation to worship false gods and a craving for illicit sexual relationships.

In the Old Testament, the prophet Isaiah condemned the Israelites for worshipping the false gods of their pagan neighbors. They were "enflaming" themselves "with idols under every green tree" (Isaiah 57:5). This refers to the pagan shrines where their idolatry occurred.

In the New Testament, the word refers to out-of-control sexual desire. This craving can be so strong that Jesus issued a strong warning against it in the verse above. He probably did not mean that lustful thoughts were equal to the actual act of adultery. He indicated that such strong desires, if given free rein, would lead to sexual sin.

The apostle Paul issued a similar warning to Timothy, his young missionary associate, when he told him to flee from "youthful lusts." This temptation could be overcome by focusing on such positive Christian virtues as faith, love, and peace (2 Timothy 2:22).

Learn More: Romans 1:27 / Ephesians 2:3 / Titus 2:12 / James 1:14–15 / 1 John 2:16

MAJESTY

To the only wise God our Saviour, be glory and majesty. Jude 25

The author of Jude ended his brief New Testament book with a beautiful benediction on the power and glory of Jesus. Because of His majesty and power, He is able to protect believers and present them blameless before His heavenly Father.

The word *majesty* describes a person or thing with supreme power and authority. It is used as a title for earthly monarchs, as in "his majesty the king." When the term is applied to God, it means He is the supreme ruler of the universe. He stands above and beyond all earthly authority. He rules the world, His own creation, with unlimited power.

When the psalmist thought about this truth, He declared that the very name of God was infused with dignity and greatness. "O Lord our Lord," he declared, "how excellent [*majestic*, niv] is thy name in all the earth!" (Psalm 8:9).

The divine title "King of Kings" (Revelation 19:16) is another declaration of the Lord's supreme greatness and majesty.

Learn More: 1 Chronicles 29:24–25 / Psalm 29:4; 96:6; 104:1; 145:12 / Hebrews 1:3; 8:1

MAMMON

Ye cannot serve God and mammon. Matthew 6:24

Jesus spoke these words to the disciples in His Sermon on the Mount. He warned them it was impossible to follow the values of the world and serve the kingdom of God at the same time. They had to choose one or the other—the lure of materialism or the call of their heavenly Father.

Mammon is a transliteration of an Aramaic word that means "earthly goods" or "riches." Modern translations render the term as "money," "gold," or "material possessions."

Jesus also used the word in His parable of the dishonest servant, a man who made a deal with his master's debtors to secure his own future. Jesus' point was that people of the world often do a better job of protecting their interests than believers do in advancing the kingdom of God.

The apostle Paul also cautioned against the dangers of putting money ahead of everything else in life. "The love of money is the root of all evil," he declared (1 Timothy 6:10).

Learn More: Matthew 16:26 / Mark 8:36 / Luke 12:13–21; 16:1–13

MARRIAGE

And the Lord God said, It is not good that the man should be alone. GENESIS 2:18

God established marriage when He created Eve and presented her to Adam in the garden of Eden. She was to be his helper and companion. Since then, marriage has been the bedrock of human society. This sacred relationship between a man and a woman brings mutual joy and happiness to both. Their union is also part of God's plan to bring children into the world.

Jesus placed His seal of approval on marriage when a group of Pharisees asked Him about the grounds for divorce. Jesus declared that this union should not be broken for any flippant reason, since the husband and wife were united in a sacred "one-flesh" relationship.

The apostle Paul compared the marriage union to the relationship between Christ and His church. The husband should love his wife as he loves his own body, just as Christ sacrificed His life for the church. The wife, in turn, should submit to her husband's headship and leadership, just as believers are subject to Jesus as the head of the church.

Learn More: Matthew 19:1–8 / Mark 10:6–8 / John 2:1–2 / Ephesians 5:22–33 / Colossians 3:18–19 / Hebrews 13:4 / Revelation 19:7–9

MEDITATION

His delight is in the law of the Lord; and in his law doth he meditate. PSALM 1:2

Meditation is the practice of deep reflection or concentration on some thought or idea. In this verse, the psalmist declared that meditation on divine law was a characteristic of the person who followed the Lord.

One word behind *meditation* in the Old Testament means "to murmur quietly." Some scholars suggest that the ancient Israelites meditated on passages of scripture by reciting them in a low voice. This contemplation on the character of God and His teachings deepened their faith in His provision for their needs.

If anyone ever needed assurance of God's presence, it was Joshua. Upon succeeding Moses as leader of the Israelites, he must have wondered how he could measure up to the high standards set by this revered servant of the Lord.

The prescription that God ordered for Joshua's anxiety was meditation on His law "day and night" and total commitment to His commands. This would secure His success: "For the LORD thy God is with thee whithersoever thou goest" (Joshua 1:8–9).

Learn More: Psalm 19:14; 63:5–6; 119:15, 97; 143:5 / Luke 21:14 / 1 Timothy 4:15

MEEKNESS

Blessed are the meek: for they shall inherit the earth. MATTHEW 5:5

No biblical concept is more misunderstood than meekness. To most people the term conjures up images of a weak, spineless person who is nothing but a doormat for the feet of others.

But meekness in the biblical sense has a totally different meaning. Through their dependence on the Holy Spirit, meek people have mastered the art of control. God gives them the inner strength not to strike back when they are insulted or slighted by others.

Meek people are also open and teachable—willing to admit that they don't know everything. This is probably why Jesus said the meek would inherit the earth. He came to establish the kingdom of God, a new and revolutionary concept. Those who accepted this truth and became citizens of this kingdom were heirs to a spiritual gift that might be compared to the earth itself.

Jesus is the perfect example of meekness, and He invites believers to cultivate this virtue by depending on Him. "Take my yoke upon you, and learn of me, for I am meek and lowly in heart," He declared, "and ye shall find rest unto your souls" (Matthew 11:29).

Learn More: Numbers 12:3 / Psalm 22:26; 37:11 / Isaiah 61:1 / Galatians 5:22–23 / Colossians 3:12 / 1 Peter 3:15

MERCY

The Lord is merciful and gracious, slow to anger, and plenteous in mercy. Psalm 103:8

The mercy of God is a divine characteristic similar to His grace. But while grace leads Him to forgive the guilty, His mercy is expressed as compassion toward those in difficult situations, particularly the poor and helpless. For example, when Joseph arrived in Egypt as a slave, "The Lord was with [him], and shewed him mercy" (Genesis 39:21). Other translations render the Hebrew word behind *mercy* as "kindness" or "compassion."

This attribute of God is mentioned often in the psalms. When the psalmists thought about their human weakness in comparison to the unlimited strength and compassion of God, they thanked Him for His mercy.

Since God is merciful, He expects us to show mercy to others. Jesus told a parable about a traveler who was beaten by thieves and left for dead. Two religious professionals ignored him and continued on their way. Then a Samaritan—member of a race of half-breed Jews despised by the pure-blooded Jews—happened by. He stopped and took care of the helpless man. It was clear which one of these three was the traveler's real neighbor: "He that shewed mercy on him" (Luke 10:37).

Learn More: Psalm 31:9; 109:26 / Matthew 5:7 / Luke 6:36 / 2 Corinthians 1:3 / 1 Peter 1:3

MINISTRY

As every man hath received the gift, even so minister the same one to another. 1 Peter 4:10

The words *minister* and *ministry* are often used to refer to the professional leaders of a church. But the apostle Peter's directive in this verse makes it clear that every believer is a minister of the grace of God.

Ministry is just another term for the biblical concept of sacrificial service. The idea originated with Abraham, whom God promised to make into a great nation, the Israelites. But they in turn were expected to serve as His witnesses to the other peoples and nations of the world.

The ultimate minister, or servant, was Jesus Christ. Soon after He launched His public ministry, He read from one of the prophet Isaiah's servant songs. Jesus identified with this divine messenger whom God sent to sacrifice His life for others. On another occasion, Jesus declared that He came into the world "not to be ministered unto, but to minister, and to give his life a ransom for many" (Mark 10:45).

Following the example of Jesus, all believers are called to "do good unto all men, especially unto them who are of the household of faith" (Galatians 6:10).

Learn More: Genesis 12:1–3 / Psalm 103:21 / Ephesians 3:7 / Colossians 4:17 / 2 Timothy 4:5

MIRACLE

How great are his signs! and how mighty are his wonders! Daniel 4:3

A miracle is an event contrary to natural law, performed by the Lord through His unlimited power. Other words in the Bible that mean essentially the same thing are *signs* (Exodus 7:3), *wonders* (Joshua 3:5), and *marvellous works* (Psalm 105:5).

The most spectacular miracles in the Bible occurred during the ministry of Jesus. He did not perform these signs to dazzle the crowds or showcase His power; His miracles declared that the kingdom of God had arrived, and it was being fulfilled in His mission of compassion and redemption. "The blind receive their sight," He said, "and the lame walk, the lepers are cleansed, and the deaf hear, the dead are raised up, and the poor have the gospel preached to them" (Matthew 11:5).

In addition to His miracles of healing, Jesus also demonstrated through mighty works that He was Lord over nature and death. His miraculous resurrection after His death on the cross shows that death is not the final word for those who accept Jesus as Lord and Savior.

Learn More: Mark 4:35–41 / John 3:2; 11:1–44 / Acts 3:1–16; 9:36–42 / 1 Corinthians 12:10

MORTALITY

For what is your life? It is even a vapour, that. . .vanisheth away. JAMES 4:14

This verse from the epistle of James is a dramatic statement about mortality, or the certainty of death. The Bible also compares the fragile nature of human life to water spilled on the ground (2 Samuel 14:14), a broken pot (Ecclesiastes 12:6), a flower that blooms for just a short time (Isaiah 40:6), a fog at dawn that disappears with the rising sun (Hosea 13:3), and a passing breeze (Psalm 78:39).

God created humankind originally for life not death. But Adam and Eve changed that when they rebelled against God and ate the forbidden fruit in the garden of Eden. Death has been the unavoidable destiny of all humans ever since. As the apostle Paul put it, "The wages of sin is death" (Romans 6:23).

But that is not the end of the story. Paul also added an important exception to this verse: "But," he continued, "the gift of God is eternal life through Jesus Christ our Lord." He has replaced the certainty of death with a promise of life without end for those who claim Him as Lord and Savior.

Learn More: Psalm 90:5–6, 10 / 1 Corinthians 15:21–23 / 2 Corinthians 5:4–6

MURDER

Cain rose up against Abel his brother, and slew him. GENESIS 4:8

The murder of Abel by his brother, Cain, is the first recorded homicide in the Bible. This apparently was a premeditated killing, making it an even more serious crime against the standards of a holy God.

In the Bible's creation account, the Lord made humans in His own image. He appointed us the caretakers of His physical world and granted us the unique privilege of having fellowship with Him. The high value He places on human life makes murder a crime specifically prohibited by the Ten Commandments (Exodus 20:13).

In His Sermon on the Mount, Jesus deepened this Old Testament command by tracing murder to its source in the human heart (Matthew 5:21–22). Extreme anger or hatred for another person is often the prelude to the act of murder itself.

The apostle John stated this principle in even stronger language. "Whosoever hateth his brother is a murderer," he declared, "and ye know that no murderer hath eternal life abiding in him" (1 John 3:15).

Learn More: Genesis 1:26–27 / Exodus 20:13 / Numbers 35:30 / Matthew 15:19 / John 8:44 / Romans 1:29

MYSTERY

And without controversy great is the mystery of godliness. 1 TIMOTHY 3:16

The concept of mystery appears often in the writings of the apostle Paul. In this classic passage, he declares that what had once been a mystery has been revealed in the life, ministry, and ascension of Jesus Christ.

Paul's thought on this subject may have been influenced by the prophet Daniel in the Old Testament. To Daniel, a mystery was something that could not be understood unless God chose to explain it through divine revelation (Daniel 2:17; 4:9). Some of God's mysteries were revealed to the prophet and the king of Babylon whose dreams Daniel interpreted.

Paul declared that the ways of God are no longer puzzling or beyond the limits of human understanding; they have been revealed to all the world through the redemptive work of His Son.

Jesus told His disciples on one occasion, "It is given unto you to know the mysteries of the kingdom of heaven" (Matthew 13:11). He was referring to God's eternal plan of salvation as revealed in Jesus and the spiritual kingdom that He came to establish.

Learn More: 1 Corinthians 2:7; 4:1; 13:2 / Ephesians 5:32 / Colossians 1:26–27

OBEDIENCE

To obey is better than sacrifice, and to hearken than the fat of rams. 1 SAMUEL 15:22

King Saul of Israel disobeyed the Lord's command to wipe out the Amalekites and all their property. When confronted by the prophet Samuel, he lied by claiming he planned to offer the animals he kept alive as ritual sacrifices to God.

Unfortunately, this was not the last time Saul's stubborn disobedience got him into trouble. He was eventually rejected as king when God ordered Samuel to anoint the young shepherd boy David as his replacement.

Obedience in biblical terms is closely related to the concept of hearing. To really hear God's commands is to obey what He commands us to do. His grace and favor lead His followers to seek and follow His will.

In the New Testament, the apostle Paul contrasts the obedience of Jesus with the disobedience of Adam, the first man. Adam's rebellion brought sin and death into the world, but Jesus bent His own will to that of His heavenly Father. His submission brought grace and righteousness to believers (Romans 5:19).

Learn More: Deuteronomy 27:10 / Ecclesiastes 12:13 / Romans 5:19 / Philippians 2:8 / Hebrews 11:8 / 1 Peter 1:13–14

OFFERINGS

So Christ was once offered to bear the sins of many. HEBREWS 9:28

Offerings brought to the Lord in Old Testament times were placed on the altar by officiating priests. These offerings consisted of sacrificial animals, fine wine, grain, or in some cases a complete meal. The people believed these sacrifices would atone for their sins and restore fellowship with God.

With the coming of God's Son, Jesus Christ, and His atoning death, the need for these Old Testament sacrifices no longer exists. The author of the book of Hebrews declared that Jesus is able to save all people who turn to Him in faith, "seeing he ever liveth to make intercession for them" (Hebrews 7:25).

Obedience to God's commands is the offering that He requires from modern believers. Dedication to service in the cause of Jesus and His kingdom is the "living sacrifice" that makes a difference in a dark and sinful world (Romans 12:1).

Learn More: Genesis 4:4 / Exodus 29:18 / Psalm 96:8 / Hebrews 10:6

OMNIPOTENCE

Alleluia: for the Lord God omnipotent reigneth. REVELATION 19:6

This attribute or characteristic of God refers to His unlimited and infinite power. The term is derived from two Latin words, *omni* ("all") and *potens* ("power"). Thus, God is all-powerful—the most awesome force in the universe.

The Bible is filled with examples of God's power. He created the universe from nothing by the power of His Word. He struck Egypt with ten plagues to convince the pharaoh to release the Israelites from slavery. He divided the waters of the Red Sea to allow the Israelites to escape from the pursuing Egyptian army.

The prophet Jeremiah was familiar with all these mighty acts of the Lord. "Ah Lord GOD!" he marveled, "behold, thou hast made the heaven and the earth by thy great power and stretched out arm, and there is nothing too hard for thee" (Jeremiah 32:17).

The names "Almighty God" and "mighty One of Jacob" also emphasize God's unlimited power.

Learn More: Genesis 1:1–3 / Exodus 6:1 / Deuteronomy 7:21 / Psalm 47:2 / Isaiah 49:26 / Amos 4:13 / Zephaniah 3:17

ORDINATION

I ordained thee a prophet unto the nations. JEREMIAH 1:5

To be ordained is to be set apart for special service to the Lord. Ordination is generally a ceremony performed by a church or a Christian organization, but Jeremiah was selected by the Lord as His servant even before the prophet was born.

In Old Testament times, kings were formally commissioned to their office by having oil poured on their heads. Aaron and his sons were also set apart as priests to perform sacrifices on behalf of God's chosen people, the Israelites.

Ordination was also practiced in New Testament times. When Jesus began His public ministry, "he ordained twelve, that they should be with him, and that he might send them forth to preach" (Mark 3:14). Jesus gave the twelve special training so they could continue His work through the church after His earthly ministry came to an end. Jesus Himself was sent into the world by God the Father on a special mission. So He is sometimes described as one ordained for ministry by the Lord (Acts 17:31).

Learn More: 1 Samuel 10:1 / Exodus 28–29 / John 15:16 / Acts 14:23 / Titus 1:5

PARADOX

He that loseth his life for my sake shall find it. MATTHEW 10:39

A paradox exists when two statements seem to contradict each other but both are actually true. For example, we affirm that God is sovereign or supreme in the universe. But He also created man with free will and the ability to reject His rule and authority. Both these facts are true, though they seem to be mutually exclusive.

Paradox is also evident in the life and ministry of Jesus and His continuing work of redemption in the world. He was God's Son, sharing fully in the divine essence of the Father. But He was also fully human, subject to every human emotion and the pain and suffering that led to His death on the cross.

The best we can do with such paradoxical truths is to admit the limit of our human understanding. What seems impossible from the standpoint of human logic is no problem to God. He is always true to His nature as the all-wise, all-knowing, and all-seeing Lord. He is the great "Wholly Other" whose ways we cannot fully understand.

Learn More: Matthew 11:28–30; 20:20–26; 23:12 / Luke 9:24–26 / 2 Corinthians 12:10 / 1 Corinthians 3:18

PARDON

Pardon, I beseech thee, the iniquity of this people. NUMBERS 14:19

The Israelites got some bad news when they arrived at the edge of Canaan. Upon learning that the ferocious Canaanites populated the promised land, they threatened to kill Moses and Aaron for leading them into the wilderness to die.

Only the eloquent prayer of Moses stood between the people and certain destruction at God's hands. The Lord responded to the great leader's plea with words of mercy: "I have pardoned according to thy word" (Numbers 14:20). Or as the Good News Translation puts it, "I will forgive them, as you have asked."

Pardon is another word for the Lord's forgiveness. It appears several times in the Old Testament. The term does not appear in the New Testament, where *forgiveness* can refer to both divine and human forgiveness.

Learn More: Nehemiah 9:17 / Psalm 25:11 / Isaiah 55:7 / Jeremiah 33:8–9 / Micah 7:18

PASSOVER

Keep the passover unto the Lord your God. 2 KINGS 23:21

King Josiah of Judah ordered the people to observe the Passover, a religious festival that commemorated their deliverance from Egyptian slavery many years before. This annual holiday celebrated how God "passed over" the Israelite houses in Egypt that were sprinkled with the blood of a lamb. Egyptian houses were not spared from this calamity (Exodus 12:1–14).

The Passover eventually developed into a pilgrimage festival. The Jewish people were encouraged to travel to Jerusalem to observe this annual holiday. Jesus and His disciples were in the city for this event when He turned the Passover meal that they ate together into a memorial of His approaching death.

Just as the blood of a sacrificial lamb saved the Israelites from destruction, so Jesus' blood was an agent of deliverance. He was the ultimate Passover sacrifice that saves humankind from bondage to sin. The apostle Paul expressed it like this: "Purge out therefore the old leaven, that ye may be a new lump, as ye are unleavened. For even Christ our passover is sacrificed for us" (1 Corinthians 5:7).

Learn More: Numbers 9:5 / Luke 22:15 / Hebrews 11:24–28

PATIENCE

Now the God of patience and consolation grant you to be likeminded. ROMANS 15:5

Most people think of patience as the steady endurance of some unpleasant circumstance—the very opposite of a knee-jerk reaction. But the apostle Paul makes it clear in this verse that patience is a mark of the divine character that believers should observe in their walk of faith.

Throughout the Bible, God showed patience toward His people, the Israelites, when they rebelled against Him. He sent the prophets to remind them of their mutual covenant that demanded their loyalty. The apostle Peter referred to this divine patience as "longsuffering," reminding his readers that the Lord was "not willing that any should perish, but that all should come to repentance" (2 Peter 3:9).

The author of Hebrews compared the life of faith to a marathon that requires a steady, consistent pace. Completing this race successfully demands that we keep our eyes on Jesus, "the author and finisher of our faith" (Hebrews 12:2).

Patience, or longsuffering, is cited by the apostle Paul as one of the nine fruits of the spirit (Galatians 5:22–23).

Learn More: Psalm 40:1 / Romans 5:3–4 / 2 Thessalonians 3:5 / 1 Timothy 6:11 / James 5:7

PEACE

The peace of God. . .shall keep your hearts and minds through Christ Jesus. PHILIPPIANS 4:7

Soon after His resurrection, Jesus stood among His disciples and said, "Peace be unto you" (John 20:19). These words were the common greeting used by Jewish people of that day—a wish for others' peace, wholeness, and well-being.

When the disciples heard this greeting from Jesus, perhaps they remembered His previous promise to them: "Peace I leave with you; my peace I give you. . . . Do not let your hearts be troubled and do not be afraid" (John 14:27 NIV). This assured them of His continuing presence through the Holy Spirit, even though He would no longer be with them in the physical body.

Just as believers are assured of God's peace, we are urged to pursue peace and to live peaceably with all people. This Christian virtue is one of the nine "fruits" granted to believers by the Holy Spirit (Galatians 5:22–23).

Learn More: Psalm 55:18 / John 14:27; 16:33 / Ephesians 2:14 / 2 Timothy 2:22

PERSECUTION

There was a great persecution against the church which was at Jerusalem. Acts 8:1

Hostility against Christian believers by Jewish zealots broke out in Jerusalem after the death of Stephen, the first Christian martyr. This event fulfilled the prediction of Jesus that His followers would suffer persecution because of their faith in Him and their witness to unbelievers.

Godly people have been rejected by an unbelieving world since Old Testament times. The prophet Jeremiah was imprisoned by his own people for preaching that their country was headed for destruction unless they turned back to the Lord.

Jesus Himself was persecuted and eventually killed because He dared to question the sacred traditions of the Jewish law. His disciples and early followers were also mistreated because they proclaimed that Jesus was the long-awaited Messiah who offered salvation to a sinful world.

The apostle Peter wrote his first epistle to encourage believers who were undergoing persecution. Because they were suffering for a righteous cause, they had reason to be happy, or blessed (1 Peter 3:14). In His Sermon on the Mount, Jesus had declared, "Blessed are they which are persecuted for righteousness' sake: for theirs is the kingdom of heaven" (Matthew 5:10).

Learn More: Matthew 5:10–11; 24:9 / 2 Corinthians 4:8–9 / Colossians 1:24 / 2 Timothy 3:12

PERSEVERANCE

Be ye stedfast, unmoveable, always abounding in the work of the Lord. 1 Corinthians 15:58

The dictionary defines *perseverance* as "persistence in an undertaking in spite of opposition or discouragement." This is the trait that the apostle Paul desired for the believers in the church at Corinth. He wanted them to "keep on keeping on" in following Christ so they would be fruitful witnesses for Him in a city that was known for its pagan way of life.

While salvation results from faith alone, perseverance in doing good works in the Lord's name is one indication of authentic faith. The writer of the epistle of James put it like this: "As the body without the spirit is dead, so faith without works is dead also" (James 2:26).

The model of perseverance is Jesus Himself. Though hounded by His enemies, tempted by Satan, and misunderstood by His disciples, He completed His redemptive mission with His declaration from the cross: "It is finished" (John 19:30). The author of Hebrews urged his readers to finish the race of Christian discipleship by following Jesus' example.

Learn More: 1 Corinthians 7:37 / Ephesians 6:18 / Colossians 2:5 /
Hebrews 3:14; 6:19; 12:1–2 / 2 Peter 3:17

PETITION

The Lord hath given me my petition which I asked of him. 1 Samuel 1:27

Hannah was heartbroken because she was not able to have children. She took her request for a child to the Lord, who soon blessed her with a son, whom she named Samuel (1 Samuel 1:10–20). Hannah's request involving a personal need is a special form of prayer known as petition.

Because we are finite creatures, taking our requests to God is as natural as breathing. We face difficulties that are more than we can handle on our own. Like the psalmist, we seek help from the all-sufficient Lord. "In the day of my trouble I will call upon thee," he declared, "for thou wilt answer me" (Psalm 86:7).

Sometimes our personal requests to God don't bring what we consider a satisfactory answer. The apostle Paul prayed for an affliction that he referred to as his "thorn in the flesh" to be taken away. But this didn't happen, apparently because the Lord wanted to use this human weakness to show the adequacy of His own grace in Paul's life. In His wisdom, God always answers our petitions in the way that is best for us and in accordance with His purpose.

Learn More: Psalm 20:5 / Daniel 6:13 / 2 Corinthians 12:7–10

PRAISE

I will call on the Lord, who is worthy to be praised. 2 SAMUEL 22:4

King David uttered these words as he recalled how the Lord had blessed his life. God had chosen David the shepherd boy to succeed Saul as king of Israel. He kept David safe from the king's attempts to take his life. These memories led to the long prayer of praise that appears in 2 Samuel 22. Praise like this is one of the elements of authentic prayer.

The entire book of Psalms might be called "the praise book of the Bible." It is filled with expressions of praise to God for His loving concern and kindness toward His people. The different psalm writers praised the Lord for His goodness, mercy, truth, justice, righteousness, protection, and His instructions for daily living through His written word, the Bible. The book ends with this dramatic exclamation: "Let every thing that hath breath praise the LORD. Praise ye the LORD" (Psalm 150:6).

Most of us have good things to say about people whom we love and respect. So praise to the One who holds our very lives in His hand should be as natural as taking our next breath.

Learn More: 1 Chronicles 16:25 / Psalm 67:3 / Isaiah 12:5 / Acts 16:25 / Hebrews 13:15 / Revelation 19:5

PRAYER

If we ask any thing according to his will, he heareth us. 1 JOHN 5:14

In this verse the apostle John declares that the Lord has promised to hear our prayers when they are offered in faith and humility. The apostle Peter put it like this: "The eyes of the Lord are over the righteous, and his ears are open unto their prayers" (1 Peter 3:12).

Most of us think of prayer as asking God for His blessings and benefits. This is a form of prayer known as petition, bringing our personal requests before the Lord. But there is so much more to prayer than this. In our prayers, we should offer our adoration to God simply because He is and He deserves our highest praise. Thanksgiving is also a vital part of prayer; God should receive our thanks for specific ways in which He has blessed our lives.

No prayer to God is complete without the confession of our sins and our humble plea for His forgiveness. King David modeled this element of prayer after His sin of adultery with Bathsheba. "Have mercy upon me, O God, according to thy lovingkindness," he prayed. "Wash me throughly from mine iniquity, and cleanse me from my sin" (Psalm 51:1–2).

Learn More: Psalm 4:1; 69:13 / Daniel 9:17 / Matthew 6:7 / Luke 6:12 / Philippians 4:6

PREDESTINATION

In whom also we have obtained an inheritance, being predestinated... EPHESIANS 1:11

The term *predestination* comes from a Latin word that means "to decide upon beforehand." The apostle Paul declares in this verse that God had a plan for the salvation of the human race even before time began. Since He is all-knowing (or omniscient), He knows all things, even our choices long before we make them. So He knows who will become believers and part of His kingdom.

But God's foreknowledge of what will happen does not mean that He will predestinate some people to be saved and others to be eternally lost. Because of Adam and Eve's fall in the garden of Eden, people sin by their own free choice. No person deserves God's salvation, but His love for sinners applies to everyone. Paul expressed it like this: "The gospel of Christ...is the power of God unto salvation to every one that believeth" (Romans 1:16).

Learn More: Jeremiah 1:5 / Galatians 3:8 / Romans 8:29 / 1 Corinthians 2:7 /
Ephesians 1:5 / 1 Timothy 2:4

PRESENCE, GOD'S

I am with thee to deliver thee, saith the Lord. JEREMIAH 1:8

With these words the Lord promised Jeremiah he could depend on God's presence to enable the prophet to carry out the task he had been called to do. Jeremiah would need courage to warn his people of the calamity they faced unless they turned back to the Lord.

God's presence with His people is one of the dominant themes of the Bible. He promised to bless Abraham and his offspring and make them a blessing to others if they would remain faithful to the Lord. His presence was a source of strength to Moses and Joshua, who led the Israelites to claim the land God had promised to Abraham's descendants.

God's presence reached a new level when He sent His Son, Jesus, into the world. His coming was a fulfillment of Isaiah's prophecy of the coming Messiah. His name Emmanuel means "God with us" (Matthew 1:23).

Believers feel Jesus' strength and presence through the action of the Holy Spirit. As Jesus Himself promised, "I will pray the Father, and he shall give you another Comforter, that he may abide with you for ever" (John 14:16).

Learn More: Genesis 12:1–7 / Exodus 3:12; 33:14 / Joshua 1:5 / Psalm 16:11; 139:7 / Isaiah 7:14 / Matthew 1:23

PRIDE

In lowliness of mind let each esteem other better than themselves. PHILIPPIANS 2:3

In this verse the apostle Paul encouraged the believers at Philippi to avoid pride, or a feeling of arrogance about one's accomplishments or status in life. Pride is the very opposite of humility, or putting others before oneself. Excessive pride is a serious sin because it attributes to oneself the glory and honor that belong to God alone.

Jesus told a parable about a self-righteous Pharisee and a penitent tax collector to emphasize the problem of pride. Both men went to the temple to pray. The proud Pharisee thanked God that he was not a sinner like other people. But the humble tax collector prayed, "God be merciful to me a sinner" (Luke 18:13).

Jesus made it clear which of these two men found favor in God's sight. The humble tax collector went home justified before God, Jesus noted, "For every one that exalteth himself shall be abased; and he that humbleth himself shall be exalted" (Luke 18:14).

Learn More: Psalm 10:2 / Proverbs 16:18 / Philippians 2:3–6 / 1 John 2:16

PRIESTHOOD

Ye. . .are built up a spiritual house, an holy priesthood. 1 PETER 2:5

Under the Mosaic law, the priesthood was limited to members of the tribe of Levi and the family of Aaron. But the apostle Peter in this verse declares that all Christians are priests. They belong to the universal priesthood of all believers because of the atoning sacrifice of Christ.

In Old Testament times, only the high priest was allowed to enter the holy of holies, the most sacred spot in the temple in Jerusalem. But when Jesus died on the cross, the curtain that stood before this sacred space was split from top to bottom. This showed that all people now had equal access to God's presence (Matthew 27:50–51).

The doctrine of universal priesthood also emphasizes the ministry responsibility of all believers. As priests of God, we are commissioned to reach out to others in a spirit of love. The apostle Paul expressed it like this: "Now then we are ambassadors for Christ, as though God did beseech you by us: we pray you in Christ's stead, be ye reconciled to God" (2 Corinthians 5:20).

Learn More: Ephesians 3:11–12 / Hebrews 4:15–16 / 1 Peter 4:10

PROPHECY

Holy men of God spake as they were moved by the Holy Ghost. 2 PETER 1:21

This verse from the apostle Peter makes it clear that biblical prophecy originates with God not human beings. Prophecy is a divine message to the world, inspired by the Holy Spirit and issued through the Lord's righteous spokesmen.

Throughout biblical history God raised up courageous prophets who received His commands and passed them on to others. One of the best examples of this process is the prophet Nathan. This brave messenger was sent by the Lord to confront King David about his adulterous affair with Bathsheba and the murder of her husband. Nathan also predicted that the child conceived through this affair would die. This sober message led the king to confess his sin and repent (2 Samuel 12:1–14).

Some biblical prophets were *forthtellers* as well as *foretellers*—that is, they delivered God's message for the present as well as the future. For example, the prophet Isaiah predicted the coming of the Messiah in the future. But he also delivered the good news from the Lord that King Hezekiah would not die from a serious illness (2 Kings 20:4–6).

Learn More: Jeremiah 7:25 / Amos 3:7 / Luke 13:33 / 1 Corinthians 13:2 / James 5:10

PROPITIATION

God. . .sent his Son to be the propitiation for our sins. 1 JOHN 4:10

The word *propitiation* comes from an Old English word meaning "to appease" or "to satisfy." Thus, the apostle John says in this verse that God the Father sent His Son, Jesus, to serve as the satisfaction for our sins. This word is the key to one of the classical theories of the atonement, or the sacrificial death of Jesus.

According to this view, God is a holy God who cannot tolerate sin. This puts us as humans in a dilemma because we are not capable of living a sinless life, no matter how hard we try. To make matters worse, the Lord is also a just God who is determined to punish sin wherever He finds it. So our sin separates us from Him and makes us liable to His punishment. *Hopeless* is the only word that adequately describes this situation.

But God loved us too much to allow us to remain in this situation. He sent Jesus to die to pay the penalty that He demanded from us because of our sin. Jesus was the sacrifice that covered over or atoned for our sin and restored the broken relationship between a holy God and sinful people.

Learn More: Mark 10:45 / Romans 3:24–25 / 1 John 2:2

PUNISHMENT

I will punish the world for their evil, and the wicked for their iniquity. ISAIAH 13:11

This message from the Lord through the prophet Isaiah shows His determination to punish sin and wrongdoing in the world. Since God is sovereign, He has the right to set the standards for human behavior.

In the Mosaic law of the Old Testament, specific punishments were listed for crimes committed against others. For example, a person injured in an act of violence was to be compensated for his loss of productivity. The general Old Testament rule was repayment in kind for any loss suffered, or "eye for eye" (Exodus 21:24).

Jesus' teachings on forgiveness and redemption take center stage in the New Testament, making punishment a secondary concern. But the concept of eternal punishment for those who refuse to accept Christ as Savior and Lord emerges in the writings of the apostle Paul. He declared that unbelievers will be "punished with everlasting destruction" in the final judgment (2 Thessalonians 1:8–9). The worst part of this punishment will be eternal separation from God's presence.

Learn More: Genesis 4:13; 19:24–25 / Numbers 14:26–35 / Proverbs 19:19 /
Matthew 25:46 / Acts 5:1–11 / Galatians 6:7

PURITY

Many went. . .up to Jerusalem before the passover, to purify themselves. JOHN 11:55

The Jewish people had strict rules about staying clean and pure. The Old Testament law prescribed purification rites for people who had been defiled by touching a corpse, by contact with bodily discharges, by childbirth, and by leprosy. Before they celebrated a major religious festival such as the Passover, they went through prescribed washing rituals to make sure they were worthy to stand in the presence of a holy God.

Jesus had no patience with such practices. On one occasion the Pharisees criticized Him and His disciples for not purifying their hands in an elaborate washing ritual before eating. Jesus told them, "What goes into someone's mouth does not defile them, but what comes out of their mouth, that is what defiles them" (Matthew 15:11 NIV).

To Jesus, real purity is not a matter of keeping external rules but aligning one's heart and actions with the will and purpose of God.

Learn More: Matthew 15:1–11 / Philippians 4:8 / 1 Timothy 5:22 / Titus 1:15 / James 3:17; 4:8 / 1 Peter 1:22 / 1 John 3:3

RECONCILIATION

If, when we were enemies, we were reconciled to God by the death of his Son. . . ROMANS 5:10

The basic meaning of the word *reconciliation* is "to exchange." In a spiritual sense, reconciliation is the process by which our separation from God is exchanged for a relationship of peace and fellowship. This is how the apostle Paul used the word in this verse.

This exchange is possible because of Christ's sacrifice on our behalf. Our sin barred us from fellowship with a holy God. But His Son's atoning death paid the penalty demanded by our sin and allowed us to enter into God's presence.

Our union with the Lord in a fellowship of joy comes about solely through the Lord's initiative. There is nothing we can do on our own to bring about this sense of peace in His presence. All we can do is accept in humility the reconciliation that He offers through the death of His Son. As the apostle Paul expressed it, "All things are of God, who hath reconciled us to himself by Jesus Christ" (2 Corinthians 5:18).

Learn More: Hebrews 2:17 / 2 Corinthians 5:19–20 / Colossians 1:20

REDEMPTION

Who gave himself for us, that he might redeem us from all iniquity. TITUS 2:14

The concept of redemption reflects the close family ties of Old Testament times. A near relative would sometimes "redeem" a kinsman who had fallen on hard times by paying his debt or buying back his property from foreclosure. This is what happened in the book of Ruth. Boaz, a kinsman of Naomi's deceased husband, bought back the property he had lost and restored it to Naomi (Ruth 4:1–9).

This redemption process is a good illustration of the work of Christ, who "bought us back" from sin and death through His atoning death on the cross. He was sent to earth by God the Father as the agent of His divine plan of redemption. Jesus Himself declared, "The Son of man came not to be ministered unto, but to minister, and to give his life a ransom for many" (Mark 10:45).

Jesus never wavered from His mission to redeem a sinful world. Through His suffering and death, He rescued us when we were hopeless and bankrupt, unable to help ourselves.

Learn More: Psalm 107:2 / Isaiah 43:1 / Matthew 20:28 / Romans 4:25 / Galatians 3:13 / Ephesians 1:7

REMISSION

Repent. . .in the name of Jesus Christ for the remission of sins. ACTS 2:38

The apostle Peter preached to the crowds gathered in Jerusalem to celebrate the festival of Pentecost. Convicted of their sin, many people asked how they should respond to His message that Jesus was the Messiah whom God had sent as His agent of salvation. Peter responded that repentance and acceptance of Jesus as Savior were the only ways to receive remission of their sins.

Remission is a form of the word *remit*, which means "to release" or "to relax." The Greek term behind this English word suggests that God's forgiveness is active rather than passive in nature. He has actually taken the initiative through the death of His Son to set people free from sin's bondage. Remission is often linked with repentance, as in the verse above and in the preaching of John the Baptist (Mark 1:4).

Jesus declared that His blood was "shed for many for the remission of sins" (Matthew 26:28). Most modern translations render "remission of sins" as "forgiveness of sins" (see Acts 10:43 NIV).

Learn More: Luke 1:76–77; 3:3; 24:47 / Romans 3:25 / Hebrews 9:22; 10:18

REMNANT

The remnant of Israel. . .shall stay upon the Lord. ISAIAH 10:20

The prophet Isaiah had some bad news and some good news for the nation of Judah. God would punish the people for their unfaithfulness by allowing them to be conquered by a foreign power. But a righteous remnant—a small portion—of God's people would be preserved and would eventually return to their homeland (Isaiah 1:7–9).

The first prediction occurred when the Babylonians overran Judah and the people were taken into exile. The second prophecy was fulfilled two generations later when some of the people returned and resettled their homeland.

Moses was the first person to speak of a righteous remnant of God's people. Even before they settled in Canaan, he predicted they would eventually be scattered among the nations, but a portion of them would survive and reclaim their territory (Deuteronomy 28:62–68).

In the New Testament, the apostle Paul declared that the new remnant consisted of the followers of Jesus. They continued His work of redemption through the Church, the community of the faithful for which He gave His life.

Learn More: 2 Kings 19:30 / Ezra 9:8 / Isaiah 11:11 / Jeremiah 23:3 / Ezekiel 6:8 / Romans 11:5

REPENTANCE

That they should repent and turn to God, and do works meet for repentance. ACTS 26:20

The apostle Paul made this statement in his defense before King Agrippa. Paul made it clear that repentance was the first human step toward salvation. True repentance involves confessing one's sin, turning from it, and asking God's forgiveness.

The best example of repentance in the Old Testament is that of King David. After he committed adultery with Bathsheba, he prayed to the Lord, "Wash away all my iniquity and cleanse me from my sin. . . . Create in me a pure heart, O God, and renew a steadfast spirit within me" (Psalm 51:2, 10 NIV).

In the New Testament, John the Baptist called on people to repent and turn to the Lord (Matthew 3:2). Jesus continued John's emphasis on repentance as the first step for those who wanted to enter His kingdom (Mark 1:15).

Repentance is not just for unbelievers. It is also essential for Christians who yield to temptation and fall into sin. The apostle Peter declared that God "is longsuffering. . .not willing that any should perish, but that all should come to repentance" (2 Peter 3:9).

Learn More: 2 Chronicles 7:14 / Job 42:6 / Matthew 4:17 / Luke 15:7

REST

Let us labour therefore to enter into that rest. HEBREWS 4:11

According to the dictionary, *rest* as a noun means "to refrain from action or motion." All of us have experienced the need to sit and rest after working for a while in the hot summer sun. But to the author of Hebrews, the concept of rest referred to the Lord's promise of heavenly peace to His people (Hebrews 4:1–11).

God promised His people, the Israelites, a land of rest that they could call their own. This eventually happened, although their failure to trust the Lord led to a forty-year period of aimless wandering in the wilderness. The author of Hebrews cautioned Christian believers against making this same mistake.

During His earthly ministry, Jesus told His followers, "Take my yoke upon you, and learn of me; for I am meek and lowly in heart: and ye shall find rest unto your souls" (Matthew 11:29).

The rest that Jesus promises is eternal fellowship with Him in heaven as well as peace of mind in the here and now. We can relax in the assurance that our future is in His hands.

Learn More: Genesis 2:2–3 / Exodus 33:14 / Psalm 23:3; 95:7–11 / Revelation 14:13

RESURRECTION

But if there be no resurrection of the dead, then is Christ not risen. 1 CORINTHIANS 15:13

This classic passage from the apostle Paul emphasizes the importance of the doctrine of the resurrection. Jesus' victory over death and the grave assures believers they will also experience bodily resurrection in the afterlife.

After His resurrection, Jesus spent forty days among His followers before ascending to His heavenly Father. This convinced them He was still alive and motivated them to continue His witness in the world through the church.

Even before His death, Jesus told His disciples that He would be killed and buried, only to emerge from the grave after three days (Mark 9:31). In a conversation with Martha, sister of Lazarus, Jesus assured her that He was the resurrection and the life—master over life and death. He then made good on His claim by raising Lazarus from the dead.

The apostle Peter echoed Paul's words about Jesus' resurrection and the promise of eternal life that this represented. God the Father had blessed believers with "a lively hope by the resurrection of Jesus Christ from the dead" (1 Peter 1:3).

Learn More: John 11:25 / Acts 4:33 / Philippians 3:10, 20–21

REVELATION

Neither was I taught it, but by the revelation of Jesus Christ. GALATIANS 1:12

How do we as earthbound beings come to know God, who is beyond our human experience? The apostle Paul declares in this verse that such knowledge comes through God's revelation. He has acted to make Himself known to us.

God reveals Himself in a general way through the physical world. The complexity of nature shows that He is all-powerful and that He has put order and design into His creation (Job 37:14–19).

The Lord also makes Himself known through "special revelation." His interaction with His chosen people, the Israelites, made it clear that He was a holy God who expected righteous behavior from them. But the best example of His special revelation is the Bible. It contains a record of His acts in history and His guidelines for daily living. Through scripture, His Word, we understand what God is like and how He wants us to act.

God's revelation is progressive in nature. People of biblical times dealt with their sin by offering sacrificial animals at the altar. Since the coming of Jesus, we are cleansed of sin through the redemptive death of His Son and our acceptance of Him as our Lord and Savior.

Learn More: Isaiah 40:5 / Matthew 16:17 / Romans 1:17 / 1 Corinthians 2:10

RIGHTEOUSNESS

The Lord is righteous in all his ways, and holy in all his works. Psalm 145:17

Righteousness is an attribute or characteristic of God that signifies His holiness, moral purity, justice, and acts of goodness. The term comes from a root word that means "straightness." Only God is perfectly straight or upright in "all His ways," as the psalmist put it.

The sinful nature of humans prevents them from reaching God's standard of righteous living. The apostle Paul declared, "There is none righteous, no, not one" (Romans 3:10). Since we cannot attain holy living on our own, we must depend on God to assign His righteousness to us.

This transfer is possible because of Jesus' sacrificial death on the cross. God grants the righteousness of His Son to those who place their trust in Him as Lord and Savior. As Paul stated, Jesus the sinless One was made "sin on our behalf, so that we might become the righteousness of God in Him" (2 Corinthians 5:21 nasb).

Several centuries before Jesus was born, the prophet Isaiah referred to Him as God's "righteous servant" (Isaiah 53:11). He was the Messiah who came to earth on a mission of redemption for the entire world.

Learn More: Matthew 6:33 / Romans 5:19; 10:9-10 / 2 Corinthians 5:21 / Titus 3:5

SACRIFICE

Noah. . .offered burnt offerings on the altar. Genesis 8:20

The first thing Noah did after he and his family left the ark was to build an altar and make a sacrificial offering to the Lord. The burning of an animal on the altar expressed the family's thanksgiving to God for preserving them from the great flood.

In Old Testament times, the Israelites presented many different types of sacrificial offerings. These sacred gifts were acts of worship that were thought to intercede on their behalf with God Himself. The most important sacrifice was known as the sin offering. In this ritual the blood or flesh of an animal such as a lamb or a young bull was offered to the Lord as a sort of "substitute payment" to atone for sin.

With the coming of God's Son, Jesus Christ, and His atoning death, the need for these Old Testament rituals no longer exists. The sacrifices that God desires today are acts of obedience and service. These are what the apostle Paul referred to as "living sacrifices" (Romans 12:1).

Learn More: 1 Samuel 15:22 / Psalm 116:17 / Jonah 2:9 / Hebrews 9:11-14 / 1 Peter 2:5

SAINTHOOD

Earnestly contend for the faith which was once delivered unto the saints. Jude 3

Most people think of saints as Christians honored by a church organization for their devotion to God—for example, Saint Augustine or Saint Theresa. But the word is used in the New Testament for all believers—those who have accepted Jesus as their Savior and have committed their lives to Him. This is how the author of the epistle of Jude used the term.

The apostle Paul was particularly fond of using the word *saints* in this way. For example, he told the believers at Rome that he was on his way to Jerusalem "to minister unto the saints" (Romans 15:25). He also spoke of the wonders of the Gospel of grace that had been "made manifest to his saints" (Colossians 1:26).

So according to Paul, Christians don't have to wait for centuries to be recognized for their saintly way of life or their contribution to the church. If you are a believer in Christ, you are automatically a saint.

Learn More: Matthew 27:52 / Romans 12:13 / 1 Corinthians 1:2 / Ephesians 4:11-12

SALVATION

Neither is there salvation in any other. Acts 4:12

The apostle Peter made this bold statement to the Jewish religious leaders in Jerusalem. They questioned him and the apostle John about their healing of a lame man. Peter declared that his authority came from the risen Christ. Faith in Jesus was the only way to be delivered from sin.

In the Old Testament, the word *salvation* often refers to deliverance from physical danger (Exodus 14:13). But by New Testament times, the term was used for spiritual release from the bondage of sin. Jesus' mission was to bring salvation to a lost and hopeless world.

The salvation offered by Jesus has three dimensions: past, present, and future. We *have been saved* because of our faith in Christ and His atoning death (Acts 16:31). We are in the process of *being saved* from sin's power (Philippians 2:12). We *will be saved* in the end time from the very presence of sin (Romans 13:11).

The process of salvation includes several other biblical ideas. These include Adoption, Imputation, Justification, Reconciliation, Redemption, and Repentance (see individual entries for each).

Learn More: 2 Samuel 22:47 / Psalm 18:46 / Luke 19:9 / Romans 10:10 /
Ephesians 2:8–9 / Hebrews 2:3 / 1 Peter 1:8–9

SANCTIFICATION

And the very God of peace sanctify you wholly. 1 Thessalonians 5:23

Sanctification is the process of consecrating or setting something apart for a holy purpose. The apostle Paul in this verse expressed his hope that the Thessalonian believers would be set apart by the Lord for service to others in His name.

In the Old Testament, priests, Levites, and each family's firstborn child were consecrated to the Lord. In the New Testament, sanctification was regarded as a work of grace following conversion (Philippians 1:6), a work of the Holy Spirit. The result is purification from the guilt and grip of sin.

God calls all believers to holiness and sanctification. Those sanctified are committed to God's truth and serve as witnesses to His power and grace in the world (Romans 6:11–13). Sanctification is a process that continues throughout our lives as believers. It will be completed only when we are "made perfect" in the presence of the Lord in heaven (Hebrews 12:23).

Learn More: Leviticus 20:7 / 1 Corinthians 6:11 / 1 Thessalonians 4:3, 7 /
2 Thessalonians 2:13 / Romans 6:11–13 / Hebrews 10:14

SCRIPTURE

These were more noble. . .and searched the scriptures daily. Acts 17:11

This verse contrasts the reception that the apostle Paul received in the cities of Thessalonica and Berea. The Thessalonians sent Paul away, while the people of Berea searched the Old Testament scriptures to verify his claim that Jesus was the Messiah. This shows the need for an eager and open-minded approach to God's written Word, the holy scriptures.

Paul had a high view of the Bible. "All scripture," he declared, "is given by inspiration of God" (2 Timothy 3:16). Because the Bible is of divine origin, it tells us how to live in accordance with God's will and purpose.

The scriptures are a treasury of godly wisdom to help us make good decisions. They lift us up during life's "downer" moments. They equip us to perform good works in the name of Jesus. They lead us to seek the glory of God rather than the praise of others in everything we do. They provide assurance of eternal life for those who trust in Jesus Christ as Lord and Savior.

Learn More: Matthew 22:29 / John 5:39 / Acts 8:35 / Romans 15:4 /
2 Timothy 3:16 / 2 Peter 1:20

SECOND COMING OF CHRIST

And if I go and prepare a place for you, I will come again. John 14:3

During His earthly ministry, Jesus promised His followers that He would return to earth after His death, resurrection, and ascension to the Father. But He also indicated that the time of His second coming was uncertain. This called for them to live in a state of watchful readiness. Jesus could return at any time, perhaps when His followers least expected it (Matthew 24:40–42). His second coming will be in accord with God's plan, just as He originally came to earth in the "fulness of time" (Galatians 4:4).

The second coming will happen suddenly, and Jesus will be "revealed from heaven with His mighty angels" (2 Thessalonians 1:7). He will raise the dead, destroy death, gather the redeemed, judge the world, and reward God's people.

We are not called as believers to spend our days trying to determine the exact time of the second coming. While looking forward eagerly to His return, we should be busy carrying out His Great Commission and sharing the Gospel in a dark and sinful world.

Learn More: Matthew 16:27; 24:31; 25:13 / Acts 1:8–11 / 1 Thessalonians 4:13–17

SERVANTHOOD

Behold my servant, whom I uphold; mine elect, in whom my soul delighteth. Isaiah 42:1

Several people in the Bible, including Moses, are called God's servant (Exodus 14:31). But Jesus Christ stands out above all the others who have devoted their lives to faithful service to the Lord. In this verse the prophet Isaiah predicted that humble service would be one of the marks of Jesus' ministry.

Isaiah also predicted that Jesus the Messiah would undergo great suffering while carrying out His mission (Isaiah 53:3–5). But this would be for a divine purpose. His suffering and death would provide a means of deliverance for the human race, which was trapped in sin.

On one occasion Jesus' disciples began to argue over who would occupy the places of honor in His future glory. He gently reminded them: "Whosoever of you will be the chiefest, shall be servant of all. For even the Son of man came not to be ministered unto, but to minister, and to give his life a ransom for many" (Mark 10:44–45).

Today the servant work of Jesus continues through His church. Those who belong to Him are automatically in the serving business.

Learn More: Psalm 119:125 / Matthew 23:11 / Luke 22:27 / Galatians 4:7 / Philippians 2:7

SIN

The blood of Jesus Christ his Son cleanseth us from all sin. 1 John 1:7

Sin was introduced into the human race when Adam and Eve disobeyed God in the garden of Eden—and sin has infected the human race ever since. The apostle Paul declared, "There is none righteous, no, not one" (Romans 3:10).

One of the most graphic images for sin in the Bible comes from a Greek word that means "to miss the mark." When we disobey God and fall into sin, we fall short of the goal that God intends for our lives.

Sin is not only doing what is wrong. We also sin when we fail to do what we know is right. This is sometimes referred to as the "sin of omission." The Bible also makes a distinction between *sin* and *sins*. "Sin" refers to our corrupt nature, while "sins" refers to wrong deeds or actions. Christ died for both our evil nature and our evil acts.

The consequence of sin is spiritual death, but God's gracious gift is forgiveness of our sins and eternal life through the atoning death of Jesus Christ (Romans 6:23).

Learn More: Genesis 3:6 / Job 13:23 / Matthew 26:28 / 2 Corinthians 5:21 / James 4:17 / 1 John 4:10

SOUL

God. . .breathed into his nostrils the breath of life; and man became a living soul. Genesis 2:7

The term *soul* has several distinct meanings in scripture. In this verse the word refers to Adam's inner life, his essence as a person created in God's image. As a living soul, he received a spiritual sensitivity from the Lord that made him different than the rest of the animal world.

But in other passages, soul can refer to people, as in Abraham's taking the "souls," or household servants whom he owned, to Canaan (Genesis 12:5). The term is also used in reference to oneself, as in the friendship of Jonathan, who loved David "as his own soul" (1 Samuel 18:1).

In the New Testament, the word is often used in reference to life in general. Perhaps the most famous example of this meaning is Jesus' warning against depending on the things of this world for security rather than on Him. "What is a man profited, if he shall gain the whole world, and lose his own soul?" He asked. "Or what shall a man give in exchange for his soul?" (Matthew 16:26).

Learn More: Job 19:2 / Psalm 35:9 / Lamentations 3:24 / John 12:27 / Romans 13:1 / 1 Peter 2:11

STUMBLING BLOCK

But we preach Christ crucified, unto the Jews a stumblingblock. 1 Corinthians 1:23

The Jews expected the Messiah to be a military hero who would deliver them from Roman oppression. Instead, Jesus was a spiritual leader who died on a Roman cross. This was a hindrance to belief, or a stumbling block, for many Jews of Paul's time.

In the Old Testament, the prophet Ezekiel described pagan idols as a threat to the people's belief in the one true God—and thus a stumbling block. Another prophet, Jeremiah, warned that God would use a foreign nation as a stumbling block to Judah unless the people turned back to the Lord.

A phrase that means basically the same thing as stumbling block is "rock of offence" (Romans 9:33). Paul describes Jesus with this phrase because God's grace and faith in His Son are now the keys to salvation. Jews who had always depended on works and keeping the law to make them acceptable to God found this hard to swallow.

The apostle Paul urged believers to avoid all activities that might cause weaker Christians to fall into sin. This establishes a valuable principle for modern believers: "Decide never to put a stumbling block or pitfall in your brother's way" (Romans 14:13 HCSB).

Learn More: Jeremiah 6:21; 18:15 / Ezekiel 14:3–4 / 1 Corinthians 8:9 / Revelation 2:14

SUBMISSION

Submitting yourselves one to another in the fear of God. Ephesians 5:18, 21

These two verses introduce the apostle Paul's famous passage about the need for believers to submit themselves to one another. He continues through Ephesians 6:9 to list the submissive relationships he had in mind: wives should submit to their husbands, children should obey their parents, and servants should be subject to their masters.

But Paul does not let husbands, parents, and masters off the hook. He goes on to list their responsibilities to those who are submissive to them. Husbands should love their wives, fathers should treat their children with courtesy and respect, and masters should not be cruel or overbearing toward their servants. *What's fair is fair,* Paul seems to be saying. *If you expect others to defer to you, you should reflect the spirit of Christ in your relationship with them.*

The concept of submission does not imply that some people are inferior to others. Jesus submitted Himself to God the Father, but the Son was not inferior to the Father (John 17:1–5). Even though Jesus had all power, He was the very personification of humility (Matthew 11:29). He is the example that believers should follow in all their relationships.

Learn More: James 4:7 / 1 Peter 5:5

SUPPLICATION

With my voice unto the Lord did I make my supplication. PSALM 142:1

The term *supplication* is a part of the vocabulary of prayer. In meaning, it is similar to petition, which is a request to God involving a need of the person who is calling upon God. But when the word *supplication* appears in the Bible, it seems to refer to the state of mind of the supplicant.

In the verse above, for example, the psalmist David cried out to the Lord in desperation while hiding from King Saul in a cave. David went on to acknowledge his despair and loneliness at a time when "no man cared for my soul" (Psalm 142:4).

Sometimes a prayer of supplication is one offered in humility. For example, in King Solomon's long prayer at the dedication of the temple, the word *supplication* appears several times. Solomon was overwhelmed at God's graciousness to His people and His blessings that enabled the king to complete this ambitious building project.

Learn More: 1 Kings 8:45–54 / Psalm 6:9; 31:22; 140:6 / Jeremiah 37:20 / Daniel 9:3 / Philippians 4:6 / 1 Timothy 5:5

TEMPERANCE

But I keep under my body, and bring it into subjection. 1 CORINTHIANS 9:27

The campaign against alcoholic beverages in the United States during the early 1900s was called the "temperance movement." This campaign has given the word a restricted meaning to most people. But temperance in the biblical sense is much wider in scope.

In the verse above, for example, the apostle Paul refers to the discipline he exercises over his body to assure he is a credible witness for Christ. The concept of self-control is what he had in mind. This is basically what temperance means—a calm, moderate, and balanced approach to life that leads to mastery of fleshly impulses such as sexual desire and greed.

Temperance is one of the nine virtues mentioned by Paul in his famous passage on the fruit of the spirit (Galatians 5:22–23). The appearance of the word in this context means that temperance or self-control is possible only because of the influence of the Holy Spirit in the lives of believers.

Learn More: Proverbs 25:28 / 1 Corinthians 9:25 / 1 Thessalonians 5:6 / Titus 1:8 / 2 Peter 1:6

TEMPTATION

And he said unto the woman, Yea, hath God said. . . GENESIS 3:1

This verse contains the first recorded instance of temptation in the Bible. Satan, in the form of a snake, placed doubt in the mind of Eve about the fruit that God had forbidden her to eat. She fell for Satan's trickery and ate, thus plunging humankind into a state of sin.

Temptation is any enticement to disobey God that arises in the human mind. A thought does not become a sin until a person acts on the desire. But thoughts have great power. If kept in the mind long enough, they can result in sinful actions.

For this reason, believers should monitor their minds constantly and replace tempting thoughts with reflections that are pure and uplifting. Here is how the apostle Paul expressed this idea: "Whatsoever things are true, whatsoever things are honest, whatsoever things are just, whatsoever things are pure, whatsoever things are lovely, whatsoever things are of good report; if there be any virtue, and if there be any praise, think on these things" (Philippians 4:8).

Learn More: Matthew 4:1 / 1 Corinthians 10:1–13 / Galatians 6:1 / 2 Peter 2:9 / Hebrews 4:15

TEN COMMANDMENTS

He wrote upon the tables the words of the covenant, the ten commandments. EXODUS 34:28

The Ten Commandments are the ethical commands given by the Lord to Moses on Mount Sinai. Also called the Decalogue, the Ten Commandments summarize the basic moral laws of the Old Testament. They are the very heart of the special covenant between God and His people, the Israelites. While handed down by God more than three thousand years ago, they are still authoritative in our own time.

Four of these commandments deal with our responsibilities to God: recognize the Lord alone as God, have nothing to do with pagan gods, do not misuse the Lord's name, and sanctify the Sabbath day (Exodus 20:1–11).

The last six commandments deal with obligations to other people, including honoring one's father and mother, not committing murder, not engaging in adultery, not taking another person's property, not bearing false witness, and not desiring anything that belongs to others (Exodus 20:12–17).

Jesus summed up these commandments in two great principles—supreme love for God and loving our neighbors as ourselves (Matthew 22:37–40).

Learn More: Exodus 19:16–19; 20:1–17 / Deuteronomy 5:7–22

TITHING

He gave him tithes of all. GENESIS 14:20

The concept of tithing began with Abraham. He gave a priest named Melchizedek a tenth of the spoils he had taken from several kings who had captured Abraham's nephew Lot. This gesture showed that Abraham recognized Melchizedek as a fellow worshipper of the one true God.

From that point on, the tithe was an important element in the religious practice of God's chosen people, the Israelites. The Mosaic law specified that they were to present a tenth of their crops and livestock as a special offering to God. After the people returned from exile in Babylon and Persia, the prophet Malachi accused them of willful disobedience by failing to present their tithes and offerings to the Lord.

The New Testament does not specifically command tithing. But believers should be generous in sharing their material possessions and in supporting the work of the kingdom of God. Our giving should be motivated by love for Jesus Christ, who is the model of generosity and sacrifice.

Learn More: Genesis 28:22 / Leviticus 27:30–32 / Numbers 18:21–32 /
Malachi 3:8–12 / Luke 11:42 / Hebrews 7:5–6

TRANSFIGURATION, THE

Jesus. . .was transfigured before them. MARK 9:2

The change in Jesus' appearance as He prayed before these three disciples is referred to as the transfiguration. Peter, James, and John were probably shocked when Jesus' face took on a different appearance and His clothes became "dazzling white" (Mark 9:3 NLT).

This event looked ahead to what Jesus had told His disciples several times—that He would be glorified by God the Father, be received into heaven, and then return to earth one day in all His glory (Matthew 25:31). He was giving these disciples a glimpse of His glorified body to strengthen them for the time when He would be crucified but then gloriously resurrected.

Two key Old Testament personalities—Moses and Elijah—appeared and discussed Jesus' approaching death. Their presence pointed to Jesus as the fulfillment of the Old Testament promise of the Messiah. From a cloud, God the Father spoke to the three disciples: "This is my beloved Son: hear him" (Luke 9:35).

Peter, James, and John must have taken these words seriously. After Jesus' ascension, they became faithful witnesses in the early church.

Learn More: Exodus 34:29 / Luke 9:28–36 / 2 Peter 1:16–18

TRINITY

He that raised up Christ. . .shall also quicken your mortal bodies by his Spirit. ROMANS 8:11

The doctrine of the Trinity declares that God expresses Himself through three distinct realities as Father, Son, and Holy Spirit. At the creation, God's Spirit hovered over the formless mass that He shaped into the orderly universe (Genesis 1:2). And the Gospel of John declares that Jesus the Son was active with God the Father in the creation process (John 1:1–3).

All three persons of the Trinity were also present at Jesus' baptism when He launched His public ministry. As Jesus came out of the water, "he saw the Spirit of God descending like a dove, and lighting upon him: and lo a voice from heaven, saying, This is my beloved Son, in whom I am well pleased" (Matthew 3:16–17).

The experience of believers as recipients of salvation also confirms the reality of the Trinity. God's love for sinful humankind motivated Him to send His Son, Jesus, as an atoning sacrifice. Jesus was obedient to His Father's will and died on the cross to redeem humankind from bondage to sin. Through the work of God's Spirit, people are convicted of their sin and moved to repent and accept God's generous gift.

Learn More: Galatians 4:6

TRUTH

For the Lord is good. . .and his truth endureth to all generations. PSALM 100:5

The psalmist praised the Lord because He is the sum and substance of truth. As the God of truth, He is trustworthy and dependable. He does not shift with the changing times but is the same yesterday, today, and forever.

We live in a world in which deception and half-truths abound. Businesses make false claims about their products and services. Investment hucksters cheat the elderly out of their retirement savings. Athletes take performance-enhancing drugs to give themselves an edge over their competitors. In a society like this, it's tempting to give in to despair and determine to trust no one.

But we can place our ultimate trust in the Lord. He is the source of all truth, and He always deals with us in integrity. He never makes any false claims that He cannot live up to.

Just like His heavenly Father, Jesus is the ultimate definition of truth. In the prologue to his Gospel, the apostle John declared, "The law was given by Moses, but grace and truth came by Jesus Christ" (John 1:17).

Learn More: Psalm 119:142 / John 14:6 / Romans 3:4 / Ephesians 6:14 / 1 Timothy 3:15

VANITY

Vanity of vanities, saith the Preacher, vanity of vanities; all is vanity. ECCLESIASTES 1:2

In our modern culture, the word *vanity* usually refers to people with an over-the-top sense of their own importance. When pride and conceit were handed out, they seemed to receive more than their share.

But vanity in the biblical sense refers to something that is meaningless or lacking in purpose. Throughout the book of Ecclesiastes, King Solomon of Israel used this word repeatedly to describe life as he had experienced it "under the sun." He looked for meaning in work, wisdom, knowledge, pleasure, money, and power. But he concluded that none of these things brought happiness or joy when pursued as ends in themselves.

After twelve chapters of empty searching, Solomon ended his book with a declaration on the one thing that infuses life with purpose: "Fear God, and keep his commandments," he concluded, "for this is the whole duty of man" (Ecclesiastes 12:13).

Learn More: Psalm 2:1; 127:1 / Proverbs 31:30 / Matthew 6:7 / 1 Corinthians 3:20 / 2 Timothy 2:16

WARFARE, SPIRITUAL

For we wrestle. . .against spiritual wickedness in high places. EPHESIANS 6:12

This verse is part of the apostle Paul's classic passage on spiritual warfare—or the struggle that Christians face in trying to live out their faith in a sinful world.

The apostle compares this conflict to a wrestling match in which believers do battle with the temptations of Satan. His allies are invisible demonic forces that wield great power. Their goal is to wreck the work of Christ and put a halt to the positive influence of His followers.

Just as a Roman soldier is well equipped for physical battle, Christians need an arsenal of spiritual weapons to overcome Satan's power. Paul refers to these as the "whole armour of God" (verse 13)—truth, righteousness, the assurance of the Gospel, faith, salvation, the Word of God, and prayer.

Equipped with these weapons and guided by the Holy Spirit, believers are assured of victory in this crucial battle.

Learn More: John 17:15 / Romans 12:2 / 2 Corinthians 4:4; 6:14 /
Ephesians 6:10–18 / 1 Timothy 6:12 / 2 Timothy 2:3

WITNESS

Ye also shall bear witness, because ye have been with me from the beginning. JOHN 15:27

In this verse Jesus left no doubt that the twelve disciples whom He had trained would become witnesses for Him after His earthly ministry ended. A witness gives testimony about something he has seen or experienced. The best examples of this are people who testify in a trial: their task is to tell the court what they know from personal experience that is relevant to the case under investigation.

The witness that Jesus bore about God grew out of His personal experience. He knew God like no one has ever known Him. Jesus came into the world to show that His Father is a merciful God who relates to His people in love and grace. By dying on the cross, Jesus showed just how much God the Father and God the Son love us.

Those of us who are transformed by God's love are also charged to give testimony about His love to others. This witnessing work continues through the church and individual believers. If you know Jesus as Lord and Savior, you have no choice in the matter—you are automatically in the witnessing business.

Learn More: Matthew 24:14 / John 1:8 / Acts 10:39; 22:15 / Revelation 3:14

WORD, THE

In the beginning was the Word. . .and the Word was God. JOHN 1:1

In this verse from the prologue of John's Gospel, he repeats the first three words of the book of Genesis. Just as God existed "in the beginning," so Jesus existed as the eternal Word before time began. But Jesus eventually took on the form of a man to make His dwelling on earth. As the eternal Word, Jesus is of the same substance as God the Father, who spoke the universe into being with the power of His words (Genesis 1:3).

Words are the primary units of language that enable humans to communicate with one another. In the same way, Jesus reveals the will and mind of God the Father to earthbound mortals. He is the ultimate expression of God's redemptive plan for a sinful world.

The description of Jesus as the Word is unique to the apostle John's writings. In his first epistle, John declared, "There are three that bear record in heaven, the Father, the Word, and the Holy Ghost: and these three are one" (1 John 5:7). This leaves little doubt that John thought of Jesus as the Word who was the second person of the Trinity.

Learn More: Isaiah 55:11 / John 1:1–18; 5:39 / Hebrews 11:3 / 2 Peter 3:5–7

WORK

But Jesus answered them, My Father worketh hitherto, and I work. JOHN 5:17

Several religious leaders criticized Jesus for healing on the Sabbath. They were more concerned about keeping the rules than celebrating a miracle of healing. Jesus replied that His mission was to do the work that God, His Father, had sent Him to do.

In the very first chapter of the Bible, we find a God who is at work. After creating the physical world, He formed Adam from the dust of the earth and placed him in a beautiful garden. Adam's responsibility was to take care of this paradise. So work was ordained by God as a blessing from the very beginning. But this task became burdensome after Adam and Eve disobeyed the Lord.

In spite of this, work is meaningful when it is done for God's glory. The psalmist prayed that his work would be fruitful (Psalm 90:17). This was certainly true of the work that Jesus performed. He was faithful to His redemptive task until the very end. "I have glorified thee on the earth," He declared from the cross. "I have finished the work which thou gavest me to do" (John 17:4).

Learn More: Genesis 2:2 / Exodus 20:8–11 / John 4:34 / Acts 13:2 / Ephesians 4:12; 6:6–8 / 2 Thessalonians 3:10

WORSHIP

O come, let us worship and bow down: let us kneel before the Lord. PSALM 95:6

The word *worship* comes from an Old English word *worthship*, referring to someone or something that deserves our devotion. Only the one supreme God of the universe is worthy of worship. Anything else is idolatry.

Authentic worship has several elements. The first is adoration or praise. Whether we worship God in private or in public, we should come before Him with joyful praise for His goodness and mercy.

Another element of worship is thanksgiving. When we offer our thanks to God for His goodness, we admit that we are not self-sufficient, that we need His constant presence. The apostle Paul encouraged the Philippian Christians to present their requests to God in an attitude of thanksgiving (Philippians 4:6).

Worship is not complete until we have recognized God's holiness, compared His righteousness with our sin, and confessed our shortcomings to Him. Then we can claim this promise from the apostle John: "If we confess our sins, he is faithful and just to forgive us our sins, and to cleanse us from all unrighteousness" (1 John 1:9).

Learn More: 1 Chronicles 16:29 / Psalm 99:5 / Matthew 2:2 / John 4:24 / Revelation 7:11

WRATH

For in my jealousy and in the fire of my wrath have I spoken. EZEKIEL 38:19

Through the prophet Ezekiel, the Lord declared that He would exercise His wrath against His people because of their worship of false gods. God's wrath is not an irrational fit of anger but His calm and calculated response to the problem of human sin.

God's people, the Israelites, often refused to obey His commands. In response to their waywardness, His wrath would often "wax hot" (Exodus 22:24) or be "kindled" (Numbers 11:33) against them. The purpose of His indignation was to turn them from their sinful ways and back to obedience of Him as the one true God.

In the New Testament, the wrath of God is often connected with His future judgment. For example, the apostle Paul spoke of a day of wrath to come that would condemn unbelievers. But believers would be delivered from this judgment of the Lord (Romans 5:8–11).

The Bible is clear that all people are sinners (Romans 3:23). Thus, everyone deserves God's wrath, or judgment, against sin. But the good news of the Gospel is that we may be delivered from His wrath through faith in Jesus and His atoning death (Romans 3:24–25).

Learn More: Exodus 32:11 / Psalm 21:9 / Romans 1:18; 5:9 / Revelation 6:17

THE 1-MINUTE
BIBLE
GUIDE

180 Key Questions

A listing of the 180 most intriguing
questions asked or answered in scripture.

Written by Mary Selzer
Edited by Elijah Adkins

SCRIPTURE'S FIRST QUESTION

Hath God said, Ye shall not eat of every tree of the garden? GENESIS 3:1

Scripture's first question is found in Genesis 3:1. It was posed by Satan to Adam and Eve to cast doubt upon God's command not to eat fruit from the tree of knowledge of good and evil. The devil's smooth talk worked, and Adam and Eve ate the forbidden fruit. Suddenly, their innocence was gone, and they immediately hid from God.

Satan's name means "enemy," implying he stands in opposition to the Lord. The devil's goal is to destroy any relationship between God and humanity, and his strategy is deception. In fact, Jesus said that Satan is incapable of speaking truth. Lying is his native tongue.

It should not surprise us that Satan uses the same tactic today—a little twist of God's words to sow a seed of doubt. Fortunately, scripture gives us several ways to defeat the devil: resist, stay alert, test the spirits, extinguish lies with the shield of faith, and wield the sword of the Spirit (the Word of God). God's truth will always triumph over Satan's lies. We need only to use it.

Learn More: Genesis 3 / John 8:44–45 / Ephesians 6:10–18 / Hebrews 4:12 / 1 Peter 5:8–9

A QUESTION OF ACCOUNTABILITY

Where art thou? GENESIS 3:9

The Lord never asks a question He doesn't know the answer to. When He asked Adam, "Where art thou?" He wanted Adam to verbally express the reality of his actions. God's question dug out the truth—Adam was hiding because he was afraid, and he was afraid because he was naked. This admission prompted more questions: "Who told thee that thou wast naked? Hast thou eaten of the tree, whereof I commanded thee that thou shouldest not eat?" (Genesis 3:11).

Throughout scripture, God asks more than four hundred questions, each one fulfilling a distinct purpose. For example, after Job's severe trial, the Lord asked questions to contrast Job's weak arguments with God's great power. He asked Jacob (whose name meant "deceiver"), "What is thy name?" (Genesis 32:27) so Jacob could hear himself say, "My name is liar." Then God changed Jacob's name to Israel. When Elijah escaped from Jezebel and ran to Mount Sinai, God asked him, "What doest thou here, Elijah?" (1 Kings 19:9). Then he told Elijah to go back and complete his ministry.

After David had committed the egregious sins of adultery and murder, he wrote in Psalm 51, "Behold, thou desirest truth in the inward parts" (verse 6). While Satan plants seeds of doubt, God reaches into our "inward parts" to draw out our flaws. He does this without condemnation, so there's no need to hide once we openly acknowledge the truth.

Learn More: Genesis 3–4 / Psalm 51 / 1 Corinthians 15:20–23

ABRAHAM'S QUESTION

Lord God, whereby shall I know that I shall inherit it? GENESIS 15:8

The Lord directed Abram to leave his home and take possession of land in Canaan, promising that his descendants would be innumerable. When Abram asked for confirmation, God sealed His oath with a covenant. This covenant involved Abram's bringing God a heifer, a goat, and a ram, cutting them in half, and arranging the pieces opposite each other. Traditionally, the covenant maker would then walk between the pieces as if to say, "May this happen to me if I fail to keep my oath." When Abram fell asleep, the Lord Himself appeared and walked between the pieces, solidifying His promise that Abram would possess the land.

To show the magnitude of this event, the Lord changed Abram's name, which meant "exalted father," to Abraham—"father of many." He also changed Sarai's name, which meant "princess," to Sarah, which had the deeper meaning of "the princess—the source of nations and kings."

Although Abraham didn't live to see God's promise fulfilled, he continued to believe. God counted this unwavering trust as righteous, and Abraham's descendants eventually took possession of the promised land.

Learn More: Genesis 15:1–21; 17:1–27 / Joshua 1:2–3 / Jeremiah 34:18–19 / Hebrews 6:13–15; 11:8–10

SARAH'S QUESTION

Shall I of a surety bear a child, which am old? Genesis 18:13

In Bible days, marriages were often arranged more for convenience than for love. A wife was seen as little more than property, and a barren womb could completely demolish her sense of value.

During the various encounters between God and Abraham—such as God's call for Abraham to leave his homeland and Abraham's willingness to sacrifice his only son—Sarah seems to be absent from the story. But there is one exception.

When three angels showed up at Abraham's doorstep, he told Sarah to prepare a meal for them. Curious, she sat in the doorway of the tent and eavesdropped. When she heard the angel say that she would bear a son within a year, she was understandably cynical. After all, she was close to ninety and Abraham was almost one hundred. The thought was so ludicrous that she laughed to herself.

However, just as God promised, Sarah gave birth to a son one year later. She named him Isaac, which means "laughter." But this time, her laughter was joyful and came directly from God.

Learn More: Genesis 12:1–5; 18:1–15; 21:1–7

GOD'S RHETORICAL QUESTION

Is anything too hard for the Lord? Genesis 18:14

When Abraham and Sarah heard they would have a son in their old age, they both laughed. But instead of rebuking them, God reassured them, "Is anything too hard for the Lord?" He asked (Genesis 18:14). Centuries later, the angel Gabriel told Mary, the virgin who would become the mother of Jesus, "With God nothing shall be impossible" (Luke 1:37). And decades after that, the author of Hebrews wrote, "Without faith it is impossible to please [God]" (Hebrews 11:6).

The Lord doesn't just do the impossible; He allows His created beings—both angelic and human—to participate in the process. Though only God could create the universe out of nothing, simply by His word, He steps into our world to help and allow us to accomplish things that would otherwise be impossible.

To answer God's own question: No, nothing is too hard for the Lord. When we believe Him by faith, He is pleased. . .and can do even greater works on our behalf.

Learn More: Genesis 18:11–15 / Isaiah 7:14 / Mark 6:5–6 / Luke 1:1–38

WHEN GOD ASKS QUESTIONS OF HIMSELF

Shall I hide from Abraham that thing which I do[?] Genesis 18:17

The city of Sodom was known for its arrogance, selfishness, and shameless sexual perversion. As God prepared to destroy the city, He wondered if he should tell Abraham about His plan or just let him be shocked along with the rest of the world.

The psalmist says that the Lord confides in those who fear Him. From his call to leave Haran to God's promise that he would become the father of a great nation, Abraham had enjoyed an intimate relationship with God for years. He had demonstrated his faith in the Lord and had earned God's trust, so the Lord decided to share with Abraham what was about to happen to the Sodomites.

When God reveals His secrets to people, He expects them to respond and assume necessary responsibility. For example, after God revealed the interpretation of dreams to Joseph and Daniel, they both used this knowledge to glorify God. Similarly, God gave divine insights to the Old Testament prophets so they could share them with the people. The Lord confides in those He trusts, and we earn that trust by fearing the Lord.

Learn More: Genesis 18:16–21; 41:1–40 / Psalm 25:14 / Jeremiah 33:3 / Daniel ⁞

A QUESTION OF GOD'S JUDGMENT

Shall not the Judge of all the earth do right? Genesis 18:25

The Lord sent three angels on simultaneous missions: to deliver the good news to Abraham and Sarah about Isaac's birth and to see if Sodom was wicked enough to receive God's judgment. When Abraham learned of God's plan to destroy Sodom, he worried about the safety of his nephew Lot, who lived there with his wife and two daughters. Sodom, along with its neighboring city Gomorrah, had become a thriving metropolis, and archaeologists estimate the population was perhaps in the tens of thousands. Abraham agonized in prayer for these people, asking God whether He would destroy the righteous with the wicked. Finally, God assured Abraham that if He found ten righteous people in Sodom, He would spare the city. Sadly, not even ten could be found.

Abraham knew the Lord would be fair. Even in His wrath, God had showed mercy by rescuing Lot before Sodom was destroyed.

Learn More: Genesis 18:16–33; 19:1–29 / Ezekiel 16:49–50 / Habakkuk 3:2

A PAGAN KING'S OFFENDED QUESTION

What have I offended thee, that thou hast brought on me. . .a great sin? Genesis 20:9

As Abraham and Sarah traveled toward Canaan, they briefly settled in a place called Gerar, where Abimelech reigned as king. Because Sarah was beautiful, Abraham was afraid Abimelech would kill him and take Sarah for himself. So Abraham instructed her to tell Abimelech that she was Abraham's sister. (In truth, she was his half-sister.)

Just as Abraham had predicted, Abimelech attempted to take Sarah as his wife. The Lord was displeased, so He warned Abimelech in a dream that he was living with a married woman. Because of this sin, God had made every female in Abimelech's house unable to conceive. Abimelech, terrified of God's impending punishment, agreed to return Sarah to Abraham. When he asked Abraham why he would tell such a lie, Abraham said that since there was no fear of God in the land, he was afraid the men would kill him for his wife.

To Abimelech's credit, he did show fear of the Lord by obeying God's warning. He paid Abraham twenty-five pounds of silver as compensation, and in return, Abraham prayed that Abimelech and his family would be able to bear children again. Ironically, a similar situation played out years later as Abraham's son, Isaac, dwelled in the same area. Isaac told the identical lie about his wife to a different king, whose name also happened to be Abimelech.

Learn More: Genesis 20; 26:1–11

ISAAC'S QUESTION ABOUT THE SACRIFICE

Where is the lamb for a burnt offering? Genesis 22:7

Abraham and Sarah had waited twenty-five years for a son. During that time, Abraham had repeatedly witnessed God's faithfulness, causing his trust in God to increase. But God had one final test for him: He commanded Abraham to sacrifice his long-awaited son on Mount Moriah.

Scripture doesn't indicate that Abraham argued or questioned God. He simply left with his son and two servants on the three-day journey to the mountain. Upon arrival, Abraham instructed the servants to stay with the supplies, telling them, "I and the lad will go yonder and worship, and come again to you" (Genesis 22:5). Apparently, Abraham hadn't told Isaac everything he knew, because as they ascended the mountain, Isaac asked, "Where is the lamb for a burnt offering?" (22:7). Abraham replied with confidence that God would provide the lamb. The author of Hebrews says that Abraham's faith was so strong he believed that even if he sacrificed Isaac, the Lord would raise him from the dead.

When Abraham had proved that he was withholding nothing from the Lord, an angel intervened, and God sent a ram for the sacrifice. Abraham then called that place *Jehovahjireh*, which means "The Lord Will Provide."

Learn More: Genesis 22:1–19 / Romans 4 / Hebrews 11:17–19

A QUESTION OF MARRIAGE

Wilt thou go with this man? Genesis 24:58

In Bible days, most marriages were arranged either by the father or a trusted family friend. When Isaac was forty years old, Abraham sent his servant (probably Eliezer) to find Isaac a wife among Abraham's relatives.

Eliezer set out with ten camels and several gifts from Abraham. Upon arrival, he sat by a well and prayed for a specific sign—whichever girl offered to give him and his camels a drink would be God's selection. Seemingly a far-fetched idea, but the Lord still answered his prayer. When Rebekah showed up and offered to draw water for him and his camels, Eliezer thanked God for His faithfulness.

Eliezer then told Rebekah's family about his mission, and they acknowledged that the hand of God was in it. They asked Rebekah if she would go with Eliezer to marry Isaac. She agreed, and the entourage headed back. As she and Eliezer neared Isaac's home, Isaac saw them from a distance and ran out to meet his bride. After taking her home, Isaac loved her.

Learn More: Genesis 24:1–67 / Revelation 19:7–9, 22:17

ESAU'S FOOLISH QUESTION

What profit shall this birthright do to me? Genesis 25:32

In Bible times, the birthright was significant because it gave special privileges to the firstborn son. With it came both a double portion of the inheritance and the spiritual responsibility as head or priest of the family. The firstborn son was referred to as the "first sign of his father's strength" (Deuteronomy 21:17 NIV), meaning the family was strengthened as the father's quiver was filled with arrows (children).

Isaac had twin sons. Esau, the oldest, was an outdoorsman, and Jacob, the youngest, was a homebody. One day Esau came back from a hunting trip, famished and begging Jacob for some stew. Jacob agreed but under one sly condition: Esau had to turn over his birthright. Esau, whose stomach spoke louder than his common sense, swore an oath renouncing his birthright to satisfy his immediate desire. Later, as he begged his father to bless him, Esau realized the terrible magnitude of his rash decision.

The author of Hebrews cautions that we should not be like "profane" Esau. Rendered as *godless* in the New International Version, the term means unhallowed or not blessed. If we value our spiritual "birthright" of privilege and responsibility, we will be blessed and have no regrets.

Learn More: Genesis 25:19–34 / Deuteronomy 21:15–17 / Psalm 127:4 / Hebrews 12:16–17

JOSEPH QUESTIONS A TEMPTATION

How then can I do this great wickedness, and sin against God? Genesis 39:9

Joseph was Jacob's favorite son, and his older brothers knew it. Seething with jealousy, they sold Joseph to the Midianites as a slave. He was later resold to Potiphar, an Egyptian official, who appointed Joseph as the administrator over his entire household.

Joseph, having been torn from his family and homeland, still served Potiphar with integrity, and God gave him success in all he did. Scripture describes Joseph as handsome and well-built, qualities which unfortunately drew the attention of his master's wife. Unbeknownst to Potiphar, she repeatedly made inappropriate advances on Joseph—all of which he resisted, not wanting to sin against God. One time she became exceptionally persistent, causing Joseph to pull away and run out of the house. Frustrated, Potiphar's wife falsely accused Joseph of attempted rape, and Potiphar threw him into prison. God, however, gave Joseph favor in the eyes of the prison warden, and Pharaoh eventually released Joseph to serve a great purpose.

Joseph could have easily carried on a quiet affair with his master's wife. But his devotion to God outweighed the temptation to compromise. One teacher has said the devil couldn't bring Joseph down through trouble, so he tried to overtake him with pleasure. We must remember that the devil is always on the prowl, searching for ways to exploit our weaknesses.

Learn More: Genesis 37; 39 / Galatians 5:16–17 / 2 Timothy 2:22 / 1 Peter 5:8

REUBEN'S REPROACHING QUESTION

Spake I not unto you, saying, Do not sin against the child? Genesis 42:22

Everyone carries regrets for some past misdeed, and if we don't attempt to rectify these wrong-doings, they can eat at us for years. Eventually, the consequences will catch up with us. When we repent, however, the Lord forgives, mercifully clearing our slate.

As Joseph's jealous brothers plotted to kill him, he had only one advocate—his brother Reuben. Without Reuben's knowledge, the brothers sold Joseph into slavery. Joseph ended up in Egypt, where, through God's providence, he eventually became a top official, second only to Pharaoh.

Years later, during a severe famine, Joseph's brothers traveled to Egypt for food. To their dismay, they found themselves face-to-face with the brother they had betrayed. Reuben re-minded them, "Spake I not unto you, saying, Do not sin against the child; and ye would not hear?" After all this time, the ghost of their sin had returned to haunt them. Joseph had the power to retaliate, but he instead offered mercy, assuring them of the Lord's higher purpose: "God sent me before you to preserve you a posterity in the earth, and to save your lives by a great deliverance" (Genesis 45:7).

If a mere man can forgive so generously, how much more will our heavenly Father show mercy when we show contrition? God is always willing to forgive and forget. We must be too.

Learn More: Genesis 37:12–36; 42–45 / Isaiah 43:25 / Romans 8:28 / 1 John 1:9

PHARAOH QUESTIONS THE JEWISH MIDWIVES

Why have ye done this thing, and have saved the men children alive? Exodus 1:18

The Israelites continued to multiply long after Joseph died. The new Pharaoh began worrying that they would overtake the Egyptians, so he put slave masters over them and oppressed them with forced labor. Yet their population still grew. Pharaoh ordered cruel abortions, demanding that the midwives kill all Hebrew boys at birth. But the midwives, fearing God more than man, defied Pharaoh's orders.

When confronted about their disobedience, the midwives claimed that the Jewish mothers gave birth before they could arrive to assist. The Lord rewarded these brave women with families of their own, and He increased His blessings on the Israelites.

In Acts, the apostles were ordered to stop teaching in the name of Jesus. Their response was simple: "We ought to obey God rather than men" (Acts 5:29). This is not an excuse for Christians to disobey earthly authority; rather, it serves as a guideline for those times we are tempted to compromise: obedience to God always takes priority. The Lord will reward us with increased blessing.

Learn More: Exodus 1 / Acts 4:1–20; 5:12–42 / Romans 13:1

MIRIAM'S HELPFUL QUESTION

Shall I go and call to thee a nurse of the Hebrew women? Exodus 2:7

It was a tumultuous time for the Israelites. Hoping to curb their growing population, Pharaoh had mandated that all male Jewish newborns be thrown into the Nile. During this time, a Levite woman named Jochebed gave birth to a boy, and she hid him for three months before finally placing him in a basket and setting him among the reeds on the bank of the Nile. Miriam, Jochebed's daughter, kept watch over her baby brother—and God watched too.

Pharaoh's daughter, who was more compassionate than her father, providentially happened to be walking along the bank of the river at the time, and she discovered the baby in the basket. Miriam, having witnessed the entire scene, wasted no time in offering to find a Hebrew woman to nurse him. Naturally, she chose the baby's mother. After the baby had been weaned, Jochebed released him to Pharaoh's daughter, who named him Moses—a name meaning "drawn out." And the rest is history.

Learn More: Exodus 2:1–10; 6:20 / Psalm 139 / Jeremiah 1:4–5; 29:11

A QUESTION FOR A PRIDEFUL RULER

How long wilt thou refuse to humble thyself before me? Exodus 10:3

As Egypt was slammed with terrible plagues, God gave Pharaoh ten opportunities to swallow his pride and release the Israelites from slavery. Moses warned the Egyptian ruler in advance of the looming disasters, but Pharaoh either lied, ignored him, or intentionally hardened his heart. As a powerful tyrant, Pharaoh found it easy to play with people's emotions. Even when he begged Moses to pray for him, his thoughts were centered on himself not on others. Scripture says several times that Pharaoh hardened his heart through obstinate resistance. Eventually, he became unbendable. Some passages state that the Lord hardened Pharaoh's heart, meaning God turned him over to his own stubborn defiance. Pharaoh was given several opportunities to change, but his pride was a steel cage, locking him in his own rebellion.

In Romans 1, Paul writes that those who fail to acknowledge or glorify God are turned over to their own depraved mentality—but not before they have an opportunity to know Him, since He reveals Himself plainly to everyone. The Lord revealed Himself to Pharaoh ten times, but Pharaoh's futile thinking led to his own destruction.

Learn More: Exodus 7–11 / Romans 1:18–32 / James 4:6

A QUESTION OF QUARRELING

Wherefore do ye tempt the Lord? Exodus 17:2

As the Israelites journeyed through the desert, they camped at a place called Rephidim. Thanks to God's intervention, they had already crossed the Red Sea on dry ground and enjoyed a divine supply of manna and quail. Now, at Rephidim, they were out of water, and they immediately blamed Moses and tested God. When Moses cried out to the Lord, God once again provided, this time by bringing water from a rock. This event was so significant that Moses named the place *Massah*—which means "testing"—and *Meribah*—which means "quarreling."

Testing the Lord in this fashion implied that no matter how miraculously God met the Israelites' needs, His efforts would never suffice. In effect, the Israelites were taunting Him, always urging Him to prove Himself to them. At one point they even cried, "Is the Lord among us, or not?" (Exodus 17:7).

Later, as Moses reminded them of God's faithfulness, he admonished them, "Ye shall not tempt the Lord your God, as ye tempted him in Massah" (Deuteronomy 6:16). Notice Moses referred not to Rephidim but to the place of "testing."

Learn More: Exodus 17:1–7 / Psalm 78:1–56; 95:8–11; 106:1–14

A QUESTION OF DELEGATION

What is this thing that thou doest to the people? Exodus 18:14

Despite Moses' initial resistance when God called him to free the Israelites from Egyptian bondage, he soon became a devoted leader to the Jews. However, his tendency to micromanage the people's affairs almost cost him his physical and emotional health. Fortunately, his father-in-law, Jethro, intervened.

Moses was sitting as the main judge of the people's disputes, helping them settle their differences and informing them about God's law. Imagine the chaos as hundreds of thousands of people lined up to voice each minor grievance. Moses thought he was doing them a favor; instead, he was teaching the Israelites to rely on him without trying to work through their issues first. All the while, men with leadership potential were being ignored.

Jethro's corrective approach served three purposes: (1) Moses' health was spared, (2) a workable solution was easily implemented, and (3) much of the load was delegated to qualified men. Moses was more than eighty years old by this time, but his age didn't deter his teachable spirit—he did everything Jethro suggested. In the end, Moses was relieved, his appointed leaders applied their strengths, and the people went home satisfied.

Learn More: Exodus 18 / Ephesians 4:11–1?

A QUESTION OF SEPARATION

Wherein shall it be known here that I and thy people have found grace in thy sight? EXODUS 33:16

While Moses met with God on Mount Sinai, the Israelites became impatient. Under Aaron's leadership they fashioned a golden calf and worshipped it, leaving Moses appalled when he returned. After Moses had reprimanded the people, the Lord told him to leave with, the people, but God wasn't going with them. When the people heard this, they began to mourn.

Moses told God that if He didn't go with them, they weren't leaving. After all, God's presence was the only distinguishing factor between Israel and the other nations. God assured Moses that He would honor his request and go with them. Without hesitation, Moses responded, "Shew me thy glory" (Exodus 33:18). For Moses, just talking with God wasn't enough; He wanted to *see* God. The Lord complied, giving Moses a dramatic glimpse of His back. After that day, Moses' face radiated before the people whenever he emerged from God's presence.

The world today needs to see believers being led by the Lord. If we remain in God's presence in private, His glory will radiate through us in public, sharply distinguishing us from the rest of the world.

Learn More: Exodus 32–33; 34:29–35 / 2 Corinthians 3:7–18

JEALOUS QUESTIONS

Hath the Lord indeed spoken only by Moses? hath he not spoken also by us? NUMBERS 12:2

Miriam, Aaron, and Moses were siblings who served as co-leaders of the Israelites. But after Moses married an Ethiopian woman, Miriam and Aaron spoke against him and complained that their leadership positions weren't as prominent as Moses'.

When the Lord heard their complaints, He summoned all three to the tent of meeting, where His presence descended in a cloud. God reproved Miriam and Aaron, reminding them that even though He normally communicated through visions and dreams, He spoke clearly with Moses because of Moses' complete faithfulness. He also pointed out that He and Moses met face to face, with Moses having even seen the form of the Lord. Then He asked, "Wherefore then were ye not afraid to speak against my servant Moses?" (Numbers 12:8).

Miriam and Aaron were undoubtedly stunned into silence. As the cloud lifted, Miriam found herself covered with leprosy, a contagious disease that symbolized uncleanness. The Lord instructed that she be confined outside the camp for seven days. As the priest, Aaron had to pronounce his own sister unclean and examine her later before she could return. Not only was Miriam disgraced, the entire nation couldn't move until she was declared clean.

Learn More: Numbers 12:1–16 / Leviticus 14:1–32

UNGRATEFUL, UNFAITHFUL QUESTIONS

Is it a small thing that thou hast brought us up. . .to kill us in the wilderness? NUMBERS 16:13

As if leading hundreds of thousands of Israelites through the wilderness weren't difficult enough, Moses also had to deal with complaints and rebellions. When ten of the twelve spies who scouted the promised land (described by God as flowing with milk and honey) returned with a negative report, the Israelites clamored for a leader to take them back to Egypt. They found a man named Korah, who persuaded more than 250 leaders to rebel.

Korah and his henchmen convinced the people to believe Egypt—not Canaan—was the land flowing with milk and honey. How tragic that the land of their slavery and oppression could become more appealing in their eyes than God's promises. As punishment for this blatant display of contempt for the Lord and His blessings, the Israelites spent the next forty years wandering in the desert.

Both Peter and Jude warn that in the last days scoffers—people like Korah—will bring division and doubt. Jude instructs us to build ourselves up in faith and love, praying in the Spirit while we wait for the eternal land of milk and honey.

Learn More: Numbers 13–14; 16 / 1 Corinthians 10:1–12 / 2 Peter 3:3–4 / Jude 17–21

A DONKEY'S QUESTION

What have I done unto thee, that thou hast smitten me these three times? Numbers 22:28

Balaam was a prophet for hire, meaning he would offer blessings or cursings depending on whether the recipient was a friend or enemy. Balak, king of Moab, wanted Balaam to curse the Israelites because he feared they would overtake his land. Balaam sought counsel from God, who told him the Israelites were a blessed nation—he was not to curse them.

Refusing to take no for an answer, Balak sent his most influential envoy, along with a handsome payment, to convince Balaam to change his mind. Though God had already commanded him not to go, Balaam told the entourage he would ask the Lord one more time. This was a big mistake. Knowing Balaam's covetous heart, the Lord allowed him to go but restricted what he could do.

On the way, Balaam's donkey saw an angel with a sword standing in the middle of the road, but Balaam saw nothing. As the animal frantically tried to avoid the angel, Balaam became angry and began beating the donkey. Miraculously, the donkey spoke, asking Balaam why he was beating her. Suddenly, Balaam's eyes were opened and he saw the angel, who rebuked Balaam for beating his donkey and disobeying God's initial instructions.

Learn More: Numbers 22:1–41 / Proverbs 12:15; 21:2

A QUESTION OF AUTHORITY

Must I not take heed to speak that which the Lord hath put in my mouth? Numbers 23:12

Balak, king of Moab, hired a sorcerer named Balaam to curse the Israelites. As the two men traveled to a location where Balaam would have a clear view of Israel, Balaam prayed, and the Lord gave him a message of blessing to speak over the Israelites. When Balak heard this, he became angry. He had paid Balaam to curse Israel not bless them. The king took the prophet to another location, hoping a better view of Israel would change his message. Once again, however, God put blessings in Balaam's mouth. Frustrated, Balak insisted they travel to a third site. Surely a different location would inspire a curse.

But Balaam was experiencing a miraculous awakening. Previously, he had resorted to sorcery to work his magic, but now he was discovering a strange new reliance on God. As the Spirit of the Lord swept over him, he proclaimed a third oracle of blessing over Israel.

Balak was livid and refused to pay Balaam, but Balaam wasn't finished. In his final oracle, he foretold that Israel would conquer many nations, including Moab—the very outcome the king had been trying to prevent.

Learn More: Numbers 23–24 / 2 Peter 2:15–16

A QUESTION OF TRUE PROPHECY

How shall we know the word which the Lord hath not spoken? Deuteronomy 18:21

The nation of Israel had three leadership roles: (1) kings, who governed the land; (2) priests, who followed spiritual guidelines; and (3) prophets, who spoke for God and upheld morality. Before the Israelites moved into the promised land, Moses cautioned them not to adopt the traditions or lifestyles of other nations. They would be tempted, he said, to practice sorcery or divination to know the future, but the Lord would speak to them through prophets. The test of a genuine prophet was simple—if his prediction didn't come true, it was not from the Lord, and the people could disregard both the message and the messenger.

Today, God has equipped us with His Word and spiritual gifts (such as discernment) to help us test the spirits. When Paul taught the Bereans, they responded eagerly but still searched the scriptures every day to confirm the truth of his message. We should test each "message from the Lord" in the same way. If a prophecy doesn't align with God's Word, then it's not a word from God.

Learn More: Deuteronomy 18:9–22 / Jeremiah 23:16–22 / 1 Corinthians 12:4–11 / 1 John 4:1–6

A QUESTION OF INHERITANCE

How long are ye slack to go to possess the land? JOSHUA 18:3

After forty years of wandering, the Israelites were now ready to claim their promised inheritance. Under Joshua's leadership, four of the tribes moved into the promised land and settled quickly. Surprisingly, the other seven tribes were not as eager to follow suit, causing Joshua to ask them how long they were planning to wait.

One tribe—the Levites—did not receive an allotment of land. Instead, the Lord promised them He would be their inheritance. Those who value material gain might think the Levites were cheated, but nothing could be further from the truth. Everything the land could have offered—God would become for them as they served the people.

God no longer expects His people to conquer foreign lands; instead, He invites us to move into His presence. This eternal inheritance will never perish, spoil, or fade away—and we need not wait to claim it.

Learn More: Joshua 11:23; 14–18 / Numbers 18:20–21 / Deuteronomy 12:10 / Psalm 16:5–6; 78:55; 142:5 / 1 Peter 1:3–5

QUESTION FOR A COMMANDER

Is not the Lord gone out before thee? JUDGES 4:14

While Jabin, king of Canaan, and Sisera, his commander, cruelly oppressed the Israelites, Deborah ruled as a judge. Deborah told Barak that the Lord wanted him to lead Israel's military against Sisera's army. God had promised to lure the enemy into Barak's hands, she explained, so a victory was guaranteed. After Barak agreed to go under the condition that Deborah accompany him, Deborah warned that the honor of overtaking Sisera would fall to a woman not to Barak.

Sisera, having learned that Barak's forces were approaching, gathered his army's nine hundred iron chariots in an intimidating stance against Israel. Deborah urged Barak to attack, reminding him that the Lord had already gone ahead. True to His word, God routed Sisera's army, and Barak overcame them with ease.

Because Barak requested that a woman accompany him to battle, many have accused him of a lack of manliness. However, Barak recognized that Deborah possessed the gift of exhortation—which was exactly what he and his troops needed at the moment. Barak later proved his manliness by humbly allowing Jael, a woman, to receive the honor for killing Sisera.

Learn More: Judges 4–5 / Deuteronomy 31:8

GIDEON QUESTIONS GOD'S PRESENCE

If the Lord be with us, why then is all this befallen us? JUDGES 6:13

The book of Judges recounts numerous examples of Israel's inconsistent spirituality. Under Joshua's leadership, the Israelites had continued to serve the Lord in the promised land. But after Joshua died, their spiritual fervor dissipated so quickly that the next generation had no knowledge of God.

The Lord used other nations to teach the Israelites warfare and to test their obedience to His commands. Each time a judge stepped up to lead, their passion for God was momentarily renewed. But each time the judge died, the people slipped once again into idolatry, thus incurring a new season of punishment.

One such punishment came in the form of the Midianites, who severely oppressed the Israelites for seven years by stealing their crops and killing their animals. The impoverished nation finally cried out to God, and He mercifully sent an angel to appoint Gideon as their rescuer. When the angel assured Gideon that the Lord was with him, Gideon responded, "If the LORD be with us, why then is all this befallen us?" Even though Israel's pattern of forsaking God and reaping the consequences had become obvious by now, Gideon had apparently not yet connected the dots.

Learn More: Judges 2:6–23; 3:1–6; 6:1–13

GOD'S QUESTION FOR GIDEON

Have not I sent thee? JUDGES 6:14

Even while Israel languished under Midianite oppression, God had a plan for their release. As Gideon was threshing wheat in a winepress while hiding from the Midianites, God sent an angel to tell him he must save Israel out of the hand of the Midianites. "Have not I sent thee?" the angel asked.

Gideon (whose name means "warrior") argued that he was the least in his clan and was therefore incapable of saving Israel, but the angel assured him that the Lord would lead him to victory. Somewhat convinced, Gideon asked for a sign. He presented an offering before the angel, who touched it with his staff and consumed it with fire. Later, Gideon requested two more confirmations—that the ground would remain dry while a fleece would be wet with dew, and then vice versa. Each time, the Lord patiently answered his request.

Gideon was so moved by his encounter with the Lord that he built an altar and named it "The Lord Is Peace." It was this peace that enabled Gideon to lead the Israelites to a miraculous victory against the Midianites.

Learn More: Judges 6–7

DELILAH'S NAGGING QUESTION

How canst thou say, I love thee, when thine heart is not with me? JUDGES 16:15

Samson was one of many judges over Israel. At birth, he was set apart as a Nazirite (one who has taken a vow of separation). One requirement of this vow was that a Nazirite could not cut his hair for the duration of the vow—which, for Samson, was his entire life.

Samson displayed tremendous strength at times, such as when he killed a lion with his bare hands or slaughtered a thousand Philistines (Israel's enemies) with a donkey's jawbone. Samson is never described as unusually large and muscular; rather, the secret of his strength lay within his Nazirite vow and the Spirit of God. The Philistines did not realize this, and they were determined to find the source.

To learn this secret, the Philistines bribed Delilah, Samson's girlfriend. She agreed to help and immediately began pressing Samson for information. After Samson had toyed with her by giving false claims about his strength, she began to pout, declaring that true love keeps no secrets. At last, he revealed the truth—if his head were shaved, he would lose his strength. The Philistines then cut off his hair, plucked out his eyes, and threw him in prison. However, his hair slowly regrew, and so did his strength. As the Spirit of God came over him one last time, Samson collapsed the Philistine temple, killing more enemies in his death than he had while alive.

Learn More: Judges 13–16 / Numbers 6:1–21 / Hebrews 11:32–34

NAOMI'S QUESTION TO HER DAUGHTERS-IN-LAW

Why will ye go with me? RUTH 1:11

Naomi and her husband, Elimelech, lived in Bethlehem with their two sons, Mahlon and Chilion. During a famine they moved to Moab, where Mahlon and Chilion married Moabite girls named Ruth and Orpah. Elimelech, along with his two sons, soon died, leaving the three widowed women behind.

Upon hearing that the famine in Bethlehem was over, Naomi and her two daughters-in-law set out to return there. On the way, Naomi encouraged Ruth and Orpah to go back to their families, but they refused. "Why will ye go with me?" Naomi asked. She was obviously too old to have any more sons, and the young women would never wait that long to marry them even if she did.

Orpah listened and returned to her family, but Ruth remained persistent, proclaiming that she was willing to worship Naomi's God, even if it meant leaving her own family. The Lord's timing was perfect. The two women arrived in Bethlehem at the beginning of barley harvest, ensuring a way for Ruth to provide for Naomi and herself—as well as allowing her to meet Boaz, her soon-to-be husband.

Learn More: Ruth 1 / Ecclesiastes 3:1–8

BOAZ'S QUESTION ABOUT RUTH

Whose damsel is this? RUTH 2:5

Boaz, a wealthy landowner, was related by marriage to Naomi, whose husband and two sons had died in Moab during a famine. Naomi had just returned to Bethlehem with Ruth, her Moabitess daughter-in-law.

During barley harvest, Ruth gleaned behind the harvesters, unaware that this field was owned by Boaz. After he discovered that she was related to Naomi, Boaz showed Ruth kindness and favor. He invited her to eat meals with the other workers and instructed his men to leave extra stalks of barley for her to glean.

Naomi, knowing that Boaz was their kinsman-redeemer (a close male relative who would assist them in time of need), was overjoyed to learn that Ruth had met him. One evening she instructed Ruth to go to the threshing floor and lie at Boaz's feet—a sign of submission in those days. Boaz responded to Ruth's overture, promising to assist her and Naomi in any way he could. Eventually, Ruth and Boaz were married, and Obed, their firstborn son, became the grandfather of King David—Jesus' ancestor. Ruth is one of two non-Jewish women mentioned in the genealogy of Christ.

Learn More: Ruth 2–4 / Matthew 1:1–17

ELI'S CARELESS QUESTION TO HANNAH

How long wilt thou be drunken? 1 SAMUEL 1:14

Having been barren all her life, Hannah prayed persistently for a son, promising to give the child to the Lord if He answered her prayer. One day, while she and her husband were offering sacrifices to the Lord in Shiloh, she stood to pray. Eli, the high priest, remained seated by the doorpost and watched from a distance as Hannah mouthed the words. Assuming she must be intoxicated, he bluntly told her to stop drinking. The accusation was hurtful.

Ironically, Eli's own sons "were sons of Belial [wickedness]" who "knew not the LORD" (1 Samuel 2:12). Eli did very little to correct them, and the entire nation of Israel paid for their mistakes.

God eventually answered Hannah's prayer, and she kept her vow by giving Samuel, her firstborn son, to be raised by Eli—the very man who had falsely accused her. God rewarded Hannah's devotion by giving her five more children. Despite Eli's poor record as a father and priest, the Lord watched over Samuel, and he grew to become a godly and influential leader over Israel.

Learn More: 1 Samuel 1–3 / Deuteronomy 23:21–23

THE FRIGHTENED PHILISTINES' QUESTION

What shall we do to the ark of the Lord? 1 SAMUEL 6:2

Shortly after the Israelites had left Egypt, God told Moses to build the ark of the covenant—a holy representation of His presence among humans. It was to be treated with reverence.

Under Eli's priesthood, the Israelites became reckless in their devotion to God. As a result, the Philistines defeated them in a battle, killing thousands of their men and capturing the ark. Dread spread throughout Israel as the glory of the Lord departed with the ark.

The Philistines, thinking they now possessed a magical treasure, began transferring the ark from city to city. But to their dismay, each city was afflicted by plagues upon the ark's arrival. More than once they cried out, "What shall we do to the ark of the LORD?" Even though they had captured the coveted ark, they had no way of controlling God's presence. After seven long months, they returned the ark to Israel.

Everything about God is holy. Although He has granted us permission to approach Him boldly, we must maintain an attitude of reverence. Even as His children, we should kneel in humble awe in the presence of the Lord.

Learn More: 1 Samuel 4–6 / Exodus 15:11–14; 25:10–22 / Psalm 96:9 / Hebrews 4:16; 12:28

A QUESTION FOR A REBELLIOUS KING

Hath the Lord as great delight in burnt offerings and sacrifices, as in obeying? 1 SAMUEL 15:22

Saul was the first king over Israel. Although he was chosen by the Lord, Saul had a serious flaw: he tended to do things his way not God's way. Because of the Amalekites' attack on Israel after they left Egypt, Samuel instructed Saul to "utterly destroy" the Amalekites (1 Samuel 15:3). He was to leave no survivors, neither animal nor human. However, Saul preserved the Amalekite king—along with the best of the animals—and then told Samuel, "I have performed the commandment of the LORD" (15:13).

The prophet saw through his lies, but Saul still maintained his innocence. Although he admitted he had made small exceptions to God's commandment, Saul claimed that he planned to sacrifice the best animals to the Lord. Samuel's response was sobering: God prefers obedience over sacrifice.

Perhaps Saul truly believed he had obeyed the Lord, but this act of rebellion marked the beginning of the end of his reign. Samuel left him, anointing young David shortly afterward to replace Saul as king.

Learn More: 1 Samuel 15:1–35 / Exodus 17:8–16 / Psalm 51:16–17 / Proverbs 21:3

A QUESTION OF REVERENCE

Who can stretch forth his hand against the Lord's anointed, and be guiltless? 1 SAMUEL 26:9

David had at least two perfect opportunities to kill Saul, the crazed king who had chased him for years. Although such an act may have been best for Israel and would have accelerated David's ascent to the throne, David knew Saul's position had been ordained by God.

In scripture, those who had a special calling from God—such as prophets, priests, and kings—were anointed with oil. This oil represented the Holy Spirit, thus indicating that they were set apart for a sacred purpose. By no means did the anointing imply the person was perfect; rather, the individual was expected to do everything possible to fulfill God's divine purpose. Some met these expectations—many did not.

When David found Saul in a vulnerable situation, he looked beyond Saul's imperfections and saw the holy anointing. Even as his own military men urged him to kill Saul, David refused. The Lord had instructed Samuel to anoint Saul as king. Who was David to remove him?

While we can admire David's respect for Saul, we should applaud the reverence He had for God even more.

Learn More: 1 Samuel 10:1; 24:1–7; 26:2–25 / Exodus 29:1–7 / 1 Chronicles 16:22 / Psalm 105:15

OFFENDED ABNER'S QUESTION

Am I a dog's head. . .that thou chargest me to day with a fault? 2 SAMUEL 3:8

For years, Israel's loyalty was divided between King Saul and David—the latter having been anointed king during Saul's reign. Gradually, David accumulated followers while Saul's influence weakened.

Abner, King Saul's cousin and commander of his army, remained loyal to Saul, as did Ish-Bosheth, Saul's son, who took the throne after Saul was killed in battle. Abner loyally served Saul, so when Ish-Bosheth accused him of sleeping with one of Saul's concubines, he was understandably outraged. Not only was Ish-Bosheth questioning Abner's loyalty, he was implying that Abner was a dog—someone worthless and contemptible. In his anger, Abner threatened to leave Saul's house and help David gain his rightful place as king. Ish-Bosheth regretted his accusation, but it was too late.

True to his word, Abner switched his allegiance to David, who welcomed him with open arms. But David's military general, Joab, didn't share his excitement. Years prior, Abner had killed Joab's brother in battle, leaving Joab hungry for revenge. He too thought Abner was a dog. Unbeknownst to David, Joab ambushed Abner and killed him—an action for which he was later executed by King Solomon.

Learn More: 2 Samuel 3 / 1 Kings 2:1–34

A CONVICTING QUESTION

Wherefore hast thou despised the commandment of the Lord? 2 SAMUEL 12:9

King David committed two egregious sins: (1) having an affair with Bathsheba, a married woman, and (2) plotting to have her husband, a soldier, sent to certain death on the front lines. The Lord told Nathan the prophet to confront David about his sin. This was a risky message. If David didn't like it, the prophet could face the same demise as Bathsheba's husband. Nathan wisely began with a story about a rich man who owned herds of livestock yet stole his neighbor's only lamb. Livid at such injustice, David demanded justice for this greedy man. Nathan, pointing to David, said, "Thou art the man" (2 Samuel 12:7). Then he asked David why he despised (ignored) God's commandments against murder and adultery. David immediately admitted his sin, and the Lord showed mercy.

David poured out his heart before the Lord during this time and, under the Spirit's anointing, composed Psalm 51. In verse 17 of this prayer, David writes, "A broken and a contrite heart, O God, thou wilt not *despise*"—the same word Nathan had used while confronting David. Thankfully, the Lord never treats true repentance with flippancy.

Learn More: 2 Samuel 11–12 / Psalm 51

ABISHAI'S QUESTION IN SUPPORT OF DAVID

Why should this dead dog curse my lord the king? 2 SAMUEL 16:9

After Saul died, David became king. However, he was not popular with everyone. Shimei was a relative of King Saul who vocally hated David, going so far as to openly curse him—calling him a son of the devil and pelting him and his officials with stones. Abishai, David's military official, called Shimei a dead dog and wanted to behead him for his slander. Believing the Lord would deal with Shimei, David mildly rebuked Abishai and spared Shimei's life.

Sometime later, Shimei feared punishment for his previous actions and groveled at David's feet for forgiveness. In that moment, David promised he would not take Shimei's life. But David, possibly not wanting his heir Solomon to experience the same disrespect, later told Solomon about Shimei's actions and instructed him to deal with Shimei as he saw fit. Solomon showed grace, allowing Shimei to remain in Jerusalem but warning him never to leave the city, under penalty of death.

A few years later, Shimei ignored the royal order and left Jerusalem to find his runaway slaves, thus earning his execution. Once this disloyal citizen was removed from the picture, Solomon's kingdom stood secure, and Israel enjoyed a peaceful reign.

Learn More: 2 Samuel 16:5–14; 19:18–23 / 1 Kings 2:8–9, 36–46

A CONCERNED FATHER'S QUESTION

Is the young man Absalom safe? 2 SAMUEL 18:29

King David fathered many children by different wives. His oldest son, Amnon, raped his own half sister, Tamar. Even though David was furious, he refused to punish Amnon for this egregious sin. However, Tamar's full brother, Absalom, took lethal revenge on Amnon and then fled.

Two years passed before David allowed Absalom to return to Jerusalem. Absalom lost respect for his own father and, as his influence increased, began conspiring against the king. As Absalom grew as a threat, David's emotions were torn. Should he love Absalom as a son or treat him like an enemy?

Eventually, Absalom led his men against the king, and David's military told David to stay back while they set out to fight. David, still conflicted over his son's actions, told his commanders to "deal gently" with Absalom (2 Samuel 18:5). During the battle, Absalom rode his mule under a low-hanging branch and snagged his long hair in the tree. Joab, one of David's commanders, seized the opportunity and killed him. David was heartbroken by the news.

Even though his struggle with Absalom was agonizing, David still confided in God, penning at least two inspiring psalms about his experiences.

Learn More: 2 Samuel 13:1–19:8 / Psalms 3; 7

A QUESTION OF HONOR

Was he not most honourable of three? 2 SAMUEL 23:19

King David's soldiers were known for their amazing exploits. Standing head and shoulders above the others, however, were his Three Mighty Men: Adino (chief of the three), Eleazar, and Shammah.

Scripture names another soldier, Abishai, who performed amazing exploits, even though he was not part of the Three. Abishai was the brother of Joab—the captain of David's army—and he stepped up when David asked for a volunteer to go with him into King Saul's camp. In addition to killing three hundred men with his spear, Abishai also rescued David from certain death during a battle between the Israelites and Philistines.

Contented to serve where he could have the greatest impact, Abishai didn't try to jostle or cajole his way through the ranks. But Abishai's extreme loyalty to the king eventually earned him an unimaginably high position—Captain of the Three Mighty Men.

When we faithfully serve the Lord with humility, He will raise us up in due time.

Learn More: 1 Samuel 26:1–12 / 2 Samuel 21:15–17; 23:8–19 / 1 Chronicles 11:20–21 / 1 Peter 5:6

A QUESTION OF GOD'S CHOOSING

"Is it not my family God has chosen?" 2 SAMUEL 23:5 NLT

King David's family was flawed, to say the least. David had committed adultery and murder, one of his sons had tried to overthrow the throne, and another son had raped his half sister. Even as David lay on his deathbed, his family squabbled over who would be the next king. Yet at the end of his life, David said, "Is it not my family God has chosen?" David's house wasn't "right" because of his own efforts; it was right because the Lord had promised David to make it absolute.

God's eternal covenant with David guaranteed his throne would be established forever—a messianic prophecy concerning the birth of Jesus and His eternal reign as King of kings. We might think that a perfect God would regret making promises to an imperfect person like David, but the Lord never rescinded His word.

At the end of his life, David didn't look back at his mistakes with regret. Instead, just like his ancestors, "having seen [the promises] afar off, and were persuaded of them. . .embraced them" (Hebrews 11:13). King David could rest in peace, confident that the King of kings would one day reign forever.

Learn More: 2 Samuel 23:1–5 / Psalm 89:3–4 / Hebrews 11:13–16

JOAB QUESTIONS DAVID'S CENSUS

Why doth my lord the king delight in this thing? 2 SAMUEL 24:3

King David made a serious mistake that cost Israel thousands of lives. Joab, David's own army general, advised him not to take a military census, but David ignored his warning—not because the census was necessary, but because it stroked his pride.

When Joab returned with the numbers, David realized his sin and asked for God's forgiveness. God let him pick his punishment: three years of famine, three months of being overcome and pursued by Israel's enemies, or three days of a ravaging nationwide plague. Instead of choosing, David threw himself at the mercy of the Lord.

A plague struck the land, killing seventy thousand Israelites. As an angel began to destroy Jerusalem, God instructed David to travel to a threshing floor owned by a man named Araunah, build an altar there, and sacrifice to the Lord. Araunah offered to donate the property, but David insisted on paying. "I [will not] offer," he said, "burnt offerings unto the LORD my God of that which doth cost me nothing." David sacrificed, and the Lord immediately stopped the plague.

Even though David paid the fee, a far larger price—the loss of thousands of lives—had already been paid. If only he had listened to Joab's advice, the catastrophe would have been avoided altogether.

Learn More: 2 Samuel 24 / 1 Chronicles 21 / 2 Chronicles 3:1

BATHSHEBA'S QUESTION TO THE DYING DAVID

Didst not thou. . .swear unto thine handmaid, saying, Assuredly Solomon thy son shall reign after me? 1 KINGS 1:13

While King David lay on his deathbed, Adonijah, his oldest living son, declared himself the royal successor. Eager for his father to die, Adonijah planned a public parade announcing his kingship. He also prepared a celebratory feast, inviting his brothers and supporters but excluding Solomon and any opposing leaders.

Nathan the prophet informed Bathsheba about these events, reminding her of God's promise to select David's successor. The Lord had told David, "I will set up thy seed after thee, which shall proceed out of thy bowels" (2 Samuel 7:12). This promise had come before Solomon's birth, indicating that none of the children David already had would succeed him.

Bathsheba reminded David of the promise, and he immediately ordered for Solomon to be anointed as king. When Adonijah heard the news, he was struck with fear. He had shown such disrespect for his father, and now Solomon had the power to kill him if he wanted. Adonijah bowed before Solomon, acknowledging his kingship, and Solomon spared his life and sent him home.

Learn More: Deuteronomy 17:14–20 / 1 Kings 1

A PROPHET'S QUESTION TO A POOR WIDOW

Fetch me, I pray thee, a little water in a vessel, that I may drink. 1 KINGS 17:10

God sent Elijah to Zarephath, the heart of Baal worship. Zarephath was located in Sidon (modern-day Lebanon), where Jezebel's father, Ethbaal, ruled as king. Israel's King Ahab had married Jezebel for political advantages, resulting in a surge of Baal worship throughout Israel.

Why did God send Elijah to Zarephath instead of a place in Israel? Jesus answered this question when He told the Israelites, "No prophet is accepted in his own country" (Luke 4:24). To find someone willing to listen, Elijah had to leave his own people.

While in Zarephath, Elijah met a widow who God had said would provide food for him. Elijah asked her to fetch him some water and bread—an outrageous request, given that a famine and drought were afflicting the land. These supplies were all she had, but both Elijah and the widow had enough faith to follow God's instructions.

Her response to his request was commendable. She said that even though she had no bread, she did have the necessary ingredients (flour and oil) to make it. Elijah's prompting helped the widow see beyond her dire circumstances to recognize God as her ultimate Provider.

Learn More: 1 Kings 17:1–16 / Psalm 111:5 / Luke 4:24–26 / 2 Corinthians 9:10

A POOR WIDOW'S QUESTION TO A PROPHET

Art thou come unto me to call my sin to remembrance, and to slay my son? 1 KINGS 17:18

Elijah was staying in the upper room of a widow's house. When her young son fell ill and died, the grief-stricken mother lashed out at Elijah, accusing him of punishing her for her sin. Perhaps Elijah had observed a sinful lifestyle or she carried guilt over previous wrongdoings.

Instead of countering the distraught mother's accusation, Elijah took the child to his room and prayed over him three times. Miraculously, the boy revived. The overjoyed woman became a believer, glorifying God and acknowledging Elijah's role as God's prophet.

Not every tragedy is a punishment. God often uses difficulties to show His glory. For example, the disciples once encountered a blind man and asked Jesus who had sinned—the man or his parents. Jesus answered, "Neither. . .but that the works of God should be made manifest in him" (John 9:3). As Mary and Martha grieved over Lazarus' death, Jesus ordered that the stone be rolled away from the tomb. Martha protested, but Jesus replied, "Said I not unto thee, that, if thou wouldest believe, thou shouldest see the glory of God?" (John 11:40).

Sometimes, it takes a difficult circumstance for us to open our eyes to God's power.

Learn More: 1 Kings 17:17–24 / John 9:2–3; 11:1–44

ELIJAH'S QUESTION TO ALL ISRAEL

How long halt ye between two opinions? 1 Kings 18:21

Elijah was a prophet during the reign of King Ahab. At that time, the land was undergoing a severe drought—both physically and spiritually. The Israelites vacillated between worshipping the false god Baal and serving the Lord. When Elijah confronted the people and urged them to choose, they remained silent, so he challenged the prophets of Baal to a contest that would prove who the true God really was.

As everyone gathered on Mount Carmel, Elijah set the rules: lay a bull on some wood and ask your deity to send fire and burn the sacrifice. The one who responded would be declared the true God. For an entire day, Elijah mocked the prophets of Baal as they prayed, shouted, and slashed themselves with swords and spears to no avail. That evening, Elijah repaired the Lord's altar, dug a trench around it, and ordered the altar and the trench to be filled with water. Then he simply asked the Lord to show His power, returning the people to Him.

Instantly, God sent fire that burned up the entire altar and devoured the water in the trench. The people immediately declared, "The LORD, he is the God" (1 Kings 18:39). Elijah then ordered the prophets of Baal to be destroyed, thus ending their influence. Within a short time, the drought—both physical and spiritual—was over.

Learn More: Joshua 24:15 / 1 Kings 18:16–46 / James 5:17–18

JEZEBEL'S BULLYING QUESTION

Dost thou now govern the kingdom of Israel? 1 Kings 21:7

The wicked King Ahab was easily influenced by his wife Jezebel, who was even more wicked than he. They manipulated each other—he by pouting when he didn't get his way and she by bullying him and usurping his power.

Near Ahab's palace was a vineyard owned by Naboth. That property had been in Naboth's family for generations, but Ahab wanted to buy it. His offer, however, was refused, so he went to his bedroom to sulk. When he told Jezebel about the incident, she reprimanded him for not using his power. Then, using the king's seal, she arranged for Naboth to be falsely accused and sentenced to death. After removing this innocent man from the picture, Jezebel gladly reported to Ahab that the vineyard now belonged to him. The king asked no questions. He had gotten what he wanted, and that was all he needed to know.

According to the apostle Paul, greed is just like idolatry. Ahab probably had more wealth than he could ever spend, yet it wasn't enough. With Jezebel's encouragement, Ahab became his own god, worshipping himself while expecting others to gratify his desires.

Learn More: 1 Kings 21:1–16 / Micah 2:1–3 / Luke 12:15–21 / Ephesians 5:5

A QUESTION TO A TRUE PROPHET OF GOD

Shall we go against Ramothgilead to battle, or shall we forbear? 1 Kings 22:15

The kingdom of Israel was divided, with the northern section being ruled by the wicked King Ahab and the southern part (Judah) being ruled by the God-fearing King Jehoshaphat. Ahab wanted Jehoshaphat to join him in war against the ruler of Ramothgilead, but Jehoshaphat wanted to seek counsel from the Lord first. Ahab, not caring about God's message, asked four hundred false prophets if he should fight, and all of them said yes. Unsatisfied, Jehoshaphat sent a messenger to fetch Micaiah, a true prophet of God. Micaiah had previously spoken sternly with Ahab, and Ahab hated him for it.

Upon arrival, the messenger instructed Micaiah to just agree with the others and not cause trouble. At first, Micaiah mockingly told Ahab that he would absolutely be victorious. Ahab, sensing the prophet's ironic tone, insisted he tell the truth. Micaiah then revealed that the other prophets were deceiving Ahab. If the kings went to war, Israel would lose and Ahab would die.

Ahab was livid, and he ordered the prophet to be imprisoned until he returned from war. Sadly, Micaiah's prophecy was fulfilled, and Ahab never returned alive.

Learn More: 1 Kings 22:1–40 / 2 Chronicles 18 / Job 33:14–18

ELISHA'S FIRST QUESTION AS LEAD PROPHET

Where is the Lord God of Elijah? 2 KINGS 2:14

Jeremiah the prophet says the Israelites were failing to ask one important question: "Where is the LORD?" (Jeremiah 2:6). By not following the example of Elisha—who sought God in every circumstance—the Israelites had lost their spiritual curiosity.

Elisha was Elijah's protégé. The two worked together for several years, until the time came for Elijah to depart. Near the end of their journey, they approached the Jordan River, whose waters Elijah divided by striking them with his cloak. After they had crossed on dry ground, Elijah asked Elisha if there was one more thing he could do for him, and Elisha requested a double portion of the older prophet's spirit. That request would be granted, Elijah said, if Elisha witnessed his transport to heaven. Elisha followed him to the end, witnessing his dramatic departure in a whirlwind and chariot of fire. Elijah's mantle then fluttered from the sky, signaling to Elisha that he had indeed received a double portion of the prophet's spirit.

As Elisha once again approached the Jordan River on his way home, he raised Elijah's mantle and asked, "Where is the LORD God of Elijah?" He struck the waters, parting the rivers and clearing his path. The older prophet's final miracle became the younger prophet's first—a seamless continuation of the Spirit's work through two men who saw God in every situation. By the end of Elisha's life, the number of his recorded miracles had roughly doubled that of his mentor's.

Learn More: 2 Kings 2:1–14 / Jeremiah 2:6–8

ELISHA'S QUESTION TO A DEBT-RIDDEN WIDOW

Tell me, what hast thou in the house? 2 KINGS 4:2

The poor woman in this story was being slammed from all sides. Her husband had died and left her with a major debt, and now the creditor was threatening to enslave her sons if she didn't pay the loan. In desperation, she begged Elisha for assistance.

When the prophet asked what she had in her house, she at first replied, "Nothing," then admitted that she did have a small amount of oil. Despite the woman's grim predicament, Elisha was determined to help her take advantage of what little she had left.

Elisha told her to borrow jars from the neighbors, stressing that she ask for many. Something big was about to happen. Not wanting her sons to miss the miracle, she sent them to fetch the jars, and Elisha instructed her to shut the door to prevent any distractions. He didn't tell her what to do with the oil until every vessel had been filled, maybe because he wanted her to focus on one thing at a time. Amazingly, the oil kept flowing until there were no more jars to contain it. God never stops giving—we only stop receiving.

Learn More: 2 Kings 4:1–7 / Luke 6:38 / Ephesians 3:20–21 / James 1:17

NAAMAN'S IRRITABLE QUESTION

Are not Abana and Pharpar. . .better than all the waters of Israel? 2 KINGS 5:12

Naaman, an army commander in Aram, was plagued with leprosy. So when a Jewish girl told him that a prophet named Elisha could cure him, Naaman asked the king for permission to travel to Israel. The king supplied resources for his trip, including a letter to the king of Israel. Upon arrival, Naaman reported to Israel's king, who admitted he had no idea how to cure leprosy. But Elisha, when he heard about Naaman's plight, offered to intervene.

Elisha sent his messenger out to instruct Naaman to dip seven times in the Jordan River. Having expected Elisha to perform a spectacular miracle, Naaman was furious. He had cleaner rivers in his own country! But Naaman's servants eventually talked sense into him, and he agreed to dip in the Jordan. True to Elisha's word, Naaman was cured on the seventh time he emerged.

As an army captain, Naaman approached his healing with a desire to control the way God answered his requests. We may be guilty of the same mistake at times. Thankfully, God's Word leads us into obedience to His directives—even when we feel like our plan is better.

Learn More: 2 Kings 5:1–19 / Psalm 143:10 / Isaiah 55:8–9

A QUESTION PRECEDING A MIRACLE

Where fell it? 2 KINGS 6:6

The group of younger prophets under Elisha's mentorship was rapidly growing—so much so that their meeting space had to be enlarged. As the prophets went to cut down trees by the Jordan River, they invited Elisha to come along.

One of the men had borrowed an ax head, which to his horror flew off midswing and landed in the river. Because weapons and tools were in limited supply, losing the borrowed tool was a significant problem. Surprisingly, no one dove into the water to fetch it. While the others panicked, Elisha remained calm and simply threw a stick into the water, miraculously causing the ax head to float.

Once the prophets' construction was over, the finished building undoubtedly served as a constant reminder of God's sovereign and unpredictable power.

Learn More: 1 Samuel 13:19–22 / 2 Kings 6:1–7

A SICK KING'S QUESTION

Shall I recover of this disease? 2 KINGS 8:8

The relationship between Ben-Hadad and Elisha was strained, to say the least. Ben-Hadad—king of Syria—had declared war against Israel. But as he discussed military strategy with his officers, the Lord revealed the king's battle plans to Elisha the prophet, who then informed the king of Israel. When Ben-Hadad learned about the information leak, he accused his officers of betrayal, but they told him that Elisha was privy to their conversations and was informing Israel's king. Ben-Hadad ordered his officers to find and capture Elisha. With a mass of horses and chariots, the Syrians surrounded the city where the prophet was staying, but God struck them all with blindness when Elisha prayed.

Although Ben-Hadad was certainly displeased with Elisha, he now knew where to turn if he ever needed an ally. So when he later became ill, he sent Hazael, one of his servants, to ask Elisha if he would recover. Elisha told Hazael that Ben-Hadad would not die from his illness; rather, he would be assassinated by his own trusted servant.

Despite the tension between him and Ben-Hadad, Elisha never compromised. As a result of this integrity, even his staunchest enemy could trust him in desperate times.

Learn More: 2 Kings 6:8–23; 8:7–15

JOASH'S QUESTION REGARDING GOD'S TEMPLE

Why repair ye not the breaches of the house? 2 KINGS 12:7

When King Joash (also known as Jehoash) was a toddler, his evil grandmother, Athaliah, had gone on a rampage to destroy the entire royal family. Joash's aunt, wife of Jehoiada the priest, hid him in the temple for six years during Athaliah's reign. When Joash turned seven, Jehoiada publicly declared him king. Athaliah tried to run but was overtaken and killed.

During her reign, Athaliah had encouraged Baal worship, desecrating the holy temple. Once Joash became king, he instructed the priests to collect money for the temple's restoration. The priests gladly took the money but refused to work, even after Joash's prodding. Joash took things into his own hands, placing by the temple's entrance a chest where people could drop their offerings. Then he hired workers who diligently rebuilt the structure.

After Jehoiada died, leaders in Judah influenced Joash to reinstate Baal worship, and the temple was once again abandoned. When Jehoiada's son objected, Joash had him killed. Eventually, Joash was assassinated by his own officials.

Sadly, the king had not been as diligent in restoring his heart as he was in restoring the temple.

Learn More: 2 Kings 11–12 / 2 Chronicles 24:1–16

KING HEZEKIAH'S QUESTION OF HEALING

What shall be the sign that the Lord will heal me? 2 Kings 20:8

Hezekiah was a righteous king, and the Lord blessed everything he did. At thirty-nine, he became deathly ill, and Isaiah told him he wouldn't recover. Hezekiah was stricken with grief and begged God to spare his life, so the Lord mercifully gave him fifteen more years.

During those additional years, pride seeped into Hezekiah's heart. He even allowed Babylonian envoys to tour his storehouses and armory. Isaiah rebuked him, forewarning that the day would come when the Babylonians would possess everything he owned, including his children. Hezekiah breathed a selfish sigh of relief—at least that wouldn't happen in his lifetime. Hezekiah's son Manasseh—who became king after Hezekiah's death and led the Israelites away from God—was also born during these years. We can only wonder how different Israel's story would have been had Hezekiah died at thirty-nine...had he not shared his secrets with the Babylonians...had Manasseh never been born.

However, both Hezekiah and Manasseh eventually repented of their mistakes, and the Lord showed mercy to them. Even after the biggest blunders, God is willing to forgive.

Learn More: 2 Kings 20-21 / 2 Chronicles 32:24–33; 33:1–20 / Job 14:5

SOLOMON'S HUMBLE QUESTION

Who can judge this thy people, that is so great? 2 Chronicles 1:10

Solomon's first act as king was offering sacrifices at the tent of meeting, also known as the tabernacle. The Lord honored his humility and promised to grant anything he requested. When Solomon asked only for wisdom and knowledge, God answered his request—and included a generous bonus of wealth, riches, and honor as well. Solomon ruled wisely and gained renown throughout the world. Most importantly, he built the temple—a permanent residence for God's presence.

While everyone remembers Solomon's request for wisdom and knowledge, his dedicatory prayer over the temple was even more significant. After asking the Lord to meet the people when they came to the temple to pray, worship, or ask for mercy, the king invited God to enter His "resting place." God responded by sending holy fire from heaven, consuming the burnt offering and sacrifices. The glory of the Lord that filled the temple was so overpowering that the priests couldn't even enter the building. The people, struck with awe, fell on their faces before the Lord.

As long as Solomon feared and remained faithful to the Lord, he experienced an exponential flow of wisdom. He learned quickly that the fear of the Lord is the beginning of wisdom.

Learn More: 2 Chronicles 1; 6-7; 9:23 / Proverbs 9:10

A GOOD QUESTION IGNORED

What advice give ye that we may return answer to this people. . .? 2 Chronicles 10:9

When Solomon became king, the Lord promised him a prosperous and peaceful reign—provided he remained faithful to God. Unfortunately, Solomon began supporting his wives' idol worship, thus nullifying God's promise and forcing the king to heavily tax his people.

After Solomon's death, his son Rehoboam assumed the throne. Both Jeroboam, one of Solomon's former officials, and Rehoboam's group of older consultants requested that the king lighten the tax load. But Rehoboam ignored them, following instead the advice of his younger peers and raising the tax even more. As a result, the people rebelled and sought shelter under Jeroboam's leadership. The nation of Israel split, with ten of the twelve tribes following Jeroboam, who encouraged idol worship and further alienated the people from God.

When Rehoboam was a young child, Solomon had instructed him to "Let not mercy and truth forsake thee. . . . So shalt thou find favour and good understanding in the sight of God and man" (Proverbs 3:3–4). If only Solomon would have followed his own advice, Israel need not have been divided.

Learn More: 1 Kings 11-12 / 2 Chronicles 10 / Proverbs 2:1–11; 3:1–35

AMAZIAH'S GREEDY QUESTION

What shall we do for the hundred talents. . .given to the army of Israel? 2 Chronicles 25:9

Amaziah, king of Judah, was halfhearted in his devotion to God. Upon discovering his military numbered only three hundred thousand fighting men, the king bribed a hundred thousand soldiers from the northern kingdom with almost four tons of silver to join his army. A prophet soon learned of this maneuver, however, and he cautioned Amaziah to send the men back to Israel because God was opposed to the northern kingdom. When Amaziah complained that he had just paid an exorbitant amount to hire them, the prophet replied, "The LORD is able to give thee much more than this" (2 Chronicles 25:9). The king relented and let the men return.

With God now on his side, Amaziah later went to war against the Edomites and won. Unfortunately, he slighted the Lord by bringing back foreign gods and worshipping them as his own. The Lord sent a prophet to warn him about the consequences, but Amaziah refused to listen and sent the prophet away. When the king of Israel attacked Judah, Amaziah was captured, but he hardened his heart even more against the Lord. Eventually, he was assassinated.

Learn More: 2 Chronicles 25 / Proverbs 3:5 / 1 Timothy 6:17

SENNACHERIB'S BLASPHEMOUS QUESTION

Whereon do ye trust, that ye abide in the siege in Jerusalem? 2 Chronicles 32:10

During Hezekiah's reign over Judah, the Assyrian king, Sennacherib, laid siege to Jerusalem. But the Israelites were prepared. As Hezekiah repaired broken areas of Jerusalem's wall and built a second wall as reinforcement, the Jews blocked the water supply from the Assyrians and stockpiled weapons and shields.

The Assyrians never shot one arrow. Instead, they used mental tactics, hoping to weaken the Israelites' confidence in God. Hezekiah encouraged the people not to fear, reminding them that their God was more powerful than Sennacherib's huge army. He called on the Lord and sought counsel from God-fearing people—including Isaiah the prophet, who bolstered him and the people with a direct word from the Lord. When the God of Israel intervened for His people, the only one who lost confidence was Sennacherib.

The devil loves to use mental tactics against us, but we can be prepared by "stockpiling" scripture—the sword of the Spirit—in our hearts. This will repair our broken walls of faith, eliminating any vulnerability to doubt. We must pray diligently and associate with other believers for encouragement. But most importantly, we must keep our confidence in God, who will always win our battles.

Learn More: 2 Kings 18:17–19:37 / 2 Chronicles 32:1–23 / Isaiah 36–37

A GOVERNOR QUESTIONS THE REBUILDING OF JERUSALEM

Who hath commanded you to build this house, and to make up this wall? Ezra 5:3

At the end of Israel's captivity, the Lord moved Cyrus, king of Persia, to allow the Israelites to rebuild the temple in Jerusalem. Under the leadership of Jeshua and Zerubbabel, nearly fifty thousand people left Persia, carrying temple articles that had been stolen decades earlier.

Israel's enemies offered to "help," but the Jews refused, thus sparking a campaign of sabotage as their enemies tried to frustrate their plans. After Xerxes replaced Cyrus as king, these enemies wrote him a letter that falsely accused the Israelites of a plot to turn against Xerxes once Jerusalem was rebuilt. The king immediately ordered construction to cease.

However, two prophets—Haggai and Zechariah—urged the Jews to resume the work, reminding them that the original directive had come from God through Cyrus. When Tatnai, the governor, asked who had authorized the rebuilding, the Jews told him Cyrus had. Not only did Xerxes verify their claim, he ordered Tatnai to fully cooperate and provide all their resources.

Because of the people's diligence and the prophets' encouragement, the temple was completed and worship was restored in Jerusalem.

Learn More: Ezra 1–6 / Haggai 1–2 / Zechariah 1

EZRA'S QUESTION ABOUT GOD'S JUDGMENT

Wouldest not thou be angry with us till thou hadst consumed us? Ezra 9:14

Once the temple had been rebuilt, Ezra, a Jewish law expert, returned to Jerusalem to assure that pure worship was restored. He trained descendants of Levi to attend the temple and oversee the sacrifices as priests.

Israel, having lacked strong spiritual leadership for years, had become lax in following God's commands. For example, the people had extensively intermarried with foreigners—an act which God had prohibited due to Israel's propensity toward idol-worship. When Ezra learned of this sin, he immediately called out to the Lord and repented on behalf of the people. He told God that He had every right to be angry, even to the point of obliterating the entire Jewish race, "so that there should be no remnant nor escaping."

As Ezra cried out to the Lord, the people began weeping bitterly over their own disobedience. Ezra led them in corporate confession, and the people pledged to right their wrongs and offer proper sacrifices to God.

Even though the temple had been restored, the people themselves needed restoration. Only through repentance could their worship become pure and their devotion undivided.

Learn More: Exodus 34:14–16 / Ezra 7–10 / Psalm 66:8–20 / John 4:23 / Romans 2:4

XERXES'S QUESTION FOR NEHEMIAH

Why is thy countenance sad, seeing thou art not sick? Nehemiah 2:2

Nehemiah was a Hebrew possibly born in captivity. As cupbearer to the Persian king Xerxes, he maintained an upbeat, cheerful attitude in his presence. But upon learning that the once-impregnable Jerusalem stood vulnerable and without walls, Nehemiah wept and prayed.

In his prayer, Nehemiah confessed the sins of the Israelites and asked God to remember His promise to return the Hebrews to their homeland. The Lord evidently inspired him with a plan, because Nehemiah then prayed for favor in the eyes of Xerxes. The king later noticed Nehemiah's sad countenance, and he asked what was wrong. Recognizing this as a divine opportunity, Nehemiah told the king about Jerusalem's disrepair. The king asked what he wanted, and Nehemiah immediately prayed. Then he boldly requested permission to return to Jerusalem and rebuild the walls with full backing and resources from the king. Xerxes agreed.

Nehemiah could have stayed comfortable in Babylon and delegated his responsibility to someone else. But he instead chose to carry the burden until the Lord opened a door of opportunity. Even though prayer is vital, acting on God's response to our prayer is equally important. The Lord will use anyone in any position to accomplish His purposes.

Learn More: Nehemiah 1–2 / Proverbs 21:1 / Luke 11:28 / James 1:22

SANBALLAT'S BELITTLING QUESTION

What do these feeble Jews? Nehemiah 4:2

When Nehemiah followed God's call to rebuild the walls around Jerusalem, he encountered resistance. To prevent the Jews from regaining strength and power, a Horonite named Sanballat and his friends began a campaign of ridicule, calling the Israelites feeble and questioning their ability to complete the project. It was a vain attempt to sabotage the Jews' self-confidence.

Nehemiah responded by calling out to the Lord and reminding the people of God's continual faithfulness. In turn, the Lord frustrated Sanballat's plans. But Nehemiah, knowing better than to let his guard down just yet, armed half of his men and strategically placed them along the vulnerable areas of the wall. Meanwhile, the rest of the people continued to build the wall, carrying materials with one hand and holding a weapon in the other. They didn't relax until the work was completed—fifty-two days later. The Jews weren't as feeble as Sanballat had thought.

The armor of God is a strong defense against Satan's opposition. It makes us much stronger than the devil would have us believe.

Learn More: Nehemiah 4; 6:15 / Isaiah 35:3–4; 54:17 / Ephesians 6:10–18 / 1 Peter 5:8–11

NEHEMIAH'S INCREDULOUS QUESTION

Why is the house of God forsaken? Nehemiah 13:11

The events recorded in the books of Ezra and Nehemiah are intertwined. After Nehemiah rebuilt the walls around Jerusalem, he resumed his service to Xerxes in Persia. Jeshua and Zerubbabel led the rebuilding of the temple while Ezra, a teacher and scholar, instructed the people in the Law.

During Nehemiah's absence, Eliashib the priest had given Tobiah, an enemy Ammonite, a room in the temple—a space previously used for storing grain offering materials. There were two problems with this: (1) Tobiah had vigorously opposed Nehemiah's efforts to rebuild the walls, and (2) the Lord had cautioned that Ammonites were not permitted to enter the "assembly of God" because they had hired a prophet to curse Israel.

When Nehemiah returned to Jerusalem the second time, he immediately evicted Tobiah from the temple, purified the room, and returned all the offering materials. Then, upon learning that the Israelites were neglecting God's house and repeating the sins of their forefathers, Nehemiah used extreme measures to correct them.

The walls restored protection, the temple restored worship, and Ezra and Nehemiah strived to keep both pure.

Learn More: Deuteronomy 23:2–4 / Nehemiah 13 / John 4:24 / Hebrews 12:28–29

A QUESTION OF PURPOSE

Who knoweth whether thou art come to the kingdom for such a time as this? Esther 4:14

Mordecai was one of countless Jews taken captive by the Babylonians—who were soon afterward conquered by the Persian King Xerxes. While in captivity, one of Mordecai's relatives gave birth to a baby girl named Esther. After that relative died, Mordecai raised Esther as his own daughter.

King Xerxes, having called for his wife Vashti to appear before a drunken crowd at a banquet, was furious when she refused. After deposing her, he later sought a replacement by forcing every young virgin in the kingdom to appear before him for evaluation. He chose Esther, whom Bible scholars believe was approximately fifteen years old at the time. Xerxes was around forty.

Xerxes had an ego-filled official named Haman, whom Mordecai deeply offended by refusing to bow before him as the law required. As retribution, Haman convinced Xerxes to sign a decree ordering the annihilation of all Jews, and Mordecai pleaded with Esther to use her royal position to change the king's mind. She hesitated, knowing such a move could be fatal. But Mordecai reminded her that God may have placed her in the palace for the sole purpose of saving the Jewish race.

The young girl stepped up to assume this enormous responsibility—all because Mordecai dared to believe God had a plan.

Learn More: Esther 1–4

HAMAN'S IRONIC QUESTION

What shall be done unto the man whom the king delighteth to honour? Esther 6:6

During the reign of King Xerxes, two of his officers plotted to assassinate him. But Mordecai overheard their plan and reported it to Queen Esther, his cousin. Esther then informed the king, and the two officers were hanged for treason. At the time, Persian kings often employed scribes to record the names of people who performed significant deeds. Thus, Mordecai's name and deed found their way into Xerxes' diary.

Sometime later, Xerxes requested that a servant read to him from his journal during a sleepless night. As the servant read about the foiled assassination plot, Xerxes asked if Mordecai had ever been rewarded. To the king's surprise, he had not. The king then created a plan to honor Mordecai for his heroism.

Learn More: Esther 2:21–23; 6:1–6 / Psalm 56:8; 121:3–4 / Isaiah 40:10 / Zephaniah 3:17 /
Malachi 3:16 / Matthew 16:2

A SELFISH, MISDIRECTED QUESTION

To whom would the king delight to do honour more than to myself? ESTHER 6:6

As an egomaniac who held a high position under King Xerxes, Haman expected the people to bow before him. So when a Jew named Mordecai refused, Haman prepared gallows on which to hang him, and he hatched a plan to annihilate all the Jews.

One day, Xerxes asked Haman to help him brainstorm ways he could honor the man who pleased him. Haman, unaware that the king was planning to reward Mordecai for spoiling an assassination plot, selfishly assumed this honor would be for himself. He devised a lavish plan—dress this person in the king's robe and parade him around town on the king's horse, declaring how honorable the man is. Haman's reverie was shattered when the king instructed him to implement this plan—for Mordecai. Utterly humiliated, Haman led his enemy through the streets. But this reversal was only the beginning: in the end, Haman was hanged on the gallows intended for Mordecai, and Mordecai was elevated to Haman's former position.

Prideful people are captivated with themselves; they gaze at mirrors to see only themselves. Unfortunately, Haman's self-centered mirror led to his destruction. "A man's pride shall bring him low: but honour shall uphold the humble in spirit" (Proverbs 29:23).

Learn More: Esther 6–7 / Proverbs 11:2; 16:18 / 1 Peter 5:6

A QUESTION DEMANDING ACTION

How can I endure to see the evil that shall come unto my people? ESTHER 8:6

Young Queen Esther was in a precarious position. She was married to a powerful Persian king who had just been persuaded by Haman, his top official, to sign an edict eradicating all the Jews in the kingdom. According to Persian law, a decree that was sealed with the king's ring could never be changed. The future of the Jewish people rested on Esther's shoulders.

After fasting for three days, Esther risked her life by appearing before Xerxes without being summoned—and he accepted her. She then invited him and Haman to a banquet. Haman, unaware that his evil plot was about to be uncovered, was delighted. At the banquet, Esther pleaded with Xerxes to spare her and her people, revealing Haman's plot. The king became furious and ordered Haman's immediate execution.

In yet another act of bravery, Esther asked the king to address Haman's edict. Xerxes agreed, allowing her to write a new edict that permitted the Jewish people to defend themselves from annihilation. Esther saved her people and influenced a powerful king to countermand a sealed decree, thus proving that God's will transcends human laws.

Learn More: Esther 4:15–10:3 / Daniel 6:8, 12, 15

A FOOLISH QUESTION BORN OF PAIN

Dost thou still retain thine integrity? JOB 2:9

When a person experiences a difficult trial, the pain often extends to family and friends, who sometimes speak without thinking. After Job had lost everything, his wife was deeply hurt and frustrated. She told him to drop his continued integrity, arguing that it was ultimately futile. Ironically, this integrity was one of the qualities for which God commended Job.

Integrity is defined as a sound condition able to withstand extreme pressure without breaking. People of integrity possess virtue, honesty, and high morals; however, even the most righteous people can reach a tipping point. King David, for example, composed several psalms expressing his fears and distress. More than once he asked God to destroy his enemies, sometimes even questioning if God was still with him. Yet David remained upright, and he asked the Lord to judge him according to his integrity.

Scripture gives no indication that Job's wife was punished or even reprimanded by the Lord—even when she told Job to curse God and die. It's reassuring to know that even in our least patient moments, the Lord remains patient with us.

Learn More: Job 1–2 / Psalm 7:8; 13; 55

JOB'S WISE QUESTION

Shall we receive good at the hand of God, and shall we not receive evil? JOB 2:10

Job is considered the model of patience—a man who endured the loss of children, wealth, home, servants, and health. And it all began when God mentioned Job's name to Satan.

In His talk with the devil, the Lord described Job as a blameless, upright, God-fearing man of integrity. When God gave Satan permission to wreak havoc on Job's life, the man remained faithful. He even declared at one point that he would always trust God, even if the Lord took his life. How did God know Job wouldn't defect? Maybe this wasn't Job's first trial, and his perfect track record assured God that Job would emerge from this new test as gold.

The Lord has a higher purpose for everything, including our trials. The apostle Paul writes in Romans that we should rejoice in suffering because it produces perseverance, which then creates character and hope. The psalmist indicates his afflictions were necessary to draw him closer to the Lord. And James says the testing of our faith makes us mature and complete.

Suffering is a catalyst for change. Some might call it trouble, but God calls it growth.

Learn More: Job 1–2; 13:15; 23:10 / Psalm 34:2; 119:67, 71, 75 /
Romans 5:3–4 / 1 Peter 1:3–7 / James 1:2–4

A QUESTION OF SENSE

Doth not the ear try words? and the mouth taste his meat? JOB 12:11

Throughout Job's trial, his friends overwhelmed him with their speculations about why he was being afflicted. Job, however, maintained his ability to discern, pushing back whenever they accused him of hidden sin. At one point he told his "comforters" that he was a listening connoisseur, testing their words the way the tongue tastes food.

By transmitting nerve signals to the brain, our taste buds can distinguish flavors like salty, bitter, sweet, sour, and savory—and the body reacts accordingly. Sweet food is pleasant; bitter food is not. As food affects our bodies, so people's words influence our attitude and decisions. If their words are false and bitter, we should deny them entrance into our minds, lest they secure themselves in our hearts.

Even though Job's physical health had been compromised, his spiritual sensitivity stayed keen, enabling him to reject any faith-shaking words. Paul's directive, "Whatsoever things are true. . .think on these things" (Philippians 4:8), is our safest recourse.

Learn More: Job 12; 19:23–27 / Psalm 26:2 / Proverbs 18:21

BILDAD'S RUDE QUESTION FOR JOB

How long will it be ere ye make an end of words? JOB 18:2

As Job suffered, three of his friends—Eliphaz, Bildad, and Zophar—visited him to offer sympathy and comfort. Stunned at his appearance, they sat in silence for several days until Job finally began to express his agony. Instead of listening, these men scrutinized Job's words and gave their own analyses. They accused Job of secretly living an evil life (4:7–9) and claimed his children had died because they had sinned (8:4). They called his laments "lies" (11:3) and "unprofitable talk" (15:3). Even worse, they said he didn't even know God (18:21). By judging Job's words so severely, they only rubbed salt in his wounds.

Job finally told his friends what he really needed—fewer speeches and more encouragement. Bildad, not taking the hint, asked Job when he would end his speeches and heed their words.

As Solomon says, "He that answereth a matter before he heareth it, it is folly and shame unto him." Active listening is a scriptural skill everyone should strive to develop; however, in our increasingly self-centered culture, this skill is becoming a lost art. If only Job's friends had listened with nonjudgmental ears, they would have seen that "in all this, did not Job sin with his lips" (Job 2:10).

Learn More: Job 2:10–18:21 / Proverbs 1:5; 18:13 / James 1:19

GOD'S FIRST QUESTION FOR JOB

Who is this that darkeneth counsel by words without knowledge? Job 38:2

When we experience difficulties, we sometimes question if the Lord hears our laments. But just as Job and his friends quickly discovered, God pays close attention to everything we say. Silence doesn't mean indifference.

When God finally appeared to Job, He didn't bellow loudly from the heavens; rather, He spoke out of a storm, implying He had been Job's silent partner the whole time. Then, in order to give them a proper perspective, God challenged Job's friends by asking questions of His own. Now it was their turn to listen.

The Lord asked Job more than seventy rhetorical questions—each one intended to provoke self-awareness. After hearing the Almighty speak, Job had a sobering realization: "I have heard of thee by the hearing of the ear: but now mine eye seeth thee" (Job 42:5).

The Lord always finishes what He starts. Job's trial began with a conversation between God and Satan, and it concluded with the Lord ordering Job's friends to sacrifice burnt offerings as Job prayed for them. In the end, God rewarded Job with twice the possessions he had before. He lived long enough to see his great-great-grandchildren and died "old and full of days" (42:17).

Learn More: Job 38–42 / Isaiah 40:28; 55:8–13 / Philippians 1:6

DAVID'S DESPERATE QUESTION

Why standest thou afar off, O Lord? Psalm 10:1

In no place is the longsuffering of the Lord more evident than in David's psalms. As the former shepherd boy poured out his deepest emotions, God graciously exhibited patience and understanding. David's question to God, "Why standest thou afar off?" was not a sign of disrespect—it was a display of desperation. David wanted immediate retribution toward the wicked, but the Lord seemed distant and slow to respond.

God extended His patience—both to David as he ranted and to the wicked as they ignored their Maker. What we often misinterpret as poor timing is usually God's act of extending grace. As the Lord told Ezekiel, He takes no pleasure in the death of the wicked. While we might wish for retribution, God hopes for repentance.

David begins Psalm 10 with the frustrated observation that the wicked seem to have the upper hand. Then he backpedals, acknowledging that the Lord is King forever. Even within his pleas for vengeance, David recognizes that God's timing is perfect and His ways are flawless.

Learn More: Psalm 10 / Ezekiel 18:23 / 2 Peter 3:9

A QUESTION OF ACCESS

Lord, who shall abide in thy tabernacle? Psalm 15:1

The psalms are filled with David's questions. Some he directs to God, some he asks himself, and some he even answers for himself. Today, we would label David as an external processor.

In Psalm 15, David seeks to know the qualifications for living in God's presence (His tabernacle or sanctuary). But instead of waiting for God's response, David creates the list himself: a blameless walk, righteous acts, a heart of truth, no slander, respectfulness toward neighbors, no false accusations, hatred toward evil, honor toward those who fear the Lord, determination to keep promises, no usury, and no bribery.

David concludes this psalm with a powerful statement: "He that doeth these things shall never be moved" (verse 5). Notice two key words—*never* and *moved*. *Never* contains a stronger meaning than the word *not*. It means "not under any circumstance." *Moved* means "tottered, shook, or slipped." Using these definitions, one can read the verse, "He who does these things will not, under any circumstance, ever totter or slip."

It is comforting to know that righteous living results in stability. Even greater is the assurance that we will abide in God's presence, where nothing is ever shaken.

Learn More: 2 Chronicles 16:9 / Psalm 15 / Proverbs 10:9 / 1 Corinthians 15:58

A QUESTION OF MORAL ERROR

Who can understand his errors? PSALM 19:12

In Psalm 19, David compares God's law, statutes, precepts, and commands to invaluable gold. Obedience to these instructions is enriching, satisfying, and rewarding. However, David also contrasts pure obedience with the progression of sin, which begins with error and ends with great transgression.

An error is a mistake or flaw—a blind spot that isn't always recognized. David acknowledges that it is difficult for us to perceive errors—that is why God warns us with His statutes. Once we recognize an error, we must correct it; otherwise, it can become a "secret fault" (verse 12)—a persistent imperfection that brings us guilt. Since our words and actions display our internal condition, secret faults can grow into "presumptuous [or willful] sins" (verse 13). If one keeps committing presumptuous sins, that person will eventually revolt against God—the "great transgression" (verse 13).

David concludes this psalm by declaring his desire for the words of his mouth (external evidence) and the meditation of his heart (internal condition) to be pleasing in God's sight.

The best way to avoid sin's progression is to love, cherish, and obey the law of the Lord. Otherwise, how can we understand our errors?

Learn More: Joshua 1:8 / Psalm 19; 119:11, 47–48

A QUESTION OF SUBMISSION

What man is he that feareth the Lord? PSALM 25:12

Fearing the Lord means willingly submitting to Him because we are aware of His holiness. In Psalm 25, David asks how someone who fears the Lord can be identified. The first way involves the blessings that accompany God-fearing people. David writes that these people will enjoy prosperity and that the Lord will confide in them and assure them of His promises.

But the list doesn't stop there. According to Psalm 112, people who fear the Lord will be generous and judicious in their affairs—and will prosper as a result. Psalm 128 says the God-fearer will enjoy a strong, unified family. And in Proverbs, Solomon tells us that this person will even sleep better.

Solomon indicates that the fear of the Lord is merely the beginning of wisdom and knowledge. The more we submit to His will, our longing to discover more about Him will increase. The more we know, the more we will revere Him. And the more we revere, the more we glorify God.

Learn More: Job 28:28 / Psalm 25; 112; 115:11–15; 128 / Proverbs 9:10; 16:6; 19:23

THE PSALMIST QUESTIONS HIS DEPRESSION

Why art thou cast down, O my soul? PSALM 42:5

Psalms 42 and 43 are two halves of one song, and both grapple with the subject of depression. Three times the psalmist asks, "Why art thou cast down, O my soul? and why art thou disquieted in me?" (42:5, 11; 43:5). This could simply be a musical refrain, or it could be a desperate cry from the composer's heart. Given the extended laments throughout these psalms, the latter sounds much more probable.

This psalmist had once been filled with joy, leading multitudes to God's house with singing and shouting. But now he felt rejected by God. What had sent him into this pit of despair? Whatever the cause, he was determined to crawl out.

His situation created a voracious thirst for God—which could only be satisfied by the Lord's presence. The psalmist freely expressed his frustrations, knowing God would not condemn him. He recalled the Lord's constant faithfulness through day and night, referring to God as his Rock, Savior, and Stronghold. Because of his hope in God, there *was* light at the end of the tunnel. God would bring him to His dwelling place, and once again the psalmist would play his harp and sing.

Learn More: Psalm 42–43 / Philippians 4:4–9

A QUESTION OF JERUSALEM'S PUNISHMENT

Why hast thou then broken down her hedges? Psalm 80:12

Asaph penned this psalm as a prayer for rescue when the Assyrians invaded Israel. For years, the Israelites had struck fear into the hearts of other nations as the Lord won victory after victory. Now, because of Israel's unfaithfulness, the tables had turned.

City walls were intended to shut out invaders, and the watchmen on the walls were responsible for sounding the alarm when enemies approached. Fortunately for the enemy, Israel's nonchalant spirituality had made them ripe for invasion. Why break down the walls when Israel had opened her gates? Eventually, the city lay in ruins, and anyone who passed by could plunder its vineyards.

Asaph knew that the Lord had always divinely protected Israel. But now He had lifted His hand, exposing the nation to ridicule and derision. The Israelites had compromised their own protection, and now they were paying the price.

Thankfully, the Lord does not harbor anger forever. Even when we deserve the harshest of consequences, He extends mercy. Isaiah prophesied that Jerusalem's walls would be rebuilt, allowing the people to safely enjoy their harvest. But this time, the walls would be named Salvation and Praise.

Learn More: Psalm 80; 103:9–13 / Isaiah 58:12; 60:18; 62

A QUESTION OF REVIVAL

Wilt thou not revive us again: that thy people may rejoice in thee? Psalm 85:6

In this song, the psalmist asks God to do two things: (1) to restore Israel's broken relationship with Him and (2) to revive them spiritually. Notice that he asks the Lord to restore and revive *again*. This word reveals the author's hope that Israel would finally become consistent in her devotion to God.

When an item is restored, it is brought back to its original condition. Spiritual restoration is no different. Hosea the prophet said that God would heal Israel's broken condition, eagerly restoring her relationship with Him.

The psalmist didn't want only a simple repair job. He wanted God to breathe into the lungs of a spiritually dead nation, causing them to exhale with praise and rejoicing. He wanted revival. But this time he prayed that Israel, instead of returning to her reckless living, would listen to the Lord and live. The psalmist deeply desired that God's glory would once again dwell in the land as the people rejoiced in the Lord.

Learn More: Genesis 2:7 / Job 33:4 / Psalm 85 / Isaiah 57:14–16 / Hosea 6:1–3

QUESTIONING SINNERS' SEEMING TRIUMPH

Lord, how long shall the wicked, how long shall the wicked triumph? Psalm 94:3

The composer of Psalm 94 is unknown. Yet one thing is certain: he was desperate for God to intervene on his behalf. Throughout his introspective cries of desperation, he asks nine questions, one of which especially stands out—"How long shall the wicked triumph?"

As pressures on Christians increase and evil seems to win, we can find comfort, hope, and strength in the psalmist's words. Sandwiched between his rhetorical questions are the psalmist's recognitions of God's power: the Lord knows everything that happens in our lives, our nation, and our world. He even knows our thoughts. God remains faithful to His followers, bringing relief when troubles increase. His judgment is perfect and righteous, and the upright in heart will understand when it is revealed. Even when we slip, His love supports us. The Lord replaces anxiety with consolation and joy. He is our fortress and refuge.

So, in answer to the psalmist's question, God *will* repay those who deserve His vengeance. He is always fair. We only need to trust Him.

Learn More: Psalm 94; 27:4; 73:1–20 / Habakkuk 2:3

A QUESTION OF CLEANSING

Wherewithal shall a young man cleanse his way? PSALM 119:9

Each section of Psalm 119 begins with a letter of the Hebrew alphabet, and each letter is represented by a symbol. The character for the Hebrew letter *Beth* (Psalm 119:9–16) is a house—a structure that protects people from intruders. When the author asks, "Wherewithal shall a young man cleanse his way?" he answers his own question by recognizing the need for structure. A young man must live according to God's Word, whose boundaries protect from sin's intrusion.

In these verses, the psalmist uses different words with similar meanings—commands, decrees, laws, ordinances, statutes, and precepts. Because God's ways make the psalmist feel secure, he delights—and even rejoices—as he obeys them. Just as houses have foundations, walls, ceilings, floors, support beams, and so on, we need structure to surround us from every angle, top to bottom. Our homes bring us comfort, peace, and protection—and so does God's presence.

The Lord is referred to as our dwelling place, hiding place, and refuge. Psalm 125:2 says, "The LORD is round about his people from henceforth even for ever." Only by remaining within God's presence and by securing His Word in our hearts can we cleanse our way.

Learn More: Psalm 119:9–16; 16:1; 18:2–3; 32:7; 90:1

A QUESTION OF PAST SIN

If thou, Lord, shouldest mark iniquities, O Lord, who shall stand? PSALM 130:3

How unsettling it is to imagine that God would keep record of every sin we've committed, especially given that we probably can't remember all of them ourselves. Thankfully, when we confess, He forgives us, removing our sins as far as the east is from the west.

Some Christians fear that when they stand before the Lord, everything they've said or done will be revealed, even if they have received forgiveness. While scripture teaches that everyone will give an account to God, it's not certain what will be brought up on that day. Worst-case scenario—Satan, our accuser, will level charges against us based on every sin we've committed. Should that happen, Jesus, our Defender, will speak on our behalf, refuting every charge. Best-case scenario—nothing is brought up because no record of sin exists.

If we are concerned about standing before God, we should examine our hearts for any unconfessed sins, acknowledge them immediately, and accept forgiveness. When we have a clear conscience, there's no fear or guilt because Jesus has eliminated our sin on the cross. If the Lord keeps no record of our sins, neither should we.

Learn More: Psalm 130; 103:10–12 / Acts 3:19 / Hebrews 4:13 / 1 John 2:1–6

WISDOM'S QUESTION

How long, ye simple ones, will ye love simplicity? PROVERBS 1:22

Throughout the book of Proverbs, three specific groups of people are mentioned: the simple—those who lack a clear sense of direction and are easily swayed by others; the fools—those who shun knowledge and act irresponsibly; and the mockers—arrogant scoffers who scorn correction. One Bible scholar has described these three groups as an army of evil. The simple are the recruits, the fools are the rank and file, and the mockers are the proud leaders.

It's bad enough to be labeled as one of these three; it's even worse to take delight in the lifestyle. While wisdom beckons for them to change their ways in the face of impending doom, these people turn a deaf ear to her appeal. Their obstinate hearts drive them into reckless lives without fear of consequences or even of God Himself.

Wisdom is the antidote for godless living. She instructs people to listen, watch, and wait daily at her doorstep. Those who listen will receive blessings and favor from the Lord.

Learn More: Proverbs 1:20–33; 8:1–36 / 2 Peter 3:3 / Jude 18–23

A QUESTION FOR ADULTERERS

Can one go upon hot coals, and his feet not be burned? PROVERBS 6:28

In Proverbs 6, Solomon imagines two absurd situations: a man playing with fire without expecting to be burned and a man who commits adultery without fear of consequences. Earlier, however, Solomon tells his son that God's commands will create a safety net of protection from temptation.

Scripture clearly teaches that temptation does not come from God. Instead, our own desires drag us into disobedience. Succumbing to evil desires leads to sin, and sin culminates in death. According to James, if we deceive ourselves into believing our sins have no consequences, we will throw caution to the wind. While the Lord builds, strengthens, and equips us, the devil tears down and breaches our most vulnerable areas.

In his epistle, John speaks of three types of temptation—the lust of the flesh, the lust of the eyes, and the pride of life. All three were at play when Satan tempted Jesus to turn a stone into bread after a long fast, to bow down to him in exchange for many vast kingdoms, and to prove He was the Son of God by jumping from the top of the temple. But Jesus resisted by using the Word—the safety net of protection—and the devil left defeated.

Learn More: Proverbs 6:20–32 / Matthew 4:1–11 / James 1:13–16 / 1 John 2:15–17

AN EMOTIONAL QUESTION

A wounded spirit who can bear? PROVERBS 18:14

Solomon notes that people's attitude (spirit) affects their response to physical sickness. Medical science confirms that attitudes can determine how quickly people will recuperate. If they are upbeat and optimistic, their chances of recovery are much higher. But a crushed (wounded) spirit pulls them into depression.

A person's spirit can be crushed in different ways—through disappointment, grief, hurt, loss, loneliness, and so on. While it's important to identify the reason, it's equally important to control our response. To deal with a physical illness, doctors first assess the cause and then focus on the cure. A broken spirit should be treated in the same way.

Scripture tells us how to restore a crushed spirit. First, we should avoid isolation. By asking who can bear a crushed spirit, Solomon implies outside help is needed. As Paul says, we should carry one another's burdens. Second, we should sing in our hearts. Music therapy is not just a modern phenomenon—even Saul found relief when David played his harp. Finally, we must call out to God, who embraces the brokenhearted and saves those who are crushed in spirit.

Learn More: 1 Samuel 16:14–23 / Psalm 34:17–18; 51:8 / Proverbs 17:22 / Galatians 6:2 / Ephesians 5:19

A QUESTION OF GOD'S KNOWLEDGE

Doth not he that pondereth the heart consider it? PROVERBS 24:12

In addition to being concerned for our own needs, we must also care for the needs of others. If we aren't careful, our vision can become myopic, blinding us to the people within our reach. Solomon admonishes us to make every effort to save those who are facing spiritual death. We can't claim ignorance, because God peers into the heart and perceives what we know.

Rescuing people from physical death is noble, but eternal death is a far greater threat. Imagine if the church exerted the same intensity in reaching the lost as medics exert while saving lives. To increase our passion, we must be compelled by love.

John says if we are living in love, then we are living in God and God lives in us. And if He dwells in us, our eyes will be opened to the needs around us. Therefore, when we stand before the Lord on Judgment Day, we can face Him with confidence because His love has been made complete in us.

Learn More: Romans 14:12 / 2 Corinthians 5:14–15 / Hebrews 4:13 / 1 John 4:16–21

A QUESTION OF JEALOUSY

Who is able to stand before envy? Proverbs 27:4

Solomon's proverbs cover dozens of topics, no doubt due to his interactions with people from many nations. One such interaction apparently inspired him to compare anger with envy, rendered as *jealousy* in many modern Bible translations.

Jealousy is a self-feeding machine, and rivalry is its main power source. A jealous husband may feel threatened if he believes another man is interested in his wife, or vice versa. An employee may become jealous if a new hire shows more potential than he or she does. Jealousy often manifests itself through anger, resulting in irrational decisions.

For example, Joseph's brothers sold him into slavery, lied to their father, Jacob, and hid their sin for years—all because Joseph was Jacob's favorite son. As the early Christian church grew, the priests and Sadducees began persecuting and jailing the apostles out of jealousy over the number of new converts. After Paul and Barnabas preached to crowds in Antioch, the Jews became jealous and threw them out of the city.

Anger comes and goes, but jealousy tends to fester. As part of the sinful nature that conflicts with the Spirit, jealousy can only be overcome when we actively take a stand against it.

Learn More: Numbers 5:11–31 / Proverbs 6:34 / Acts 13:44–52 / 1 Corinthians 3:3 / Galatians 5:19–26

THE QUESTION OF LIFE'S PURPOSE

For whom do I labor, and bereave my soul of good? Ecclesiastes 4:8

Solomon's reflections in Ecclesiastes differ starkly from his earlier wisdom in Proverbs. Some believe he became quite cynical in his later years, as his thoughts often smack of pessimism and disappointment. Even so, the life lessons that he liberally shares in this book can help us enjoy life as God intended.

One theme woven throughout Ecclesiastes pertains to finding enjoyment in one's work. It's no secret that many are dissatisfied with their jobs. One study has shown that people stick with jobs they don't like in order to remain in houses they can't afford. But according to Solomon, God wants people to enjoy their work. Scripture indicates that the only way to enjoy life is to fear the Lord and reverently submit to His sovereign will.

In his younger years, Solomon had said, "Better is little with the fear of the Lord than great treasure and trouble therewith" (Proverbs 15:16). By the end of his life, this wise and experienced king finally realized the purpose of life: "Fear God and keep his commandments: for this is the whole duty of man" (Ecclesiastes 12:13).

Learn More: Proverbs 2:1–6; 10:27; 19:23 / Ecclesiastes 3:12–13; 5:19; 8:15

A QUESTION OF BALANCE

Be not righteous over much. . .why shouldest thou destroy thyself? Ecclesiastes 7:16

Solomon mused over life's paradoxes in his later years, speaking at one point about a righteous man who died young and a wicked man who grew old. This observation inspired Solomon to warn about taking righteousness and wisdom to extremes.

Righteousness and wisdom are given by God with a measure of faith. Paul instructs us to use these gifts with "sober judgment"—not beyond the bounds God has established (Romans 12:3-4). God granted Solomon the gift of wisdom, making him wiser than any other human being. Unfortunately, his wives coerced him into supporting idol worship, thus compromising his relationship with God and opening his heart to pride. It's possible that he took his wisdom for granted, forgetting the One who gave it to him.

In Proverbs, Solomon says, "Pride goeth before destruction, and an haughty spirit before a fall" (Proverbs 16:18). When a person depends more on the gift than on the Giver, the results will never be good.

Learn More: 1 Kings 4:29–34 / Ecclesiastes 7:15–18 / Romans 3:21–22

GOD'S QUESTION TO ISAIAH

Whom shall I send? Isaiah 6:8

Isaiah served as a prophet to King Uzziah. Most of Uzziah's reign was blessed by God; however, pride eventually crept into the king's heart, inciting him to offer incense in the holy place of the temple—an action reserved only for priests. When confronted about his sin, Uzziah became angry and God struck him with leprosy. He was confined away from his palace until he died.

The king's death must have impacted young Isaiah, who marked that year as a reminder of his vision and calling. As Isaiah admitted his own uncleanness in the Lord's holy presence, did he recall Uzziah's actions in the holy place? While the prophet struggled with his unworthiness, a seraph touched his lips with a burning coal and declared him guiltless. At that moment, God asked "Whom shall I send?" Without hesitation, Isaiah exclaimed, "Here am I; send me" (Isaiah 6:8). His mission was to keep warning the Israelites—who were unable to see, hear, or discern the truth—about the coming judgment until the land was completely forsaken.

Even though his task seemed futile, Isaiah obeyed. Nearly fifty years later, at the end of his ministry, Isaiah penned one of the most beautiful messianic prophecies ever recorded, thereby giving hope for Israel. We may be pleasantly surprised by the outcome whenever we respond, "Send me!"

Learn More: 2 Chronicles 26 / Isaiah 6; 9:6–7; 40:28–31; 51–55

A QUESTION OF FASTING

Is it such a fast that I have chosen? Isaiah 58:5

The Israelites had turned their fasting into spiritual obligation instead of acts of worship. Their food deprivation made them irritable to the point of striking each other. God told them if their hearts had been right, they would have been more sensitive to the needs of others.

Fasting is a way of seeking direction (2 Chronicles 20:3; Acts 13:1–3); practicing spiritual discipline (Matthew 6:16–18); preparing for ministry (Matthew 4:1–2; Acts 14:23); and showing repentance (1 Samuel 7:6), desperation (Esther 4:3), grief (1 Samuel 31:13), and humility (Ezra 8:21–23). When people deny their bodies food, their spirits become more sensitive, making God's voice easier to hear. Fasting should never be a legalistic formality—it is a way to increase one's spiritual appetite.

The Israelites, who were trying more to impress God than to humble their hearts, complained that the Lord didn't notice their fasting. They were similar to the hypocrites in Jesus' day who fasted to impress people with their piety. The Lord is very aware when we fast, but He is more concerned about how we have changed once the fast is over.

Learn More: Isaiah 58:1–10 / Zechariah 7:1–10 / Matthew 6:16–18 / 1 Corinthians 10:31

AN UNASKED QUESTION

Where is the Lord? Jeremiah 2:8

Scripture occasionally highlights questions that nobody asked. Two of them are recorded in Jeremiah 2, where God charges the Israelites with forgetfulness. First, He mentioned their ancestors, who even though they had been led out of Egypt, through the desert, and into the promised land, still quickly forgot God's faithfulness. The Lord also pointed to the priests who had failed to ask, "Where is the Lord?" By taking their focus away from God, these spiritual leaders held the door wide open for rebellion, false prophesies, and idol worship.

Moses cautioned the Israelites to "keep thy soul diligently" (Deuteronomy 4:9), lest they forget their miraculous experiences. They were to keep these memories fresh by telling future generations. Samuel also had a method of preserving memories. After the ark of the Lord had been taken from Israel, the Israelites repented and began sacrificing to the Lord. So when the Philistines tried to attack again, God intervened, rewarding the Jews with a miraculous victory. Samuel set up a stone as a reminder, calling it "Ebenezer"—which means "stone of help."

Learn More: Deuteronomy 6:12; 8:11; 32:7 / 1 Samuel 7:1–13 / Jeremiah 2:1–9

A QUESTION OF VAIN THINKING

How long shall thy vain thoughts lodge within thee? JEREMIAH 4:14

Jeremiah warned Israel frequently about impending judgment for their wickedness, but to no avail. "Wash thine heart from wickedness, that thou mayest be saved. How long shall thy vain thoughts lodge within thee?" he cried, but nobody listened. Their "wickedness" was their devotion to false gods instead of the Lord, and their "vain thoughts" kept them in a state of denial. Thanks to the lies of false prophets, the Israelites had become convinced of their safety. They were certain that Jeremiah's dire warnings would come to naught.

When something is "lodged," it is held securely in place. The New International Version uses the word *harbor* in Jeremiah 4:14, indicating an anchored ship. The anchor that secured the Israelites' vain thoughts was self-deception. Jeremiah cautioned them more than once about this self-deceit, noting that "the heart is deceitful above all things. . .who can know it?" (17:9). It's difficult for people to be fully aware of their own hearts' condition. But if that's true, then what hope do we have?

Thankfully, God has a solution. He told the Israelites, "I the LORD search the heart" (17:10). If we frequently invite the Lord to inspect our hearts, He will reveal hidden sin—and remove the anchor that holds it in place.

Learn More: Job 10:6–7 / Jeremiah 4:5–18; 29:8–9; 37:9 / 1 Corinthians 3:18

A QUESTION OF SPIRITUAL HEALING

Is there no balm in Gilead? JEREMIAH 8:22

Prior to Israel's seventy-year captivity, God gave several warnings through Jeremiah about the people's spiritual unfaithfulness. Unfortunately, many of Israel's scribes, priests, and prophets played a role in leading the people away from the Lord. God described Israel's spiritual condition as a deep wound that needed to be healed lest it become fatally infected.

Jeremiah felt the people's pain, but the popular false prophets simply declared, "Peace, peace," to appease the people (Jeremiah 8:11)—just like sticking an adhesive bandage over a gaping wound. Jeremiah lamented Israel's injuries, proclaiming that even Gilead, the major producer of medical balm, seemed to have depleted its supply.

Jeremiah was more than a prophet—he was an intercessor. The Lord responded to his prayers by encouraging him when he needed it the most. As soothing as Gilead's balm might have been on the surface, the Lord promised to bring a lasting cure. This remedy from the Sun of Righteousness would penetrate deep into the spiritual infection, bringing ultimate restoration.

Learn More: Isaiah 58:8 / Jeremiah 8; 33:1–18 / Malachi 4:2

A QUESTION OF TRANSFORMATION

Can the Ethiopian change his skin, or the leopard his spots? JEREMIAH 13:23

At first glance, the answer to this question would be no—outside of drastic means, people cannot change their skin color. Jeremiah used this question to drive home a point: the Israelites had become so accustomed to doing evil that they were incapable of doing good. Yet there is always hope because God *can* transform the internal person and renew his or her mind.

While speaking of transformation, the apostle Paul uses the Greek word for metamorphosis—a term that often describes a caterpillar's changing into a butterfly. As amazing as this alteration is, the renewing of the human mind is even more miraculous. Old habits can be erased and replaced with new ones. As the psalmist testifies, the most effective way to renew the mind is through scripture meditation. Meditating on the Word not only helps us avoid evil, it causes us to hate it.

Despite Israel's penchant for sin, God still promised plans for future hope. Our hope for change rests in Christ, who specializes in reshaping the old into something new. Once He begins, He won't stop until the change is permanent.

Learn More: Psalm 119:97–104 / Isaiah 43:18–19 / Jeremiah 29:11 /
Romans 12:2 / 2 Corinthians 4:16; 5:17 / Philippians 1:6

A QUESTION FROM A REBELLIOUS KING

Is there any word from the Lord? Jeremiah 37:17

Babylon's King Nebuchadnezzar made Zedekiah king over Judah. According to scripture, Zedekiah was a stiff-necked king with a hard heart, rebelling against the Babylonian ruler and ignoring Jeremiah's prophecies during his eleven-year reign.

Although he refused to obey, Zedekiah couldn't resist knowing his future, so he secretly asked Jeremiah if he had any word from the Lord, thus treating the prophet like a fortune-teller. Jeremiah told him if he surrendered to the Babylonians, he and his family would be spared and Jerusalem would not be destroyed. Unsurprisingly, Zedekiah did not heed the warning. Even after Nebuchadnezzar had held Jerusalem under siege for two years, Zedekiah remained defiant. Finally, he abandoned Jerusalem with his army, but it was too late. The Babylonians captured him, slaughtered his children before his face, put out his eyes—so that the sight of his dying family would be forever engraved in his mind—and placed him in prison until he died.

Today, our Word from the Lord is the Bible, which teaches, rebukes, corrects, and trains us in righteousness. While we may not always like what God tells us, every word He speaks is for our good. Obedience is always the best response.

Learn More: 2 Chronicles 36:11–14 / Jeremiah 37; 38:14–28; 52:1–11 / 2 Timothy 3:16–17

JEREMIAH'S RHETORICAL QUESTION

Out of the mouth of the most High proceedeth not evil and good? Lamentations 3:38

Jeremiah's deep love for the Israelites and his tendency to cry over their sins and punishment has earned him the title of "weeping prophet." His book of Lamentations gives readers a deeper look into his heart. In chapter 3, Jeremiah begins by listing every unfair challenge that his opponents had thrown at him. Then he writes, "This I recall to my mind, therefore have I hope" (verse 21)—a reminder to keep God foremost in our thoughts, no matter what. The prophet then stunningly contrasts his opponents' unjust actions with God's justice.

Acknowledging how we blame God for misfortune, Jeremiah stresses personal responsibility, urging us to examine our hearts and confess our waywardness before we fault God. The wicked may affect others with their sin, but that doesn't make them all-powerful. Jeremiah says, "All our enemies have opened their mouths against us" (Lamentations 3:46); however, the Most High has spoken too, and nothing can happen apart from His decree.

So, to answer the prophet's rhetorical question, both calamities and good *do* come from the Lord—but never without purpose and always within His control.

Learn More: Isaiah 45:7 / Lamentations 3 / 1 Corinthians 10:13

A QUESTION OF RESPONSIBILITY

What mean ye, that ye use this proverb concerning the land of Israel. . . ? Ezekiel 18:2

The Israelites often quoted a proverb: "The fathers have eaten sour grapes, and the children's teeth are set on edge." Some believe this referred to Adam, who cursed humankind by eating the forbidden fruit in the garden, while others believe it was a way for children to blame their sinful tendencies on their elders.

In Ezekiel 18, the Lord describes three generations of people who make choices—both good and bad. Each person, God says, is responsible for their own actions. Twice in this chapter, the Lord says, "The soul that sinneth, it shall die" (verses 4 and 20). A righteous son born to a wicked father will not be punished for the father's sins. Moreover, a virtuous father whose son makes bad decisions should not blame himself, especially if he has set a godly example.

God's explanation about responsibility for sin also means a wicked son born to a righteous father will be punished. As one seasoned minister has said, "You can't get to heaven on your father's coattails." We will each be held accountable for our actions, and the decision of whether or not to follow Christ rests in our own hands.

Learn More: Jeremiah 31:27–34 / Ezekiel 18:1–20 / Romans 14:12

A QUESTION OF GOD'S FAIRNESS

Have I any pleasure at all that the wicked should die? EZEKIEL 18:23

The Israelites accused God of being unjust for chastising sinners. What the Lord had called "accountability," the Israelites called "unfair." Apparently, they thought God enjoyed doling out punishment; on the contrary, God wanted people to repent and walk in righteousness.

What the Israelites really wanted was instant forgiveness and a license to do anything they pleased. But God explained that all people will be judged according to their choices. If righteous people return to a life of sin, they choose death, but if wicked people turn from their evil ways, they receive life. It's a choice we all must make. God is not willing for anyone to perish, no matter how grave the sin. He wants everyone to repent. Even though God's mercies are everlasting and His anger is short-lived, He will punish wickedness someday.

After the Israelites accused God of being unjust, He offered an olive branch, promising them that if they would repent and turn to Him, He would both forgive them and give them a new heart and spirit. Doesn't that sound fair?

Learn More: Deuteronomy 30:19 / Psalm 30:5 / Isaiah 54:8 / Ezekiel 18:23-32 / 2 Peter 3:9

GOD'S QUESTION TO EZEKIEL

Son of man, can these bones live? EZEKIEL 37:3

Ezekiel was a prophet during the Babylonian captivity, and he had frequent visions that either warned or encouraged God's people. In one such vision, he found himself in a valley full of bones. At God's command, Ezekiel prophesied to the bones, watching as they joined together with tendons, flesh, and skin. Then Ezekiel spoke breath into them, and the motionless bodies suddenly stood, creating a massive army. This vision foretold that Judah's captivity would end and that the people would return to their homeland with new life.

Centuries before Ezekiel, Israel had split into two competing nations: a northern kingdom still called Israel and the southern kingdom of Judah. But as Ezekiel's vision showed, this division would not be permanent. Israel would become a united country, ruled by the eternal King, Jesus Christ. Through this union, other nations would witness God's restorative work.

According to the apostle Paul, the church's head is Christ and its life is the Spirit. Each body part has a different role, yet we all work toward one goal—to show Jesus to the world.

Learn More: Ezekiel 37 / John 17:23 / Romans 15:5-13 / 1 Corinthians 1:10; 12:12-13 / Galatians 3:26-29 / Colossians 1:18

A BABYLONIAN STEWARD'S NERVOUS QUESTION

Why should he see your faces worse. . .than the children which are of your sort? DANIEL 1:10

Jeremiah the prophet foretold that the Israelites' Babylonian captivity would last seventy years. He instructed them to settle in Babylon and live normal lives without compromising their devotion to the Lord. Among the first captives was Daniel, whose name means "God is my judge." He and the other young Jewish men were teenagers at the time. The Babylonians, hoping to quickly conform these men to a foreign lifestyle, changed their names. Daniel was renamed Belteshazzar, meaning "Bel [a Babylonian god] protect his life."

The king treated Daniel and his companions royally—even serving them his own rich food. Daniel knew this food was both unhealthy and against Hebrew law, so he requested only vegetables and water. At first, the steward—who was responsible for presenting these men before the king—balked. If they looked unhealthy, the steward would be held accountable. God, however, turned the steward's heart, and he agreed to serve the food they requested. Much to the steward's astonishment, Daniel and his friends looked healthier and better nourished than the others after ten days of the leaner diet.

Daniel remembered God was his protector.

Learn More: Proverbs 1:10 / Jeremiah 29:4-14 / Daniel

DANIEL'S QUESTION ABOUT NEBUCHADNEZZAR'S DECREE ———

Why is the decree so hasty from the king? Daniel 2:15

Shortly after Daniel, Shadrach, Meshach, and Abednego were taken into Babylonian captivity, King Nebuchadnezzar had a dream. He called for all the magicians, sorcerers, and astrologers not only to interpret his dream but to tell him what it was. If they didn't, they would all be "cut in pieces" (Daniel 2:5) and their houses burned down. When they protested that the king's request was impossible, Nebuchadnezzar threatened to have every wise man in the land executed—including Daniel and his three friends.

Upon hearing about this rash decree, Daniel requested time to interpret the dream. He and his friends met together to seek God's mercy and insight, and the Lord granted Daniel the interpretation. Daniel appeared before the king, clarifying that nobody on earth could fulfill the king's request, but "God in heaven" had revealed the mystery. Then, Daniel proceeded to correctly share the dream and its interpretation.

Nebuchadnezzar was so impressed that he declared, "Your God is a God of gods, and a Lord of kings, and a revealer of secrets" (2:47). He then honored Daniel and his friends by making them administrators over Babylon and by putting Daniel in charge of all the wise men.

Learn More: Daniel 2:1–49 / Amos 4:13

NEBUCHADNEZZAR'S INCREDULOUS QUESTION ———

Did not we cast three men bound into the midst of the fire? Daniel 3:24

Nebuchadnezzar had an ego bigger than himself. After erecting a ninety-foot golden statue, he commanded everyone to bow down and worship it. . .or be cast into a blazing furnace. However, as hundreds planted their faces on the ground before a lifeless, man-made creation, three Jewish men, Shadrach, Meshach, and Abednego, boldly stood.

These men had been elevated to leadership positions in Babylon, so when Nebuchadnezzar learned of their defiance, he was furious. When he confronted them, they responded by proclaiming their God was able to save them. "But if not," they said, "we will not serve thy gods, nor worship the golden image which thou hast set up" (Daniel 3:18). The king ordered the furnace, perhaps a brick kiln or ore smelter, to be heated seven times its normal intensity, and Shadrach, Meshach, and Abednego were bound and thrown inside. But suddenly, Nebuchadnezzar saw a fourth Man walking in the fire—a Man who looked "like the Son of God." The king's heart changed immediately, and he publicly acknowledged the power of God.

Learn More: Exodus 20:1–6 / Psalm 91 / Isaiah 43:1–3 / Daniel 3

KING DARIUS'S HOPEFUL QUESTION ———

Is thy God, whom thou servest continually, able to deliver thee from the lions? Daniel 6:20

Daniel was young when he was taken captive by the Babylonians, and by the time he was in his eighties, the Medes and Persians had conquered Babylon. Darius, king of the Medes, was so impressed with Daniel's leadership skills that he appointed Daniel as an administrator—first over 120 governors and then over the entire kingdom.

When the other leaders heard of Daniel's upcoming promotion, they formed a plan to prevent it. They knew Daniel was devoted to God, so they asked the king to sign a decree requiring everyone to pray to Darius alone for one month. Those who disobeyed would be thrown to the lions. This idea resonated with the king, and the law—which could not be repealed—was put into effect.

Daniel continued his prayer routine. His opponents caught him in the act and reported him to Darius, who had no choice but to throw Daniel into the lions' den. After a sleepless night, Darius checked on Daniel and was overjoyed to learn God had spared him.

In the end, Daniel's accusers were thrown to the lions, Daniel prospered, and Darius glorified God.

Learn More: Psalm 5 / Daniel 6 / Hebrews 11:6

A QUESTION OF DANGER

Will a lion roar in the forest, when he hath no prey? Amos 3:4

Amos was a shepherd who—through divine inspiration—issued prophetic warnings to Judah, the southern kingdom, for her idolatry and to Israel, the northern kingdom, for her immorality, selfishness, and reckless living.

Amos begins his admonition with several rhetorical questions: Can two people who disagree walk together? Can a bird be trapped if a trap hasn't been set? Does a trumpet sound when no danger looms? And finally, will a lion roar when it has no prey in his sights? All four questions were symbolic: Israel had walked without God, the enemy had set a trap, many prophets had sounded the trumpet, and now the lion was roaring. Doom was imminent, but the people paid no heed.

As persistent as Israel was in her sin, the Lord was more persistent in His warnings. In Amos 4 He reminded them of several methods He had used to draw them back to Him, and the words "Yet have ye not returned unto me" are repeated five times (verses 6, 8, 9, 10, and 11).

Learn More: Amos 3–4 / 1 Thessalonians 5:6

JONAH'S POUTING QUESTION

O Lord, was not this my saying, when I was yet in my country? Jonah 4:2

The story of Jonah is fascinating. At first glance, its emphasis seems to be upon the Ninevites, Israel's sworn enemies; however, a closer look reveals that the story is more about Jonah's need for change. God could have chosen any prophet, but He specifically called Jonah—twice—to preach repentance to the Assyrians.

Jonah's epiphany happened while he was inside a huge fish. Not once, however, did he ever pray for the Ninevites, who were facing God's wrath. When the Lord told him again to go to Nineveh, he obeyed, albeit grudgingly. Walking through the city, he warned the Ninevites of the upcoming disaster that was coming if they didn't repent. To Jonah's dismay, they *did* repent, and God showed mercy.

Jonah then revealed his true desire. Instead of simply returning home after delivering his message, he parked outside the city, hoping to see the fireworks of divine retribution. When none arrived, the prophet directed his frustration toward God, criticizing Him for being gracious, compassionate, and loving.

The book concludes with no indication that Jonah changed. Ironically, his message of repentance connected with the Ninevites—but not with himself.

Learn More: Jonah 1–4 / Matthew 12:38–41

MICAH'S TIMELESS QUESTION

What doth the Lord require of thee? Micah 6:8

Many people believe the way to earn God's favor is through hard work and sacrifice. While God does call His saved people to good deeds, the primary way in which we show our love to Him is through the obedience of a humble heart.

Micah the prophet corrected the Israelites for routinely offering sacrifices without changing their lives. He used extreme illustrations to drive home his point. Were the youngest, best calves enough to take away sin? What about thousands of rams? If so, how many thousands? Would rivers of oil suffice? Or would it take the ultimate sacrifice—the firstborn child?

Micah then gave three actions the Lord requires. The first is to "do justly." This means being fair with others and not falsely accusing or taking advantage of the less fortunate. The second is to "love mercy." We should eagerly search for ways to show kindness to others—forgiving not because we *have* to but because we *want* to, just as God showed mercy to us. And the third is to "walk humbly with thy God." Humility is shown through submission, so we should put God and His desires above our own.

Learn More: Micah 6:6–8 / John 14:15 / Ephesians 4:2 / James 4:10 / 1 Peter 3:8–11; 5:6

GOD'S QUESTION THROUGH HAGGAI

Who is left among you that saw this house in her first glory? HAGGAI 2:3

God's prophets had many vital roles. They foretold future events, exposed sin, gave warnings, and offered insight, wisdom, and encouragement. Haggai and Zechariah were instrumental in encouraging Jeshua and Zerubbabel to rebuild the temple in the face of opposition, and the Israelites prospered under the two prophets' ministries.

Centuries earlier, God had given King David plans for the temple. David amassed tons of resources for the job and gave them to his son Solomon. Solomon's temple was magnificent, adorned with precious stones and overlaid with gold. It contained an inner sanctuary called the Most Holy Place, where the ark of the covenant—the presence of the Lord—resided. When the temple was destroyed, however, the ark disappeared.

Jeshua and Zerubbabel's temple paled in comparison to Solomon's. As the Israelites watched them build, the younger people who had never seen the original structure rejoiced. But the older ones wept, remembering the beauty of the first temple. Sensing their sorrow, Haggai assured them that God's presence was not confined to a mere building; rather, He would now manifest His glory in a greater way than before, and the new structure would be filled with His peace.

Learn More: 1 Chronicles 28–29 / 2 Chronicles 2–5 / Ezra 3:7–13; 5:1; 6:14 / Haggai 1–2

A QUESTION OF SIGNIFICANCE

Who hath despised the day of small things? ZECHARIAH 4:10

Zechariah was one of the prophets who encouraged Zerubbabel while the temple was being rebuilt. Although the second structure's size and splendor paled in comparison to Solomon's temple, God did not look at the building itself. Instead, He focused on the purpose behind the reconstruction—to restore worship in Jerusalem.

While Zerubbabel led reconstruction, Zechariah shared his God-given visions of hope. One such revelation involved a golden lampstand with seven lights. Since the inner chamber of the temple had no windows, the lampstand provided the only light source—which foreshadowed the coming of Jesus, the Light of the world. In another vision, all mountains and obstacles became flat land. While progress on the temple may have seemed slow and the structure unimpressive, the force behind it was invincible.

God often uses small things to accomplish impossible tasks: David defeated Goliath with a single stone, a young boy's small lunch fed thousands, and Jesus proclaimed that faith the size of a mustard seed can move mountains.

Learn More: Proverbs 30:24–28 / Zechariah 4 / Luke 17:6

SINFUL ISRAEL'S QUESTION TO GOD

What profit is it that we have kept his ordinance? MALACHI 3:14

The book of Malachi is an oracle in which God points out two offenses that the Israelites needed to address. First, they had robbed the Lord by not paying tithes and offerings. He said if they would honor Him by bringing their entire tithe, He would give them an uncontainable flood of blessing, including an abundance of healthy crops.

Second, the Israelites were speaking harsh words against God, saying it was pointless to serve Him. "What profit is it that we have kept his ordinance?" they asked. If wrongdoers were prospering, what was the point of obedience? Unfortunately, the Israelites were oblivious to their own wrongdoing. "Wherein have we robbed thee?" they asked (3:8).

Thankfully, a remnant of God-fearing people cared about Israel's indifference. As they shared their concerns with each other, the Lord listened and recorded their conversation. Then He promised to remove any confusion about righteousness and wickedness. Their fear of the Lord protected them from the spiritual lethargy that had gripped the rest of the nation.

Learn More: Malachi 3 / Romans 12:11 / Philippians 1:9–10

A QUESTION ABOUT WORRY

Which of you by taking thought can add one cubit unto his stature? MATTHEW 6:27

The Sermon on the Mount was Jesus' first major teaching. In the middle of this discourse, Jesus spoke about worry. Hoping to give His audience a clearer perspective, He asked an absurd question about what difference worrying makes. Does it have enough power to increase a person's height or lengthen someone's life? Of course not.

Jesus here refers to God as "your heavenly Father" (Matthew 6:32) for the first time in scripture. The possessive pronoun *your* is key: if your heavenly Father feeds the birds and clothes the flowers, imagine how much more He will provide for you, His children. What a beautiful contrast between life's angst and the Father's affection.

The apostle Paul encourages us not to be anxious about anything but to present all our needs to God and even thank Him in advance. Paul doesn't promise that we will receive everything we ask for, since some requests spring from a worried mind and not from an expectant heart. However, the Lord will give what we need the most—His peace. As we rest in His calming presence, we may realize that the object of our anxiety was never worth worrying about.

Learn More: Psalm 94:19 / Matthew 6:19–34 / Philippians 4:6–7 / 1 Peter 5:7

QUESTIONS JESUS REJECTS

Lord, Lord, have we not prophesied in thy name? MATTHEW 7:22

In His Sermon on the Mount, Jesus described false prophets as wolves in sheep's clothing. The sign of authentic ministry, He said, is the condition of the fruit. Pure motives produce good fruit, while corrupt motives yield rotten fruit. As for the latter group of people, Jesus said He wouldn't even acknowledge them or their works.

Some people mimic supernatural gifts for personal benefit. Others may be unaware of their wrong motives, deceived by their own pride into believing that success is measured by the number of their followers.

The apostle Paul teaches that the only way to avoid gratifying our flesh is by walking in the Spirit. As we internally develop the fruit of the Spirit, it will be manifested in our external works. Paul also instructs us to periodically test ourselves, making sure we are on the right track. One way is to ask the Lord to reveal any bad fruit we might be producing. Some hesitate to ask because they're afraid of what might be revealed; however, being examined now is better than being judged later—when it's too late.

Learn More: Matthew 7:15–29 / Luke 6:43–49 / 2 Corinthians 13:5 / Galatians 5:16–25

A QUESTION OF BAD SEED

Didst not thou sow good seed in thy field? MATTHEW 13:27

Jesus gave a parable about the kingdom of heaven, which He later explained to His disciples. A farmer (the Son of Man) sowed wheat seeds (believers) in his field (the kingdom of heaven). During the night, his enemy (the devil) sowed weeds (sons of the evil one) among the wheat, but no one realized until the plants began to grow. The farmer told the workers that the harvesters (angels) would collect the weeds at harvest time (the end of the age) and throw them into the furnace (eternal punishment). The wheat would then be harvested and stored in the barn (God's kingdom).

Today, as wickedness seems to increase, Jesus' words offer us valuable insight. According to the parable, this increase is an outgrowth of the "evil seeds" the enemy has scattered over the years. The closer we get to the Lord's return, the more wickedness will continue to surge.

When the angels harvest, they will differentiate the "weeds" from the "wheat," just as farmers do today. When fully grown, wheat heads cause the plants to bow—unaffected by the weeds. However, weeds stand fully erect, making them easy to identify and remove. By bowing in humility before God, we will be protected from evil influences, thus assuring our place in heaven.

Learn More: Matthew 13:24–30, 36–43 / James 4:6–10 / Revelation 14:15

A QUESTION OF RESOURCES

How many loaves have ye? MATTHEW 15:34

The book of Matthew gives two accounts of Jesus feeding the multitudes. In Matthew 14, in which a large crowd follows Him until evening in a remote place. When the disciples urged Christ to send the people away to find food, He told His disciples to feed them—even though all they had were five loaves of bread and two fish. Jesus blessed the food, broke it, and used it to feed five thousand men—plus women and children. The leftovers filled twelve baskets.

In Matthew 15, Jesus performs miracles before yet another multitude. Jesus knew that the people were hungry, but as the disciples pointed out, they were in a "desolate" place with hardly any food in sight. Once again, Jesus asked how many loaves they had, and this time they counted seven loaves and a few small fish. Jesus then broke the bread and fed a crowd of four thousand men—plus women and children. The leftovers filled seven baskets.

The Lord later referenced these two incidents to remind His disciples of His miraculous power. Apparently, some miracles were intended more for growing the disciples' faith than for benefitting the people.

Learn More: Matthew 14:13-21; 15:29-38; 16:5-12 / John 6:1-14

A QUESTION OF JESUS' IDENTITY

Whom say ye that I am? MATTHEW 16:15

Jesus was a master conversationalist. His questions always inspired self-examination—especially within His disciples. These twelve men had traveled with Jesus, heard His teachings, and witnessed His miracles. Yet did they really *know* Him?

One day, Jesus suddenly asked His disciples how people identified Him. Some thought He was Elijah, some John the Baptist, and others Jeremiah. Some have suggested the Pharisees believed that deceased people reappear in other forms to complete their work. Even Herod had thought Jesus was John the Baptist, back from the dead.

Before this moment, the disciples had referred to Jesus as Lord, Master, Teacher, or Rabbi. But when He asked them their own opinion on who He was, Peter immediately exclaimed, "Thou art the Christ, the Son of the living God" (Matthew 16:16). One can only imagine Peter's exuberance as he declared for the first time that Jesus was the Anointed One. His declaration became even more significant when Jesus told him it was a revelation directly from God the Father.

The Jews were hoping for a king, but Jesus wanted to be seen first as Savior and Lord. His mission was to seek and save the lost not to reign on a throne—not yet, at least.

Learn More: Matthew 16:13-20 / Mark 8:27-30 / Luke 9:18-21; 19:10 / 1 Timothy 6:14-15

A QUESTION OF FORGIVENESS

Lord, how oft shall my brother sin against me, and I forgive him? MATTHEW 18:21

The Jews believed that it was enough to forgive someone three times. So, when Peter asked if he should forgive up to seven times, he probably thought he was being generous. But Jesus responded that a person should forgive until "seventy times seven"—a clever way of saying "infinity." The Lord then told a parable about a man whose debt of millions of dollars was written off. However, when it was his turn to forgive a friend who owed him a few dollars, the man demanded immediate payback.

If we could put a monetary price on the sins for which God has forgiven us, what would be the total? Now compare that total to the price of the wrongs we've received from others. Obviously, the Lord's mercy far outweighs our own. By forgiving in the way Jesus instructs us, we will gain many more brothers and far fewer offenders.

Learn More: Matthew 6:12-15; 18:15-35 / Luke 23:34-35 / Colossians 3:12-17

A QUESTION OF APPROPRIATE APPAREL

Friend, how camest thou in hither not having a wedding garment? Matthew 22:12

While teaching about the kingdom of heaven, Jesus told the story of a king who sent three invitations for his son's wedding banquet. The first two were ignored, so the king sent his servants out with a come-one-come-all invitation to anyone they could find. These citizens gladly accepted and showed up at the celebration.

In the first century, wedding guests were required to wear certain garments. Often, the groom's father would provide specially made wedding robes, which the attendees would wear over their clothing upon arrival. So when the king in the story arrived at the banquet and noticed one guest who was not wearing the designated clothing, he confronted the man. The guest gave no explanation for his intrusion, so the king cast him out.

There is only one entrance to the marriage supper of the Lamb, and that entrance is Jesus, the Bridegroom. Isaiah says the Lord will provide us with garments of salvation on that day. He will not ask us, "How did you get in here?" but will instead say, "Welcome! Come and share in the happiness!"

Learn More: Isaiah 61:10 / Matthew 22:1–14; 25:21 / Revelation 16:15

A QUESTION OF JESUS' RETURN

What shall be the sign of thy coming, and of the end of the world? Matthew 24:3

We don't know the exact day of Jesus' return, but He has told us about the signs that will precede it. When the disciples asked for details, Jesus described unrest, famines, and worldwide weather changes—which He called "the beginning of birth pains" (Matthew 24: 8 niv).

When a woman first goes into labor, the pains aren't severe and the contractions are irregular. But as the time of birth approaches, the pains increase in intensity and frequency. Similarly, the world's calamities will grow more frequent and intense, but these pains are only the beginning. Jesus also warned about upcoming persecutions, deceptions, and wickedness—not to frighten but to prepare His followers.

First, He instructs us that we should stand firm in our faith, enduring to the end. The world may fall apart, but we can rest secure in God's sovereignty. Second, we must keep watch and refuse to slumber, even if He doesn't return as quickly as we hope. If we begin each day anticipating His return, life's difficulties will not dismay us—and we will not be unprepared when His words come to pass.

Learn More: Matthew 24:3–44 / Mark 13:32–37 / Luke 18:8 / 2 Timothy 3:1–5

THE DISCIPLES' INAPPROPRIATE QUESTION

To what purpose is this waste? Matthew 26:8

This story of the woman and her alabaster jar is told in three Gospels. While some of the details differ, the core remains the same—a grateful woman anoints Jesus with a valuable substance and is criticized for being wasteful.

In those days, a woman would often save spikenard (an extremely expensive oil) and anoint her groom with it on their wedding night, symbolizing her love and devotion. So by breaking the jar and pouring its contents on Jesus' head, the woman in this story was pouring out her future. Rather than recognizing her action as a sacrificial act of worship, however, some of the disciples became indignant, complaining that the woman should have sold it to benefit the poor instead. Their criticism was offensive for two reasons: (1) It implied that the woman had made a poor choice by anointing the Messiah, and (2) it suggested that the Lord wasn't worthy of such an outpouring.

Jesus reminded them that the poor would always exist, but He would soon be leaving. Furthermore, because this type of oil could be used for preparing bodies for burial, her act foreshadowed Jesus' death. Giving to the needy is crucial, but it shouldn't replace our worship. Pure worship with pure motives is never a waste.

Learn More: Matthew 26:6–13 / Mark 14:3–9 / John 12:1–8

A QUESTION OF WATCHING

What, could ye not watch with me one hour? Matthew 26:40

Jesus often slipped away to pray in the garden of Gethsemane on the Mount of Olives. On the night of His arrest, He took His disciples there, confiding to Peter, James, and John that His soul was overwhelmed to the point of death and asking them to keep watch while He prayed. When Jesus returned, all three had fallen asleep. He asked them, "What, could ye not watch with me one hour?" The question was probably addressed specifically to Peter, who not long before had boldly declared that he would never deny Christ—even to the point of death.

Jesus told the disciples to watch and pray, lest they fall into temptation. "The spirit indeed is willing," He said, "but the flesh is weak" (Matthew 26:41). What temptation was Jesus talking about? Maybe surrendering to anger by impulsively slicing off the ear of the high priest's servant. Or perhaps deserting Jesus in fear as He was taken away. The disciples may have had the spirit to endure, but their flesh took control.

If Jesus—the perfect Son of God—asked His Father for strength to endure the cross, how much more should we pray for strength to carry ours?

Learn More: Matthew 26:17–56 / Luke 14:27; 21:37

JESUS' AGONIZING QUESTION

My God, My God why hast thou forsaken me? Matthew 27:46

When Jesus uttered these words, He was quoting from Psalm 22, a song composed by David after he was betrayed by his son Absalom. Unbeknownst to David, his words prophetically pointed to Jesus' crucifixion.

It's difficult to imagine how the heavenly Father could forsake His only Son in His darkest hour. However, God actually turned His back on the *sin* that Jesus willingly took upon Himself. Jesus, who had no sin, bore the shame and guilt of all our sins to redeem humanity.

Jesus didn't just redeem us—He reconciled us to God. In Isaiah 59, the prophet writes that God's arm isn't too short to reach down and save. Then he says, "Your iniquities have separated between you and your God, and your sins have hid his face from you, that he will not hear" (verse 2). By agonizing on the cross, Jesus filled the gap between humanity and God the Father.

Because Jesus was forsaken by the Father, we are accepted into God's family. What great love!

Learn More: Psalm 22 / Isaiah 53 / 2 Corinthians 5:21 / Colossians 1:12–14, 19–22

THE DEMONS' QUESTION

What have we to do with thee, thou Jesus of Nazareth? Mark 1:24

One of Jesus' first miracles was delivering a demoniac. The demons who controlled the man recognized Jesus as the Holy One of God, even calling Him by name. But Jesus silenced them and commanded them to leave. The spirits obeyed and fled, proving Jesus' authority over evil. This was not the only time Jesus confronted evil spirits—on another occasion He cast them out with a single word—*Go.*

Some people elevate the devil to a higher status than he deserves—which is exactly what he craves. The devil is not God's counterpart; he is a created being who, because of his pride, was cast out of heaven with a third of the angels. These angels now serve Satan by trying to lead the world astray.

However, Christians have been given authority over the forces of darkness, so we can foil Satan's plans with the same command to "go." As the letter of James teaches, "Resist the devil, and he will flee from you" (James 4:7).

Learn More: Matthew 8:28–34 / Mark 1:21–28 / Luke 10:18–20 / Revelation 12:3–4, 7–9

THE DISCIPLES' INSULTING QUESTION

Master, carest thou not that we perish? Mark 4:38

Jesus wasted no time in teaching His disciples the importance of trusting Him, and this lesson can be found in Matthew, Mark, and Luke. Having spent all day ministering to a large crowd, Jesus told His disciples that they should cross the lake. Mark writes, "They took him even as he was in the ship" (4:36). Exhausted, Jesus immediately fell asleep.

A storm began to brew on the lake, but Jesus still slept. Panicking, the disciples woke Him and asked, "Carest thou not that we perish?" (4:38). Given that the disciples had spent all day witnessing Jesus' compassion toward huge crowds of people, this question seems insulting. Of course, He cared—but more importantly, He wanted their faith to rest in Him. Standing up, Jesus simply said, "Peace, be still," to the storm (4:39). Immediately, the storm ceased, and Jesus reproved them for their lack of faith.

Because of God's sovereignty, we too can have peace—no matter how intense the storm.

Learn More: Matthew 8:23–27 / Mark 4:1, 35–41 / Luke 8:22–25

JESUS' QUESTION TO A HEALED WOMAN

Who touched me? Mark 5:31

The bleeding woman's story is tucked within the story of a dying girl. The girl's father, Jairus, pleaded with Jesus to come to his house and heal her, and a mass of people followed them there. One of these people was a woman who had suffered for twelve years. She made her way through the jostling crowd, convinced she could be made whole by just touching Jesus' clothes. The woman finally touched His robe, and she was immediately healed. The story could end there, but it doesn't.

Even though Jesus was on a mission, He still stopped when He felt power go out from Him. Several had bumped into Him, but only one had touched Him with the intention of being healed. Realizing that she couldn't slip away, the woman fell at Jesus' feet and publicly told her story, and the Lord acknowledged her faith and confirmed her healing. Meanwhile, however, Jairus's daughter died.

Had the woman not "interrupted" Jesus, the girl might have lived, saving Jairus and his family unnecessary sorrow. However, the Lord never sees our needs as interruptions. To Him, everyone is important—which is why He raised Jairus's daughter from the dead shortly afterward. In Jesus' mission, no one is left behind.

Learn More: Matthew 10:30–31 / Mark 5:21–43 / Luke 8:40–56

THE QUESTION THAT KILLED JOHN THE BAPTIST

What shall I ask? Mark 6:24

King Herod was married to Herodias, his brother's wife. When John the Baptist told Herod this marriage wasn't lawful, Herodias took offense, and the king had John imprisoned. But Herodias apparently wasn't satisfied. She wanted him dead.

One day, Herod threw himself a lavish birthday party, and Herodias's daughter danced before the crowd. Herod was so pleased with her performance that he publicly vowed to grant her any request—up to half his kingdom. Caught off guard by such a generous offer, the girl asked her mother what she should ask.

Herodias saw her chance. Without hesitating, mother told daughter to ask for John's head on a platter. This request troubled the king, but he had sworn an oath before the crowd. He sent an executioner to the prison, and John was beheaded. His head was presented on a platter to the girl, who then carried it to her mother. Herodias now had her revenge.

When they are nursed, grudges can turn into irrational hatred, and hatred isn't satisfied without retribution. Sadly, Herodias included her young daughter in her revenge—an experience that probably traumatized the girl for life.

Learn More: Leviticus 19:18 / Proverbs 10:12; 19:11 / Mark 6:14–29

A QUESTION FOR A BLIND MAN

"Do you see anything?" MARK 8:23 NIV

This story about a blind man stands out from other miracles for several reasons. First, the man did not ask for his own healing; other people begged Jesus to touch him. The Lord responded by taking the blind man's hand and leading him away from the village. Imagine how frightened he must have felt as a stranger took him into an unfamiliar area.

Second, this is one of the few accounts in which the Lord uses spit to heal. Some Jews believed that the saliva of the first-born male carried healing powers that came through the father not the mother. Thus, Jesus demonstrated that His power flowed directly from His heavenly Father.

Third, the man's healing required a second touch. After the first touch, Jesus asked if he saw anything, and the man responded, "I see men as trees, walking" (Mark 8:24). Jesus then touched him again, and the man's sight became clear. The Lord instructed him not to return to the village—his familiar place. Instead, he was to move on with clarity of vision.

Had the man not put blind trust in the perfect Stranger, his sight would have never been restored.

Learn More: Mark 7:31–37; 8:22–26 / John 9

JESUS' ULTIMATE QUESTION

What shall it profit a man, if he shall gain the whole world, and lose his own soul? MARK 8:36

Jesus met with the disciples to prepare them for what was to come—His arrest, death, and resurrection three days afterward. Peter, however, immediately rebuked Jesus, insisting these things would never happen. But the Lord reproved Peter for his shallow thinking. Peter was so fixated on Jesus' execution that he overlooked His promise about resurrection. Christ gave hope even when speaking of death.

The Lord then said that anyone who wants be His disciple must deny himself, take up his cross, and follow Him, even to death. This is the first time in scripture that the cross is mentioned. Jesus' audience would have understood this as a reference to crucifixion—the common form of capital punishment—but to us, the cross represents any suffering we endure for following Christ. Jesus clearly taught that His followers would pay a price—but what would a prosperous, pain-free life matter if one's own soul were lost?

Jesus' words are certainly sobering; however, the fact that He endured the cross, knowing that the joy ahead was worth the price, bolsters our faith. Even in death, we have hope.

Learn More: Matthew 10:38–39; 16:21–28 / Mark 8:31–38 / Luke 9:18–27 / Hebrews 12:1–3

A QUESTION OF PRIDE

What was it that ye disputed among yourselves by the way? MARK 9:33

Jesus' disciples were sincere, but they were far from perfect. One day, thinking they were out of earshot of Jesus, they began disputing over who was the greatest. Perhaps Peter, James, and John bragged about their place in Jesus' inner circle. Judas might have boasted about being treasurer. Or maybe Andrew reminded everyone that he had found the Messiah before Peter had. Whatever the subject was, it was foolish enough to embarrass them into silence whenever the Lord asked them what they were arguing about.

Jesus then sat down and explained, "If any man desire to be first, the same shall be last of all, and servant of all" (Mark 9:35). The Greek word translated *servant* can have a meaning of "to raise up dust by moving quickly to serve others." Jesus modeled everything He taught, as seen by the time He washed the disciples' feet—a task normally relegated to the lowest servant in the household. Interestingly, although Peter initially resisted having his feet washed by Jesus, not one of the disciples offered to wash the Lord's feet.

Allowing someone else to come first can be humbling. However, the more we "move quickly" to serve, the more we will resemble Jesus—a goal far better than being first.

Learn More: Matthew 18:1–5; 23:11–12 / Mark 9:2–9 / Luke 9:46–48 / John 13:1–17

A VERY IMPORTANT QUESTION

Good Master, what shall I do that I may inherit eternal life? Mark 10:17

As the rich ruler kneeled before the Lord, he asked this desperate and sincere question about eternal life. In response, Jesus encouraged him to keep the commandments, but the ruler claimed he had followed them all his life. Out of the Ten Commandments, Jesus named only six—all of which pertain to our relationship with others, not with God. Perhaps Christ wanted him to realize that merely being a good person does not guarantee eternal life.

To uncover the man's priorities, the Lord tested him further: "Go thy way, sell whatsoever thou hast, and give to the poor" (Mark 10:21). Being extremely wealthy, the man left sadly. Jesus no doubt recognized the man's internal struggle between eternal life and earthly possessions, so watching him walk away must have been difficult. However, Jesus made no effort to soften the bargain. The way to eternal life is non-negotiable.

Ironically, the sound of riches drowned out the words of the Messiah—the only One who could have fulfilled this man's request for eternal life.

Learn More: Matthew 6:19–21; 19:16–30 / Mark 10:17–31 / Luke 18:18–30

A QUESTION OF WORSHIP

Is it not written, My house shall be called of all nations the house of prayer? Mark 11:17

The temple was where God's presence dwelled and where His people came to worship. So when Jesus saw people exchanging money and selling animals there, He became furious and drove them out. Jesus declared that His Father's house was to be a house of prayer for all nations—not just for Jews—but these merchants had invaded it, turning it into a den of thieves. They were robbing people—and God—of their worship.

A house is a haven for familial love, nourishment, and rest, but a den is a hiding place for thieves and animals. Jesus wanted worshippers to find safety and security in God's presence, but instead, the merchants and their herds of animals had brought chaos and triviality.

Centuries before Jesus, David composed several "psalms of ascent," which were to be sung or recited as people journeyed to the temple, preparing their spirits to enter God's presence. If we will prepare our hearts before praising God, neither party will be robbed of a meaningful worship experience.

Learn More: Psalms 120–135 / Isaiah 56:7 / Jeremiah 7:11 / Matthew 21:12–13 / Mark 11:15–17

ZACHARIAS'S DOUBTING QUESTION

Whereby shall I know this? Luke 1:18

Zacharias, who was an elderly priest, and Elizabeth, his wife, had prayed for years for a child. While Zacharias was serving at the temple one day, an angel appeared. It seems that Zacharias's priestly duties had become so routine that he no longer expected God's presence, because the angel's appearance sent him into shock. However, the angel calmed his fears and gave him good news: Elizabeth would indeed give birth to a son, and this child would work in the spirit of Elijah by reconciling people to God.

Zacharias's response—"Whereby shall I know this?"—revealed his doubt. Not only had this priest lost hope of witnessing God's presence in the temple, he seemed to doubt that God would ever answer his prayer.

The angel rebuked Zacharias, proclaiming that the news about Elizabeth's pregnancy had come from God Himself. Because of his doubt, Zacharias was made mute for nine months. However, upon his son's birth, the priest's mouth sprang open into a song about the faithfulness of God.

Learn More: Psalm 106:12 / Luke 1:5–25, 67–80 / 2 Corinthians 1:20

MARY'S QUESTION TO THE ANGEL GABRIEL

How shall this be, seeing I know not a man? LUKE 1:34

Luke gives two accounts of angelic visitations before Christ's birth. The first angel appeared to Zacharias the priest, and the second angel, Gabriel, visited Mary. While Zacharias was shocked, Mary was unflustered. However, when Gabriel said, "Hail, thou that art highly favoured, the Lord is with thee: blessed art thou among women" (Luke 1:28), Mary became troubled. How could she a young, inexperienced teenager, be "blessed among women"?

Gabriel then informed Mary that she would give birth to the Son of God. Instead of responding with doubt asked, Mary how this could be possible since she was a virgin. It would be a miraculous conception, the angel responded, by the Holy Spirit.

When the angel left, Mary went to the home of her elderly relative Elizabeth, Zacharias's wife. Before Mary even entered the house, Elizabeth sensed the holy presence that Mary now carried. Under the anointing of the Holy Spirit, Elizabeth affirmed Mary's faith by saying, "Blessed is she that believed" (1:45).

As Gabriel eloquently proclaimed, "With God nothing shall be impossible" (1:37).

Learn More: Isaiah 7:14 / Matthew 1:18–25 / Luke 1:26–56

A QUESTION OVER A MIRACLE BABY

What manner of child shall this be! LUKE 1:66

John the Baptist's birth was a miraculous event. His parents, Zacharias and Elizabeth, were an elderly couple who had prayed for a child for years. One day an angel told Zacharias that their prayers would be answered. When Zacharias showed doubt, he was struck mute.

Eight days after the baby was born, friends and relatives showed up for his circumcision and ceremonial naming—a duty normally performed by the father. However, since Zacharias couldn't speak, the relatives took the responsibility upon themselves. Leaning toward tradition, they named the baby after his father; the old priest, however, knew his son would carry a special calling. Zacharias wrote on a tablet that the baby would be called John, overturning his relatives' decision and fulfilling the words of the angel. Immediately, the new father regained his speech.

Everyone was awestruck by the extraordinary events: an elderly woman's giving birth, Zacharias's inability to speak, the child's unique name, and the elderly priest's speech miraculously restored. No wonder they pondered the child's future.

The angel's prophecy was eventually fulfilled, and John the Baptist—with the Lord's hand upon him—became the forerunner of Christ.

Learn More: Matthew 3 / Luke 1:57–80

JAMES AND JOHN'S ANGRY QUESTION

Lord, wilt thou that we command fire to come down from heaven? LUKE 9:54

For centuries, the Jews and Samaritans had lived at odds with one other—a rivalry stemming back to the Assyrian captivity. The Assyrian king had taken non-Jews—who were unfamiliar with God's requirements for worship—from surrounding cities and settled them in Samaria. Then the king instructed a Jewish priest to teach the foreigners how to worship the Lord. The result was a mishmash of worship styles that highly offended the Jewish people.

One long-standing point of contention between the Jews and Samaritans was the location of the temple: the Jews believed it belonged in Jerusalem while the Samaritans thought it belonged on Mount8 Gerizim. As Jesus and His disciples journeyed toward Jerusalem, they traveled through a Samaritan village, whose residents refused to let them pass. James and John became irate and offered to call down fire from heaven, but the Lord instead reprimanded His followers and led them in a different direction.

Often, our response to an offense can be worse than the offense itself, and anger only exacerbates the situation. However, we can avoid this disaster by following Jesus' example: simply walk away.

Learn More: 2 Kings 17:24–34 / Luke 9:51–56

MARTHA'S FRUSTRATED QUESTION

Lord, dost thou not care that my sister hath left me to serve alone? Luke 10:40

Mary and Martha were close friends of Jesus and often opened their doors to Him. During one such visit, Martha worked feverishly in the kitchen while Mary sat at the Lord's feet, listening to Him teach. Martha became upset, insisting that Jesus tell Mary to help in the kitchen.

We might be tempted to fault Martha for being too bossy or busy, but Jesus did not. Instead, He focused on her tendency to worry and become upset. Maybe she was trying too hard to impress Jesus, or perhaps she envied Mary's serenity. Whatever the reason, Martha needed to realize that the kitchen was her wheelhouse and hospitality was her gift.

In Romans 12, Paul explains that believers are part of the body of Christ, with each member having a different function. God has gifted everyone differently, so we should not expect everyone to be just like us. Instead, we should use our own gifts while allowing others to use theirs.

Jesus later revisited the sisters' home, but this time Martha served without complaint while Mary poured perfume on Jesus' feet, demonstrating her gift of giving.

Learn More: Luke 10:38-42 / John 12:1-3 / Romans 12:4-8

JESUS' QUESTION ABOUT HEALING ON THE SABBATH

Is it lawful to heal on the sabbath day? Luke 14:3

The Lord had given the Israelites a list of commandments, but the Pharisees had added many, many more. Their laws subjugated their followers to people rather than to God, and the religious leaders thrived on this power—until Jesus began upsetting their authority. Feeling threatened, they embarked on a campaign to undermine everything Jesus did, including His actions on the Sabbath.

One Sabbath, Jesus healed a man with dropsy (today, we would say edema) as the Pharisees watched, and then He asked them if it was lawful to heal on the Sabbath. They remained silent. The Lord then pointed out their hypocrisy—if one of their animals fell into a ditch on the Sabbath, they would rescue it. Did a trapped animal carry more value than a human life to them?

Jesus taught that the Sabbath was made for man, not vice versa. Just as God had rested on the seventh day, people needed to do the same. Unfortunately, the religious leaders had created such a heavy man-made burden of laws that the people struggled beneath it all seven days. Now that Jesus has revealed Himself as the Lord of the Sabbath, we can find rest because His burden is light.

Learn More: Matthew 11:28-30; 12:1-14 / Mark 2:23-28 / Luke 6:1-11; 13:10-17; 14:1-6

JESUS' QUESTION ABOUT LOST THINGS

Having an hundred sheep, if he lose one of them, doth not leave the ninety and nine? Luke 15:4

Jesus often kept company with social outcasts, much to the Pharisees' consternation. In response to their criticism, Jesus told them a three-part parable.

First, He spoke of a shepherd who left ninety-nine sheep to rescue one that had wandered off. Next, He told of a woman with ten coins (probably a wedding dowry), who after losing one in the house, searched diligently until she found it. In the third story, the youngest of two sons demanded that his father give him his inheritance, offhandedly implying that he wished his father were dead. The father complied and the son left. However, upon squandering his inheritance, losing his friends, and ending up with the pigs, the son finally came to his senses. The parables' message is clear: wandering "sheep" and lost "coins" don't even know they're lost. To be found, they must be sought. Rebellious "sons," however, often come to their senses only when they find themselves in a pigpen.

But Jesus also had a more subtle point: the Pharisees were so lost in their legalism that they couldn't see the sinners who needed to be rescued. Jesus, however, came to seek and save the lost. That is why He socialized with outcasts.

Learn More: Matthew 9:9-13 / Luke 15; 19:1-10

A QUESTION OF OWING

How much owest thou unto my lord? LUKE 16:5

To teach the importance of serving God rather than money, Jesus told a story about a shrewd manager who oversaw his wealthy employer's assets. Upon checking the books, the employer discovered the manager had been wasting opportunities that could have increased his wealth, so he fired him. The manager, realizing the importance of having friends in his time of need, discounted the amount each creditor owed to his employer—thus winning their favor.

This manager could have stolen from his employer, gouged the debtors with a high interest rate to get revenge on his master, or simply deserted his job. Instead, he focused on his relationships—which were far more important at this point than getting rich. The master was impressed and commended him for being shrewd.

As "managers" responsible for building God's kingdom, we should invest our gifts, opportunities, and resources into serving others. Jesus calls this true wealth. If a dishonest manager can understand the value of relationships, how much more should we, the children of light, value human souls over wealth.

Learn More: Ecclesiastes 5:10 / Luke 16:1–15 / Romans 14:12 / 1 Timothy 6:6–10

A QUESTION OF PERSEVERING PRAYER

When the Son of Man cometh, shall he find faith on the earth? LUKE 18:8

Jesus often used parables to make a point. To stress that people should never give up on praying, He told the story of a persistent widow who continually begged a wicked judge for justice against her adversary until he finally relented and granted her request. Jesus said that if an unjust judge can do the right thing, how much more will God grant justice for those who continually plead their case before Him.

Some people teach (falsely) that believers need to present a request to the Lord only once and that praying multiple times about something shows a lack of faith. However, this parable teaches precisely the opposite.

Jesus concluded His parable by saying, "Nevertheless, when the Son of Man cometh, shall he find faith on the earth?" By linking this final statement with the parable's initial purpose, we can conclude that the Lord *wants* us to continue asking and believing.

Just as the widow experienced adversity, we will face similar hardships. Jesus said, "He that shall endure unto the end, the same shall be saved" (Matthew 24:13). When we endure in unflagging faith and diligent prayers, we can know God will come to our defense.

Learn More: Matthew 24:3–13 / Luke 18:1–8 / Ephesians 6:18 / 1 Thessalonians 5:17

A QUESTION OF STEWARDSHIP

Wherefore then gavest not thou my money into the bank. . . ? LUKE 19:23

Luke's and Matthew's versions of this parable have different details but parallel endings. In Luke's account, a nobleman leaves on a journey and entrusts each of his ten servants with ten "pounds" (around three months' wages). When the nobleman returns, he calls for the servants to give an account. Two report that they have received healthy profits by investing the pounds, and they are rewarded with promotions. A third servant, however, reveals he has hidden his pound, and he returns it to the king, saying, "I feared thee, because thou art an austere man" (19:21). The master calls him a wicked servant, giving his pound to the one who had earned ten more.

In Matthew's account, the master has the wicked servant thrown into outer darkness. While this punishment sounds harsh, a closer reading reveals that the servant portrays the nobleman as a hard-to-please man who strikes fear in others—a false assessment that prevents the servant from even *trying* to please his master.

Jesus said, "I am the good shepherd, and know my sheep, and am known of mine" (John 10:14). Knowing the One we serve will kindle our motivation to please Him.

Learn More: Matthew 25:14–30 / Luke 19:12–27 / John 10:14–18, 27

A QUESTION OF PROPHECY UNDERSTOOD

Did not our heart burn within us. . .while he opened to us the scriptures? Luke 24:32

In the forty days between His resurrection and ascension, Jesus appeared to hundreds of people, but many didn't recognize Him immediately. Mary Magdalene, who discovered the empty tomb first, had no idea she was talking with Jesus until He spoke her name. When Jesus later appeared to the disciples, He opened their minds so that they could understand the prophecies in scripture.

Also, as Cleopas and his friend walked seven miles to Emmaus, Jesus explained that the Old Testament messianic prophecies pointed to Himself. But these men didn't recognize Him until Christ broke bread with them. Suddenly, their eyes were opened and their hearts burned. They had been hearing the Word of God from the Son of God.

All these individuals had experienced trauma. Jesus, the One in whom they had placed their hope, had been killed and buried, and now His body was missing from the tomb. None of them expected Jesus to appear, and their overwhelming circumstances kept them from seeing, hearing, and understanding when He did. But when they turned their attention to the Word, the eyes of their hearts were opened, and they understood.

Learn More: Jeremiah 20:9 / Luke 24:13–49 / John 20:1–20 / Ephesians 1:18

A SAMARITAN WOMAN'S QUESTION ABOUT JESUS

Is not this the Christ? John 4:29

Jesus loved spending time with social outcasts, and the woman at the well was no exception. Respectable women came to the well in the early morning or late evening, but this one was drawing water in the middle of the day. As a Samaritan (a race hated by the Jews) who had been married five times and was currently living with a man, she was obviously a *persona non grata*—yet Jesus remained cordial and did not condemn, giving her spiritual hope.

Near the end of their conversation, the disciples showed up. The woman was so impacted by Jesus' words that she left her water jar and raced back to town, exclaiming, "Is not this the Christ [Messiah]?" to her fellow Samaritans. Intrigued, many people left town and came to the well.

Meanwhile, Jesus told His disciples that the fields were ready to harvest. "Lift up your eyes," He said, "and look on the fields" (John 4:35)—referring to people not crops. The disciples looked up to behold the spiritually thirsty Samaritans headed their way. After only a couple of days in Christ's presence, the townspeople were convinced that He truly was the Messiah. One conversation between a flawed woman and the perfect Lord transformed an entire town.

Learn More: John 4:4–42

JESUS' QUESTION TO A LAME MAN

Wilt thou be made whole? John 5:6

In Jerusalem there was a certain pool named Bethesda—meaning "house of mercy" or "flowing water"—near the marketplace. The physically handicapped would wait by the pool where, according to tradition, an angel would come from time to time and stir up the waters. The first one into the rippling pool would receive healing.

One Sabbath, Jesus entered the pool area and saw a man who had been an invalid for thirty-eight years. Jesus asked him if he wanted to get well, but the man never gave a direct answer. Instead, he gave reasons why he had been unable to get into the pool first for thirty-eight years. The Lord then instructed him to pick up his mat and walk, which the man miraculously did. However, Jewish law limited the distance people could travel on the Sabbath to a little more than half a mile. Imagine waiting thirty-eight years to be healed, then being restricted by the law of distance!

Later, when Jesus encountered the same man in the temple, He instructed him to stop sinning, lest something worse happen to him. As wonderful as physical healing is, spiritual healing is far more urgent.

Learn More: Exodus 16:29 / John 5:1–18 / Acts 1:12

A QUESTION OF JESUS' CHOOSING

Have not I chosen you twelve? John 6:70

One day, as Jesus taught a large group of His followers, He called Himself the "bread of life," saying that anyone who would "eat of this bread" (accept Jesus and His teachings) would live forever. Upon hearing this, many people walked away, murmuring that this teaching was too difficult to accept. Jesus, looking at the remaining twelve, asked if they were going to leave too, but Peter assured Him they had nowhere else to go. They knew His teachings were true. The Lord then reminded them that they hadn't chosen Him—He had chosen them.

The fact that Jesus handpicked His disciples is significant. According to Jewish custom, the student would request to be discipled by a certain rabbi, who would then interview the student and test his knowledge of the Law. If the rabbi thought the young man was worthy and knowledgeable enough, he would accept him as a pupil. If not, the young man would return to his family business.

The disciples were unschooled men, unworthy of following a rabbi. But because they were willing to learn, Jesus invited them to join Him. Thankfully, none of us need to pass a test to follow Christ—we just need to obediently believe.

Learn More: John 6:26–70 / Acts 4:13 / Ephesians 2:1–9

A QUESTION DEFENDING JESUS

Doth our law judge any man, before it hear him, and know what he doeth? John 7:51

Because they misunderstood Jesus' teachings and feared His influence on the people would surpass their own, the chief priests and Pharisees spent more than three years trying to bring Jesus down. During the Feast of Tabernacles, Jesus went to the temple courts to teach, and many people put their faith in Him. Upon seeing this response, the religious leaders ordered the temple guards to arrest Jesus. These leaders claimed to be experts in the law, but they were ready to convict Jesus without a trial.

Nicodemus, a Pharisee, was sympathetic toward Jesus. He referred the priests and Pharisees to the Mosaic law, which demanded a just trial. Was it fair, he asked, for a person to be condemned without allowing him to defend himself? But the religious leaders responded with sarcasm. Even when the guards returned without arresting Jesus, the priests and Pharisees protected their own egos and accused the guards of being deceived.

Sadly, the Pharisees and chief priests couldn't recognize the truth because of their own prideful and biased hearts—and that was their folly and shame.

Learn More: John 7:1–53 / Exodus 23:1 / Leviticus 19:15 / Deuteronomy 1:16–17; 19:15

A QUESTION OF MERCY

Hath no man condemned thee? John 8:10

As Jesus taught in the temple early one morning, religious leaders brought in a woman caught in adultery. Standing her in front of the crowd, they challenged Jesus about the law of Moses, which stated such a woman should be stoned. However, they conveniently omitted the part that commanded the adulterous man—who was mysteriously absent—to be put to death also. They were less concerned about punishing sin than they were about trapping Jesus.

Jesus, aware of their motives, simply ignored their badgering questions as He stooped to write something on the ground. Nobody knows what He wrote—some suggest it was the Ten Commandments while others speculate it was the religious leaders' own sins. Finally, Jesus presented to them a challenge: the one who had never sinned should cast the first stone. One by one, the crowd dissipated, leaving Jesus alone with the woman.

When the Lord asked who had condemned her, she responded, "No man" (John 8:11). Jesus assured her that He didn't either; however, He also instructed her to leave her life of sin.

Often, a narrow brush with severe punishment can be a wake-up call to repentance. It is too bad the adulterous man was missing—he could have received mercy too.

Learn More: Leviticus 20:10 / John 8:1–11

THE DISCIPLES' MISTAKEN QUESTION

Master, who did sin, this man, or his parents, that he was born blind? John 9:2

The disciples' question reveals a false belief that some Jews held. In Psalm 51:5, David writes, "Behold, I was shapen in iniquity; and in sin did my mother conceive me." David here refers to humanity's natural propensity to sin. However, the Jews used this and other Old Testament passages to extrapolate a belief that all people born with a malady were suffering for their own pre-birth sin or the sin of their parents. But how can unborn babies sin?

Jesus told the disciples that, in this case, no one had sinned—instead, God was about to display His glory. Then, even though it was the Sabbath day, Jesus healed the man, much to the religious leaders' consternation. These leaders challenged the authenticity of this miracle, telling the formerly blind man that Jesus was a sinner. The man argued back that Jesus was obviously from God; otherwise, He would be unable to work miracles. The Pharisees threw him out of the synagogue, declaring, "Thou wast altogether born in sins" (John 9:34).

Later, Jesus encountered the man again, this time granting him spiritual rather than physical sight. If only the religious leaders had opened their ears to the truth, their eyes would have opened as well.

Learn More: John 9

A QUESTION OF JESUS' MESSIAHSHIP

How long dost thou make us to doubt? John 10:24

Having languished for centuries under oppressive empires—Babylonian, Persian, Greek, and Roman—the Jews longed for a Messiah who would establish His kingdom on earth immediately and restore the nation of Israel. When Christ appeared, many hoped He would rescue the Jews. Jesus gave Himself several titles—including Son of God, Bread of Life, Light of the World, and Good Shepherd—but "revolutionary leader" was not one of them.

Several Jews challenged Jesus to end the suspense and plainly state if He was the Christ (or Messiah). The Lord reminded them that He had revealed His identity many times and that His miracles could speak for themselves; however, He said, the people were unable to believe because they were not His sheep. Only sheep could hear and understand the voice of the shepherd.

Jesus was everything the people needed—but not what they wanted. These Jews didn't want a shepherd—they wanted an army commander. They sought a revolution, but Jesus sought a relationship. One day, Jesus *will* reign eternally as King, and the sheep who have followed Him now will reign with Him. That is a revolution worth waiting for.

Learn More: Matthew 22:41–46 / Luke 1:30–33; 19:11; 24:21 / John 10:1–42 / 2 Timothy 2:11–12

THE CHIEF PRIESTS' FRUSTRATED QUESTION

What do we? John 11:47

The Pharisees and chief priests opposed Jesus' ministry from day one. Although everything He did was for the good of the people, the religious leaders feared they would lose power if He gained popularity. Never mind that Jesus' ministry positively impacted the Jews—the religious leaders wanted to save their positions at the people's expense.

After Lazarus was raised from the dead, many Jews followed Jesus. This was the tipping point for the religious leaders. They called the Sanhedrin to an emergency meeting, frantically asking what they were accomplishing. Caiaphas, the high priest on duty, replied, "It is expedient for us, that one man should die for the people, and that the whole nation perish not" (John 11:50). By getting rid of Jesus, he implied, they could keep their power. But little did he know, his words were prophetic.

When Jesus was arrested, He stood before Caiaphas, who was probably elated that this Man would finally die. After Jesus' ascension, Peter and John were arrested for healing a crippled man. Ironically, they also stood before Caiaphas—who had to realize by now that the Man's influence was continuing to spread, even after the Sanhedrin had put Him to death.

Learn More: John 11; 18:12–14, 19–24 / Acts 4:1–21

PILATE'S TIMELESS QUESTION

What is truth? John 18:38

When Pilate asked Jesus if He was King of the Jews, Jesus said yes but added that His kingdom wasn't of this world. "For this cause came I into the world," He said, "that I should bear witness unto the truth. Every one that is of the truth heareth my voice" (John 18:37). Pilate flippantly responded, "What is truth?" and then abruptly left to address the people. Too bad Pilate couldn't realize that he was standing in the presence of truth Himself (John 14:6).

While Pilate didn't believe Jesus was the Son of God, he did know Christ was not guilty. However, his craving for popularity outweighed his acceptance of the truth.

Scripture warns that those who do not love the truth may subject themselves to a stronger delusion. But if we cling diligently to Jesus' teachings, we will know the truth—and that truth will set us free.

Learn More: Isaiah 59:14–15 / John 18:28–40; 8:31–32 / Romans 1:25 / 2 Thessalonians 2:10–12 / 2 Timothy 3:12–17

JESUS' PROBING QUESTION

Simon, son of Jonas, lovest thou me? John 21:16

During Jesus' trial, Peter adamantly denied Christ three times and then wept over his actions. Jesus appeared to Peter multiple times after His resurrection, but not once did this topic come up—until now.

In one of His last interactions with His disciples, Jesus intentionally broached the issue. Jesus didn't use the name *Peter*, which means "rock" and was given by Jesus Himself; instead, He addressed His disciple by his family name—*Simon*, which means "a reed swaying in the wind."

Twice, Jesus asked, "Simon, son of Jonas, lovest thou me?" Here, the word *love* is the Greek *agapao*—which implies obedient devotion. Both times, Peter responded, "Yea, Lord; thou knowest that I love thee" (John 21:15–16), using the Greek word *phileo*—which means "close friends." The third time, however, Jesus used Peter's word, asking in effect, "Simon, are we good friends?" Peter got the message, and Jesus once again called Peter to follow Him.

Peter was now more than a fisher of men—he would soon feed Jesus' sheep by leading in the early church. Peter later encouraged believers to "Love [*agapao*] each other deeply, because love covers over a multitude of sins" (1 Peter 4:8 niv). This love doesn't just forgive—it restores.

Learn More: Matthew 16:13–18 / Luke 5:1–11 / John 21

AN ANGEL'S QUESTION TO JESUS' DISCIPLES

Men of Galilee, why do you stand gazing up into heaven? Acts 1:11

The disciples experienced an emotional roller-coaster following Jesus's death and resurrection. Judas, one of their own, had betrayed Christ and committed suicide. All of them except John had deserted Jesus in His hour of need. Then, when they thought Jesus was dead, He suddenly appeared at random times and places.

Jesus interacted with His disciples for forty days after His resurrection. One day, they asked if He would now restore the kingdom to Israel. But Jesus deflected the question, saying it wasn't for them to know the times and dates the Father had established. However, He left them with a command—remain in Jerusalem and wait for the promised Holy Spirit. Remembering previous conversations, they realized He had to leave before the Spirit could come.

As Jesus ascended into heaven, the disciples gazed upward until a cloud blocked their vision. Suddenly, two angels appeared, snapping them back into focus. The angels assured the disciples that Christ would return the same way He ascended. But for now, their mandate was to pick up where Jesus left off.

Learn More: Luke 21:27 / John 14:23–31; 16:5–8; 20:19–31 / Acts 1:1–11

A QUESTION FOR ANANIAS AND SAPPHIRA

Why hath Satan filled thine heart to lie to the Holy Ghost? Acts 5:3

When the early church began, the believers shared with one another by selling land and houses and distributing the proceeds among the less fortunate. Ananias and his wife, Sapphira, sold some property too, but they kept a portion for themselves. So when Ananias brought the proceeds to the church elders, he lied, claiming it was the entire amount. Peter, sensing the deceit, asked why Ananias had lied to the Holy Spirit, and Ananias immediately dropped dead. Later, Sapphira came, unaware of her husband's demise. She too lied to Peter—and met the same fate as her husband. As this news spread, the people were gripped with fear.

While such a punishment for withholding profit may seem harsh, the deeper sin lay in the couple's deceitfulness. God always begins His work by building on a pure foundation. Had the apostles ignored this dishonesty, it could have spread throughout the newly established church.

Paul the Apostle cautions us to never build on any foundation but Jesus. Since He is pure in every way, everything we do for Him should also be pure.

Learn More: Leviticus 6:1–7 / Isaiah 33:6 / Acts 4:32–37; 5:1–11 / Ephesians 2:19–22

THE ETHIOPIAN EUNUCH'S QUESTION

How can I [understand], except some man should guide me? Acts 8:31

As Christians in Jerusalem scattered in the face of persecution, Philip went to Samaria. There, he preached and performed miracles, leading many people to Christ. In the middle of this revival, the Lord instructed Philip to leave the crowds and travel to a desert road between Jerusalem and Gaza. On the way he met the treasurer for Queen Candace of Ethiopia.

The Spirit prompted Philip to approach the Ethiopian, who was sitting in his chariot reading from Isaiah. Philip asked him if he understood what he was reading. "How can I," the man replied, "except some man should guide me?" Philip climbed into the chariot and explained to him that Isaiah's prophecy foretold of Jesus, the Messiah, and of the salvation He would bring. They eventually came to a body of water, and the Ethiopian asked Philip to baptize him. As they emerged from the water, the Spirit of the Lord transported Philip to a city sixty miles away.

The Ethiopian returned to his home country, probably unaware of the vital role he would play in spreading the Gospel on another continent. Jesus' words were already being fulfilled: the disciples were witnessing in Jerusalem, Judea, Samaria, and the ends of the earth—even in Africa.

Learn More: Acts 1:8; 8:1–40

THE PHILIPPIAN JAILER'S QUESTION

Sirs, what must I do to be saved? Acts 16:30

When Paul, Silas, and Luke arrived in Philippi, they went to the river to pray. There they met Lydia, a prominent, God-fearing businesswoman. The Lord opened her heart to the Gospel, and she and her household were saved and baptized.

Sometime later, Paul cast a demon out of a slave girl. Her owners, upset that their means of income had been erased, had Paul and Silas arrested under false charges. Despite being stripped, beaten, and imprisoned, these two prayed and sang into the night. God then caused an earthquake that shook the foundation of the prison, releasing the prisoners from their shackles.

Knowing he would face execution if any prisoners escaped under his watch, the jailer frantically grabbed his sword to kill himself. But Paul assured him that no one had fled. The jailer was so moved that he asked how he could be saved. "Believe on the Lord Jesus Christ," Paul replied (Acts 16:31). That night, the jailer and his whole household believed and were baptized, and then they took care of the disciples' physical needs.

Paul and Silas then went to Lydia's house, where other converts had gathered. After encouraging one another, the two went to another city, leaving behind the newly planted seeds of the Philippian church in the home of Lydia—the first European convert.

Learn More: Acts 16:11–40 / Philippians 1 / 1 Thessalonians 2:2

THE ATHENIAN PHILOSOPHERS' QUESTION

May we know what this new doctrine, whereof thou speakest, is? ACTS 17:19

While in Athens, Paul encountered a group of Epicurean and Stoic philosophers who spent most of their time talking about and listening to new ideas. When they heard Paul preaching about Jesus' death and resurrection, they accused him of advocating foreign gods and took him before the Areopagus—a court that heard religious topics. The court politely asked Paul to explain this "new" teaching.

Even though Paul wasn't shy about the Gospel, he remained respectful. Having taken the time to acquaint himself with Athenian customs, Paul told the court that he had noticed several objects of worship, including one marked TO THE UNKNOWN GOD. Even with their intellect and their exhaustive collection of gods, these theorists recognized that something was missing. Paul filled in the blank, preaching to them this "unknown" One. Although he lost some of the group when he mentioned the resurrection, a few people did believe.

According to scripture, we must be prepared to give a reason for our salvation with gentleness and respect. Spreading the Gospel is always worthwhile, even if only a few believe.

Learn More: Acts 17:16–34 / 1 Peter 3:15–16

A DEMON'S HUMBLING QUESTION

Jesus I know, and Paul I know; but who are ye? ACTS 19:15

During his two-year stay in Ephesus, Paul mentored several Christians, leading them in lecture hall discussions and teaching about the kingdom of God. Through Paul, the Lord performed extraordinary miracles—in fact, even the handkerchiefs and aprons he had touched were used to heal the sick and cast out evil spirits.

Some Jews tried to mimic Paul's performance, using Christ's name as a spell to exorcise demons. At the time, a man named Sceva was the chief priest. He had seven sons, all of whom were self-proclaimed exorcists who charged people for their services. During one exorcism, an evil spirit spoke through the possessed man, saying to them, "Jesus I know, and Paul I know; but who are ye?" The demon then overpowered them, leaving them beaten and astonished.

Before long, word of this incident had spread throughout Ephesus. Although the people were gripped with fear, they determined to uphold the name of Jesus. Many were convicted by the Spirit, openly confessing their sins and bringing their magic scrolls to be burned. As a result, the word of the Lord spread quickly and the church began to thrive in Ephesus.

Learn More: Acts 19:1–20 / Ephesians 1:15–23; 2:1–10

A QUESTION OF IDOL WORSHIP

What man. . .knoweth not how that the city of the Ephesians is a worshipper of the great goddess Diana? ACTS 19:35

The apostle Paul took several missionary journeys through Asia Minor and Europe. One trip took him to Ephesus (located today in western Turkey), where God performed extraordinary miracles, convincing many people to renounce their sorcery and convert to Christianity.

Demetrius was an Ephesian silversmith who made and sold miniatures of the goddess Diana (also named Artemis). With Christianity's growth threatening his lucrative business, he convinced other tradesmen to join a campaign against Paul's ministry. They stirred up the Ephesians by loudly chanting, "Great is Diana of the Ephesians" (Acts 19:28). The entire city rushed to the theater, where they chanted the goddess's praises for two hours. Finally, the city clerk calmed the crowd by reminding them that Ephesus remained the guardian city of the "great goddess Diana." Appeased, the crowd dispersed.

Paul wisely kept his distance during the chaos, and after the uproar ended, he set out for Macedonia. However, the seed of the Gospel had been planted, and the Ephesian church was soon firmly established in the heart of Diana's domain.

Learn More: Acts 18:19–21; 19:1–20:1 / Ephesians 1:1–18

PAUL'S QUESTION TO EPHESIAN CHRISTIANS

What mean ye to weep and to break mine heart? ACTS 21:13

In his final travels, Paul revisited the churches he had planted, exhorting believers and bidding them farewell. Paul told them the Holy Spirit had forewarned him of imminent imprisonment. Even though the Spirit confirmed it to them, the believers didn't want to hear it. They wept and pleaded with Paul not to go to Jerusalem, but he was determined to make the journey, knowing it would be his last.

Some Bible scholars believe Paul's trip to Jerusalem was an act of disobedience, making his martyrdom unnecessary. However, scripture clearly says that the believers surrendered the situation into God's hands. God could have prevented Paul from going, but His plan included an expansion of Paul's ministry from Rome. While in prison, Paul wrote four epistles (Ephesians, Philippians, Colossians, and Philemon) and influenced the entire palace guard as well as Caesar's household. Furthermore, because Paul was in chains, other brothers were encouraged to fearlessly share the Gospel.

When God speaks, He may say things we don't want to hear. But once we learn the rest of the story, there's always a reason to rejoice.

Learn More: Acts 20:13–38; 21:1–16 / Ephesians 6:19–20 / Philippians 1:12–14; 4:22 / Colossians 4:3–4 / Philemon 8–9

KING AGRIPPA'S QUESTION TO THE APOSTLE PAUL

"Do you think that in such a short time you can persuade me to be a Christian?" ACTS 26:28 NIV

After one of his missionary journeys, Paul reported to the church elders in Jerusalem about the many Gentiles getting saved throughout the region. While he was in the temple, the people accused him of opposing Jewish law and defiling the temple. They tried to kill him, but the Roman soldiers pulled him into the barracks, where Paul informed them that he was a Roman citizen.

Paul's citizenship enabled him to appeal to Caesar; however, he first had to appear before the high priest, governors Felix and Festus, and King Agrippa. Unfortunately, these leaders were more concerned with appeasing the people than with releasing Paul. When he came before Agrippa, Paul shared his conversion story, appealing to Agrippa's Jewish heritage and knowledge of the prophets. Agrippa bristled, telling Paul it would take much more to persuade him to accept Christianity. The king abruptly left the room but privately declared Paul innocent. However, Paul's appeal to Caesar had necessitated his journey to Rome.

Had Paul been released early, he would not have had a personal audience with the king. Only eternity will tell if Agrippa ever seized his opportunity to follow Christ.

Learn More: Acts 21:27–40; 22–26

A QUESTION OF SECURITY

Who shall separate us from the love of Christ? ROMANS 8:35

Some have wondered why, if God loves us so much, He doesn't keep us from hardships. These people often interpret adversity as a sign of God's anger or punishment. But even though our correction may sometimes be well-deserved, the Lord can also use difficulties to help us develop our character, deepen our faith, and discover more about His nature. Romans 5:1–4 tells us that our sufferings produce perseverance, which develops character, which yields hope. Hope never disappoints, because God has poured His love into our hearts. God's love is unchanging, perfect, and complete. His love can't get any stronger because God *is* love.

But what about our love for Him? Is it so fragile that it cracks under pressure? Our love for the Lord will grow as we strive to learn more about Him and to pursue Him with all our heart, soul, mind, and strength. But the true test of our love is obedience. Hopefully, our own selfishness will never come between us and Him.

Learn More: John 14:15 / Romans 8:28–39; 5:1–8 / James 1:2–8 / 1 John 4:7–12

A QUESTION OF SIN IN THE CHURCH

Know ye not that a little leaven leaveneth the whole lump? 1 CORINTHIANS 5:6

In his first letter to the Corinthians, Paul addressed the issue of a man who was sleeping with his father's wife. The apostle wasn't concerned only with the immorality in the church; he was deeply disturbed over Corinthians' attitude—they were proud! It's doubtful that they were boasting about the sin itself; rather, they were perhaps feeling smug in their moral superiority over this man. As Paul said, they should have been grieving instead.

Paul recommended that the church remove this man from the congregation. The punishment may seem extreme, but Paul knew that any sin, if left unchecked, could spread through the entire church like yeast in a batch of dough.

Later, Paul wrote to the Corinthians again, readdressing the subject of the immoral man. The Corinthians had performed the apostle's suggested discipline, so Paul instructed them to forgive the man and reaffirm their love so he wouldn't be overwhelmed with sorrow. While Paul didn't want the Corinthians to tolerate sin, he did want them to react in a balanced manner. Both extremes—being too lenient or too severe—can cause more harm than good.

Learn More: Matthew 13:33 / 1 Corinthians 5; 10:12 / 2 Corinthians 2:5–11 / Galatians 6:1–5

PAUL'S QUESTION FOR COMPETING CHRISTIANS

Why do ye not rather take wrong? 1 CORINTHIANS 6:7

The Corinthian Christians needed a lesson in how to settle disputes. Things had gotten so out of hand that they were suing each other, and unbelievers were settling their cases. The fact that they had lawsuits among themselves, Paul said, implied the presence of a deeper, potentially disastrous issue. They might have been competing with one another, but no one was winning—so they were cheating each other in the process. Paul asked, "Why do ye not rather take wrong? why do ye not rather suffer yourselves to be defrauded?"

After reminding the Corinthians of their previous lifestyle of wickedness, greed, slander, and swindling, Paul said, "And such were some of you" (1 Corinthians 6:11). Since this past had been erased, Paul taught, they should have been living peacefully with one other, showing their righteous testimonies in the presence of unbelievers. If this meant a victory for the opponent, so what?

If anyone has ever been cheated, it was Jesus. But when He was falsely accused and put on trial, He didn't sue or command angels to defend Him. His surrender to the cross brought victory over death—and all believers are winners as a result.

Learn More: John 13:35 / 1 Corinthians 6:1–11 / Philippians 2:3–11

PAUL'S QUESTION ABOUT THE SPIRIT'S TEMPLE

Know ye not that your body is the temple of the Holy Ghost? 1 CORINTHIANS 6:19

The temple was a man-made edifice that became a permanent dwelling for God's presence. There, people worshipped and sacrificed while the priests supervised and offered aromatic incense to God. Everything about the temple was holy—even the outer courts, where Gentiles could pray and worship.

If our bodies are temples of the Holy Spirit, then every part of our lifestyle must be devoted to the Spirit. The same activities that were performed at the temple in Jerusalem should be part of our daily lives. We *sacrifice* by resisting fleshly lusts. We *worship* by honoring God with our thoughts, decisions, and actions. And since He has made us priests, we *supervise* our minds and bodies.

In Bible times, people traveled to the temple to worship. But now, as temples of the Holy Spirit, we carry His presence everywhere. As people approach us—entering our "outer courts"—the aromatic fragrance of the Spirit within will hopefully draw them near to Him.

Learn More: Psalm 116:19; 134; 135:1–2 / 2 Corinthians 2:14–15 / 1 Peter 2:4–5

A QUESTION OF CONSCIENCE

*Shall not. . .him which is weak be emboldened to eat those
things which are offered to idols?* 1 CORINTHIANS 8:10

Paul encourages believers to set an example that is motivated by love. Addressing a conflict in
the Corinthian church, he began by writing, "Love builds up" (1 Corinthians 8:1 NIV).

Some believers in Corinth still struggled with issues pertaining to idol worship. Often,
after offering meat to idols, people would then eat the meat in a celebratory feast. Any leftovers
were sold in the marketplace. The "mature" Corinthians reasoned that idols were lifeless and the
sacrifices meaningless—besides, it was good meat being sold at a reduced price. However, those
with weaker consciences believed any meat offered to idols was defiled and should be avoided.

Rather than criticize the weaker brothers, Paul admonished those with a stronger conscience
to set an example of love. Setting the bar high, he offered to utterly disavow meat rather than
to risk causing his brother to stumble. Paul was not legalistic—he was loving. He knew that
love never fails, especially when it involves self-sacrifice.

Learn More: Romans 14:13–21 / 1 Corinthians 8; 11:1; 13

A QUESTION FOR RUNNERS

*Know ye not that they which run in a race run all,
but one receiveth the prize?* 1 CORINTHIANS 9:24

The popular Isthmian athletic games took place every few years near Corinth. Before they
could even qualify for the games, participants had to undergo months of extreme training and
harsh diets. The prize was a vine or branch that was twisted into a crown. This crown—plus
bragging rights—made the intense training worth the effort.

Paul uses the race metaphor, knowing it would resonate with the Corinthians, to make a
specific point: believers should put more effort into the spiritual race than athletes put forth for
the games. In the spiritual race, we don't compete against everyone else; instead, we compete with
ourselves by reckoning our fleshly desires as dead so we can surrender to the Spirit. Just going
through the motions is not enough—this race requires intentionality, discipline, and endurance.

Paul tells us to run with perseverance and keep our eyes on Jesus, who waits eagerly for the
moment when we will run across the line and into His arms. He's the prize worth running for.

Learn More: Acts 20:24 / 1 Corinthians 9:24–27 / Galatians 5:16–18 / Philippians 3:13–14 /
2 Timothy 4:7–8 / Hebrews 12:1–3

A QUESTION OF DEATH'S POWER

O death, where is thy sting? 1 CORINTHIANS 15:55

The Corinthian church was confused about the resurrection of the dead, so Paul broached the
topic logically. First, he pointed out that Jesus appeared after His resurrection to more than
five hundred individuals, all of whom witnessed His glorified state. Second, he argued that
if the Corinthians denied Christ's resurrection, there was nothing left for them to believe.
Their faith would have been futile and his preaching vain. By denying the resurrection, the
Corinthians were giving death more power than it deserved.

When Lazarus died, Jesus comforted Mary and Martha by revealing that He is the resurrection and the life. When He asked Martha if she believed this, she affirmed that He was
Christ; however, she said nothing about His being the resurrection. Instead of watching with
anticipation as the stone was rolled from Lazarus's tomb, she protested that her brother had
been dead for four days. When Lazarus revived, Jesus proved His resurrecting power even
before His own resurrection!

Death will be the final enemy that is defeated. It will be utterly annihilated as it is cast into
the lake of fire. Just knowing that death is temporary is enough to rob it of its sting—even
when we face it directly.

Learn More: Isaiah 25:8 / Hosea 13:14 / John 11:17–44 / 1 Corinthians 15 / Revelation 20:14

A QUESTION OF PLEASING

For do I now persuade men, or God? or do I seek to please men? GALATIANS 1:10

The apostle Paul planted several churches in Galatia, laying a solid scriptural foundation. However, shortly after he had left, the churches quickly succumbed to a perverted gospel that emphasized works over grace. Whoever led the Galatians astray also maligned Paul's reputation, planting seeds of doubt about his credibility.

Some believe the Galatians were accusing Paul of being a crowd pleaser who followed a man-made gospel. They also wondered if his prior motives for persecuting the church may have been merely to impress others, thus calling into question the sincerity of his devotion to Christ. Paul refutes this argument, however, by reminding the Galatians of his life-changing encounter with Jesus.

In his Gospel, John mentions some Jewish believers who kept their faith quiet because they feared the Pharisees might expel them from the synagogue. John describes these "closet Christians" as those who "loved the praise of men more than the praise of God" (John 12:43).

When we become too focused on winning people's approval, we become ensnared in a paralyzing crowd-pleasing mentality. To avoid such a trap, remember Paul's self-reflection: "If I yet pleased men, I should not be the servant of Christ" (Galatians 1:10).

Learn More: Galatians 1:6–24

PAUL'S QUESTION OF THE GALATIANS' RACE

Who did hinder you that ye should not obey the truth? GALATIANS 5:7

In a race, runners are required to stay in their own lanes. If they swerve into the others' lanes and cut them off—either accidentally or intentionally—they are disqualified.

The Galatians had been running well, being faithful and obedient to Paul's Gospel message. However, someone with a foreign doctrine persuaded them to swerve from the lane of truth. The apostle pointed out that they had been influenced too easily, comparing them to a large batch of dough that was leavened by a little yeast.

While Paul expressed concern over the Galatians' quick departure from the truth, he also gave a warning of judgment to whoever had caused them to swerve. He might have said this to caution the Galatians to be more critically aware in the future.

To keep the misdoings of others from removing our attention from God, we must push forward and apprehend the goal. Finishing a race takes intense focus and determination.

Learn More: Galatians 5:7–10 / Philippians 3:12–14 / Hebrews 12:1–3

A QUESTION FOR ASPIRING CHURCH LEADERS

If a man know not how to rule his own house, how shall he take care of the church? 1 TIMOTHY 3:5

In 1 Timothy, Paul referred to Timothy, his young protégé, as "my own son in the faith" (1:2). He told Timothy that seeking a leadership position in the church, particularly the role of an overseer, is a noble endeavor—but certain requirements must be met. Paul then listed these requirements—one being the ability to manage one's own family. Otherwise, he asked, how can the overseer take care of God's church?

Households in Bible days extended beyond the spouse and children—they often included parents, descendants, extended relatives, and servants. Managing a household involved many aspects: husbands were instructed to love their wives unselfishly, and wives were encouraged to submit to and respect their husbands. Fathers were not to rile their children but were to train and instruct them in the Lord. Masters were commanded to treat their servants with kindness not with favoritism.

Love, submission, respect, training, instruction, and kindness remain vital ingredients for managing a household as well as for leading a church. If they are practiced in the home, they will automatically flow everywhere else.

Learn More: Ephesians 5:21–33; 6:4, 9 / 1 Timothy 3:1–16

A QUESTION OF SALVATION

How shall we escape, if we neglect so great salvation? Hebrews 2:3

Salvation is God's most valuable gift to humankind. It offers us eternal life for free, but it cost Him His only Son. Salvation through Jesus is the only way to escape punishment for our sin. If we ignore His gift, we will pay the price.

Some believe they must work for eternal life. However, when a group of people asked Jesus how they could fulfill God's requirements, He responded, "This is the work of God, that ye believe on him whom he hath sent" (John 6:29). The Pharisees, with their legalistic adherence to the law and heavy expectations for their disciples, had missed the point entirely. As Jesus told them, they were neglecting justice and God's love.

We should never ignore God's great salvation; rather, the author of Hebrews instructs us to grow up in our spirituality. We begin as spiritual infants who thrive on pure spiritual milk, but maturity eventually brings a craving for solid food. Then, as spiritually mature adults, we can teach others about His great salvation so they too may find the way of escape.

Learn More: Luke 11:42 / 1 Corinthians 3:1–2 / Ephesians 2:8–9; 4:11–16 / Hebrews 5:13–14

A QUESTION OF DISCIPLINE

What son is he whom the father chasteneth not? Hebrews 12:7

We often consider discipline from God as negative, but in reality, it is one of the best things that can happen to us. As Job said, "Happy is the man whom God correcteth" (Job 5:17).

In the New Testament, the Greek word for discipline means "instruction that trains someone to reach full development." This instruction is proactive, just like regular study or exercise, and it can include mentoring, accountability, and self-discipline. But it can also be uncomfortable, involving stretching, consistency, and obedience. God was proactive when He gave the Israelites the Ten Commandments—He set the ground rules and left the choice up to them. Parents implement proactive discipline by encouraging children to play outside. The child may be annoyed for the moment, but the results are worthwhile.

Discipline, however, can also be reactive. If someone intentionally disobeys ground rules, consequences must follow. For example, because the Israelites disobeyed God, they were forced to wait forty years outside the promised land and spend seventy years in captivity—just as God had warned.

Discipline is unpleasant while it is happening, but the righteousness and peace that come from our loving Father make it worthwhile.

Learn More: Deuteronomy 8:1–6 / Hebrews 12:1–13

A QUESTION OF FAVORITISM

Do not rich men oppress you, and draw you before the judgment seats? James 2:6

In the Old Testament law, God had labeled favoritism toward the rich as a perversion of justice. Centuries later, James wrote that the wealthy people whom his readers were trying to impress were cheating them through exploitation and lawsuits. Meanwhile, the poor—who truly needed help—were being ignored.

James referenced the commandment "Thou shalt love thy neighbour as thyself" (2:8), suggesting that the core issue is a lack of love. To remedy this issue, James speaks of three types of love: compassionate, corrective, and confident. Compassionate love is shown to the poor and forgotten. Corrective love should be displayed to those who have manipulated others with their wealth. And confident love is shown when we love our neighbor as we love ourselves.

Confident love allows us to know what's best for everyone—whether it's compassion or correction—and to meet these needs without showing bias.

Learn More: Leviticus 19:15–18 / Deuteronomy 10:17–18 / 1 Timothy 5:21 / James 2:1–1

A QUESTION ABOUT THE TONGUE

Doth a fountain send forth at the same place sweet water and bitter? JAMES 3:11

James doesn't mince words when speaking about the tongue. He describes it as an unruly, destructive, evil, and untamable force that—although it's one of the tiniest members of the body—resembles a small rudder that controls a large ship. James also asks thoughtful rhetorical questions, teaching that whatever lies at the source will be manifested in the outflow: fresh water sources only produce fresh water, fig trees bear only figs, and grapevines exclusively produce grapes. Anything else would run contrary to nature's design and purpose.

Cool water satisfies thirst and energizes the body, but salt water dehydrates and makes the body unhealthy—two types of water from two different sources. According to Jesus, our speech is not a tongue issue. It's a heart issue. "Out of the abundance of the heart," He says, "the mouth speaketh" (Matthew 12:34). Bitter hearts produce bitter words. Kind hearts, kind words.

Solomon writes, "Keep thy heart with all diligence; for out of it are the issues of life" (Proverbs 4:23). By setting watch over our hearts, we can tame our tongues, thus guaranteeing wholesome words.

Learn More: Proverbs 10:19; 15:28; 18:21 / James 3:1–12

A QUESTION OF CONFESSION

Is any sick among you? JAMES 5:14

At the end of James's letter, he encourages believers to deepen their prayer life. Those who are suffering should pray for themselves, but they should also ask the elders of the church to anoint them with oil and pray in the name of the Lord. According to James, that person will then be restored.

But physical healing isn't everything. God also wants to provide spiritual healing by forgiving our sins—which might be why James instructs us to confess our sins to each other. While James probably isn't referring to public confessions before an entire congregation, he does emphasize the importance of honesty about one's shortcomings. The psalmist says that the Lord doesn't hear the prayers of those who purposely hide their sin, and James confirms this. He gives three remedial steps: confess, pray, and receive healing.

Those who pray don't have to be perfect beforehand; otherwise, this prayer would be pointless. However, they *are* expected to be righteous—innocent before God. Praying people should be the first to confess: only then can they lay hands on others and pray effective prayers of faith—prayers which the Lord will eagerly answer.

Learn More: Psalm 66:18–20 / John 9:31 / James 5:13–18 / 1 Peter 3:12 / 1 John 3:21–22

A QUESTION OF JUDGMENT

What shall the end be of them that obey not the gospel of God? 1 PETER 4:17

Most Bible scholars believe that Peter's question refers to one of Ezekiel's visions. In this vision, God took the prophet inside the temple, where men and women were committing idolatry by bowing to the sun god and mourning the death of the Phoenician god Tammuz. After appointing an angel to go through Jerusalem and place a mark on the foreheads of the Israelites who had rejected this detestable idolatry, God sent other angels to destroy everyone without this mark—beginning in the temple and moving through the city. Judgment began in the house of the Lord.

We as Christians are not exempt from suffering. In fact, we should expect it. But Peter encourages believers to think of persecution as a compliment: by suffering for Christ's sake, we bear the marks of Christianity.

As both Ezekiel and Peter teach, judgment will begin with us—and we can face that day with confidence. However, we should also mourn the fate of those who do not bear the mark of Christ.

Learn More: Proverbs 11:31 / Ezekiel 8–9 / 1 Peter 4

A QUESTION OF LIVING IN LIGHT OF THE SECOND COMING ⸺

What manner of persons ought ye to be? 2 Peter 3:11

Peter's description of the day of the Lord is quite vivid. The heavens will disappear "with a great noise"; the elements—which many believe are the heavenly bodies—will burn with an intense heat; and the earth will be utterly consumed (2 Peter 3:10). That day will come when least expected—like a thief. So, Peter asks, since we don't know when that day will happen, what kind of lives should we live as we await it?

First, Peter says we should strive to be spotless—morally unblemished and full of faith and love. Then he says we should seek to be blameless—reconciled and at peace with God. It's up to us to eliminate anything that might stain our moral character. Peter also cautions us to guard against those who distort scripture and lead people astray. Staying immersed in God's truth enables us to perceive deception quickly.

The apostle's advice for preparing for the day of the Lord is spot-on. If we want to be found spotless then, we must begin the process now.

Learn More: Mark 13:32–37 / Luke 21:34–36 / 2 Peter 3 / 1 Peter 2:1–3

A QUESTION OF SELFLESSNESS ⸺

How dwelleth the love of God in him? 1 John 3:17

John wrote three epistles and one Gospel. He and his brother James, when they were young disciples, once became so angry with Samaritans who had disrespected Jesus that they wanted to call down fire on their village. But now John was in his nineties, writing of God's power to soften hearts and quench tempers through love. In his first letter, John uses the word *love* more than twenty times—quite the contrast from a man once nicknamed "son of thunder."

John addresses the hypocrisy of those who say they love the poor while closing their hearts—and wallets—to them. This section echoes Jesus' teaching about selfless love—the willingness to lay one's life down for another.

Though it would be rare for any of us to die for another person, our lives are full of opportunities for *inconvenient* love, in which we place the needs and interests of others above our own. Our actions will express our love much louder than words. Remember, God loved so much that He gave—and so should we.

Learn More: John 3:16–17; 15:9–17 / Romans 5:8 / 1 John 3:11–24

A QUESTION OF WORTHINESS ⸺

Who is worthy to open the book, and to loose the seals thereof? Revelation 5:2

End-times prophecies stretch back into the Old Testament, including the book of Daniel. God commanded Daniel to seal the words of his vision in a scroll until the opportune time, and Daniel asked God what the outcome would be. The Lord responded, "Go thy way, Daniel: for the words are closed up and sealed till the time of the end" (12:9).

Fast-forward to John's vision on the isle of Patmos. He saw a sealed scroll—whose time had come to be opened—sitting in God's right hand. A powerful angel then asked who was worthy to break the seals. Only one could be found—the Lamb of God, now standing as the victorious Lion of Judah. He is not just the First and Last—He is the One and Only.

The word *worthy* means having sufficient weight or moral character. Jesus, having fulfilled God's mission by rising again to conquer death, was worthy both to open the scroll and to execute its commands. As each seal was broken, the scroll never left Jesus' hands.

Regardless of what may transpire, everything lies within Jesus' control. Only He can carry the weight.

Learn More: Daniel 12 / Revelation 4–6

THE 1-MINUTE
BIBLE
GUIDE

180 Key Figures of Speech

An alphabetical listing of the 180 most
interesting phrases and word pictures of scripture.

Written by George W. Knight
Edited by Paul Kent

ACTS NOT DONE IN A CORNER

For this thing was not done in a corner. ACTS 26:26

The apostle Paul made this bold declaration before a Roman ruler known as King Agrippa II. Paul was being held as a prisoner after being accused of blasphemy by Jewish religious leaders. In his defense, Paul recounted his glorious conversion when Jesus appeared to him in a vision on the Damascus road (Acts 9:3–6). Then known as Saul, he was transformed from a persecutor of the church into a zealous preacher of the Gospel.

Since his about-face, the apostle declared, he had witnessed about Jesus openly and forthrightly to anyone who would listen. He had nothing to hide from Agrippa or any other Roman official. The New Life Version renders Paul's words as "These things happened where everyone saw them."

Paul's forthright testimony of his conversion must have made a favorable impression on this Roman official. He told the apostle, "Almost thou persuadest me to be a Christian" (Acts 26:28).

Learn More: Acts 9:1–7; 22:6–10 / Philippians 3:4–7

ANCHOR OF THE SOUL

Which hope we have as an anchor of the soul. HEBREWS 6:19

In this verse, the hope of which the author speaks is confidence in the promise of eternal life. This hope belongs to all who accept Jesus as Lord and Savior.

This anchor is not made of steel nor dropped to the ocean floor to steady a ship. It is a spiritual reality that Jesus has planted "within the veil" of the heavenly sanctuary where He dwells with God the Father. Before His crucifixion, resurrection, and ascension, He told His followers, "In my Father's house are many mansions: if it were not so, I would have told you. I go to prepare a place for you" (John 14:2).

A sign of safety and security, the anchor was a popular symbol in the early days of the church. Its shape is similar to the cross on which Jesus was crucified. Anchor images appear on the tombs of many Christian martyrs in the catacombs beneath the city of ancient Rome.

Learn More: Psalm 31:24 / Romans 5:3–5; 15:13 / 1 Thessalonians 4:13

APPLE OF GOD'S EYE

He kept him as the apple of his eye. DEUTERONOMY 32:9–10

These verses are part of the chapter of Deuteronomy known as the Song of Moses. It describes the nation of Israel in poetic imagery as people chosen by the Lord for His special blessing and His divine purpose in the world.

The phrase "apple of the eye" refers to the pupil of the human eye—the most precious part of one of the most important organs of the body. Thus, a person or thing considered the "apple of one's eye" is something highly esteemed and very precious. This imagery refers to God's deep love for Israel as His chosen people.

Other English translations render this phrase as the Lord guarding Israel "as he would guard his own eyes" (NLT) and "as those he loved very much" (NCV).

Learn More: Psalm 17:8 / Proverbs 7:2 / Zechariah 2:8

APPLES OF GOLD

A word fitly spoken is like apples of gold in pictures of silver. PROVERBS 25:11

The message of this proverb from King Solomon is that an appropriate word spoken at just the right time is a thing of beauty. Words like this have been known to lift up the discouraged, rally troops in battle, and inspire a football team to come from behind and win a close game.

The image of "apples of gold" was inspired by carvings of golden apples in a highly polished silver frame. These ornate decorations were displayed in the homes of kings and other wealthy people in Bible times.

The phrase "watch what you say" does not appear in the Bible, but it expresses a biblical truth. Words, once spoken, cannot be taken back. Even if we apologize for a critical remark we make of another person, it leaves its mark on that relationship. The words of the psalmist should be front and center in the thoughts and prayers of every believer: "Let the words of my mouth, and the meditation of my heart, be acceptable in thy sight, O LORD, my strength, and my redeemer" (Psalm 19:14).

Learn More: Job 6:25; 33:3 / Psalm 12:6 / Matthew 12:36 / James 3:5

ARM OF GOD

Thou hast made the heaven and the earth by thy great power and stretched out arm. JEREMIAH 32:17

The prophet Jeremiah warned the people of Judah that their sins would lead to their captivity and deportation by a foreign nation. But he also comforted God's people by saying that they would eventually be restored to their homeland. The Lord would bring about both these events through the power of His mighty arm.

The metaphor of God acting with His arm occurs throughout the Bible. With His arm He delivered His people from slavery in Egypt (2 Kings 17:36). He also used His arm to send lightning in a thunderstorm (Isaiah 30:30); to gather His people to Himself (Isaiah 40:11); and to scatter the proud (Luke 1:51). When God "bares His arm," He takes swift, decisive action (Isaiah 52:10).

When King Hezekiah of Judah was threatened by the Assyrians, he contrasted their "arm of flesh" with the spiritual power the Lord could wield with His arm. God rescued His people by sending a deadly plague among the enemy army (2 Chronicles 32:8, 21)

Learn More: Deuteronomy 33:27 / Psalm 44:3 / Isaiah 48:14; 51:5

ARMOR OF GOD

Take unto you the whole armour of God, that ye may be able to withstand. EPHESIANS 6:13

The apostle Paul wrote Ephesians while in prison in Rome. During this ordeal he probably saw many Roman soldiers in full military dress. So it was natural for him to compare the spiritual battle that Christians faced with the physical armor worn by these warriors.

The apostle went on to specify six items of spiritual armor that believers could rely on: the belt of truth, the breastplate of righteousness, the shoes of peace, the shield of faith, the helmet of salvation, and the sword of the spirit (verses 14–17).

Paul knew that Satan never lets up in his attempts to derail believers from their commitment to the Lord. But God has made available the spiritual armor to help Christians even the odds in their spiritual battle. Although Satan is a determined foe, he is no match for the all-powerful God who protects His people.

The apostle John assured believers they have the upper hand when standing against Satan's false teachers. "Greater is he that is in you," he declared, "than he that is in the world" (1 John 4:4).

Learn More: Romans 16:20 / Ephesians 6:12 / James 4:7 / 1 John 2:13

ARROWS OF THE ALMIGHTY

For the arrows of the Almighty are within me. Job 6:4

Job had lost all his earthly possessions, his children, and his health. On top of that, his three friends began to criticize him rather than offer comfort. No wonder he felt like a person who had been targeted by God, wounded by arrows from His divine arsenal.

Job's complaints were echoed by the prophet Jeremiah. He felt that God had set him up for a life of misery by calling him to preach an unpopular message of judgment to His wayward people. God had "bent his bow," Jeremiah lamented, "and set me as a mark for the arrow" (Lamentations 3:12).

Because of their ability to inflict pain and death, arrows are apt images for various unpleasant experiences mentioned in the Bible. Critical words were like arrows shot from one's tongue, causing distress and misery (Psalm 57:4). Failure of crops brought on the "arrows of famine" (Ezekiel 5:16). But on the positive side, children of one's youth were like "arrows...in the hand of a mighty man" (Psalm 127:4).

Learn More: Psalm 7:13; 38:2; 64:3 / Proverbs 25:18 / Jeremiah 9:8 / Zechariah 9:14

BACKSLIDING HEIFER

For Israel slideth back as a backsliding heifer. Hosea 4:16

The prophet Hosea proclaimed God's message to the people of the northern kingdom of Israel during the chaotic final days before it fell to the nation of Assyria. Hosea was unrelenting in his declaration that the Lord would punish His people unless they turned from their worship of false gods.

Hosea compared Israel to a young cow that refuses to follow the direction in which it is being led. It pulls back ("backslides"). This is an apt image for falling into sin, which the prophet applied to the people of Israel. They were deliberately stubborn and disobedient, refusing to follow the Lord's commands.

The term *backsliding* also occurs in the writings of Jeremiah. This famous prophet preached to the citizens of Judah, Israel's sister kingdom that was also conquered and carried into captivity by a foreign nation. God's people paid a high price for their willful rebellion.

The second part of Hosea 4:16 is translated as a rhetorical question by several modern English translations. Because of Israel's stubbornness, the New International Version reads, "How then can the LORD pasture them like lambs in a meadow?"

Learn More: Jeremiah 3:6; 14:7; 31:22 / Hosea 11:7; 14:4

BAG WITH HOLES

He that earneth wages earneth wages to put it into a bag with holes. Haggai 1:6

The prophet Haggai addressed the nation of Judah after their return from captivity of the Babylonians and Persians. God's people needed encouragement because they were struggling to rebuild their homes, restore their homeland, and get back to life as they knew it before the exile.

But they also needed to be prodded to rebuild the worship customs that set them apart as God's chosen people. They were busy building their homes while the temple remained in ruins. This shrine, which represented the presence of God, had been destroyed by their enemies several decades before. Haggai declared that all their efforts to restore the nation would be futile unless they first rebuilt this sacred place of worship.

The prophet declared that their misguided efforts would amount to nothing—like hard-earned money placed in a bag that couldn't hold anything. This is a good reminder of the futility of all human effort apart from the Lord. The psalmist put it like this: "Except the LORD build the house, they labour in vain that build it: except the LORD keep the city, the watchman waketh but in vain" (Psalm 127:1).

Learn More: Job 14:17

BALM IN GILEAD

Is there no balm in Gilead; is there no physician there? JEREMIAH 8:22

This verse from the prophet Jeremiah is a good example of an ironic statement. The people of Judah knew that faithfulness to the Lord was the antidote for their sinful tendencies. All they had to do was commit to Him and His commands, but they refused to do so.

The prophet compared their refusal to turn to the Lord to a sick person's unwillingness to be treated with a well-known remedy. Known as the balm of Gilead, this ointment came from the sap of trees that grew in a mountainous region near the Sea of Galilee.

This medicine was exported from Israel to surrounding nations (Ezekiel 27:17). The traveling merchants who bought Joseph and sold him as a slave in Egypt traded in this precious substance (Genesis 37:25). Jeremiah was implying that even pagan nations recognized the value of Israel's God, while the Israelites themselves were rejecting Him to worship false deities.

Learn More: Numbers 32:29 / Jeremiah 46:11

BED TOO SHORT

For the bed is shorter than that a man can stretch himself on it. ISAIAH 28:20

Anyone who has ever tried to sleep on an uncomfortable bed can identify with the prophet Isaiah's imagery in this verse. There's nothing worse than tossing and turning in discomfort for hours on end, unable to fall asleep.

The prophet's reference to a bed that was too short apparently refers to an alliance the leaders of Judah had made with Egypt. They hoped this agreement would provide protection in the event of an attack from Assyria. The Assyrians were on a campaign to conquer surrounding nations and become the dominant power in the region.

Isaiah declared that this alliance with Egypt was futile. It would provide no protection from Assyria, just as a short bed failed to give full support to a human body. The only source of safety for the nation of Judah was the Lord, who required the people to turn from their sin and pledge undivided loyalty to Him.

The prophet continued to counsel against trusting in Egypt throughout his book. In one passage he characterized the nation as one whose only strength was "to sit still" (Isaiah 30:7).

Learn More: Isaiah 30:3; 31:1; 36:6, 9

BEULAH AND HEPHZIBAH

Thou shalt be called Hephzibah, and thy land Beulah. ISAIAH 62:4

Through the prophet Isaiah, the Lord delivered this message to the nations of Judah and Israel. Although they would fall to their enemies as punishment for their sins, God had not forgotten His people.

Because of the devastation of their land, the Israelites seemed "forsaken" by the Lord. But they would be referred to as Hephzibah in the future. This word means "my delight is in her," showing they would be restored to God's favor.

"Desolate" Israel would also be transformed into a land known as Beulah—a term meaning "married." This name declares that Israel would be restored to a loving relationship with the Lord in which He would provide abundantly for His people. This change of names by the Lord symbolized radical change and the opportunity for a new beginning.

The term *Beulah* has been immortalized in a hymn entitled "Beulah Land," which was written more than a century ago. The phrase in this song refers to heaven.

Learn More: Genesis 32:28 / 2 Kings 21:1

BLIND LEADING THE BLIND

If the blind lead the blind, both shall fall into the ditch. Matthew 15:14

Jesus used this phrase for the Pharisees after they criticized Him and His disciples for not washing their hands before eating. As the "blind leading the blind," they were leading people astray through their insistence that people keep this burdensome Old Testament law.

The Pharisees thought a person who did not practice this purification ritual was made unclean and thus unacceptable to God. But Jesus declared that keeping one's heart pure and undefiled was what really mattered in the Lord's sight. He told His disciples, "Not that which goeth into the mouth defileth a man; but that which cometh out of the mouth, this defileth a man" (Matthew 15:11).

The Pharisees also accused Jesus of violating the Sabbath by healing people on that day of rest. On one occasion He reminded them that the Old Testament law made allowance for acts of mercy, such as rescuing a sheep, to be done on the Sabbath. Then He healed a man's handicapped hand after declaring, "How much then is a man better than a sheep? Wherefore it is lawful to do well on the sabbath days" (Matthew 12:12).

Learn More: Matthew 23:16–26 / Luke 6:39 / John 9:25, 40–41

BLIND WATCHMEN

His watchmen are blind: they are all ignorant. Isaiah 56:10

The prophet Isaiah had no patience for the leaders of Israel who were leading the people astray. They were pretending that the nation was secure and had nothing to fear from its enemies. At the same time, they were ignoring the widespread idolatry among the population. The prophet compared these leaders to "blind watchmen." They were oblivious to the danger that loomed on the horizon.

Watchmen, or sentinels, were key elements in the defense system of the walled cities of Bible times. These guards were rotated regularly so they were always fresh and alert. Their job was to sound the alarm to the city's defenders when they spotted suspicious activity. Isaiah's message was clear. How could Israel's leaders warn about the dangers they were incapable of seeing?

As if the image of watchmen without eyesight were not strong enough, the prophet also compared the nation's leaders to "dumb dogs" that couldn't bark. His description of these canines conjures up an image of a house being plundered by a burglar while the guard dog lies sound asleep on the floor.

Learn More: Psalm 127:1 / Ezekiel 3:17; 33:7

BONES OUT OF JOINT

I am poured out like water, and all my bones are out of joint. Psalm 22:14

This psalm is generally interpreted as messianic in nature, referring to the crucifixion of Jesus. As He hung on the cross, He quoted its first verse: "My God, my God, who hast thou forsaken me" (Psalm 22:1).

It's hard to imagine a more painful experience than having one's bones pulled out of joint. We know from the Gospels that not a bone of Jesus' body was broken when He was crucified (John 19:36). So His statement about out-of-joint bones probably refers to the feeling of abandonment that He suffered on the cross.

In the Bible, bones are often spoken of in a figurative sense. The psalmist felt mocked by his bones (Psalm 22:17). One's bones could be dried up by a spirit of sadness or remorse (Proverbs 17:22). The prophet Jeremiah confessed that the message of God's judgment that he proclaimed was like "a burning fire shut up in [his] bones" (Jeremiah 20:9). The prophet Ezekiel had a vision of dry bones coming to life, symbolizing God's restoration of His people to their homeland (Ezekiel 37:1–11).

Learn More: Numbers 24:8 / Job 30:30 / Psalm 6:2; 102:3 / Isaiah 58:11

BOOK OF LIFE

And with other my fellowlabourers, whose names are in the book of life. PHILIPPIANS 4:3

In this verse the apostle Paul mentioned several people who had assisted him in his ministry. He added that their names were recorded in "the book of life." This book, a metaphor for eternal life, includes those who have accepted Jesus as Lord and Savior. They will enjoy fellowship with God the Father and Jesus the Son in heaven after their earthly days are over.

The concept of a book of life may have originated with Moses. This godly leader prayed for mercy for the wayward Israelites. He asked God to erase his own name from "thy book" instead of wiping out His people for their sin of idolatry in the wilderness (Exodus 32:32).

In one of the apostle John's visions in the book of Revelation, the book of life is in the hands of God. But He gives the book to the Lamb, a symbol for Jesus. He alone is worthy to open the book. This shows that all authority and power in heaven and earth has been committed to Jesus the Son.

Learn More: Psalm 69:28 / Revelation 5:1–9; 13:8; 17:8; 20:15; 21:27

BORN OUT OF DUE TIME

Last of all he was seen of me also, as of one born out of due time. 1 CORINTHIANS 15:8

Immediately before this verse, the apostle Paul recalled the appearances that Jesus made to several people after His resurrection. Then Paul thought about his own glorious conversion on the Damascus road. He also saw Jesus—the last of His recorded appearances in the New Testament.

Jesus commissioned Paul to preach the Gospel of grace, just as He had earlier chosen twelve disciples for this task. This personal call from the Lord Himself is why Paul is referred to as an apostle. His late-to-the-table experience may have caused him to wish that He had been one of the twelve who knew Jesus in the flesh. The Contemporary English Version renders his words like this: "Finally, he appeared to me, even though I am like someone who was born at the wrong time."

Paul considered himself inferior to the original Twelve. In the next verse, he declared, "I am the least of the apostles" (verse 9). His humility is commendable, but Paul was second to no one when it came to spreading the Gospel, particularly to unbelievers in the Gentile world.

Learn More: Acts 9:1–6, 15 / Romans 11:13 / 1 Corinthians 1:1 / Ephesians 3:8 /
1 Timothy 2:7 / 2 Timothy 1:11

BOSOM OF GOD

He shall gather the lambs with his arm, and carry them in his bosom. ISAIAH 40:11

This chapter launches the second major division of the book of Isaiah. The prophet spent the earlier chapters emphasizing God's judgment against His wayward people. Chapters 40–66 are known as the "comfort" section of the book. Here, Isaiah portrays the Lord as a loving Father who cares deeply for His people.

Isaiah used familiar imagery to show this tender side of the Lord. He compared God to a shepherd who watched over all his sheep with great care. But newborn lambs needed special attention, lest they wander away from the flock. The shepherd would take these helpless little ones in his arms and hold them close to his bosom, or chest, to keep them safe and secure. One modern translation says the shepherd holds these lambs "close to his heart" (NLT).

The imagery of God's bosom appears one other time in the Bible. The fourth Gospel declares, "No man hath seen God at any time," but "the only begotten Son, which is in the bosom of the Father, he hath declared him" (John 1:18)

Learn More: Numbers 11:12 / Psalm 74:11 / Luke 16:22

BOWELS OF COMPASSION

Whoso. . .shutteth up his bowels of compassion from him,
how dwelleth the love of God in him? 1 JOHN 3:17

Every student of human anatomy knows that the term *bowels* refers to the internal organs that break down and digest food. But the Greek word behind the term in this passage refers to the body's internal organs in a general sense. The Bible often uses *bowels* to indicate feelings or emotions that come from a person's inner being. Thus the apostle John declared that a person without "bowels of compassion" has no empathy or pity toward those in need.

The prophet Jeremiah even portrayed God as having "troubled bowels" for His people, the nation of Israel. Although He punished them for their sin, He never rejected them. The New Revised Standard Version says the Lord was "deeply moved," and He would show mercy toward the Israelites in spite of their sin (Jeremiah 31:20).

Job in his misery declared, "My bowels boiled, and rested not." The New International Version reads, "The churning inside me never stops" (Job 30:27).

Learn More: Jeremiah 4:19 / Lamentations 1:20 / 2 Corinthians 6:12; 7:15 / Philippians 1:8; 2:1 / Colossians 3:12

BRASEN WALL

And I will make thee unto this people a fenced brasen wall. JEREMIAH 15:20

The Lord called the prophet Jeremiah to a daunting task: he must preach an unpopular message to the nation of Judah. The country would fall to a foreign invader unless the people turned from their worship of false gods. But God's call carried with it a comforting promise—that He would strengthen the prophet to endure the persecution and isolation he would face. Jeremiah would be like a wall that stood against his enemies. This image refers to the massive defensive walls around biblical cities. Built of stone, they were almost impregnable. But attackers could batter down such defenses during a prolonged siege against a city.

But Jeremiah would be a "brasen wall." The term refers to brass, a hard metal that was used for cooking utensils and weapons. With such security, the prophet had nothing to fear from his enemies. He claimed God's promise, stood firm against all opposition, and proclaimed God's message of judgment for more than forty years.

Learn More: Deuteronomy 33:25 / Job 6:12 / Psalm 18:2; 28:7 / Mark 7:4

BRAY A FOOL IN A MORTAR

Though thou shouldest bray a fool in a mortar. . .yet will not his foolishness depart.
PROVERBS 27:22

A mortar was a stone cup in which grain was crushed into flour. This was accomplished by pounding the grain with a heavy stone object known as a pestle. To bray, or crush, a fool in a mortar is a figurative way of describing the futility of trying to reform a fool. Even if you could grind him in a mortar, you wouldn't be able to separate him from his foolish ways.

This is only one of many colorful expressions in the book of Proverbs about human folly and the people who behave foolishly. A fool:

- hates wisdom and instruction (1:7),
- will serve those who are wise (11:29),
- is filled with pride (14:3),
- has an explosive temper (14:17),
- despises his father's instruction (15:5),
- stirs up strife and contention (18:6), and
- speaks without thinking (29:11, 20).

Learn More: Ecclesiastes 10:14 / Romans 1:22

BREATH OF GOD

Were the heavens made; and all the host of them by the breath of his mouth. Psalm 33:6

The Bible's account of the creation of the universe declares that God brought everything into existence through His spoken commands (Genesis 1:1–3). The stars, or "host" of heaven, were created in the same way. Thus, the breath of God in this passage is best interpreted as a figure of speech for His unlimited power.

Breathing is a natural, normal function of the human body. Similarly, God in His awesome power simply breathed the world into being from nothing. In contrast to pagan gods, which were powerless, He just had to speak, and the material world appeared.

On the final day of creation, God created Adam and "breathed into his nostrils the breath of life; and man became a living soul" (Genesis 2:7). This marked humankind as the crown of His creation.

Because we are created in the image of God and we breathe the air He provides, we should live our lives in thanksgiving to Him. Job acknowledged his gratitude when He declared, "The spirit of God hath made me, and the breath of the Almighty hath given me life" (Job 33:4).

Learn More: Exodus 15:8 / Job 37:10 / John 20:22

BROKEN CISTERNS

My people have. . .hewed them out cisterns, broken cisterns, that can hold no water. Jeremiah 2:13

The prophet Jeremiah knew a bad deal when he saw one. The people of Judah had traded the one true God for the false gods of the pagan nations. He compared this to rejecting the fresh water from a gushing fountain and drinking instead from a leaking cistern that held stagnant water. The Contemporary English Version translates "broken cisterns" as "cracked and leaking pits dug in the ground."

Cisterns were holding tanks that collected rainwater. They filled up during the rainy season and then were drawn down during the dry months of the year. Stored water like this was drinkable, but it came in a poor second to the fresh water that flowed from underground wells and natural springs.

In the book of Proverbs, the image of a cistern refers to marital faithfulness. King Solomon urged men to "drink. . .out of thine own cistern" (Proverbs 5:15). The Contemporary English Version translates this verse as "You should be faithful to your wife, just as you take water from your own well."

Learn More: 2 Kings 18:31 / Isaiah 36:16

BUILDING OF GOD

Ye are God's building. 1 Corinthians 3:9

In this verse, the apostle Paul addressed the factions that existed in the church he had founded at Corinth. Members of the church disagreed on which human leaders to follow. Paul tried to convince them that they should be working toward the common goal of honoring the Lord. They were the field ("God's husbandry") in which the Lord was sowing seed, as well as the building He was constructing to bring honor and glory to Himself.

Paul went on to explain that he had laid the foundation of this building when he gathered the people together to establish the Corinthian church. Other leaders who came after him had added to this base. But none of them could claim credit for the church's existence. This was God's work, and they should join hands in the business of reaching unbelievers and helping the church to grow. Paul cautioned them, "Let every man take heed how he buildeth thereupon" (verse 10).

The image of God's people as a building that belongs to Him also appears in the Old Testament. The psalmist declared, "Except the Lord build the house, they labour in vain that build it" (Psalm 127:1).

Learn More: 2 Corinthians 5:1 / Ephesians 2:21 / Hebrews 9:1

BULL IN A NET

Thy sons. . .lie at the head of all the streets, as a wild bull in a net. Isaiah 51:20

In Bible times nets were used to trap animals, particularly birds and other small prey. But this verse describes a wild bull stuck in a net. To the prophet Isaiah, it was a perfect picture of the nation of Judah on the road to disaster. He had already witnessed the fall of Israel, Judah's sister nation. He warned that the same thing would happen to Judah if it continued to tolerate idol worship.

Bull imagery was also cited by the psalmist. He complained that he had been surrounded by his enemies, whom he characterized as "strong bulls of Bashan" (Psalm 22:12). The region of Bashan in northern Israel near the Sea of Galilee contained lush pastureland that produced prime livestock.

Names of animals in the King James Version are interpreted in different ways by modern translations of the Bible. For example, "wild bull" in Isaiah 51:20 is rendered as "antelope" in the Contemporary English and New International Versions. Either way, the verse conjures up images of wild thrashing and helpless struggling that awaited the nation of Judah unless it turned back to the Lord.

Learn More: Jeremiah 50:11

BUY THE NEEDY FOR A PAIR OF SHOES

That we may buy the poor for silver, and the needy for a pair of shoes. . . Amos 8:6

The prophet Amos was a lowly shepherd from the village of Tekoa in Judah. God called him to deliver a message to Israel, Judah's sister nation to the north. Amos is known for condemning the wealthy class of Israel for its oppression of the poor.

The rich were cheating their helpless neighbors with dishonest business practices and seizing their property when they fell into debt. They were even selling the needy into slavery for nothing more than the price of a pair of shoes. This graphic image showed how far short they fell of the Lord's command to His people: "Thou shalt open thine hand wide unto thy brother, to thy poor, and to thy needy, in thy land" (Deuteronomy 15:11).

Amos also used another colorful figure of speech to describe the wives of these wealthy Israelites. He called them "kine [*cows:* NIV] of Bashan" (Amos 4:1). They were just as guilty as their husbands because they encouraged the men to oppress the poor to support their extravagant lifestyle.

Learn More: Deuteronomy 24:15 / Nehemiah 5:1–5 / Job 29:12; 34:28 / Psalm 35:10

BYWORD AMONG THE HEATHEN

Thou makest us a byword among the heathen. Psalm 44:14

This psalm was apparently written after the Israelites had been defeated by an enemy. The psalmist was puzzled by this setback because it occurred during a time when the nation was following the Lord. Why had God allowed them to fall into such humiliation? They had become a byword—an object of ridicule and disgust—in the eyes of other nations.

Several modern English translations resort to modern images to render the meaning of the term *byword.* The Christian Standard Bible reads, "You make us a joke among the nations." The New Living Translation says, "You have made us the butt of their jokes." These images make it clear that this defeat was particularly humiliating for God's people.

Perhaps the greatest takeaway from this passage is that setbacks and disappointments are a normal part of life. But faith in the Lord's goodness enables us to rise above those times and remain faithful to Him. The psalmist, after registering his complaint, went on to make this declaration of faith: "Our heart is not turned back, neither have our steps declined from thy way" (Psalm 44:18).

Learn More: Deuteronomy 28:37 / 1 Kings 9:7 / 2 Chronicles 7:20 / Job 17:6; 30:9

CAMEL THROUGH A NEEDLE'S EYE

*Easier for a camel to go through the eye of a needle, than for
a rich man to enter into the kingdom.* Matthew 19:24

Jesus made this statement to His disciples after His encounter with the rich young ruler. The young man's wealth was more important to him than following Jesus and finding the eternal life he sought.

The disciples would certainly have realized the impossibility of a camel worming its way through the eye of a needle. Jesus' words were a deliberate exaggeration to drive home a truth: wealthy people have a hard time releasing their grasp on the things of this world in order to focus on the spiritual realities that give meaning to life.

The disciples asked Jesus how anyone could enter the kingdom of heaven if the rich could not make it. They probably reflected the common belief of Bible times that wealth was a sign of God's favor. He replied, "With men this is impossible; but with God all things are possible" (Matthew 19:26). In other words, earthly impossibilities can come to pass through the power of God's Spirit.

Learn More: Matthew 6:21, 24 / Mark 10:23–24 / Luke 18:24 / 1 Timothy 6:17

CANDLE UNDER A BUSHEL

Is a candle brought to be put under a bushel? Mark 4:21

After Jesus explained the parable of the sower to His disciples, He told them this brief parable. Just as the seed that fell on good ground multiplied abundantly, His teachings should bear fruit in the lives of His followers. They should bear witness of these truths to others, not just hide them away for their own personal enrichment.

Jesus used the image of a "candle under a bushel" to drive home His point. A candle should not be hidden away but placed in the open where it could light up a room. The word *candle* refers to the tiny oil-burning lamps that were used to illuminate homes in Bible times. Most modern translations render this phrase as "lamp. . .under a bowl" (NIV).

Jesus was speaking of Christian influence. Those who have been redeemed by the Lord have a responsibility to pass along the good news of the Gospel to others. In His Sermon on the Mount, Jesus stated this principle clearly and succinctly: "Let your light so shine before men, that they may see your good works, and glorify your Father which is in heaven" (Matthew 5:16).

Learn More: Luke 8:16–18

CAST GOD BEHIND THE BACK

For thou. . .hast cast me behind thy back. 1 Kings 14:9

The prophet Ahijah condemned King Jeroboam for leading his people to worship false gods. Jeroboam became king of the northern region after the ten Jewish tribes rebelled and formed their own nation, known as Israel. He established shrines in two cities in his territory to replace the temple as the place of worship in the sister kingdom of Judah. This act eventually led to widespread worship of false gods throughout Israel.

Ahijah characterized the king's act of rebellion as "casting God behind his back." This was a way of saying that Jeroboam had turned his back on the Lord. The prophet went on to declare that God's judgment would fall on the king as punishment for his sin. Jeroboam was eventually defeated by King Abijah of the southern kingdom (2 Chronicles 13:19–20).

A figure of speech similar to this is withdrawing the shoulder. During the restoration of the law under Ezra, a group of Levites accused the people of this act as well as hardening their necks against the Lord's commands (Nehemiah 9:29).

Learn More: 2 Chronicles 29:6 / Jeremiah 2:27; 32:33 / Ezekiel 23:35 / Zechariah 7:11

CHAFF BLOWN BY THE WIND

The ungodly are not so: but are like the chaff which the wind driveth away. PSALM 1:4

In this brief but well-known psalm, the psalmist contrasts the behavior of those who follow the Lord with the acts of the ungodly—those who ignore God and do as they please. The godly rest on a firm foundation, "like a tree planted by the rivers of waters" (verse 3). But the wicked are rootless and empty. They are like chaff, or the useless stems tossed aside after being stripped of grain. With nothing to hold on to, they are blown away by the wind.

Chaff is mentioned several times in the Bible as a symbol of things that have no substance. For example, God would cause the pagan nations to flee like "the chaff of the mountains before the wind" (Isaiah 17:13). John the Baptist described Jesus as coming to the earth in judgment to separate the grain from the chaff. The grain represented true believers, while chaff symbolized those who refused to acknowledge Jesus as the Messiah (Matthew 3:12).

Learn More: Job 21:18 / Psalm 35:5 / Isaiah 17:13 / Hosea 13:3 / Luke 3:17

CHILDREN OF BELIAL

And there came in two men, children of Belial. 1 KINGS 21:13

These two false witnesses were part of a plot to take over property that belonged to a man named Naboth. Jezebel, wife of King Ahab of Israel, initiated this crime. The king wanted the land for a vegetable garden.

"Children of Belial" is a good name for these witnesses because *Belial* means "worthless" or "useless." What could be worse than sending an innocent man to his death by making false statements against him? Modern English versions render this term as "scoundrels" (NIV), "wicked men" (CSB), and "troublemakers" (NCV).

The sons of Eli the priest are two other men in the Bible to whom this term is applied. They abused their privileges as priests by confiscating animal sacrifices and committing adultery with women who came to the altar to pray (1 Samuel 2:12–22). The apostle Paul referred to Satan as Belial—a schemer and a liar (2 Corinthians 6:15).

Learn More: Deuteronomy 13:13 / Judges 19:22 / 1 Samuel 10:27 / 2 Chronicles 13:7

CHILDREN OF LIGHT

Ye are all the children of light, and the children of the day. 1 THESSALONIANS 5:5

The apostle Paul wrote these words to the believers at Thessalonica. He pointed out that the second coming of Christ would be a time of judgment for unbelievers. But as Christians, these church members walked in the light they received from the Lord. The return of the Lord would be a time of joy and eternal reward for them.

Light is one of the most popular images in the Bible. It represents righteousness, truth, purity, and God's redemptive work. It is often contrasted with darkness, which symbolizes humankind's sinful tendency and refusal to follow the Lord.

The psalmist declared that the Lord was his light and salvation (Psalm 27:1). The coming Messiah would shine like a bright light on those who walked in darkness (Isaiah 9:2). Jesus, as the light of the world, is the very image of spiritual illumination that comes from God the Father. He urged His followers as children of light to bear their positive influence in a dark world: "Let your light so shine before men, that they may see your good works, and glorify your Father which is in heaven" (Matthew 5:16).

Learn More: Luke 16:8 / John 12:36 / Ephesians 5:8

CIRCLE OF THE EARTH

It is he that sitteth upon the circle of the earth. Isaiah 40:22

This is the only place in the Bible where this image of God appears. But it is only one of many biblical figures of speech that show the omnipotence of the Lord—His unlimited and infinite power. The God who sits on "the circle of the earth" created the universe, and He is in total control of His creation.

This image of God outside but looking over the earth argues against a view known as pantheism. According to this theory, God and the universe are one and the same; He has no separate existence apart from the physical world. But the Bible is clear that God created the world as a separate entity (Genesis 1:1). He is both separate from and superior to His creation, and He continues as its sovereign ruler.

In the verse above, the prophet Isaiah used two additional images to show God's awesome power as Creator: He stretched out the heavens as easily as a person would hang a curtain or pitch a tent.

Learn More: Job 38:4 / Jeremiah 32:17 / Hebrews 1:10

CIRCUMCISION OF THE HEART

Circumcision is that of the heart, in the spirit, and not in the letter. Romans 2:29

In his letter to the Christians at Rome, the apostle Paul declared that people were justified in God's sight by faith alone. This was a bitter pill for some Jews to swallow because they thought keeping the Jewish law was the route to salvation. One of the most cherished parts of the law was undergoing circumcision—removal of the foreskin from the male sex organ. This signified the covenant between the Lord and His special people, the Jews.

In this verse from Romans, Paul declared that one's birth as a Jew and physical circumcision were not important. What really mattered was "circumcision of the heart"—or spiritual transformation of a person's basic nature as a sinner. The New Living Translation renders the apostle's words like this: "True circumcision. . .is a change of heart produced by the Spirit."

Paul affirmed this truth several times during his ministry. "Circumcision is nothing, and uncircumcision is nothing," he declared to the Corinthian believers, "but the keeping of the commandments of God" (1 Corinthians 7:19).

Learn More: Jeremiah 4:4 / Acts 7:8 / Romans 2:28; 3:1 / Galatians 5:6 / Colossians 2:11

CITY WITHOUT WALLS

He that hath no rule over his own spirit is like a city. . .without walls. Proverbs 25:28

The massive stone walls around biblical cities provided protection against enemy attacks. A city without such a defense could be easily captured. The writer of Proverbs applied this image to people who lacked self-control. A quick temper left a person defenseless, subject to ridicule and manipulation by others. The Good News Translation renders the verse like this: "If you cannot control your anger, you are as helpless as a city without walls, open to attack."

Jerusalem, Judah's capital, was left defenseless for more than a century after the Babylonian army broke down the wall, razed the city, and carried the people into exile. After the Israelites returned to their homeland, a man named Nehemiah rallied the people to rebuild the wall in less than two months (Nehemiah 6:15).

The writer of Proverbs speaks often of the virtue of self-control. In another passage that uses the imagery of a city, he declares, "He that is slow to anger is better than the mighty; and he that ruleth his spirit than he that taketh a city" (Proverbs 16:32).

Learn More: Ezekiel 38:11 / Zechariah 2:4

CLAY IN GOD'S HANDS

O Lord, thou art our father; we are the clay, and thou our potter. ISAIAH 64:8

Isaiah 64 draws an ugly portrait of God's people. They had rebelled against the Lord and worshipped false gods. But all was not lost. God had not forsaken them. Like clay in His hands, they could still be shaped into instruments of righteousness by returning to Him.

Clay is a fine soil with a high concentration of sand. In Isaiah's day, potters turned clay on a spinning wheel to mold the substance into a dish or cooking pot. They had total command over the objects they wished to create, just as God was the sovereign ruler of His people.

The Lord drove home this lesson to another prophet by sending him to watch a potter at work. The first vessel molded by the craftsman was faulty. But he reshaped the same clay into another object that was perfect in every way. This led to a declaration from the Lord: "Cannot I do with you as this potter? saith the LORD. Behold, as the clay is in the potter's hand, so are ye in mine hand, O house of Israel" (Jeremiah 18:6).

Learn More: Job 10:9; 33:6 / Isaiah 45:9 / Nahum 3:14 / Romans 9:21

CLOUDS WITHOUT WATER

Clouds they are without water, carried about of winds. JUDE 12

The epistle of Jude contains some of the New Testament's strongest language against false teachers. The teachers whom Jude condemned in these two verses may have been claiming to be free in Christ while continuing in sin and debauchery. Jude compared them to clouds that promised to bring rain but produced nothing but wind.

Three additional images for these false teachers also appear in this passage. To Jude they were like trees that produced no fruit; like churning waves that left nothing but foam in their wake; and like wandering stars that had no fixed orbit among the other heavenly bodies.

Clouds appear as metaphors in many passages of the Bible. For example, Israel's goodness and commitment to the Lord could disappear like a morning cloud (Hosea 6:4). God's truth reached as high as the clouds (Psalm 57:10). The Lord rode on a swiftly moving cloud—an image for His judgment (Isaiah 19:1).

Learn More: Proverbs 25:14 / Ecclesiastes 11:3 / Isaiah 5:6 / 2 Peter 2:17

CORDS OF SIN

He shall be holden with the cords of his sins. PROVERBS 5:22

This verse is one of many proverbs that warn against adultery. Sexual involvement with someone other than one's wife or husband is like a snare from which a person cannot escape or a cord that holds people captive to their illicit desires. The Good News Translation renders the verse like this: "The sins of the wicked are a trap. They get caught in the net of their own sin."

The best example of this is King David of Israel. He committed adultery with his neighbor Bathsheba, who became pregnant. Then he tried to cover up the affair by bringing her husband home from the battlefield to sleep with his wife. When this failed, the king had the soldier sent to the front lines, where he was killed (2 Samuel 11:3–17). Although David received divine forgiveness for this crime, his own family was torn apart by jealousy and resentment.

The image of being held captive by one's sin also occurs in the New Testament. When Simon the sorcerer tried to buy the gift of the Holy Spirit, the apostle Peter declared, "I perceive that thou art in the gall of bitterness, and in the bond of iniquity" (Acts 8:23).

Learn More: Job 36:8 / Isaiah 5:18

COTTAGE IN A VINEYARD

And the daughter of Zion is left as a cottage in a vineyard. Isaiah 1:8

The phrase "daughter of Zion" in this verse refers to the city of Jerusalem. The prophet Isaiah predicted that this capital of the land of Judah would be devastated by an enemy nation unless the people turned from their sinful ways. It would be torn apart and looted, then left like a "cottage in a vineyard."

The word *cottage* refers to the flimsy huts built from tree branches that were used as guard shacks in Bible times. Farmers would post family members in these enclosures to protect their crops from predators and thieves. After the harvest, these fragile structures would soon fall into ruin.

Old Testament prophets used many figures like this to describe the plight of Jerusalem after its devastation by a pagan nation. It would be left like a wilderness, plowed like a field, and covered by the Lord with a cloud. Wild animals like foxes would walk throughout the city.

But this was not the end of the story. The prophet Jeremiah declared that the city would be gloriously restored after the people returned from exile (Jeremiah 31:6).

Learn More: Isaiah 64:10 / Jeremiah 26:18 / Lamentations 2:1; 5:18

COVENANT WITH DEATH

We have made a covenant with death, and with hell are we at agreement. Isaiah 28:15

The prophet Isaiah issued this warning to the northern kingdom of Israel during its chaotic final days. The Assyrians were threatening to overrun Israel, as well as other surrounding countries. The Israelites and the Egyptians had signed an agreement to provide military support for one another in the event of an Assyrian attack.

The prophet saw this pact as a hopeless move. He referred to it as a "covenant with death," implying that Egypt would fall quickly to Assyria and that Israel would be next on their hit list. In essence, Israel was hiding its head in the sand by seeking safety in false hopes.

Isaiah called on the people of Israel to turn from their sinful ways and place their confidence in the Lord as their safe haven. The prophets of the Old Testament often delivered this message to God's people when they depended on military might rather than the Lord for protection.

Learn More: Exodus 15:19 / Psalm 20:7; 24:8 / Isaiah 31:1 / Zechariah 4:6 / Romans 13:1

CROWN OF RIGHTEOUSNESS

Henceforth there is laid up for me a crown of righteousness. 2 Timothy 4:8

This spiritual crown cited by the apostle Paul represents the righteousness that belongs to every believer. We do not become righteous—people worthy of fellowship with God—through our own strength or because of our moral character. This is something transferred to us when we accept Jesus as Savior and become His followers.

Paul expressed this truth in another familiar passage about the process of salvation. God made Jesus, who had no sin, "to be sin for us," the apostle declared, so that in him we might be made "the righteousness of God" (2 Corinthians 5:21).

A crown was a symbol of a king's authority. The imagery of this royal headpiece was often cited by Paul to express our privileges and responsibilities as believers. For example, our hope in Christ is a "crown of rejoicing" (1 Thessalonians 2:19), and we will receive an incorruptible crown—one that will never fade away—as our eternal reward in heaven (1 Corinthians 9:25).

Learn More: Psalm 103:4 / Isaiah 62:3 / Zechariah 9:16 / James 1:12 / 1 Peter 5:4 / Revelation 2:10

CRUMBS FROM THE TABLE

Truth, Lord: yet the dogs eat of the crumbs which fall from their masters' table. MATTHEW 15:27

A Gentile woman responded to Jesus with these words when He told her His main priority was to minister to the Jewish people. "It is not meet to take the children's bread, and to cast it to dogs," He told her (verse 26). Jesus knew that most of the Jews thought of Gentiles as dogs, or hopeless sinners who were not worthy of God's love.

This woman was desperate for Jesus to heal her sick daughter. So she threw herself on His mercy. She said, in effect, *I'm not asking for a full loaf—just toss me and my daughter a few crumbs from your bountiful table.* Impressed by this woman's faith, Jesus then healed her daughter.

This desperate mother was not the only Gentile whose faith impressed Jesus. On one occasion a Roman centurion asked Him to heal his servant. He believed Jesus could do so without even coming to his house. Jesus healed the servant from a distance, then declared of this military officer: "I have not found so great faith, no, not in Israel" (Matthew 8:10).

Learn More: Matthew 15:21–28 / Mark 7:24–30

CUP OF WATER IN JESUS' NAME

Whosoever shall give you a cup of water to drink in my name. . . shall not lose his reward. MARK 9:41

This saying from Jesus shows how He often turned minor things into matters of great significance. A cup of water costs little when measured on the scale of earthly value. But to offer a cup of refreshing water to a person in the name of Jesus is to render a valuable service on His behalf. The reward of such a gesture is the awareness of believers that they have borne witness to the love and sympathy of their Lord and Savior.

People in vocational Christian ministry—preachers, evangelists, and teachers—usually receive praise and recognition for their efforts. But Jesus reminds us in this verse that the simplest acts of ministry, such as showing kindness and hospitality to others, are just as important in the work of spreading the Gospel throughout the world.

Learn More: Isaiah 6:8 / Mark 9:35 / John 20:21 / Acts 20:35 / Romans 12:10–11 / Galatians 5:13 / James 2:15–16 / 1 Peter 4:10

DEER PANTS FOR WATER

As the hart [deer: NIV] panteth after the water brooks, so panteth my soul after. . .God. PSALM 42:1

Many interpreters believe this psalm expresses the despair of King David after he went into exile to escape the wrath of his rebellious son Absalom. Miles from Jerusalem and the temple, he longed for better times. He especially desired a closer relationship with God in this dark time.

The king compared his spiritual longing to a deer that looks for a brook from which to slake its thirst after wandering in the dry countryside. This longing was not just for any god; only the living, authentic God could meet this deep need of his soul (verse 2).

By the end of the psalm, David claimed the assurance that God had not forsaken him. "Hope thou in God," he reminded himself, "for I shall yet praise him who is the health of my countenance, and my God" (verse 11).

David's thirst for the Lord is reflected in the words of an old hymn, "Break Thou the Bread of Life," written by Mary A. Lathbury:

> *Beyond the sacred page I seek Thee, Lord;*
> *My spirit pants for Thee, O living Word!*

Learn More: Nehemiah 9:15 / Psalm 63:1; 143:6 / Isaiah 55:1 / Matthew 5:6 / John 4:14

DEN OF THIEVES

My house shall be called the house of prayer; but ye have made it a den of thieves. MATTHEW 21:13

This event happened the day after Jesus made His triumphant entry into Jerusalem. When He came to the temple, He was angered by the buying and selling that was occurring in the outer courts of this holy place. Merchants were changing foreign money into Jewish coins and selling doves for the people to offer as sacrifices.

The phrase "house of prayer" comes from the prophet Isaiah (56:7). This contrasts dramatically with the words that Jesus used to describe what was going on. Unscrupulous businessmen had turned the sacred precincts of the temple into a "den of thieves." This strong statement makes it clear that the people were coming out on the short end of the stick in these business transactions.

This phrase is still a metaphor for an unethical place of business. Most people know to stay clear of a firm that has such a reputation.

Learn More: Mark 11:15–19 / Luke 19:45–47 / John 2:13–25

DISH TURNED UPSIDE DOWN

I will wipe Jerusalem as a man wipeth a dish. . .turning it upside down. 2 KINGS 21:13

The Lord was not pleased with the ungodly acts of King Manasseh of Judah. During his long reign of fifty-five years, he encouraged the worship of false gods, dabbled in occult practices, and even sacrificed his own son to a pagan deity (2 Kings 21:1–7). This had led the entire country to forsake the Lord.

God served notice in this verse that Judah would pay for its sins, just as the northern kingdom, its capital city Samaria, and the evil kings who followed Ahab had already suffered judgment. The imagery of a dish showed the severity of God's punishment: Judah's capital city, Jerusalem, would be emptied of its inhabitants as easily as a person could wipe a dish clean and turn it upside down.

That is exactly what happened about a hundred years after the Lord issued this warning. The Babylonian army captured Jerusalem and carried the leading citizens of Judah into captivity. Divine judgment against sin does not always happen immediately, but its certainty is assured.

Learn More: 2 Chronicles 33:10–11 / Jeremiah 39:1–8

DOUBLE-MINDED PEOPLE

Purify your hearts, ye double minded. JAMES 4:8

The writer of the epistle of James had no patience with believers who were not totally committed to the Lord. In this verse he called on double-minded believers—those who were divided in their thinking, wavering between two choices—to get off the fence and declare their complete loyalty to Jesus as Lord. In its rendering of this verse, the Easy-to-Read Version accuses these people of "trying to follow God and the world at the same time."

This was also a problem in Old Testament times. The prophet Elijah called on God's people to choose between worshipping false gods and the one true God. "How long halt ye between two opinions?" he thundered. "If the LORD be God, follow him: but if Baal, then follow him" (1 Kings 18:21).

Other biblical terms similar to double-minded are *double-tongued* and *double-hearted*. Depending on their context, they refer either to divided loyalty or to hypocrisy—saying one thing and meaning another.

Learn More: 1 Chronicles 12:33 / Psalm 12:2 / 1 Timothy 3:8 / James 1:8

DROP IN A BUCKET

Behold, the nations are as a drop of a bucket. ISAIAH 40:15

A "drop in a bucket" is one of those biblical figures of speech that is still heard today. It refers to something that is small and insignificant. For example, "What Becky paid for that antique desk was like a drop in a bucket compared to what she sold it for."

This image was coined by the prophet Isaiah, who compared the pagan nations of his time to the incomparable greatness of the one true God. These pagan peoples were proud of their culture, their accomplishments, and the numerous false gods they worshiped. But their countries were nothing in comparison to the God who created the universe and controls its destiny.

Another image that appears in this verse is "dust of the balance." Compared to the Lord, the nations of the earth were nothing more than a speck of dust that would not tip by a single ounce the scales on which they were weighed.

Learn More: 2 Samuel 7:23 / 1 Chronicles 16:31 / Psalm 22:28; 72:11; 113:4 / Isaiah 40:12; 41:2; 52:10 / Jeremiah 10:10 / Habakkuk 3:6 / Revelation 7:9

DUST AND ASHES

I have taken upon me to speak unto the Lord, which am but dust and ashes. GENESIS 18:27

These words came from Abraham, who pleaded with the Lord to spare the cities of Sodom and Gomorrah. By referring to himself as "dust and ashes," Abraham declared that he was a weak and worthless human being in comparison to the awesome and all-powerful God. But still, he stood firmly before the Lord and begged Him to spare the city if as many as ten righteous people lived there. Tragically, that many could not be found, so God destroyed Sodom.

When Jonathan's lame son, Mephibosheth, was honored by King David, he used another interesting metaphor to signify his unworthiness. He asked the king, "What is thy servant, that thou shouldest look upon such a dead dog as I am?" (2 Samuel 9:8).

The words *dust* and *ashes* are often used figuratively in the Bible. God promised Abraham that his descendants would be as numerous as the dust of the earth. The psalmist expressed his profound sorrow by declaring that he had "eaten ashes like bread" (Psalm 102:9).

Learn More: Genesis 13:16; 18:22–33 / 2 Samuel 13:19 / Job 10:9; 30:19; 42:6 / Psalm 102:9; 103:14

DUST OF GOD'S FEET

The Lord hath his way in the whirlwind. . .the clouds are the dust of his feet. NAHUM 1:3

The prophet Nahum pronounced divine punishment against Nineveh, capital city of the Assyrian empire. He portrayed God as coming in judgment swifter than a whirlwind, stirring the clouds as if they were dust under His feet.

This poetic imagery shows a God who is superior to all pagan gods of the ancient world. They were identified with various elements of nature, such as the sun, moon, and stars. But the one true God existed above and beyond the natural order. He actually used the elements of nature to work out His purpose.

Many images from nature drive home this biblical truth. The Lord is portrayed as walking on the wings of the wind (Psalm 104:3); riding on a swift cloud (Isaiah 19:1); watering the hills from his heavenly chambers (Psalm 104:13); and stretching out the heavens like a curtain (Isaiah 40:22).

None of these images can top that from the psalmist: the Lord not only counts the number of stars He created, but "he calleth them all by their names" (Psalm 147:4).

Learn More: 1 Samuel 2:8 / Psalm 18:9; 68:33 / Isaiah 40:12, 22 / Hebrews 1:10

DUST SHAKEN OFF THE FEET

When ye depart out of that house or city, shake off the dust of your feet. MATTHEW 10:14

Jesus gave these instructions to His twelve disciples when He sent them out on a witnessing mission. The time had come for them to put into practice what they had learned from His teachings. Their assignment was to spread the good news about the arrival of the Messiah in the person of Jesus.

The Jewish people had a custom of shaking dust from their sandals on leaving Gentile territory. This symbolized their separation from those whom they considered sinful pagans. Jesus instructed His disciples to follow this custom when they talked to people who rejected their message. It carried a warning of judgment against unbelievers. The disciples were not to waste time arguing or debating with people but should move on to witness to those who were open to their message.

The book of Acts contains an example of this practice. The missionaries Paul and Barnabas found a ready audience among Gentiles in the city of Antioch of Pisidia. But the Jews of the city rejected their witness, and they "shook off the dust of their feet against them" and moved on to Iconium (Acts 13:51).

Learn More: Mark 6:11 / Luke 9:5; 10:11

EARS OF GOD

Samuel. . .rehearsed them in the ears of the Lord. 1 SAMUEL 8:21

Samuel served as the moral conscience of the nation of Israel during a time of transition. The people grew weary of their tribal form of government with its lack of centralized authority. So they asked Samuel to appoint a king as their ruler.

After thinking this over, Samuel approached the Lord and told Him what the people wanted. The phrase "rehearsed them in the ears of the Lord" is rendered by the New American Standard Bible as "repeated them in the LORD's hearing." Samuel must have prayed fervently to determine the Lord's will in this crucial matter.

The phrase "ears of the LORD" appears often in the Bible, particularly in the book of Psalms. The psalmist was confident that God's ears were always open to the cry of the righteous (Psalm 34:15). Although he felt "poor and needy," he knew the Lord would honor him as a person of dignity and worth by hearing his prayers (Psalm 86:1).

The prophet Isaiah expressed this same quiet confidence when he declared, "The LORD's hand is not shortened, that it cannot save; neither his ear heavy, that it cannot hear" (Isaiah 59:1).

Learn More: Psalm 116:2; 143:1 / Isaiah 37:29 / 1 Peter 3:12

EYE HATH NOT SEEN

Eye hath not seen. . .things which God hath prepared for them that love him. 1 CORINTHIANS 2:9

This verse is the apostle Paul's loose quotation of Isaiah 64:4. Paul's version is an eloquent expression of the truth that God's ways are beyond human understanding. Our eyes, ears, and heart—or mind—are incapable of grasping God's gracious provision of salvation for a sinful world.

But the next verse (verse 10) declares that God has sent a tutor to enlighten our understanding of such matters. This tutor is the Holy Spirit, the very one who, according to Jesus, would guide us "into all truth" (John 16:13). God's Spirit has unlimited wisdom and understanding, and He reveals these divine truths to us.

We are not able to see the Holy Spirit with our physical eyes. But our faith and experience tell us that He is at work in the world. He points people to Jesus and leads us to worship the living God and Jesus His Son.

Learn More: Deuteronomy 11:7 / 1 Samuel 12:16 / Job 42:5 / Psalm 119:18 / Isaiah 40:21

EYES OF GOD

His eye seeth every precious thing. Job 28:10

In this verse Job described a living God who sees everything that happens in the world. This imagery of the eyes of God is one of the richest figures of speech in the Bible.

The biblical writers describe a God whose eyes are on the righteous (Psalm 34:15) as well as those who are haughty and filled with pride (2 Samuel 22:28). His eyes behold the nations (Psalm 66:7), and they are particularly focused on the nation of Israel, His chosen people (Deuteronomy 11:12). To do what was right "in the eyes of the Lord" (1 Kings 15:5) was to follow His commands. Our thoughts and actions may not be seen by others, but they are always "before the eyes of the Lord" (Proverbs 5:21).

Hagar, the servant of Abraham's wife, Sarah, learned this truth in a dramatic way. She was close to death in the wilderness when the Lord appeared. He promised to bless her and others through the life of her unborn child. Hagar responded by saying, "Thou God seest me" (Genesis 16:13).

Learn More: 1 Kings 9:3; 15:5 / 2 Chronicles 16:9 / Psalm 11:4 / Proverbs 5:21 / Jeremiah 16:17 / 1 Peter 3:12

FACE OF GOD

Pour out thine heart like water before the face of the Lord. Lamentations 2:19

The book of Lamentations records the prophet Jeremiah's lament, or cry of despair, over the destruction of Jerusalem by the Babylonian army. The prophet called on the people to join in this cry and to pour out their sorrow before the Lord's face.

The phrase "face of the Lord" appears several times in the Bible. It is a figurative way of describing God as a deity who is personally involved with His creation. He is more than an abstract theory or an ethereal spirit. He cares for His people, and He interacts with them on a personal level.

The psalmist asked the Lord, "How long wilt thou hide thy face from me?" (Psalm 13:1). He felt as if the Lord had abandoned him. Perhaps he had been through a traumatic experience that caused his faith to waver.

The cure for such a feeling is renewed commitment to God and total reliance on His promise: "If my people [will]. . .seek my face, and turn from their wicked ways; then will I. . . forgive their sin, and will heal their land" (2 Chronicles 7:14).

Learn More: Numbers 6:25–26 / Psalm 34:16; 80:19 / Jeremiah 21:10 / 2 Corinthians 4:6

FACE SET LIKE FLINT

Therefore have I set my face like a flint, and I know that I shall not be ashamed. Isaiah 50:7

This verse belongs to one of the "Servant Songs" in the book of Isaiah (42:1–9; 49:1–55:13). Israel had failed to carry out God's mission of world redemption. So the prophet declared that the Lord would accomplish this goal through His Servant, the Messiah.

Isaiah used the image of a hard stone known as flint to describe the Servant's work. This substance was shaped into knives and saws and other cutting tools. Jesus, the future Messiah, would "set His face like flint," refusing to be turned aside from the mission God the Father would send Him to do.

This prophecy was fulfilled during the closing days of Jesus' earthly ministry. He had faced the stark reality of His approaching death in His agonizing prayer in the garden of Gethsemane (Matthew 26:36–39). He knew that His enemies were gathered in Jerusalem to celebrate the annual Passover. Here they could arrest Him and bring Him to trial. In spite of the danger, "he stedfastly set his face to go to Jerusalem" (Luke 9:51).

Learn More: Job 41:24 / Isaiah 5:28 / Ezekiel 3:9 / Zechariah 7:12 / Luke 9:53

FALLOW GROUND

Sow to yourselves in righteousness, reap in mercy; break up your fallow ground.
HOSEA 10:12

The prophet Hosea proclaimed God's message to the nation of Israel, the northern Jewish kingdom. He condemned the nation for its slide into idolatry, but he also preached a message of hope. It was not too late for them to repent and realign their lives with the Lord's standard of behavior.

In this verse Hosea used an agricultural image to carry his message. Like fallow ground that had been out of cultivation for a while, the people had ignored righteousness and mercy for too long. It was time for them to return to these virtues that God demanded from His people.

Hosea probably drew this image of fallow land from the Old Testament law. It specified that selected plots of ground should lie idle every seventh year to allow the soil to renew its fertility. This was called "a sabbath of rest unto the land" (Leviticus 25:4).

Learn More: Exodus 23:10 / Jeremiah 4:3

FEET OF THE WICKED

Their feet run to evil, and they make haste to shed innocent blood. ISAIAH 59:7

Chapter 59 of Isaiah contains a graphic description of the sin of God's people in the prophet's time. Parts of their physical bodies—hands, fingers, lips, and tongue (verse 3)—showed the depths to which they had sunk. And their feet had strayed from the path of righteousness and were on the road to ruin. The verb *run* shows how eager they were to indulge their desires.

Feet are often cited in the Bible as a symbol of one's way of life. Feet that "run to evil" describe a person who deliberately disobeys God and follows his own path. But one's feet can also be energized and directed by the Lord. The prophet Habakkuk declared, "The LORD God is my strength, and he will make my feet like hinds' feet, and he will make me to walk upon mine high places" (Habakkuk 3:19).

The feet of God is another familiar image in the Bible. The apostle Paul declared that in the end time He will put all enemies under His feet—a symbol of victory over the forces of evil (1 Corinthians 15:25).

Learn More: Proverbs 1:16 / Romans 3:15 / Ephesians 1:22

FINGER OF GOD

Tables of stone, written with the finger of God. EXODUS 31:18

This verse refers to God's deliverance of the Ten Commandments to Moses. The Lord first spoke these laws in the hearing of Moses on Mount Sinai. Then He inscribed them on two stone tablets to show they would last forever. Since they were written by God Himself, they also carried divine authority.

The reference to God's finger in this verse symbolizes His omnipotence. Just as He brought the universe into being through His spoken word, He established these guidelines for human behavior by writing them with His own finger.

Even the Egyptian pharaoh's pagan magicians were impressed with God's power when He caused a series of plagues to strike the land. They admitted to the king, "This is the finger of God" (Exodus 8:19).

Jesus was once accused of healing people through the power of Satan. But He replied that His power came from God alone. "If I with the finger of God cast out devils," He told His critics, "no doubt the kingdom of God is come upon you" (Luke 11:20).

Learn More: Exodus 20:1–18 / Psalm 8:3–4

FLY IN THE OINTMENT

Dead flies cause the ointment. . .to send forth a stinking savour. ECCLESIASTES 10:1

This expression is still heard today, centuries after it was first recorded by King Solomon in the book of Ecclesiastes. For example, someone might say, "Their new house is beautiful, but the sinkhole that developed in the back yard is like a fly in the ointment." The expression refers to something that spoils what is perfect in every other way.

King Solomon was making the point that a person who is wise and honorable may have a character defect, or "folly," that makes his wisdom and honor ineffective. The Good News Translation renders the verse like this: "Dead flies can make a whole bottle of perfume stink, and a little stupidity can cancel out the greatest wisdom."

The book of Ecclesiastes is known for its colorful language of contrast and comparison. For example, all rivers run into the sea, but the sea is never full (1:7); there is nothing new under the sun (1:9); a poor but wise child is better than an old and foolish king (4:13); wisdom is better than the weapons of war (9:18).

Learn More: Proverbs 16:22

FOOTSTOOL OF GOD

Exalt ye the Lord our God, and worship at his footstool. PSALM 99:5

A footstool was a piece of furniture on which people rested their feet. It is spoken of in many symbolic ways in the Bible. Some interpreters believe this verse in the Psalms refers to the sanctuary in Jerusalem where God's people gathered to worship. This interpretation is supported by Lamentations 2:1, a verse that refers to either the temple or Jerusalem itself.

Others believe this verse from Psalm 99 was a command to fall at God's feet in humble adoration and submission. This is how the Contemporary English Version renders the passage: "We praise you and kneel down to worship you, the God of holiness!" Mention of the footstool in some passages does symbolize God's dominion and superiority. For example, the Lord declared through the prophet Isaiah, "The heaven is my throne, and the earth is my footstool" (Isaiah 66:1). To make one's enemies a footstool was to put them under the feet, a symbol of total victory.

Whatever the exact interpretation of this verse, one thing is clear: the holy, supreme God deserves our worship, and we should come into His presence with humble submission.

Learn More: 1 Chronicles 28:2 / Psalm 110:1; 132:7 / Matthew 5:34–35 / Mark 12:36 / Hebrews 10:13

FOUNTAIN OF TEARS

Oh that my head were waters, and mine eyes a fountain of tears! JEREMIAH 9:1

The prophet Jeremiah did not hold back when condemning the people of Judah for their many sins against the Lord. He was also equally blunt about their punishment; they would be defeated and taken into exile by a foreign nation.

But the prophet took no pleasure in issuing these bleak messages from the Lord. He spoke to his people from a broken heart. He is known as the "weeping prophet" of the Old Testament because of this sensitivity to the plight of God's people. In this verse he wished that his head was a stream of water and his eyes were a fountain of tears so he could cry constantly over the plight of his fellow citizens.

As it turned out, Jeremiah's weeping did not change his people's race toward destruction. But the Lord dried his tears to send the message that they would eventually be restored to their homeland. "Refrain thy voice from weeping, and thine eyes from tears," He told the prophet, "for thy work shall be rewarded. . .and they shall come again from the land of the enemy" (Jeremiah 31:16).

Learn More: Jeremiah 9:18; 13:17; 14:17

FRUITFUL BOUGH BY A WELL

Joseph is a fruitful bough, even a fruitful bough by a well. Genesis 49:22

Near the end of his life, the patriarch Jacob gathered his twelve sons, gave them his blessing, and predicted their future. Their offspring would grow into the twelve tribes that made up the nation of Israel.

Some of these sons did not fare so well in Jacob's evaluation. But he had nothing but praise for Joseph. This son's descendants would be particularly fruitful, like a bough by a well—or, as the New Century Version puts it, "a healthy vine watered by a spring."

This prediction came true when Joseph's two sons, Ephraim and Manasseh, became the nucleus of two of the twelve tribes. The phrase "whose branches run over the wall" refers to Joseph's godly character and his continuing influence among God's people for many generations. His forgiveness of his brothers for selling him into slavery sets an example in mercy and grace for all believers (Genesis 50:15–21).

This image of a fruitful tree or vine appears often in the Bible. To the psalmist, a person who followed the Lord was "like a tree planted by the rivers of water, that bringeth forth his fruit in his season" (Psalm 1:3).

Learn More: Psalm 92:12 / Isaiah 61:3 / Jeremiah 17:8 / Matthew 12:33

FRUIT OF THE LIPS

Let us offer the sacrifice of praise to God continually. . .the fruit of our lips. Hebrews 13:15

The author of Hebrews refers to sacrifices of many different kinds. He declared that Old Testament animal offerings had been replaced with the once-for-all atoning death of Jesus Christ (Hebrews 10:10). The sacrifice that he describes in 13:15 is the praise that believers should offer to God for divine mercy and love. To present this praise as the "fruit of our lips" is to utter words of thanks for His goodness.

Fruit is a common figure of speech in the Bible. Children are described as the "fruit of the womb" (Genesis 30:2). Believers should be filled with the "fruits of righteousness" (Philippians 1:11). God's people would be judged "according to the fruit of your doings," or actions (Jeremiah 21:14).

To sin was to deceive oneself and to eat "the fruit of lies" (Hosea 10:13). The "fruit of the spirit" were godly virtues that the Holy Spirit cultivated in the lives of believers (Galatians 5:22–23). Jesus declared that members of His kingdom would be recognized by their fruits, or godly actions (Luke 6:44).

Learn More: Deuteronomy 7:13 / Isaiah 3:10 / Jeremiah 6:19 / James 3:18

FULL OF YEARS

Abraham. . .died in a good old age, an old man, and full of years. Genesis 25:8

Abraham had lived a remarkable life. In his early years, he was called by the Lord to leave his home to enter a land he knew nothing about. He received God's promise that His descendants would become a great nation. He fathered a son in his old age. He was indeed "full of years" when he died at the age of 175.

But this phrase implies something more than just a long life span. The New Living Translation says he died "at a ripe old age, having lived a long and satisfying life." He never lost faith in God's promise, and he always obeyed the Lord's commands. He could look back over the years with joy because they had been devoted to the Lord's service.

Years later Abraham's son Isaac died "old and full of days." He followed the godly example that his father had set, remaining faithful to the covenant between God and His chosen people.

Learn More: Genesis 35:29 / 1 Chronicles 23:1; 29:28 / 2 Chronicles 24:15 /
Job 42:17 / Jeremiah 6:11

GATES THAT NEVER CLOSE

Therefore thy gates shall be open continually. Isaiah 60:11

Cities of Bible times were surrounded by massive stone walls. Some of these structures were more than thirty feet high and ten to twelve feet thick. Residents of the city would retreat behind these walls when under attack by an enemy army.

The gates of these walls were made of huge wooden beams, reinforced with iron. When closed, the gate would be secured by sliding heavy timbers or iron bars across its surface from inside.

These gates were closed at night as a security measure. The prophet Isaiah used the image of gates that never closed to describe the reign of the Messiah. In that coming time, God would be all the protection His people needed.

The psalmist used this image of a city gate in two different ways. He prayed for God to lift him up from the "gates of death" (Psalm 9:13). He also called on the Lord to open to him the "gates of righteousness" (Psalm 118:19). Then he vowed to enter these gates and to praise God for His goodness.

Learn More: Deuteronomy 3:5 / Psalm 24:7, 9; 107:18 / Isaiah 60:18

GIRD UP THE LOINS

Thou therefore gird up thy loins, and arise, and speak unto them. Jeremiah 1:17

The prophet Jeremiah needed to be strong to resist the opposition he would face as God's messenger to the people of Judah. So the Lord commanded him to "gird up his loins," a figurative way of saying "take courage" or "get ready for battle." The New Living Translation renders the phrase as "get up and prepare for action."

This expression comes from the outer garments that people wore in Bible times. They would tuck these full-length robes into their belts—or gird up the loins—to make it easier to do strenuous work. The term *loins* refers to the lower abdomen and the reproductive organs of the human body.

In the New Testament, Jesus told a parable in which guests at a wedding were urged to be ready for the arrival of the newlywed couple. He applied this to believers who should be expectantly waiting for His return. "Let your loins be girded about," He cautioned, "and your lights burning" (Luke 12:35).

Learn More: Exodus 12:11 / 1 Kings 18:46 / Job 38:3 / Proverbs 31:17 / 1 Peter 1:13

GNASHING OF TEETH

There shall be weeping and gnashing of teeth. Matthew 8:12

Jesus uttered these words as He reflected on the faith of a Roman centurion. Although this man was a Gentile, he believed that Jesus could heal his servant. This contrasted starkly with the unbelief of many of Jesus' own Jewish countrymen. He referred to them as "children of the kingdom," or members of God's favored people, the Jewish nation.

In the end time, Jesus declared, people like these doubters would gnash their teeth—or grind them together—in frustration at being excluded from God's heavenly kingdom. The phrase "outer darkness" refers to the place reserved for those who reject Jesus as Lord and Savior.

The grinding of one's teeth, when directed against another person, could express anger, disappointment, frustration, hate, and pain—or perhaps a combination of all of these emotions. Stephen's charges against those who executed Jesus led to a raging fury among his hearers until they "gnashed on him with their teeth" and stoned him to death (Acts 7:54).

Learn More: Job 16:9 / Psalm 35:16; 112:10 / Lamentations 2:16 / Matthew 13:42, 50; 25:30 / Luke 13:28

GOING OUT AND COMING IN

I know thy abode, and thy going out, and thy coming in. 2 KINGS 19:27

The prophet Isaiah spoke these words of assurance from the Lord to King Hezekiah of Judah. An Assyrian army led by King Sennacherib of Assyria was at Judah's doorstep. The prophet knew that only the living, all-powerful God could save the nation from disaster.

Isaiah used the poetic phrase "going out and coming in" to let Hezekiah know that God had the situation in hand. He knew all about the pagan king and his mighty army, and the Lord would act on Judah's behalf. Before Sennacherib could launch an attack, his forces were decimated by "the angel of the LORD," and he withdrew in humiliation and defeat (2 Kings 19:35–37).

To admit that God knows our "going out and our coming in" is to declare His awareness of everything about us. This divine characteristic is known as His omniscience, or perfect knowledge. The psalmist expressed this truth with these inspiring words: "Thou compassest my path and my lying down, and art acquainted with all my ways. For there is not a word in my tongue, but, lo, O LORD, thou knowest it altogether" (Psalm 139:3–4).

Learn More: Deuteronomy 33:18 / 1 Samuel 29:6 / 2 Samuel 3:25 / Psalm 121:8 / Isaiah 37:28

GO THE WAY OF ALL THE EARTH

This day I am going the way of all the earth. JOSHUA 23:14

Joshua, the great warrior-leader of Israel, lived to the age of 110. Not long before he died, he called the nation's leaders together to give them some final instructions. His statement that He was "going the way of all the earth" shows that he was aware of his approaching death. But he gave no evidence of regret or remorse. He had a quiet confidence that he had accomplished the work he was destined to do.

Joshua took up the reins of leadership after Moses died, leading God's people to conquer the land of Canaan. He also supervised the division of the land among the tribes of Israel. Now as he bid his people farewell, he urged them to remain faithful to the Lord, who had blessed them with a land of their own.

This expression for death is similar to one used by Job: "When a few years are come, then I shall go the way whence I shall not return" (Job 16:22).

Learn More: Joshua 13:1; 24:1, 19 / 1 Kings 2:2

GRAPES OF GALL

Their grapes are grapes of gall, their clusters are bitter. DEUTERONOMY 32:32

This verse is part of a passage known as the "song of Moses" (Deuteronomy 32:1–43). In this long poetic discourse, he reviewed the history of the Israelites, emphasizing God's faithfulness to His people in spite of their disobedience. He also predicted that the Lord would chasten His people if they disobeyed His commands.

Moses compared God's people to a vine that yielded grapes of gall—fruit that was bitter and inedible [*filled with poison:* NIV]. He also reminded them of Sodom and Gomorrah, twin cities destroyed by the Lord because of their wickedness. This was a warning to the nation of Israel that disloyalty to God would result in His judgment.

The term *gall* is often used in the Bible to symbolize anything that is undesirable or distasteful. The prophet Jeremiah spoke of his misery after Jerusalem was destroyed by the Babylonians as "the wormwood and the gall" (Lamentations 3:19). Wormwood was a desert shrub from which an intoxicating drink was made. It was known for its strong smell and bitter taste.

Learn More: Psalm 69:21 / Jeremiah 8:14; 9:15; 23:15 / Lamentations 3:5 / Matthew 27:34 / Acts 8:23

GRAVEL IN THE MOUTH

*Bread of deceit is sweet. . .*BUT AFTERWARDS HIS MOUTH SHALL BE FILLED WITH GRAVEL. PROVERBS 20:17

King Solomon uses the images of food and gravel in this verse to condemn dishonesty. He declares that a person may cheat and lie to obtain something to eat, but the food will provide no nourishment: it will be like gravel in his mouth—tasteless and unappetizing. The Good News Translation renders the verse like this: "What you get by dishonesty you may enjoy like the finest food, but sooner or later it will be like a mouthful of sand."

This technique of contrasting something good with something bad appears often in the book of Proverbs. For example:

- The fear of the LORD prolongeth days: but the years of the wicked shall be shortened (10:27).
- A false balance is abomination to the LORD: but a just weight is his delight (11:1).
- A soft answer turneth away wrath: but grievous words stir up anger (15:1).

Learn More: Isaiah 48:19 / Lamentations 3:16

HAMMER THAT BREAKS ROCK

Is not my word. . .like a hammer that breaketh the rock in pieces? JEREMIAH 23:29

Jeremiah often clashed with false prophets. They assured the people of a rosy future, while God's real prophet declared that the Lord would punish the nation of Judah unless the people turned back to Him. In this verse Jeremiah contrasts the comforting words of these counterfeit prophets with the Lord's authentic message.

God's Word was like a hammer that would break stone into small pieces—an apt metaphor for His coming judgment. The prophet also characterized God's Word as fire, another familiar biblical image for God's reaction to unrighteousness.

The Bible also describes the Word of God as a lamp (Psalm 119:105). It lights the way for believers, guiding them on a path that honors the Lord. As a double-edged sword, God's Word cuts deeply, judging not only our actions but "the thoughts and intents of the heart" (Hebrews 4:12).

Finally, God's Word is eternal, the standard of truth in a wavering world: "The grass withereth, and the flower thereof falleth away," the apostle Peter declared, "but the word of the Lord endureth for ever" (1 Peter 1:24–25)

Learn More: 2 Samuel 22:31 / Psalm 12:6; 119:103 / Jeremiah 50:23 / John 10:35 / 2 Timothy 3:16

HAND OF GOD

And the Lord said unto Moses, Is the Lord's hand waxed short? NUMBERS 11:23

Although Moses was a great leader of the Israelites in the wilderness, he had his moments of frustration. He complained to the Lord that the people were demanding meat after eating nothing but manna for some time. God reminded Moses that His hand was not too short to deliver another miracle for His people. This was a figurative way of asking Moses, "Haven't you yet realized that there is no limit to My power?"

The phrase "hand of God" appears often in the Bible. It symbolizes His unlimited power at work. For example:

- The psalmist felt consumed by a blow from God's hand (Psalm 39:10).
- God opens His hand and provides generously for His people (Psalm 145:16).
- God's people are the work of His hand (Isaiah 64:8).
- The Lord will uphold His people with His hand of righteousness (Isaiah 41:10).

Isaiah was another great leader who ministered among God's people. Like all believers, Isaiah felt secure "in the shadow of [God's] hand" (Isaiah 49:2).

Learn More: Exodus 13:3–4 / Deuteronomy 6:21 / 1 Chronicles 29:12 / Joshua 4:24

HAND OPEN TO THE POOR

Thou shalt not. . .shut thine hand from thy poor brother: But thou shalt open thine hand wide. DEUTERONOMY 15:7–8

Taking care of the poor has been a priority for people of faith since ancient times. In this verse from the Old Testament law, God's people were directed to open their hands wide toward the unfortunate. This figure of speech is still with us today. People who give generously to others are said to be "open-handed"—the very opposite of a stingy, "tight-fisted" spirit.

Jesus took this Old Testament law a step further. He declared, "When thou doest alms [*give to the poor*: NASB], let not thy left hand know what thy right hand doeth" (Matthew 6:3). In other words, give without calling attention to the act.

Our hands are front and center in almost everything we do. So the Bible speaks often of human hands in symbolic terms. To have "clean hands" was to be committed to righteousness as a follower of the Lord (Psalm 18:20). To lift one's hands "unto the LORD" was to pray to Him in a spirit of devotion and humility (Genesis 14:22).

Learn More: Deuteronomy 15:11; 24:19 / Job 5:15; 20:10 / Psalm 82:4; 109:31

HARDNESS OF HEART

Pharaoh's heart is hardened, he refuseth to let the people go. EXODUS 7:14

This is one of several statements in the book of Exodus about the Egyptian pharaoh's response to Moses' demand to release the Israelites from slavery. After each plague against the land, the king would seem to soften in his determination to keep the people captive. Then his heart would grow harder than ever.

Today, we apply the term *hard-hearted* to a person who has no sympathy or feelings of concern for others. But in the Bible it usually refers to stubborn refusal. God's chosen people, the Israelites, were often guilty of this sin. They repeatedly refused to obey His commands and even slipped into worship of false gods on many occasions.

Sometimes hard-heartedness refers to lack of faith or understanding. For example, Jesus' disciples failed to see the spiritual significance of the miracle of the feeding of the five thousand because "their heart was hardened" (Mark 6:52).

To harden one's neck or to be stiff-necked also expresses the idea of stubborn refusal to follow the Lord. The prophet Jeremiah charged that the people of Judah had "hardened their necks" against the Lord's commands (Jeremiah 19:15).

Learn More: Deuteronomy 15:7 / 1 Samuel 6:6 / 2 Kings 17:14 / Nehemiah 9:16 / Hebrews 3:8

HARMLESS AS DOVES

Be ye therefore wise as serpents, and harmless as doves. MATTHEW 10:16

This verse is part of Jesus' instructions to His disciples when He sent them out among the Jewish people. Their mission was to announce that the kingdom of God was at hand with Jesus' arrival as the Messiah.

The spirit and attitude with which the disciples proclaimed this news was crucial. Jesus wanted them to use their cleverness and ingenuity to secure a hearing ("wise as serpents"). But they were also to be innocent and blameless at the same time—as harmless and gentle as doves. They were not to argue, debate, or bicker with people. As representative of Christ, they should treat everyone they met with kindness and respect.

Because of its gentle nature, the dove is a common religious symbol in the Bible. A dove returned with an olive leaf in its mouth to show Noah it was safe to leave the ark. At His baptism, the spirit of God descended from heaven like a dove and landed on Jesus to affirm His identity as the Messiah, God's Anointed One. Then God the Father declared, "This is my beloved Son, in whom I am well pleased" (Matthew 3:17).

Learn More: Genesis 8:11 / Psalm 55:6 / Isaiah 59:11

HEART OF GOD

I will plant them in this land assuredly with my whole heart. JEREMIAH 32:41

The Lord delivered this promise through the prophet Jeremiah. After His people had spent several decades in exile in a foreign land, they would return to their own country.

This was a spectacular promise because God would put His heart—His entire being—into making this happen. The Contemporary English Version catches this nuance by rendering the verse "With all my heart I promise that they will be planted in this land once again." This is similar to the compliment paid people today for superhuman effort, as in "The coach put his heart into developing a championship team."

The heart is portrayed in the Bible as the center of human emotions. To attribute a heart to the Lord is to declare that He is a feeling God, not an impersonal deity who has no concern for humankind. His heart's desire is for a just and righteous world. As the psalmist expressed it, "The counsel of the LORD standeth for ever, the thoughts of his heart to all generations" (Psalm 33:11).

Learn More: Genesis 6:6 / 1 Chronicles 17:19 / Psalm 78:72 / Isaiah 63:4 / Jeremiah 30:24

HEATH IN THE DESERT

He shall be like the heath in the desert, and shall not see when good cometh. JEREMIAH 17:6

The heath plant was a spindly shrub that grew in desert areas of Israel. Its deep roots enabled it to live in these barren regions, but it was almost leafless and had no commercial value. The prophet Jeremiah cited the plant as a symbol of those who failed to follow the Lord. They had cut themselves off from the spiritual blessings that God promised to His people.

Jeremiah continued this imagery by declaring that these people lived in a "salt land." Salt was used as a seasoning and a preservative, but it could become destructive in the hands of an enemy. The judge Abimelech, son of Gideon, captured the city of Shechem and sowed salt in the fields around the city. This made the soil barren, threatening famine and starvation for the city's inhabitants (Judges 9:45).

In contrast to the ungodly, Jeremiah declared, those who obeyed the Lord would flourish like "a tree planted by the waters" that would always bear fruit, even in drought conditions (Jeremiah 17:8).

Learn More: Jeremiah 48:6 / Ezekiel 47:11

HIGHWAY OF HOLINESS

And an highway shall be there. . .and it shall be called The way of holiness. ISAIAH 35:8

The prophet Isaiah peered into the future and saw a glorious future for the people of Judah who had been exiled to a foreign country. After more than fifty years in captivity, they would go back to their homeland. This symbolic highway of holiness on which they would travel showed that the Lord Himself had prepared the way for their return.

This passage has also been interpreted as a reference to the coming kingdom of God. In the end time, Jesus the Messiah has provided a way that all believers can follow to enter their heavenly home and enjoy eternal fellowship with Him.

Several passages in Isaiah's book refer to this spiritual highway. He declared, "Prepare ye the way of the LORD, make straight in the desert a highway for our God" (Isaiah 40:3). In the New Testament, this passage is applied to John the Baptist, who prepared the way for the coming of Jesus Christ (Luke 3:4–5).

Learn More: Isaiah 11:16; 49:11

HIP AND THIGH

And he smote them hip and thigh with a great slaughter. JUDGES 15:8

Samson is known as the strongman of the Bible. He was one of a series of judges, or military champions, who delivered Israel from her enemies before kings began to rule over the nation. A people known as the Philistines felt the brunt of Samson's superhuman strength. On one occasion he wiped out a thousand of their warriors by using a jawbone from the carcass of a donkey (Judges 15:15).

The phrase "hip and thigh" is a poetic way of saying that Samson struck the enemy down right and left in a ferocious attack. The Christian Standard Bible says he "tore them limb from limb."

In other superhuman feats against the Philistines, Samson burned their crops and ripped the gate from the wall of one of their cities. Betrayed by a Philistine woman, he was eventually captured and enslaved. He died, along with many of his enemies, when he pulled down the pillars of a pagan Philistine temple.

Learn More: Judges 15:4–5; 16:3–30 / Hebrews 11:32

HOLD ONE'S PEACE

But Jesus held his peace. MATTHEW 26:63

After Jesus was arrested, he appeared before the Jewish high court. Two false witnesses accused Him of blasphemy. But He "held his peace," or refused to speak in His own defense. This fulfilled an ancient prophecy from Isaiah about the coming Messiah: "He was oppressed, and he was afflicted, yet he opened not his mouth: he is brought as a lamb to the slaughter, and as a sheep before her shearers is dumb, so he openeth not his mouth" (Isaiah 53:7).

To "hold one's peace" was to keep quiet or say nothing, especially in situations that seemed to call for a verbal response. This phrase appears several times in the Bible:

- Aaron held his peace when God destroyed two of his sons for offering an illicit sacrifice (Leviticus 10:2–3).
- The people of Judah held their peace at boastful threats from the king of Assyria (2 Kings 18:36).
- The psalmist held his peace when he considered his unworthiness to stand before the Lord (Psalm 39:2).

Learn More: Genesis 24:21 / Nehemiah 5:8 / Job 33:33 / Mark 3:4 / Luke 19:40

HONEY TO THE SOUL

Eat thou honey. . . . So shall the knowledge of wisdom be unto thy soul. PROVERBS 24:13–14

Wisdom is the ability to apply one's knowledge and understanding to practical situations. The writer of Proverbs used the image of honey to show how important wisdom is to the spiritual life of believers. Honey was known for its sweet, appetizing taste. Thus, divine wisdom would enrich the lives of those who follow the Lord and give them a rewarding future in His service.

The Bible uses many different figures of speech to describe this wisdom that comes from above. It is more desirable than gold, silver, or rubies. It is like deep waters or a flowing brook. It is more desirable than the weapons of war. It makes a person stronger than ten armed defenders of a walled city.

How does a person gain such wisdom? The writer of the epistle of James in the New Testament has the answer: "If any of you lack wisdom, let him ask of God, that giveth to all men liberally. . .and it shall be given him" (James 1:5).

Learn More: Job 28:18 / Psalm 19:10 / Proverbs 8:11; 16:16; 18:4 / Ecclesiastes 7:19; 9:18

HOOK IN THE NOSE

I will put my hook in thy nose, and my bridle in thy lips. 2 KINGS 19:28

Sennacherib, king of Assyria, was threatening to overrun the nation of Judah. King Hezekiah of Judah sought counsel from the prophet Isaiah. The Lord assured Hezekiah that Judah had nothing to worry about. Sennacherib would return to Assyria with a "hook in his nose," an image of defeat and utter humiliation.

Hooks and bridles were used in Bible times to control draft animals such as oxen and horses. But the cruel Assyrians used this technique to subdue prisoners of war. When tethered to these devices, captives offered little resistance to their enemies. Monuments discovered at ancient Assyria show these unfortunate victims linked together and being pulled along by a rope.

This image for total domination appears several times in the Bible. In His description of the creature known as leviathan, God assured Job that no one was capable of putting a hook in its nose. This symbolizes the Lord's power as Creator of all life on earth.

Learn More: Job 41:2 / Isaiah 37:29 / Ezekiel 29:4 / Amos 4:2

HORSE RUSHING INTO BATTLE

Every one turned to his course, as the horse rusheth into the battle. JEREMIAH 8:6

The prophet Jeremiah drew a bleak picture of the future of the nation of Judah. The people had been warned repeatedly of the coming judgment of the Lord unless they turned back to the Lord. But they were stubborn and unyielding, like a trained war horse that charged headlong against the enemy with no concern for its own safety. The New Living Translation renders the prophet's words like this: "All are running down the path of sin as swiftly as a horse galloping into battle!"

In the next verse, Jeremiah cited the example of several other animals to show the spiritual apathy of his countrymen. The stork, turtle (dove), crane, and swallow knew when winter was coming on, "but my people know not the judgment of the LORD" (verse 7). They would be shocked into reality when God raised up a foreign nation to take them into captivity.

Learn More: Jeremiah 12:5; 20:4; 24:1; 29:11; 34:2

HOUSE DIVIDED

A house divided against a house falleth. LUKE 11:17

Jesus directed these words to a group of people who were looking on as He cast demons from a deaf man. Some of these onlookers thought He was driving out the evil spirits by the power of Satan.

Jesus knew their thoughts, so He addressed them with a bit of logic: Why would Satan want to rid people of the very demons that he himself had placed within them? Such a situation would be like a house divided against itself—a problem that would cause the structure to collapse.

This figure of speech was immortalized by Abraham Lincoln in a speech in 1858 while campaigning for a U.S. Senate seat from Illinois. The nation was in turmoil over the slavery issue. Lincoln declared that "a house divided itself cannot stand"—that it would eventually have to endorse either slavery or freedom for all the states.

A "house divided" is still used as a metaphor for sharp disagreement among members of an organization, threatening its stability.

Learn More: Mark 3:22-26 / Luke 11:14-18

HOUSE OF CLAY

He put no trust in his servants. . . . How much less in them that dwell in houses of clay? JOB 4:18–19

These words from Eliphaz are part of the first cycle of speeches in the book of Job. Eliphaz was replying to Job's complaint that he was being treated unjustly by the Lord. The point of the passage is that humans are imperfect, like clay houses that eventually crumble when subjected to the rain and wind. So what right did a flawed man like Job have to grumble against a just and righteous God?

Clay is cited several times throughout the book of Job as a symbol of humankind's weakness and the uncertainty of life. Later on in the book, Job admitted he was made from clay and would return to dust when he died (Job 10:9).

The tent is another biblical figure of speech for the frail human body. These makeshift dwellings could be taken down and moved from one place to another. The apostle Paul declared, "We know that if our earthly house of this tabernacle [*tent*: NIV] were dissolved, we have a building of God, an house not made with hands, eternal in the heavens" (2 Corinthians 5:1).

Learn More: Job 13:12; 33:6 / Isaiah 64:8

ITCHING EARS

Shall they heap to themselves teachers, having itching ears. 2 TIMOTHY 4:3

Second Timothy is one of the three "pastoral epistles" of the apostle Paul; the other two are 1 Timothy and Titus. These epistles deal with matters of church leadership. Paul wrote his second letter to Timothy, his young missionary associate, to encourage him to stand firm in his commitment to Christ in the midst of troubling times.

In this verse the apostle reminded Timothy of his responsibility as a preacher of the Gospel. Drawing from the teaching of Jesus, He was to declare the truth, even though this might not be pleasing to some people. He warned against false teachers who would preach a watered-down Gospel by telling people, as the Contemporary English Version puts it, "only what they are itching to hear."

To have an "itch" for something is an idiom still heard today. It refers to a strong desire. The problem with such urges is that they can lead to poor decisions and indulgence of sinful desires. Paul had the answer for such cravings: "Set your affection on things above, not on things on the earth" (Colossians 3:2).

Learn More: Jeremiah 7:8 / Romans 16:17 / Ephesians 4:14 / 2 Peter 2:1

JEWEL IN A PIG'S SNOUT

As a jewel of gold in a swine's snout, so is a fair woman. . .without discretion. PROVERBS 11:22

Pigs were detestable animals to the Jewish people. So it is not surprising that the pig appears in this proverb to show how some things just don't seem to go together. The Contemporary English Version renders the statement like this: "A beautiful woman who acts foolishly is like a gold ring on the snout of a pig."

The Amplified Version adds this clarifying note: "Her lack of character mocks her beauty." The Message avoids any reference to gender by stating, "Like a gold ring in a pig's snout is a beautiful face on an empty head."

This verse reminds us of Queen Jezebel, a woman of noble bearing who was ugly in every other way. She conspired to have an innocent man killed in order to take his land for her husband, King Ahab. Jezebel also led the people of Israel to worship the pagan god Baal. She threatened the life of the prophet Elijah. But she met a grisly death when dogs ate her body after she was thrown from her palace window.

Learn More: 2 Kings 9:30–37 / Job 40:10 / Proverbs 31:30

KISS THE CALVES

Let the men that sacrifice kiss the calves. HOSEA 13:2

This declaration from the prophet Hosea is one of the strongest denunciations of idolatry in the entire Old Testament. Hosea issued his criticism against the northern kingdom of Israel. The phrase "kiss the calves" symbolized the affection of the people for these false gods.

The prophet may have been referring to the two calf idols that King Jeroboam erected along opposite borders of Israel about two centuries before (1 Kings 12:25–30). The purpose of these shrines was to draw his subjects away from devotion to the temple in Jerusalem, capital city of the sister kingdom of Judah. This step in the wrong direction eventually led to widespread worship of many false gods throughout the nation of Israel.

Paying homage to a calf idol was an unfortunate part of Israel's history. While camped in the wilderness during the Exodus several centuries before, they bowed down before a golden calf. This was probably an image of Apis, a sacred bull worshipped by the Egyptians.

Learn More: Exodus 32:3–6 / Deuteronomy 9:16 / Nehemiah 9:18 / Psalm 106:19

LAMP OF SALVATION

And the salvation thereof as a lamp that burneth. Isaiah 62:1

In this verse, through the prophet Isaiah, God declared His determination to bless His people. Although they had been disobedient and would experience His punishment, He would ultimately shower His favor upon them and make them a blessing to the rest of the world. His salvation would be like a lamp that lit the path for them to follow.

The lamp in this passage refers to the tiny oil-burning vessels that were used for lighting houses and public buildings in Bible times. It is an apt image of God's saving power on behalf of His people.

A lamp also symbolized insight and understanding that come from the Lord, as well as the divine commandments that provide guidance for daily living. Sometimes the Lord Himself is portrayed as a lamp, as in this line from a song of David: "Thou art my lamp, O LORD: and the LORD will lighten my darkness" (2 Samuel 22:29).

In the New Testament, John the Baptist was like "a burning and shining lamp" (John 5:35 NLT) that prepared the way for the arrival of Jesus the Messiah.

Learn More: Leviticus 24:2 / Proverbs 6:23 / Psalm 119:105

LAND FLOWING WITH MILK AND HONEY

Unto a good land and a large, unto a land flowing with milk and honey. Exodus 3:8

God made this promise when He called Moses to deliver the Israelites from Egyptian slavery. The Lord would bring them to a "land flowing with milk and honey"—an idiom for a fertile and productive place where God's people would be happy and content.

When the Israelites reached the border of this land known as Canaan, Moses sent twelve scouts to explore it. They returned with a huge cluster of grapes and other fruit to show that God had made good on His promise. "Surely [the land] floweth with milk and honey," they declared; "and this is the fruit of it" (Numbers 13:27).

But the people did not have the faith to claim the land at this time. They were afraid of the fierce peoples who inhabited Canaan. So the Lord sentenced them to forty years of wandering in the wilderness. Most of them did not live to set foot in this bountiful place. His promises always require something from His people—the faith to reach out and claim them.

Learn More: Exodus 3:17; 13:5; 33:3 / Jeremiah 11:5; 32:22

LAND OF THE LIVING

Thou art my refuge and my portion in the land of the living. PSALM 142:5

This figure of speech is still heard occasionally today. When asked about his health after an extended illness, a person might reply, "I'm still in the land of the living." That is basically the meaning of the phrase in this psalm, written by David as he reflected on the experience of hiding in a cave to escape the wrath of King Saul (see psalm title). David knew the Lord had kept him safe, and he was glad he still existed in the "land of the living."

This poetic phrase appears several times in the Bible:

- Job declared that true wisdom was not found in the land of the living (Job 28:13).
- The psalmist vowed to walk before the Lord in the land of the living (Psalm 116:9).
- The prophet Isaiah declared that God's servant, the Messiah, would be cut off from the land of the living (Isaiah 53:8).
- In his prophecies of divine judgment against the nations, Ezekiel said the Egyptians would be snatched from the land of the living (Ezekiel 32:32).

Learn More: Psalm 52:5 / Isaiah 38:11 / Jeremiah 11:19

LEAP OVER A WALL

By my God have I leaped over a wall. PSALM 18:29

According to the title of this psalm, it was written by King David to express his thanks to the Lord for leading his armies to victory. If not for the phrase "by my God"—or through the Lord's strength—this verse would seem as if David were boasting about his superior abilities.

But the king always gave credit to the Lord for his accomplishments. To "run through a troop" and "leap over a wall" are poetic ways of saying that God enabled David to become a valiant warrior and military leader.

The Bible is filled with supernatural, "wall-leaping" events that God brought about on behalf of His people. These include David's victory over the Philistine giant Goliath; the destruction of pharaoh's army in the Red Sea; the fall of the walls of Jericho; and Gideon's defeat of a large army with a handful of warriors.

The prophet Jeremiah was amazed at what the Lord could accomplish with His unlimited power. "Ah Lord GOD. . .thou hast made the heaven and the earth by thy great power," he declared, "and there is nothing too hard for thee" (Jeremiah 32:17).

Learn More: Exodus 14:27–28 / Joshua 6:20 / Judges 7:19–21 /
1 Samuel 17:49–50 / Matthew 17:20 / Philippians 4:13

LEOPARD CANNOT CHANGE ITS SPOTS

Can the Ethiopian change his skin, or the leopard his spots? JEREMIAH 13:23

The prophet Jeremiah used two rhetorical questions to get the attention of the people of Judah. They had to admit that it was impossible for a person to change the color of his skin. And it was equally true that a leopard could not alter the spots in its coat.

These questions symbolized a deep-rooted problem. The people had sinned so blatantly for so long that they had lost sight of right and wrong. Had they reached the point where it was impossible for them to turn back to the Lord? The New Living Translation catches this nuance in the prophet's words. Just as these two things could not happen, Jeremiah declared, "Neither can you start doing good, for you have always done evil."

This is a shocking indictment. Continuing in sin can dull a person's sensitivity to the Lord and His influence for good in our lives. The apostle John had the cure for those times when sin creeps into our lives: "If we confess our sins, he is faithful and just to forgive us our sins, and to cleanse us from all unrighteousness" (1 John 1:9).

Learn More: Isaiah 1:25 / Hebrews 9:14

LIFE IS A VAPOR

What is your life? It is even a vapour, that appeareth for a little time. JAMES 4:14

This is one of the Bible's best known passages on the brevity and uncertainty of life. James compares our lives to a vapor that is visible for only an instant before disappearing and leaving no trace of its existence.

In the larger context of this verse, James warned his readers about planning for the future without including God in their projections. He knew that the future is a giant question mark for everyone. But if the Lord walks with us along the way, we are in good hands. The psalmist David put it like this, "Yea, though I walk through the valley of the shadow of death, I will fear no evil: for thou art with me" (Psalm 23:4).

Several modern translations express this truth from James in different imagery, replacing *vapor* with such phrases as "morning fog" and "puff of smoke." Perhaps the most graphic rendering comes from the Amplified Version: "You are *merely* a vapor [like a puff of smoke or a wisp of steam from a cooking pot] that is visible for a little while and then vanishes [into thin air]."

Learn More: Psalm 90:4 / Hosea 13:3 / 1 Peter 1:24

LIFTING UP HOLY HANDS

I will therefore that men pray every where, lifting up holy hands. 1 TIMOTHY 2:8

This verse is part of the apostle Paul's instructions to Timothy on public prayer (1 Timothy 2:1–8). Those who lead in prayer should do so respectfully and in a spirit of confidence that God will hear and answer their requests.

The phrase "lift up holy hands" describes the posture that many people in Bible times took when praying. They would stand looking up and lifting their open hands toward the sky as they made their requests to the Lord. This stance reflected an attitude of humility and respect.

King Solomon "spread forth his hands toward heaven" (1 Kings 8:22) during his long prayer at the dedication of the temple. When Ezra led a covenant renewal ceremony in Jerusalem, the entire assembly lifted their hands in prayer as they worshipped the Lord (Nehemiah 8:6).

The hands are prominent in most activities, so they symbolize total devotion to the Lord. The psalmist asked, "Who shall ascend into the hill of the LORD?" Then he gave the answer: "He that hath clean hands, and a pure heart; who hath not lifted up his soul unto vanity, nor sworn deceitfully" (Psalm 24:3–4).

Learn More: Psalm 28:2; 119:48; 141:2 / Luke 24:50

LIFT UP THE EYES

Get thee up into the top of Pisgah, and lift up thine eyes. DEUTERONOMY 3:27

God spoke these words to Moses as he looked into the land the Lord had promised to His people. Moses was prohibited from entering Canaan because of an act of disobedience as the Israelites wandered in the wilderness (Numbers 20:9–12).

To "lift up one's eyes" implies more than a casual glance. The Lord wanted the great leader to look long and hard over the land because this was as close as he would get to it. The Good News Translation expresses this distinction perfectly: "Look carefully at what you see, because you will never go across the Jordan."

Several people in the Bible are said to lift up their eyes. Perhaps the most interesting example is that of Isaac and Rebekah. Their marriage had been arranged by relatives, and they had never seen one another. Upon their first meeting, as Rebekah was still a distance away, they lifted up their eyes toward each other. This was probably more than a brief look. Both must have been anxious to check out the person with whom they would spend the rest of their lives.

Learn More: Genesis 13:10; 24:63–64 / Isaiah 37:23

LIGHT THAT NEVER GOES OUT

The Lord shall be thine everlasting light. ISAIAH 60:20

This is a classic passage from the prophet Isaiah about the future glory of Jerusalem and the coming Messiah. The image of the sun and the moon that never stop shining emphasizes the consistency and dependability of the Lord. When He appeared in all His glory, He would be all the light His people needed.

Light is one of the most popular images in the Bible. It was the first thing the Lord created when He began to call the universe into existence (Genesis 1:3). It represents His presence, protection, and salvation. God used a pillar of fire to light the way for the Israelites in the wilderness. His presence was like a lamp that drove away the darkness.

But the greatest light the world has ever seen was Jesus, whose life reflected the love of God the Father. "I am the light of the world," He told His followers. "He that followeth me shall not walk in darkness, but shall have the light of life" (John 8:12).

Learn More: Exodus 13:21 / 2 Samuel 22:29 / Psalm 27:1 / Proverbs 4:18 / Philippians 2:15 / Revelation 22:5

LINE STRETCHED OVER JERUSALEM

Stretched out a line, he hath not withdrawn his hand from destroying. LAMENTATIONS 2:8

Lamentations was written by the prophet Jeremiah. The book is a sad lament over the destruction of Jerusalem by the Babylonian army in 587 BC. The prophet had warned the people repeatedly that this would happen unless they gave up the worship of false gods and turned back to the Lord.

This verse speaks to the collapse of the city's massive defensive wall. Jeremiah used the image of a measuring line to show that God was determined to carry out His plan of bringing the city to its knees. The New Century Version renders the phrase like this: "He measured the wall and did not stop himself from destroying it."

A measuring line was similar to a tape measure used by modern carpenters. It appears several times in the Bible as a symbol of God's judgment. For example, God warned that He would stretch a line of judgment over Jerusalem just as He had caused the fall of its sister city, Samaria, in the northern kingdom of Israel (2 Kings 21:13).

Learn More: Isaiah 28:17 / Jeremiah 31:39 / Zechariah 1:16

LION IN A DEN

He lieth in wait secretly as a lion in his den. PSALM 10:9

This psalm is a cry of protest against wicked people who oppress the poor and innocent of society. The psalmist compares these evildoers to lions that hide in their dens, waiting for their unsuspecting prey to pass by so they can make an easy kill.

Lions were known for their savage nature. They are mentioned several times in the Bible as symbols of strength. The prophet Jeremiah compared the Babylonian army that would devastate the nation of Judah to a lion that was on the hunt (Jeremiah 4:7). In the New Testament, the apostle Peter compared Satan to a "roaring lion [that] walketh about, seeking whom he may devour" (1 Peter 5:8).

A second image in this verse—a net—also underscores the problem of being lured into a trap. Nets made of cords were used to catch small animals such as birds and fish. In his suffering, Job felt like he was being punished unjustly. He protested that God had surrounded him with His net (Job 19:6).

Learn More: Job 10:16 / Psalm 22:13; 57:4 / Proverbs 22:13 / Jeremiah 50:17 / 2 Timothy 4:17

LOWER PARTS OF THE EARTH

*Shout, ye lower parts of the earth. . .*FOR THE LORD HATH REDEEMED JACOB. ISAIAH 44:23

These two verses make up one of the greatest praise passages in the entire Bible. In poetic symbolism, the prophet Isaiah calls on the entire universe to break out in song to express unrestrained joy at His gift of redemption.

This praise should stretch from the heavens above to the "lower parts of the earth," a poetic phrase meaning "as far as the imagination can penetrate into the earth beneath our feet." The Easy-to-Read Version renders the phrase like this: "Earth, shout for joy down to your deepest parts!"

The prophet calls on mountains and forests to join in this enthusiastic song of praise to the gracious Lord of redemption. This includes not only the forest as a whole but every single tree that grows there. In another passage, the psalmist expressed this call for universal praise of the Lord from His creation like this: "Let every thing that hath breath praise the LORD" (Psalm 150:6).

Learn More: Psalm 48:10; 66:4; 69:34; 96:10–11; 98:4; 148:1–13

MILK OF THE GENTILES

Thou shalt also suck the milk of the Gentiles. ISAIAH 60:16

In this verse the prophet Isaiah provided a glimpse of the future glory of Jerusalem. Although God's people would be exiled to a foreign nation because of their sin, they would eventually be restored to their homeland. All nations would recognize that Israel was God's chosen people, and they would bow down to worship the Lord.

To "suck the milk of Gentiles" was a poetic way of saying the nations would provide everything God's people needed to flourish and prosper. The Good News Translation renders the phrase like this: "Nations and kings will care for you as a mother nurses her child." The term *Gentiles* is often rendered as "nations" in modern English translations.

Since infants were sustained by milk, it is often cited as a symbol of dependence and the need for deeper understanding. "I have fed you with milk, and not with meat," the apostle Paul told the Corinthian believers, "for hitherto ye were not able to bear it, neither yet now are ye able" (1 Corinthians 3:2).

Learn More: Isaiah 66:11 / Ezekiel 25:4 / 1 Peter 2:2

MILLSTONE AROUND THE NECK

It were better for him that a millstone were hanged about his neck. . . MATTHEW 18:6

Jesus made this statement in response to the question of His disciples, "Who is greatest in the kingdom of heaven?" (Matthew 18:1). He placed a little child in their midst and told them that the spirit of humility and trust modeled by this child represented true greatness. Anyone who wanted to enter God's kingdom must have this childlike attitude.

Then Jesus applied this figure of a little child to new believers. He emphasized that anyone who discouraged those who sought to follow Him were committing a great wrong. Such sin deserved the worst possible punishment—having a heavy stone tied around one's neck and being tossed into deep water. The millstone to which He referred was a heavy object used for grinding grain.

The figure of a "millstone around one's neck" is still used today. It refers to a troubling situation or a heavy problem from which there seems to be no escape.

Learn More: Job 41:24 / Mark 9:42 / Luke 17:2

MOAB AS GOD'S WASHPOT

Moab is my washpot. PSALM 60:8

This psalm was written after the nation of Israel had suffered a humiliating defeat at the hands of her enemies. The psalmist lamented that God had made His people "drink the wine of astonishment" (verse 3). But he also prayed for God to intervene on Israel's behalf again and give the nation victory over her adversaries.

The psalmist was convinced that one of these enemies, the Moabites, would eventually be reduced by the Lord to the status of a washpot, a container in which dirty hands and feet were cleaned. Foot-washing was usually done by the servants of a household, so this was a poetic way of saying that Moab would become lowly servants of the Israelites. King David did eventually defeat the Moabites, but they regained their strength in later years.

Moab occupied the territory along the eastern shore of the Dead Sea. The Israelites passed through this land while traveling to Canaan. The king of Moab hired a magician named Balaam to put a curse on God's people, but the Lord intervened and caused him to bless the Israelites instead.

Learn More: Numbers 22:1–6 / 1 Samuel 25:41 / 2 Samuel 8:2 / Psalm 108:9 / John 13:5

MOTE IN THE EYE

How wilt thou say to thy brother, Let me pull out the mote out of thine eye? MATTHEW 7:4

These words of Jesus are some of the most familiar from His Sermon on the Mount. He was cautioning against harsh judgment of others. Jesus knew that people tend to condemn other individuals for their small faults (the mote in others' eyes) while ignoring even greater deficiencies in themselves (the beam in their own).

The New International Version picks up this dramatic contrast perfectly in its rendering of the verse: "How can you say to your brother, 'Let me take the speck out of your eye,' when all the time there is a plank in your own eye?"

Rendering such harsh judgment of others is a good example of self-righteousness and hypocrisy. Jesus had harsh words for both these human foibles, particularly as expressed by the scribes and Pharisees.

On one occasion He called them out for their attempt to stone a woman who had been accused of adultery. "He that is without sin among you," He charged them, "let him first cast a stone at her" (John 8:7). They turned and walked away, "being convicted by their own conscience" (verse 9).

Learn More: Matthew 23:1–38

MOUTH OF GOD

The Lord giveth wisdom: out of his mouth cometh knowledge and understanding. PROVERBS 2:6

This verse uses the imagery of God's mouth to emphasize His authority. If something comes from His mouth, we know that it's correct—not a half-truth or a baseless rumor. This passage is just one of many throughout the Bible that speak of the mouth of the Lord. For example:

- People do not live by bread alone, but by every word that comes from the Lord's mouth.
- The words from God's mouth are more valuable than food.
- God will judge the earth with the rod of His mouth.

God often delegated messages to His spokesmen known as the prophets. When they spoke His commands under divine inspiration, it was as if their words were coming from the mouth of the Lord Himself.

The prophet Jeremiah tried to stop preaching the Lord's unpopular message of judgment to the people of Judah. But he found that God's truth overcame his ability to resist its power. "But his word was in mine heart as a burning fire shut up in my bones," he declared. "I was weary with forbearing, and I could not stay" (Jeremiah 20:9).

Learn More: Deuteronomy 8:3 / Job 23:12 / Isaiah 11:4 / Matthew 4:4

MOUTH TO MOUTH

He shall speak with thee mouth to mouth, and thou shalt go to Babylon. JEREMIAH 34:3

This message from the Lord was delivered through the prophet Jeremiah to Zedekiah, the last king of Judah. The prophet declared that the king would not escape the wrath of the Babylonian army when it ransacked the city of Jerusalem. Zedekiah would be captured and taken to Babylon, where he would stand "mouth to mouth" before the pagan ruler. Several modern translations render this phrase as "face to face."

It happened just as Jeremiah prophesied. When the city fell, Zedekiah and his sons fled the city but fell into enemy hands. His sons were killed, and he was taken into exile, blinded, and imprisoned. He died as a captive among the pagan Babylonians.

This phrase is used in a more complimentary way of Moses, the great leader of God's people during the Exodus. After Moses' siblings, Aaron and Miriam, questioned his leadership, God scolded them for their disobedience. Moses was the divinely chosen leader with whom the Lord spoke "face to face," and "not with hidden meanings" (Numbers 12:8 NCV). He should be obeyed without question.

Learn More: Jeremiah 32:4

NAIL IN A SURE PLACE

And I will fasten him as a nail in a sure place. ISAIAH 22:23

This verse refers to Eliakim, a royal official under King Hezekiah of Judah (2 Kings 18:18). The prophet Isaiah compared Eliakim to another aide in Hezekiah's court who was building an elaborate tomb for himself (Isaiah 22:15–17). This tomb builder, known as Shebna, would not survive the coming invasion of the Babylonian army, while Eliakim, as a "nail in a sure place," would be secure in his position for a while longer.

But two verses later, Isaiah reversed himself and declared that Eliakim's security would not last forever. He would fall from his important position when the Babylonians breached Jerusalem's defensive wall and destroyed the city (Isaiah 22:25). The nail in these verses refers to the wooden pegs that were used to fasten structural timbers together in Bible times. Once fastened in place, these pegs were difficult to remove, but they could be smashed and broken by an army on the rampage.

This reversal of fortune described by Isaiah has an important lesson. Life is fragile, and disaster can strike quickly. Only the Lord is the ultimate "sure place" in a perilous world.

Learn More: Ezra 9:8 / Psalms 18:2; 46:1; 57:1; 91:2

NEST AMONG THE STARS

Though thou set thy nest among the stars, thence will I bring thee down. OBADIAH 4

In this brief prophetic book, Obadiah condemned the Edomites, ancient enemies of the Israelites. The Edomites had participated in the destruction and looting of the city of Jerusalem when it fell to the Babylonian army in 587 BC. Because of this despicable act, Obadiah declared, the Edomites would be destroyed by the Lord.

In verse 4, Obadiah condemned the Edomites for their pride, using the image of "nesting among the stars" to show their exalted opinion of themselves. They considered themselves invincible in their fortress cities in the mountainous territory near the Dead Sea. They had exhibited this arrogant attitude several centuries before Obadiah's time by refusing to let the Israelites pass through their territory while they traveled toward the land of Canaan (Numbers 20:14–21).

The prophet Jeremiah also used the image of an exalted nesting place to portray the pride of another pagan nation, Phoenicia. He described this country north of Israel as making its "nest in the cedars," referring to the majestic trees of Lebanon—a point of Phoenician pride Jeremiah 22:23).

Learn More: Jeremiah 48:29; 49:16 / Proverbs 16:18 / Zechariah 10:11 / Habakkuk 2:9

NOSE OF GOD

There went up a smoke out of his nostrils. 2 SAMUEL 22:9

This verse appears in David's song of thanksgiving, which he recorded after becoming the undisputed king of Israel. He expressed thanks to God for keeping him safe from King Saul and for giving him victory in battle. Through the imagery of smoke from God's nostrils and fire from His mouth, David draws a vivid picture of the all-powerful God who had protected him from all his enemies.

References to God's nose in the Bible have several additional meanings. The sweet smell He sensed from Noah's burning of incense implied that this offering was pleasing and acceptable to Him. A blast from His nostrils portrayed His punishment of wickedness and injustice. A strong wind from His nostrils also showed His awesome power—the ability to roll back the waters of the Red Sea to deliver His people from Pharaoh's pursuing army.

Eliphaz reminded Job that evil people may seem to rule the earth, but God is the ultimate judge of unrighteousness. "By the blast of God they perish," he declared, "and by the breath of his nostrils are they consumed" (Job 4:9).

Learn More: Genesis 8:21 / Exodus 15:8 / Psalm 18:8, 15 / Isaiah 65:5 / Amos 5:21

OFFSCOURING OF ALL THINGS

We. . .are the offscouring of all things unto this day. 1 CORINTHIANS 4:13

In the first few verses of this chapter of 1 Corinthians, the apostle Paul used irony to scold the Corinthian believers about their exalted opinion of themselves. Then he contrasted this attitude with that of the apostles, who preached the Gospel in a spirit of meekness and humility.

These messengers of the Lord did not strike back when persecuted. By the standards of the world they were considered nothing but garbage, or the "offscouring of all things" [*scum of the earth*: GNT].

This verse echoes another famous statement from the apostle as he thought about his earthly accomplishments as a learned Pharisee. He counted all these things "but loss for the excellency of the knowledge of Christ Jesus my Lord. . .and do count them but dung, that I may win Christ" (Philippians 3:8).

Paul had learned that serving the Lord was more valuable than any shallow rewards offered to those who live by earthly standards. He also advised the Corinthian Christians, "Be ye stedfast, unmoveable, always abounding in the work of the Lord, forasmuch as ye know that your labour is not in vain in the Lord" (1 Corinthians 15:58).

Learn More: 1 Corinthians 15:9 / Philippians 4:11

OIL OF GLADNESS

God, thy God, hath anointed thee with the oil of gladness above thy fellows. PSALM 45:7

This psalm celebrates a royal marriage. But it has been interpreted as a messianic psalm. The Messiah, as the instrument of righteousness, will be anointed with the "oil of gladness." Kings were anointed by having oil poured on their heads, so this figure of speech refers to the Messiah's reign. His universal kingship will bring unlimited joy and gladness to God's people.

The oil of Bible times came from the fruit of olive trees. It was used in sacrificial rituals. The patriarch Jacob, after his dramatic encounter with an angel on a ladder, set up an altar of stones and covered it with oil. This was his way of expressing thanks to God for making the same covenant promises to him that the Lord had made originally to his grandfather, Abraham.

Oil was also used as a healing agent. In one of Jesus' parables, a kind Samaritan helped a stranger who had been robbed and beaten by putting oil on his wounds. The writer of the epistle of James instructed believers to care for the sick by treating them "with oil in the name of the Lord" (James 5:14).

Learn More: Genesis 28:18 / 1 Kings 1:39 / Luke 10:34 / Hebrews 1:9

ONE STEP AWAY FROM DEATH

There is but a step between me and death. 1 SAMUEL 20:3

David and King Saul's son, Jonathan, had developed a close friendship. This frustrated the king because he was on a mission to eliminate David as a claimant to the throne. David knew his life was in danger, but he had to convince Jonathan that his own father was out to kill him. With these words to his friend, David probably referred to his close shave with death when he dodged a javelin thrown by the king. A quick step to the side saved his life.

The Bible contains many similar colorful expressions for physical death. Dying is characterized as being cut down, as water spilled on the ground, as the disappearance of our earthly house, as being gathered to one's people, and as returning to dust.

Physical death is inevitable, but believers know that dying is not the end of our existence. As the apostle Paul declared, "The wages of sin is death; but the gift of God is eternal life through Jesus Christ our Lord" (Romans 6:23)

Learn More: Genesis 49:33 / Deuteronomy 31:16 / 2 Samuel 14:14 / Job 14:2; 16:22 / Psalm 89:48; 104:29 / 2 Corinthians 5:1

OUTER DARKNESS

Take him away, and cast him into outer darkness. MATTHEW 22:13

This phrase from the mouth of Jesus occurs in His parable of the wedding feast. One guest appeared at this celebration not wearing the appropriate clothes. The king ordered his servants to expel this person and cast him into "outer darkness." The phrase refers to Jesus' judgment of disobedient people who refuse to acknowledge Him and His authority.

Earlier in the parable, some people who had been invited to the feast failed to attend. So the king authorized his servants to summon people off the streets to join the festivities. Jesus' words "Many are called, but few are chosen" (Matthew 22:14) show that His own countrymen, the Jewish people, had rejected Him as the Messiah. So the kingdom of God that Jesus had come to establish was now broadened to include the Gentiles.

In later years, after Jesus ascended to God the Father, this principle of "whosoever will" was made even more explicit through the missionary work of the apostle Paul. He asked, "Is he the God of the Jews only? is he not also of the Gentiles? Yes, of the Gentiles also" (Romans 3:29).

Learn More: Matthew 8:12; 25:30

OVEN OF GOD'S WRATH

Thou shalt make them as a fiery oven in the time of thine anger. PSALM 21:9

This psalm is a song of praise to the Lord for giving the nation of Israel victory over their enemies. The psalmist portrays the wrath or judgment of God as a hot oven that consumes those who tried to destroy God's people.

The anger of Israel's adversaries was intense, but they became the victims of a fury that was even hotter—the wrath of the holy God. The New Living Translation renders the phrase like this: "You [God] will throw them in a flaming furnace when you appear."

God's wrath was not always directed against Israel's enemies. Sometimes His anger would "wax hot" (Exodus 22:24) or be "kindled" (Numbers 11:33) against His own people for their waywardness and disobedience. The prophets often spoke of God's wrath being directed against His people because of their worship of false gods (Habakkuk 2:19).

Learn More: Hosea 7:4, 6, 7 / Malachi 4:1

OWL OF THE DESERT

I am like an owl of the desert. PSALM 102:6

The title of this psalm gives us a hint about its content and the meaning of this particular verse. The title reads, "A prayer of the afflicted, when he is overwhelmed, and poureth out his complaint before the Lord." The psalmist may have written this lament while alone and far from home—an exile with God's people in the pagan nation of Babylon.

The author cited the image of an owl in the desert to show his spirit of despair. The Israelites considered the owl an unclean bird. They often portrayed it as a solitary creature that lived in isolated areas. The other birds cited in this verse also conjure up the image of loneliness and a longing for the familiar.

Even for the most outgoing and genial people, life does have its lonely moments. But the psalmist teaches us that we have help at hand during those challenging times. He directed his prayer, as another psalmist did, to the God who is "our refuge and strength, a very present help in trouble" (Psalm 46:1).

Learn More: Job 30:29 / Isaiah 13:21 / Jeremiah 50:39 / Micah 1:8

PAVILION OF GOD

For in the time of trouble he shall hide me in his pavilion. PSALM 27:5

This untitled psalm is attributed to King David. Some interpreters believe he wrote it while on the run from his son Absalom, who was trying to take over the throne by force. No matter who penned it, it is a strong affirmation of God's protection in a time of trouble.

The term *pavilion* refers to any temporary shelter such as a tent, a tabernacle, or a hut made of tree branches. Several modern English translations render the word as "tent." The psalmist felt safe and secure in the promise that God provided shelter for His people.

Two other poetic figures in this verse are *tabernacle* and *rock*. The tabernacle, or tent of meeting, was the sacred place of worship built by the Israelites during the Exodus from Egypt. It represented the Lord's presence. A rock, as an object that cannot be moved, symbolized His eternity, dependability, and never-changing nature. As the author of the epistle of James put it, He "does not change like shifting shadows" (James 1:17 NIV).

Learn More: Psalm 31:20 / Malachi 3:6 / James 1:17

PEACE LIKE A RIVER

O that thou hadst hearkened. . .then had thy peace been as a river. ISAIAH 48:18

No one likes to hear the phrase "if only," but sometimes it's necessary. In this verse the Lord used the phrase to remind His people what might have been if they had only listened to Him. The New International Version renders the verse like this: "If only you had paid attention to my commands, your peace would have been like a river, your well-being like the waves of the sea."

The prophet Isaiah delivered this message to God's people as if the Babylonian army had already overrun the nation of Judah. Their disobedience would lead to their captivity by a pagan nation, but this could have been avoided if they had remained faithful to the Lord.

Peace "like a river" is a poetic way of referring to unlimited joy and happiness. The image of a free-flowing river occurs often in the Bible to represent the abundant blessings provided by the Lord. Sometimes God Himself is described as a river. Isaiah declared that God's people would eventually be restored to their homeland, where "the glorious LORD will be unto us a place of broad rivers and streams" (Isaiah 33:21).

Learn More: Psalm 1:3 / Isaiah 43:19 / Jeremiah 31:9 / John 7:38

PECULIAR PEOPLE

The Lord hath avouched thee this day to be his peculiar people. DEUTERONOMY 26:18

In modern English the word *peculiar* means "odd" or "strange," perhaps even "weird" or "eccentric," in certain contexts. But this was not what the term meant when the King James Version of the Bible was published in 1611. In those days it meant "one's very own." It was sometimes applied to property that belonged to an individual, as opposed to property owned in common by the entire community.

This word is rendered by modern English translations as God's "own special treasure" (NLT), "His treasured possession" (ESV), and God's "very own people" (NCV). The idea is that God's people belong exclusively to Him, so He has the right to demand their loyalty and obedience.

This expectation of obedience comes through clearly in the Lord's command to the Israelites during the Exodus: "Now therefore, if ye will obey my voice indeed, and keep my covenant, then ye shall be a peculiar treasure unto me above all people: for all the earth is mine" (Exodus 19:5).

Learn More: Deuteronomy 14:2 / Psalm 135:4 / Titus 2:14 / 1 Peter 2:9

PILLARS OF THE EARTH

The pillars of the earth are the Lord's, and he hath set the world upon them. 1 SAMUEL 2:8

This verse is part of Hannah's song of thanksgiving to the Lord for a birth that bordered on the miraculous. Her son, Samuel, was born in answer to her prayer after she had been unable to conceive for many years.

Hannah interpreted this event as more than just another birth. She saw it as a blessing that God had poured out on all His people. Indeed, Samuel went on to become one of the greatest leaders in Israel's history, encouraging the people to follow the Lord.

In poetic symbolism, Hannah praised the God of creation who brought the world into being and set it upon supporting pillars. We moderns know that the earth floats in space without any underpinning. But is this any less miraculous than the idea that the world stands on literal pillars created by an all-powerful God? Faith leads us to believe that the Lord is at work behind the scenes, keeping watch over His creation and those who live in it.

Learn More: 2 Samuel 22:8 / Job 38:4 / Psalm 102:25 / Isaiah 48:13 / Hebrews 1:10

PLAY THE FOOL

Behold, I have played the fool, and have erred exceedingly. 1 SAMUEL 26:21

Saul was determined to kill David, a young warrior who had been selected by the Lord to replace Israel's first king. David got close enough to assassinate Saul on two occasions, but he refused to do so. When Saul realized his brush with death, he addressed these words to his rival.

What the king said seemed to be a genuine confession of how foolish he had been, but his actions spoke louder than his words. He had owned up to his misguided actions on other occasions, only to continue his campaign to take David's life.

To "play the fool" is to take on the role of an undiscerning person, to be blinded by one's emotions and reckless desires. The New Century Version renders Saul's words like this: "I have been very stupid and foolish."

The image of playing a role through foolish actions was also used by the prophet Jeremiah. He accused the people of Judah of worshipping false gods and thus "play[ing] the harlot with many lovers" (Jeremiah 3:1).

Learn More: Proverbs 14:7; 26:8; 27:3

PLOWING INIQUITY

Even as I have seen, they that plow iniquity, and sow wickedness, reap the same. Job 4:8

This verse appears in the response of Eliphaz to the suffering Job's initial protest of his innocence. Eliphaz was bothered by Job's suggestion that godly people sometimes suffered while wicked people seemed to prosper.

This man called on his experience to answer Job's protest. Eliphaz had noted that people who "plowed iniquity"—or committed sin and wrongdoing—would inevitably reap the results of their behavior.

The agricultural image of plowing occurs often in the Bible. The prophet Hosea declared that the people of the northern kingdom of Israel had plowed wickedness and they would reap iniquity. The psalmist complained that his enemies had brought him low by plowing long furrows on his back. The prophet Micah proclaimed that God would punish the city of Jerusalem for its sin by causing it to be plowed like a field—a reference to its destruction by the Babylonian army.

This image is closely related to another agricultural figure of speech: sowing or planting. Perhaps the best known example in the Bible comes from the apostle Paul: "Whatsoever a man soweth, that shall he also reap" (Galatians 6:7).

Learn More: Psalm 129:3 / Hosea 10:13 / Micah 3:12 / 1 Corinthians 9:10

PLUMBLINE AMONG GOD'S PEOPLE

I will set a plumbline in the midst of my people Israel. Amos 7:8

This verse records one of the three visions of the prophet Amos in chapter 7 of his book. The other two were a horde of locusts (verses 1–3) and a consuming fire (verses 4–6). All three visions represented the devastation that would strike the northern kingdom of Israel unless the people turned back to God.

In this particular vision, the prophet saw the Lord standing on a wall holding a plumbline (verse 7). This tool was used by carpenters to keep a wall straight and true while it was under construction. The message of the vision was unmistakable: the Lord had measured the nation of Israel and found it to be faulty—crooked and out of alignment with His will and purpose. Unless they straightened up, they were headed for God's judgment and a dramatic change of fortune.

Unfortunately, the nation did not change, and it fell to the Assyrian army in 722 BC. Many of its citizens were taken into exile and settled in this pagan land.

Learn More: 2 Kings 18:9–11

PURGED WITH HYSSOP

Purge me with hyssop, and I shall be clean. Psalm 51:7

Hyssop is a plant that belongs to the mint family. In Egypt, the Israelites used bunches of this plant to sprinkle blood on the doorposts of their houses to keep them safe from the final plague (Exodus 12:22). Hyssop was also used in purification ceremonies.

King David probably had these facts in mind when he wrote Psalm 51. He had committed adultery with Bathsheba and then tried to cover up his crime by having her husband killed. To be "purged with hyssop" was his poetic way of pleading with the Lord for full forgiveness of this heinous sin.

David also used the image of snow to express his desire for divine cleansing power. His sin was like a dark blot on his conscience, and he wanted to feel thoroughly clean again so he could enjoy fellowship with the Lord. This is a vivid reminder of God's message to His wayward people through the prophet Isaiah: "Come now, and let us reason together, saith the Lord: though your sins be as scarlet, they shall be as white as snow" (Isaiah 1:18).

Learn More: Numbers 19:18 / Psalm 65:3 / Isaiah 6:7 / 1 Corinthians 5:7 / Hebrews 9:19

REED SHAKEN BY THE WIND

What went ye out into the wilderness to see? A reed shaken with the wind? Matthew 11:7

John the Baptist sent two of his disciples to Jesus to determine if He was the Messiah whose arrival John had announced. Jesus assured them that He was indeed this messenger from God. Several bystanders apparently heard this conversation and wondered why John was expressing uncertainty over who Jesus was.

Jesus' response to the crowd left no doubt as to His opinion of His forerunner. When people went into the desert to hear John preach, they had not seen a "reed shaken with the wind"—a symbol of frailty and weakness. They had witnessed a courageous spokesman for the Lord who called on them to repent and turn to God. John had not changed; he was still the messenger whom God had sent to announce the arrival of His long-awaited Messiah.

The Old Testament prophet Ahijah also used this image to express God's judgment. The Lord would strike Israel and its king, Jeroboam, "as a reed is shaken in the water" (1 Kings 14:15) because they had provoked His anger by worshipping false gods.

Learn More: Luke 7:24

REMOVED LIKE A SHEPHERD'S TENT

Mine age is departed, and is removed from me as a shepherd's tent. Isaiah 38:12

King Hezekiah of Judah uttered these words after he almost died. The Lord had extended Hezekiah's life when he prayed in a spirit of repentance after receiving news of his serious illness. The king compared the uncertainty of life to the tents that shepherds lived in while watching over sheep. These dwellings could be taken down quickly and moved to other grazing spots. The Contemporary English Version renders Hezekiah's words like this: "My life was taken from me like the tent that a shepherd pulls up and moves."

This passage emphasizes three undeniable truths: (1) Life is uncertain; it can be taken from us at any time. (2) Death plays no favorites; it happens to kings as well as commoners. (3) Because of the first two truths, we need to be ready to meet the Lord at any time. Jesus cautioned us, "Watch therefore, for ye know neither the day nor the hour wherein the Son of man cometh" (Matthew 25:13).

Learn More: Isaiah 40:22 / 2 Corinthians 5:1

REND THE HEART

And rend your heart, and not your garments. Joel 2:13

The prophet Joel proclaimed God's message during the final days of the nation of Judah. His prophecies of divine judgment were intermingled with words of hope. God's people could avoid this disaster, he declared, by turning from their wicked ways.

In poetic symbolism, Joel called for the people to repent by rending their hearts. This image reflects a biblical custom known as rending—or tearing—one's clothes. People would sometimes grab the garments they were wearing and rip them with one forceful motion to express their deep distress.

To rend one's heart instead of one's clothes was to repent, turn from sin, and seek the Lord. The Contemporary English Version renders the phrase like this: "Don't rip your clothes to show your sorrow. Instead, turn back to me with broken hearts."

The human heart is one of the richest figures of speech in the Bible. God is more impressed with a person's heart, or character, than physical appearance. King Solomon had "largeness of heart" or great wisdom and understanding. To have a "pure heart" is to be godly in thoughts and actions.

Learn More: 2 Samuel 3:31 / 1 Kings 4:29 / Esther 4:1 / Psalm 24:3–4

RICHES MAKE WINGS AND FLY AWAY

Riches certainly make themselves wings; they fly away as an eagle. PROVERBS 23:5

Anyone who has tried to save money or invest some of their income can identify with this verse. Anyone can see their money take flight because of an unexpected expense or a downturn in the stock market. One modern translation renders the verse like this: "In the blink of an eye, money can disappear, as if it grew wings and flew away like a bird" (ERV).

In the preceding verse, the writer of Proverbs cautioned against laboring to become rich (verse 4). He probably knew that great wealth has a tendency to make people prideful and self-sufficient rather than humble and dependent on God. The apostle Paul put it like this: "For the love of money is the root of all evil: which while some coveted after, they have erred from the faith, and pierced themselves through with many sorrows" (1 Timothy 6:10).

Jesus also taught that it is impossible to serve God while placing ultimate trust in riches (Luke 16:13).

Learn More: Psalm 52:7 / Proverbs 11:28 / Jeremiah 9:23 / Mark 10:23 / 1 Timothy 6:17

RICH IN GOOD WORKS

That they do good, that they be rich in good works. 1 TIMOTHY 6:18

Most people think the early church consisted only of poor people. But these words from the apostle Paul to Timothy, his young missionary associate, tell us otherwise. Some members of the church at Ephesus, where Timothy was ministering, were apparently "rich in this world." But Paul wanted them to be counted wealthy in another way—in service to the Lord and in the good works they performed for others in His name.

The Bible is clear that salvation comes through God's grace alone. We cannot work our way into heaven through our deeds, no matter how unselfish they may be. But it is equally true that godly actions flow naturally from our commitment to Christ after we become members of His kingdom.

Paul went on to specify what being "rich in good works" meant for the wealthy members of the Ephesian church: they should be "generous to those in need, always being ready to share with others" (NLT).

Learn More: Ephesians 2:8–10 / 1 Timothy 5:25 / Titus 3:8 / Hebrews 10:24

ROBE OF RIGHTEOUSNESS

He hath covered me with the robe of righteousness. ISAIAH 61:10

The prophet Isaiah looked forward to better times for God's people. After a period of captivity in a foreign nation, they would return to their homeland. Here they would be dressed in "robes of righteousness"—a dramatic contrast to their sinful actions that had brought on the Lord's punishment.

In Bible times, a robe was an outer garment, reaching from head to toe, worn by both men and women. As with this piece of clothing that covered the entire body, the people of Judah would be enveloped by a new sense of purpose from the living God, who required righteous behavior from His people.

Several additional images for the concept of righteousness appear in the Bible. The psalmist prayed for the "gates of righteousness" to be opened so he could enter and enjoy fellowship with the Lord. The coming Messiah would be known as the "Sun of righteousness." When resisting Satan, believers should put on the "breastplate of righteousness."

Learn More: Job 29:14 / Psalm 132:9 / Isaiah 11:5 / Malachi 4:2 / Ephesians 6:14 / Revelation 7:9

SATAN AS A ROARING LION

The devil, as a roaring lion, walketh about, seeking whom he may devour. 1 PETER 5:8

The apostle Peter wrote his first letter to believers who were suffering persecution from Roman authorities. During these perilous times, he wanted them to depend on the Lord for protection. He also warned them to be on guard against the wiles of Satan.

This "roaring lion" could plant doubt in their mind and cause them to waver in their commitment to Jesus. Peter knew all about this possibility because he had denied the Lord in a moment of weakness on the night of His arrest (Matthew 26:74–75). Peter's words "be sober, be vigilant" are rendered by one modern translation as "discipline yourselves, keep alert" (NRSV). Resisting Satan requires that believers never underestimate his power.

The Bible uses several other names and images to describe Satan. He is also called "the tempter," "the god of this age," "the wicked one," "Beelzebub," "the son of perdition," "the prince of the power of the air," and "that old serpent, called the Devil, and Satan, which deceiveth the whole world" (Revelation 12:9).

Learn More: Matthew 12:24; 13:19 / 2 Corinthians 4:4 / Ephesians 2:2 /
1 Thessalonians 3:5 / 2 Thessalonians 2:3

SEE THROUGH A GLASS, DARKLY

For now we see through a glass, darkly; but then face to face. 1 CORINTHIANS 13:12

This verse is part of the famous "love chapter" of the Bible written by the apostle Paul. He declared that no spiritual gift exercised by believers is superior to love. All our good deeds, unless exercised in love, amount to nothing.

The apostle realized that understanding spiritual concepts like unselfish love is a challenge for earth-bound believers. He called on the image of the mirrors of Bible times to illustrate this truth. These metal mirrors gave a poor reflection not a clear vision of a person's facial features. But one day we will understand all spiritual matters more clearly when we are face-to-face with the Lord in heaven.

No matter how mature we may be in our faith, we have an imperfect understanding of God and how He works in the world. But the path of love will take us to the time when He reveals Himself completely. Then we will have full insight into His nature, just as He has known us so perfectly during our life on earth.

Learn More: Deuteronomy 29:29 / Isaiah 40:5 / Luke 12:2 / 1 Peter 5:1

SERVANTS OF CORRUPTION

While they promise them liberty, they themselves are the servants of corruption. 2 PETER 2:19

The apostle Peter wrote his second letter to condemn heretical teachings in the church. False prophets had wormed their way into the fellowship, convincing people that their freedom in Christ allowed them to sin as much as they liked. These teachers did not live up to the ethical demands of the Gospel but gave in to the worst impulses of human nature. To Peter these misguided people were "servants of corruption." Touting Christian liberty, they were actually slaves to their own lust.

During His earthly ministry, Jesus spoke to this problem by declaring, "Whosoever committeth sin is the servant of sin" (John 8:34). The New Century Version makes an important distinction with this rendering of the verse: "Everyone who *lives* in sin is a slave to sin" (italics added).

Sin inevitably creeps into every life. But true believers don't continue in their wrongdoing; they confess their failures and seek Jesus' cleansing forgiveness. The apostle John expressed it like this: "If we confess our sins, he is faithful and just to forgive us our sins, and to cleanse us from all unrighteousness" (1 John 1:9).

Learn More: Romans 6:17–20 / James 5:16

SHEEP OF GOD'S PASTURE

So we thy people and sheep of thy pasture will give thee thanks for ever. Psalm 79:13

Psalm 79 laments the destruction of Jerusalem and the scattering of God's people. Yet the psalmist was confident that the Lord had not abandoned His people. They were still the "sheep of His pasture" who looked to Him for leadership. The image of God's people as sheep appears often throughout the Bible.

- The Israelites often disobeyed the Lord and were like sheep without a shepherd.
- God led His people like sheep during the Exodus from Egypt.
- The psalmist confessed that he had gone astray like a lost sheep.
- The prophet Jeremiah condemned Judah's leaders who led God's sheep into idolatry.

Jesus picked up on many of these images from the Old Testament and gave them new meaning. He condemned the Pharisees and Sadducees as the Jewish leaders who were misleading the people of His time. He offered Himself as the ultimate guide who would never lead people down the wrong path. "My sheep hear my voice," He declared, "and I know them, and they follow me" (John 10:27).

Learn More: 1 Kings 22:17 / Psalm 74:1; 78:52; 95:7; 100:3; 119:176 / Jeremiah 23:1 / Matthew 9:36

SHINE LIKE THE STARS

They that turn many to righteousness as the stars for ever and ever. Daniel 12:3

The prophet Daniel ministered in Babylon during the exile of God's people to that pagan land. He is known for his wisdom and his predictions of the last days and the second coming of Christ.

In this particular verse, the prophet had encouraging words for believers during the final days of world history. In contrast to the dark future that many will experience, believers will shine like the stars. Their eternal destiny is assured because of their commitment to Jesus Christ as Lord and Savior.

Those believers who "turn many to righteousness" during these perilous times are especially commended by Daniel. Until the very end of time, Jesus' followers have an obligation to proclaim the message of the Gospel to a lost and dying world.

The stars of heaven are a favorite poetic image of biblical writers. The Lord assured Abraham that his descendants would be as numerous as the stars. The final days of divine judgment were described as a time when the stars would not shine. The psalmist called on all the stars to praise the Creator of the universe.

Learn More: Genesis 15:5 / Psalm 148:3 / Joel 2:10

SINS CAST INTO THE SEA

Thou wilt cast all their sins into the depths of the sea. Micah 7:19

The prophet Micah delivered his message to God's people at about the same time as the prophet Isaiah. Micah made it clear that the nations of both Judah and Israel would be punished by the Lord for their sin and rebellion. But God would eventually restore them through a remnant of people who remained faithful to Him.

The prophet called upon the strongest possible imagery to describe this process of redemption. To cast something into the sea was to remove it as far away as possible, never to be seen again. The Lord's forgiveness, based on the repentance of His people, would have no strings attached. They would be restored to full fellowship with Him.

This image is similar to one used by Isaiah. The Lord declared that He would sweep away the sins of His people "like a cloud that disappears into the air" (Isaiah 44:22 ncv). Both these figures of speech looked forward to the Gospel age, when the redemptive death of Jesus provided forgiveness and salvation for those who claim Him as Savior and Lord.

Learn More: Psalm 32:1; 103:10 / Isaiah 1:18 / Jeremiah 31:34 / Romans 6:23

SIN WRITTEN WITH AN IRON PEN

The sin of Judah is written with a pen of iron. JEREMIAH 17:1

This verse contains one of the prophet Jeremiah's most graphic descriptions of the sin of the people of Judah. It was as if someone had taken an iron pen, or stylus, and engraved their sins on their rebellious hearts. The implication is that their wrongdoing was so grievous that it could not be easily blotted out or erased. The only cure for their deep-rooted evil was to forsake their worship of false gods and turn back to the one true God.

As a spiritual symbol in the Bible, iron depicts hardness, permanence, or durability. For example, people who trusted in the Lord would be outfitted with shoes of iron. A yoke or iron on one's neck depicted helplessness and submission.

In their stubborn refusal to follow the Lord's commands, the Israelites had necks of iron. The iron teeth of the fourth successive beast in Daniel's vision symbolized the formidable power of the future nation of Rome. The Lord made the prophet Jeremiah like an iron pillar so he could stand his ground as he delivered his unpopular message of divine judgment to the nation of Judah.

Learn More: Deuteronomy 28:48; 33:25 / Isaiah 48:4 / Jeremiah 1:18 / Daniel 7:7

SITTING DOWN AND RISING UP

Behold their sitting down, and their rising up; I am their musick. LAMENTATIONS 3:61, 63

The book of Lamentations is appropriately named. Written by the prophet Jeremiah, it is a sad lament over the destruction of Jerusalem by the Babylonian army. The prophet was ridiculed and imprisoned for warning the nation of Judah about this coming punishment from the Lord. Sometimes, as in this verse, he voiced his own frustration over being taunted and treated as an outcast by his fellow citizens. He resented their constant hounding—whether they were sitting or standing—and serving as a target of "their mocking songs" (NLT).

Jeremiah is known both for his poetic language and the physical acts he performed to drive home the Lord's message. For example, he wore a yoke around his neck to demonstrate that Judah should submit to the pagan nation of Babylon (Jeremiah 27:2).

But to show that he was more than a pessimistic killjoy, Jeremiah bought a piece of property in Judah. This plot would certainly lose value during the Babylonian occupation. But the prophet's act declared that the land would eventually become fruitful again when the people returned from exile in a foreign land (Jeremiah 32:8–9).

Learn More: Job 30:9 / Jeremiah 20:7 / Lamentations 3:14

SKIN OF THE TEETH

I am escaped with the skin of my teeth. JOB 19:20

These words from Job to his three friends show a desperate man in deep grief over the losses he had experienced. All his earthly possessions had been destroyed, and his ten children had died in a tragic accident.

In addition to all these tragic events, Job's entire body broke out in troublesome sores. He was reduced to sitting on an ash heap, scraping his itching skin with a shard of pottery. No wonder he felt miserable and at the point of death. The Good News Translation renders his words like this: "My skin hangs loose on my bones; I have barely escaped with my life."

The idiomatic phrase "by the skin of my teeth" is still heard today. A student might say, "I passed that course by the skin of my teeth." It refers to the razor-thin margin between failure and success—some action accomplished but just barely so.

The Bible contains other "skin of my teeth" accounts. For example, Joseph was almost killed by his brothers but was sold into slavery instead. God preserved his life and ultimately used him to save the rest of his family from starvation.

Learn More: Genesis 45:3–7 / 1 Samuel 20:3

SLEEP WITH ONE'S FATHERS

So David slept with his fathers, and was buried in the city of David. 1 KINGS 2:10

When David died, he had reigned as king for about forty years—seven years over the southern tribe of Judah and thirty-three years over all the tribes of Israel. The phrase "slept with his fathers" is a poetic way of saying he joined his ancestors who had died before him. His burial in the city of Jerusalem was considered a great honor, since bodies were usually interred outside the walls of cities in Bible times.

Several other Israelite kings who followed David were also said to sleep with their fathers after they died. These included Joash, Jotham, Hezekiah, and Jehoiakim. Sleep was a common biblical euphemism for death, comparable to statements that people "pass away" or "go to their heavenly reward" that are commonly heard today.

Jesus also used the image of sleep for the daughter of Jairus who had died. "The damsel is not dead, but sleepeth," He told the crowd (Mark 5:39). Then He raised her from the dead and presented her to her parents. The apostle Paul also assured the Christians at Thessalonica that they would eventually join other believers who had died, or were asleep.

Learn More: 2 Kings 13:13; 15:38; 20:21; 24:6 / Acts 7:60 / 1 Corinthians 15:6 / 1 Thessalonians 4:13

SMOOTHER THAN BUTTER

The words of his mouth were smoother than butter, but war was in his heart. PSALM 55:21

This psalm was written by a person who had been betrayed by a close friend. This becomes clear in verses 12 and 13: "It was not an enemy that reproached me; then I could have borne it. . . . But it was thou, a man mine equal, my guide, and mine acquaintance." This person apparently assured the psalmist with comforting words—they were "smoother than butter"—but then betrayed him by his actions.

Some interpreters believe this psalm was written by King David after he was betrayed by Ahithophel, one of his closest advisors. Ahithophel joined David's son Absalom in his attempt to seize the throne from his father. The revolt failed. Ahithophel knew his days were numbered so he committed suicide (2 Samuel 17:23).

Ahithophel is the very personification of hypocrisy—to say one thing while doing the opposite. Students of the Bible have noted the parallel between him and Judas, the disciple who betrayed Jesus. Judas also assured Jesus of his loyalty but sold the Lord out to the Jewish authorities for thirty pieces of silver. Like Ahithophel, Judas also took his own life.

Learn More: Matthew 26:48 / Mark 14:11

SNARE OF THE DEVIL

That they may recover themselves out of the snare of the devil. 2 TIMOTHY 2:26

The apostle Paul's second letter to Timothy is one of his three "pastoral epistles." The other two are 1 Timothy and Titus. They are called "pastoral" because they deal with issues of church leadership. They show the apostle's concern for effective church organization and administration.

In this verse Paul told his young missionary associate how to deal with believers who had fallen into sin. He was not to be argumentative in his approach but to deal with them patiently to show them the error of their ways. The goal was to lead them to repent of their sins and escape from the devil's trap into which they had fallen.

A snare was a net made from cords, used to trap birds and other small animals. The devil, or Satan, uses every trick in his book—half-truths, outright lies, and manipulation—to draw people into his snare. Christians are not immune to his tactics. Once the trap springs shut, nothing but confession, repentance, and turning to the Lord for forgiveness can free believers from the devil's grasp.

Learn More: Psalm 141:9 / Proverbs 29:6 / 1 Timothy 3:7; 6:9

SOAR LIKE AN EAGLE

But they that wait upon the Lord. . .shall mount up with wings as eagles. Isaiah 40:31

In this verse the prophet Isaiah peered into the future and described the future restoration of God's people. After being exiled in a foreign land, they would be energized and renewed back in their own country. The prophet called on three familiar images—walking, running, and soaring like an eagle—to symbolize this glorious restoration.

Eagles were majestic birds admired for their ability to soar for hours on wind currents. King Solomon marveled at "the way of an eagle in the air" (Proverbs 30:19). This familiar sight led Moses to declare that God led the Israelites out of Egyptian slavery "on eagles' wings" (Exodus 19:4). Job complained that his earthly life seemed to slip away as swiftly as "the eagle that hasteth to the prey" (Job 9:26).

The prophet Jeremiah used eagle imagery to describe God's judgment. He declared that the nation of Judah would be defeated by warriors from Babylon whose horses would be "swifter than eagles" (Jeremiah 4:13).

Learn More: Deuteronomy 28:49 / 2 Samuel 1:23 / Psalm 103:5 / Ezekiel 17:7 / Revelation 4:7

SOUL OF GOD

Your new moons and your appointed feasts my soul hateth. Isaiah 1:14

The people of Isaiah's time were practicing the externals of religion but living as they pleased. God declared in strong language that He hated what they were doing. His "soul," in this context, refers to His total personality. Thus, the New International Version renders His words as "your appointed festivals I hate with all my being."

Several other references to the soul of God appear in the Bible. His soul detested idolatry among His people. His soul was grieved for Israel when they suffered hardship during the period of the judges. After the exile, He would restore His people with His whole heart and soul.

In other contexts in the Bible, the word *soul* has a variety of meanings. It can refer to an individual, as in God's declaration that "all souls are mine" (Ezekiel 18:4); to the spiritual side of human nature, as in the soul of the psalmist longing for the Lord (Psalm 42:1); and to a human life, as in Jesus' question "What is a man profited, if he shall gain the whole world, and lose his own soul?" (Matthew 16:26).

Learn More: Leviticus 26:11, 30 / Judges 10:16 / Psalm 11:5 / Jeremiah 5:9; 13:17

SOW THE WIND

For they have sown the wind, and they shall reap the whirlwind. Hosea 8:7

The prophet Hosea spoke these words to the wayward people of the northern kingdom of Israel. Because of their worship of false gods, they would experience God's wrath. Their evil deeds, which Hosea characterized as "sowing the wind," would be gathered as a harvest of disaster—a whirlwind of destruction. His prediction was fulfilled several decades later when Israel was invaded by the Assyrian army.

In modern usage, to "sow the wind and reap the whirlwind" is to experience a disastrous result from an act that seemed perfectly harmless. This principle of sowing abundantly from planted seeds was an apt metaphor in the agricultural society of Bible times. The image is usually applied to sin and its inevitable results.

In his response to Job's claim that he was suffering unjustly, Eliphaz declared, "They that plow iniquity, and sow wickedness, reap the same" (Job 4:8). But another Bible writer turned this principle around and put it in more positive terms: "The wicked worketh a deceitful work: but to him that soweth righteousness shall be a sure reward" (Proverbs 11:18).

Learn More: Proverbs 22:8 / Hosea 10:12 / Galatians 6:7

SPEECH SEASONED WITH SALT

Let your speech be always with grace, seasoned with salt. COLOSSIANS 4:6

The apostle Paul gave the Colossian believers good advice on how to interact with others, especially nonbelievers who might question them about their faith. They were to be gentle, respectful, and graceful in their replies. But at the same time, they were to flavor their words with a touch of salt. This is a poetic way of saying they should be enthusiastic in their witness in order to win a hearing for the Gospel.

Many nonbelievers think of the Christian faith as a dull, stagnant enterprise. And too many Christians contribute to this misunderstanding by their I-dare-you-to-drag-a-laugh-out-of-me approach to life. Followers of Jesus should be the most zealous people on the block because of the meaning and purpose that He brings to their lives. And this inner glow should show on their faces and in their relationships with others.

Like the apostle Paul, King Solomon knew the value of a positive attitude and an optimistic approach to life. "A merry heart doeth good like a medicine," he declared, "but a broken spirit drieth the bones" (Proverbs 17:22).

Learn More: Psalm 19:14 / Proverbs 16:24; 18:21; 25:11; 29:20 /
2 Timothy 2:14 / James 3:5-8

SPRING OF THE DAY

It came to pass about the spring of the day, that Samuel called Saul. 1 SAMUEL 9:26

The Lord had revealed to the prophet Samuel that Saul was His choice to serve as the first king of Israel. The two got up early and set off together. As they traveled, Samuel anointed Saul by pouring oil on his head.

The phrase "the spring of the day" is a poetic way of referring to the first light of early morning. Most modern translations render the phrase as "dawn" or "daybreak." Samuel apparently wanted to get an early start on this historic day that marked a turning point in the history of the nation of Israel.

This poetic imagery is also used in one of the titles by which Jesus is known. Zacharias, father of John the Baptist, called the coming Messiah "the dayspring from on high" (Luke 1:78). The word means "a rising up," and it referred to the rising of the sun as well as the first appearance of stars at night. Thus, Zacharias identified Jesus as the bright light that God was sending into a dark world.

Learn More: Judges 19:25 / Job 38:12

STIFF-NECKED PEOPLE

I have seen this people, and, behold, it is a stiffnecked people. EXODUS 32:9

While Moses was receiving the Ten Commandments from the Lord, the Israelites were creating a calf idol from the gold they had taken out of Egypt. Ironically, this was a flagrant disobedience of the first commandment that God issued to Moses: "Thou shalt have no other gods before me" (Exodus 20:3). The Lord condemned their action, calling them a "stiffnecked people."

This word refers to a stubborn, arrogant, and unyielding attitude. It was used of draft animals such as oxen. Sometimes they were difficult to yoke, and they refused to follow directions while pulling a plow. It was a perfect image of the tendency of God's people to rebel against Him rather than follow His commands.

This phrase appears several times in the Bible. The prophet Jeremiah urged the people of Judah not to harden their necks against the Lord. In the New Testament, Stephen was stoned to death by a crowd of Jewish zealots after he accused them of being "stiffnecked and uncircumcised in heart and ears" when they put Jesus to death (Acts 7:51). The word *stiff-hearted* expresses the same idea.

Learn More: 2 Kings 17:14 / Psalm 75:4-5 / Jeremiah 7:26; 32:33 / Ezekiel 2:4

STRANGERS AND PILGRIMS ON EARTH

They were strangers and pilgrims on the earth. Hebrews 11:13

Hebrews 11 is known as the great "faith chapter" of the Bible. Several heroes of the faith from the Old Testament are mentioned to encourage the readers of Hebrews to remain strong in their own faith. These people are called "strangers and pilgrims on earth" because their relationship to the Lord was more important to them than riches or fame or any other earthly prize.

To use another biblical image, they were "in" the world, but they lived as citizens of another kingdom—the kingdom of God. The apostle Paul expressed the principle like this: "Set your affection on things above, not on things on the earth" (Colossians 3:2).

The apostle Peter also referred to believers as "strangers and pilgrims" whose hope was set on spiritual matters and not on worldly affairs. Since they had been redeemed from slavery to sin, they were to "abstain from fleshly lusts" that threatened to drag them back into the worldly life from which they had been delivered (1 Peter 2:11).

Learn More: John 15:19; 18:36 / Romans 12:2 / Ephesians 2:12 / Colossians 2:8 / Titus 2:12

STUMBLING BLOCK TO THE WEAK

Take heed lest. . .this liberty of yours become a stumblingblock. 1 Corinthians 8:9

In this chapter the apostle Paul dealt with the problem of meat sacrificed to pagan gods. Some believers at Corinth felt that eating this meat was no problem for followers of Christ. But others felt the practice condoned the sin of idolatry. Paul urged the people not to eat the meat if doing so was a "stumblingblock" to weaker believers. The Good News Translation says the more mature believers should not let their "freedom of action make those who are weak in the faith fall into sin."

The word *stumbling block* appears several times in the Bible. Literally, it was a rock or similar obstacle that caused people to fall. The Lord showed His compassion for the handicapped by ordering His people not to deliberately place such an object in the path of the blind.

In a figurative sense, the word refers to setting up the conditions that prevent a person from doing the right thing. The apostle Paul put it like this: "No man [should] put a stumblingblock or an occasion to fall in his brother's way" (Romans 14:13).

Learn More: Leviticus 19:14 / Isaiah 57:14 / Jeremiah 6:21 / Ezekiel 14:4 / 1 Corinthians 1:23 / Revelation 2:14

SUN OF RIGHTEOUSNESS

Unto you that fear my name shall the Sun of righteousness arise. Malachi 4:2

The prophet Malachi looked forward to the future day of the Lord and second coming of the Messiah. God would punish the wicked with wrathful fire, but the righteous remnant would experience the gentle warming that radiates from the wings of the "Sun of righteousness."

This prophecy was fulfilled with the healing ministry of Jesus. Most of His miracles were performed for people who were suffering from various physical problems—blindness, deafness, leprosy, and possession by evil spirits. But in many of His miracles, He went beyond healing the body to healing the soul and spirit through forgiveness of sin. For example, after healing a paralyzed man, Jesus said, "Son, be of good cheer; thy sins be forgiven thee" (Matthew 9:2).

This title of Jesus, Sun of righteousness, brings to mind His role as a never-failing source of strength and guidance for believers, just as the sun is a constant presence in the sky. This awareness should lead us to praise Him, just as the psalmist directed: "From the rising of the sun unto the going down of the same the Lord's name is to be praised" (Psalm 113:3)

Learn More: Psalm 148:3 / Matthew 13:43

SWORDS BEATEN INTO PLOWSHARES

They shall beat their swords into plowshares. . .neither shall they learn war any more. ISAIAH 2:4

This verse is part of Isaiah's prophecy about the end time. In that future day, Jerusalem will become the center of the earth. All nations will flock to this ideal place to learn about the ways of the Lord. It will be a time of universal peace when all weapons of war will be fashioned into tools of peace.

The prophet Joel reversed this imagery in his look toward that future time. The tables would be turned against the wicked when the righteous beat their agricultural implements into weapons and declare, "I am strong" (Joel 3:10).

War and its devastation are mentioned often in the Bible in both literal and symbolic terms. The Lord denied David the privilege of building the temple because he had been "a man of war" (1 Chronicles 28:3). King Solomon declared that the pursuit of wisdom was "better than weapons of war" (Ecclesiastes 9:18). The psalmist was confident that God had the power to cause war "to cease unto the end of the earth" (Psalm 46:9).

Learn More: Ecclesiastes 3:8 / Micah 4:3 / Matthew 24:6

TABERNACLE FOR THE SUN

In them hath he set a tabernacle for the sun. PSALM 19:4

This psalm is filled with wonder at the sky and its heavenly bodies. "The heavens declare the glory of God," the psalmist declares in the first verse, "and the firmament [the dome formed by the sky] sheweth his handywork." Although the heavenly bodies were silent, their imposing appearance sent a message "through all the earth," bearing witness to the awesome Creator who brought them into being.

The psalmist was particularly impressed that God provided a tabernacle, or tent, as a dwelling place for the sun. It seemed to go into this shelter at night then emerge the next morning. We moderns realize that the rising and setting of the sun is caused by the rotation of the earth on its axis. But this scientific explanation seems bland and boring in comparison to the psalmist's more vivid expression.

The term *tabernacle* is used in several other figurative ways in the Bible. For example, the apostle Paul referred to our material bodies as impermanent tabernacles. But, he declared, believers have a "house not made with hands, eternal in the heavens" (2 Corinthians 5:1).

Learn More: Job 11:14; 36:29 / Psalm 46:4 / Hebrews 9:11 / 2 Peter 1:14

TALE THAT IS TOLD

We spend our years as a tale that is told. PSALM 90:9

This is the only psalm in the book of Psalms attributed to Moses. He may have written it while the Israelites were wandering aimlessly in the wilderness. God directed that an entire generation would die there as punishment for their lack of trust in Him (Numbers 14:22–23). As Moses watched these people perish, he lamented the brevity and uncertainty of life, comparing our brief earthly existence to "a tale that is told."

Most modern English translations of this phrase have life ending with either a "sigh" (NRSV) or a "groan" (NLT), based on the original Hebrew text. But the King James rendering has persisted into modern times. It has been immortalized in Hamlet's words in the play by William Shakespeare:

Life's but a walking shadow, a poor player
That struts and frets his hour upon the stage
And then is heard no more: it is a tale
Told by an idiot, full of sound and fury,
Signifying nothing.

This pessimistic view of life stands in contrast to the biblical view. Life is more than a tale that is told when it's dedicated to the Lord and His service.

Learn More: Matthew 6:25 / Luke 12:15 / John 6:35 / Romans 6:4 / 1 Timothy 4:8

TEETH SET ON EDGE

The fathers have eaten a sour grape, and the children's teeth are set on edge. JEREMIAH 31:29

The prophet Jeremiah refused to let the people of Judah make excuses for their sin. He denied the proverb that sour grapes eaten by parents would cause their children to have a bitter taste on the edge of their teeth. The people of Judah had no one but themselves to blame for their wrongdoing.

In later years this principle was echoed by the prophet Ezekiel. He ministered among God's people while they were in exile in a foreign land. "The son shall not bear the iniquity of the father," he declared, "neither shall the father bear the iniquity of the son" (Ezekiel 18:20).

Teeth are often spoken of in a figurative sense in the Bible. The teeth of the wicked are compared to swords. In his suffering, Job felt as if the Lord were gnashing His teeth against him—a symbol of disgust and rejection. The nation that would devastate Judah was characterized as having the teeth of a lion.

Learn More: Job 16:9 / Proverbs 30:14 / Joel 1:6

THIEF IN THE NIGHT

The day of the Lord so cometh as a thief in the night. 1 THESSALONIANS 5:2

When and how Jesus will return is the theme of Paul's first letter to believers in the city of Thessalonica. Paul used the image of a thief who strikes during the night to show that Jesus' second coming would happen when no one expected it. Just like the break-in of a burglar when no one is home, Jesus' return will be a total surprise.

During His earthly ministry, Jesus told the parable of the wise and unwise wedding guests to emphasize this point. Five of these women brought oil for their lamps in case they had to wait for the bridegroom to appear. But the other five did not bring any oil, so they missed the opportunity to welcome the groom. Jesus' point was clear: believers should be watchful and ready for His return at any time. "Watch therefore," He cautioned, "for ye know neither the day nor the hour wherein the Son of man cometh" (Matthew 25:13).

Learn More: Matthew 24:43; 25:1–12 / Luke 12:39 / 1 Thessalonians 5:4 / 2 Peter 3:10 / Revelation 3:3; 16:15

THORN IN THE FLESH

There was given to me a thorn in the flesh, the messenger of Satan. 2 CORINTHIANS 12:7

In the verses just before this passage, the apostle Paul describes several visions that the Lord had revealed to him. In spite of these heavenly revelations, he was suffering some mysterious malady that he referred to as his "thorn in the flesh."

This may have been some physical problem, such as malaria, epilepsy, migraine headaches, or poor eyesight. All these possibilities have been suggested by Bible interpreters. Or the affliction may have been some strong temptation that he struggled to resist or perhaps opposition from his enemies. Whatever it was, it was painful, and Paul asked the Lord to remove it.

God refused this request, but He gave the apostle something even better: the grace to live with the problem. This led to Paul's conviction that God's power is made perfect in human weakness. "Most gladly. . .will I rather glory in my infirmities," he declared, "that the power of Christ may rest upon me" (2 Corinthians 12:9). He could endure this affliction because of the victorious power of Christ in his life.

Learn More: 1 Corinthians 9:22 / 2 Corinthians 6:10; 12:8 / Philippians 4:13

TINGLING EARS

I will do a thing. . .at which both the ears of every one that heareth it shall tingle. 1 SAMUEL 3:11

The Lord delivered this message to the boy Samuel, who was living with Eli, the high priest. Eli's two priestly sons were using the privileges of their office to commit adultery and to steal meat offered as sacrifices by the people.

The Lord told Samuel that He would discipline these priests for their sins. He would also punish their father, Eli, because he had failed to correct his sons. Divine intervention would be so severe that the ears of all the people would tingle when they heard about it.

This idiom of "tingling ears" is similar to a modern expression. A person who has a frightening experience can feel the "hair stand up on the back of his neck." The Contemporary English Version renders the Lord's words like this: "I am going to do something in Israel that will shock everyone who hears about it!"

The Lord made good on His promise. In a battle with the Philistines, Eli's two sons were killed. When he heard the news, Eli fell backward and died from a broken neck.

Learn More: 1 Samuel 4:10–18 / 2 Kings 21:12 / Jeremiah 19:3

TO AND FRO

They are the eyes of the Lord, which run to and fro through the whole earth. ZECHARIAH 4:10

Zechariah is one of three prophets in the Old Testament known as "postexilic" prophets. The other two are Haggai and Malachi. They delivered their messages during the turbulent period after God's people returned to Judah following their period of exile in a foreign land.

Zechariah is known as a prophet of hope and encouragement. The people had started rebuilding the temple under the leadership of a man named Zerubbabel. But their enthusiasm had begun to lag. Zechariah called on them to get busy and finish the job. The eyes of the Lord ran "to and fro" throughout the earth—that is, He knew everything that happened in the world. Surely they could complete this important project under His watchful eyes.

The Lord told the prophet Jeremiah to run "to and fro through the streets of Jerusalem" to see if he could find one person who remained faithful to the Lord (Jeremiah 5:1). This imagery shows how deeply the sin of rebellion against divine authority had infected God's people.

Learn More: Job 1:7 / Zechariah 1:10

TONGUE STUCK TO THE ROOF OF THE MOUTH

If I do not remember thee, let my tongue cleave to the roof of my mouth. PSALM 137:6

This psalm was written while God's people were in exile in a foreign land. The psalmist expressed his anguish at being separated from the things he valued most, especially the city of Jerusalem and the temple where the people worshipped the Lord.

The writer prayed that Jerusalem would never fade from his memory. If this should happen, his ability to speak ought to be taken away—expressed as having his tongue stick to the roof of his mouth. The Good News Translation expresses his thought like this: "May I never be able to sing again if I do not remember [Jerusalem]."

To "hold one's tongue" is another metaphor for silence in the Bible. Job promised to hold his tongue if the Lord would help him understand why he was being subjected to such suffering. And Queen Esther refused to remain silent when her people, the Jews, were threatened by the evil Haman's execution campaign.

Learn More: Esther 7:4 / Job 6:24; 29:10 / Psalm 22:15 / Ezekiel 3:26 / Amos 6:10 / Habakkuk 1:13

TOSSED LIKE A BALL

He will surely violently turn and toss thee like a ball into a large country. ISAIAH 22:18

These words from the prophet Isaiah refer to Shebna, an official in the administration of King Hezekiah of Judah. Isaiah prophesied that Judah would fall to a foreign nation. But Shebna went about his duties as if the nation had nothing to fear. He actually built an ornate tomb for himself that he expected to be buried in one day (Isaiah 22:15–16). The prophet declared that he would never use the burial chamber. Instead he would be "tossed like a ball" into a foreign country, where he would meet his death. This poetic expression shows that he would lose his power and offer no resistance to a superior military force that would overrun the nation of Judah.

In these verses Shebna is identified as a treasurer, leading to speculation that he was one of the chief aides to King Hezekiah. Isaiah's blunt assessment of Shebna's future shows the courage with which he spoke the Lord's message to the most powerful people of his day. He was equally forthright in delivering bad news to the king himself.

Learn More: 2 Kings 20:1

TREASURE IN EARTHEN VESSELS

But we have this treasure in earthen vessels. 2 CORINTHIANS 4:7

The apostle Paul realized what a precious thing the Gospel was because it had transformed many lives, including his own. Equally amazing to him was the fact that God had placed the proclamation of this message in the hands of weak human beings.

Believers were responsible for spreading the good news of the Gospel to others, although they were subject to the sins and temptations of the flesh. This was like a priceless treasure being stored in a common clay pot. As the New Living Translation renders his words, "We now have this light shining in our hearts, but we ourselves are like fragile clay jars containing this great treasure."

This amazing fact meant that believers should not take credit for the lives that were changed as a result of their witnessing efforts. This happened because of the power of God, not as a result of their persuasive words. Jesus expressed the same truth when He encouraged His followers to depend on Him when they witnessed to others and were subjected to persecution. He promised that the Holy Spirit "shall teach you in the same hour what ye ought to say" (Luke 12:12).

Learn More: Romans 1:16; 12:3

TREE BY THE WATER

And he shall be like a tree planted by the rivers of water. PSALM 1:3

This verse compares the righteous person to a tree that flourishes in a well-watered spot. In the hot, dry climate of Palestine, this was an apt description of those who followed the Lord. They would be abundantly blessed because of their faithfulness.

Trees are often spoken of symbolically in the Bible. For example, the psalmist was shocked to see wicked people enjoying prosperity like a flourishing tree. The writer of Proverbs noted that positive and wholesome words were comparable to a healthy tree. The prophet Isaiah predicted better days for God's people after their exile in a foreign land came to an end; they would be renewed by the Lord, just like a willow tree beside a flowing stream.

All trees, representing the entire natural world, are encouraged to add their voices to the universal song of praise that the Lord deserves. "Sing. . .O forest, and every tree therein," the prophet Isaiah declared, "for the LORD hath redeemed Jacob, and glorified himself in Israel" (Isaiah 44:23).

Learn More: Psalm 37:35; 52:8; 92:12 / Proverbs 13:12; 15:4 / Isaiah 61:3

TRUSTING IN A SPIDER'S WEB

Whose hope shall be cut off, and whose trust shall be a spider's web. JOB 8:14

These verses were spoken by Job's friend Bildad in response to Job's claim that he was being punished unfairly by the Lord. Bildad believed that all suffering was a direct result of a person's sin. He had some dire words for those who placed their trust in anything other than the mighty God who could do no wrong.

Bildad compared this misplaced confidence to a familiar image from nature. The New Living Translation renders his words like this: "Their confidence hangs by a thread. They are leaning on a spider's web."

Trusting the Lord rather than depending on things that are destined to fail is a familiar refrain throughout the Bible. The latter include riches, military might, alliances with foreign nations, and human wisdom and understanding. The psalmist had discovered a source of strength that would never let him down: "They that trust in the LORD shall be as mount Zion, which cannot be removed, but abideth for ever" (Psalm 125:1).

Learn More: 2 Kings 18:20–21 / Job 15:31 / Psalms 16:1; 20:7; 44:6; 49:6 / Proverbs 3:5–6; 11:28 / Jeremiah 17:5

TRY THE REINS

I the Lord search the heart, I try the reins. JEREMIAH 17:10

The word *reins* in this passage comes from a Hebrew word that means "kidneys." It is used here in a figurative sense to express a person's inner being, just like we speak of the heart today as the center of human emotions and feelings. An expression like "he has a big heart" doesn't refer to the physical organ in the body but to a person's generosity toward others.

The Lord delivered this verse through the prophet Jeremiah. It expresses the idea that God was probing deeply into the consciousness of the people of Judah to test their loyalty. Could He count on their faithfulness, or were they on the verge of turning aside to worship false gods?

Three modern words in the English language—heart, mind, and soul—express the same meaning as the biblical *reins*. The phrase "try the reins" is rendered by two modern translations as "examine the mind" (NIV) and "test the heart" (CSB).

Learn More: Job 16:13 / Psalm 26:2; 139:13 / Proverbs 23:16 / Revelation 2:23

TURN NOT TO THE RIGHT OR LEFT

Ye shall not turn aside to the right hand or to the left. DEUTERONOMY 5:32

The Greek word behind the title *Deuteronomy* means "second law." The book consists of a series of speeches from Moses, who led the Israelites out of their Egyptian slavery. He used the imagery of "turning not to the right or left" to encourage the people to remain faithful to the Lord. They were to obey the commands the Lord had laid down for His people at Mount Sinai.

Moses knew the people would be surrounded by a pagan culture once they entered the land of promise. He warned them against the danger of these false worship systems. In modern terminology, we would put Moses' words something like this: "Don't compromise your beliefs. Stay true to what you have been taught by the Lord."

This image of not turning aside may have been a familiar proverb in Old Testament times. King Solomon declared in his book of wisdom sayings, "Turn not to the right hand nor to the left: remove thy foot from evil" (Proverbs 4:27).

Learn More: Deuteronomy 28:14 / Joshua 1:7; 23:6 / 2 Kings 22:2 / 2 Chronicles 34:2

TWINKLING OF AN EYE

We shall all be changed. . .in the twinkling of an eye. 1 CORINTHIANS 15:51-52

These verses from the apostle Paul deal with the resurrection of believers at the second coming of Christ. Some people in the church at Corinth wondered whether this resurrection would be physical or spiritual in nature. Paul made it clear that the physical bodies of believers would be raised and that it would happen instantly at Jesus' return—in the "twinkling of an eye."

This is the only place in the Bible where the word *twinkling* appears. The Contemporary English Version renders this phase as "quicker than the blink of an eye." But the human eye is spoken of in a figurative sense throughout the Bible.

- Any Canaanites left in the land would be like pricks in the eyes of the Israelites.
- To do what was right in one's own eyes was to disobey the Lord.
- To find favor in the Lord's eyes was to be approved by Him.
- To have lofty eyes was to be puffed up with pride.

Learn More: Numbers 33:55 / Judges 17:6 / 2 Samuel 15:25 / Psalm 131:1

VAIN JANGLING

From which some having swerved have turned aside unto vain jangling. 1 TIMOTHY 1:5-6

The apostle Paul's first letter to Timothy opens with a warning not to pay attention to certain false teachers in the church. They were concentrating on "fables and endless genealogies" (verse 4) that were causing divisions. Paul urged his young missionary associate to ignore their talk and to emphasize the things that really mattered: love, a pure heart, and a genuine faith in the Lord.

Paul used the phrase "vain jangling" to describe these troublemakers. This description is only one word in the Greek text. It refers to something that is empty and useless. The modern translations show great creativity in their rendering of the word: "fruitless discussion" (HCSB), "empty talk" (CEV), "useless talk" (NCV), "idle talk" (NKJV), and "talk that doesn't mean anything" (CEB).

Paul used the same Greek word in his letter to Titus, another missionary associate. The apostle described the false teachers whom Titus was dealing with in the church on the island of Crete as "vain talkers" (Titus 1:10). The Common English Bible refers to them as "loudmouths."

Learn More: 1 Timothy 6:3 / 2 Peter 2:17 / Jude 12-13

VINE AND FIG TREE

Judah and Israel dwelt safely, every man under his vine and under his fig tree. 1 KINGS 4:25

Solomon succeeded his father, David, as king over all the tribes of Israel. Solomon was noted for his wisdom and administrative ability, the expansion of trade with other countries, and the construction of the temple. His forty-year reign was a time of peace and prosperity for the nation and its people.

During this period, according to the writer of 1 Kings, every man lived "under his vine and under his fig tree." These were two major crops of Israel's economy. With every person enjoying a harvest of grapes and figs from these plants, things were going very well indeed. To put it in modern terms, "The economy was booming, and everyone was making good money."

This same figurative phrase appears several other times in the Bible. For example, the prophet Micah predicted that the Messiah would usher in a time when every man would sit under his vine and fig tree—an image of blessing for God's people through the person of His Son.

Learn More: 2 Kings 18:31 / Isaiah 36:16 / Joel 2:22 / Zechariah 3:10

VINEYARD GONE BAD

What could have been done more to my vineyard, that I have not done in it? Isaiah 5:4

This verse is part of a passage known as the prophet Isaiah's "Song of the Vineyard" (Isaiah 5:1–6). He described a man who planted a vineyard in fertile soil and cultivated it with loving care. He also built a winepress in anticipation of harvesting the grapes and processing them into wine for his family's enjoyment. But all this came to naught when the vines produced nothing but wild, bitter grapes.

This parable is actually an indictment of the nation of Israel. The Lord had chosen the Israelites as His special people, bringing them out of slavery and giving them a land of their own. He charged them with the responsibility of serving as His witnesses to the other nations of the world. But they rebelled against Him, ignoring His commandments and worshipping false gods.

When Israel failed the Lord, He sent the Messiah, Jesus Christ, to serve as His ambassador of love. He did not fail in this mission. He is the "true vine" who brings the light of redemption to a sin-stained world.

Learn More: Psalm 80:8 / Jeremiah 2:21 / Hosea 10:1–2 / John 15:1–5

WALKING IN THE LIGHT

If we walk in the light, as he is in the light, we have fellowship one with another. 1 John 1:7

In this verse the apostle John combines two of the most familiar images of the Bible—the concept of walking with God and the light represented by the presence of Jesus.

Walking, as used figuratively in the Bible, refers to one's behavior and way of life. Noah, for example, was a righteous man who "walked with God" during a time when the world was infected with evil. In other passages, to "walk in the ways of the Lord" is to obey His commands. To "walk in darkness" is just the opposite—to reject the Lord and to follow one's own path.

The apostle John may have had these Old Testament figures in mind when he described following Jesus as "walking in the light." Jesus was the eternal truth foretold by the prophets of the past. As the light of the world, He has promised that those who follow Him "shall not walk in darkness, but shall have the light of life" (John 8:12).

Learn More: Genesis 6:9 / Deuteronomy 5:33 / 1 Kings 2:3 / Psalm 82:5 / Isaiah 9:2 / Ephesians 5:8

WATCH IN THE NIGHT

A thousand years in thy sight are but as yesterday. . .as a watch in the night. Psalm 90:4

In this verse the psalmist pointed out how limited humans are in their understanding of God and how He works in the world. A millennium seems like a long time to us, but it is nothing to the Lord but one day after it has disappeared into the mist of the past. A thousand years of history to the Lord is nothing more than the few hours of duty—or a "watch"—for sentries who kept an eye out for suspicious activity during the night.

Jesus also referred to the watch in a figurative way in one of His parables. He told about a man who had been away at a wedding. His household servants didn't know the exact time when he would be home. But they were anxiously waiting, ready to welcome their master as soon as he arrived. "And if he shall come in the second watch, or come in the third watch," Jesus said, "and find them [ready], blessed are those servants" (Luke 12:38).

Jesus' message is clear: believers should be ready and eagerly waiting for the Lord's return at any time.

Learn More: Judges 7:19 / Psalm 63:6 / Matthew 27:66

WATERED GARDEN

And their soul shall be as a watered garden. JEREMIAH 31:12

Chapter 31 of Jeremiah contains prophecies about the restoration of God's people. They will return to their homeland after a period of exile in a foreign land. Their spirit will be like a watered garden—prosperous and content in the land that God promised to give them several centuries before.

This image of a watered garden may harken back to the garden of Eden in the book of Genesis. God created this home for Adam and Eve after He brought the physical world into being. He provided everything they needed to live here in comfort, even providing a river to water its plants and trees. But Adam and Eve were cast out of this paradise because they disobeyed God and ate fruit from a tree He had declared off limits (Genesis 3:22–24).

Perhaps Jeremiah was reminding the people of Judah of the consequences of rebellion against God. Now that they were beginning again in a symbolic new garden, they should renew their dedication to follow His commands.

Learn More: Job 5:10 / Psalm 65:9 / Isaiah 51:3 / Ezekiel 36:35

WAX OLD, WAX STRONG

Joshua waxed old and stricken in age. JOSHUA 23:1

Joshua succeeded Moses as leader of the Israelites. He led the people to take the promised land from the Canaanites. Then he supervised the division of the territory among the twelve tribes. By the time all this had been accomplished, he was an old man. Just like Moses, he had served his purpose, and his leadership of the people would pass to others.

The statement that Joshua "waxed old" is just a poetic way of saying that Joshua was now in his declining years, the common lot of every human being. *Wax* is an obsolete Old English word for "grow" or "become." Thus, the Amplified Version renders the phrase as "Joshua had grown old and advanced in years."

This verb appears numerous times throughout the King James Version. God's anger sometimes "waxed hot" against His people because of their disobedience. The hands of the king of Babylon "waxed feeble," causing him to fall before his enemies. Jesus "waxed strong in spirit" during His growing-up years. Paul and Barnabas "waxed bold" in their witness to Gentiles.

Learn More: Exodus 22:24 / Jeremiah 50:43 / Luke 2:40 / Acts 13:46

WIND OF IDOLATRY

Their molten images are wind and confusion. ISAIAH 41:29

One of the strongest temptations for God's people, the Israelites, was to worship the false gods of the surrounding pagan nations. This always drew the condemnation of God's prophets, including Isaiah. In this verse the prophet described the images of these objects of pagan worship as fakes that had no power. They were nothing but "wind and confusion." In the words of two modern translations, they were "less than a passing breeze" (CEV) and "empty as the wind" (NLT).

Isaiah used even stronger language for false worship in chapter 44 of his book. It was ridiculous, he declared, for human beings to fashion such idols from wood or stone then bow down to worship these objects of their own creation. In a sarcastic tone, the prophet asked, "Shall I fall down to the stock of a tree?" (Isaiah 44:19; *a block of wood*: HCSB).

Wind is cited several times in the Bible as a symbol of vanity and emptiness. Job declared that his life was as fleeting as the wind. The prophet Hosea characterized Israel's rebellion against the Lord as "feed[ing] on wind" (Hosea 12:1).

Learn More: Exodus 20:3 / Job 7:7 / Isaiah 44:9–20 / Jeremiah 5:13 /
1 Corinthians 10:14 / Ephesians 4:14

WINGS OF GOD

The children of men put their trust under the shadow of thy wings. PSALM 36:7

Since the Psalms is a book of poetry, we can safely say that this verse is a purely poetic expression for the guidance and protection of the Lord. To rest under the shadow of God's wings is to find in Him all we need to feel safe and secure.

This image of the wings of God may have been inspired by the eagle, a majestic bird that was a common sight in Israel. Through His spokesman Moses, the Lord reminded His people that He had brought them out of Egyptian slavery "on eagles' wings" (Exodus 19:4). A mother eagle on the nest, feeding its young and teaching them to fly, also conjures up the imagery of the Lord's loving care and protection (Deuteronomy 32:11–12).

In the New Testament, Jesus used a different version of this figure of speech. He expressed his regret over Jerusalem's rejection of His messiahship with a plaintive cry: "O Jerusalem. . . how often would I have gathered thy children together, as a hen doth gather her brood under her wings, and ye would not!" (Luke 13:34).

Learn More: Psalm 36:7; 57:1; 63:7 / Malachi 4:2

WOLVES IN SHEEP'S CLOTHING

Which come to you in sheep's clothing, but inwardly they are ravening wolves. MATTHEW 7:15

This is one of the most familiar figures of speech from Jesus in His Sermon on the Mount. He warned His disciples against false teachers who would lead them astray. These imposters would look as gentle and harmless as sheep. But the false doctrines they spread made them more dangerous than vicious wolves.

Religious counterfeits have always been a danger to authentic faith. The prophet Jeremiah's message of divine judgment was denied by court prophets who told the kings of Judah what they wanted to hear. The apostle John also condemned the false teachers of His day who taught that Jesus was strictly a divine being who did not exist in the flesh. But John declared, "Every spirit that confesseth not that Jesus Christ is come in the flesh is not of God" (1 John 4:3).

Charles H. Spurgeon, the great nineteenth-century British preacher, used words just as colorful as Jesus' image of "ravening wolves" for false teachers. They undercut the truths of the Gospel, he declared, until there was not enough left to make "soup for a grasshopper."

Learn More: Jeremiah 14:14 / Matthew 24:11, 24 / Mark 13:22 / 2 Peter 2:1 / 1 John 4:1

YOKE OF BONDAGE

Be not entangled again with the yoke of bondage. GALATIANS 5:1

The apostle Paul founded several churches in an area known as Galatia. He learned later that these believers were on the verge of falling away from the Gospel he had taught. False teachers were claiming that faith in the grace of Christ was not sufficient for salvation. They insisted that believers should also obey the Old Testament law, which involved submitting to circumcision and observing Jewish holy days.

Paul told these believers in strong language that they were in danger of taking on the "yoke of bondage" from which the Gospel of Christ had freed them. The old Jewish law had been replaced by the grace of Christ. Nothing else was necessary for this new way of life that Christ offered.

A yoke was a wooden beam placed on the neck of an ox, to which farming implements were attached. This was burdensome and uncomfortable for the animal, so this was an apt metaphor for the old Jewish law and its endless regulations. By contrast, believers enjoy liberty in Christ through faith in Him alone and their commitment to Him as Lord and Savior.

Learn More: Matthew 11:29 / Acts 15:10 / Romans 8:21 / 2 Corinthians 3:17

BIBLE TRANSLATIONS QUOTED IN THIS BOOK ———————————

STEP INTO THE BIBLE TIME MACHINE

The 5-Minute Visual Guide to the Bible makes scripture easier to approach...and come alive when you do. This guide keys beautiful, full-color illustrations—classic paintings, landscape and artifact photos, maps and charts—to a helpful chronological time line, allowing you to get more from your time in God's Word.

Paperback / 978-1-64352-889-2 / $14.99